SEMPER
FIDEL

To my parents

Without whose support
nothing would have
been possible

SEMPER FIDEL

FIDEL

AMERICA

&

CUBA

1776-1988

BY

MICHAEL J. MAZARR

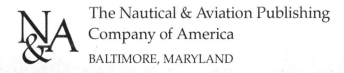
The Nautical & Aviation Publishing
Company of America
BALTIMORE, MARYLAND

Published by The Nautical & Aviation Publishing Company of America, Inc.,
101 W. Read Street, Suite 314, Baltimore, Maryland 21201.

Library of Congress Catalog Card Number: 88-22537

Mazarr, Michael J. 1965-
Semper Fidel / by Michael J. Mazarr.

ISBN 0-933852-74-6

1. United States—Foreign relations—Cuba. 2. Cuba—Foreign relations—United
States. I. Title.
E183.8.C9M29 1988
327.7307291—dc19

Sol
E
183,8
C9
M29
1988

Printed in the United States of America

CONTENTS

PART FOUR
RESPONSES TO REVOLUTION—CRISES AND COVERT ACTION

PART FIVE
RELATIONS SINCE 1974

PART SIX
ASSESSMENTS

Acknowledgements

The author wishes to acknowledge the kind support provided by a number of scholars of Cuban history and Cuban-American relations, and by several current and former U.S. policy-makers, who reviewed portions of the draft.

Louis A. Perez, Jr., Juan M. del Aguila, Jorge I. Dominguez, and *Jaime Suchlicki* all provided useful and extensive comments, primarily on the earlier chapters. *Stuart Lippe* and *Kenneth Skoug* of the United States Department of State's Office of Cuban Affairs were also enormously helpful, providing a wealth of original source materials and reviewing several chapters, especially the one on the Reagan years, from the perspective of those actively engaged in making U.S. policy toward Cuba.

Mr. Jose Manuel Casanova gave generously of his time and wealth of knowledge of Cuban affairs.

That said, the author, most naturally, retains all responsibility for the contents of the book—its opinions, biases, and errors included.

1

Preface

The history of U.S.-Cuban relations is an exciting one, filled with fascinating characters, wars, revolutions, and watershed foreign policy decisions. Perhaps in no other individual case is the history of American diplomacy so accurately summarized in microcosm.

An account of that relationship between these two countries sounds most of the key themes of American foreign policy: intervention, isolationism, economic sanctions, diplomatic and military intimidation, colonial competition with Europe, anti-Communism, popular and unpopular wars. To a surprising degree, current American policies in Latin America mirror policies that the U.S. government has pursued since the eighteenth century.

PART
ONE

EARLY RELATIONS

Spanish Imperialism and American Growth

1

REVOLUTIONARY RELATIONS AND THE MONROE DOCTRINE

The United States and Cuba, 1762-1824

"The multitude of palm trees and various forms, the highest and most beautiful I have ever met with, and an infinity of other great and green trees; the birds in rich plumage and the verdure of the fields; render this country. . .of such marvelous beauty that it surpasses all other in charms and graces as the day doth the night in lustre. I have been so overwhelmed at the sight of so much beauty that I have not known how to relate it."
Columbus, on sighting Cuba, to Ferdinand and Isabella

"The Monroe Doctrine. . .is more fundamental than the Constitution itself."
U.S. Congressman R. Walton Moore

Through the first quarter of the nineteenth century, American relations with Cuba were characterized by two overriding considerations: trade and a fear of European meddling in the Hemisphere. Until about 1810, trade was the more significant, as first the British colonies and then the young American republic strove to develop commerce. Cuba played a significant role in sixteenth and seventeenth century European conflicts, and later in the war of independence of the British colonies. After that time, as European powers became more interested in monopolizing Caribbean trade and security, the United States faced its first crucial diplomatic test.

Successive American administrators promoted the interests of the United States as best they could. Protectionist and mercantilist, the Founding Fathers pursued a form of power politics and a balance of power to deflect the threats they faced from the Old World. Commercial and strategic concerns were interrelated to the extent that early U.S. administrations attempted to use trade to play France, Spain, and Great Britain against one another and thereby create a balance of power that would protect the young nation.[1] These policies were reflected in early U.S. Cuban policy.

CUBA'S EARLY HISTORY

Cuba is a small island which lies some ninety miles off the Florida Keys. The island is 750 miles long from East to West, and ranges from 25 to 125 miles in width. It is ringed with 2,500 miles of coastline, and includes a total of 42,827 square miles of territory.

The land has a varied nature. The provinces of central Cuba— Havana, Matanzas, Santa Clara, and Camaguey—consist mostly of rolling plains and low hills broken by shallow stream valleys. Most of the country's sugar and tobacco is grown in the rich and healthy soil there. Other parts of the island are mountainous, forested, or swampy. The provinces of Pinar del Rio in the west, and Oriente in the east, are quite rugged.

Cuba lies in the trade wind belt, so its climate is semi-tropical, with temperatures ranging from 70 to 80 degrees fahrenheit. The average temperature is 77 degrees, and it rarely rises to 100. The rainfall varies; on the coasts it averages 45-50 inches per year, while the interior receives over 60. Cuba's natural beauty became well-known to expeditions of the 16th and 17th centuries, as did its wealth of rich soil and its excellent climate for agriculture.[2] Before 1492, Cuba was inhabited by three tribes of varying degrees of primitiveness. None had a written language, and all later perished of disease or abuse during the Spanish occupation.

The *Guanahatabeyes*, the oldest tribe of the three, were a quiet, reticent people, a "shell culture" of fruit pickers who did some hunting and lived, for the most part, in caves. Cuba's first governor, Diego Velazquez, said that they lived "like savages, without houses of towns, and eating only the meat they were able to find in the forests as well as turtles and fish."[3]

The *Ciboneys* were slightly more advanced, part of the Arawak group of Indians prevalent in Latin America. They probably migrated to Cuba somewhere in South America, though some have suggested they came down Florida into Western Cuba. Theirs was a stone-age culture, and they fished, hunted, and constructed small towns near rivers or the sea. They also practiced some basic agriculture, and were generally gentle and unwarlike.[4]

Another branch of the Arawak tribe, the *Tainos*, the most advanced of the three groups, produced advanced stone implements and pottery, lived in well-built villages, and played games, including one like modern-day soccer. They also bound the foreheads of their offspring, which produced slightly mis-shapen heads with wide crania. The *Tainos* used a relatively advanced agricultural system, and cultivated *yucca*, which was baked into *cassava*, a sort of unleavened bread. They also grew corn, beans, peanuts, and other crops. The relative advancement of the *Tainos* allowed them to conquer and subjugate the *Ciboneys*.

By 1492 the *Tainos* had been attacked by the *Caribs* (''cannibals'') who made a number of raids into Cuba, eating their victims and generally terrorizing the population. The *Caribs* were eventually driven away by the Spanish.

The Arrival of Columbus

Looking, as almost everyone knows, for the Far East and its riches, Christopher Columbus stumbled upon North America instead. On October 27, 1492, he sighted Cuba. Columbus sailed around various parts of the Cuban coastline, but never managed to get all the way around, and never realized it was an island. Following his discovery, several attempts to establish permanent colonies failed, and by 1494 only the nearby island of Hispaniola (the island that is now Haiti and the Dominican Republic) had been colonized.

The Indians, generally peaceful, at first welcomed the Spanish, greeting the first two Spanish envoys with gifts of food and Indian artifacts. In the early sixteenth century, various gold speculators and explorers ventured to Cuba to seek their fortune, though few found anything of value. Diego Velazquez set out to conquer the whole island, but found resistance stiff. The famous chieftain Hatuey led the rebellion for a time, outclassed by Spanish weapons but nevertheless fighting on.

* * *

Hatuey was a young Indian chieftan, leader of the tribe called the *Guahabas* on the island of Hispaniola. Stories of Spanish atrocities made him suspicious of the alien interlopers, and when Columbus landed on the island Hatuey did not welcome him as had other tribes. Realizing that his small tribe of 400 men, women, and children was no match for the warriors from the Old World, Hatuey took his people to the bigger island of Cuba, hoping to establish an organized resistance.

At first the Cuban Indians, thinking Hatuey's tribe to be *Caribs*, fled into the mountains, but they eventually returned. Hatuey told the Cubans that a Spanish invasion was imminent, and that the Spanish were a "cruel and wicked people" who worshipped gold and riches. He called for resistance to the "tyrannical" Spanish, and asked the tribes to throw their gold into the sea to remove the object of Spanish attention, as Hatuey had done.

The Indian chieftains, however, were suspicious. They found Hatuey's stories of Spanish brutality difficult to believe, and they feared that a young chief was using the issue as an excuse to bend the Cuban tribes to his will. Except for a few small groups, therefore, no Cubans joined his rebellion.

But Hatuey would not be deterred. In the first engagement of the war, he ambushed the Spanish shortly after they had landed on Cuba, but was driven off by the better-armed conquistadors. Recognizing the fruitlessness of conventional tactics, Hatuey decided on a strategy of guerilla warfare, designed to frustrate the Spanish and eventually to force them to quit the island. Small groups of Indians constantly harried the Spanish and kept them confined to fixed, fortified positions, preventing a true occupation of the island.

An enemy of Hatuey among the Indians, however, eventually betrayed the position of the chief's headquarters, and he was captured by the Spanish. They demanded to know where his tribe's gold had been hidden, and offered to spare Hatuey's life if he told them; he refused. On February 2, 1512, he was brought out to be burned at the stake. Again the Spanish offered to spare him if he revealed the location of the gold. Again he refused.

Just before the flames were lit, a Spanish priest asked Hatuey if he wished to become a Christian and be baptized before he died. When informed that it would mean he would go to a Christian heaven, Hatuey reportedly replied, "If the Christians do go to heaven, I do not want to go to heaven. I do not wish ever again to meet such cruel and wicked people as Christians who kill and make slaves of the Indians."[5]

Hatuey met his death among the flames, and after a time the leaderless Indian revolt was crushed by the Spanish. In many ways, his revolt established a pattern for the history of Cuba; spurred by the injustice of paternalistic, and sometimes brutal, occupation by larger powers, Cubans would be fighting for their liberty for centuries to come. There would be gaps in the revolutionary process: periods of especially great prosperity or repression, which alternately discouraged or crushed rebellions. But the battle for freedom and independence had begun. It would last some four hundred years.

* * *

The Spanish established what became known as the policy of *encomiendas*, by which Spanish settlers were given Indian slaves if they promised to Christianize them. The system was fraught with abuse, and many Spaniards spent less time Christianizing their charges than they did beating them. The Spanish crown, angry at this insult to religious principles, attempted to end these cruelties with several sets of laws, but failed. Even by the mid-sixteenth century, the Indians—weakened by mistreatment and Spanish diseases—had already begun to die out, and were too few and too weak to serve as reliable labor. The Spanish turned to the importation of black slaves from Africa, and the slave trade was soon booming. By 1544 the population of the island was about 7,000: 660 Spanish, 800 black slaves, and 5,000 Indians.[6]

By the end of the century, the Caribbean had begun to teem with commerce. Spanish monopolies on regional trade gave rise to a huge smuggling system, and the Cubans, paid handsomely, often aided the smugglers. Violent raids by profiteers were also commonplace; Havana was sacked and burned in 1555. The Cuban settlers, for their part, merely wanted to trade freely, and this desire established a running feud with the Spanish government, which routinely imposed severe duties on Cuban trade in an attempt to monopolize its profits.

British influence in the Caribbean grew during the seventeenth century, with Francis Drake, Oliver Cromwell, and others turning their gaze toward the region. They had little success at first, capturing only Santo Domingo and Jamaica for short periods of time. But eventually British Caribbean commerce expanded. This period also witnessed the development of the buccaneers, captains and crews who "served European nations in times of war and plundered for themselves in times of peace."[7] The desire of European powers to end the practice led to several important treaties of the mid- to late-seventeenth century.

The first half of the eighteenth century was marked by huge European wars, in which the Caribbean colonies were used as pawns. Cuba, for example, served the Spanish as a source of agricultural products and thus income, and as a base of operations in the region. Trade grew and fell in cycles depending on who was fighting whom, and where. Cuba, the "Pearl of the Antilles," was prized by Spain as one of the jewels of her colonial crown, and no one could have predicted the enormous trouble it would later cause for Madrid.

THE UNITED STATES AND CUBA FROM 1762 TO 1800

The period 1762-1800—from the British occupation of Cuba until the beginning of the Jefferson Administration in the United States—was distinguished by the overriding importance of trade relations. The colonial powers clashed in the Caribbean largely over trade issues, and both the rebellion of the British colonies and the recurring revolts of the colonists in Cuba were motivated by unfair taxes, trade monopolies, and other economic concerns.

Until 1762, the crippling Spanish trade restrictions on Cuba continued in full force. The advent of increasingly profitable sugar and tobacco prompted the Spanish to institute a series of taxes and trade tariffs, which culminated in 1740 when The Royal Company of Commerce was established; it held a complete monopoly on the island's trade. Spain's Cuban colonists complained vehemently about such restrictions to no avail.[9]

The sugar industry began to develop into the enormously valuable business that would later draw U.S. interest and involvement. Mills that had begun to expand in the mid-18th century multiplied, so that by the 1780s Cuba was the world's fourth largest sugar producer. Increasingly, and especially after the Revolutionary War, Cuba looked to the United States as a market. The industry's expansion continued at a rapid pace, so that by 1815, ''Cuba stood on the threshold of world leadership in sugar production.''[10]

From 1745 to 1762, Cuba was governed under the benign direction of Felipe Fons de Viela, Marquis de la Torre. Under his leadership, the standard of living in Cuba rose markedly. Improvements in health, public buildings, paved roads,and education, and the abolition of such oppressive institutions as 'party judges', brought Cuba into a new Golden Age. With the sugar industry blossoming, the stage seemed set.[11] In 1762, however, this process was interrupted by a British invasion.

The British Invasion

As early as 1710, the British had cast envious eyes upon Cuba. Cuban colonists expected a British invasion several times during the 17th and 18th centuries; in the summer of 1741, British colonial soldiers actually attempted to attack the island but failed. Finally, in 1759, the French and Spanish made a pact to restrict and harry British trade in America, and in response the British in June 1762 carried out the plans for the invasion of Havana originated by Lord Pitt. By August the Spanish had capitulated; their forces had refused to believe an invasion was imminent, and thus unprepared for the attack mounted only an ill-equipped and poorly organized defense. The campaign was not easy, however, and the battle for Morro Castle was particularly bloody.[12] British forces also drove the Spanish from Portugal and the Philippines.

American colonists assisted the British in their invasion with men and supplies. The reaction in the colonies to the British victories was exultant: the governor of Boston announced that "above all, with hearts full of gratitude and amazement we must contemplate the glorious and important conquest of Havannah [sic]," and towns all across New England celebrated with general revelry, drinking, and gun salutes.[14] British officers involved in the invasion also profited heavily.[15]

Trade ramifications of the invasion particularly pleased American colonists. Not only would the Cuban market be opened up, but "the fall of Havana freed the people of the south from the ravages of the privateer,"[16] many of whom had found a home in Cuba. The British immediately eliminated the Spanish trade restrictions, and exchanges between Cuba and the British colonies boomed.

The occupation, however, was short-lived. In 1763, after a sharp debate in Parliament, the British traded Cuba—which had weathered a year of harsh and money-grubbing rule by Lord Albemarle—back to Spain for Florida, and Spain acquired Louisiana from France. The British saw advantages in fixing firmly the Southern tip of their colonial possessions, and were also happy to get the French out of the southern United States.

These maneuvers carried significant implications for the later Revolutionary War. Had Britain kept Cuba, it would have robbed the Americans and their allies of one of their key ports of refuge and bases of operations. The possession of Cuba would also have assisted British attempts to establish a blockade around the colonies. In short, British possession of Cuba would have hampered the efforts of the American colonies to a significant degree, and might possibly have helped alter the outcome of the war.[17]

At first, Madrid found it difficult suddenly to reimpose the trade restrictions that had been relaxed by the British.[18] For a short period, the British and Spanish, each for their own reasons, attempted to prevent Cuban-American trade, but by 1765 many of the original monopolies had still not been reimposed. The sugar industry continued to grow; for example, by 1778 the number of ships trading between Spain and Cuba had grown to 200, from 6 in 1762.[19] British levies on their own colonies, meanwhile, began to create the tensions which would lead eventually to the Revolutionary War.

The Revolutionary War and Its Effects

The Revolutionary War, of course, produced the United States of America, and so it can be said that in a definitional sense, U.S.-Cuban relations were inaugurated with the Declaration of Independence. But in many other ways as well, the War contributed to growing Cuban economic and political ties with the North American mainland, and hastened the day when the Spanish would be evicted from the island. One commentator has concluded that Cuba "was at the very center of the French and Spanish involvement in the American war of independence.''[20]

In an important sense, the model of the revolutionary American colonies encouraged the dissatisfied Cuban colonists to consider similar means of obtaining their self-determination. The independence of the United States would serve as precedent for later Spanish colonial uprisings, especially insofar as it was based on principles of economic freedom.

The war also precipitated a boom in the Cuban economy. Madrid had originally remained impartial, and in August 1776 they issued a Royal Order of Neutrality, barring both British and American ships from their harbors except in extreme cases. Eventually, however, the Spanish permitted Americans to trade with Spanish Caribbean colonies, and a Spanish Royal Order of November 5, 1776, allowed American ships to purchase supplies in Cuba. The Continental Congress soon dispatched the first official U.S. delegate to Cuba, Robert Smith, to undertake trade negotiations. Thereafter Cuba imported foodstuffs and other materials from the United States, and American privateers used Cuba as a base, purchasing supplies and weapons there.[21]

An American request for trade with and aid from the Spanish colonies, and Cuba in particular, was delivered to the Spanish at New Orleans in September, 1776, by one George Gibson. Part of the Spanish response consisted of a November declaration of open trade with the Americans, but the Spanish also began to plot various military adventures with the colonists. In December, 1776, the governor of Louisiana was told to encourage the Americans to take Pensacola from the British, with the promise of supplies sold to the Americans through Havana.[22] Bernardo de Galvez, the Spanish governor of Louisiana at the time, favored war with England; his presence, and the situation as a whole, raised Anglo-Spanish tensions to the boiling point, although the two nations were not yet at war.

In 1778, Galvez revived the plan for a colonial expedition against the British in Florida. He broached the subject to Oliver Pollock, an American representative in Cuba who would replace Robert Smith. Galvez told Pollock to inform the Continental Congress that if the Americans would undertake such an expedition, ''he [Galvez] would furnish your troops with cash and in short anything in his power they may stand in want of.''[23] Some Americans were tempted by such offers; George Morgan, the colonial commander at Pittsburgh, for example, began investigating ways to assemble a force to attack Florida, and in July, 1777, he wrote a memorandum to the Continental Congress recommending such a course of action.[24] The Congress never implemented the proposal.

In 1779, however, Spain decided to declare war against Britain in any case, and so the secretive operations of Galvez and others became operational plans for Spanish troops in the New World. In these efforts, the Spanish expected the help of colonial troops, but the Americans could not spare scarce troops or supplies for Spanish projects. British commanders in America, moreover, pressed their Georgian campaign with vigor, putting the colonial troops there on the defensive; offensive operations, against Florida or elsewhere, were out of the question.[25]

During the war, U.S.-Cuban trade increased substantially. Even during this period of great demand, however, high duties were still in force, 30 per cent import and 10 per cent export taxes not being unusual. U.S. ships were often arbitrarily denied docking rights, which caused cargoes to spoil. Nevertheless, at the height of wartime trade, more than 40 vessels regularly transversed the Philadelphia-Havana route, and smaller trade lines existed elsewhere.[26]

In late 1779, John Jay, the U.S. minister to Spain, attempted to use the Spanish declaration of war to American benefit. He managed to secure small amounts of aid but not much substantial assistance. Spain, unsympathetic toward the upstart Americans who were challenging a monarchical authority, allowed little progress in Spanish-American relations until the 1780s.[27]

Post-War Tensions: Relations 1780-1800

Once the war was over, however, the rationale for freer trade was gone, and the 1780s witnessed a significant increase in Spanish protectionism. Robert Smith accomplished little in the way of promoting trade, and Oliver Pollock did not fare much better; in fact, he was initially denied entry to Cuba, then detained as an accused smuggler for over a year until Galvez, whom Pollock knew, returned and set him free. In January, 1784, the Spanish crown issued decrees ending the open trade period, banning all Cuban trade except that with Spain, and expelling all foreigners from Cuba, including U.S. representative Pollock.[28] American negotiators made a strong plea for the exemption of the new United States from such barriers, but to no avail. From 1785 to 1789, trade between Cuba and the U.S. was essentially nonexistent, apart from some contraband smuggled in on slave ships.[29]

In 1793, another European war—this one pitting British and Spanish monarchies against Republican France—again isolated Cuba and created the need for increased trade with America. The trade did not flow without restrictions, however. Spanish administrators still imposed fees on what trade they could control, often pocketing the money they received. Privateers from France and elsewhere harried ships sailing between Cuba and Philadelphia or other American ports. And by 1795, when the European war had ended, Spain again closed Cuban ports; by July of that year, trade was again negligible.

Less than a year later, however, in August, 1796, Spain was back at war with Britain and the revolving door of Spain's colonial trade policy continued with the reopening of trade relations with America. Spanish monopolies continued, run by one Count Jaruco and his associates, who amassed huge personal fortunes as a result. Trade increased gradually.

The war did not go well for Spain, and when in 1797 the British drove the Spanish from the Americas, Cuban ports were thrown wide open. "Within a year," one later observer concluded, "the high levels of trade of the preceding period were doubled."[30] By 1798 U.S. trade with Cuba had risen to nearly $50 million, an enormous sum for the time, though the exchange was still severely hampered with duties. The French and Spanish were convinced that the United States was aiding Great Britain in the European war, and they determined to damage U.S. trade as much as possible. French privateers and the Spanish navy seized U.S. ships and often left the crews on deserted islands to die.

The U.S. government, meanwhile, sent representatives to Spain's American ports, though the Spanish at first refused to accept any official American consulates. Josef Maria de Yzardni, U.S. consul at Cadiz, was sent to Cuba on other business, and remained there for several months in 1797 to look after U.S. interests and try to provide what protection of sailors he could muster. President Adams, meanwhile, furious at the Spanish consulate policy, went ahead and appointed two consuls: Daniel Hawley at Havana in December 1797, and Josiah Blakely at Santiago in 1798. Both were allowed to remain, though neither was recognized as a consul or provided any privileges. Hawley accomplished little; he "spent more of his time in getting trade permits and taking advantage of his fellow men than in looking after U.S. interests or seamen."[31] John Morton eventually replaced Hawley and called for greater protection against French privateers and for an end to illegal slave trade. But there was still no sign that Spain would recognize these men as official consuls, and in 1799, motivated by a desire for greater profits and hoping to impress their French allies, the Spanish closed all their American ports to trade once again.

In France, Napoleon had come to power in a 1799 coup. Unwilling to waste precious resources confronting ships of the growing American Navy in the Caribbean, he pulled out most of the privateers, and by mid-1800 privateering had nearly ended. The sudden calm allowed Morton to take a leave of absence, and in the spring of 1801 his brother, George, who had been left in charge, reported from Cuba that "the wealth and importance of this colony has increased during the few years that it has been open to the American trade in a most astonishing degree."[32]

By 1800, however, Napoleon had acquired Louisiana, and he contemplated the reestablishment of a French colonial empire in the Mississippi Valley. His intention was to make Gulf of Mexico a "French lake."[33] The treaty promising Louisiana to France renewed European involvement in North American affairs, involvement that would expand in the next century and the implications of which disturbed American officials. The importance of Central America as a land bridge between the two oceans was significant, as were the commercial opportunities in the New World territories. European powers set out to surround and strangle the United States—whose government was still seen as disturbingly revolutionary—and to reassert their own influence in the region. The American response to these efforts would form the basis of U.S.-Cuban policy for the next century, a policy that would be institutionalized in the Monroe Doctrine.

THE JEFFERSON ADMINISTRATION

If there was any doubt left at the beginning of the Jefferson Administration that Cuba would become a crucial issue in the foreign policy of the developing United States, it was quickly dispelled. Many of the most significant policy issues in the first two-thirds of the century were directly related to Cuba; the single most important U.S. foreign policy proclamation of the era, the Monroe Doctrine, stemmed from Cuban concerns, and the Cuban issue became tied to the problem of slavery that would rend America.

As Willis Fletcher Johnson wrote in his "History of Cuba," the nineteenth century demonstrated once and for all that the names 'Cuba' and 'America' had become "inseparable." He wrote:

> Every page and line and letter of Cuban history in the nineteenth century is colored by the fact that the United States of America had arisen as the foremost power in the Western Hemisphere. Through the inspiration which it gave to the French Revolution, the United States was chiefly responsible. . . for the complete collapse of Spain as a great European power. Through its example and potential influence as a protector it was responsible for the revolt and independence of the Spanish colonies in Central and South America. Then through its assertion of special interests in Cuba. . . it determined the future destinies of [Cuba].[34]

Not all the special interests the United States would assert would be benign, however, and the destiny they determined for Cuba was ambiguous at best.

At the turn of the century, Thomas Jefferson was probably the most ardent advocate of the annexation of Cuba in the U.S. government. His maneuvers as President were limited by his desire to keep the fledgling United States out of foreign wars, but he took what steps he thought prudent to further the acquisition of Cuba. Many years after his term in office, he would write that, "I candidly confess that I have ever looked on Cuba as the most interesting addition which could ever be made to our system of states."[35] His desire was tempered with the realization that he could not obtain Cuba without a war with Spain, and he hoped to avoid foreign involvement at virtually any cost. Later, as an adviser to subsequent presidents, he would argue for more ambitious efforts at annexation.

Jefferson was an unceasing advocate of expansion; his desire to augment the size of the United States (and to rid the continent of European influence) led to the Louisiana Purchase in 1803-4. Later, in 1807, Jefferson's Caribbean envoy, James Wilkinson, summarized his president's policies thus: keep European influence out of the hemisphere, take Florida, and occupy Cuba. Jefferson caused the Congress of Cuban Historians to conclude in 1947 that "the precursor of the annexation of our island to the United States was President Thomas Jefferson. . . [who was] a constant spokesman for the incorporation of Cuba into the Union."[36] By 1803, indeed, his trepidation waning, Jefferson discussed risking war with Spain because at the time Cuba might be an "easy conquest."[37] These plans also included a possible invasion of the Spanish Florida territory. Jefferson even sent Henry Hill to Havana to report on Spanish military deployments on the island.

Eventually, Jefferson recognized that such a war would not be in the U.S. interest. Indeed, so long as Cuba remained a Spanish colony, it was little threat; the Spanish empire was on the wane, and its Caribbean possessions did not pose a serious danger to the United States. Jefferson therefore formulated the principle that would guide U.S. policy toward Cuba for nearly a century, and would later be expanded and institutionalized in the Monroe Doctrine. He warned Cuba that "if you remain under the dominion of the Kingdom and family of Spain, we are contented; but we should be extremely unwilling to see you pass under the domination or ascendance of France or England."[38] An English or French Cuba would constitute a threat and could not be tolerated; an American Cuba, however, was still something Jefferson desired. In 1807, in an oft-quoted statement, he said that if he could acquire Cuba he would "inscribe on [Cuba's southern limit] a *ne plus ultra* as to us in that direction. . . .Cuba can be defended by us without a navy, and this develops the principle which ought to limit our views."[39]

Accordingly, in 1807 he began meeting with Cuban annexationists, a group that influenced U.S. policy for decades. The annexationist groups included a varied set of anti-Spanish plotters: Cuban slaveowners worried about the future of slavery in the Spanish empire, and desirous of incorporating Cuba into the South; businessmen intent on expanding commercial ties with the United States, which were still circumscribed by Spanish tariffs and corruption; and true Cuban patriots hoping that alliance with the United States would lead to eventual independence. Jefferson, after discussing the island's future with these and other groups, concluded that in case of war with Spain Cuba might well "add itself to our confederation." In 1808, Jefferson sent Wilkinson to discuss annexation with Captain General Someruelos, Spain's appointed colonial governor.[40]

Developments in Europe magnified the growing threat to American interests in Latin America. In 1808 Napoleon deposed the Spanish monarch and placed his brother Joseph on the throne. The remains of the Spanish government sought aid from the British, who imposed yet more obstructions on Cuban trade with America. Spain's weakness had become even more manifest, and Britain and France emerged as the key threats to the United States. Fear of their interference in hemispheric affairs, and in Cuba in particular, guided U.S. policy for most of the remainder of the century and led to the Monroe Doctrine and other demands for European non-intervention. Napoleon's takeover in Spain also led to revolts among Spanish colonies unwilling to "accept rule by the conquering dynasty"[41] and hungry for independence from an exploitive—and tottering—colonial system.

Thus the revolt of Spanish colonies—which would eventually spread to Mexico, Chile, Colombia, and others—offered opportunities to the United States. Jefferson thought he could annex the former Spanish territories which lay on American borders. He also foresaw trade openings with the newly-free countries, and an end to significant European influence in the New World. He used diplomatic means to promote these interests.[42]

Jefferson's machinations were also guided by an imminent threat of European involvement in the hemisphere, the sort of involvement of which his earlier proclamation had warned. Cuba, he worried, could become a base of British or French operations against the United States in a future war, and there were some signals that European powers intended to transform that fear into a reality. The American diplomat Albert Gallatin wondered in 1808 if, given a revolution in Cuba, "will not Great Britain in that case take possession of Cuba?" Aaron Burr reported from England that the British desired Cuba as well as Florida as colonies. British naval forces were reported in the West Indies, and Jefferson feared imminent invasion.[43]

Jefferson and his Cabinet made clear to "influential persons in Cuba" that any European control of the island would be unacceptable. The United States would not offer to protect the island, the Cabinet's message stated; it would only say that should you choose to declare independence, we cannot now commit ourselves by saying we would make common cause with you but must reserve ourselves to act according to the then existing circumstances, but in our proceedings we shall be influenced by friendship to you, by a firm belief that our interests are intimately connected, and by the strongest repugnance to see you under subordination [of European powers].[44]

A week later he wrote to Governor William Claiborne of the Orleans Territory, and said that American and Spanish interests regarding Latin America were largely the same: "the object of both must be to exclude European influence from this hemisphere."[45]

The threatened British invasion, however, never materialized. Meanwhile, U.S. commerce with Cuba was declining; Spain continued to refuse to recognize American commercial agents in Cuba, and the official tariffs were often multiplied by corrupt port officials. The United States in retaliation imposed a trade ban in 1807-8, but it proved to be totally ineffective; within a year 104 U.S. vessels had violated it. Trade continued to be an irritant in developing U.S.-Cuban relations.[46]

THE MADISON ADMINISTRATION

James Madison was Thomas Jefferson's hand-picked successor, and as such he won easily despite the Federalist challenge to Republican dominance. Madison's term in office was marked by many crises, including the War of 1812; he proved a rather weak president, being carried by events rather than dictating their outcome. Madison's interest in Cuba, however, continued Jefferson's; he wished to acquire it if he could, but his paramount concern was to prevent its becoming a British or French colony. With Napoleon's rise to power in Europe, the prospect of a French operation against Cuba loomed large. Madison himself admitted that "Cuba will, without doubt be a cardinal object with Napoleon."[47] For its part, France feared U.S. operations against its Caribbean colonies and Florida.

Madison still harbored fears of a British invasion, and Jefferson suggested that, to preempt European action the United States should take advantage of the disarray of the Spanish government to seize Cuba. Gallatin warned from England in 1810 that Britain was ready "to take possession of Cuba." In the same year Madison wrote that he hoped the European powers would stay out of American affairs; "the position of Cuba," he argued, "gives the United States so deep an interest in the destiny, even, of that Island, that although they might be an inactive, they could not be a satisfied spectator of its falling under any European government, which might make a fulcrum of that position against the commerce and security of the United States."[48] This amounted to a nearly complete statement of the Monroe Doctrine thirteen years before the latter was formulated. European powers, especially Britain and France, were warned that interference in the hemisphere would result in political and perhaps military confrontation with the United States.

Like Jefferson, Madison flirted with acquiring Cuba, and sent representatives to Cuba to sound out annexationist sentiment. William Shaler, the U.S. consul in Havana, was told to determine whether Cubans favored annexation to the United States; one writer has concluded that Shaler was instructed to "foment" such sentiment.[49] Shaler met some favorable reactions, particularly from wealthy Cuban planters who wanted to protect their slave industries. On the whole the Cubans were still too timid to risk conflict with Spain,[50] but in 1811 the planters gathered the will to ask for U.S. protection against British interference should the Cubans start an insurrection against the Spanish. Among any fears of the Cuban planters wary of revolution was that Britain might use such a conflict as an excuse to intervene.

This fear was magnified by England's growing tilt toward the abolition of slavery. In 1807 abolition was declared for British dominions, and by 1833 England abolished slavery in its colonies as well. Led by William Wilberforce, British abolitionists possessed a strong voice in their government, and England became perhaps the leading advocate of abolition in the world. Cuban landowners knew that if Britain regained control of Cuba, their slave system—and the wealth it generated—would be destroyed.

Shaler initially agreed to protect the planters against that eventuality, but Madison, unwilling to risk war with Britain, rescinded the offer. Later in 1811 Spanish authorities in Cuba, suspicious of Shaler's dealings with alleged revolutionaries, expelled him from the island.

Slavery in Cuba

Slavery in Cuba was a varied and sometimes brutal institution. The growth of sugar, tobacco, and coffee industries, and the extermination of most of the native Indians, created the need for outside labor, and slaves filled this need. Most slaves brought to Cuba came from the parts of Africa now comprising Togo and Cameroon, and were employed on Cuba overwhelmingly in rural occupations; 80 per cent of the slaves imported from 1840 to 1860 went to the plantations.

Slaves were shipped to Havana and other ports and sold to Cubans in huge auctions. Between 1521 and 1791, some 90,000 slaves were imported; by 1854

644,000 had been brought in. One writer describes the conditions of slaves on the auction block:

> Here the droves of dazed savages were confined, awaiting sale—as many as 200 at a time. Either completely naked or almost so, their emaciated bodies, as well as their agonized faces, were stamped with the horrors of the ocean crossing. . . . Half-perished with hunger and thirst, they sat mumbling to their heathen gods, speculating on the ultimate destiny of their dead companions whom they had seen raked out of the ship's bottom and dumped over the side like offal.

Slaves were often treated well at first, because it had been found that if they were abused from the start many would quickly commit suicide, believing that death would allow them to return to Africa. Such suicides were costly, and to help forestall their occurrence the planters took to burning the bodies of the suicides and scattering their ashes, in full view of the remaining slaves, over the fields; the slaves believed burning prevented the return home. Those slaves who revolted or attempted to escape were burned alive.

Conditions for slaves varied according to where they worked. Urban slaves were lucky; they had relatively regular work hours, frequently enjoyed close relations with their owners, and had opportunities to purchase their freedom. There were even small taverns and clubs that catered to a slave clientele, and the slaves possessed certain rights, protected by the *sindico* or slave overseer. On the plantations, life was different and much more harsh: the work was hard, the hours long, and the slaves were often monitored by cruel overseers who ran plantations for absentee owners. Health conditions and the quality of food and housing were uniformly odious.

By mid-century, the constant interaction of the races, promoted by the end of the slave trade and the need to rely on self-sustaining slave communities, had improved conditions somewhat for all slaves. Julia Ward Howe, the American writer, poet, and author of the "Battle Hymn of the Republic," travelled to Cuba, and she commented on the conditions of slaves there in the middle of the nineteenth century. She noted that in Cuba, the races were far more mixed by blood than in the United States, and that this contributed to better race relations; she was speaking of the Creoles, the mixed blood planters and farmers who constituted much of the middle class. As a result, "the negro cannot be so hated, so despised" as in the United States. "There is a great familiarity between the children of the two races," she added. "They play, and run about, and are petted together."

In 1888 slavery was finally abolished in Cuba in accordance with an 1879 order of Captain General Martinez Campos. By that time contract labor had become less expensive than owning slaves in any case; indeed the ironic result of abolition was that living standards for most newly-freed slaves actually fell. The institution quietly died away, a marked contrast to the abolitionist process in the United States.[51]

Continuing U.S. Diplomacy

American attempts to precipitate a revolt in Cuba that would lead to annexation continued. In 1881, Secretary of State Monroe discussed annexation with Jose Alvarez de Toledo, a Spanish naval officer who promised to lead a revolution in Cuba and annex it to the United States, first economically and eventually politically as well. Toledo claimed that he was "ready to face any danger for the welfare of my native land and these United States." Monroe and other U.S. leaders were enthusiastic about the plan, but the war of 1812 intervened, Toledo left to fight in the Mexican wars, and his plan was laid aside. It would reappear in many guises and under many leaders, however, over the next several decades.[52]

Another key U.S. goal was the removal of European influence in the region, and the government made continuing efforts to achieve it. The U.S. Congress, in January, 1811, approved a policy toward newly- independent Spanish colonies. Called the "No-Transfer Resolution," the legislation expressed the feeling of Congress that the "United States, under the peculiar circumstances of the existing crisis, cannot without serious inquietude see any part of the said territory pass into the hands of an foreign power."[53] European powers, in other words, should keep their hands out of Latin America.

The War of 1812 led to familiar disagreements between the United States and Spain over the use of Cuban ports by British warships. The British did use Havana on occasion, but not extensively, and the war was over before the U.S. claims could be resolved. Interestingly, the British troops that landed near New Orleans to fight General Jackson, in the famous American victory that occurred after the treaty of peace had been signed, sailed from Havana.[54]

Meanwhile, revolts in many of Spain's other American colonies had begun around 1810; this movement eventually destroyed the Spanish colonial empire, pulling Argentina, Chile, Venezuela, Ecuador, Colombia, Peru, Bolivia and Mexico from Madrid's control. Continuing government crises—coups, countercoups, and instability surrounding Ferdinand VIII's return to the throne—prevented Spain from responding quickly or decisively to the insurrections in its colonies. U.S. popular opinion strongly supported the democratic revolutionary events, and was guided in part by opinion-makers such as the Philadelphia *Aurora*, the New York *Colombian*, and the Washington *Gazette*, who "gave tongue in English to the patriots of the South."[55]

The American government, however, unwilling to risk its relations with Spain, maintained a policy of "strict neutrality" and would not recognize the independent colonies for over a decade. Many conservatives in the United States, especially Southern slaveowners, were skeptical; the *Southern Patriot* contended that "the people of these provinces are not duly prepared for the enjoyment of that great boon and blessing—well-regulated freedom."[56] Those wary of Spanish American independence were influenced by various considerations; the U.S. government wanted to maintain good relations with Spain to acquire Florida and reduce tariffs on Cuban trade; American merchants wanted stability to support trade; Southern slaveowners distrusted any "revolutionary" process that threatened another slave system. Proponents of independence responded with virulent attacks on these "opponents of liberty."

Henry Clay, Speaker of the House, was a important figure in the development of U.S. policy toward these independence movements, and toward Cuba as well. An engaging man called "Harry of the West," Clay was an early "hawkish" advocate of expansion to the West Coast and he became a strong advocate of Western interests, especially the promotion of U.S. commerce. This led him to a somewhat progressive endorsement of independent South American states, and he spoke of a Pan-American federation designed to guarantee freedom from European intervention—and free markets for American products. Clay wrote that "at the present moment the patriots of the South are fighting for liberty and independence—for precisely what we fought for. . . .The moral influence of such a recognition, on the patriots of the South, will be irresistible."[57]

Later, as Secretary of State, Clay became somewhat more conservative, and admitted occasional disillusionment with the South America nations. He was therefore hesitant at times to argue for complete recognition, though he did support the idea of sending delegates to the Panama Congress, a meeting of representatives from many of the newly independent Latin American states. As with many American policymakers, too, Clay was concerned about the implications of recognition for the slave states. He said of Cuba in 1826 that

> no subject of our foreign relations has created with the executive
> government more anxious concern than that of the condition of the
> island, and the possibility of prejudice to southern states, from the
> convulsions to which it might be exposed. . . .The slave holding
> states cannot forget that they are now in a minority, which is in a
> constantly relative diminution, and should certainly not be the first
> to put a principle of public action by which they would be the
> greatest losers.[58]

Clay's personal sentiments lay with the independent states, but the realities of the times delayed U.S. recognition until 1822 and impeded true assistance thereafter. As of 1824 Clay was still forced to maintain that the United States preferred that "Cuba and Puerto Rico should remain dependent on Spain. This government desires no political change in that condition."[59]

THE MONROE ADMINISTRATION AND THE "EVER FAITHFUL ISLE"

Rufus King, the last Federalist presidential candidate, suffered from other disadvantages in the 1816 campaign than his somewhat laughable name. His party was in a steep decline, and its machinery was no match for that of the Republicans, whose candidate, James Monroe, won easily. Monroe, like Madison before him, was the handpicked successor of the incumbent president.

Monroe was generally a strong, confident president, though weakened by disputes within his party. He was not the brightest of men but he was surrounded by a competent cabinet. He faced various crises: a banking collapse, an assertive Marshall Supreme Court, and the continuing slavery debate, which would be "resolved" by the Missouri Compromise in 1820. In terms of foreign policy, however, the key concern of the United States continued to be territorial disputes on its own continent and the affairs of Central and South American countries. Cuba played a prominent role in these debates. The revolt of the Spanish American colonies, meanwhile, proceeded, though it did not yet include Cuba, whose fidelity earned it the nickname of the "Ever Faithful Isle." The disarray in the Spanish government had ruptured the foundations of her strong American policy.

In the United States, sentiment continued to run strong for revolutionary movements. Some favored actual intervention, others merely financial or diplomatic support. Thomas Jefferson and many members of Congress endorsed the idea of an inter-America alliance comprising the United States and the newly independent Spanish colonies. While President Monroe merely sent several officials to investigate the situation, his claim of neutrality was called into question by repeated expeditions in support of the revolutionaries from U.S. shores. The British, whose own diplomacy in the region moved at a snail's pace, would later describe the U.S. position toward Latin American independence as "Yankee ultra-liberalism."[60]

The collapse of the Spanish colonial system opened up further opportunities for U.S. expansion, most notably in Texas. Trade restrictions were somewhat relaxed and led to growing trade with Cuba by 1820. British officials were worried by increasing American prosperity at Spain's expense, and in 1820 discussed occupying Cuba as a response to the U.S. acquisition of Florida. The London *Morning Chronicle* and the *Times* both called for such an invasion.[61] On the diplomatic level, the British began a decades-long drive to obtain a non-intervention treaty for Cuba involving themselves, the Americans, and the French. The Monroe administration, however, would not cooperate; it felt that the natural course of events would lead to an annexation of Cuba, and did not want to sign a treaty that might interrupt that process. This reluctance made U.S. policy clear; the Monroe administration was willing to warn European powers off intervention in Cuban affairs, but wished to retain the right to intervene as it saw fit.

At about the same time, under pressure from England and other countries, the Spanish Cortes (its legislative assembly) considered abolishing slavery in the colonies, but rejected this as impractical. The effect of this process was to cause Cuban planters increasingly to look to the United States for salvation, in the form of annexation, from this abolitionist trend. Slave revolts in Haiti and Jamaica had fed the fear that slavery was a dying institution, and the Cubans felt that attaching themselves to the South was one way to prolong its life. Cuban planters, moveover, could look forward to an end to U.S. tariffs on their sugar, should they become part of the Union.[62] The drive for annexation thus grew significantly during the period.

The U.S. government continued to investigate these sentiments. Early in 1822, the American commerce agent in Havana, John Warner, wrote that "two-thirds to three-fourths" of white Cubans supported annexation "as a state."[63] From this and other reports, the American government and some private citizens as well made exaggerated conclusions about the viability of annexation. In September, Cuban annexationists sent an official agent under the pseudonym of "Mr. Sanchez" to Washington to plead their case. He offered possession of Cuba if the United States would intervene and strip the island from Spanish possession. President Monroe, interested but wary, called a cabinet meeting to discuss the letter. John Quincy Adams recorded the resulting discussion:

> The question was discussed what was to be done. Mr. Calhoun has a most ardent desire that the island of Cuba should become part of the United States, and says that Mr. Jefferson has the same. There are two dangers to be averted by the event: one, that the island should fall into the hands of Great Britain; the other, that it should be revolutionized by the Negroes. Calhoun says Mr. Jefferson told him two years ago that we ought, at the first possible opportunity to take Cuba, though at a cost of war with England; but as we are now

not prepared for this, and as our great object must be to gain time, he thought we should answer this overture by dissuading them from their present purpose, and urging them to adhere at present to their connection with Spain.[64]

U.S. policy, in short, would remain publicly restrained.

Some Cubans, though, were definitely ready to revolt; one U.S. diplomat said at the time that "if any nation would come forward and offer the protection, with a competent naval force, the island would be declared independent in a month or less." It was the American fear that the nation might be England. Guided by the desire to avoid war with England, Monroe gave a polite public "no" to Sanchez; but he secretly sent an agent to Cuba to investigate the real chances a revolt with have of succeeding.[65]

British Foreign Minister George Canning was himself concerned about U.S. designs on Cuba. Hearing of Monroe's continuing interest in fomenting a revolution, he warned the British cabinet that American acquisition of Cuba would be disastrous to British Caribbean interests, and he persuaded them to send a naval force to the area to forestall such a development. The United States, which as we have seen was unwilling to risk war with England, had no such immediate plans for intervention, but the British naval force worried them. It was a classic misunderstanding: both sides sent forces to the region to respond to the other side's deployments, and both interpreted these defensive reactions as offensive moves. The American government warned the British not to intervene in Cuba, citing national interests of the highest degree.

President Monroe outlined these interests in a letter to Jefferson in June 1823. Arguing that the Cubans wanted annexation, he wrote:

> I have always concurr'd with you in sentiment, that too much importance could not be attached to that Island, and that we ought, if possible, to incorporate it into our Union. . . .The acquisition of it to our Union, was of the highest importance to our internal tranquility, as well as our prosperity and aggrandizement.[66]

Jefferson himself emphasized the importance of Cuba when he admitted that it "alone seems at present to hold up a speck of war to us. Its possession by Great Britain would indeed be a great calamity to us."[67]

By 1822, the United States had recognized the other independence movements in former Spanish American colonies, though its support for them was still lukewarm. In 1823, perhaps encouraged by these murmurs of pro-revolutionary sentiment, more Cuban revolutionary and annexationist groups appealed to the U.S. government for help. The Cubans said that, for the time being, they were satisfied, but should Spain redouble its efforts to repress the island and monopolize its commerce, the Cubans would have no choice but to seek an exit from the Spanish empire. At that point, Cuban representatives in Washington claimed, they would apply first to the United States for annexation, and if refused would apply to Great Britain. Sentiment grew once again in America for the recognition and support of the Cuban insurrectionists who remained strange bedfellows: slaveowners, businessmen, and freedom fighters. In March, 1823 some in the Cabinet were pressuring Monroe to support the groups, but Adams put a damper on this feeling, believing that the Cuban revolutionaries were as yet far too weak to undertake even a moderately successful revolution.[68] The Monroe government still saw annexation as the long-term goal, though, and maintained as a top priority the exclusion of European influence.

The Monroe Doctrine

In the period from 1818 to 1823, continuing Spanish domestic instability had kept U.S. Caribbean policy *ad hoc*. By 1822 the lack of Spanish action forced the Monroe administration to recognize the independence of the Spanish colonies in the New World; in 1823 France invaded Spain once again and put the conservative King Ferdinand back on the throne. Ferdinand was dedicated to the preservation of the Spanish empire and to rejection of reform in the colonies.[69] Thus Monroe was forced to rethink his Cuban policy, as the threat of British or French intervention in Cuba had been magnified. Sentiment in the Cabinet and in Congress ran to support for Cuban annexationists, perhaps immediate intervention, and to war with England if necessary. Continuing doubts over the true strength of the rebels led the government to send Thomas Randall to Cuba, to reiterate the U.S. position that Cuba should remain Spanish and to investigate the nature of the revolution.

Secretary of State John Quincy Adams soon spelled out U.S. policy in a reiteration of Madison's position and a precursor of the Monroe Doctrine. The policy was known to Cubans as ''la fruta matura'' (''the ripe fruit'') because it essentially committed the United States to preserving Cuba on the Spanish vine until, like a ripe fruit, it fell into the American lap.[70]

In 1823 Great Britain tried again to obtain a treaty providing for regional nonintervention by itself, the United States, and whatever other parties it could persuade. This enterprise seems to have been directed more at enlisting the U.S. government in a diplomatic agreement demonstrating British leadership with regard to other European powers, than at stopping U.S. encroachment in the region.[71] Monroe, however, seeing little imminent risk of either Cuba or Texas annexing themselves to Great Britain, saw no need for such a treaty. Once again, he wanted to preserve what he felt would be the natural course of events, which would culminate in the incorporation of Cuba into the Union.

At the same time, however, Monroe wanted to make sure that Britain, and any other European power which might covet Cuba, Texas, or any newly independent American nations, understood that the United States would not tolerate European intervention in the hemisphere. He was also influenced by Adams's suggestion to establish this principle unilaterally rather than to follow "as a cock-boat in the wake of the British man-o-war."[72] These desires led to the enunciation of the famous Monroe Doctrine in the president's 1823 annual message; because Europe was not directly involved in North or South American affairs, he argued, it should stay clear of them. Regarding the independence of the former Spanish colonies (which, recall, the United States had done little if anything to support), Monroe said, "we could not view any interposition for the purpose of oppressing them. . . . by any European power in any other light than as the manifestation of an unfriendly disposition toward the United States."[73] To a large degree, then, the Monroe Doctrine was merely a reiteration of what had been official U.S. policy for some time. (It is perhaps surprising that this famous doctrine, the basis of so much later U.S. policy—and so much debate and interpretation—originated as a few small sentences in the annual message of a president.)

The Doctrine was received with predictable ire in Europe.[74] Spain made a half-hearted attempt to rally European support for a rejection of the Doctrine but failed, due primarily to waning European interest in the New World. France and Britain in any case already supported Latin American independence. The Spanish media depicted the United States as a brazen youth, stealing the territorial possessions of a legitimate authority; there was some fear of an American invasion of Cuba.

Latin American nations resented the new doctrine, perceiving it as a justification for American interference in their internal affairs, and indeed it would be used for this purpose on many occasions. Latin American leaders also felt that their ability to cultivate good European relations had been compromised.[75]

Monroe wanted to increase U.S. influence and commerce in Latin America without going to war with any European powers, and the Doctrine allowed him to pursue both goals. But as with all U.S. governments, the Monroe administration was also strongly influenced by domestic political considerations, and Ernest R. May has emphasized these in his study of the formulation of the Doctrine. Monroe wanted his administration, May notes, to be respected by others in his party, and he did not want his successor to trump him by creating something like the Doctrine. Adams, Calhoun, and Clay each wanted to further their personal campaigns for the presidency, and smaller figures had their own motives. Monroe beat them to the punch by stating strongly the U.S. case for a virtual monopoly of influence in the region. "Foreign policy," May concludes, "can be determined less by the cleverness or wisdom of a few policymakers than by the political structure which determines their incentives." In short, May believes that the Monroe Doctrine "may be said to have epitomized the foreign policy of a democracy."[76]

The Doctrine has had a continuing effect on U.S.-Latin American diplomacy. One analyst has called it the "sheet-anchor of American foreign and defense policy," and the quotes at the beginning of the chapter give some indication as to its hallowed place among American diplomatic pronouncements.[77] Especially in the decades immediately following its formulation, it was used as a justification for all manner of interference in Latin American affairs. Even at the end of the 1980s, more than 160 years after the Doctrine's explication, some American policy-makers called for its reassertion in the face of growing Soviet influence in the Caribbean.

The Monroe Administration ended with a few more desultory suggestions for invasions or blockades of Cuba. Pirates operating from the island were a constant nuisance to U.S. shipping, and some suggested a blockade or a landing to punish the privateers, but no agreement was reached and the president was left to work the matter out with the Spanish. Spain gradually became somewhat more amicable, but as a result of U.S. support for the independence of its colonies had still not recognized U.S. consuls.[78] Cuba was ruled by a military government with repressive powers, and continued to languish in the decaying slave empire of Spain. But the Spanish colonial system was soon to be rocked with the ultimate denouement of the revolutions in its colonies: the virtually complete annihilation of Spanish power in the Americas, brought about by a liberation army led by Simon Bolivar.

REFORM AND RADICALISM IN CUBA

Bolivar's success was in part the result of a growing Latin American sense of nationalism. Tired of Spain's repressive rule and desiring independence, many nations in the hemisphere would overthrow their Spanish colonial administrations and achieve self-determination.

Throughout the seventeenth and eighteenth centuries, economic, political, and intellectual trends in the Caribbean began to establish the context for later rebellions against outside influence and colonialism. Twentieth century revolutions in Cuba did not occur spontaneously; in many ways they issued from a long tradition of radicalism and revolt, itself a product of a history of Caribbean thought that promoted regional independence and collective economic solutions to poverty and underdevelopment.

The polyglot nations of the Caribbean suffered from domestic social stratification and ingrained inequalities, based primarily on race. In part because of this, as Gordon Lewis has recognized, it was impossible for any of the countries, including Cuba, to develop any real sense of community or shared values. It was impossible "for such a society to develop into a genuine community, with common interests binding all of its members into a coherent civic whole."[79] As a result, Cuban society remained fragmented well into the twentieth century, and hence, when faced with revolutionary threats, mounted only *ad hoc* defenses of the existing social order.

Colonial race bias also left in its wake feelings of insecurity, inferiority, and dependency that would plague Caribbean societies for two centuries. Without a strong, generally-held set of national or cultural values, the ex-slave societies would find the path to independence a difficult one.

Without necessarily relying on Marxist analysis, moreover, it is possible to argue that the Caribbean was a region constantly exploited by colonial powers for economic benefit. The natural resources of the islands (especially, of course, sugar), which in the absence of outside interference would have allowed Caribbean countries to achieve enormously high standards of living, were instead exploited by distant imperial powers. Local economic conditions were not often desperate, but uniformly far worse than they might have been without European involvement. And the slave culture, of course, also served to imprison hundreds of thousands of people in horrible economic conditions from which they had no real hope of escape. The "common experience of suffering and oppression," Gordon Lewis concludes, "gave birth to a common experience of resistance"—against colonial influence of any sort, including the later U.S. meddling in Cuban affairs.[80]

Such resistance originated in the resentment felt by colonial officials and intellectuals against the mother country, resentment fed by the sort of inferiority complex mentioned above. Proper administrative officials and army officers remained loyal to their respective crowns, but after a time even they began to favor local interests over colonial ones. Lewis notes that

> there is a general principle involved in all of this that is well known to
> all students of colonialism. The Creole settler, or the 'old hand,'
> feels an instinctive jealousy of the bureaucratic official; the soldier
> on the spot resents what he regards as the purely academic ideas of
> the 'office wallah' at home; the resident official. . .identifies himself
> with an oppressed subject-people as against the officials of the
> home office who seek merely to enforce policies based on general
> theories of how 'natives' should be treated.[81]

Of course, the same process was at work in the British colonies in North America, and their eventual rebellion against the crown established a precedent for later Caribbean revolutions.

The intellectual tradition of the whole of Latin America and the Caribbean also began to be formed during this time, and it was a tradition rich in respect for liberty, independence, and the value of every human being. As against colonial values of profit, social order, and control, thinkers in the New World posited values of human dignity, progressivism, and independence. Many Caribbean intellectuals were strongly influenced by classical liberalism, but many, reacting against European capitalism, were also drawn already to the radical, indeed socialistic, ideas of such Utopians as More. Many stressed collective, social-planning solutions to problems of poverty and underdevelopment.

These ideas were influential in late-eighteenth and nineteenth-century Cuba. Individual Cuban thinkers, like Felix Varela y Morales and Jose Augustin Caballero, stressed values of freedom, independence, and economic equality. Organizations promoting independence, such as the Economic Society of the Friends and the Sun and Rays of Bolivar, sprang up, as did a nascent labor movement. In 1829 the Society of Sailors and Fisherman was founded, inaugurating what would become a large and powerful labor movement in Cuba.[82]

For a time, discussion and acceptance of these ideas was limited to a few intellectuals. But the Cuban intelligentsia, including crucially the university community, would later serve as the core of several rebellions against Spanish and American authority. Over time, moreover, the general themes of freedom, independence, and human dignity would become popularized to some degree. Even in 1800, the seeds of Castro's revolution were being sown.

2

MANIFEST DESTINY AND FILIBUSTERS

Relations to the American Civil War

"It is our manifest destiny to lead and rule all nations."
James Gordon Bennett

"Any people anywhere, being inclined and having the power, have the
right to rise up, and shake off their existing government, and form a new
one that suits them better. This is a most valuable, a most sacred right—a
right, which we hope and believe, is to liberate the world."
Abraham Lincoln

"If Cuba pass from [Spain], it shall not pass into any other hands but
ours. . . because it is indispensable to the safety of the United States that
this island should not be in certain hands."
John C. Calhoun

American diplomacy of the mid-nineteenth century
shed the defensiveness of the Monroe Doctrine in favor of an expansionist
policy of land acquisition and broadening regional influence. Guided by the
advent of the notion of Manifest Destiny in the 1840s, the United States would
engage in a war with Mexico and risk conflicts with European powers over
Cuba and other hemispheric interests. From the United States would sail the
filibusters, groups of adventurers with a mixed bag of goals, many of whom

set their sights on Cuba. But the young nation was not prepared to risk war with the Old World, and its own internal problems were driving it toward a Civil War that would distract all attention from foreign adventures. Until that time, however, those who advocated the acquisition of Cuba held the upper hand.

THE ADAMS ADMINISTRATION AND BOLIVAR'S WAR FOR INDEPENDENCE

John Quincy Adams came to the presidency in 1824 amid a huge electoral dispute: though Andrew Jackson had received the most popular votes and electoral votes of any candidate, neither he nor Adams held a strict majority of electoral votes. The election was therefore decided in the House, where Henry Clay held the deciding votes. Fearful of his Western rival Jackson, Clay cast his votes for Adams.

Adams himself was an unfriendly, rude, arrogant man. He named Clay to the position of Secretary of State in a deal for Clay's support that became known as the "Corrupt Bargain." Adams's unpopularity, combined with the general feeling that the election had been "robbed", rendered his presidency ineffectual. Andrew Jackson resigned his senate seat to begin a four-year campaign to bring the presidency back "to the people," and from the start Adams was perceived as a lame-duck president.

By 1825, meanwhile, Latin America's battle against Spanish colonialism was in full swing, led by a legendary hero of the fight for freedom: Simon Bolivar. Daniel O'Leary, a friend and compatriot of Bolivar, described him as the "standard of South American independence." Bolivar was born of Spanish parents in Venezuela in 1783, and grew into an athletic, impish youth with a quick mind but not much discipline to apply it. In 1797 he received a commission as a Spanish militia officer but by 1799 he went to study in Europe. As the son of well-to-do parents, he traveled Europe in some style, and was invited to Napoleon's coronation, among other events.[1]

By 1802 Bolivar was back in Venezuela, where a revolution against Spanish rule began in 1810. Bolivar was given the rank of colonel and sent to England as a diplomatic envoy. Returning to Venezuela, he took part in several battles, and the rebel forces eventually secured independence from Spain. Bolivar had by now become completely committed to the cause of Latin American independence, and became involved in the region-wide fight against Spanish rule.[2]

Those in Cuba who desired true independence appealed to Bolivar for his assistance. Would he not free them also from the Spanish yoke? Bolivar was interested but as of 1823 he felt his forces were insufficient for an invasion of the island. He wanted to persuade the Spanish to leave by threat of invasion; failing that, he admitted that an intervention might eventually be necessary. In 1824, he asked Vice President Santander of Colombia if "anything can be done against Cuba,"[3] but as yet the answer was still no. In 1825, several of his generals pressed for an invasion, and Santa Maria offered 6,000 Mexican troops for the task. President Victoria of Mexico allowed exiled Cubans to establish the Junta for the Promotion of Cuban Liberty, and to begin forming military cadres with Cuban and Mexican volunteers. Victoria notified Santander of his desire to unite with Colombian forces and force a resolution of the Cuban issue. But Bolivar, aware of the risks of overextending his young armies, argued that "it would not be to our advantage. . . [to] attempt to liberate Havana."[4]

During these years, and especially in 1825 as the Mexican and Colombian pressure for an invasion of Cuba increased, the United States tried to discourage adventures on Bolivar's part. This U.S. caution was dictated by a consideration that would crucially affect its Cuba policy before the Civil War: fear of the controversial nature of Cuban slavery. If the United States were to intervene, it would have to decide whether to retain slavery, and if so in what form; the decision would no doubt be hotly contested. Southern states favored annexing Cuba as slave territory, while Northern states desired an abolitionist Cuba. It was feared that carefully worked-out compromises between North and South would founder on the rocks of Cuban annexation.

In order to slow Bolivar's campaign, the United States urged Spain to recognize the independent colonies—eventually including Argentina, Chile, Ecuador, Venezuela, Mexico, Colombia, Peru, and Bolivia—and appealed to friendly European governments for help in persuading the Spanish of this requirement. Spain refused, and Britain as a counter-proposal brought up its old U.S.-British-French non-intervention treaty, which Adams rejected for the same reasons articulated by his predecessors: he wanted to keep U.S. options open, and the Monroe Doctrine had already indicated a desire to bar European involvement while promoting that of the United States. Besides, such a pact would not address the greatest imminent threat of intervention, which lay in Bolivar's forces in Mexico and Colombia.

This final U.S. rejection of a non-intervention pledge settled for Simon Bolivar the issue of U.S. intentions. He was dissuaded from serious consideration of an invasion of Cuba by U.S. and British warnings to avoid such a course, and the American government seemed dedicated to the acquisition, not the independence, of Cuba. American goals were again tested by Mexican President Victoria, who did not believe, or did not want to believe, that the United States opposed Cuban independence. When informed that America feared a Mexican invasion, Victoria promised that he would not launch such an operation, and would put that pledge in writing if the United States would support independence; U.S. Minister Pointsett rejected the proposal, again demonstrating U.S. resolve to keep the possibility of annexation open. Meanwhile, the United States sent agents to the Panama Conference, a meeting of representatives from regional governments including many newly independent countries; the U.S. delegates, however, arrived too late to participate, and when they did get there they gave the departing delegates the impression that the American government was opposed to Cuban independence.[5]

The reputation of the United States as an advocate of freedom and self-determination had been seriously damaged. Cuban historian Evelio Rodriguez Lendian concluded, in a way that mirrored the perception of many in Latin America at the time, that the United States "frustrated" the independence of Cuba: "had not the United States intervened," he writes, "the liberating forces of Colombia and Mexico would have established Cuba as an independent nation." In short by 1826 the United States had become, in British Foreign Minister George Canning's words, an "object of suspicion" in Latin America.[6]

U.S. policy had thus changed little since the early years of the century; it was still "to let Spain keep the island until the United States could get in, without risk of losing it,"[7] while attempting to avoid war with Britain in the process. At the same time, some in Congress raised the old annexation flag, and discussed, in lieu of such an expedition, a plan to build a canal across Florida to provide an alternate waterway should Cuba be occupied by a hostile power. Cuban exiles in Mexico and Colombia, meanwhile, were plotting a revolution in Cuba, and by now had begun seriously considering asking the British, rather than the Americans, to be their protectors. The conservatism and acquisitiveness manifest in U.S. policy had already begun to work against it.

British leaders, however, still balked at the idea of an invasion. Through 1825 and 1826 they maintained their offers of a multilateral non-intervention treaty. In December 1826 U.S. Minister Gallatin wrote Clay from England to say that while "reports of an intention on the part of this government to attack Cuba are still in circulation," they were more indicative "of popular feeling than of the views of the ministry." But no U.S. action was forthcoming.[8] The Adams administration thus closed with a whimper: it had succeeded in alienating many Latin American countries, and had accomplished nothing toward either the independence or the annexation of Cuba.

CALM BEFORE THE STORM: THE JACKSON, VAN BUREN, AND HARRISON/TYLER ADMINISTRATIONS

For the next fifteen years, American policy toward Cuba lay in a fallow state. The Monroe Doctrine continued to dictate most U.S. decisions, and the four presidents who served during the period made few initiatives in Cuban policy. The relative quiet of this first portion of the century, however, was to be lost in the explosion of expansionist sentiment during the Polk administration.

Andrew Jackson's four-year campaign to return the presidency to the people and to oust the "Judas of the West," Adams, came to fruition in the 1828 election, a resounding success for Jackson. He would come to be known as the "people's president," a man of humble origins unlike the aristocrats who had so far occupied the White House.

At once Jackson was faced with a difficult situation in Latin America. Mexico and Colombia continued to stir rebellion in Cuba, sending a mission to Haiti to help in this purpose. They continued supporting Cuban expatriates, and considered an invasion. A primary method to incite rebellion was the use of slave resentment, a form of revolution which played into the fears of Spaniards and U.S. slaveowners.

Neither Spain nor the United States felt it could tolerate such a rebellion. Cuban landowners, terrified at the prospect of a general revolution that might loose the fury of their slaves against them, in 1829 asked Spain to invade Mexico and pacify the revolutionary movement at its source, but by then Spain was far too weak to contemplate such adventures. Spain actually pulled back further from its colonies, accepting the *de facto* independence of those which had revolted already while still refusing to recognize them officially.

U.S. officials were caught in something of a bind; they wished to recognize the independence of the Latin American states, but for the time being saw continued Spanish rule in Cuba as beneficial. Yet how could the United States endorse colonialism in one area and oppose it in others? The revolts in Latin America also posed difficult questions for America in relation to the slave issue. Jackson decided simply to accept the contradiction and support Spanish rule in Cuba, while demanding in return more favorable trade agreements (though the Spanish did not live up to their part of the bargain). U.S. Secretary of State Van Buren ordered a careful study of the situation in Cuba, and concluded that the United States should not interfere with Mexican and Colombian actions unless they fomented a slave revolt, which was unacceptable to the American government.[9]

By 1833, with Texas added to the insurrectionary colonies and the United

States pressing for a settlement of that territory, Spain finally gave in and recognized the independent South American states. It also negotiated the transfer of Texas to the United States. By 1836, Jackson could claim favorable relations with Spain, except for the outstanding trade disputes. The ascension to power in Spain of King Ferdinand's widow in the aftermath of the Carlist wars, however, guaranteed a continuation of Spain's essentially conservative colonial policy.

Martin Van Buren had emerged as a skillful politician during the Jackson presidency, helping Jackson resolve the Eaton scandal and other domestic affairs. Eventually Van Buren become Jackson's appointed successor, and won election in 1836.

The annexationist cause had by now come truly into its own. There were supporters of union between Cuba and the United States in both countries. Some were Cuban patriots who, outraged at the despotic rule of Spanish captain generals, hoped that annexation would lead to reforms and eventual independence. Other annexationists, as we have seen, were guided by more sinister motivations, seeking to protect Cuban slavery; the beginnings of slave insurrections in the early 1840s intensified these fears. Some businessmen desired the broadened trade that annexation would bring.

A number of influential voices were raised against these arguments. Many slaveowners contended that once the revolutionary process was begun, it would become uncontrollable; there was no way to guarantee a regulated revolt which would remain under wealthy landowner leadership. Once Spanish rule was expelled, there was nothing to prevent the slaves from fighting for their freedom. These arguments, of course, did not influence those Cubans seeking true independence, but the numbers of such individuals were still small and their influence weak compared to the land barons.

The issue was decided, at least for a time, in 1849. In that year the Spanish captain general allowed a fake communication to leak in which he reported to his superiors that he would free the slaves at the first sign of a successful revolution. With the object of their fears so cleverly guaranteed, Cuban slaveowners turned away from revolution as an immediate mechanism to bring about annexation.[10]

British policy was still committed to the promotion of instability in Cuba. Dedicated to world-wide abolition as well as the pursuit of its own geostrategic interests, the British government felt that an abolitionist revolution in Cuba might well spin the island into her orbit. Some in England cautioned that such an enterprise would prove costly, as Britain might have to compensate slaveowners who had been deprived of their "possessions" and livelihood, and this dampened enthusiasm somewhat. But, like the United States— though to a lesser degree and with an opposite object (abolition)—the British sought ways to make Cuba their own. British interest in Cuba intensified during the Harrison and Tyler years, 1840-45. In 1840 the British consul in Havana, David Turnbull, was accused of intriguing with revolutionaries, and after an investigation the American government reiterated its refusal to tolerate British influence in the island.

At the same time, a rapid succession of changes of government in Spain made consistent diplomacy difficult. In 1841 Espartero was made regent, but others who coveted his position immediately began to plot against him. Rapid changes in the Spanish cabinet led Washington Irving, a U.S. representative there, to remark that "to carry on negotiations with such transient functionaries is like bargaining at the window of a railroad car—before you can get a reply to a proposition, the other party is out of sight."[11]

Spain carried a huge debt to American banks, and often had trouble making the interest payments alone. The Spanish loss of empire had coincided with, and contributed to, economic ruin at home. The United States would eventually use this debt as a lever to attempt to force a Spanish sale of Cuba, but for the time being, since most of what hard currency Spain earned came from Cuban plantations, American banks had an interest in a stable and profitable Cuba. This formed another barrier to a favorable U.S. response to revolutionary movements on the island.

In January 1843, more rumors emerged of a planned British invasion of Cuba, which would come on the heels of a slave revolt. The United States reaffirmed the Monroe Doctrine and considered aiding Spain materially against British intervention. President Tyler claimed he would counterattack by invading Cuba if such steps were necessary to repel the British.

More rational heads, however, argued that such grandstanding was unnecessary, as Britain would probably not take drastic action. John Quincy Adams studied the issue closely and concluded that the English did not really intend to invade. Washington Irving recognized, too, that the Spanish were not likely to approve of British meddling; he wrote from Spain that he was satisfied that "from all that I can judge of the present tone of feeling of the actual cabinet and of the people at large, in respect to England, there is no danger of any views she may have in regard to the island of Cuba meeting with any encouragement [in Spain]."[12]

THE POLK ADMINISTRATION: ANNEXATIONISM INSTITUTIONALIZED

It was only a matter of time before the expanding, expansionist United States began to undertake more active measures to obtain Cuba, and latent desires and designs for annexation sprang to life in the Polk administration. Polk, his subordinates, and private American citizens tried virtually every trick, above-board and otherwise, to acquire the Island; the Polk administration was "filled with projects for the acquisition of Cuba, ranging from filibustering expeditions to proposals for a purchase of the island."[13] The U.S. minister to Spain, Pierre Soule, attempted to acquire the island "by purchase; by favor of the Spanish Court; by threat of war; by revolution in Spain; by favor of the Spanish democrats; by the republicanizing of Europe."[14] But all the plans would founder on the unwillingness of a dying empire to surrender the last shining jewel in her colonial crown.

The first serious governmental proposals for the annexation of Cuba came from Senator Yulee in 1845. Northern states were immediately wary of such plans because they suggested the incorporation of a new slave territory, but some in Congress and a few representatives of the Polk administration persisted. In 1845 Vice President Dallas spoke of the necessary "annexation of Cuba," and that same year Congress resolved that the United States should attempt to buy the island. Polk, still worried about the implications of Cuban slavery, balked for a time, though he would later approve attempts to purchase Cuba.

O'Sullivan and Beach: Early Annexationists

Attempts to arrange annexation directed by individuals outside the government also proliferated up to the time of the U.S. Civil War. By 1847 the most prominent U.S. private citizens to support, seriously and openly the annexationist cause had begun working toward that end. These citizens were John L. O'Sullivan and Moses Yale Beach.

O'Sullivan was the author of the phrase "Manifest Destiny" and was one of its strongest proponents. A believer in the superiority of the Anglo-Saxon race and all it meant for policy, O'Sullivan became a champion of Southern expansionism and a defender of slavery.[15] In the late 1840s, O'Sullivan's main concern was the promotion of Cuban annexation.

Moses Yale Beach was an old hand at fomenting anti-Spanish revolutions. In 1847 he went to Mexico, financing and promoting a clerical revolt in Mexico City to divert attention from General Scott's Vera Cruz landing. Also an ardent advocate of American expansion, Beach was persuaded by Cubans that an expedition against Cuba was worthwhile.

O'Sullivan and Beach were both newspaper owners, and they used their wealth and position to support the annexationist cause. They offered $100 million toward a plan for the purchase of Cuba, and allowed their printing presses to be used by Cuban exiles who supported annexation. Powerful men, they used their connections and prestige to good effect.[16]

O'Sullivan and Beach reopened the annexationist issue in their papers, though the reaction was not immediately favorable. Most of the Eastern press "responded with ridicule and apathy,"[17] feeling that the issue was dead and its slave implications far too controversial. Eventually, realizing Northern support would not be forthcoming, the two abandoned any hope of acquiring aid from that quarter and restated their argument in a way more likely to gain the full support of the South; they admitted their pro-slavery intentions and made protection of Cuban slaveowners a positive part of their proposal.

U.S. Purchase Attempts Continue

In early 1848 the negotiations for the U.S. purchase of Texas came to fruition in the Trist treaty. Advocates of Manifest Destiny were happy, but not overjoyed; they felt that the treaty provided for the acquisition of an insufficient amount of territory, and argued that the United States should look elsewhere for new objects of annexation. O'Sullivan, naturally, chose Cuba, and he pressured Buchanan to influence the government to invade or purchase the island. Polk, however, was not close to Buchanan, whose own presidential aspirations were well known, and the latter's advice meant little. Buchanan, for his part, wanted to reserve the great moment of the acquisition of Cuba for his own presidency.

In May 1848, Senator Lewis Cass, a longtime advocate of annexation, renewed purchase proposals in Congress. On May 10, the same day Cass introduced these bills, O'Sullivan went directly to President Polk to appeal for the annexationist cause; Polk later wrote that while he (Polk) "express[ed] no opinion" he was "decidedly in favor" of buying Cuba. On May 22, Cass was nominated to the presidency by the Democrats, and with the Northern abolitionists thus defeated, Polk saw that he had little to lose politically from purchasing Cuba. On May 30 he proposed this course to his Cabinet, a plan some Cabinet members endorsed. Buchanan begged caution, reminding Polk of the potential election problems stemming from the slavery issue and risks of war with Britain and France; his real motive was to put off the purchase until he himself could accomplish it as president.[18]

Polk overrode Buchanan's objections, however, and by June, Romulus M. Saunders, the U.S. minister to Spain, was informed that the Polk administration desired to purchase Cuba. Saunders replied that he did not feel the weak Spanish government could withstand such a sale; Spanish public opinion, in the words of the Spanish minister of state, "would prefer to see [Cuba] sunk in the ocean" than transferred to any other power. In July, nevertheless, Buchanan authorized Saunders to offer up to $100 million for the island.[19]

Meanwhile, events in Cuba supported U.S. desires to purchase the island.

In May 1846 Narciso Lopez, an adventurous Cuban of whom we will learn more later, organized a revolt in Cuba for June 29, 1848, after which he planned to request annexation, though whether Lopez's eventual goal was incorporation or independence is a matter of dispute. At about the same time, the Havana Club, composed of wealthy Cuban landowners most of whom wanted annexation to protect their slave systems, offered General William Jenkins Worth and 5,000 U.S. veterans of the Mexican war some $3 million to invade Cuba. The Club's goal was unquestionably incorporation into the South. Lopez, persuaded by the Havana Club to await Worth's arrival, set the date of his revolution back to July.

Some in the U.S. government, however, viewed these developments with trepidation. Though O'Sullivan and some others proposed an intervention to aid Lopez and his group, the Southern-oriented Polk administration feared that even a controlled revolution in Cuba could easily lead to a slave uprising, which would have disturbing implications for the United States. The administration therefore ordered General Butler to stop Worth, who was quickly transferred away from Mexico, and warned the Cuban annexationists that a failed revolution would do much damage to long-term annexation progress. Buchanan, to prove his good intentions to Spain, betrayed Lopez's plans to the Spanish minister in Washington, and Lopez barely escaped. Some of his co-conspirators were not so lucky. They were captured, tried, and killed.

The summer of 1848 saw repeated and futile U.S. attempts to convince Spain to sell Cuba. Spain remained adamant regarding such a sale. "No [Spanish] government could exist," it declared, "that should be capable of taking into consideration the transfer of the island of Cuba." When in October the word of purchase negotiations leaked in Spain, the Spanish people were furious that their government would even be in the process of discussing the subject. U.S. Minister Saunders rejected that the Spanish people "regard Cuba as their most precious gem" and that only "extreme necessity" would cause them to part with it.[20]

Motives for U.S. Expansionism

A number of sociological and political factors contributed to the explosion of expansionist sentiment during the Polk administration. Southern slave-owners were concerned about the repercussions of an abolitionist Cuba on their own system, and wanted to annex the island to prevent such a development. American businessmen also had an interest in any policy which would serve to eliminate the high Spanish tariffs, and incorporation into the Union would certainly accomplish that.

The American government saw immense strategic value in Cuba, a value that had been emphasized since Jefferson's time. In May 1848 John C. Calhoun made a speech in which he disparaged the role of Mexico, but concerning Cuba he argued:

> There are cases of interposition where I would resort to the hazard of war with all its calamities. Am I asked for one? I will answer. I designate the case of Cuba. So long as Cuba remains in the hands of Spain . . . [U.S. policy should be] to let Cuba remain there . . . [and] if Cuba pass from her, it shall not pass into any other hands but ours; this not from a feeling of ambition, not from a desire for the extension of dominion, but because that island is indispensable to the safety of the United States; or rather, because it is indispensable to the safety of the United States that this island should not be in certain hands.[21]

Calhoun thus re-stated the traditional American "no transfer" policy.

Psychologically, however, the most potent force guiding American acquisition efforts around the turn of the century was Manifest Destiny: the very desire "for the extension of dominion." The doctrine held that the Anglo-American race was naturally superior and destined to conquer all of North America, and eventually probably the world as well. The acquisition of Texas and the Mexican War of 1846-1848 fostered the growth of this expansionist sentiment, and Cuba soon became one of its focuses.[22]

Set against the strong desire for acquisition was an equally powerful set of arguments against the incorporation of Cuba. Some U.S. slaveowners shared the fear of Cuban landholders that a revolt would lead inevitably to slave rebellions and instability. Others argued that incorporation would pose insurmountable political problems for a nation that had only recently hammered out the Missouri Compromise to settle its slave disputes. Would Cuba be treated as a slave state or a free one? The debate could be expected to be acrimonious.

On the other side of the spectrum, political liberals argued that the expansionist adventurism of Manifest Destiny was exploitive, expensive in resources and men, and a break from the traditional Jeffersonian policy of neutrality. Abolitionists rejected the incorporation of a slaveowner-dominated Cuba. Some raised the continuing spectre of conflict with Spain, Britain, or France over the island. The expansionists generally dominated the debate, which would be re-created at the end of the century, when a "New" Manifest Destiny would exert its full influence on Cuba.

Continuing Negotiations

The Polk administration, however, was guided by the pro-annexation arguments, and its negotiations to purchase the island—and plans to foment insurrection in case those negotiations failed—continued. In October 1848 these schemes were broached to the world, possibly by deception. A secret envoy travelling under an assumed name approached Vice President Dallas and claimed to have been sent by Queen Isabella II of Spain with an offer to sell Cuba. Polk foolishly told Dallas to inform the person that negotiations were already underway, which the envoy surely would have known if he were truly a representative of the Spanish government. The messenger disappeared when asked for credentials of his position, and it is altogether possible that, whoever he was, he then leaked the existence of the ongoing negotiations. Once the Spanish public was informed of the proceedings, their continuing opposition to the sale of Cuba immediately became apparent.[23]

The November 1848 presidential election in the United States drove the last nail in the coffin of the Polk administration plans to purchase Cuba. Expecting a new and perhaps more accommodating administration, the Spanish saw little need to deal with Polk's agents. Congress remained slightly in favor of purchase, due to the influence of the slave states; in January 1849 a resolution of purchase passed 23 to 19 in the Senate, with 21 Democrats and 16 slave states supporting Polk.[24] (Polk's negotiations were still secret, but Congress, guessing correctly at his intentions, supported the undeclared policy in any case.) But continuing Spanish intransigence prevented the consummation of a sale.

THE TAYLOR AND FILLMORE ADMINISTRATIONS

The Mississippi slaveowner and hero of the Battle of Buena Vista Zachary Taylor was brought to the White House in 1848 by a split within the Democratic party engineered by the "Free Soilers" and Van Buren. Free Soil Democrats joined with liberal Whigs and abolitionists to form the Free Soil Party. This split diluted Democratic strength enough to allow the Whig Taylor to win. Taylor's support lay heavily with Southern Democrats, but by 1850 he became disillusioned with expansionism, especially that motivated by desires of slaveowners. His sudden death in 1850 brought Millard Fillmore to power.

Taylor-Fillmore policies regarding Cuba were a withdrawal from the aggressive Polk diplomacy, and created a diplomatic lull before the advent of the Pierce administration and another series of annexation attempts. Taylor and Fillmore awaited Spanish proposals to sell Cuba, which, given the Spanish attitude, was destined to be a fruitless process. Meanwhile, they continued to reaffirm the Monroe Doctrine and its no-transfer rule. Fillmore would also continue to reject British and French plans for a multilateral declaration of intent to keep Cuba in Spain's hands.

The Taylor administration was thus mostly indifferent to Cuban annexation schemes. John Clayton, the Secretary of State, implemented this indifference using expansive rhetoric to appease the advocates of Manifest Destiny, while doing nothing. He was determined to repudiate the annexationist-purchase policy of Polk, Buchanan, and Saunders.[25]

In the summer of 1849 the administration sent Benjamin E. Green to investigate the situation in Cuba. He reported that revolutionary sentiment indeed existed on the island, and that rich Cuban slaveowners in particular financed insurrectionary activities they hoped would lead to annexation. Taylor, however, was not willing to risk a confrontation with Spain, and he declined to press the situation. In 1850, James Robb, a New Orleans banker, offered to finance a purchase attempt, but Taylor again refused. Meanwhile in May 1849 Clayton openly repudiated the Polk-Saunders policy in an attempt to cement ties with Spain; he pledged to recall Saunders, to leave Cuba to Spain, and to take actions to end the U.S.-Spanish tariff war.

For the first time, then, a U.S. administration had made at least a partial pledge of non-intervention in Cuban affairs, and the Taylor administration seemed determined to follow a hands-off policy. The issue would not lay dormant, however, and reemergent annexationist sentiment led the *New York Times* to conclude by October 1852 that "the Cuban question is now the leading one of the time."[26] Taylor's policy continued to equivocate; Cayton's instructions to the new U.S. minister to Spain, Daniel M. Bauringer, told him not to offer purchase and to make clear that any U.S. pledges to maintain Cuba in Spain's possession by force must end. "Whilst this government is resolutely determined that the island of Cuba shall never be ceded by Spain to any other power than the United States," Clayton wrote, "it does not desire, in future, to utter any threats, or enter into any guarantees, with Spain, on that subject."[27] Barringer's primary duty was to end the tariff wars.

Events were beginning to unfold in Cuba, however, which would make a shambles of the Taylor and Fillmore administrations' quiet policy. The most significant attempt yet at armed annexation was about to begin, led by a brave, determined, quixotic figure: Narciso Lopez.

The Lopez Expeditions and Cuban Society of the Time

Narciso Lopez was a Venezuelan-born Spanish general who lived in Cuba in the early 1840s. Lopez was one of the first "filibusters," who would attempt to invade or otherwise annex Cuba (and other countries or regions) to the United States. He was an imposing and impressive figure; a *Mobile Tribune* writer said that "his full dark eyes, firm, well-formed mouth, and erect head, crowned with iron grey hair, fix the attention and convince you that he is no ordinary man." An American who accompanied Lopez on his first expeditions agreed; Lopez, he wrote, "is a fine looking old gentleman, appears to be about 50 years of age, 5 feet 8 inches high, well set; to look at him, you would conclude at once, he is capable of enduring much hardship." That Lopez would seek support from the South was natural, as Lopez himself supported slavery; he wrote that

> Domestic slavery is not a primitive social phenomenon of Cuba
> alone, nor is it incompatible with the liberty of the citizen body.
> Ancient and modern history shows us that, and nearby you have the
> example of the United States, where three million slaves do not
> impede but rather reinforce the most liberal institutions of the
> world.[28]

Lopez received most of his military experience with the Spanish armies opposing Bolivar; later, as a military commissioner on Cuba, he proved himself a stern disciplinarian. After failing at several businesses, he determined to begin the revolutionary process that would eventually join Cuba to the United States. In this enterprise, his motives are the subject of dispute. Some see him as a true Cuban patriot who saw annexation as a precursor to independence, while others condemn him as a tool of American expansionism. Either way, he was an indefatigable warrior against Spanish influence, and his adventures inaugurated a period of annexationist sentiment that, in one form or another, would last the rest of the century.

As we have seen, Lopez's first plans to foment an insurrection in 1846 were uncovered, and he was forced to flee to Rhode Island. There, he attempted to enlist the aid of other Cuban-Americans and form filibustering parties to invade Cuba. He received some monetary support and began to form a force for invasion.

Local Cuban government of the period was organized around city councils (*Ayuntamientos*) and courts (*Audiencias*). Both branches of government, and the judiciary in particular, were corrupt, and briberies from merchants and landowners were rife. (Such corruption was a staple of the Spanish administrative government, and the tradition would be passed down to independent Cuban governments after 1900.) Cuba was denied political participation in the Spanish government itself, and this lack of rights extended to individual Cuban citizens, who were denied freedom of speech, assembly, movement, and the like by successive captains general.[29]

Cuban society, like the Spanish system after which it was in many ways modeled, was organized aristocratically, with 29 marquises and 30 counts at its head. Their power, in turn, rested mainly on ownership of the island's various agricultural productions, especially sugar. These industries in turn depended upon the slave trade. The population of the island was nearly one million, comprised of half a million whites, 150,000 free blacks, and some 300,000 slaves.

Cuban intellectuals continued to emphasize themes of freedom and independence, and the radicalization of political discussion in Cuba was reinforced. During the mid-nineteenth century, moreover, as open U.S. annexationism and covert filibustering expeditions threatened to replace one colonial government with another, the resentment and fear of foreign influence characteristic of the more progressive Cuban intelligentsia began to be transferred from Spain to the United States. The Cuban labor movement also expanded, as the poet Alfredo Torroella, the periodical *La Aurora*[1], and growing unions (such as the Tobacco Workers' Society of Havana, founded in 1866), pressed for workers' rights. [30]

To attack Cuba, Lopez attempted to enlist the services of Jefferson Davis, who was offered $200,000 to lead the expedition against Cuba; he rejected the offer, but suggested that Lopez contact an experienced and competent Army officer: Robert E. Lee. Lee was interested, but thinking it dishonorable to leave one's own army for that of a foreign nation—even a revolutionary government—he declined also. Lopez was undeterred; he felt the South would still support an invasion, so he decided to lead it himself, with the assistance of several American officers. He therefore gathered a group of soldiers-for-hire at Round Head, Louisiana, and began training for an invasion, promising $1,000 and 160 acres of liberated Cuban soil to each man who joined.

Lopez's supporters raised some $80,000, and with this money he bought supplies and obtained three steamships: the *Fanny*, the *Seagull*, and the *New Orleans*. Lopez promised his fundraisers that he would add "the star of Cuba to those which shine in the glorious flag of the American Union." His actions were beginning to brush up against the Neutrality Act of 1818, which forbade (and still forbids) attacks from American territory against countries with which the United States is at peace. Once Spanish agents got wind of Lopez's plans, they asked the Taylor administration to enforce its laws and disband his expeditionary force. Taylor did issue a strong proclamation forbidding such an attack, and he also sent warships to blockade Round Island.

The Taylor administration's objectives were relatively simple: to prevent a confrontation with Spain, and to avoid the severe sectional disputes in the United States that would result from a U.S. annexation of Cuba. Taylor had no particular quarrel with Lopez, but the latter had become caught in a vortex of domestic and international strife that severely hampered his efforts to seize Cuba.

Taylor nevertheless suffered heavy criticism from Democratic and Southern Whig papers for these actions, which ran counter to the spirit of expansionism so prevalent in the country. Cuban expatriates were divided and demoralized, unsure of what to do next; their efforts in future filibustering expeditions would be subordinate to those of American adventurers. *De Bow's Review*, for example, an expansionist Southern paper, summarized the popular feeling of the day, which considered the Lopez expeditions to be in the proper and honorable military/expansionist tradition then developing in the nation. Many thought that the United States had "a destiny to perform," the paper explained, "a 'manifest destiny' over all Mexico, over South America, over the West Indies and Canada....The gates of the Chinese empire must be thrown down by the men from the Sacramento and the Oregon." Japan and Europe would also fall, and "a successor of Washington [will] ascend the chair of universal empire!" These, *De Bow's* concluded, "are the giddy dreams of the day." (Surprisingly enough, *De Bow's* argued against this course of action, which it believed would only harden the Spanish against parting with Cuba, and which was not "honorable." The paper suggested conventional purchase schemes as a respectable alternative.)[31]

In Cuba, the ranks of dedicated annexationists were further thinned by defections, on moral or practical grounds. By October 1849 most of Lopez's recruits in the United States had deserted, and in that month the expedition was given up.

Lopez, however, was undeterred, and in December 1849—barely two months after his first expedition disbanded—he formed a New York group to raise funds and support for Cuban independence. Moving his operations to New Orleans, Lopez offered the command of his new expedition to John Quitman, governor of Mississippi. Quitman declined, but encouraged Lopez with a pledge to come to Lopez's aid with troops once the Cuban had established a viable fighting force on the island.

From late April to early May, 1850, Lopez brought the final pieces of his expeditionary puzzle together, and sailed from New Orleans with three ships and some 1,000 men—a paltry force, but one that Lopez hoped would be aided by revolutionary elements in Cuba. On April 25, the *Georgiana* left for Cuba carrying several hundred troops under the command of Colonel O'Hara and Captain Benson; they received arms and ammunition from a fishing boat after they left port.[32]

Spanish intelligence—aided by Lopez's almost total lack of concern for secrecy—had learned of the expedition, and the warships *Pizarro* and *Habanero* were sent to search for it. Lopez's party managed to avoid them, however, and on May 18 he landed at Cardenas, Cuba, and seized the town. Most of his troops were Southern mercenaries, not Cuban "freedom fighters," and his expedition was greeted with much fanfare in the Southern press, which saw Lopez as a great liberator. The first U.S. invasion of Cuba was underway.

Lopez's victory was short-lived, however. The promised insurrection was nowhere to be seen, and after some time a large force of Spanish troops arrived and chased the filibusters off. The Americans made a hasty and panicked retreat and crowded aboard the *Creole*, which could barely hold them; with men covering the decks and clinging to anything they could hold, the ship made for Key West. It pulled into the harbor there just minutes ahead of the *Pizarro*, and the Lopez party abandoned the boat hurriedly to avoid arrest by U.S. port authorities. Largely due to the influence of favorable public opinion, Lopez was acquitted of Neutrality Act violations.

In retrospect it is little wonder that a force of less than one thousand American mercenaries with a few Cubans along for show, intent on annexing Cuba to an alien power as a slave state, failed to excite the imagination of the Cubans. But in 1851, Lopez was plotting once more. His third expedition was momentarily delayed when U.S. officials seized the steamer *Cleopatra* in New York, but the Southern detachments of the force flourished, thanks in part to intentionally lax enforcement of the neutrality laws by Southern port officials.

Spanish diplomats continued their efforts to persuade the U.S. government to stop Lopez. By this time, however, Millard Fillmore had come into office, and Fillmore, unwilling to risk the ire of Southern expansionists so soon after the delicately balanced slave compromise of 1850 had been hammered out, denounced the expedition but did not act firmly to destroy it. He did despatch two ships in April 1851 to intercept Lopez, and later, in August, returning hurriedly to Washington to deal with the Cuban crisis, sent the *U.S.S. Saranac* to Havana. But he did not catch Lopez.

On July 4, 1851, two small insurrections sprang up in Cuba, both proslavery, both favoring incorporation into the United States. Unable to gather much support from average Cubans or slaves, the revolts were quickly put down by Spanish authorities. Excited by the news, however, and unaware the uprisings had been crushed, Lopez sailed prematurely in August, 1851, his expectations raised by Spanish agents. On the very day when Joaquin Aguero, one of the leaders of the revolt, was executed—August 11—Lopez landed, bringing some 430 men and a pledge to hold a vote to determine whether the island would be annexed to the United States.

Lopez was attacked by a large body of Spanish troops, and his force was split in half. One portion was chased off through the jungle, where some of the sick and wounded were left to die in the mire; the rest were either killed or captured as they attempted to reach a number of small boats. Those taken prisoner, including the leader of the detachment, the American W. H. Crittenden, were soon summarily shot, and a crowd gathered in Havana to mock and deface the dead and dying. Thirty minutes before he was killed, Crittenden wrote a bitter letter to his friend Lucien Hensley, in which he asked Hensley to care for his family and lamented, ''We have been deceived grossly. . . during my short sojourn on this island I have not met a single patriot.'' But he concluded, ''I will die like a man. My heart has not failed yet, nor do I believe it will.'' Indeed, it did not; Crittenden refused to die with his back to his executioners, and demanded to kneel facing them. The Havana press reported that his dead body, along with those of his compatriots, was thrown into the crowd, dragged through the streets, and horribly mutilated.[33]

During this massacre, press reports in the United States were trumpeting Lopez's huge success. Expecting that he could not fail, the Southern papers announced that thousands of Cubans had rallied to his side and that he was marching on Havana. The annexation of Cuba was near, they claimed.

* * *

The reality was that at that very moment Narciso Lopez and several score of his sick, tired, and hungry men were barely holding out in the jungle. His half of the force had temporarily evaded the Spanish, but conditions were bad enough to try the commitment of Lopez's most devoted followers. Growing desperation exacerbated by lack of food and water, the constant pressure of the heat, and gradually spreading disease were by punctuated by regular firefights and ambushes. On August 17, Lopez met Spanish troops at Las Frias in one such pitched battle.

Lopez deployed his men behind a thicket of mango trees, which with their dense foliage made a natural barrier. A Spanish officer arrived at the adjacent plantation, and after a short delay ordered his 150 cavalry and several hundred supporting infantry to attack Lopez's position. Lopez had ordered his men not to fire, thinking the Spanish were going to defect to his cause; when the charge came not all the rebels fired, but enough did, and with masterful enough accuracy, to drive off the Spanish. But only some 250 filibusters remained, and Lopez withdrew to a nearby hill.

After a short delay, Lopez decided to press on. One writer described the developments:

> [That night] the rain fell in torrents, and it was impossible to keep up the fires sufficiently to cook the meat which had been secured. The majority of the men marched on the next day without food. . . .That

evening a halt was made near a saw mill, where ammunition could
be kept dry in spite of the torrents of rain. Two oxen were killed and
with the abundant growing corn the men were able to enjoy a good
meal again. . . . [The next day] the road was now almost impassable.
Men walked in mud to their knees.

By the time the column approached San Cristobal, the men had been spread
out over five miles of road, and some had dropped dead from exhaustion or
sunstroke. The troops were in tatters; many had thrown away their rifles to
conserve strength, and by August 19 only 90 still carried weapons.

The Americans in the party, understandably, demanded that Lopez inform
them of his plans; they had begun to doubt whether the revolt would succeed,
as no Cubans seemed to be coming to their aid. On the evening of August 19,
then, unable to push his men further, Lopez allowed them to set up a defensive position with felled trees near San Cristobal, and the next morning he
ordered a retreat to the mountains, where he hoped to avoid Spanish patrols.
On the 21st, as Lopez's men ate breakfast, they were surprised by some 400
Spanish infantry, and after a short, sharp fight in which several Americans
were killed, Lopez's group fled the field, their retreat covered by rain and
made necessary by the lack of weapons and dry ammunition.

Eight years later, an American who had been in Cuba just after the Lopez
expeditions recounted the mood in the island during the battles. Their impact
was considerable: "a far greater impression than is commonly supposed in
the United States." The government had been panicked by exaggerated
reports of Lopez's strength. As far as Lopez and his men were concerned,

> their little force of a few hundred broken-down men and lads,
> deceived and deserted, fought a body of eight times their number
> and kept them at bay, causing great slaughter. The railroad cars
> brought the wounded into Havana, car after car; rumors of defeat
> filled the city; artillery was sent out; and the actual loss of the
> Spaniards, in killed and wounded, was surprisingly large.

But Lopez and his exhausted men could run only so far. They trekked on into
the mountains, eating Lopez's horse, palmetto roots, and other material to
keep alive. They were exhausted and starving; "the only possibility seemed
to be to wander about the mountains until death brought relief." Lopez still
held out hope of reinforcements from the United States, but none arrived.

The next day the rains stopped, and the party set out to find a village or
home where they might obtain some nourishment. Finding none, they
decided to undertake a desperate, bold attack on San Cristobal; but on their
way a Spanish cavalry unit fell on the column and dispersed it, capturing many,

including Lopez himself. Scattered groups of filibusters were rounded up by the Spanish over the next several days. Many were shot on sight, until August 26, when the Spanish captain general ordered all prisoners spared and brought to Havana.

Lopez was brought to the capital to be publicly executed. An American in the city described his approach:

> Lopez, after being taken prisoner, walked several miles escorted by
> a few soldiers, and not even a dozen patriots endeavored to wrest
> him from the grasp of his murderers. . . . Lopez was exhausted from
> weariness, hunger and thirst; he walked barefoot for a long distance,
> limping and bleeding from his lacerated feet; while the soldiers who
> guarded him embittered his sufferings by insulting and mocking
> words.

As the time approached for his death, many Spaniards looked forward to a glorious killing, after which they would feast around a glass bowl filled with Lopez's blood "to enjoy the smell." Rumors of a last-ditch rescue attempt proved false, and Lopez was taken out to be executed. The U.S. writer Hudson Strode described Lopez's final moments.

> Lopez's martyr-lit eyes turned to right and left searching the crowd
> and the near landscape for sympathizers, for someone into whose
> hands he might pass the torch. "Ah, Cubans!" he doubtless
> thought, as he died alone. His last audible words, however, were
> prophetic: "My death will not change the destinies of Cuba!"

Other reports claimed Lopez's final words were, "I die for my beloved Cuba." His head was lopped off, and for a time the filibustering threat to Cuba ended.[34]

* * *

Southern papers in the United States, predictably enough, called for immediate revenge and a new expedition. Huge riots broke out in New Orleans, with men who had been waiting to join Lopez taking out their frustration on the Spanish members of the community. Police, for the most part, stood aside. The Spanish consulate was sacked, an action that led to the ironic situation of the U.S. Congress apologizing to Spain for the incident. Later, in February, 1852, Fillmore secured the release of ninety American prisoners held in Spain.[35]

Despite this clamor for action, the fervent period of annexationism had already passed. Its dregs would live on until the Civil War, when the abolition of slavery in the South would destroy the primary Cuban motivation for annexation. Many thought Lopez was merely the first of many expeditioners to Cuba, and in a strict sense he was. But his was also the last expedition with any real chance of success.[36]

THE PIERCE ADMINISTRATION

The election of 1852 brought Franklin Pierce into office. On the eve of the Civil War, the amiable Pierce's primary mandate was maintaining the tenuous slave compromises that stood as the last barriers to sectional conflict. The Cuban issue was inextricably linked with the larger question of slavery, a linkage reinforced in writing by the Ostend Manifesto. U.S. commercial interests in the island had also expanded; America imported flour and sugar from Cuba, and exported to it machinery for the sugar mills.

Duties on trade, however, soon provided another argument in the annexationist repertoire. This interest centered in the South, mostly around New Orleans. *De Bow's Review* trumpeted the U.S. commercial stake in Cuba. The paper and its supporters were sometimes moderate in their proposals, advocating a simple purchase of Cuba; but at other times they mirrored the most racist versions of Manifest Destiny by arguing that "it is by war that you conquer an ignorant and barbarian people."[37]

The annexationism that began in the 1852 election continued throughout the remainder of the decade in various groups and expeditions. The "Order of the Lone Star" was established in some Southern cities and in New York to promote revolution in Cuba and subsequent annexation, and soon claimed tens of thousands of members. Others took an indirect approach, attempting to promote a war with Spain which they felt would lead to the acquisition of Cuba. It was this sort of strategy that led to the *Crescent City* episode.

George Law, president of the U.S. Mail steamship company, thought a plan to foment war with Spain might succeed in wresting Cuba away from the European power. He owned the *Crescent City*, a steamer that plied the Cuban routes, carrying mail and other cargo. Spanish officials had suspected its purser, William Smith, of smuggling insurrectionary materials into Cuba and of otherwise aiding the annexationist cause; they therefore made it clear that they would not let the ship land with Smith on board.

Law, seeing an opportunity to provoke the Spanish and an angry U.S. response, sent the ship to Havana with Smith on board, and when it was turned away he demanded war. Pierce did not yet feel confident enough to risk conflict, however, and he ordered Law to cease his adventures. Law nevertheless sent a newer ship back to Cuba, a ship that carried no cargo, no passengers, and that had no real purpose other than the ferrying of purser Smith and the resultant provocation of the Spanish. Smith, however, undercut Law's plans by agreeing that he would spread no more illegal documents, and the Spanish let him land. President Fillmore finally threatened Law with legal and military action, and the episode came to a quiet close, never having held out any serious prospect of war.

When John Quitman, the former governor of Mississippi, was offered the leadership of a Cuban expedition for a second time, he gave it more serious thought. After deliberating for three months, he decided that he could acquire the support of the Pierce administration in the enterprise, and so in August 1853 he signed an agreement with the *Junta Cubana* of New York. The *Junta* was the representative body of wealthy Cuban landowners who still hoped for annexation, and so it was not surprising that one proviso in Quitman's agreement stipulated that he would maintain slavery on the island after he captured it.

Quitman himself had far more ambitious goals than the Junta. He was a Manifest Destiny proponent of the most virulently racist tone; Senator William N. Gwin once described him as "one of the most bigoted egotists I ever met," with "all his life eaten up with ambition."[38] Quitman hoped to establish a southern slave empire, a conglomeration of several Central and South American nations—as well as the U.S. slave states—under a military government (with Quitman, of course, at its head).

Quitman believed he had Pierce's support in part because the latter had been his subordinate in the Mexican War, and Quitman had given favorable reports to the press during the election of Pierce's performance in battle. Other of Quitman's friends and associates from the Mexican war were in the Pierce cabinet, and Quitman felt their sympathies lay with him and his mission.

To a certain degree, Quitman was correct; the administration did assume, and many in it hoped, that he would take Cuba from Spain. Pierce, committed to annexation, in his inaugural address promised to pursue the acquisition of territory unrestrained "by any timid forebodings of evil from expansion." He had thus already become the first president to openly proclaim expansion as a goal of his administration from its outset. Pierce confirmed these indications of expansionist intent by appointing Pierre Soule as minister to Spain; Soule was known as an advocate of the acquisition of Cuba, and had participated in anti-Spanish, pro-Cuban rallies. Observers, especially in the Spanish government, correctly perceived his appointment as a signal that Pierce intended to resurrect plans to obtain the island. In this sort of atmosphere a project like Quitman's could not but be viewed favorably.[39]

Soule meanwhile was making his own attempts to convince Spain to sell the island. Though he spent much of his time in such frivolous pursuits as shopping for clothes and dueling, Soule did manage to work hard promoting the acquisition of Cuba. In March 1854 he offered a loan to help Spain sustain its enormous debts, with Cuba as collateral.[40] At about the same time he tried to convince the Spanish queen mother, who held almost sole ownership of Cuba, that selling the island would be a good idea. Indeed, he met with her so often that rumors of an affair began to circulate. None of these plans brought any success, however.

Pierce also attempted to obtain Cuba by threat of war. The American steamer *Black Warrior* was seized by the Spanish in Havana Bay for violations of various trade regulations. The Pierce administration, in a reversal of its *Crescent City* policy, rallied U.S. opinion against Spain; Pierce's message to Congress regarding the affair was unusually strong, promising to "vindicate the honor of our flag." Some papers and congressmen began calling for an invasion of Cuba, and administration officials suggested to Spain that unless she ceded the island, war might result.[41]

The U.S. Congress, however, was dominated by anti-annexationist forces, and the administration's attempts to whip up a war-making mood in the United States soon collapsed. Spain, meanwhile, apparently unconvinced that there was any real threat of war, remained intransigent. Pierce decided to return to diplomacy, though Soule did demand a $300,000 indemnity from Spain for the *Black Warrior*.

It was at about this time that the "Africanization" scare jolted Cuban slave-owners into a renewed drive for annexation. There was some fear among wealthy, land-owning Cubans that Spain, responding to pressure from England, France, and elsewhere, would emancipate blacks on the island. This plan was referred to as "Africanization." William Robertson, the U.S. consul at Havana, influenced by the landowners' fears, urged Pierce to send in U.S. troops. In March 1854, to determine to veracity of these reports, Secretary of State Marcy sent Charles Davis to investigate the situation; Davis surprised even Marcy by reporting that the British and French were indeed arguing for Africanization, a policy which would lead, in Davis's opinion, to a violent revolution.[42]

On April 3, Marcy told Soule to inform the Spanish that Africanization was an unacceptable policy, and that the United States still wished to purchase Cuba. He authorized Soule to offer $130 million. In the absence of such a sale, Marcy threatened to "detach" Cuba, a curious phrase that meant the United States would promote its independence if it could not own the island. Soule had his own preoccupations during this time; he was plotting with Spanish revolutionaries against the Spanish government, hoping to obtain Cuba in the bargain. Again, he failed.[43]

Annexationist calls for war continued. On May 1 Senator Slidell urged an exception to the neutrality laws for Quitman's expedition, but nothing came of it. Quitman for his part was afraid to wait for the administration to act; he felt the United States might well purchase Cuba only after the island had been emancipated, making its acquisition anathema to Quitman and his slave-empire cohorts. By late May Quitman, with George Law's help, had acquired a ship, weapons, money, and troops, and he continued to believe he enjoyed the tacit support of the Pierce administration.

Pierce, however, influenced by Spanish pressure and domestic opposition to war, would not allow Quitman to sail. On May 31 his administration announced its intention to prosecute anyone violating the neutrality laws. Meanwhile by 1856 a reformist revolution in Spain, led by General Leopoldo O'Donnell (another former captain general of Cuba) and assisted by Soule, had been crushed, and with reactionaries back in power there was little chance that Pierce's purchase proposals would meet with success.

The Ostend Manifesto

In October 1854, Soule, Buchanan, and Mason—the U.S. ministers to Spain, France, and England, respectively—met in Ostend, Belgium to discuss the Cuban situation. The result of their discussions—the Ostend Manifesto—was intended as a confidential dispatch to Marcy. It urged the immediate U.S. acquisition of Cuba, and would become one of the most famous—or infamous—documents of U.S. diplomatic history. One commentator concluded that "in its fervid style, its astonishing proposals, and its naive excuses it stands unrivaled."[44]

The Manifesto began with a recommendation to purchase Cuba if possible. Indeed, the authors expressed their opinion that Spain needed hard currency so badly that "under the circumstances we cannot anticipate a failure" to convince Spain to sell. Given later developments, and indeed what was then known of the mood of the Spanish government, the idea that Spain would be willing to sell seems completely misguided; so much so, in fact, that the possibility may have been held out by the Manifesto's authors as a ruse to convince policy makers that their efforts to acquire Cuba would stop short of war.

Continuing with an analysis of Cuba's importance to the United States, the Manifesto stressed economic and geopolitical considerations. "It must be clear to every reflecting mind," it argued,

> that, from the peculiarity of its geographical position, and the considerations attendant on it, Cuba is as necessary to the North American republic as any of its present members, and that it

belongs to us naturally. . . . [The United States] can never be
secure, but must ever be endangered whilst Cuba is a dependency
of a distant power in whose possession it has proved a source of
constant annoyance and embarrassment to their interests.

"Indeed," it concluded, "the Union can never enjoy repose, nor possess
reliable security as long as Cuba is not embraced within its boundaries."

But the Manifesto did not stop there. It noted that the United States would
also significantly increase its Caribbean commerce if it were to acquire Cuba
and lift the Spanish duties. This economic motive, combined with strategic
concerns, meant that the United States, if it could not purchase the island or
otherwise secure its transfer by peaceful means, was justified in "wresting"
the island from Spain. Such a suggestion could only imply warfare. And Soule
in private correspondence went even further, urging an immediate war to take
Cuba from Spain and to reassert the Monroe Doctrine.[45]

Subsequently it has become clear that probably the only signator who really
believed the Manifesto's exhortations was Soule, and even he was perhaps
skeptical. Some historians have speculated that the Manifesto was designed
to convince conservative Democrats of Buchanan's toughness and so to help
win him that party's nomination for the presidency in the next election; if this
were indeed the purpose, the document had its intended effect. In the United
States, Marcy was somewhat embarrassed by what his representatives had
sent him, and for his part did not want war.

Immediately, a political scandal erupted over the Manifesto. It arrived in
Washington just as the Democrats were being badly beaten in mid-term elections. Pro-annexation forces lost power throughout the nation, and the generally hostile public mood was incited even further when the details of this new
"Manifesto of the Brigands" were released. Public opinion strongly opposed
the ideas expressed in the document, and on November 13 the administration
was forced publicly to repudiate most of the Manifesto's proposals. The
Pierce government, while attempting to distance itself from the Manifesto,
tried to hold open a glimmer of hope for a purchase or takeover of the island
by arguing such actions would become necessary should Cuba threaten
"immediate peril to the existence" of the United States. Public opinion, however, had already tried and convicted the administration of expansionist and
pro-slavery sentiment, and the connection of the first to the second was reinforced by the Manifesto.

The Pierce administration was finally forced to give up its designs on Cuba.
Later in November, 1854, Soule was told to break off the negotiations for the
purchase of the island; he resigned in protest. The administration gave up any
thought of aiding expeditions such as Quitman's.

Despite this late setback, the Pierce administration had used every possible mechanism to promote annexation.[46] It continued the by-then traditional U.S. Cuban policy: deny the island to any other power, prevent abolitionist reform, and seek ways for the United States to absorb the island. The first two goals were realized, the last was not—with the result that Cuba remained oppressed and abused by a despotic Spanish colonial government.

Meanwhile, on Cuba, a succession of captains general fell victim to continuing Spanish opposition to reform. Captain General Pezuela had begun registering and tracing slaves as an administrative prelude to abolition, but Cuban slaveowners, acting in concert with conservative Spanish authorities, forced him out and replaced him with Don Jose Gutierrez Concha, who eliminated the registration system. Concha was no reactionary, but his own efforts to end the slave trade (as opposed to slavery itself) came to naught, however, and in December 1859 he resigned in frustration. He was succeeded by Senor Serrano, a moderate reformer who also attempted to crack down on importation of slaves and who cultivated close ties with middle- and lower-class Cubans.[47]

Meanwhile Quitman, who had still not given up his dreams of conquest, had amassed over $1 million and some 10,000 volunteers, and he informed his commanders to prepare to embark for Cuba. In November 1854, however, just as the Pierce administration's diplomatic efforts were crashing down, an independent filibustering group, dissatisfied with Quitman's pace, launched their own invasion, which was quickly annihilated. It did, however, serve the purpose of putting then-Captain General Concha on his guard, and he discovered a plot on the island led by Ramon Pinto, whose insurrection was set to correspond with Quitman's landing. Pinto and many of his group were arrested and some were executed, and Quitman now realized his expedition would be hopeless. Responding also to pressure from Pierce to give up his plans, on April 30, 1855, Quitman publicly did so. The *Junta Cubana*, one of the largest annexationist front organizations in the United States, was disbanded.

That same year, the last of the true filibustering expeditions, undaunted by the continuing failure of annexationism, set out for Cuba. It was led by two tough adventurers: Domingo Goicuria and William Walker.

Goicuria was a 56-year-old Cuban exile who boasted a long grey beard and a checkered history of mercenary activities. He painted himself as a Cuban patriot, claiming he would never end his fight until Cuban independence was achieved. His real motives may have been less pure, however, and he was willing to discuss the annexation of Cuba to the United States as a "prelude" to its independence.

Walker was one of the most colorful characters of the time. Called the "grey-eyed man of destiny," he was a failed doctor and lawyer, and had taken a job as the editor of the New Orleans *Crescent*. In 1853 he led an expedition against part of Mexico, and obtained a general reputation as an adventurer. After Quitman gave up his plans, Southern annexationists turned to Walker as their savior.

In February, 1856 Walker and Goicuria invaded Nicaragua with several hundred men, as a first step toward other Caribbean expeditions. Easily overwhelming the weak and primitive government, Walker set himself up as autocrat. With a tiny force, he had essentially acquired a kingdom for himself. Southerners expected him to eventually continue to Cuba. On May 15, 1856, in one of the truly idiotic actions in American diplomatic history, the Pierce administration recognized the ludicrous Walker regime in Nicaragua, thereby earning the enmity of all legitimate Latin American governments, who were not amused at the prospect of being conquered by Yankee slave mercenaries operating with the tacit approval of the U.S. government.

Walker ruled for a time, and through his increasingly megalomaniacal statements made it clear that he did not intend to invade Cuba at all—at least not for some time. Walker's dream as with Quitman and others before him was the creation of a federation of Central American slaveowner-dominated military dictatorships, which would eventually merge with the South into a huge slave empire. Secession was already in the wind, and Walker and men like him dreamed of shifting the "true" United States to the south through military conquest. Accordingly, Walker in September 1856 re-established slavery in Nicaragua.[48]

Goicuria, angered and perhaps more than a little frightened by his comrade-in-arms's despotic rule, broke from Walker. Goicuria knew that England, given its opposition to the slave trade and slavery in general, would never permit the establishment of the sort of empire Walker wanted, Monroe Doctrine or not; and it certainly would not permit Walker to invade Cuba, if he ever saw fit to do so. Goicuria therefore left and went in search of others to support Cuban independence.

Legitimate Central American governments, meanwhile, had mobilized against Walker, and in March and April of 1857 he was defeated by a Costa Rican army. In May he surrendered to U.S. naval forces, who removed him from the area. Walker had followed a "scorched earth" policy and had reduced much of Nicaragua to ruins. He destroyed the once-beautiful capital city of Granada, and thrust a lance bearing the inscription "Here Was Granada" into the rubble-strewn ground.

Walker returned to the United States and once again used the Cuban issue as a clarion call to obtain support. He organized another invasion of Nicaragua: one which would this time be followed, he promised, by a prompt incursion into Cuba. He landed in Honduras, but true to Goicuria's prediction, was captured by the British, turned over to the Honduran government, and shot. Latin American governments breathed a collective sigh of relief—they had, at one point, been considering placing themselves under the protection of Britain, France, and Sardinia to avoid being conquered by U.S.-supported filibusters like Walker. The threat was not nearly so great as they thought, but once again the United States had pursued a confused policy in the area which gained them nothing and lost the trust of virtually all Latin Americans.

THE BUCHANAN ADMINISTRATION

James Buchanan came into office as a compromise choice of the Democrats, who were unwilling to offend the party with more controversial choices such as Pierce or Douglas. Buchanan, whose strength was mainly in the South, won the presidency over the split coalitions of John C. Fremont and Millard Fillmore. Buchanan's political dependency on the South would significantly shape his Cuba policy; as we have seen, he used the Ostend Manifesto to rally support of expansionist Democrats. Indeed, while the contents of the Manifesto may have been more ambitious than Buchanan himself would implement, he was nevertheless determined to acquire Cuba. He had opposed the island's purchase in earlier administrations with the secret motive of reserving that accomplishment for his own.

Traditional channels seemed closed. In 1855 the new U.S. minister to Spain, Mr. Dodge, reported that the Spanish government was too weak to sell Cuba and survive the public opinion backlash which would inevitably follow. But Christopher Fallon, a Philadelphia banker, had another idea: he offered to use his influence with the European banks that lent the huge sums of money Spain required to keep refinancing its $400 million external debt. Fallon would attempt to get these bank to force Spain to sell Cuba for hard cash.

Buchanan approved the plan. Fallon went to Europe, but reported that even if the banks pressured Spain she would not give up the colony. Bank influence was not enough; bribes of Spanish officials would be required. Fallon suggested that a new minister be sent to Spain carrying large sums of cash, which could be distributed to the appropriate officials. Buchanan agreed and proposed August Belmont, a convenient choice since Belmont had been in favor of bribery schemes to acquire Cuba for years. The U.S. Senate, however, perhaps sensing something fishy, rejected the appointment, and Buchanan had to settle for William Preston, a former Kentucky congressman.

Buchanan had his plan in place, his briber in office, his banker ready to apply the pressure. All he needed now was the money. On December 6, 1858, in a display of bold underhandedness, Buchanan gave his annual address to Congress, in which he proposed a purchase of Cuba which might require "an advance [payment] to the Spanish government" before the Senate had actually ratified the treaty of sale; he asked for a "large" appropriation. On January 10, 1859, John Slidell of Louisiana introduced a bill to provide for such funds.[49]

The Foreign Relations committee of the Senate agreed, noting that Cuba must eventually leave Spanish hands, that possession by a European power would be disastrous, and that a purchase by the United States was therefore logical. It recommended a $30 million appropriation. Republicans on the Senate floor, however, would have none of it. They began a filibuster to prevent a vote on the bill, a vote which the Democrats might well carry.

Outside the Congress, meanwhile, opposition to Buchanan's scheme grew. Northerners, abolitionists, and others who had traditionally opposed the annexation of Cuba continued to do so. Even Southern support was diluted; Buchanan had felt compelled to promise an end to the slave trade in Cuba in his December message, a pledge his opponents did not believe but which did manage to alienate many of his Southern supporters. This latter problem was resolved when one senator proposed a bill to guarantee slavery in Cuba after annexation; when attached to the appropriation this provision formed a package acceptable to all Southerners, who now supported the "30 Million Dollar Bill."

Republicans, however, though numbering less than one-third of the senate—20 of 62 seats—managed to prevent a vote on the bill. Preston continued to report that the $30 million, combined with bank pressure, would enable him to secure Cuba, and Buchanan redoubled his efforts. On December 19, 1859, he again called for the money, and the Democrats in the Senate made another effort, but the Republicans still managed to block the vote. By June 1860, however, the nation was on the brink of civil war, and the "30 Million Dollar Bill" faded to back page news and never again approached passage. The North saw no reason, on the verge of a secession, to add to the territory opposing it.

The Campaign of 1860

As the campaign of 1860 unfolded, the Cuba issue emerged as a significant one. Stephen Douglas and Abraham Lincoln differed sharply. Douglas placed emphasis on Cuba, and argued for its annexation to placate Southern slaveowners by balancing the seventeen free states.[50] Though not adamantly proslavery, Douglas's primary concern was tempering the sectional conflict which threatened to tear the young republic apart, and he felt that attempting to placate the southern states—with such promises as the preservation of a slave Cuba—was the best means to achieve this. Douglas was nevertheless perfectly happy to accept allies in the Manifest Destiny camp, who wanted to annex Cuba for their own reasons; such men as George Law and the leaders of the Young America Movement found in Douglas a convenient tool for the promotion of their goals.

Lincoln opposed annexation, and felt that the nation must come to terms with its slavery dispute, not try to conceal it with compromises and political niceties. Arguing that ''a house divided against itself cannot stand,'' Lincoln urged the country to resolve the slave issue once and for all.

These views were reflected in the two candidates' notions of what to do with Cuba if it indeed became, by purchase or otherwise, part of the United States. Lincoln was against its incorporation as a slave state. Douglas concluded in the Lincoln-Douglas debates that ''the time may come, indeed has now come, when our interests would be advanced by the acquisition of Cuba. When we get Cuba we must *take it as we find it*, leaving the people to decide the question of slavery for themselves.'' That meant incorporating it as a slave territory.[51]

With Abraham Lincoln's victory the course the nation would take became clearer, and the imminent Civil War would to some degree distract American diplomatic attention from the Cuban issue. But the island, as we shall see, did play a role in the Civil War.

The Verge of a New Age

Cuban American relations—which in many ways were really still Spanish-American relations—had weathered more than a decade of American annexation attempts. Such expansionism would disappear in the 1860s, as American leaders became preoccupied with the Civil War and its aftermath. From both Cuban and American perspectives, moreover, the U.S. Civil War would do much to eliminate annexationist sentiment: Cuban landowners could no longer look to the United States as a potential guardian of their slave system, and U.S. filibusters would, with abolition, be robbed of their goal of a slave empire.

Yet the relative calm characteristic of Spanish-Cuban-American relations during and after the U.S. Civil War would be short-lived. Cubans were disillusioned with Spanish rule, and shortly after the end of the American Civil War they would begin a revolution of their own. This war would constitute a serious challenge to American diplomacy, as U.S. leaders groped for an adequate response to Cuban cries for freedom. By the end of the century, American expansionism was again on the rise, and Cuba became a focal point of America's emergence to true world power status.

In 1860, however, Americans were obsessed with growing calls for secession and with the imminent civil war threatening to tear their nation apart. Cuba, though it would play some role in the developing conflict, was in general not a priority of either Federal or Confederate policymakers.

Thomas Jefferson

Daniel Edgar Sickles

Pierre Soule

William Walker

Leonard Wood

Elihu Root

Hamilton Fish

John A. Quitman

Orville Hitchcock Platt

3

CIVIL WAR AND IMPERIALISM

Relations 1861-1890

"Who draws his sword against the prince must throw away the scabbard."
English Proverb

"The right of revolution is an inherent one. When people are oppressed
by their government, it is a natural right they enjoy to relieve themselves
of the oppression, if they are strong enough, whether by withdrawal from
it, or by overthrowing it and substituting a government more acceptable."
Ulysses S. Grant, *Personal Memoirs,* Volume I

The second half of the nineteenth century saw American policy toward Cuba develop from an issue of minimal significance, lost amid the overriding considerations of a bloody civil war, to one of paramount importance. The end of the century brought a new wave of American expansionism, and with it burdens of empire that many in the young nation found distasteful. By 1898, the United States had irrevocably committed itself to the maintenance of domestic Cuban stability, and this responsibility would plague it for decades afterwards. In mid-century, however, Cuba possessed relevance only in relation to the key crisis facing the United States: the American Civil War.

CUBA AND THE CIVIL WAR

As the 1860s began, the United States was on the verge of a war whose toll, in terms of both human lives and psychological impact, has not been matched by any subsequent conflict involving the country. Both the Union and the Confederacy struggled for international recognition and geostrategic position, and with regard to both goals the island of Cuba, and more generally relations with Spain, became important.

On the eve of the Civil War, a conflict over the small island of Santo Domingo further damaged U.S.-Spanish relations, which were already strained due primarily to Spain's anger over American policy toward its colonies. In 1860 Spanish troops sent from Cuba invaded Santo Domingo. The United States protested; it was willing to let Spain keep Cuba, but not expand further in the Caribbean. Santo Domingo requested U.S. aid, but the beginning of the Civil War prevented it.[1] The hostile U.S. stance angered Spain.

With the outbreak of the war, this and other disputes between Spain and the Federal government caused Spain to favor the Confederacy. Whatever their disagreements with the Federals, however, Madrid should perhaps have recognized the dangers a Southern victory would create. Southern slaveowners were the spiritual and financial inspirations for the filibustering expeditions against Cuba, and as long as slavery lived in the United States, Cuban slaveowners would have a reason to favor annexation. U.S. Minister to Spain Perry emphasized these facts, and Spain reconsidered an early predisposition to recognize the Confederacy.

Still, Spain generally favored the South. The Spanish government believed, in the words of Minister Perry, that if the North won, the United States would take all the Gulf, "and then quietly draw into the open jaws of that great serpent the fascinated and powerless islands of Cuba without efforts and without defense."[2] Spain was also angry about Union bullying over the *Black Warrior* and other issues, and held some sympathy for the underdog South. Strong economic ties between the prewar South and Cuba had also bred some familiarity.[3]

Spain's official policy gradually evolved into one of neutrality guided by her own commercial interests—interests that allowed Cuba to admit Confederate traders and privateers. Captain General Serrano granted Confederate agents free travel on the island and expressed his wish that Spain would recognize the Confederacy.

Many in Cuba, however, did identify themselves with the North. One such group was the Reformist Party. Even though only timidly abolitionist they deified Abraham Lincoln; *El Siglo*, the paper of the Reformists, editorialized that "the name of Lincoln is destined to occupy a glorious page in the book of great men, and the place which he occupies in history is already fixed by the passions and miseries of the present moment."[4] Reformists favored the North due to a desire for industrial development, and because they felt a Northern victory would undermine Spanish authority in the island.[5] Cuban creoles who opposed slavery also looked to the North for guidance and assistance.

Cuban policy had posed a problem for Lincoln in the pre-war months. Opposed to an intervention that would bring a slave-holding Cuba into the Union, Lincoln nevertheless felt that, in order to stave off war, annexing Cuba to placate the South might be worth the cost. In January 1861 he wrote that "a year will not pass till we shall have to take Cuba as a condition upon which they [the Southern states] will stay in the Union."[6] Before that year was up, however, the Civil War had begun.

In the early years of the war, the Confederacy made repeated attempts to reassure Spain of its peaceful intentions. In 1861, *De Bow's Review*, which had supported annexation, even proposed guaranteeing Cuba to Spain in exchange for Spanish aid in the war. In July of that same year, Jefferson Davis sent his agent C. J. Helm to meet the Captain General of Cuba, bearing a letter that claimed the South no longer desired the island. The Southern states contended that they had supported the filibusters only because they perceived Cuba, a vassal of Spain, as a threat, and wished to dilute the "dominant majority" of its government. Since this had changed, the Southerners argued—since Spain was no longer dangerous—they no longer wanted Cuba. The South also appealed to the common "pariah state" status of Spain in regard to the slave issue. "Spain being the only European nation interested in the same social system which pervaded the Confederate states"—i.e. feudal slavery—it was important, and some thought possible, for the Confederacy to have close relations with Spain.[7] Some in Spain, and many slaveowners in Cuba, were responsive to such appeals.

By 1862 Confederate ships used Cuba regularly as a port of call. Confederate captains seemed confident that they could obtain landing rights whenever they needed them, and the U.S. government obtained evidence of this use, but its protests, as usual, were of little avail. The United States at one point warned that it would not tolerate Cuban-Confederate trade but it never consummated the threat.[8]

The Emancipation Proclamation was greeted with predictable ambivalence by Cubans. Slaveowners naturally despised it, and even reformers felt unease over its central message of immediate abolition. It was seen, however, as necessary for a Northern victory, and as such was welcomed by liberal elements of Cuban society. Cuban slaves, of course, were ecstatic. Lincoln's later death caused much grief on the part of the slaves and liberals, including the 12-year-old Jose Marti, the man whose name would later become synonymous with Cuban liberation.

REVOLUTION IN CUBA AND AMERICAN POLICY

Hard on the heels of the American Civil War came a revolution in Cuba, the Ten Years' War. American policy toward Cuba, and its parent country Spain, was severely tested during this period, and the constant American refusal to recognize the rebels in Cuba angered many Americans and Latin Americans. But the risks of confronting Spain over Cuba were significant, and the United States was in no mood or condition to risk an international conflict. While it would eventually drive the Spanish from their last refuge in the Caribbean, the United States needed a generation to recover from its wounds before contemplating such an adventure.

Developments in Cuba

The Cuba of the mid-1860s possessed a reformist spirit. Captain General Serrano, and later Dulce, followed a ''policy of attraction'' or accommodation to quell revolutionary sentiment. It was during this period that the Reformist Club and its offshoot, the Reformist Party, were formed, even though opposition parties were officially banned. The captains general were determined to rob potential insurrectionists of their grievances, rather than crush them through military repression. Conservative landowners formed the Unconditional Spanish Party to oppose all reform; but Serrano and Dulce remained committed to change. In January, 1865, Serrano recommended that Cuba be granted representation in the Cortes, Spain's legislative assembly, and also proposed changes in the tariff system and other reforms.

Slavery was still a huge business, however. During the Civil War there were almost half a million slaves on the island, along with 730,000 whites and 221,000 free blacks. Spanish abolitionists continued to tread softly and wield little influence. The seeds of the decline of the slave industry, however, were slowly being planted, and Rebecca Scott has analyzed them in her excellent *Slave Emancipation in Cuba*. Some historians contend that the growing mechanization of the Cuban sugar industry rendered continued resort to slave labor both unprofitable and unnecessary; while this view has some merit, Scott cautions, ''the issue. . .is a complex one.'' She advances several other important causes of the decline of slavery: an increasingly effective U.S. and British suppression of the international slave trade, so that by 1867 no slaves were being brought into Cuba; and a general opposition to Spanish rule in all its forms, including the slave system.[9] Slavery itself survived another 20 years in Cuba, but unquestionably its days were numbered.

By this time, however, the moderate captain general Francisco Serrano had been succeeded by Francisco Lersundi. Harsh, stern, at times cruel, Lersundi suspended the reforms that had been implemented and opposed others. Despite Reform Commission recommendations, he steadfastly opposed change and championed the status quo. He met the small, occasional outbursts of opposition he encountered with overwhelming and brutal displays of force.

Lersundi's tactics and the apparent hopelessness of reform fed the growing insurgency, and many Cubans turned to organized opposition. Even some middle-class whites and more wealthy planters favored a revolution involving blacks, and eventual abolition of slavery, to the then-current state of affairs. In September, 1868, the "Glorious Revolution" in Spain brought a progressive government to power and created the conditions for a possible overhaul of Spain's repressive colonial system in Cuba. At the head of the revolutionary Spanish government was Serrano, the former captain general of Cuba. On May 21 the Cortes voted to return Spain to its traditional Monarchical government, but they needed a king. They found Amadeo I, who presided over a shifting, unstable government. After an 1872 assassination attempt, Amadeo abdicated, and in 1873 the Cortes approved the transition to a republican government.[10]

The Beginning of the Ten Years War

The new government in Spain promised reforms for the colonies, but the Cubans were accustomed to unfulfilled Spanish promises. Many small revolutionary groups had formed, and after a time they began coordinating their efforts; by 1868 the forces opposing Spanish rule in Cuba had grown to significant proportions. They set a tentative date for a revolution against Spanish colonial authority: December 24, 1868.

By late September, however, harsh Spanish tax demands on Cuba had already pushed the insurgents to the breaking point, and they considered immediate revolution. But the wife of one of the conspirators revealed the plan to her priest, who promptly informed the Spanish authorities of the impending insurrection. Many of the conspirators were arrested, and it seemed that the revolution had been dealt a death blow.

The remaining insurgents, however, determined to go ahead, and on October 10, 1868, Carlos Cespedes, proclaimed the independence of Cuba from his plantation in Yara, freed his slaves, and assembled a rag-tag guerrilla force. Encouraged by the change of government in Spain, Cespedes thought he would eventually have Madrid on his side. Cespedes could not have known it, but he had put into motion the forces which would keep Cuba at war for a decade. The "Ten Years' War" for Cuban independence had begun.

Inspiration for the revolution sprang largely from coffee planters, cattle ranchers, and other groups of the Cuban landowning class, especially those in eastern Cuba. Facing economic ruin at the hands of Spanish duties, they were determined to rid Cuba of its colonial yoke. They were not joined by all landowning Cubans. The sugar producers, most notably, and many western planters, did not necessarily favor the conflict, and many slave-owners agreed. The revolution's ambiguous position on abolition was in part conditioned by this split coalition, and conservative planters distrusted the movement because they feared its anti-slavery bias. Eventually, the mass reaction to the war produced new rebels and new rebel leaders, and some who fought were true Cuban patriots, fighting merely for independence and basic freedoms. A few still hoped that a revolution would lead to eventual annexation to the United States, though of course the Civil War had destroyed the notion of a U.S.-protected Cuban slave system.[11]

The movement in Cuba grew rapidly under Cespedes's control. From the first group of about 150 it expanded to 4,000 by October 12, 1868; nearly 10,000 by early November; and 12,000 by the latter part of the month.[12] On October 19 these forces captured the city of Bayamo after a number of smaller victories. Rebel units (not guerrillas—during the nineteenth century "guerrilla" was a term for Cubans fighting for the Spanish, while the term "gerrilleros" often referred to anti-Spanish Cuban insurgents) were assisted by Dominican exiles, including Maximo Gomez, who had learned their tactics in the Dominican wars for independence. With this assistance, Cespedes's forces soon seized much of eastern Cuba, and other insurrectionary groups rose up across the island.

Madrid's colonial administrators initially underestimated the threat posed by the insurrection, but by late October they could not ignore it any longer. Lersundi, still captain general, sent a strong column against Bayamo, initiated martial law, and cracked down with brutal efficiency on supporters of the revolution.[13]

Lersundi also established one of the most infamous groups in Cuban history: the *Voluntarios*, or Volunteer Corps. The Volunteers were civilians who supported the Spanish colonial government and who aided it by serving as garrison troops in towns and cities. This freed Spanish forces to pursue the rebels. Their role sounded innocent enough. But in fact they were reactionaries of the most brutal variety—mostly wealthy merchants, small manufacturers, bankers, and their dependents—who opposed change of any sort and fought to preserve slavery and the status quo. Essentially nineteenth century versions of modern reactionary death squads, Volunteers beat, tortured, raped, and killed many civilians who supported the revolution, and killed many suspects merely to strike fear into the hearts of potential revolutionaries. One observer concluded that "there can be little doubt about the ruthless character of these Cuban hostilities."[14] Madrid bought 90,000 Remington rifles from the United States to equip the Volunteers; thus armed they wreaked havoc and terror throughout the island.

Spain eventually replaced Lersundi with a more progressive captain general, Don Domingo Dulce, in January, 1869. Dulce, like Serrano before him, was determined to woo the revolutionaries back into the fold with soft talk and concessions. The rebels had recently suffered a few military setbacks, and Dulce issued various concessions to convince them of his good intentions: a general amnesty, an offer of talks with Cespedes, an end to press censorship and martial law, and others.[15]

The Volunteers, for their part, would have nothing of Dulce's reforms. They continued their murderous activities. At the end of January they staged a three-day reign of terror in Havana, looting and killing. The Spanish had unwittingly turned loose a force that was subverting their own policy. Though Dulce tried to accommodate them, by June they had him dismissed.

Madrid went through the motions of appointing a new Captain General— Antonio Caballero de Rodas—but it was the Volunteers that really exercised control, and Rodas merely assented to their policies. Reaction and violence became the order of the day, and both sides of the conflict increasingly tried to make terror their ally. The Volunteers, seeing no end in sight to the conflict, decided upon a "war of extermination" to simply wipe out all supporters of the revolution.

Advent of the Grant Administration

The U.S. war hero Ulysses Grant won a surprisingly close election from Horatio Seymour in 1868. Like his predecessor, he was confronted with painful issues of reconstruction and domestic reconciliation after the Civil War. Ill-equipped to handle international diplomacy, Grant was faced with a severe test in regard to U.S. Cuban policy, a test born of the burgeoning Cuban revolution. Events moved quickly, and the war was as complex as it was brutal. Grant was simply not up to the task of formulating an innovative policy; for the most part he acceded to the recommendations of his Secretary of State, Hamilton Fish.

Fish's role in U.S. policy toward Cuba during the Ten Years' War is hotly disputed. There is no doubt that he discouraged U.S. recognition of the independence movement, and that, given strong U.S. popular support for the revolutionaries, at times only Fish's opposition prevented U.S. recognition or even intervention. What is questionable is his motive. Was Fish a brilliant diplomat, determined to avoid a war with Spain so soon after America's own Civil War, or was he an anti-reformist attempting to protect U.S. business interests?

Fish was a tall, "leonine" statesman, and a quiet, aristocratic man. His admirers, including Richard H. Bradford, have argued that Fish's prevention of war with Spain amounted to "the greatest achievement of statecraft, the prevention of trouble rather than the continuing of some splendid conflict." Grant himself was inexperienced in politics and "seemed not to understand what was going on during his presidency." In fact, Fish was responsible for "whatever successes were achieved in foreign affairs during the general's time in office."[16] Fish's supporters admit that he was influenced by some slightly shady motives; his son-in-law, Sidney Webster, was legal counsel for the Spanish government, and Fish certainly took American business interests into account. But his overriding motive, they claim, was prevention of conflict.[17]

Fish's detractors, on the other hand, label him a lackey of American business, a man who personally barred the U.S. recognition which might have meant the difference in the Ten Years' War. While Cubans were fighting and dying for their independence, Fish lived well in Washington, allowing interests of profit and trade to determine his decisions, these critics contend. And some see Fish as motivated more by a desire to preserve America's opportunity to annex Cuba than a desire to grant the island independence.

The U.S. Minister to Spain during this period was the equally controversial—but more universally condemned—Daniel Sickles. Sickles was a pompous, ungracious, rude man who caused diplomatic trouble wherever he went. While attending a state dinner as a member of the U.S. London delegation in 1853-54, Sickles caused an uproar by refusing to toast the Queen before he had toasted George Washington. In 1859, his wife had an affair with Philip Key, the son of Francis Scott Key; and though Sickles himself had been unfaithful, he hunted down, shot, and killed the hapless Key in Lafayette Square, within shouting distance of the Executive Mansion. After serving in the Civil War, Sickles accepted an appointment from Grant as minister to Spain.[18] Even in Spain, after the death of his wife, his actions stirred controversy, and following in the path of former American ministers, he took part in various plots to overthrow the government. There were rumors of an affair with Queen Isabella II, the former Spanish Monarch then living in exile in Paris. In short, Sickles was a better newsmaker than diplomat.

At the end of the 1860s, a number of Americans, including Secretary of War Rawlins, pressed for recognition of the Cuban revolutionaries. Fish decided to open negotiations with Spain and promote reforms to help bring an end to the conflict, and bankers on the Continent reported that Spain might be willing to sell Cuba to a consortium of Cuban buyers. The *Junta Cubana* (a group of Cuban exiles and sympathetic Americans, based in New York, promoting Cuban independence), unsure whether to take the offer seriously, finally agreed to put up $100 million to purchase the island. Fish proposed a five-point plan: the independence of Cuba, abolition on the island, payment of the $100 million to Spain, a U.S. guarantee of this payment, and a cease-fire during the negotiations.

Sickles was told to forward the proposal to the Spanish government, along with the threat that if it were not accepted the United States would recognize Cuba's right of belligerency. (The importance of recognition was obvious to everyone involved. It would allow the United States to negotiate directly with the rebels as a government and legal sales of arms and ammunition to them. Americans sympathetic to the Cuban cause would no longer need to skirt the Neutrality Act.) Fish attempted to demonstrate United States's good intentions to Spain by cracking down on filibusters; a June, 1869 expedition started by the *Junta* was stopped and its 1,000 members disbanded. Sickles arrived at the Spanish court on July 21 amid rumors that the Spanish government might demand $150 million. Generally, however, indications were favorable.[19]

Marshal Prim, head of the Spanish government, attempted to persuade his cabinet of the wisdom of the sale, but was unsuccessful. The cabinet was influenced by Spanish business interests, which saw Cuba as the last remaining outpost of profit in the empire. Prim, realizing the sale would not be approved, attempted to use the U.S. plan as a tool to achieve a cease-fire in any case, and demanded that the insurgents unilaterally lay down their arms. He offered an amnesty, followed by an election of Cuban members to the Cortes, and later by a general referendum in Spain on Cuban independence, which Prim promised would bind the government.

Cuban rebel leaders were naturally suspicious, especially of the provision for what amounted to unilateral disarmament in the face of a brutal foe. They deliberated, but in September, 1869 the plan was exposed by Prim's opponents who opposed a sale, and a backlash in Spain against the sale of Cuba forced Prim to formally renounce it. The Cuban insurgents now had no choice but to keep fighting.

Grant, meanwhile, in fulfillment of the U.S. threat, was ready to recognize Cuban belligerency, and arguably such an action would have been worthwhile. Spanish intransigence, now bolstered by the arguments of domestic business interests, continued to be the major barrier to independence.

Fish, however, still argued against recognition, and succeeded in dissuading

Grant. In December Grant made his position clear: there was to be no recognition. He released some thirty gunboats to Spain that he had been holding back because of the public controversy in the United States over Spain's policy in Cuba. And in his annual message, he argued that the Cubans did not deserve recognition as legitimate belligerents because the conflict "at no time assumed the conditions which amount to a war in the sense of international law."[20]

In the early months of 1870, the Spanish tried a new tactic: they attempted to argue that the war in Cuba was essentially over, that the rebels were near exhaustion, and that there was hence no cause for concern. The American public was skeptical, however, and soon reports of continued fighting dispelled the Spanish claim. Fish, however, whether intentionally or not, aided the Spanish policy by telling a friend at the New York *Herald* that the insurgency was almost at an end; the paper editorialized that this meant it was time for the United States to drop any consideration of recognition. Some other papers followed the *Herald*'s lead.

Many other papers refused to believe these claims, however, and the reports of fighting gave the lie to Fish's claim. The *Junta Cubana* also helped publicize the continuing war. By February, 1870 resolutions were afoot in both the House and the Senate to recognize Cuban belligerency, and dozens of editorials from major papers urged Congress to pass them.

Fish continued to stymie these efforts. He drafted a message for Grant to give to Congress, which was relayed on June 14. Its rationale for opposing recognition was the same as Grant's December message: that the war was still not a war. The House, influenced by this message, defeated a recognition bill on June 16 by a vote of 100 to 70.[21]

Madrid did not help matters by rejecting nearly all proposals for reform. The Moret Law of 1870, which was intended to achieve abolition, was weak, and even Hamilton Fish recognized it as such. Another stumbling block to the reform demanded by the U.S. government was the Volunteer Corps. The Volunteers vetoed much of the proposed reform in 1871-72, and their continuing power made the vetoes stick. They felt reforms would legitimize the cause of the rebels and begin a trend that would end in the total destruction of the class system in Cuba.

In a sense, this fear was justified; the war had already begun to lend credibility to the rebel cause. The United States, though trying to maintain a conservative stance, nevertheless could not avoid taking action. Fish notified Sickles that the Moret law—weak as it was—was not being enforced, and told him to inform the Spanish that if some action were not taken the U.S. position might change. Finally, when the Grant administration directly threatened a sugar boycott, Spain agreed to some reform, and promised various changes in the slave system. But as it had so many times in the past, Spain was making empty promises.

* * *

Late in 1873 an event transpired that brought the United States and Spain closer to war than perhaps they had ever been. On October 31, the steamer *Virginius*, sailing with an American and English crew, was caught by the Spanish attempting to smuggle arms to the Cuban rebels. The ship's party was led by William Ryan, a tall, dashing soldier of fortune, a veteran of the Civil War, gallant and daring. The captain of the *Virginius* was Joseph Fry, a U.S. Navy man of fifteen years before he had joined the Confederacy and fought on its side in the Civil War. Both had been contracted to deliver arms, but both were present at least partially for reasons of pure adventure.

The *Virginius* never reached its destination in Cuba; it was intercepted on the way by the Spanish warship *Tornado* and pursued. The *Virginius* was well-known to the Spanish as a smuggler's ship, and they were not about to let it slip through their fingers again. After fleeing for several hours, Fry finally realized that the engines of his elderly ship could not take the strain, and the *Virginius* stopped. The *Tornado* crew searched the American vessel, discovered the arms, and took the ship into custody, towing it into Santiago harbor.

The U.S. consul at Santiago, Arthur W. Young, was out of the country at the time. His assistant, Emil Schmitt, tried desperately and unsuccessfully to get some confirmation from the Spanish about the state of the *Virginius*'s crew. Spanish General Don Juan N. Burriel kept Schmitt isolated, and put the American prisoners on trial, a mere formality whose outcome had been decided as soon as the arms had been discovered. Fry, Ryan, and their crew were quickly convicted of various charges which amounted to gun-running and aiding the rebels. Schmitt went to see Burriel, to no avail; the General pleaded ignorance and innocence, and sent the American minister home.

The next morning, November 4, 1873, Ryan and three Cubans were brought out to be shot. Ryan, adventurer to the end, dressed nattily with his best hat, lit a cigar, faced his executioners, and wished his fellow prisoners well. Spanish soldiers tried to force Ryan and the Cubans to kneel and face away from the guns, but like Crittenden of the Lopez expeditions before them, they protested and were allowed to face their executioners. A volley flashed and the four were killed as Ryan "flung away his cigar." Four of the slain men were decapitated, their heads impaled on poles and exhibited to the public.

Schmitt continued his efforts to contact or free the men still imprisoned, but the Spanish, intent on carrying out their sentence, obstructed all his efforts. At the urging of the United States and Great Britain, President Castelar of Spain cabled Burriel to stay the remaining executions. But no telegraph station had been installed in Santiago, and the message got only as far as Havana. The British, too, were attempting to forestall the killings, and had sent the warship *Niobe* with a representative to intervene on the sailor's behalf. But it had not yet arrived, and Burriel was determined to carry out his sentence before it did.

On November 7, more men, including Fry, were brought out to be killed. He and dozens of his crewmen were led through the streets of Santiago to the wall where they would be shot. Schmitt was forced to stand aside and watch the men go to their deaths.

It is worth quoting the poignant description by Richard Bradford, author of *The Virginius Episode*, at length:

> When the men reached the wall, the firing squad was restingarms in a long line. A sergeant wasted no time running among the prisoners pushing each man by his shoulders against the wall. Fry was the only man not bound. . . .The crew knelt and in an emotional scene Fry went down the line saying goodbye. When he reached the end he took off his cap and seemed to be offering a prayer which was punctuated by commands from the firing squad officer. A ragged volley flashed toward the men. Fry fell forward, dead at the first fire. Others were still standing, leaning against the wall. Some bent forward. Many were on the ground in agony. Poor marksmanship and nervousness had made a butcher's job. Some of the squad rushed forward to administer the *coup de grace* and shoved muskets into the men's mouths. Shooting continued for five minutes until thirty-seven men lay dead in heaps before the wall. To American sailors in Santiago harbor it sounded like fireworks on the Fourth of July. A wagon drove up, the bodies were piled on hastily, and it drove off.

Captain Sir Lambton Lorraine, commanding the *Niobe*, finally arrived, and with impressive boldness forced the Spanish to cease the executions. Fifty-three men had already met their deaths.[22]

* * *

Americans of almost all political affiliations joined in calling immediately for war. Southerners were especially insulted by the affront to American honor, and called for an invasion. On November 14, 1873, large anti-Spanish rallies were held in New York and other big cities. In Madrid, Sickles demanded satisfaction, and threatened that the United States might close its embassy in Spain, a statement tantamount to a threat of war. The Spanish government by now tired of Sickles's rudeness and emotionalism, refused to deal with him, and negotiated instead through their Washington minister.

Fish did not favor military action, still believing that a war with Spain would be unwise for the United States. The two governments, speaking through Spain's Washington representative, signed a protocol providing for indemnity payments and punishment of the Spanish officers in question, but this insubstantial act failed to placate American public opinion. The economic collapse of 1873, however, which had already begun, diverted attention from the *Virginius* affair, and in the end the United States took no further action.

Perhaps most significant in dissuading the United States from going to war over the *Virginius* was the influence of Hamilton Fish. Fish used every bit of his political skill and considerable influence to steer the country clear of conflict. As we have seen his motives for opposing recognition of the Cuban rebels are in dispute, but in the case of the *Virginius* he clearly did the nation a great service, preventing a spur-of-the-moment decision to enter an unwise war. He wrote in a letter to his son, of the "tens of thousands of wives who might have been made widows, and of the hundreds of thousands of children who might have been made orphans, in an *unnecessary* war undertaken for a dishonest vessel." While the incident was unfortunate, he argued that "unless the national honor, or the national existence, require war. . .then the nation should do all that it can to avoid the terrible evil. That is what I have endeavored to do."[23]

There is no guarantee, moreover, that the United States would have won this conflict. The U.S. army had been reduced to less than 30,000 men in the demobilization which dominated the post-Civil War era, and at the time was heavily involved in the Indian Wars of the west. The Spanish army and navy, meanwhile, were experienced from their own civil wars and had retained their size. A Spanish-American war in 1873 might well have been a drawn-out affair for both countries, and Fish was probably right that the United States needed an end to bloodshed for a time.

The *Virginius* episode also indicated that "nothing had really changed in Cuba's colonial situation."[24] The Spanish were still adamantly attached to the island, and ruled it with an iron hand; they were still more than willing to throw their declining weight around in the region. Such tactics—guided perhaps more than anything by a sentimental attachment to empire—would bring on a true war at the end of the century.

The Continuing Cuban War

Meanwhile, several Central and South American republics, led by Colombia, attempted to secure independence for Cuba. In September 1872 Colombia proposed a multilateral action with aid from the United States to detach the island from Spain's control, and all Latin American governments agreed to the plan, provided the United States went along.

It would not. Fish's official rationale for rejecting the proposal was rather weak; it rested on procedural grounds. Fish claimed the United States had not been consulted during the formulation of the plan so he would refuse to grant an *ex-post-facto* endorsement. Some claim Fish's opposition to Cuban independence in almost any form was manifest in this opposition to the Latin American peace plan. Marxist historian Philip Foner has written of Fish's opposition:

> Thus with the life of the Cuban Republic and the freedom of
> hundreds of thousands of Cuban slaves at stake, the U.S. secretary
> of state rested on the niceties of diplomatic procedure to doom a
> project which had the greatest possibility thus far in the Ten Years
> War to achieve an end to the bloody conflict, the independence of
> Cuba, and the emancipation of its slaves.[25]

On the other hand, there is no guarantee that the plan would have worked. The Spanish would probably have been as intransigent as ever, and it may be true, as Fish suspected, that it would have taken a war to wrest Cuba from their control. The United States did continue to pressure Spain, obtaining French, British, Austrian, and Russian help in an attempt to force Spain to settle her differences with the Cubans.

Meanwhile, the Ten Years' War raged on in Cuba. Spain sent 35,000 veteran troops in a final attempt to crush the rebellion. The rebels fought with what they could beg and borrow from abroad, and what they could steal from the Spanish. By 1870, however, outside supplies were dwindling, in part because of active U.S. enforcement of its neutrality laws.

Generals Maximo Gomez and Calixto Garcia were the top rebel leaders of the time, battle-hardened Cuban patriots. They were assisted by a brave young officer, a military leader of legendary proportions in Cuba who later became known as "The Bronze Titan": Antonio Maceo. Maceo was born in 1845, the son of two free blacks; his mother was light-skinned, so Maceo qualified as a "mulatto" in Cuban culture. He would have clearly been viewed as a black in the United States, and he thought of himself as a man of color.

Born in Venezuela, Maceo's basically pro-Spanish family emigrated to Santo Domingo and then to Cuba, in part to avoid the continuing revolutionary wars in Spanish colonial America. At 16 he began work, hauling fruit and doing other chores. He learned horsemanship and gained a knowledge of the countryside, and his father taught him the use of firearms and the Cuban machete; those skills would serve him in good stead as an insurgent leader. His friendship with Don Ascencio de Ascencio, a Cuban lawyer, granted Maceo access to the highest levels of Cuban society, and he learned much in discussions with merchants, planters, and intellectuals.

These discussions confirmed what Maceo had believed for a long time: Spanish rule was unjust and detrimental to Cuban interests. His own conscience had already taught him to hate Spanish slavery and oppression. And so in 1864, when Maceo was in his early twenties, and as the opposition to Spanish rule in Cuba grew, he joined a secret revolutionary group, one of many then emerging on the island.

Maceo was a leader of enormous bravery, one of the greatest cavalry and guerrilla commanders in history. He was tough and uncompromising; he wrote that "liberty is not begged for; it is conquered," and in accordance with this theory carried the fight to the enemy with astonishing skill, elan, and occasional brutality. Maceo would lead his men into the teeth of overwhelming odds—sometimes as great as ten to one and somehow emerge victorious, though often wounded. By the time he had reached his early thirties his body was scarred with the results of hundreds of battles. Maceo would prove one of the most steadfast of the revolutionary leaders, refusing to abide by the compromise pacts which the Spanish proposed and unwilling to surrender no matter how badly his forces were depleted. He also serves as a good example of the sort of educated young Cuban who embodied the Caribbean characteristics outlined in Chapter One. He was one of the heroes of the Cuban revolution, and a great warrior for liberty.[26]

The revolutionary army had its own problems. It was racked with internal squabbles between two groups: the conservative class of wealthy landowners, and the middle- and lower-class farmers, slaves, and artisans. Racial tension resulted from a belief on the part of some slaves that the rebel leadership discriminated against Maceo because of his color. Various arguments erupted about what ought to constitute proper rebel strategy, especially on the question of slavery.

By 1875, however, rebels under Gomez had seized de facto control of most of Oriente and Camaguey provinces, and, pursuing a long-standing goal, he invaded Las Villas province, intending to smash the sugar mills there and destroy the material base of the Cuban economy, and, to a significant degree, of the Spanish economy as well. After some initial successes Gomez had burned nearly 100 sugar mills.

In the United States, Fish still opposed recognition, but the tide of public and congressional opinion was turning against him. By November, 1875 the administration, prodded by strong support among the American people for the rebels, had begun to talk about the right and duty to intervene "with the view of bringing to an end a disastrous and destructive conflict, and of restoring peace in the interest of all.''[27] In that same month Fish himself wrote the Spanish government, urging reforms and offering veiled threats regarding U.S. actions in the absence of such change. Fish pulled no punches: ''Spain was arraigned on almost as many charges as were solemnly paraded against George III in the Declaration of Independence.''[28] Caleb Cushing, U.S. minister to Spain, was told to inform the Spanish that the U.S. government was strongly considering intervention, and the cooperation of several European nations, especially England, was sought.

By November 15 Spain was again forced to offer concessions, but they were for the most part insubstantial. Cushing wrote Fish that if England sided strongly with the United States, Spain might be forced to capitulate completely on the Cuba issue, but he warned that many in Spain wanted a foreign war to divert attention from domestic problems. It might be more than willing to take the United States on if America stood alone.

In December, England expressed tentative support for the U.S. position based on its opposition to slavery. Cushing believed even this partial statement would force Spain to give in, but others were not so sure; Grant's annual message in December contained strong words about the devastation of Cuba in war but no proposals for specific remedies or demands for reform. Apparently he was not sufficiently convinced that the Europeans were on his side. Indeed, by January, 1876, it was clear that the Europeans would not support the United States wholeheartedly, and so on January 11, Fish announced that the Spanish had responded ''satisfactorily'' to U.S. demands for change—a politically convenient claim designed to cover up the American diplomatic failure.

Congress was doubly concerned over these machinations; it both desired action on Cuba and feared a U.S. abandonment of the Monroe Doctrine, signaled by a willingness to allow European participation in hemispheric affairs. On January 17 the House of Representatives requested from the administration the diplomatic correspondence pertaining to the issue.[29] Congress need not have worried; the only European nation seriously considering a joint intervention was England, and by January 25 it had become so unenamored of the plan that it said it would only intervene with the United States *and Spain*, an unlikely scenario.

Negotiations over reforms continued through 1876 while the Spanish kept a careful eye on U.S. military deployments. The Americans had sent a fleet to Port Royal. But by this time the fading European enthusiasm had already doomed the projected invasion; Cushing finally realized the obvious and in March he wrote Fish, ''We can do much with Spain, but it will have to be done on our own ground. We have no cause, in my belief, to expect aid from the European powers, not even from Great Britain.''[30]

On March 20 the Spanish Carlist civil wars came to an end. As noted, the Quadruple Alliance restored Ferdinand's wife to the throne. One of the major implications of the end of the Carlist wars was that Spain could now turn its full attention to the Cuban problem. By summer 1876, the Spanish had sent General Martinez Campos, the former captain-general of Cuba, and 25,000 battle-hardened troops to the island to reinforce the formidable forces already there. Within a year these fresh units, the continuing dearth of outside help, and the costs of an eight-year war began to tell seriously on the rebels, and their activities declined. In August, 1877, Fish resigned, but his policy remained in place, and the last few rebel attempts to gain U.S. recognition of belligerency failed.

Through these dark times Maceo was the spiritual as well as military leader of the opposition, and kept his troops fighting amid the surrenders of other groups. Spanish agents reportedly tried to kill, bribe, and defeat Maceo, all to no avail.[31] By 1878, however, the revolution had sputtered and stalled, and ground nearly to a halt; Gomez and other leaders of the insurrection had agreed to the Pact of Zanjon, an agreement that again promised Spanish reforms in exchange for a rebel surrender. Maceo was persuaded to go to New York in an attempt to raise support, but on May 21 the rebel government capitulated in Cuba and Maceo was forced to end his efforts. He returned to Jamaica, and began to plan for future revolutions.

The Ten Years' War was significant for a number of reasons. Though many Cubans died, thousands of others became battle-hardened veterans, instilled with a deep hatred of the Spanish and ready to fight again, as they would do a decade and a half later. Thousands of Cubans fled the island to avoid the devastation, and various Cuban independence groups sprang up in the United States and elsewhere, establishing a base of political and material support which would prove invaluable. Once slavery was abolished in Cuba, moreover, those of the Cuban planter class who opposed uprisings against the Spanish would lose their major fear—that of a slave rebellion—and many would join the ranks of those fighting for independence. The war also contributed to the growth of sentiment in the United States opposing Spanish rule and favoring Cuban independence, sentiment that would eventually contribute to the call for war at the end of the century.

Within Cuba, the period of the Ten Years' War also witnessed a further development of the progressive thought that encouraged revolt against Spanish influence and would later contribute to rebellions against the American role in Cuba. Much of this thought developed in the Cuban exile communities in the United States. Jose Marti was its chief proponent, and (as we shall see) his view was a natural outgrowth of earlier Caribbean intellectual trends. While the harsh Spanish rule from 1868 to 1878 destroyed many of the unions that had sprung up (in 1866 a Tobacco Union and some other groups had emerged), by the early 1880s the Cuban labor movement began to re-emerge. Social developments continued that would culminate in the rejection of foreign influence by the Cuban intelligentsia and large sections of the general population during the twentieth century, but quietly, incrementally, and below the generally observable surface of Cuban politics. The implications of these developments would not be fully realized for another hundred years.[32]

RELATIONS 1877 TO 1890

U.S. relations with Spain and Cuba were relatively stable during the period from 1877 to 1890. Most disputes between the United States and Spain had been resolved. Differences of opinion about the Ten Years' War and its aftermath continued, however, and through 1884 pressures on Spain to reform and demands for reparations for American property that had been destroyed constituted major topics of discussion. Between 1884 and 1890, moreover, Madrid continually demanded that the United States more firmly enforce its neutrality laws against filibusters that the Spanish knew to be forming expeditions in Key West and elsewhere. The United States responded promptly to these requests.[33]

By 1880 only trade problems lingered to qualify a description of U.S.-Spanish relations as ''cordial.'' Spanish tariffs accounted for the fact that in the period 1876-1891, U.S. imports from Cuba amounted to $923 million, while exports to the island totaled only $189 million. In 1884, the United States signed a reciprocity treaty with Spain that opened Cuban ports to some extent. American negotiators saw the treaty as a significant step toward expanding American influence in Cuba; chief negotiator John W. Foster called it ''the most perfect reciprocity treaty our government has ever made,'' and felt that it would give the United States a virtual monopoly over Cuban commerce. Foster happily reported that signing the treaty was tantamount to ''annexing Cuba in the most desirable way.''[34]

The United States also experienced a temporary renewal of the annexationist sentiment of the 1840s and 1850s, a ''momentary return of the traditional Democratic desire for the annexation of Cuba.''[35] In 1887 John Sherman was sent to Cuba to observe the situation, and reported that the depressed economy and generally poor state of affairs contributed to limited annexationist sentiment on the island. Some desultory purchase attempts were made, but none succeeded. Spain was still unwilling to part with its jewel.

In Spain, meanwhile, Martinez Campos had risen to a high position in the government. A powerful political figure in Spain even before he served as captain-general of Cuba, Martinez Campos recognized that only fundamental changes in Spanish colonial policy could prevent a recurrence of revolution. He therefore recommended sweeping reforms in that policy, especially with regard to tariffs and taxes. While in Cuba he undertook to accomplish what changes he could with his somewhat limited authority.

At the time, however, a dictatorship under Canovas ruled Spain. Canovas was a political rival of Martinez Campos, and the ongoing feud between the two men produced a deadlock on the proposed reforms. Martinez Campos became head of the Spanish government for a short time, but his cabinet and many other parts of the government were beholden to Canovas. Thus "the cause of Cuban reform had foundered on the shoals of internal Spanish politics."[36] Repressive Spanish rule continued and lack of reform set the stage for the 1895 revolution and the Spanish-American War.

Jose Marti: An Emerging Patriot

Jose Marti was born in 1853, the son of simple, uneducated parents: a Spanish artillery sergeant and his wife. An outstanding student, Marti soon emerged as an eloquent and forceful writer and speaker. His thought, again, was a development of the growing trend among Caribbean intellectuals in favor of independence.[37]

Marti entered politics as early as 1869 with the publication of *The Limping Devil*, a humorous pamphlet making light of press censorship, and *Our Free Country*, a patriotic paper that lasted only one issue. At the tender age of 17 he was arrested for anti-government propaganda, and was sentenced to six years hard labor. After serving a number of months of that sentence, he was lucky enough to be reassigned, through the intercession of his father, to a prison on a friend's estate, where he was treated well enough. But Marti would retain permanent physical and psychological disabilities from his period of imprisonment and labor. In 1871 he was sent into exile in Spain.

Marti began a colorful career fighting for Cuban independence. He started newspapers, aided Cuban exile groups, and founded an organization in New York to promote Cuban independence. He would eventually return to Cuba to wage war for the freedom he held so dear.

Marti's writings reveal a man deeply committed to liberty and respect for individual autonomy. "Respect for the freedom and ideas of others," he wrote, "of even the most wretched being, is my fanaticism. If I die, or am killed, it will be because of that." Liberty, for Marti, was "the essence of life," and politics ought to consist of an attempt to achieve the highest degree of liberty and fairness possible; it is "the art of raising unjust humanity towards justice." Marti's revolutionary spirit was based on an essential optimism about human nature. Once exposed to the good, Marti felt, men could not resist it; by nature, he wrote, ''man is noble and inclined to what is best.''[38]

Marti's views on the United States have been the subject of much debate. Marxist and anti-imperialist historians have taken his comments as a stinging critique of American society. Others, such as historian Carlos Ripoll, have argued that Marti was not anti-American per se, but merely opposed the interventionist nature of American foreign policy.[39] (Marti's views on the United States, and the influence of those views on Castro's revolution, are examined in Chapter Nine.)

The "Little War": A Prelude to Revolution

Marti and other Cuban leaders had been planning a new revolt since the end of the Ten Years' War. In 1879 their plans were still in infancy, but through an elaborate and efficient network of spies and fifth-columnists infiltrated into Cuban units, Spanish authorities learned of the plot. Revolutionary leaders in Cuba, acting independently, felt they needed to move immediately, before the whole revolution was completely compromised.

On August 29, 1879, then, the ''Little War'' began, a premature revolt led by Maceo and others in the field, with Marti manning the political headquarters of the opposition in Havana. At first there was little fighting, but by early September the Spanish were worried enough to arrest Marti and deport him to Spain, where he escaped and sailed to New York. Other rebel leaders were also arrested and sent off the island, and without leadership the insurgency quickly collapsed. By September 1880, after much planning and little actual fighting, the revolt was pronounced officially dead.

The ''Little War'' highlighted the fact that of recurring problems still undercut the efforts of the insurgents. One was racism. Maceo had been passed over for overall command of the rebel forces, and this infuriated both him and his free black troops. Support from the United States—either from its government or from illegal gun-runners or filibusters—had been virtually nonexistent. And the exile communities in the United States and elsewhere remained divided over the proper conduct of the war.[40] These problems also hampered Cuban revolutionaries during the 1895 revolution.

As the final revolution against Spanish authority approached, Cuban exile groups, led by Marti, continued to raise funds and support. Two small rebellions in the mid-1880s were easily crushed by the Spanish. In 1884 the first meeting of Marti, Maceo, and Gomez—the three great leaders of the impending revolt—occurred. There were persistent personality clashes and severe disagreements over the proper conduct of the impending war for independence. Marti left the meeting in a huff after being told by Gomez to "limit yourself to obeying orders." The result was a Marti-Gomez split that took some time to heal.[41]

By 1890, however, the drive for independence had taken on a virtually unstoppable momentum. Cubans were by then accustomed to war, and dedicated to the goal of throwing off the Spanish colonial yoke. The coming conflict would see the application of the most brutal counterinsurgency tactics by the Spanish, and terrible loss of life among the Cuban civilian population. Eventually, the United States, encouraged by a renewed sense of mission and national *hubris*, would step in, send the Spanish packing, and rebuild the island in several short months. But until that time, every Cuban became familiar with the deprivations and horrors of war.

PART
TWO

THROWING OFF THE YOKE
OF DOMINATION

The Spanish-Cuban-American War
to Castro's Revolution

4

THE GREAT REVOLUTION AND AMERICAN EXPANSION

Relations 1890-1902

"Every war is its own excuse. That's why they're all surrounded with ideals. That's why they're all crusades."
Karl Shapiro, *The Bourgeois Poet*

"War should never be entered upon until every agency of peace has failed."
William McKinley, Inaugural Address, March 4, 1897

"[We must] prevent in time the expansion of the United States in the Antilles, and their descending, with their additional strength, upon the lands of America. . . . I have lived in the monster, and know its entrails; and my sling is that of David."
Jose Marti, May 18, 1895

Since the pact of Zanjon ended the Ten Years' War in 1878, U.S. economic interests in Cuba had risen sharply. By 1896, U.S. investment in Cuba totalled over $45 million. From 1892 to 1894, trade between the two countries averaged $100 million, despite continuing Spanish tariffs. The United States became the chief importer of Cuba's sugar, tobacco, and manufactured products, and by the end of the 1880s trade with Cuba constituted one-quarter of the U.S. total.[1]

Meanwhile, as the last decade of the nineteenth century began, a new expansionism was sweeping America: the "New Manifest Destiny." A number of factors contributed to this renewed exertion of national will: the U.S. frontier had been conquered, and the nation looked to other areas for expansion; the industrial revolution created a need for foreign markets; and the influential thought of Alfred Thayer Mahan and others, who argued that a maritime empire was America's destiny, had a significant effect on public consciousness.[2]

At the same time, various exiled Cuban leaders, not broken by their defeat in the Ten Years' War, began to plan a new revolution. Jose Marti was the most famous of these, and he formed the Cuban Revolutionary Party in Tampa and Key West on January 5, 1892, later moving the group to New York. His primary tasks were to unify the quarrelling exile groups and to paper over his own dispute with Gomez. In March he started the newspaper *Patria*, and by the same month had rallied all the official Cuban exile "clubs" around him.[3] The seeds of a new revolution had been planted, and stagnant economic conditions in Cuba would provide them with fertile soil.

These three developments would be chiefly responsible for the Spanish Cuban-American War and the attendant U.S. intervention in Cuba. Driven by a desire for commercial markets, by the new expansionist mood—and by a true humanitarian concern for the Cuban people—the United States would finally break the bonds of its traditional isolationism and begin the journey to the status of a true world power. Cuba would be the primary catalyst for this change. The Harrison administration was the first to be significantly influenced by the "New Manifest Destiny," though its expansionism was expressed through diplomatic and economic, as opposed to military, channels. Not until William McKinley's administration would the expansionist sentiment reach its height.

By 1893, the general worldwide depression had done serious damage to the Cuban economy. Since about 1890 Spain's colonial government had done little to promote the economic well-being of the island, and conservatives who opposed reform held sway in Havana. The economic slowdown that resulted was compounded with high Spanish taxes and an increase in banditry and guerrilla actions. In 1891 the economy was briefly revived by the Foster-Canovas agreement discussed earlier, but the Wilson Tariff of 1894 reversed this progress by restricting Cuban imports to the United States.[4] These economic problems would serve the nascent Cuban rebel movement well, helping them to recruit thousands of volunteers, men who had lost their jobs and who otherwise might have been too afraid for their livelihoods to risk open revolt.

THE 1895 REVOLUTION BEGINS

In 1895, a new revolution began in Cuba which would eventually drive the Spanish from the island. Led by veterans of earlier wars—Antonio Maceo, Maximo Gomez, Calixto Garcia—and by Jose Marti, the revolution developed into an enormously bloody conflict, described by one author as "an orgy of pillage and destruction."[5] Even before the revolution itself, Spain sent agents to assassinate Maceo in Costa Rica; though wounded by a bullet, he survived to play an important role in the upcoming conflict.[6]

As noted, the depressed economic conditions on Cuba contributed heavily to the insurrection. The collapse of the sugar industry created tens of thousands of rural unemployed ripe for revolt.[7] Rebel leaders decided upon a strategy of crop destruction, reasoning that if they could annihilate the economic base of the island they could achieve two objectives: create desperate recruits for their army, and make the island worthless to Spain. The rebels rarely met the Spanish head-on in battle, preferring to stage raids designed to cripple the island's economic and governmental institutions.

The rebel forces did not operate without occasional cruelty. On April 21, 1895, Maceo ordered the hanging of all Spanish peace envoys, claiming that "our motto is to triumph or to die."[8] The rebels used the traditional farming knife, the *machete*, with brutal efficiency in combat, and it was said that a strong man could take off an opponent's arm with one stroke. In 1896, Maceo also ordered the killing by *machete* of all black Cubans caught fighting with the Spaniards.

Spanish officers responded with brutalities of their own. Spanish troops were alleged to have committed beatings, tortures, and rapes, on a scale seldom before seen in warfare. Faced with the classic problem of guerrilla warfare — a freely-moving insurgent group supported by the populace like fish in water — the Spanish resorted to tactics designed to drain the water, rather than catch the fish.[9] They moved much of the population into garrisoned towns or, in the rural areas, resettlement camps, in a policy called *reconcentracion*. They burned crops and pursued a scorched-earth policy in the uncontrolled areas, hoping to starve the rebels of support and supplies.

In the process, the Spanish nearly annihilated the whole Cuban population. Conditions for the *reconcentrados*, the people held in the camps, were, to say the least, inhumane; tens of thousands starved or perished of various diseases—the Spanish themselves estimated almost half a million such deaths—and thousands more were executed for alleged support for the rebels. In June, 1896 Secretary of State John Sherman called the Spanish policy "uncivilized" and President William McKinley would later say of the camp strategy that "it was not civilized warfare. It was extermination."[10]

The Spanish captain general for much of the revolution was Martinez Campos. Known and respected as the tough but fair man who had crushed the Ten Years' revolt two decades earlier, Martinez Campos nevertheless had his problems. The insurgency proved difficult to control, and Spanish leaders faced a problem that would be confronted by colonial powers for generations: determined national resistance movements, using well-executed guerrilla tactics, can frustrate larger and better-equipped forces and keep them at bay for years.

Martinez Campos was replaced in January, 1896 with the distinctly more brutal Valeriano Weyler. Martinez Campos had realized that the sorts of policies required to defeat the insurgency were beyond his moral capacity to implement, and wrote Madrid that they might want to replace him with someone possessing such capacities. "In Spain," he wrote, "only Weyler has them." Weyler, for his part, believed his reputation to be undeserved, and looked upon himself as a soldier following orders and recognizing the cruel realities of then-modern warfare.

A former leader of the hated *Voluntarios*, Weyler was reputed by the rebels to have "a face like a reptile, the body of a dwarf, the instinct of a jackal, and soul of a dog."[11] Weyler's conduct brought him the nickname of "The Butcher," and one Cuban general remarked that his rule brought "mass acts of barbarism," which were claimed to include massacres of wounded and captured Cubans as well as unarmed civilians. It was during Weyler's tenure that the *reconcentracion* policy began to be implemented in earnest.

American papers reacted violently to Weyler's appointment. He was called a "bloodthirsty" soldier who was "charged by his own countrymen with representing the spirit of extreme cruelty."[12] His tenure as captain general provided even more fodder to the interventionist press.

Even within Cuba, Weyler's arrival caused a wave of fear. Thousands of Cubans attempted to flee the island, afraid of the devastation Weyler's rule might cause. Ships leaving Cuba were booked solid for weeks after the announcement of Weyler's appointment; "it makes no difference whither the ship is bound," one paper noted. "The main thing is to get away before the arrival of Weyler."[13]

* * *

An American riding with Gomez's forces in Cuba, Grover Flint, reported the results of one of Wyler's atrocities. The Cuban peasantry lived in a "dull unceasing dread" of Spanish attacks, he wrote, an emotion born of long, hard experience. At the ruins of the Olayita plantation in Las Villas province, Flint witnessed for himself the "ghastly" results of a Spanish raid.

At Olayita, at the end of February 1896, a small unit of Cuban rebels skirmished with two Spanish columns, and after a sharp fight retired through the Olayita plantation. The Spanish troops charged and seized the sugar production facility and the surrounding houses and buildings, now empty except for some twenty-three *pacíficos*, or innocent civilians. Apparently the Spanish decided to take revenge for the battle of these defenseless Cubans.

First to die was Mr. Duarte, the administrator of the plantation. He was dragged from his bed, where he lay terrified, by Spanish troops, who hacked him to death with machetes. Then ''an indiscriminate slaughter of the plantation hands and their families'' was begun.

> Men, women, and small children [Flint wrote] were dragged from
> their homes and cut down in the usual brutal manner. The. . .build-
> ings [of the plantation] . . . were set on fire, and the bodies of the vic-
> tims, dead or dying, were thrown among the flames. Only one
> escaped, a Chinese coolie, who succeeded in making the woods
> nearby with six Mauser bullet holes in him.

Three months after the massacre, Flint was still able to view the grim results. The plantation was destroyed, many of the buildings totally razed, others reduced to rubble. In the sugar-house itself he counted seven bodies piled near the driving wheel of the machinery.

> Uppermost of all, wedged between the wheel and the masonry, lay a
> negro woman, with a baby in her arms. Her clothing had been
> turned away, but the charred flesh remained, and a portion of one of
> her leather slippers. . . .The negress lay in an almost natural posi-
> tion, clasping the infant tight to her breast with a hugging, clutching
> embrace that death had only intensified.

In other parts of the buildings lay more charred bodies, some bearing machete wounds. One coolie had been forced by machete blows into a furnace chamber, where he burned alive, his body ''writhed in intense agony,'' his face ''fixed in an expression of extreme horror.'' Nor was the Olayita massacre a unique event; Flint heard reports of shootings, machete killings, and any number of other brutalities and estimated that in every town big enough ''to have its name on the map'' twenty or more civilians had been murdered by the Spanish. And all these brutalities occurred *before* the *reconcentracion* policy was implemented, which was in itself, in Flint's words, ''a greater destruction of peasant life than one can recall in the annals of medieval warfare.''[14]

* * *

Somewhat earlier, Jose Marti had been ambushed and killed by Spanish troops. On May 19, 1895, Marti, though ordered by Gomez to keep well behind the lines, attempted to ride up to the scene of an ongoing battle. In the process, he was ambushed by a Spanish patrol and shot. Marti left a stirring example, some 70 volumes of writings, and a prophetic warning: Cuban leaders, he said in his last letter, which lay in his camp while he was killed, must "prevent, by the independence of Cuba, the United States from spreading over the West Indies and falling, with that added weight, upon other lands of our America." The Cubans must not underestimate the threat from the North, he emphasized; "I have lived in the monster and know its entrails."[15]

The *Alianca* Episode

As had been the case during the Ten Years' War, during the first years of the 1895 revolution the United States directed most of its concern to the security of its property in Cuba.[16] Rebel bands repeatedly attacked American-controlled sugar, tobacco, and coffee plantations, as part of their continuing strategy to bring the island's economy to a halt. American consuls received reports of mistreatment of pro-rebel American citizens by Spanish authorities, and a number of Americans were even arrested or killed.

In March 1895, a controversy over a U.S. mail steamer contributed to the renewed growth of widespread anti-Spanish opinion in the United States. The steamer *Alianca* was headed to New York from the Caribbean; off Cuba it was fired upon by a Spanish ship. Apparently the Spanish thought it might be another in the long procession of U.S. arms smugglers supporting the Cuban rebels. U.S. Secretary of State Walter Gresham demanded an apology on behalf of the administration, and after a month the Spanish finally responded, claiming a simple mistake.[17]

The U.S. Congress, however, was not satisfied. Since 1893, Madrid had been almost totally intransigent with regard to debts and reparations owed the United States; U.S. Minister to Spain Hannis Taylor had no success attempting to persuade the conservative Spanish government to accede to U.S. demands and this history of stubbornness caused American policy-makers to expect little in the way of compromise from Madrid. Congress was also enraged by reports of Spanish atrocities in the Cuban war. Some senators even called for an invasion of the island. Annexationist and expansionist sentiment, dormant for several decades, began to reappear in relation to Cuba, and the press fanned the flames, claiming that the "American flag has been insulted." Governor Atkinson of Georgia wrote that "Cuba should cease to be Spanish and become American," and some papers echoed his call, noting the availability of American fleets for the purpose.[18] The Cleveland administration did its best to defuse the issue.

At about the same time, a series of small filibustering expeditions began to form in Florida and other locations in the southern United States, especially in Key West. The Spanish made repeated and urgent requests to the Cleveland administration to stop these groups, and in June, 1895 Cleveland declared that all violations of neutrality laws would be "rigorously prosecuted." Spanish efforts to stop the filibusters led to some tensions, however; in 1896, for example, the schooner *Competitor* was seized for gun-running, and the United States was forced to make extensive diplomatic efforts to ensure the safety of the crew, who had been sentenced to death.[19]Most Americans did not believe Spanish claims of reform, moreover, and had the impression that nearly all Cubans were fighting with the rebels in an heroic battle against oppression.[20] This feeling was whipped into a virtual frenzy by the press, which trumpeted Spanish abuses and made rebel exploits legendary. The U.S. government was not immune to such sentiments; in September 1896, Secretary of State Richard Olney investigated the situation and came to conclusions similar to those of the press. The revolution, he wrote, commanded "the sympathy, if not the open support, of the great bulk of the population affected," and the rebel coalition was nearly capable of forming "an established, constitutional government."[21]

Congress responded with calls for recognition of the rebels as a legitimate representative of the Cuban people. In January 1896 the Senate and House passed resolutions indicating that "a condition of public war" existed between Spain and Cuba. But this legislation had no force, and Cleveland did nothing. Olney still favored neutrality, but wanted the United States to give the rebels a hearing. Cleveland, also pressured by U.S. businessmen who owned property in Cuba, resisted calls for stronger support of the rebels. Despite Olney's view, the administration determined that the rebels were incapable of self-government, and so in July, Cleveland rejected a proposal to aid the insurgents.

Traditional U.S. conservatism with regard to Cuban insurrections no doubt influenced Cleveland, but his true motives are open to some dispute. He feared war with Spain, and was skeptical about the viability of the rebels. It is important to remember that the New Manifest Destiny, like the old version, was tinged with racial bigotry, and the Cubans were seen as uneducated savages: hardly a democracy-loving people ready to accept the responsibilities of true independence. Any U.S. intervention on the rebels' behalf, moveover, would end payments Spain was making to the United States for capital losses in Cuba. In addition, long-term Spanish control would guarantee eventual stability and a favorable business climate.[22]

Some commentators have suggested a distinct pro-Spanish, anti-Cuban line in Cleveland's policies. In June and July, 1895, he certainly did take the by-now routine action of stopping filibusters headed for the island with supplies.[23] Moveover, he allowed Spain to buy, in Philip Foner's words, "all the arms and munitions she needed in her effort to crush the revolution."[24] Critics point to the influence of Edwin Atkins, a U.S. planter operating in Cuba, who supplied much of the information the Cleveland administration possessed about the revolution. In short, critics contend that the Cleveland administration's Cuban policy supported Spanish rule in a number of ways, and thereby hampered a potential victory by the Cuban rebel forces.

The public, meanwhile, was pressing even more loudly for action. The Cuban *Junta* in New York had become virtually the sole source of day-to-day public information on the war, and of course its stories were highly biased, though because they were exciting they were often reprinted verbatim in American papers. This sentiment was translated to Congress.[25]

As early as April, 1886, the United States had begun to pressure Spain in a serious fashion, demanding an end to the war or at least the atrocities. Olney informed the Spanish that it was the opinion of the United States that the war would not end soon. The U.S. government, he said, had information indicating the insurgents were 60,000 strong and unwilling to compromise. Olney decried the devastation of land (and U.S. property with it) and called for reforms aimed at a democratization of the island.[26]

Cleveland's annual message in December, 1896 reflected his ambivalence. Neither side, he said, held a clear upper hand in the Cuban war. Cleveland stressed U.S. commercial interest in Cuba, noting that U.S. investments amounted to $30- $50 million and that trade ran to $100 million annually. He suggested autonomous Cuban rule under Spain. The United States must still remain neutral, with the understanding that, if no satisfactory scheme for governing the island peacefully could be evolved, "a time may arrive when a correct policy. . .will constrain our Government" to take action, by which he meant intervention.[27] For the time being, however, he made no promises and no commitments.

The public was outraged by this position; many felt Cleveland was exhibiting weakness, and one paper noted that he had "stood up so straight" in defending proper conduct "that he leans backward."[28] As we have seen, Congress had passed resolutions calling for recognition of the belligerent status of the Cuban insurgents. Olney responded that only the President could make such foreign policy decisions, and that in any case the practical implications of the resolutions meant inevitable war with Spain.

Meanwhile, in Cuba, Antonio Maceo was killed. In early December, 1896, Maceo was surprised at his command post by a Spanish attack. The assault was repulsed, but in pursuing the attackers Maceo was shot twice and killed.[29] The greatest leader of the Cuban revolutionary movement was dead.[30]The last months of the Cleveland administration saw some hope for the home-rule proposal. Some Cubans suggested that a relatively liberal autonomy offer would be accepted by the bulk of the rebels, and the U.S. government followed up on these reports. Autonomy plans became common topics of discussion over the next years, as Cuban, American, and Spanish negotiators attempted to find an agreeable compromise between independence and unfettered Spanish rule. Gomez, however, informed Olney that he would not agree to such plans, and the U.S. efforts came to naught.

THE MCKINLEY PRESIDENCY

On March 4, 1897, William McKinley became the 25th president of the United States. American business interests, fearful of the progressivism of William Jennings Bryan, helped engineer McKinley's election. A former army officer and businessman, McKinley presented just the right image of conservative patriotism.

With regard to Cuba, McKinley proved a more aggressive president than Cleveland had been. Where Cleveland was cautious and unwilling to risk war, McKinley was determined to resolve the Cuban question. One of his election planks called for the United States to "actively use its influence and good offices" to "restore peace and give independence to this Island." In his first annual message, however, McKinley qualified this commitment by saying, "I speak not of forcible annexation, for that can not be thought of. That, by our code of morality, would be a criminal aggression."[31]

In that same message, McKinley spelled out various courses his administration might take. It could recognize the belligerent status of the Cuban rebels, more ambitiously recognize the *de facto* independence of the island, or pursue a "neutral" but decidedly military intervention. For various reasons, mostly duplicating the previous concerns expressed by Cleveland, McKinley rejected all three of these courses. He left a clear impression, however, that any or all might become possible in the absence of Spanish reforms. His goal was still an end to the war in Cuba, achieved in a fashion which would not lead to war with Spain. He replaced U.S. Minister to Spain Hannis Taylor with Stewart Woodford, a quiet, dutiful lawyer and former Civil War general whom McKinley could trust to follow his orders. McKinley saw U.S. economic interests in the island as an overriding justification for an end to the war, and was appalled by reports of Spanish abuses.[32]

Woodford recommended, and McKinley approved, a firm but progressive negotiating stance. But the key divergence from past policy was that McKinley was now truly willing to risk war with Spain, though he preferred to avoid such a conflict. Woodford made the new U.S. resolve clear in conversations with Spanish officials. Spain offered familiar promises of reform, autonomy for the rebels under Madrid's control, and an end to the war; in return they expected the rebels to lay down their arms. Rebel leaders predictably rejected the Spanish proposals as inadequate.[33] Madrid believed that McKinley would be unable to take decisive action before the November 1897 elections. Spanish minister to the United States de Lome wrote his government that "it is indisputable that today he [McKinley] is trying to have the solution of the Cuban question effected in a way that will result in triumph for his personal politics."[34]

Another change in the Spanish government offered a brief hope for reform in Cuba. Under its July, 1876 constitution, Spain alternated its governments between two parties — the Liberals and the Conservatives. When in October, 1897 the conservative Prime Minister Canovas was assassinated and the Liberal Praxedes Sagasta came to power, some speculated Spain would be more forthcoming on the Cuba issue. But while this new government wanted to appease the United States, and made several concessions including the recall of Weyler, his representatives still argued that they could not assent to "foreign interference in our domestic affairs with our colonies."[35]

The United States was becoming increasingly impatient with these delays. McKinley demanded that the Red Cross be allowed into Cuba, which it finally was in December, 1897. In June of that year the administration wrote to the Spanish government to protest the "deliberate infliction of suffering on innocent noncombatants," and "the cruel employment of fire and famine," among other abuses.[36] Woodford demanded concrete reforms by November, and transmitted a letter demanding an end to the war, and if possible a truly "honorable settlement" involving extensive autonomy guarantees for Cuba. If Spain did not provide this, Woodford explained, the United States would act in a way "which the time and the transcendent emergency may demand."[37] American concerns were still guided to a great degree by the continuing destruction of U.S. property. Meanwhile, some private U.S. citizens attempted to take matters into their own hands and arrange a purchase scheme, but it fell through.[38]

The Sagasta government tried a number of avenues to appease the McKinley administration. They claimed to have eliminated the *reconcentrado* policy, and offered another Cuban autonomy scheme. The offers were relatively generous, for the Spanish, and one U.S. official — responding to a general administrative desire to dampen public demands for U.S. intervention — was moved to say that "thus far Spain has surrendered everything asked of her, and the policy of the administration has been completely vindicated.'' In December McKinley's annual message asked the American public to give the Spanish reforms a chance to work, and it promised action if they did not.[39]

MOTIVES FOR U.S. EXPANSIONISM

On the threshold of a new century, the United States stood flushed with expansionist sentiment. Most historians place the starting point of U.S. emergence to great power status at about the time of the Spanish-Cuban-American war; U.S. intervention in Cuba and the Philippines would pave the way for decades of worldwide interventionism.

The New Manifest Destiny was founded on tenets similar to those that had infused American thought in earlier decades; they could be summed up as ''progress and mission.'' U.S. expansion would bring liberty, economic development, and the paternalistic hand of the Anglo-Saxon race to the various countries lucky enough to be chosen. The New Manifest Destiny differed from the old, as Julius Pratt has recognized, in that between 1840 and 1890 ''much had been done to provide this emotional content with a philosophical backing. The expansionists of the 1890s were able to cite the lessons of science and history in support of their doctrine.''[40]

Social Darwinism and Expansion

One such ''scientific'' lesson was provided by Charles Darwin's theory of evolution and those who (wrongly) applied it to human social development within single generations. This ''Social Darwinism'' allowed advocates of American expansion both to trumpet the philosophy of the ''white man's burden'' to support their political views and to justify expansion as the ''natural'' domination of weaker races by stronger ones.

From the beginning, a blatant streak of racism ran through much of the expansionist literature. In 1885, historian John Fiske, a disciple of Darwin, wrote that ''the two great branches of the English race have the common mission of establishing throughout the larger part of the earth a higher civilization and more permanent political order than any that has gone before.''[41] Similar sentiments were expressed by many other expansionists.

Julius Pratt analyzed the influence of Social Darwinism on U.S. expansionism in his landmark study, *Expansionists of 1898*. Darwinian science, propounded by such men as Fiske, Josiah Strong, and Columbia Professor John W. Burgess, encouraged Americans to fulfill their rights and duties as a ''superior'' race. ''If the survival of the fittest was the law of nature and the path of progress," as Pratt phrases the basic tenet of the Social Darwinists, "surely the more gifted races need offer neither apologies nor regrets when they suppressed, supplanted, or destroyed their less talented competitors."[42] Bouyed by such theories, and the scientific imprimatur they purported to bestow upon expansionism, the imperialists felt free to expand.

The Humanitarian Motive

Many Americans were undoubtedly motivated by a genuine concern for the welfare of the Cuban people. The American press highlighted Spanish atrocities and the economic devastation suffered by the island, and many Americans supported intervention for humanitarian motives. A war that had caused a quarter of a million casualties among a population of about one million could not be allowed to continue unchecked, these observers argued.

Clergymen played a particularly significant role in fostering American sentiment for the Cubans, and some combined humanitarian religious fervor with expansionism. Josiah Strong, in *Our Country*, achieved just such a synthesis, and he and other religious figures argued that God had chosen the American people to civilize the world. The Protestant press was one of the most consistent advocates of intervention, and explicitly claimed humanitarian motives.

President McKinley made special reference to humanitarian concerns in his various messages regarding Cuba. Whether or not they constituted his primary motive, he certainly claimed that sympathy for the Cuban people was high among his reasons for recommending war.

Events of the Times

A unique set of events together caused various segments of society to support expansion and war. As Walter Mills notes in *The Martial Spirit*, the loss of the frontier, the power generated by a U.S. naval buildup, the financial panic of 1893, and the growth of business—especially in terms of political influence—all contributed to an expansionist mood.[43]

Ernest May has emphasized the importance of the splintering of American national leadership, and the coincidence that many of the "splinters" found themselves, for one reason or another, advocating expansionism. The lack of acceptable alternatives to invasion—continued Spanish rule not being one—and the economic hardships of the time also contributed to a desire for an outward push. Only when brought to fruition by these developments, May stressed, did the humanitarian, racial, political, and other concerns cause a blossoming of expansionism.[44]

Richard Hofstadler has concluded that these events created a "psychic crisis" in the American mind, a growing fear that the United States was losing its frontier, its markets, its spiritual vigor, a fear that expressed itself in an almost panicked desire to expand. In a psychological sense, Americans were trying to "escape" from the "reality" of their domestic concerns, Hofstadler believes, by directing their energies outward. And in this they were at least partially successful.[45]

The Commercial Argument

More often than any other single motive, however, the desire for overseas markets has been proposed as a major contributor to U.S. expansionist sentiment.

Perhaps the best known historian who advocates this view is Walter La-Feber. In *The New Empire*, he notes that businessmen pressured the McKinley administration to expand for five primary reasons: commerce would benefit from an annexation of Cuba; businessmen were uncertain about the threat of war with Spain and wanted to resolve the question for good; they realized that the United States had acquired enough gold reserves to fight a war if one came up; the fear of European intervention on Spain's behalf had been overcome; and businessmen thought that the United States possessed sufficient military superiority to win a war against Spain.[46]

One important theme is that of *overproduction*: U.S. industry, growing at an incredible rate, had begun to produce far more products than it could sell on the domestic market. Therefore industry required foreign markets, and expansionism could provide them. As LaFeber argues, the United States went to war "as a means to acquire markets for the glut of goods pouring out of highly mechanized factories and farms."[47] In a similar vein the New York State Bankers' Association wrote at the time that

> Our capacity to produce far exceeds our capacity to consume. The home market can no longer keep furnaces in blast or looms in action. That capital may earn its increment and labor be employed, enterprise must contend in the markets of the world, for the sale of our surplus products.[48]

William Appleman Williams and other scholars have amassed a huge body of evidence suggesting that economic considerations strongly influenced, if they did not decide, all major public policy decisions during the period.[49] Charles Beard's economic analyses of the Constitution place these influences in an historical perspective.[50] And writers at the time recognized these motives. In a book published in the 1920s, Leland Jenks argued that the

United States was obviously guided by economic motives in its occupation of Cuba; "we wrap the American flag about our dollar investments," he concluded.[51]

The Marxist historian Philip Foner naturally agrees. The Spanish-American war was "an imperialistic war, fought for imperialistic reasons," he writes. More specifically, "the Cuban policy of the United States culminating in the use of force against Spain had its root in the rise of monopoly capitalism and its drive for markets." Other motives merely "reenforced economic factors," which were "predominant."[52]

But some have cautioned against a strictly economic interpretation of expansionism. "An American desire for territorial expansion," historian John Dobson argues, "was as old as the Union itself." The newfound strength of industry could not be solely responsible for expansionism because "territorial aggrandizement must be considered a dominant tradition in American history." A perception of the superiority of United States-style democratic self-government developed into a missionary zeal to spread that sort of government.[53] It is indeed debatable how much of the war pressure on Congress from the American people stemmed from economic concerns—most Americans were simply horrified at Spanish brutalities and whipped into a nationalistic frenzy over the *Maine* and de Lome incidents.

In fact, Foster Rhea Dulles argued that economic motives played a minor role in the promotion of expansionism. "Economic considerations had little to do with the popular sentiment of 1898," he concluded in 1965.

> American investments in Cuba amounted to some $50 million, and the annual trade between Cuba and the United States totalled $100 million. But, while the insurrection had led to widespread property destruction and the almost complete disruption of trade, even those Americans suffering directly from these developments did not favor intervention. They sought American diplomatic protection for their property rights, but on highly practical grounds feared that their losses would be still greater should the United States become involved in actual hostilities.

The business community "generally opposed war," Dulles concluded. The economic shakiness of the times prompted conservatism, not expansionist desires, he argues. And he relates a well-known story of Theodore Roosevelt "shaking his fist at Senator Mark Hannah," a spokesman for the business community, "and shouting, 'We will have this war for the freedom of Cuba in spite of the timidity of the commercial interests'."[54]

The truth undoubtedly lies somewhere between these two extremes.

Many U.S. businessmen favored a war, many were opposed; but either way it is hard to conclude that economic factors—or at least the direct pressure of industry—were the only real considerations sparking the war. Romantic idealism, Social Darwinism, great-power *realpolitik* sentiment, and humanitarianism all played a role. Certainly the war of 1898 was caused by the combination of a particular set of domestic developments and the convergence of a number of disparate motivations—economic, political, racial, altruistic—which, taken together, constituted an overwhelming case for expansion. The economic motive may have been the dominant driving force but it was not the only one, particularly for the average American.

A great number of influential thinkers also added their voices to this growing chorus favoring intervention in Cuba and expansionism in general. Supporters included philosophers, historians, politicians, and clergymen. Perhaps the three most outstanding, however, were Theodore Roosevelt, Henry Cabot Lodge, and Alfred Thayer Mahan.[55] Sensationalist newspapermen like Randolph Hearst used the Cuban insurrection as a tool to infuse the nation with a lust for war.

THE ANTI-IMPERIALISTS

The arguments in favor of expansionism were opposed by many thoughtful observers who felt that such a course was inadvisable. The historian Frederick Merk has argued that the Manifest Destiny school has contended historically with the "Mission" school of American thought, which sees the United States's proper role as an example to other nations rather than a great power imposing its will throughout the world. Similar tensions arise in U.S. foreign policy debates today, and to some degree they shaped discussions at the end of the nineteenth century: believers in the "Mission" school argued vehemently against expansionism.[56]

Various groups joined the anti-imperialist bandwagon. They were led by the "mugwumps," a set of abolitionist, anti-business, advocates of reform whose most significant characteristic was their non-partisan nature; they were renowned for switching parties quickly and often. Cultural gadflies, the mugwumps were also elitist and, as we shall see, in some cases racist. Leading mugwumps were William James, Charles Francis Adams. and James Russell Lowell.[57]

These and other anti-imperialist advocates had seven major objections to U.S. imperialism. First, they argued that imperialism was unconstitutional in that it violated principles of democratic rule for the countries in question. Second, they charged that the economic benefits of expansion were vastly exaggerated, and that trade did not require intervention; we shall hear more of this argument later. Third, anti-expansionists pointed out that international adventures violated the time-honored principle of non-entanglement, and harmed U.S. security through their toll on the domestic front. Fourth, critics argued that it was simply immoral to subjugate other peoples. Fifth, an overt racism caused some critics to view the peoples in question as unfit for inclusion in the United States; many of the mugwumps, in addition to opposing imperialism, argued for strong immigration laws. Sixth, foes of expansion contended that it was politically unwise; a republican government should not be a colonial one. Seventh and finally, anti-imperialists argued from historical evidence that expansion and colonization led inevitably to the decay of civilization and, eventually, imperial ruin along Roman lines.[58]

Writing at the time, Senator Gray summarized many of these arguments in a cable from Europe:

> [The] policy proposed introduces us into European politics and the entangling alliances against which Washington and all American statesmen have protested. . . . But even conceding all benefits claimed for annexation, we thereby abandon the infinitely greater benefit to accrue from acting the part of a great, powerful, and Christian nation.[59]

Some historians have elaborated the second argument, emphasizing that anti-imperialists were really in favor of *economic* interventionism, but did not want the nation to go as far as the colonial policy advocated by some.[60]

In this sense anti-imperialists opposed colonial expansion but not commercial expansion, and some would favor *de facto* U.S. political and economic control of smaller nations if not actual intervention.[61]

John Dobson concurs to some extent. He notes the U.S. tactic of establishing "protectorates" rather than explicit "colonies" in the areas into which they did expand. Dobson uses the Platt Amendment (which will be discussed below) as an example of such a policy: "it obviated," he says "the need for the United States to make a colony out of Cuba while simultaneously guaranteeing that American political influence would prevail in the island republic."[62]

Anti-imperialists thus possessed motives from simple, principled opposition to expansion to more complex (and sinister) racist and elitist theories of national purity. And while some anti-imperialists saw their ultimate goals achieved, many were frustrated by the 1898 war and felt that the "imperialists" had won out. As it was, in early 1898 the voices of those cautioning against intervention were drowned out by the overwhelming cry for war.

THE UNITED STATES APPROACHES INTERVENTION

By early 1898, U.S. tolerance for Spanish delays had nearly reached its limit. Increasingly, Madrid would give in to more and more of the American demands, but the Spanish history of intransigence and other factors contributed to a pro-war momentum in the United States that was almost impossible to stop. Many Americans believed that the time had come for the United States to intervene, and on the arrival in Cuba of Weyler's replacement—captain general Ramon Blanco—the American consul there, Fitzhugh Lee, sent a message to his government which would prove fateful indeed. He wrote that "uncertainty exists whether Blanco can control the situation. If demonstrated that he cannot maintain order, preserve life, and keep the peace, or if Americans and their interests are in danger"—and here was the crucial request—"*ships must be sent*, and to that end should be prepared to move promptly."[63]

President McKinley honored this recommendation and dispatched the U.S. battleship Maine to Cuba. At the time, it seemed a perfectly reasonable and proportionate response to the threat to U.S. interests in Cuba. But the presence of the U.S. warship, combined with several other developments in the first months of 1898, triggered the Spanish-American War.

The de Lome Letter

The first of these developments was the theft of a personal letter from Enrique Dupuy de Lome, Spanish Minister to the United States, by a rebel sympathizer in Havana. The letter was printed by the *New York Journal* on February 9, 1898. The letter strongly implied that the Spanish government's autonomy grant was a trick and claimed only a complete military victory over the rebels would suffice. It also criticized McKinley, calling him "weak and a bidder for the admiration of the crowd." At very least, the letter clearly showed the Spanish to be negotiating with all parties—both the U.S. government and the rebels—in bad faith, and to possess absolutely no desire to reform or compromise.[64]

The effect of these revelations was immediate and electric. The savvy de Lome resigned before the United States could even call for his removal, but the U.S. public was furious. American public opinion had turned even more forcefully—and irrevocably—against the Spanish.

But the de Lome letter would soon be forgotten.

The *Maine* Incident

At 9:35 p.m. on Tuesday, February 15, the battleship U.S.S. *Maine* swayed quietly at anchor in the harbor of Havana. The *Maine* was an impressive ship, 6,682 tons, 314 feet long, and carrying a main armament of 10-inch guns, huge for the period. Being in a potential war zone, the ship was at a higher stage of alert than usual: no visitors were allowed without escorts, all approaching boats were challenged, and the marines on board carried ready ammunition for their weapons. The *Maine*'s captain, Charles Sigsbee, commanded a symbol of American power, sent to overawe the Cubans and Spanish alike, and he expected little trouble.[65]

As the gentle strains of taps floated out onto Havana harbor at 9:30, Sigsbee sat quietly at his desk in the state room on the *Maine*, writing to his wife. Most of his crew had already gone to bed, and lay in their bunks throughout the ship. Suddenly, at 9:40, several explosions rocked the ship; the bow lifted out of the water and huge concussions shook its spine. Lying in shallow water, the *Maine* began to sink quickly, and soon settled to the floor of Havana bay. 266 of the 354 sailors and marines on board perished.

For decades scholars debated the true cause of the explosion on the *Maine*. Two separate boards of inquiry concluded that the *Maine* had been sunk by an external explosion. Later evidence, however, strongly suggests that the *Maine* was destroyed by the spontaneous combustion of its bituminous coal fuel—something that was a recognized phenomenon on ships of the period—which in turn ignited the ship's ammunition magazines.[66] Certainly, the Spanish had no motive to do something that would undoubtedly provoke the United States into a military response.

In the charged atmosphere of the period, however, Spain was tried and convicted of the "attack" of the *Maine* in both the American press and in the public mind. The demand for war became deafening. The Spanish government immediately offered an armistice in Cuba and reparations in a frantic bid to avoid war. Cuban rebel leaders, realizing that a continuing conflict on the island virtually guaranteed U.S. intervention, refused.[67]

Pressure on the Administration

These incidents brought the expansionist and pro-war feelings in America to a head. There was admittedly a good degree of skepticism of annexing, as the New York *Evening Post* put it, a "mongrel race"[68] of Cubans incapable of self-government. These arguments were opposed by expansionists like Randolph Hearst, who saw in the Cuban situation a perfect excuse to begin America's inexorable southward march.

At the end of March the situation reached a climax. On the 17th, Senator Redfield Proctor, known not as a vehement expansionist but rather a quiet pragmatist, delivered his report of a recent informal visit to Cuba. He referred to "the worst misgovernment of which I ever had knowledge," related that the *reconcentracion* policy was still in effect, and noted that thousands of Cubans were still dying. He also pointed out that Captain General Blanco was powerless to end the war, and that Cubans detested Spanish rule as much as ever. Two days later the *Maine* inquiry board reported that the cause of the explosion had been a mine, which everyone immediately assumed to have been Spanish. Two of the primary motives for war—sympathy for the Cubans and hatred of the Spanish—had been reinforced.

The McKinley administration had finally reached a point of decision. On March 19 Roosevelt urged war, and at the end of the month McKinley gave the Spanish an ultimatum: end the war or the United States would act. McKinley demanded an end to the policy of *reconcentracion*, Cuban self-government, an indemnity paid to the island, and of course an immediate end to hostilities. Spain agreed to many of the conditions but could not bring itself to commit to Cuban independence, perhaps fearing adverse domestic reactions to the surrender of its last significant Caribbean jewel. It offered the same old autonomous rule proposal.[69] From the American standpoint, not even a settlement of the *Maine* issue would now suffice. The Department of State argued in late March that although "relations will be much influenced" by the Spanish government's position on the *Maine*, "general conditions must not be lost sight of."[70] Those general conditions were impelling the two nations to war.

James Truslow Adams summarized the pressures affecting the administration at the time:

> An idealism in the people at large that could be easily aroused in favor of any people supposed to be oppressed and struggling for freedom; a really bad and difficult situation in Cuba; a group of powerful business men and politicians bent on imperial expansion; a group of newspapers callously searching for sensational news which could be translated into circulation; and a shining new gun in our hands of which we were proud.[71]

The decades of hesitant U.S. policy toward Cuba—and generations of pacific American foreign policy as a whole—were about to come to a sudden, irrevocable, violent halt.

* * *

Various American adventurers joined the Cuban rebel forces, and several of them survived to write accounts of the war from the Cuban standpoint. Two such men were Grover Flint and Frederick Funston.

Flint was a writer interested in traveling with Gomez's forces, and he eventually did so after avoiding Spanish troops in a trip to Cuba. We have already heard Flint's account of the Olayita massacre; he also wrote of battles and about the insurgents themselves.

Flint joined a semi-independent rebel group shortly after reaching Cuba, and spent some time in a hospital camp. The camp was guarded by a detachment of rebel troops, and Flint described them as "scantily clad in ragged cotton clothing, exposed skin swarthy as bronze under every rent; though some appeared proudly in white linen coats," freshly washed by "*pacifiquita*" or attractive young ladies sympathetic to the rebel cause. Flint concludes that the Cubans "were a courteous, genial lot of outlaws, and passed the time of day cheerily."

Frederick Funston was an American adventurer who later became famous, rising from the position of civilian with no war experience to general in the U.S. Army without being subjected to a day of formal military training. He had wanted to go to Cuba, and had shown good faith by mastering and teaching the art of handling artillery, a skill that eventually gained him access to Gomez's command. Funston was short, described during his college years by a fraternity brother as seeming to have decided "to overcome his runty size by laughing at himself. . . . He walked swiftly but not too steadily, indulged in no athletic sports whatever, was a good rifle shot, [and] had absolutely no sense of fear." Funston would prove his fearlessness again and again, first in Cuba and later in the U.S. campaigns in the Philippines.

When Funston joined the Cuban rebels, he was taken to General Gomez, who was interested to meet his new artillery expert. Funston described Gomez as a "stern, hard-hearted man, with a violent temper." Gomez "resembled exactly the many pictures of him. . .was a thin, wiry man with snow-white moustache and goatee, and was of pure Spanish descent, having the swarthy complexion of most Latins." Flint noted other characteristics upon meeting Gomez:

> He is a grey little man. His clothes do not fit well, and, perhaps, if you saw it in a photograph, his figure might seem old and ordinary. But the moment he turns his keen eyes on you, they strike like a blow from the shoulder. You feel the will, the fearlessness, and the experience of men that is in those eyes, and their owner becomes a giant before you.

Funston also had the privilege of meeting Calixto Garcia. Like Gomez, Garcia possessed snow-white hair and a moustache, but was a heavily-built man over six feet tall. He bore a large scar on his forehead, obtained during the Ten Years' War when he tried to kill himself to avoid imminent capture by the Spanish. But the bullet, which entered his lower jaw, exited through his forehead without doing fatal damage. As Funston noted, ''to the day of his death, nearly twenty-four years later, the would never entirely healed, and he always carried a small wad of cotton in the hole in his skull." Despite this injury, and the horrible experiences it connoted, Garcia was a ''courteous and kindly gentleman," and "all who came into close contact. . . had for him a feeling of affection."

Funston was appointed to the position of artillery officer with the revolutionary army, and took part in a number of skirmishes and large battles. One such battle was the fight for the town of Guimaro.

The Spanish held the town, which was defended by various blockhouses and trench systems. After Funston and his artillery had shelled the defenses for some time—without much noticeable effect—the Cubans decided to charge the town. Funston described the attack:

> Anxious to see the charge, Pennie and I hastened back to our old stand, and had hardly got settled down when a bugle rang out in the edge of the woods a hundred yards to our left, there were a number of briskly given commands, some faint cheering and a rattle of shots, and a company of men, mostly negroes, led by Garcia's chief of staff, Colonel Menocal, began to climb the grassy slope. Ordinarily chiefs of staff do not lead charges, but no chances were being taken on some bungler making a mess of this job. The slope was so steep and the grass so high and dense that the attack was made at a walk, the men in single line, firing and yelling excitedly.

Funston and his friend Pennie joined the attack, and rushed for the blockhouse with revolvers drawn. By the time they reached the top of the hill, the blockhouse had been seized, and the Spanish infantry had fled to another set of fortifications, some 700 yards away. The Cubans on the top of the hill were now exposed, and Spanish sharpshooters from surrounding buildings and fortifications brought the hill under fire.

The Spanish flag remained on a pole atop the blockhouse, and the Cubans concluded that ''this would never do." One Lieutenant Miranda volunteered to take it down, and climbed up the eighteen-foot pole, in full view of all the surrounding Spanish troops; ''bullets hissed and cracked all about, and beat a constant tatoo on the blockhouse. The pole above or below him was hit several times." The other Cubans begged Miranda to come down, but he would not; finally he reached the flag, cut it down, and slid down the pole. ''It would be difficult to imagine a feat of more reckless daring," Funston concluded.

That night, General Garcia ordered Funston and the other artillery officers to bring a cannon into the captured blockhouse. As dawn broke Funston and Major Osgood, his commander, directed a constant fire on the Spanish emplacements around Guaimaro, which lay below the commanding hill the Cubans now held. A Spanish sharpshooter tried repeatedly to put bullets into the hole through which the Cuban cannon fired; finally, when Osgood was stooping over the cannon, a bullet found its mark, striking him "with a sound like a base-ball being thrown against a building. . . . [Osgood] sank across the tail of the gun, unconscious, and was lifted from it by his horror-stricken comrades." In four hours Osgood was dead; for Funston the event was a moving one: "bound together by ties of race and language, and sharing the daily dangers and privations," he wrote of his remaining American comrades in arms, "we had become closer to each other than men ordinarily do in years of acquaintanceship under different circumstances, and now felt that the war was coming home to us."

Flint described a different sort of battle that occurred as he accompanied Gomez and some 200 mounted rebel troops. At three o'clock in the afternoon, a trooper rode up to Gomez and excitedly reported the approach of a large Spanish column, preceded by one hundred pro-Spanish Cuban guerrillas.

Directly ahead of the Cuban column lay a thick palm forest, "where sunlight brought out the white trunks against the shade within." Between the column and this forest lay a smaller palm grove. As the Cubans approached the Spanish force appeared, "drawn up in two white lines, facing us." Gomez immediately attacked this force with sixty of his cavalry, driving at the Spanish "diagonally from the trail, . . . opening as they advanced into a wide, irregular skirmish line, shouting to one another, repeating the order, 'Deploy! open wide! deploy!'" Another portion of the Cuban column split off toward the palm grove.

Flint later recalled the action:

> The Spaniards saw our column split, and their movements became
> hurried and ant-like; they might still have extended to occupy the
> palm grove before Guerra's men got there—but they did not. The
> infantry squirmed itself into a square, the last stragglers of the
> marching line closing up at a jog trot.

The Spanish guerrilla cavalry turned and deployed within and behind the Spanish infantry, which was now formed into a square designed to repel cavalry charges. "There was a white flutter of a hundred legs as the guer-rilleros swung from their saddles, and stood to horse in the very center of a solid square" that Flint described as a magnificent target, "one that would make any American marksman's trigger finger quiver up to his elbow."

One Cuban column had now reached the palm grove, and the other had approached to within 200 yards of the Spanish. Flint describes the charge as it reached the Spanish:

> [When the first volley went off] a sparkle of moving steel ran along the bluish-grey line, then the line wavered in a thin mist of explod-ing, smokeless powder, and a crash came like the swift tearing of a giant strip of carpet. Another crash! and another! Five distinct crashes; and the five cartridges that each Spanish rifle carried in its magazine were expended. The popping of our men, who shot from their saddles, seemed slight and puny.   The Spanish volleys now came irregularly, swelling to a rah! rah! rah! sound, like a confused succession of college cheers. The sun caught the waving blades of officers, who were threatening and slapping the soldiers to preserve the alignment.

The Spanish line, men arrayed shoulder to shoulder and firing as they reloaded their rifles, began to waver "like cane swayed by the wind." The Cubans in the grove took the Spanish under a flanking fire. All the while the Spanish cavalry, heavily outnumbering Gomez's and "near enough to sweep through us before we could possibly have rallied for a solid front," did noth-ing. Eventually the Cubans retired, covered by the group in the grove, rejoined their pack train and supply troops, and after a mile march, had a sup-per of beef strips, and turned in." During the whole action, the Cubans suffered one dead and perhaps a half-dozen wounded.[72]

* * *

The United States Enters the War

McKinley's Cuba policy had now become relatively clear. He wanted to end the war and supply the Cuban people with the food, medicine, and economic assistance which were required to rebuild the island.[73] After that, he desired to establish stability and order on the island, whether by transfer of power to a self-determining Cuban government or through an indefinite U.S. military occupation. Such stability, he felt, would help secure U.S. strategic and com-mercial interests in the region.

McKinley resisted the impulse to go to war in the aftermath of the *Maine* disaster. He and his staff attempted to arrange another purchase scheme, this one allowing the Cubans to buy the island from Spain, and proposed in the event of its failure an extensive plan for Cuban autonomy. But Spain refused to commit itself to any of these options.

Nevertheless, at the end of March, McKinley pursued compromises designed to avert imminent war between America and Spain. His public message about the *Maine* guarded and non-inflammatory. On the 27th, he gave Madrid one last proposal, transmitted through Assistant Secretary of State William R. Day. It demanded an end to *reconcentracion*, an armistice, and peace negotiations with the Cubans. As a McKinley telegram to Woodford reveals, the U.S. government's goal was clearly the independence of Cuba, something to which McKinley had been committed since his inauguration.

Spain was faced with a dilemma. If it accepted the American conditions, it risked a domestic uproar; if it refused it risked war. Madrid made a hasty attempt to rally other European powers behind it, but a combination of sympathy for the Cuban cause and a lack of desire to tangle with the increasingly powerful United States prevented that course from bearing fruit. On March 31, Spain therefore gave its reply: it would end the *reconcentracion* policy and provide for both an armistice and negotiations with Cuban leaders. On April 9, that armistice was declared, and the following day Woodford cabled that a solution might be in sight.

Nevertheless, in the first days of April, McKinley began to put the United States on a war footing, activating the Navy and taking other preparatory actions. He had chosen for April 6 for a national call to action to precede an actual war declaration, but Fitzhugh Lee cabled from Cuba that if the president waited until the 11th Lee could arrange for the safety of U.S. nationals on the island, and moveover that negotiations with Spain were still underway. Last-minute mediation efforts by outside parties, including Pope Leo XIII, failed.

On April 11, 1898, McKinley delivered his message to Congress. Though it was not a request for a declaration of war, it made clear that such a course was virtually inevitable. McKinley outlined four justifications for intervention into Cuba: humanitarian concerns, protection of Cuban citizens, provision for the safety of American property in Cuba, and the long-term demands of world peace. "In the name of humanity, in the name of civilization," McKinley concluded, "in behalf of endangered American interests which give us the right and the duty to speak and to act, the war in Cuba must stop."[74] These words, read by congressional clerks to the Congress, brought waves of applause.

The call for war was a foregone conclusion. McKinley waited to assess the reaction to his message of April 11, and satisfied that the American people supported intervention, he requested a declaration of war. On April 25 the Congress formally noted that a state of war had existed since the 21st; Spain had already declared war on the United States.

Presidential Leadership: The Turpie-Foraker and Teller Amendments

At about this time, a number of congressmen attempted to rob McKinley of policy leadership. Many had delayed action to see what McKinley would do, but his April 11 message, which while essentially calling for war still did not recognize the Cuban belligerents, convinced them that they had to act. On April 13, William Jennings Bryan openly opposed McKinley on the recognition issue, and that same day congressional Democrats introduced a resolution providing for recognition. It failed, however, 190 to 150 in the House, which instead passed a resolution approving the president's April 11 message and authorizing him to act as he saw fit.

In the Senate, a similar resolution of approval was afoot, but proponents of recognition attempted to attach an amendment to it. The Turpie-Foraker amendment, which recognized "the Republic of Cuba as the true and lawful government of the island,"[75] passed 51 to 37 in the upper chamber, where the Democrats were stronger. McKinley naturally opposed the amendment, and argued that it constituted a *de facto* recognition that undermined his flexibility and authority.

Sponsors of the amendment, in many instances, were not supporters of Cuban independence; they were using the legislation largely as a tool to attack McKinley and impugn his authority. Votes on the amendment thus quickly became a test of presidential leadership in foreign policy, and congressmen divided on the issue largely on partisan grounds. Those who opposed the amendment claimed it might lead "directly to war" by provoking the Spanish and committing the United States irrevocably to support for Cuban independence.[76]

At the same time, Senator Teller introduced his own revolution, which was intended to serve as an alternative to pending legislation on Cuba in the Senate, including the Turpie-Foraker amendment; Teller's amendment provided for U.S. non-intervention but not explicit Cuban independence. The Teller amendment was passed. On Monday, April 18, the two sides faced each other in reconciliation proceedings: the process whereby House and Senate legislation is "reconciled" into a coherent bill. Since the House had not yet passed the Turpie-Foraker amendment, its status was uncertain. McKinley had campaigned hard over the weekend, and on Monday made clear his intention to veto any form of the amendment. He won, and the Turpie-Foraker amendment was struck from the legislation; the Teller Amendment passed through the process. McKinley had won a significant victory, both for himself and for the foreign policy powers of the presidency.[77]

Senator Henry M. Teller of Colorado had once been an annexationist, but he now opposed that policy, at least insofar as it would bring Cuba into the Union, and in part because of the sympathetic ear he lent to Cuban representatives in Washington. His resolution included provisions essentially granting McKinley freedom of action. Teller's amendment added a stipulation that the United States had no intention to keep Cuba permanently. With little debate—perhaps occasioned by the resort to Teller's legislation as a way to resolve the crisis of presidential leadership—the amendment passed.

In its final form, the Teller Amendment read: ''Resolved: That the United States hereby disclaims any disposition or intention to exercise sovereignty, jurisdiction, or control over said island except for the pacification thereof, and asserts its determination when that is accomplished to leave the government and control of the island to its people.''

This amendment, despite its apparently clear language, meant different things to different people, and was not nearly as unqualified a statement of non-intervention as some have supposed. To outright isolationists, it constituted a U.S. commitment to reject the possibility of annexing Cuba. To others—anti-imperialist but pro-business—it simply indicated that the United States would not *officially* govern the island. It was assumed that U.S. commercial interests would have free reign, and that the United States' overwhelming military superiority would give it a *de facto* veto power over Cuban foreign and domestic policy.

It was in this latter form that the Teller Amendment would function. Its exception of the goal of ''pacification'' from the non- intervention pledge was disingenuous, and though many of these voting for the amendment probably viewed it as a simple promise of non-interference, it would not fulfill that purpose. Indeed, given subsequent U.S. interventionist policies, any thought that the amendment would effectively preclude U.S. interference in Cuban affairs would be soundly disproven.

Critiques of McKinley's Role

The debate over McKinley's role in these events is hotly contested. The controversy is the product of the seemingly ironic timing of events: just two days after Spain granted an armistice in Cuba, and one day after the U.S. minister in Madrid expressed his hope for a peaceful settlement, McKinley called for war. This series of events led many scholars to depict him as weak-willed, dragged into the war by a tide of public opinion and sensationalist journalism he found impossible to stem. It is claimed that McKinley brought on the conflict by his abdication of true leadership.

Another, more vehement school sees McKinley as a calculating, "Machiavellian" politician, absolutely aware of what he was doing and why, ruled by big business and launching a war to further U.S. commercial interests. Philip Foner has documented the apparent influence of shipping and industrial powers on the president. McKinley's initial instructions to Woodford, Foner points out, stressed that U.S. "business and...prosperity" were being damaged by the Cuban revolution. From this and other evidence Foner concludes that "McKinley's policy was being controlled by what General Sherman had called 'commercial interests rather than...sympathy with a people struggling for liberty.'"[78]

Walter LaFeber essentially agrees. McKinley eventually assumed an "inflexible position" regarding Cuban independence because, although he wanted to avoid war itself, "he did want what only a war could provide: the disappearance of the terrible uncertainty in American political and economic life, and a solid basis from which to resume the building of the new American commercial empire."[79]

Against these arguments, other scholars have marshalled different historical evidence to support a more benign image of McKinley. McKinley as we have seen, did take enormous pains to avoid war as long as he thought feasible, proposing numerous compromise schemes until the last minute. Some historians contend that indeed, if anything, Spanish intransigence, not McKinley's belligerence, can be blamed for the war. McKinley's stance was certainly not "inflexible."

Though the public cry for war eventually brought one on, moreover, McKinley succeeded in delaying the conflict and beginning it on his terms. In fact, as one defender of McKinley has concluded,

> The Spanish-American War was not the result of presidential weakness or cowardice in the face of public hysteria. McKinley sought to persuade Spain to relinquish Cuba peacefully and then turned to war when it became apparent that Madrid would never acquiesce. His diplomacy in 1897/98 was tenacious, coherent, and courageous.[80]

Other defenders of McKinley point out that his policy was perfectly consistent, and this point is perhaps the most persuasive. The key aspect of the Cuban problem, for McKinley as well as the American public, was Cuban independence. The administration's commitment to this result was longstanding and explicit. When the Spanish repeatedly refused to withdraw — even though they did give in on many other issues — the American reaction was predictable. As we have noted, a variety of motivations were impelling the United States toward war; McKinley was influenced by these; to blame him for not rejecting them—when they seemed so cogent—is perhaps too easy in hindsight.

The War

At the outset of the war, the military forces of the United States were in varied conditions.[81] The Navy, thanks to the efforts of such proponents of naval power as Alfred Thayer Mahan and Stephen Luce, was in relatively good shape. The Army was less well off; its average size in the post-Civil War years 1865-1898 was just 26,000, and most of these troops were spread out over vast distances, garrisoning towns and fighting Indians. The Army had conducted almost no operations since 1865 in which large units were forced to function as a cohesive whole. Immediately, the government called for 200,000 volunteers, and authorized the expansion of the regular army to 65,000. By the war's end the actual numbers inducted would stand at 216,000 volunteers and 59,000 regulars.

The initial U.S. strategy called for a blockade of Cuba and the supply of arms, ammunition, and food to the Cuban insurgents, who were then expected to win the war. The Army slowly began to assemble a contingency force of some 80,000, in case that strategy proved ineffectual. Public demands for action soon rendered the blockade-and-wait strategy impracticable, and Secretary of State Alger ordered the relocation of U.S. training camps into the southern United States as the first step toward an eventual intervention.

Admiral George Dewey's Asiatic squadron was massed at Hong Kong for a strike at the Philippines. After a short naval battle at Manila Bay, during which the Spanish fleet was entirely destroyed, Dewey shelled the harbor guns into silence and blockaded the Bay for two months awaiting the arrival of U.S. Army forces. Dewey brought the Philippine guerrilla leader Emilio Aguinaldo from exile in Hong Kong to aid operations against the Spanish, and provided him and his troops with what supplies could be spared.

Meanwhile, the U.S. Navy was aware of the presence of a Spanish fleet under Admiral Cervera somewhere around Cuba, but they did not know its exact location. Finally in May it was learned that his fleet was moored in the bay of Santiago de Cuba. U.S forces, under the general command of Admiral Sampson, but immediately led by Commodore Schley, initially attempted to block the harbor entrance by sinking a collier, the *Merrimac*, in its mouth. When this scheme failed the American commanders sent marines ashore to establish a naval base, and they captured Guantanamo Bay in the first land skirmish of the Cuban campaign.

It was imperative for the U.S. naval forces to neutralize Cervera's force, because General Shafter was about to sail from Tampa with thousands of troops for an invasion, borne in slow, vulnerable transport ships. On June 7 the U.S. fleet bombarded the Santiago fortifications, and established a blockade of the bay; several huge U.S. warships lay at anchor in a rough semi-circle outside its mouth, forming a wall of steel through which the Spanish would have to sail to escape or to attack Shafter's vulnerable fleet of transports. Between the 14th and the 20th of June, Shafter's convoy sailed to Santiago, carrying 18 regular and 2 volunteer infantry regiments; 10 regular and 2 volunteer cavalry squadrons, dismounted, and one mounted cavalry squadron; and artillery and gatling guns. On the 22nd, following Calixto Garcia's suggestion, the Americans disembarked at Daiquiri, east of Santiago, and the invasion had begun.

American troops immediately moved on Santiago de Cuba. Their goal was to seize the port, thereby depriving Cervera's fleet of its supplies and docking areas and forcing it out onto the guns of the waiting American fleet. Capture of the port would also provide American forces with a much-needed base of operations. Two major Spanish redoubts, however, stood in the way of the advance to Santiago: El Caney and San Juan Hill.

* * *

Just before the battle of San Juan Hill, General Lawton led four brigades of U.S. troops—almost five thousand men—against the heavily fortified Spanish positions at El Caney. The battle would prove that the Spanish, whose mettle was in doubt, could indeed fight well and stubbornly, in the proper circumstances.

The village of El Caney was a small, concentrated town about four miles northeast of Santiago. In its southwest corner was a steep hill, on whose summit stood an elderly stone fort; the rest of the village had been fortified with redoubts and trenches. American infantry approached the village and mounted a ridge on its northeast side. A British military attache traveling with the Americans, Captain Arthur Lee, described the scene:

> From the crest of the ridge we could look right down into the village, its thatched and tiled roofs half hidden by the large shade-trees. . . . In the village itself profound quiet reigned, and there was no sign of life beyond a few thin wisps of smoke that curled from the cottage chimneys. Beyond lay the fertile valley with a few cattle grazing, and around us on three sides arose, tier upon tier, the beautiful Maestra Mountains, wearing delicate pearly tints in the first rays of the rising sun.

In the village the Americans could see the Spanish flag gently lapping at its pole, and around it a group of Spanish soldiers lounging lazily. An American artillery battery set up a mile to the left of the ridge.

The battle opened at about six-thirty in the morning with U.S. artillery fire directed against the Spanish fortifications; as Lee noted, there was a "white puff from Capron's battery, and before the report reached our ears" the lounging Spanish had made for cover. The artillery kept up fire for twenty minutes or so, but it was largely ineffective.

American infantry gradually closed to a range of about six hundred yards, firing and taking fire from Spanish sharpshooters; Spanish troops ducked in and out of their fortifications and trenches, and as their gunpowder was "absolutely smokeless" the Americans could not pick out their locations. The battle evolved into a rifle duel. But, as recalled by the young author George Kennan (a distant ancestral relative of the diplomat George F. Kennan), the American infantry "was suffering far more loss than they were able to inflict, for the reason that they could find little or no shelter, while the Spaniards were protected by loopholed walls and deep rifle-pits." Lee recalled that the Spanish fire had "deadly effect," and that the Spanish marksmen "knew every range perfectly and picked off our men with distressing accuracy if they showed as much as a head." The U.S. infantry, nevertheless, pressed forward, though suffering heavy casualties: some 300 killed and wounded. The battle raged for hours, and by 1:30 in the afternoon it appeared that the attack might fail.

At about this time Lee made his way over to the Seventh Infantry, which lay in a vulnerable position exposed to a vicious crossfire. As he neared the sunken road where the regiment had taken cover, he noticed "that it was full of men lying down." He asked an officer if those were reserves, and the officer's reply "was startling—'No, Sir, by God, they are casualties.'" And indeed they were—over 100 killed and wounded. "There was a strange silence among these men," Lee explained, "not a whimper or a groan, but each lay quietly nursing his wound with closed eyes and set teeth, only flinching when the erratic sleet of bullets clipped the leaves off the hedge close above their heads."

At the height of the battle, General Lawton was ordered to break off the attack and support the actions around San Juan Hill. But, in Kennan's words, "believing that a retreat at this juncture would be disastrous. . .General Lawton disregarded this order and pressed the attack with renewed vigor." Kennan continues:

Capron's battery [of U.S. artillery], about this time, got the range of the stone fort, shot away its flagstaff, amid vociferous cheers from our men, and soon began to make great breaches in its massive walls. General Chaffee, who had been directed to make a final assault on the fort when, in his judgement, the proper time had come, then gave the order to charge; and the Twelfth Infantry, closely followed by several regiments from General Miles's brigade, and the brigade of General Bates. . . . swarmed up the steep slope of the hill, drove the Spaniards out of their rifle-pits, and took the fort by storm. The first man inside its walls was Mr. James Creelman, a war correspondent, who was shot through the shoulder while recovering the Spanish flag.

Lee witnessed the same action. The Twelfth Infantry "had long been straining at the leash," he reported, "and needed no second word." The regiment "moved quickly through a ravine which skirted the village, and on emerging from its cover swung right and charged up the hill. "Another moment and they swarmed over the wire fences and trenches beyond like a hive of angry bees," Lee wrote, "and amidst the cheering of the rest of the line drove the enemy helter-skelter over the crest of the hill." Spanish dead littered the place, in the fort and in the surrounding trenches; Lee described them as being in "horribly contorted attitudes and with sightless, staring eyes." Those Spaniards who had been in the trenches when hit, since only their heads were vulnerable, had "all [been] shot through the forehead, and their brains oozed out like white paint from a color-tube."

Casualties on both sides were considerable (though overall casualties in the war were exceedingly light), especially among the Americans, who lost 88 killed and 356 wounded. The Americans displayed enormous daring in charging up an exposed hill into heavy enemy fire; one Spanish officer remarked after the battle that "I have never seen anything to equal the courage and dash of those Americans, who, stripped to the waist, offering their naked breasts to our murderous fire, literally threw themselves on our trenches—on the very muzzles of our guns." Although the Spanish "mowed them down by the hundreds," the Americans "never retreated or fell back an inch. As one man fell, shot through the heart, another would take his place, with grim determination and unflinching devotion to duty in every line of his face. Their gallantry was heroic."

Colonel Teddy Roosevelt was a man in search of adventure. The former Undersecretary of the Navy, he had become known for his dash and adventurism. A strong advocate of expansion, he backed up his words by joining a regiment of volunteer cavalry for the war. He would eventually write of his experiences, and his description of the attack on San Juan Hill—while its accuracy has been disputed—is nevertheless a fascinating account.

Now Roosevelt's chance for glory was at hand. He was part of a force which had been ordered to take San Juan Hill, and though his Rough Riders (except for the officers) had been forced to embark without their horses, they now lay at the bottom of the hill, awaiting orders to take it. Many other units were dispersed around the battlefield, all laying down and taking no action. Roosevelt decided that "in my judgement we could not take these hills by firing at them, and that we must rush them," but a captain on the scene said the standing orders were to stay put.

"Where is your Colonel?" Roosevelt asked.

"I don't know, sir," the captain replied.

"Then I am the ranking officer here," Roosevelt said, "and I give the order to charge."

When the captain hesitated, unsure of whether to follow the commands of this upstart Colonel of the Volunteers, Roosevelt determined to lead by example. "Then let my men through, sir," he said, and led the grinning Rough Riders through the ranks of prostrate infantry. Unable to stay still and watch Roosevelt's men carry the attack through, however, "tired of waiting, and eager to close with the enemy, [the whole line] was straining to go forward"; and the American troops gradually all joined in the charge, "running forward between shots."

Roosevelt proceeded to gallop to and fro along the line, making sure all his troops were in proper order, as the charge continued up the hill. He then wheeled and resumed his charge up the hill:

> Being on horseback I was, of course, able to get ahead of my men on foot, excepting my orderly, Henry Bardshar, who had run ahead very fast in order to get better shots at the Spaniards, who were now running out of the ranch buildings....Some forty yards from the top I ran into a wire fence and jumped off Little Texas, turning him loose....As I ran up to the hill, Bardshar stopped to shoot, and two Spaniards fell as he emptied his magazine. These were the only Spaniards I actually saw fall to aimed shots by any one of my men, with the exception of two guerrillas in trees.

Roosevelt and the other U.S. troops reached the summit, and San Juan Hill was taken.[82]

* * *

The U.S. Navy won another major victory when the Spanish fleet attempted to sail out of Santiago harbor; the American ships pulverized their opponents, and destroyed or ran aground the entire Spanish force. Soon afterwards, Spanish resistance in Santiago collapsed. After some small further campaigning, the island began to fall to the Americans in huge chunks. On July 21 General Miles, with 3,000 troops, invaded Puerto Rico, and by mid-August had occupied the whole island. Meanwhile in the Philippines U.S. troops had arrived, and in August they took Manila.

Relations During and After the War

If there was any hope at the beginning of the Spanish-Cuban-American War that the United States would enjoy good relations with the Cubans, it was quickly dispelled. American officers found the Cuban insurgents unreliable and sometimes cowardly, a perception fostered by the Cubans' different ways of waging war; essentially a guerrilla army, the Cubans were unaccustomed to set-piece battles and hence did not excel in that context. Frequently, too, racist American officers treated Cuban units assigned to them poorly, and the Cubans in turn occasionally refused to fight. Many Cubans, guided by the nationalist sentiments of Jose Marti and others, were already suspicious of the American presence, and the tensions described above established the context for an often strained relationship.

One exception to this rule was Charles Johnson Post, a private with the U.S. forces in Cuba. Post had an affection for the Cubans and a respect for their fighting ability, bolstered by conversations with Funston, who warmly praised the Cubans with whom he fought. Post himself wrote that the Cubans, "barefoot, or only in rawhide sandals. . .could outmarch any of the professional armies." He expressed amazement at the fighting ability of the Cubans, who carried a motley assortment of weapons and very little ammunition. (In fact, Post noted, Cuban prostitutes obtained a great supply of Spanish ammunition by demanding it rather than money in exchange for their services: 100 cartridges from a common soldier, 200 from a noncommissioned officer, and 1,000 or more from an officer.) On the whole, Post concluded, the Cuban rebels were a brave and efficient fighting force.[83]

The Settlement of the War

At the end of July, 1898, the Spanish asked the McKinley government for peace. The resulting Treaty of Paris guaranteed an end to hostilities and a Spanish exit from the island, but neither saddled Cuba with Spanish war debts nor the United States with the perpetual responsibility to maintain order on the island. The Spanish for their part actually wanted to see the island become a part of the United States, feeling that such a development would best foster long-term stability and the health of Spanish economic interests in the Caribbean. The peace treaty of December, 1898 granted Cuba its independence and ceded Puerto Rico, Guam, and the Philippines to the United States, the latter for a payment of $20 million. On New Year's Day, 1899, Spain finally withdrew from Cuba.

The U.S. Occupation Begins

McKinley dispatched Robert P. Porter, a newspaperman and old friend, to Cuba to make policy recommendations. Porter suggested, and the administration implemented, some sensible changes: it lowered Spanish tariff rates by over 60 per cent, reasoning that the enhanced trade would more than make up for the lost tariff revenues. It made tariffs non-discriminatory. And it generally worked to promote the economic interdependence of the two countries.

One continuing problem was the status of the Cuban army. McKinley, concerned about problems the army might pose, met with a delegation of Cuban officials led by Calixto Garcia in 1898. The Cubans, for their part, wanted to determine what McKinley's intentions were. Various schemes were discussed to provide the soldiers of the Cuban army of liberation with back pay, and when Garcia requested only $3 million to pay off the Cuban army (over the protests of other Cubans who wanted more), McKinley jumped at the offer. The president also suggested that the United States keep 10,000 Cuban soldiers on permanent payroll as civil patrols and civil service officials.[84] Negotiations on these issues dragged on for months.

Meanwhile, McKinley's December annual message stated that he wished to provide for Cuban independence as quickly as possible. The U.S. military occupation, he claimed, would last only as long as necessary to allow the establishment of a Cuban government.

U.S. Military Rule Begins

On January 1, 1899, General John Brooke became the first U.S. military commander of the occupation forces in Cuba. Brooke was 60, a major general who had been in the military since 1861. He had seen action in the Civil War and later in Puerto Rico. His rule would be characterized by controversy, infighting among American leaders, and increasingly volatile relations with the Cubans.

Brooke faced a challenge in General Leonard Wood, a politically powerful departmental commander in Cuba. Wood wanted more independent control of his area, and wrote the War Department requesting it to order Brooke to give him more independence, to decentralize control of the island. The department rejected Wood's ideas, but the stage had been set for continuing squabbles between Wood, Brooke, and other U.S. officers in Cuba.

Bands of Cuban soldiers remained in the interior, refusing to be disbanded or surrender their arms. McKinley was worried about parallels with the Philippines, where an initially friendly guerrilla movement had assisted the United States in evicting the Spanish and then had turned against the U.S. military occupation forces. Even the modest Filipino forces staged an effective resistance, and McKinley was in no mood to fight another war of pacification in Cuba. General Gomez, the senior remaining Cuban commander, held out in the island's dense jungles, refusing to emerge until the McKinley administration dealt with him in what he considered a fair fashion.

In early 1899 McKinley sent Porter back to Cuba, and on February 1 he met with Gomez. Gomez was cooperative, agreeing to the $3 million figure and other considerations. Porter for his part expressed the American hope that amicable U.S.-Cuban relations could be re-established. After the meetings a ball was held, replete with speeches by the various diplomats present. For a fleeting moment, it seemed that warm relations might indeed issue from the meetings.

But it was not to be. The first complication came on February 11, during the official burial of Calixto Garcia. A U.S. cavalry unit mistakenly forced itself into the procession line where the Cuban insurgents were supposed to be; when the Cuban commanders appealed to the U.S. officers present, they were told essentially to "go to the back of the line." Furious, the Cubans left and pulled back into the interior once again.

Cuba was in a terrible state at the time, and Brooke instituted far-reaching relief and reconstruction programs. He created various Cuban government departments to oversee all manner of public programs. His troops doled out tens of thousands of meals, but by July of 1899 almost no direct food relief was required: "once allowed back on the land, their fertile soil and tropical climate allowed the Cubans to feed themselves again in a startlingly short time."[85] Brooke's men also provided medical care and huge cleaning programs, at one point engaging in a house-by-house cleaning of Havana. In just a few months Cuba was on its way to a nearly full recovery.

Despite their programs, banditry and disillusionment continued. While many areas of Cuba were quickly recultivated, the devastation wrought by the war did create an agricultural crisis of sorts. The arrival of foreign (especially American) carpetbaggers and the demobilization of the Cuban army complicated economic matters still further. and many Cubans turned to theft as a livelihood. U.S. administrators created a Rural Guard, a sort of military police force, to help keep the peace; immediately the United States distanced itself from the Cuban population, as the Rural Guard served to defend American economic interests against Cuban ones. The Rural Guard's occasional brutality and disregard of legal procedure also set a bad precedent.

When the U.S. government eventually disbursed its promised payments to Cuban veterans, the Cuban army was disbanded without serious incident. U.S. commanders from various districts reported that the Cubans were almost uniformly cooperative in surrendering their arms and returning to their homes. With the dissolution of the rebel army, the U.S. military government in Cuba ruled without any serious challenge to its authority, backed by the force of the Rural Guard.[86]

Confusion About Cuba's Status

Through the first months of U.S. occupation, debates raged over what role the United States should play in Cuba's future. Advocates discussed proposals ranging from annexation to immediate withdrawal.

The arguments of those who opposed Cuban independence are neatly summarized in two articles published in *The Atlantic Monthly* around the turn of the century. In July, 1900, J.D. Whelpley traveled to Cuba to report on conditions there. During the revolution and subsequent U.S. intervention, he noted, information about Cuba was plentiful, but after a year of U.S. rule it had never been "more difficult...for the people of the United States to obtain a correct view of conditions on that island." He reported that while the U.S. occupation forces had done an admirable job of taking care of the island, the Cuban people were still quite unable to govern themselves. Rather, "a continuation of the present conditions in Cuba will be possible for some time without serious trouble." But if "the experiment of a free Cuba" were tried, it would "inevitably result in another intervention." In fact "the only thing which seems absolutely remote, improbable, and almost impossible from every point of view is a free and independent Cuban republic." The only way Cuba could become independent, Whelpley claimed, was with U.S. tutelage and education. Once given such benefits, however, "these people will not desire separate political existence, for they will realize the greater benefits of free social and commercial intercourse with a mighty nation of which they are part."[87]

Herbert Pelham Williams, writing in 1899, was even blunter. "We must base our dealings with the Cubans," he began,

> on the understanding that they are as yet but children. The word
> describes them almost exactly. Ignorance, delight in owning petty

trifles, curiosity, the tendency to tell an untruth whenever telling
the truth may have unpleasant results, cruelty, wanton destruction
of inanimate things which have been obstacles in their path...These
are the attributes of children.

The Cubans were also characterized by "docility" to the point of being "to some degree like a race of slaves."[88] "Permanent American control," Williams thus concluded, "seems to be the most probable future for Cuba. We are responsible for good government in the island, and it is doubtful if this can be established in any other way." The only ones who denied this were "unruly elements and...those persons who have nothing to lose and everything to gain by a state of affairs in which the shrewdest and most unscrupulous man wins, and who still cling to the old fetish of 'Cuba Libre.'" America could rule Cuba in two ways, Williams argued: either stay and "keep the island under our control," or leave—at which point

the result, as every one except a few Cubans will admit, will be disorder, fierce contention between the leaders, and then civil war of the old familiar kind, degenerating into butchery; and we shall have to come back and take up the regeneration of Cuba from the beginning.

Even if Cubans would vote for independence, Williams argued, the United States should not be impressed because "all, or nearly all the people whose convictions deserve respect" wanted the United States to stay.[89]

Williams argued that when looked at squarely, the situation was relatively clear. "Our possession of the island is growing more firmly rooted every week" because of growing economic and commercial ties, he wrote. "With every life and every dollar we send to Cuba our hold on the island is being strengthened." The result is that "we shall stay to take care of our own, and thus, by imperceptible stages, the present situation will glide into permanent control."[90]

Williams's final conclusion was decidedly incorrect, but on the necessity for further interventions, as we shall see, Williams was extraordinarily prescient.

The McKinley administration did little to resolve the controversy over Cuba's status. Administration statements were arcane and sometimes contradictory. McKinley refused to take a strong stance on any position. Henry Adams was prompted to complain in 1899 that "the government lets everything drift."[91]

Following closely on the heels of the U.S. troops who landed at Santiago Bay were a host of corporations and entrepreneurs, determined to make a profit from the famous little island in the Caribbean. Dozens of companies flooded into Cuba and set up operations. This was a confirmation of what many saw as the true U.S. motive for intervention—extension of commerce—and it led to an explosion of banditry and a reinforcement of anti-American sentiment in Cuba.

The lack of administration policy pronouncements on the issue led Senator Joseph Foraker to propose his famous amendment banning the United States from granting business concessions or franchises on the island. He was not so concerned about "capitalist expansionism" as he was that if the United States allowed such business enterprise it would still be in Cuba "in a hundred years." The amendment passed, and the official imprimatur of the government could not be extended to business ventures in Cuba.

The calls to remove Brooke from his post began in earnest in early 1900. Theodore Roosevelt, worried that Brooke's light touch as governor was insufficient to guarantee stability, recommended Wood to replace him. Brooke could no longer count on his subordinates faithfully to implement his orders, and was thought by some to be "too old" and not vigorous enough to push the occupation to its goals. Differences of opinion among U.S. officers of the occupation force regarding the proper U.S. role in Cuba's future continued, with Wood and General Ludlow quietly arguing for a more substantial U.S. presence, and James Wilson and others advocating an immediate and almost total withdrawal.[92]

Even as these debates went on, however, McKinley had himself taken independent action that would resolve the Cuban quarrels once and for all: he had appointed Elihu Root to be his new secretary of war.

Root's Policies

The appointment of the lawyer Elihu Root as secretary of war to replace the inefficient Russell Alger surprised many, including Root himself. He said it would be "absurd" to accept the post because he knew "nothing about war and nothing about the army." But McKinley replied, through an intermediary, that Root's appointment had little to do with running the army per se; it had everything to do with the problems in Cuba and the Philippines. Root's inexperience with military affairs, McKinley said, was irrelevant, because he was not looking for a military man, only "a lawyer to direct the government of those Spanish islands."[93]

Thus armed with a definition of his primary task, Root took office on August 1, 1899. In his orderly, legal fashion, he interviewed many participants in the debates over Cuba. He also requested that several studies be made—censuses and the like—to determine what sort of population the United States was guiding in Cuba. He required department commanders on the island to submit "civil affairs" reports on their areas.

The result confirmed the course that the debate over Cuba had been taking for some months. Wood and Ludlow spoke in thinly veiled advocacy of a continued U.S. presence, while Wilson and U.S. consul Fitzhugh Lee wanted the United States to pull out and allow Cuban self-determination. The two sides of a decades-old debate in the United States confronted each other on the island which was the subject of their discussions. Both sides began to focus their arguments on the new secretary of war.

Wood and Ludlow continued to advocate a strong U.S. presence in letters to Root. Wilson, for his part, modified his general proposal somewhat and described to Root a plan for an apparent U.S. withdrawal that would leave in place numerous mechanisms of control, to assure that the United States would direct the affairs of Cuba when it needed to. He suggested independence qualified by a U.S. right of intervention in case of Cuban domestic instability, economic interdependence leading to eventual Cuban-advocated annexation, and the presence of U.S. naval installations on the island. "Such a treaty," Wilson wrote, "would practically bind Cuba, hand and foot, and put her destinies absolutely within our control." Though Root made no immediate reply, Wilson's ideas constituted a remarkably accurate prediction of the direction taken by American policy.

Root's motivations have been analyzed by his chief biographer, Philip C. Jessup. Root did not hold the Cubans in particularly high esteem. He referred to them as "ingrates" and poor governors, though he did feel that they deserved "pity rather than anger" because "their attitude was the inevitable result of their lack of development under Spain's strict military domination." Approaching his task without an apparent political motive of his own. Root acted in many ways on strict principle, severing a number of business ties to Cuban firms to avoid the appearance of impropriety.

Recognizing that McKinley's desire was to end the American occupation, Root dutifully implemented what he knew to be the president's intent. In fact, Root himself, Jessup concludes, was "steadfastly opposed" to annexation, although he hoped to use provisions in the Cuban constitution allowing U.S. control of the island's affairs to obstruct foreign influence on the island and preserve the stability of Cuban governments. Nevertheless, Root did believe that the United States should grant the nation independence, and given that other of the strongest personalities on the Cuban issue, especially Leonard Wood, leaned toward strong continued American role, Root's influence was critical. Jessup concludes that, in fact, "Root's steadfast determination was *the main factor* in preventing Cuban annexation or absorbtion."[95]

Accordingly, when Root's report appeared on December 1, 1899, and argued strongly for independence and against the developing consensus for

American control, it caused a mild uproar. U.S. interference, Root argued, "should not be, and of course will not be, continued any longer than is necessary to enable that people to establish a suitable government."[96] U S. occupation forces would set up elections, Root suggested, based on the recently completed census, and municipal and local elections would be followed by a national constitutional convention to establish a Cuban government. After this government was satisfactorily operating, the United States would remove its military presence and establish working relations, especially in the area of trade, with its new southern neighbor.

It must be emphasized again, however, that Root supported these provisions for Cuban independence with the understanding that U.S. negotiators were at work institutionalizing *de facto* U.S. control of Cuban economic and political affairs. Without these qualifications to Cuban independence, it is debatable what Root and others like him—dedicated to supporting both American business interests and Cuban domestic stability, perhaps at the cost of Cuban liberty—would have done.

Many Cubans were pleased with Root's statement, but were still wary of U.S. intentions in the long run. Their doubts were confirmed four days later when President McKinley released his annual message. Much more cloudy than Root's report, it left U.S.-Cuban ties mostly undefined: "the destinies of Cuba," McKinley wrote, "are in some rightful form and manner irrevocably linked with our own, but how and how far is for the future to determine in the ripeness of events." Those "ripe events," given McKinley's vague language, could just as easily justify annexation or indefinite military occupation as the transfer of power to a Cuban government. Cubans were outraged by this announcement, while the Wood coalition took some solace that the president apparently had not been fully persuaded by Root's isolationism.

In 1900, McKinley finally replaced Brooke with Wood. Leonard Wood was a forceful, energetic Army officer who was accustomed to getting what he wanted. One of his biographers describes him as "strong and in splendid physical condition. He stands about five feet ten or eleven inches, and weighs close to two hundred pounds. He is a powerfully built man with the bulging muscles of one who has done manual work." Though unpretentious, Wood managed to carry a distinct air of authority. "His eyes are blue," the biographer continued, "and his hair is of a neutral light color and looks as if the sun, rather than age, had faded it."[97]

Now fully in charge, Wood continued many of Brooke's health and food programs. He conducted a massive anti-yellow-fever campaign, disinfecting all the homes in Havana and dispensing inoculations by the thousand. Wood also took a number of steps to placate the Cubans. He tried to place influential Cuban leaders in positions in the nascent Cuban civil service. He called a meeting, upon assuming power, to reassure Cuban leaders that "on his honor" the United States had always favored, and continue to favor, Cuban independence as soon as that was feasible. And he tried to rule with what he considered a stern but kindly paternalistic hand. Most significantly, Wood called a Cuban constitutional convention for July 25, 1900, "to frame and adopt a Constitution for the People of Cuba, and, as a part thereof, to provide for an agreement with the Government of the United States upon the relations to exist between that Government and the Government of Cuba."[98]

To an uninformed observer, this was a surprising act for a man who had so clearly advocated continued U.S. presence in Cuba. But it would soon become clear that Wood had something up his sleeve: the agreement "upon the relations" between the United States and Cuba, so quietly included in Wood's call for a convention, would be one designed to allow total U.S. interference whenever Washington judged it was required. Any remaining myths about U.S. good intentions—or at least such intentions on Wood's part—would be exploded when Congress passed an almost unprecedented legislative justification for interference in the affairs of another state: the Platt Amendment.

5

THE "PLATT AMENDMENT REPUBLIC"

U.S. Domination, 1902-1932

"Rebellion, revolution—the appeal to arms to redress grievances; these
are measures that can only be justified in extreme cases. It is far better to
suffer any moderate evil, or even a very serious evil, so long as there is a
chance of its peaceable redress, than to plunge the country into civil war. . . .
Between the Scylla of despotism and the Charybdis of anarchy there is
but little to choose; and the pilot who throws the ship upon one is as
blameworthy as he who throws it on the other. But a point may be reached
where the people have to assert their rights, be the peril what it may."
Theodore Roosevelt

"I am going to teach the South American republics to elect good men."
Woodrow Wilson

By 1901, the U.S. government was determined to
implement its Root-guided policy and pull out of Cuba. When it held elections
for an independent Cuban government, and when the formation of a "Cuban
Republic" was subsequently declared in 1902, there was much celebration
in Cuba and much relief in Washington. It appeared that the United States had
decided eventually to grant the island self-determination and independence.
Strong commercial and diplomatic ties were expected to help Cuba develop
into a healthy, stable, sound American ally in the Caribbean.

But this tranquil course of development was not to be. Cuba faced numerous upheavals, coups, and revolutions over the next several decades, and the United States was forced to intervene repeatedly—either militarily or diplomatically—to pull Cuban fat from the fire. Apart from a short lapse during the Hoover administration, American policy toward Cuba from 1902 to 1933 was guided by an interventionist predisposition: the United States would either interfere "preventively," meddling in Cuban politics to prevent the circumstances that would require military intervention, or, at least for the first several years of the period, it would intervene directly with futile attempts to establish a workable Cuban government.

THE PLATT AMENDMENT: ORIGINS, DEVELOPMENT, AND RESULTS

The United States found a legal basis for these interferences in what became known as the Platt Amendment. It granted American leaders the right and duty to intervene in Cuba to maintain a government capable of keeping order. That meant, in the final analysis, preserving the sort of political stability in which American economic interests could flourish and which could provide for Cuban independence. As might be expected from a young power just embarking on a controversial course toward globalism, the right to intervene was exercised fitfully, the duty to allow and create stability often ignored.

Prelude to the Platt Amendment

At the turn of the century, most Americans felt that the Cubans were completely unprepared for self-government, a conclusion on which there was a considerable consensus. General Shafter, influenced by the supposedly traitorous conduct of Cuban troops in the war, said "those people are no more fit for self-government than gunpowder is for hell." Generals Brooke and Wood agreed, as did many members of Congress and the McKinley administration.[1]

American business interests also had a hand in pressuring the government to establish some form of U.S. protectorate. Edwin Atkins and other influential businessmen feared how independence might affect their holdings, and demanded a U.S. policy that left the true reins of power in Washington.

The U.S. government implemented this strategy in various ways; one was to bring "friendly" Cubans to power. Many American leaders were of the opinion that educated Cubans favored U.S. influence, and that only the "ignorant" lower classes wanted independence. One way to silence the unwanted views was to restrict suffrage, and this the United States did. In the June 1900 municipal elections, to be eligible to vote, a voter had to be at least 21 years of age and meet one of three conditions: be able to read and write, own more than $250 worth of property, or have served in the Cuban Liberation Army prior to July 1889.[2] This restricted voting to only *five percent* of the population. Despite these effects, the National Party, which favored independence, still won.

When the second set of elections was held, therefore, in late summer 1900, General Wood himself campaigned hard to promote the benefit of what he called the "better classes." He referred, naturally, to those landed interests that supported U.S. involvement and that, in the eyes of the U.S. government, best promoted political stability. Wood's influence was not particularly great, however; the radical, pro-independence factions still made a strong showing. The American attempt to favor those Cubans who agreed with its goals encompassed several strategies, summarized by Peter Abel. As he notes, the attempt

> turned the 'responsible leadership' and 'better classes' against the rest of the Cuban populace, flattered the surviving [pro-independence] military leaders into consenting to the disbandment of the *ejercitos libertadores*, favored the expatriate leadership at the expense of its domestic counterpart [that is, Estrada Palma over such men as Gomez and Garcia], courted former Spanish office-holders and ex-autonomists while excluding separatists, and promoted ethnic divisions both by denying black veterans access to the officer corps. . .and by imposing a male suffrage with strict property and literacy qualifications.[3]

The stubborn assertiveness of pro-independence factions within Cuba, however, further undermined U.S. confidence in the ability of elected Cuban officials to maintain public order. Wood outlined the distinction in December 1900 when he said:

> I do not mean to say that the people are not capable of good government; but I do mean to say, and emphasize it, that *the classes to whom we must look for the stable government of Cuba* are not yet sufficiently well represented to give us that security and confidence which we desire.[4]

The "confidence" to which he referred, as we have seen, related almost exclusively to the confidence of American businessmen in the investment climate of the island. Yet U.S. economic interests did not yet dominate the

Cuban marketplace, in large part because Wood did not aid American carpetbaggers with schemes to make quick money; he actually "made many permanent enemies in America because of his protection of Cuban interests."[5] Throughout, the American goal—that of Wood, Root, McKinley, and Roosevelt—was a strong Cuban economy which was "essential to the political stability that could provide an enduring Cuban independence."[6]

Leonard Wood's biographers portray his actions as guided by altruism. John Holme argued that Wood's work in Cuba was a "brilliant success," guided by "sound common sense."[7] Taking a destitute nation and building it into a prosperous, developing one, Wood's administration was "unique in the annals of colonial history. . . . nothing like it has ever been accomplished."[8] Holme concludes that Wood was a stern, frugal, energetic defender of Cuba and its people.[9] Hermann Hagedorn essentially concurs. While not praising Wood as openly as Holme does, Hagedorn nevertheless leaves the distinct impression that Wood was a strong, honest man doing his best in the circumstances. Upon the departure of Wood and his wife from Cuba, there was an "outpouring of multitudes in [his] honor."[10]

There is no doubt, however, that Wood did favor the eventual annexation of Cuba, simply because he felt it would be best for both countries. He wrote that Cubans would eventually "become intensely loyal to us and our methods," and when that occurred, "I do not believe you could shake Cuba loose [from the United States] if you wanted to."[11] At another time Wood argued that "All Americans and all Cubans who look ahead know that the Island is going to be a part of the United States."[12]

By early 1901, however, both American and Cuban leaders were beginning to grow tired of the continuing occupation. Demands for political and economic protection notwithstanding, Americans had become unhappy with the moral and financial burdens of the intervention; the latter was taxing the U.S. treasury to the tune of half a million dollars a month. Many Cubans had also begun to demand independence. The pressure on the McKinley administration, in particular, was mounting: Congress was demanding compliance with the Teller Amendment, and some critics were beginning to speculate that the administration had no intention of leaving the island. The issue of imperialism had loomed large in the 1900 U.S. presidential election, with the Democrats under Bryan decrying McKinley's policies.[13] And it had become clear that Root favored withdrawal.

Development of the Platt Amendment

The United States was ready to withdraw from Cuba by 1901. The administration, however, outlined several conditions to be met before it would do so.

In early 1901 Root specified four: (1) the United States would reserve the right to intervene to preserve "maintenance of a stable government adequately protecting life, property, and individual liberty;" (2) no Cuban government would be allowed to enter into foreign relations which "would tend to impair or interfere with the independence of Cuba;" (3) the United States would retain naval stations in Cuba; and (4) all acts of the U.S. military government and "all rights acquired thereunder" would be ratified and protected.[14]

Root, Wood, Platt, and others saw such specific legal mechanisms as necessary because they wished to protect political stability in Cuba, and with it a favorable climate for U.S. economic interests and for U.S. security in the region. Left to "free and uncontrolled" negotiation, however, as some suggested, the matter of Cuban independence might not be adequately resolved; a radical, anti-American government might come to power which would doom both U.S. interests and Cuba's stability. The pro-independence forces in Cuba and anti-expansionist ones in the United States were strong enough to place in doubt any quasi-colonial relationship. By mid-1901, then, the McKinley Administration was ready to try to force Root's four qualifications onto the Cubans in exchange for independence.[15]

To provide the framework for the implementation of these Cuban laws, Root and Wood approved the formation of a convention to frame the constitution of Cuba, and on July 25, 1900, U.S. Civil Order No. 31 provided for the September election of 32 delegates to a convention to begin in November 1900.

It has been seriously questioned whether the convention was independent or representative. Even at the time, some observers doubted the sincerity of Wood and Root's commitment to Cuban independence. Writing in October 1900, Charles Warren Currier warned of American intentions with regard to the convention and the island's independence. After the war, he argued— once the prospects of glory and conquest were gone—"the republic was entirely ignored, its flag was not permitted on the palace at Santiago, and its soldiers were dismissed with the grant of a few dollars."[16] The conduct of the imminent constitutional convention was dubious; why was it set for the first Monday of November, he asked, "the day before the Presidential election?" And the small number of delegates rendered "independent action more difficult," and facilitated "outside pressure." While Currier respected McKinley's personal motives, he feared expansionists were weaving a "network of influences" around him.[17]

The convention, moreover, was charged to frame *and adopt* a constitution—when in most democratic systems the convention would frame it and the *people* would adopt it. Here was another way to guarantee the opposition of the Cuban masses. Also, the very call for a convention demanded that relations with the United States be a precondition of constitutional decision making. Most independent governments, obviously, do not labor under such requirements. Even the *New York Times* was dubious.[18]

Convening on November 5, 1900, the assembly began to hammer out a draft constitution for the incipient republic. On November 6, McKinley was swept back into the White House by a huge margin over Bryan. Theodore Roosevelt, hero of the recent war, was the new vice-president. The Cuban convention continued its work, and by January 30, 1901, a draft was finished, modelled after the American constitution. It provided for a republican government led by a president, and included a bicameral legislature, judicial review, and many other features of the American system. It did not, however, directly address relations with the United States. On February 11, 1901, the convention voted to approve the constitution.

The fears of those who doubted the McKinley administration's good intentions, however, were borne out even as the convention completed its deliberations; Wood and Root were already at work to dictate the conditions of its final product. The United States generally approved of the draft constitution, though it was skeptical of certain measures, including universal suffrage. But administration officials were determined to make the American conditions stick. On February 5, Senator Orville Platt proposed legislation in the U.S. Congress to remedy the Cuban convention's omission of articles dealing with relations with the United States, and to give some "notion" as to "what the United States is going to insist on."[19]

On February 15, 1901, Root sent a letter to the convention, delineating five stipulations that the United States hoped would be included in the constitution. These were similar to his earlier four-point plan: (1) Cuba would not sign a treaty denying Cuban independence or giving concessions in regard to Cuban status to other nations without U.S. permission; (2) Cuba would promise to keep its national debt low and (3) to allow the United States to intervene to aid Cuba when political stability collapsed; (4) the new Cuban government would ratify all laws of the interim military government; and (5) it would also provide for U.S. naval bases on the island.

Root's motivation in this matter was primarily geostrategic, based in a continuing belief in the Monroe Doctrine. He felt that anarchy and potential European influence were still dangerous threats, and without the guarantee of an American legal right to intervene in Cuban affairs the United States would be in a "worse position as to her own interests than she was when Spain held the sovereignty of Cuba."[20] National self-interest was Root's key consideration; as one commentator has concluded, "the evidence concerning the intent of the 'Platt' Amendment overwhelmingly indicates that its sole purpose was strategic."[21] Root certainly had close ties to business, though, especially the sugar industry, and these connections undoubtedly influenced his policies as well.

Reaction to these conditions in Cuba was predictable. Cuban sugar magnates and planters favored continuing U.S. influence to provide stability, but the mass of Cubans strongly opposed American meddling. Havana in late February was alive with celebrations commemorating the sixth anniversary of the 1895 revolution, and these soon became fora for anti-American protests. Many Cubans argued that the provision of naval stations was just as odious a condition as the intervention clause, as it would be tantamount to a surrender of Cuban sovereignty.[22]

Delegates at the convention, however, anxious to secure their independence, were disposed to agree to all of these conditions except the third, which provided for the indefinite threat of U.S. military involvement. Root tried to assure them that this clause was in their interest, that it was provided solely to guarantee political stability, and that it did not refer to military intervention, but the Cubans were not convinced. The assembly—which had already approved a new constitution and was left debating only the American conditions—now began to fear for Cuba's future. Some of its members were certain that McKinley, Root, and Wood desired, if not outright annexation then at least control over Cuban affairs. There was only one hope left, as one Cuban conventioneer expressed it: that "the opinion of Mr. McKinley and of his Secretary Root might not be that of Congress."[23]

While pursuing contacts with the U.S. Congress, the convention officially accepted some of the proposals. Its committee on foreign relations, however, reported after study and debate that "some of these stipulations are not acceptable," so the Cubans made a counter-proposal. This accepted all conditions except the intervention clause. And even in regard to that the Cubans were prepared to abide by the findings of the Treaty of Paris, which had ended the Spanish-Cuban-American War and which provided for American "protection" of Cuba.

Though Wood had nearly given up on the Cuban constitution as a means to enforce the U.S. will, meanwhile, he had another plan. For contrary to the convention's "last hope," the American Congress was not necessarily on their side. It would soon write into U.S. law what the Cubans would not yet agree to include in their own: the United States would enjoy *de jure* as well as *de facto* control over Cuban affairs for the indefinite future. In fact, the infamous Platt Amendment was being written even before the Cuban convention rejected Root's five conditions.

Passage of the Amendment

On February 25, 1901, the Platt Amendment was introduced into the U.S. Senate. Though it bore the name of Senator Platt, it was in fact merely a restatement of Root's earlier conditions on Cuban independence. It noted that the United States would leave Cuba as soon as an adequate government had been established, and it defined the conditions of future U.S.-Cuban relations in eight articles. These provided that Cuba should not surrender its independence to foreign powers or contract a public debt; that the United States reserved the right to intervene to preserve the maintenance of a "government adequate for the protection of life, property, and individual liberty"; that laws already passed, and programs planned, by the U.S. military government—such as sanitation—should be enforced and carried through; and that Cuba, whose territory was said to exclude the Isle of Pines, agreed to provide the U.S. Navy with coaling stations and base facilities.[24]

The amendment thus institutionalized all the interference many Cubans and anti-interventionists had feared. There was significant opposition on the Senate floor; Senator John Morgan, among others, recommended that the United States at least await the results of the Cuban constitutional convention. Attempts were made to alter the Amendment's language. But it was seen as the only way to guarantee the near-immediate withdrawal of U.S. troops, and so it passed on March 2, 1901, 161-137 in the House and 43-20 in the Senate; the split was along party lines.

Cubans—both the general public and the delegates at the convention—were enormously disturbed at this development. In an attempt to allay these fears, Root on March 29 issued his soon-famous corollary to the Platt Amendment. He argued, in a letter to Wood, that article three of the amendment was not a demand for a U.S. right to "meddle" in Cuban affairs; intervention in the article was not "synonymous with intermeddling or interference with the affairs of a Cuban government." The United States was only exercising its right to "stand between" Cuba and other nations in order to "protect the independence of Cuba."[25] In other words, Root was defining the third section of the amendment in a fashion which presumably excluded the American right to exercise capricious interventions. American troops would only be sent, he claimed, if the independence of Cuba were threatened or the country came to be ruled by a state of general anarchy. Root's interpretation, with its emphasis on defense against external threats rather than promotion of U.S. interests within Cuba, was a reflection of his primarily geostrategic perspective.

Wood replied that if he could officially make this pledge under the imprimatur of the U.S. government, he could persuade the Cubans to accept the amendment. Root authorized him to do so, noting that his interpretation of the conditions was also the president's. Wood made the policy public. This declaration greatly reassured the Cubans, but in April a Cuban delegation went to the United States to get direct confirmation. Its members spoke with McKinley, members of his cabinet, and congressmen. McKinley assured them that the "sole purpose" of the amendment was to protect the "independence of Cuba," and that it had "no other object," and Senator Platt agreed. In a lengthy meeting with Root, the Cubans were assured that their government would "enjoy absolute independence" and that "intervention will only be made possible in the event of a foreign threat against the Cuban government, or in combination or alliance with the Cubans, or in the absence of any government in Cuba." Root also said that "military intervention on the island will never take the character of occupation."[26]

Cuban negotiators, satisfied with these qualifications, returned home. The report of the visiting group was given to the convention on May 6, and it exonerated "those who gave their votes for the approval of the amendment," because "clear and precise interpretations" had been added to the legislation which were "sufficient to allay all fears as to any future distortion of the Amendment's letter and spirit."[27] On June 12, 1901, the convention voted to add the language of the Platt Amendment to the new Cuban constitution.

Results of the Amendment

Most commentators analyzing the Platt Amendment in the years and decades following its adoption were critical. The amendment represented, they argued, a clear attempt at domination with no regard for the independence or sovereignty of Cuba. It would also play a key role in fomenting domestic disturbances inside Cuba, because any prospective rebel was virtually promised a U.S. intervention if he disturbed the peace. Immediate public reactions to the amendment were accordingly harsh.[28]

Detailed critiques were more measured and scholarly, but came to the same conclusions. Harry Guggenheim, the U.S. ambassador to Cuba from 1929 to 1933, admitted that the United States used the Platt Amendment, and the later Permanent Treaty of Relations, to suit its own interests. His study of the treaty's applications showed that "the United States had not been consistent in the applications of the Treaty and had not strictly adhered to the official interpretation of Article III," the Root interpretation of the intervention clause.[29] This inconsistency stemmed in part from American ambivalence toward expansion. Having created for itself the legal justification—however suspect—for intervention, the United States was then loath to resort to such actions in practice. As we shall see, even those military and political interventions that occurred did so, with few exceptions, accompanied by great reluctance on the part of American policy-makers.[30]

Cosme de la Torriente, a soldier in the Cuban army of liberation, wrote in *Foreign Affairs* in 1930 that thirty years after the amendment's passage, "people both in the United States and in Cuba still insist on interpreting it in senses contrary to the intentions of its author and of [Root]."[31] Torriente recommended a revision of the amendment to eliminate the intervention clause along with some others, and said that if this were done

> nothing would more greatly enhance the glory of the United States in the eyes of all civilized humanity than for her to continue giving, as she has given in the past, evidences of her high sense of international justice; and no better opportunity for doing so could exist than that of affording the Cubans the occasion for permanently welding a friendship which our close proximity requires should be eternal.[32]

Other analysts, however, defended the amendment; even within Cuba there was no consensus on its effects. Writing in a legal journal, Pedro Capo-Rodriguez insisted that "for any one who is conversant with the facts, the conclusion will be inevitable that the Platt Amendment has really been a blessing for the Cuban people."[33] It prevented social unrest by the threat of U.S. intervention, Capo-Rodriguez argued, unrest that might otherwise have destroyed the island. Capo-Rodriguez did caution that "Cuban affairs are essentially Cuban" and that therefore American policy-makers should make very sure that "American interventions are always undertaken in a noble spirit of helpfulness."[34]

An anonymous article in a 1928 issue of *Foreign Affairs* came to similar conclusions. Listed only as "O," the author was most probably a Cuban or U.S. citizen or official sympathetic to the then-current Cuban government. "O" admitted that the Platt Amendment was not popular in Cuba; Cubans found U.S. dominance "irksome," and "agitation against the Platt Amendment is perennial in Cuba."[35] Even Cuban President Machado was against it.

But as annexation was out of the question, and the chance of political instability was still high, there was little choice but to allow the Platt Amendment to continue functioning. Indeed "many Cubans are willing in their frank moments to acknowledge that this guarantee of public order [the Platt threat of U.S. intervention] is to the benefit of their own country." Anti-debt provisions of the amendment had also benefitted the Cuban economy, O. argued. American and Cuban leaders should simply let the amendment gradually cease to be necessary; "as for the Platt Amendment," he concluded, "time and the political maturity of the [Cuban] Republic will automatically dispose of its limitations on the national sovereignty."[36]

In the end, the Platt Amendment can be seen as a mechanism of indirect control, and one's opinion of the amendment must rest largely on one's view of American dominance of Cuban affairs. Even the Teller Amendment can be seen as part of a veiled attempt by the United States to exercise influence over Cuba, but if the Teller Amendment was veiled, the Platt Amendment was as overt and direct as could be imagined, notwithstanding Root's clarifications. At the same time, it demonstrated the American desire to control Cuba from a distance, to avoid the costs and burdens of actual occupation.

Louis A. Perez, a historian who has written extensively (and superbly) on Cuba, agrees. The Platt Amendment, he argues, was "something of a substitute for annexation," in that it allowed the United States to influence economic and political policies in Cuba without maintaining a burdensome occupation. "In the end," Perez concludes, "nonintervention served the same purpose as intervention," namely the commercial, political, and military control of Cuba by the United States.[37]

The Continuing Occupation

The later stages of American occupation were generally quiet ones. U.S. occupation forces continued their work in education, sanitation, legal reform, and other fields, and the Cuban political scene began to blossom with activity in anticipation of the upcoming elections. By 1901, American procedures had become routine.[38]

However, an economic process was at work that would eventually wreak havoc on U.S. interests in the region. American intervention began to reshape the Cuban economy toward instability; small, middle-class Cuban planters began to lose their tenuous position in the economy to huge, mostly U.S.-controlled land-and-factory combines (called *latifundia*). This destroyed the emerging native Cuban middle class, both in economic and psychological terms. Having lost or become "alienated from" their land, the planters possessed little in the way of a vested interest in the stability of their own country. As one author concludes, "the poverty of culture of the Cuban middle class was a function of U.S. imperialism in Cuba."[39] (The word "imperialism" carries many perhaps unnecessary connotations, but the general conclusion is clear.) At the same time, the Cuban government gradually became the key support for the upper classes of the country, both by providing them with jobs and by catering to their interests; one result was that Cuban governments would be both corrupt and inefficient.

Equally destructive were the socio-political effects of the Platt Amendment and the various economic agreements. As Antoni Kapcia recognizes, the amendment "denied any real autonomy to either any Cuban government or, by implication, the Cuban state itself." The result of dependence on the United States was thus a loss of legitimacy and an "institutional vacuum" created by the impotence of political parties, the army, and the Church. Without true power, Cuban leaders turned to graft; as Kapcia explains, "corruption became a logical outgrowth of a system that produced extensive wealth while denying any real moral purpose to political power. Finally, Cuban nationalism foundered on the American dominance institutionalized in the Platt Amendment.[40]

This situation would prove disastrous. Eventually, the lack of a stable middle-class independent of the Cuban government would doom the country to instability and eventual revolution in the 1950s. Later U.S. policymakers, such as Brooke and Taft, would recognize that the development of a middle-class was crucial to Cuban stability. But they apparently could not recognize the degree to which U.S. economic policies were undermining that goal.

Cuban reactions to this outside dominance reflected the resentment of a people whose great crowning achievement, the seizure of liberty and self-determination from a despotic colonial power, was tarnished with an increasingly intrusive American assertion of a veto power over Cuban actions. The radicalization and anti-Americanism in the thought of the Cuban intelligentsia was unified, and drew much from Jose Marti, whose final letter—a warning about "the monster" United States and its designs upon Cuba—was taken up as a clarion call. After the turn of the century, pro-independence organizations like the Anti-Platt League began to be formed, and the crystallization of Cuban thought around themes of true economic and political independence, social concern, and radical economic solutions, continued.[41]

THE END OF THE OCCUPATION

The United States occupation of Cuba formally ended on May 20, 1902. An election in Cuba brought Don Tomas Estrada Palma, a longtime leader of the Cuban independence and revolutionary movement and great friend of the United States, to power. Estrada Palma was rushed into candidacy, and was "without a program in a campaign without an opponent," a situation brought about by the withdrawal of the opposition party from the election because of alleged fraud. But he was relatively popular, and despite the threat of U.S. involvement embodied in the Platt Amendment, Cubans celebrated their new independence.

Estrada Palma immediately attempted to pursue reconciliation and establish a stable, popular government. He appointed officials from all classes and backgrounds to his government, and spoke in conciliatory terms to all Cubans. One of his first speeches to the new Cuban Congress was a call for stability and economic progress tempered with social justice.[42]

The First Palma Administration

Tomas Estrada Palma, affectionately known as "Don Tomas," was born in Oriente province in 1835, studied law in Spain, lived for a time in France, and returned to Cuba in 1868 to take part in the Ten Years' War. In 1877 he was named president of the Cuban republic, but was captured and sent to Spain. Released in 1878, he went to Honduras and then spent twenty years in the United States. During the 1895 revolution he managed the *Junta* in New York, collecting money and supplies for the rebels.

But Estrada Palma placed tremendous emphasis on law and order, and admitted that annexation to the United States might be necessary if the Cubans could not adequately run their government. Without hesitation, he argued that "a political dependence which assured us the fecund boons of liberty is a hundred times preferable for our beloved Cuba to a sovereign and independent republic discredited and made miserable by the baneful action of periodic civil wars."[43] Estrada Palma thus firmly supported the requirement for American guidance until Cuba achieved the ability to govern itself, and for this some observers consider him astonishingly prescient.

Estrada Palma's first administration was a generally peaceful one, dedicated to rebuilding the country and establishing political consensus. In this sense it represented perhaps the best period of the republic to date.[44] Relatively minor disputes continued to complicate Cuban-American relations at this time, especially arguments over a trade treaty.

Both Cuba and the United States had desired for some time to establish a reciprocity treaty granting special trade concessions, to ensure that each nation would remain the other's market. In September, 1901, the hero of the late war, Theodore Roosevelt, had come into office in the United States. After some delay, Roosevelt overrode U.S. sugar interests and passed such a treaty in December, 1903; it stipulated that Cuban tariffs would be reduced between 25 and 40 per cent, American ones 20 per cent or more.[45]

This treaty, though delayed more than Estrada Palma would have liked, helped get the Cuban economy moving, and combined with the relative stability provided by the Platt Amendment guarantees, created a favorable climate for investment in Cuba. A period of relative prosperity followed. Some observers have argued that the Roosevelt administration pursued the treaty with selfish motives, attempting to increase exports and gain control of the Cuban economy. But as Dana Munro has recognized, "neither the official record nor their private correspondence" indicate that Roosevelt or Root had "ulterior motives in pressing for reciprocity."[46] Nevertheless, whatever their reasons, American officials—as they would continue to do for decades—had established a trade relationship that served to reinforce the dominance of

"King Sugar" in Cuba and hence hamper the development of a diverse Cuban business class.[47]

Besides demanding certain courses of action on these and a few other issues, the United States eschewed interference in Cuban affairs during the first Estrada Palma administration, following Roosevelt's plan of allowing the Cubans to make an attempt at self-determination, and respected Cuban concerns in regard to the removal of marines and the conduct of consular activities. After a time, the trial seemed to be working, and Roosevelt could say in his 1904 annual message that if "every country" in the Caribbean "would show the progress in stable and just civilization" exhibited by the Cubans, "all questions of interference by this Nation with their affairs would be at an end."[48]

Two years would not yet have passed before these words had become meaningless.

Development of the Roosevelt Corollary

Theodore Roosevelt's policy toward Latin America was guided by his own interpretation of how best to enforce the Monroe Doctrine. His beliefs were expressed in what has become known as the "Roosevelt Corollary" to the Monroe Doctrine, and which would form an integral aspect of U.S. Latin American policy.

Extending the Monroe Doctrine's implications, Roosevelt argued that the United States must undercut the *causes* of European intervention in the region, in addition simply to opposing such intervention. He specified political instability and financial mismanagement, in particular, as two bases of European interference. The corollary was developed after the 1902-1903 Anglo-German blockade of Venezuela.[49]

Formulation of this policy was guided by Roosevelt's desire to develop a forceful role for the United States, one worthy of a great power. He believed it was the right and duty of large nations to impose their will on smaller ones that had gone astray. If stability were preserved, he wrote, countries "would fear no interference from the United States", but "chronic wrongdoing" or destruction of society might "ultimately require intervention by some civilized nation."[50] As Howard Hill phrases it, Roosevelt's attitude toward Cuba resembled that of "a father who takes pride in the achievements of his child but does not hesitate, if need arises, to admonish and discipline his offspring."[51]

This discipline, however, would be applied in ways *other than intervention*. Roosevelt remained dedicated to allowing Latin American nations to exercise their sovereignty, and only wished to guide them in a suggestive way. He steadfastly opposed American interference in Cuban affairs, and when forced to intervene in 1906 he expressed severe disappointment with the Cubans. Roosevelt's policy-making was infused with an enormously strict sense of values: he was strongly committed to national adherence to morality, and believed the nation should adhere to the Golden Rule; he opposed discriminatory treatment of peoples; and he felt himself to be strictly bound by his word. His commitment to the independence of Cuba is indisputable, as is the fact that he indeed endeavored to "keep his word" and provide the island with its opportunity for independence.[52]

Meanwhile, in July, 1905 Root became secretary of state. He agreed with Roosevelt's general policies, though he took the non-intervention pledge even further, and hoped to avoid in any way bullying Latin American leaders. Root summarized the U.S. attitude toward Cuba in three sentences: "First. We do not want to take them for ourselves. Second. We do not want any foreign nations to take them for themselves. Third. We want to help them."[53] On the personal level, Root liked Latin Americans a great deal and enjoyed dealing with them.

Once again, however, for all of Roosevelt's desire to preserve a distant U.S. role of detached but concerned observer, instabilities in Cuba would demand direct U.S. intervention.

The Second Estrada Palma Administration

In 1905, ready to run for a second term the following year, Estrada Palma recognized that active opposition forced him to choose a specific political party and utilize its electoral machinery. He decided on the Moderates, and his government soon became a patronage organization designed to promote Moderate interests. This favoritism and corruption set an unfortunate precedent for later Cuban governments.[54]

The National Party under Alfredo Zayas and Jose Miguel Gomez's Republicans combined to form the Liberal Party to oppose Palma, and they appointed Gomez as their presidential candidate. Appealing to nationalist sentiment, the Liberals drew strength from peasants, lower class workers, and ex-soldiers. Estrada Palma responded to the growing pressure by "purging" the government in April, 1905 of all non-Moderates, an act of circling the wagons that worried both U.S. officials and Estrada Palma's own supporters. His administration became characterized by huge amounts of graft and corruption, and his opponents began to attack him furiously. A U.S. representative remarked at the time that Estrada Palma could "fairly be charged with too great partisan activity after following a neutral policy for nearly three years."[55] The stage was set for the first great crisis of the new Cuban regime, and the first invocation of the Platt Amendment.

THE 1905 INTERVENTION

The political situation in Cuba was not nearly as stable as some American officials thought. Unaccustomed to even limited self-rule, dissatisfied with continuing American meddling, and lacking a true, indigenous middle class to preserve stability, the Cubans soon fell to squabbling and graft. Anarchy gradually began to creep into the Cuban political scene. This instability would set the stage for the second U.S. military intervention.

Background: The Election Crisis of 1905

Estrada Palma desired fair elections; he was essentially an honest man. One commentator said "he had a reputation for financial integrity never repeated thereafter by any Cuban administration" before the 1959 revolution.[56] But he had made the mistake of appointing a corrupt cabinet, and many of the lieutenants undertook fraudulent campaign tactics without his knowledge. In fact, Palma did not even want to run for a second term; he "allowed" himself to be persuaded into running, and "practically all writers and the many living witnesses interviewed agree that Estrada Palma did not desire a second term."[57] Estrada Palma was not completely blameless: once he did enter the race, he proved stubborn and his honesty was tarnished by a growing willingness to tolerate self-serving electoral abuses.

Nominating a ticket of Jose Miguel Gomez and Alfredo Zayas, the Liberals made immediate abrogation of the Platt Amendment the focus of their campaign. The Moderates rested on Palma's record and mobilized the resources available to the incumbent government; by the time of the September, 1905 local electoral board contests, the Moderate political machine was in place. It engineered a complete Moderate sweep through the use of bribery, tampering with results, and other methods of fraud. Liberal candidates were harassed, and occasionally even shot at. On September 22 the Liberal candidate Enrique Villuendas was assassinated.

By September 23, the date of the elections, the context for a Moderate theft of the election had been established. Government troops prevented Liberals from voting in many areas. Election officials had been hired or fired based on their loyalty to the Moderates. Liberals also used violence, intimidating Moderate candidates, burning government buildings, and the like, but they had no organized system to support them. Predictably enough, the Moderates won a huge victory; in many strongly pro-Liberal areas, only small turnouts for the Liberals were reported. In many areas the Moderates received well over one hundred per cent of the known voting block.

To protest these irregularities, Liberal leaders withdrew from the December

1 general elections, hoping to discredit them. They denounced the preliminary elections and argued that the later national elections would be fraudulent as well. Gomez fled to New York and tried to provoke an American intervention. Estrada Palma, however, went ahead with the December elections; he added 150,000 fake names to voting lists, and claimed total victory. No Liberal candidate won anywhere. The Liberals had not merely engaged in a momentary fit of rage, however; in Latin America, the withdrawal of an opposition party had come to symbolize one thing: revolution was imminent.[58]

The Liberal Revolt

On the night of February 24, 1906, a group of disaffected Liberals attacked the army barracks at Guanabacoa outside Havana, killing several guards and shooting up the area. This revolt was quickly smashed, but it was a precursor of what was to follow. Estrada Palma, apparently unwilling to believe a real revolt was possible, took little action. On August 16, when General Faustino Guerra Puente, a Liberal congressman, raised the true flag of general revolt in Pinar del Rio, Estrada Palma's government was ill-prepared for an insurgency.[59] Besides ordering an immediate and somewhat successful arrest of many rebel leaders, Estrada Palma was able to do little, and his Rural Guard proved hopelessly inefficient in battle. The Liberals soon had 25,000 to 30,000 rebels in the field.

Theodore Roosevelt had no intention of again becoming embroiled in Cuban politics. He had already made a new rhetorical commitment to regional noninterference, and regarding the action of intervention he said ''we emphatically do not want it. . . nothing but direct need could persuade us to take it.'' On September 26 he wrote that the Estrada Palma government was ''evidently bent to force us to an armed intervention,'' though he wanted none of it.[60] And he wrote at the time that

> At the moment, I am so angry with that infernal little Cuban republic
> that I would like to wipe its people off the face of the earth. All we
> have wanted from them was that they would behave themselves and
> be prosperous and happy so that we would not have to interfere.
> And now, lo and behold, they have started an utterly unjustifiable
> and pointless revolution and may get things into such a snarl that we
> have no alternative [but] to intervene.[61]

Roosevelt's sentiments were echoed by Acting Secretary of State Bacon, who opposed intervention because he feared it would become a self-perpetuating, counterproductive habit. When the United States did intervene, according to later U.S. ambassador Harry Guggenheim, it did so "with the greatest reluctance."[62]

Cuban rebels and government troops carried on their "war" in an unusual fashion, and many commentators described it as a poor excuse for a conflict. The rebels, in many cases motivated by a desire to steal food and valuables, camped in what one writer has described as a "picnic atmosphere,"[63] and many fled when real battle presented itself. Government troops fought poorly and only occasionally.

Roosevelt did order the army to make ready for an invasion if one proved necessary. He asked Generals Bell and Funston for their recommendations about the campaign; both provided disturbing reports. Cuban guerrillas could hide in the hills and stymie U.S. operations much as the Philippine insurgents had, they argued, creating a long and costly campaign of attrition.[64] Roosevelt was upset by these estimates, and so he was not willing to support Estrada Palma, for if he did so, he might later be forced to undertake exactly the sort of intervention he hoped to avoid.

On September 1 a group of Cuban army veterans led by Mario Menocal, later president of Cuba, sought to mediate between the government and the Liberals. By September 8, Menocal believed both sides were ready for a compromise, but none was forthcoming. At this crucial juncture, the Cuban government asked U.S. consul Frank Steinhart to intervene and decide the issue. Steinhart, in Cuba since 1899, was a strong supporter of Wood's elitist view of Cuban government, and his sympathies thus ran to Estrada Palma. On September 8, he sent a strong request for U.S. warships to back the Cuban president. On the 10th, after another urgent cable from Steinhart requesting a reply, Roosevelt, through Acting Secretary of State Bacon, agreed and said the ships were on the way, though cautioning that actual intervention was "out of the question."[65]

Steinhart cabled again on the 12th, saying the revolt was getting out of hand and that "the Cuban government has no elements to contend it, to defend the towns and prevent the rebels from destroying property."[66] On that same day, Estrada Palma, as Steinhart had said he would, formally requested intervention, asking for 2,000 or 3,000 U.S. troops, and the cruiser U.S.S. *Denver* arrived in Havana harbor and put ashore 125 marines. But Roosevelt told the officials on the scene that they "had no business to direct the landing of those troops" and ordered them re-embarked. Their deployment, however, had already raised the hopes of all those on the island who wanted intervention, which included most of the Cuban political leaders on both sides.[67]

Roosevelt finally announced that he was sending Taft and Assistant Secretary of State Bacon to Cuba to arrange for the "permanent pacification" of the island. Though Roosevelt clearly hoped for a form of diplomatic intervention that would forestall the need for military action, the implications of his new policy were far from clear. Indeed, as in the past and the future, the failure to define a clear policy led both sides in the Cuban dispute to believe that the Americans might support them. Meanwhile Roosevelt now authorized the landing of troops to aid Taft and Bacon, and the intervention—small from at first—had begun.

The United States Takes Over: The Marines and Taft Government

Secretary of War Taft was far from pleased with his new assignment. Besides his earlier reservations about the ability of the United States to win a war against the Cuban insurgents, Taft harbored doubts about his own ability to deal with the situation. He complained that his lack of information on the Cuban scene made it "quite embarrassing" for him to go there and act as mediator. He knew that something had to be done quickly, though, as the Cuban situation was like a "house of cards." Nor was Roosevelt happy at having to allow the sort of interference he so abhorred; he wrote:

I did not send Taft and Bacon to Havana until [Estrada] Palma had repeatedly telegraphed us that his unalterable purpose was to resign forthwith. . . .I have, I need hardly say, a horror of putting what is in effect a premium upon insurrection by letting the insurrectionists receive benefit from their action; but [Estrada] Palma's utter weakness. . .to do anything effective toward quelling the revolt. . .made it absolutely imperative that I should take some step unless I wished to see chaos come to the Island.

Roosevelt also expressed his fear that the United States might be forced "to exercise a more immediate control over Cuba," a course he worked strenuously to avoid.[68]

The situation grew increasingly severe. Earlier in the month U.S. charge Jacob Sleeper had warned that by the 15th "the rebels will begin burning foreign property." On the 15th, Taft told Roosevelt that 18,000 men could be quickly readied for intervention. But many U.S. officers quietly told the press that they believed 100,000 U.S. troops would be necessary to quell the revolt, and the *New York Times* and *Washington Post* even suggested that the U.S. forces would be forced to resort to Weyler's *reconcentracion* policy.[69]

As this situation disintegrated, however, the U.S. intervention continued to expand. By September 22, the naval presence had grown to three battleships and four cruisers, which carried a total of 2,000 marines.

Taft began formal negotiations between the two sides on September 19, amid reports of growing anarchy in many places on the island. Taft, Bacon, and U.S. consul Steinhart interviewed dozens of Cubans from both sides. The rebels in particular were hard to deal with because they continued to lack central leadership. Lack of progress led to the landing of more U.S. troops on the 20th. The condition of government forces was desperate, and Havana itself was surrounded by ill-equipped but hostile rebels. The arrival of Taft and Bacon, however, brought a temporary end to the fighting, and the two men now tried to arrange a permanent solution.

Taft and Bacon soon realized that the 1905 elections had been fraudulent and that the revolt was a protest against this abuse. Estrada Palma's government now enjoyed little support, and the insurgents were defeating the Rural Guard forces at many points. The United States, they concluded, could not therefore support the existing government. They did not want to force Estrada Palma out of office immediately; on the 22nd Taft wrote Roosevelt arguing that Estrada Palma would be valuable because of his perceived honesty and his acceptability to landowners. They therefore made agreement on Palma's second term the basic plank of a compromise solution, figuring that all sides recognized that he did not personally control the election fraud. Other provisions of the compromise included the resignation of all officials elected in the 1905 elections, the establishment of new municipal and electoral laws, redress for Liberals ousted from office unfairly, and new elections.[70]

Liberal leaders accepted these conditions, but the Moderates did not, claiming that they affronted the "dignity and honor" of the party and were therefore unacceptable. On the 24th Estrada Palma noted that such conditions would force him to resign, as they ran against his "personal decorum" and the "dignity of the government over which I preside."[71] This threat undercut American plans to use Estrada Palma as the centerpiece of a grand compromise, and Roosevelt, still hoping to avoid occupation, on the 25th asked Estrada Palma to stay on. He refused, but even then Roosevelt would not allow full intervention. He wrote that he did not believe the United States "should, simply because Estrada Palma has proven obstinate, put ourselves in the place of his unpopular government and face all the likelihood of a long, drawn-out and very destructive guerrilla warfare."[72]

On September 28, 1906, Tomas Estrada Palma convened the Cuban Congress to tender his resignation and those of his cabinet. Other Moderate leaders tried to meet and appoint a new president, but failed to reach agreement; Estrada Palma meanwhile had delegated his authority to Taft and Bacon. On the 29th, with Roosevelt's reluctant approval, Taft issued a proclamation to "the Cuban people" explaining the American intervention. Taft noted the lack of Cuban government required American action, but explained that the provisional American government "will be maintained only long enough to restore order and peace and public confidence.'' Taft announced that the government would remain, in name at least, a Cuban one (the United States would keep up the facade of Cuban sovereignty throughout the coming occupation) and that "the Cuban flag will be hoisted" over government buildings.[73]

Roosevelt authorized the landing of more marines. The Americans were once again in charge.[74]

AMERICAN OCCUPATION: THE MAGOON ADMINISTRATION, 1906-1909

At first, many Cubans welcomed the American forces. As we have seen, some of them had hoped for this development. Arriving Americans were cheered and treated in a friendly and cooperative manner. Cuban politicians in Havana collected money to erect a statue of Roosevelt; U.S. naval officers received watches and bouquets.[75]

Taft governed until October 13, 1906, when he turned the provisional government over to Charles Magoon. While in charge, Taft sought to disband rebel groups, and the rebels, expecting U.S. mediation of their complaints, agreed to lay down their arms; by October 8 almost all groups had been disarmed. Taft appointed a commission to investigate the 1905 elections, and deployed 6,000 U.S. troops to maintain the peace. He also released political prisoners and granted a general amnesty.

Meanwhile, Americans and Cubans alike began discussing the possibility of an outright annexation of the island. U.S. citizens in Cuba, selected Cuban planters, and the Northern U.S. press all argued that the United States might as well stay and establish permanent stability. Roosevelt, however, rejected these suggestions, and said he would give Cuban self-determination one last try. He claimed he had "no wish" to annex Cuba.[76]

Charles Magoon was a successful American lawyer and diplomat who, in 1906, had just finished rendering an outstanding service to the United States government in Panama. Root recommended him for the post as head of the U.S. provisional government in Cuba, and Roosevelt appointed him on October 6. On the 13th, Magoon took over the provisional government from Taft and Bacon, who were sent off with great fanfare. A large man with thick blonde hair and a small moustache, Magoon had had some experience in Cuba, having worked for McKinley in 1899 on legal aspects of the Cuban occupation. He was known as a friendly, hearty, if somewhat simple diplomat.

Magoon was destined to become one of the most controversial figures in the history of U.S.-Cuban relations, and if anything, it was his basic naivete and honesty that undid him. A country lawyer from the farming Midwest, Magoon was in many ways unsuited to the corrupt, power-based Cuban political system and the cheats, liars and schemers who pervaded it. He was not a military man like Wood or even the simpler Brooke, and his belief in conciliatory mediation and the achievement of compromise did not suit the Cuban political scene.

As Taft left, he surveyed the Cuban political situation, and his predictions were not optimistic. The key problems, he observed, were a constant series of rhetorical and military attacks on the government, occasioned for the most part by a degree of bitterness in political debates uncommon in true democracies, and the "aloofness and lack of political influence of the conservative and property-holding classes." Taft's main fear on leaving was the lack of development of a "sound ruling class,"[77] and he despaired at the prospect for the establishment of one. As we have seen, his doubts were well founded.

Magoon, for his part, continued the facade of Cuban independence referred to in Taft's original intervention proclamation. He allowed the Cubans to sign treaties on their own authority, to send a representative to the Hague peace conference, to fly the Cuban flag from government buildings, and to pursue other small aspects of "independence."[78]

Magoon's tasks in Cuba were simple in concept but enormously difficult to achieve in practice. He was to formulate new electoral and municipal laws, hold fair elections, and pull out as quickly as possible. Forced against his will to intervene, Roosevelt was not going to leave Cuba under American rule any longer than was absolutely necessary.

In attempting to settle the Liberal claims of fraud in recent elections, Magoon made the mistake of placing himself in the position of arbiter of political patronage, a role that would condemn him in the eyes of many. He reinstated Liberal municipal governments in many areas, and reviewed the claims of various individual Liberal leaders who demanded positions in the government. Magoon was an honest man, and decided the issues as best he could, but his actions inevitably led many Cubans to suspect he was doing someone's bidding.

U.S. troops stationed on the island again pursued public works and sanitation programs, and Magoon's administration undertook other reforms as well. In December, 1906 he appointed an Advisory Law Commission to formulate fair electoral and municipal laws. The Commission found a chaotic set of overlapping Spanish, Cuban, and American laws; its various subcommittees set out to correct this system, and developed, debated, and approved various changes. It eventually extended its reforming eye to provincial law as well, and met hundreds of times through January, 1909. Its work won general praise, and many of the laws it wrote stayed on the books until the 1930s and 1940s.

Magoon also pursued extensive public works programs. The quality of roads in the country improved markedly, U.S. medical troops engaged in huge vaccination and sanitation campaigns, and dozens of government buildings were constructed. In part due to these efforts, by the end of the occupation the Cuban crude death rate had fallen to 12 per 1,000, one of the lowest in the world at the time.[79]

Responding to Roosevelt's desire to quit Cuba as quickly as possible, Magoon wanted to hold elections for a new Cuban government rapidly, and he initially scheduled them for January, 1907. Problems with Cuban party politics, however, forced a postponement until May, then later. In April Taft visited the island, and to forestall notions that the postponement of elections might signal a U.S. intention to keep the island indefinitely, agreed with Magoon on a strong statement of continued intent to hold elections leading to independence. Taft formulated a set of conditions for a U.S. pullout, which included a new electoral law, an accurate census, municipal and provincial elections followed by national ones, and most significantly, a reference to the necessary "tranquility" of the country. This last requirement offered annexationists in Cuba one last chance to stir trouble and make necessary an indefinite U.S. presence—and some tried, confirming Roosevelt's fear that he had put a "premium upon insurrection." One was the Cuban Juan Masso Parra, a schemer whose September 1907 rebellion was designed to "fight the United States into annexation."[80] (He failed.)

Cuban elections were eventually set for November 14, 1908. Political parties in Cuba began to flesh out in anticipation of the elections; the Conservatives supported Menocal, while the Liberals support was split between "Miguelistas" and "Zayistas": those supporting Jose Miguel Gomez and Alfredo Zayas, respectively. Smaller independent parties, whether nationalist, black, or leftist, also formed. During this period the United States also recommended and oversaw the creation of an official Cuban army (besides the Rural Guard), a force that would later seriously complicate Cuban politics.[81]

The Formulation of Post-Occupation Policy

During 1908, the U.S. government began to develop a policy to follow once it had withdrawn from Cuba. In late January of that year Roosevelt met with Magoon and Crowder to discuss the subject; Magoon accurately summarized the U.S. intent when he noted that the purpose of the meeting was to provide a plan for "exercising [the] power of the United States in Cuba" after a withdrawal, in a less troublesome manner than outright intervention. Some, including U.S. Cuban consul Steinhart, recommended significant U.S. control of Cuban affairs, including the continued presence of troops and economic and political advisors.

Magoon disagreed vehemently. On April 16, 1908, he replied with a conclusive summary of his views, arguing that the United States must adhere to the strict Root interpretation of the Platt Amendment and withdraw from the country. He claimed that Cuban politics, bolstered by the U.S.-designed electoral reforms, were advanced enough that whatever government was elected in 1908 would be able to rule in an orderly fashion. A continued U.S. presence, Magoon noted, would disturb the "moral peace" and lead to resentment.[82] Two developments in particular, he contended, would ensure stability: an end to the massive and occasionally violent tradition of criticism of the Cuban government, i.e., a move toward consensus in the political sphere; and the entry into politics of the previously dormant property-owning and commercial classes.[83] Roosevelt backed Magoon, and the elections proceeded.

It is interesting to note that Magoon's analysis of the requirements for stability in Cuban politics mirrored those of Taft: the development of consensus on the basics of the political process, and the emergence of a stable ruling elite out of the middle class. The difference was that Taft despaired of these developments while Magoon expected them. In fact, Magoon's conclusions were, like much of his opinion, hopelessly naive. The Cubans were not anywhere near the establishment of a stable political arena, with the result that the upcoming elections would only usher in another period of instability.

On August 1, the first municipal elections were held, and though the Conservatives did relatively well, the Miguelistas and Zayistas immediately realized that if they pooled their resources they could win the upcoming national elections easily. Gomez and Zayas set aside their differences and joined on a single ticket, with Gomez nominated as president and Zayas as vice president. The Conservatives nominated Menocal. True to expectations, when the national elections occurred on November 14, the Liberals won, not only the presidency but also majorities in both houses of the Cuban congress.

The election was generally agreed to be as fair as could be expected, and in his December, 1908 annual message Roosevelt said that "in Cuba our occupancy will cease in about two months' time; the Cubans have in an orderly manner elected their own governmental authorities, and the island will be turned over to them." Magoon departed, and in January, 1909, the new Cuban government began to assemble; the transfer of power to the independent Republic of Cuba was soon complete. The Cubans were ready to give democracy and self-governance a second try, and the United States was ready to let them.[84]

Critiques of Magoon's Role

As he departed Havana Harbor on January 29, to the cheering of a huge crowd, Magoon could not have known how controversial his work in Cuba would become. Critics have labeled him a mere "dispenser of patronage," a mediocre administrator who viewed the Cuban political situation with incredible naivete and simply failed to correct the underlying causes of instability in Cuba.

Cuban nationalists also blamed Magoon for the graft and corruption that came to characterize later Cuban governments; Carlos Manuel Trelles, for example, contended that Magoon had "profoundly corrupted the Cuban nation"; other Cubans charged that Magoon invented the *botelles* (soft jobs), that he took bribes, favored U.S. businesses, and was, in short, a "lazy, miserly, good-for-nothing slob."[85] Even some American observers have argued that Magoon left behind him "an ominous cloud of distrust, disillusion, contempt, and downright hatred for America's administrative officers."[86]

Magoon's defenders stress that his basic service was excellent. He was an efficient, if not insightful, administrator, and was well-liked by most Cubans. He was scrupulously honest, and not a single shred of evidence for any embezzlement or graft on Magoon's part has been unearthed. Nearly all who knew Magoon praised him; General Pershing, for example, called him a man of "strong character and great ability," and said he "could not speak too highly of him."[87]

Many contemporary views of the intervention agreed. One editorial in a law journal of the time hailed the "earnest purpose" that the United States had shown in fulfilling its pledge of Cuban independence.[88] Many American papers, and many of the people who read them, believed likewise: persuaded by Roosevelt's confidence, they felt the Cuban "problem" had been, to large extent, "solved." And one later chronicler of Roosevelt's Caribbean policy, Howard Hill, argued that "whatever the future may hold for the Pearl of the Antilles, the record indicates that the second American intervention was a period of advance by the Cubans in the mastery of the difficult art of self government," a period that would make the need for a third intervention "less likely."[89]

Yet it must be admitted that as a simple country lawyer, Magoon came to Cuba ill-equipped to deal with the hucksterism, corruption, and outright brutality of the island's politics. His expectations for the Cubans ran far ahead of what any realistic observer would have hoped for. Taft knew better, as did many of the U.S. officers of the army of occupation. In a sense, then, Magoon serves as an accurate microcosm of the faults of the larger U.S. policy toward Cuba. The real problem with the second American intervention was that it did not truly address the underlying causes of Cuban instability. Magoon pursued no economic or land reform, did not attempt to establish two stable political parties, and allowed a politically dangerous army to be formed, failing then to imbue it with a respect for civilian leadership. While this was more a result of his lack of imagination than his subservience to any special interests, its effect was nevertheless damaging. Economic development accelerated by American rule came in an imbalanced and therefore destabilizing fashion, and the basic inequity of Cuban society remained unchanged.

One American officer of the occupation, Lt. Col. Bullard, summarized the situation, betraying more insight than that displayed by Magoon, Roosevelt, or the American press. Cuba had been invaded but not really altered, Bullard argued, and Cubans would inevitably again rise up again in revolts spurred, at base, by inequitable political, social, and economic structures. Bullard's analysis was not free of the cultural prejudice so common among American observers of other countries: ''with the domineering, grandee spirit of Spanish blood,'' he wrote, ''no Cuban in power can abstain from squeezing his fellows, from making them feel his power and authority.'' But his conclusion was undoubtedly accurate. ''The United States will have to go back. It is only a question of time.''[90]

THE SECOND REPUBLIC: 1909

When the United States ended its second intervention in 1909, it left in place a set of mechanisms that would allow it to exercise considerable political and economic influence over the island. Most Cubans were by now too wary of American intentions to believe that the year 1909 signalled a significant watershed in their drive for independence, and events would bear out their skepticism.

Cuban Government and Continued American Influence

Upon the United States withdrawal, the Liberals returned to power in Cuba and immediately reinstated the practices of graft, fraud, and patronage characteristic of earlier Cuban governments. Some have speculated that the United States was partially to blame for this development; with the constant threat of U.S. intervention hanging like a condescending parent's threat over the politically immature Cubans, the latter might not have felt much incentive or need to behave responsibly. In any case, while the American intervention of 1906-09 did re-establish a Cuban government of some stability, it certainly did not succeed in creating an honest one.

Meanwhile, in 1808 William Howard Taft had come into power in the United States. Roosevelt's hand-picked successor, Taft had, as we have seen, already demonstrated his administrative and political skills during terms as governor of Cuba and as Secretary of War; he also helped administer the Philippines during the American occupation there. With his secretary of state, Philander C. Knox, Taft would generally follow a policy of "preventive diplomacy," designed to forestall the development of circumstances requiring intervention. Like Roosevelt, Taft hoped to avoid the sometimes costly and often counterproductive process of recurring American interventions in Latin American nations. As one commentator described it, Taft pursued a "preventive policy, calculated to ward off such occurrences in Cuba as might lead to a new revolution and therefore to an intervention."[91] In many cases this practice took the form of directly dictating policies to Cuban governments.

The United States indeed had no intention of simply leaving the Cuban government to its devices. American economic interests in the island, in particular, dictated a strong involvement to protect the Latin American markets so crucial to U.S. exports. Knox was a former corporate lawyer, and his concern for business interests would color U.S. policy toward Cuba.[92] The United States became increasingly involved in the economic affairs of Cuba and other Latin American states.

This promotion of economic interests would soon become known as "Dollar Diplomacy." Hoping to stay away from direct intervention, the Taft administration hoped that economic development could serve as the centerpiece of a renewed effort to restore stability to Cuba and the rest of Latin America. In this sense the policy represented a continuation of the Roosevelt Corollary to the Monroe Doctrine, in that it attempted to provide for financial responsibility and progress as key components of Latin American domestic stability. While Knox and Taft were influenced by economic considerations, however, they were not necessarily in business's pocket; as Dana Munro has concluded, the primary purpose of Dollar Diplomacy was "to promote the political objectives of the United States, not to benefit private financial interests."[93]

This general set of policies can be seen as another attempt to exercise control without bearing the burdens or costs of true occupation or colonization. As Louis Perez has noted, Dollar Diplomacy created a "wider sanction for greater intervention" which in turn established "a new infrastructure of hegemony."[94] The United States could quietly but firmly tell the Cubans to keep their noses clean, and back up these demands with the constant threat of intervention, always hinted at but never, after 1909, actually used, except in some relatively minor cases. "Preventive diplomacy" was just another weak substitute for annexation, a policy dictated by the ambivalent nature of U.S. foreign policy.

In order to justify this political interference, the State Department issued another reinterpretation of the Platt Amendment. It asked rhetorically if "intervention" meant only "actual occupation of Cuban territory by American forces," or whether it had a "broader" meaning "which comprehends the giving [of] advice or the making of demands or requests by diplomatic representation."[95] State's answer to this question was a strong affirmation of the latter interpretation. American policy-makers also linked sections two and three of the amendment, making economic pragmatism a precondition for the good government which was in turn required as a guarantee against U.S. intervention. Reference to fiscal irregularity became another justification for U.S. diplomatic interference in Cuban affairs.

This political influence was in turn used to support American economic interests. The State Department lodged numerous protests against Cuban public works programs that contracted work to non-U.S. companies. It opposed railway construction, swampland development, salvage operations, and other projects not bearing a strong U.S. imprint. In fact the State Department "protested virtually every bill involving the disbursement of public funds and the creation of public contracts that favored local interests over U.S. enterprise." And this in turn helped retard the development of a true Cuban middle class, a process that rendered Cuba perpetually vulnerable to rebellions.[96]

The Crisis of 1912

In 1912, Gomez was coming to the end of his term as Cuban president. He had presided over an administration characterized by fraud and corruption, and many segments of Cuban society opposed his rule. In May 1912 two disaffected groups rose up against him: blacks and the military.[97]

The United States reacted immediately. As long before as 1910 Secretary of State Knox had expressed U.S. dissatisfaction with the political problems of Cuba.[98] Conditions demanding intervention were rapidly developing, and American leaders had no desire to follow such a course. To incite Gomez to find a solution to the insurrection, Knox warned that the United States would intervene if Gomez could not put down the revolt while at the same time preserving a republican government. (Thus the Taft administration continued the ironic U.S. practice of *threatening* intervention to *avoid* intervention—a fine idea, except when those you are threatening want you to intervene.) But the fighting continued, with blacks and other rebellious groups battling Gomez's Rural Guard.

The rebels, led by General Evaristo Estenoz, made the key mistake of calling for the destruction of foreign property, as had been done in earlier revolutions. This time it merely provoked the United States. Knox called for the deployment of 500 marines to protect American lives and property, and Gomez acquiesced and agreed to aid their operations. Making clear that U.S. policy remained "preventive", Knox said that "This is not intervention."[99]

Gomez was eventually able to put down the revolt on his own. The marines were unnecessary, but Taft, not confident in the Cuban leader's stability, did not withdraw them; he merely moved them to the U.S. naval base at Guantanamo.

WILSONIAN DIPLOMACY: 1913-1917

Woodrow Wilson was elected in 1912 largely because a rift in the Republican Party split votes between Taft and Theodore Roosevelt. Long a progressive—when president of Princeton University he had tried to break up the elitist dining clubs there—Wilson was a scholarly idealist. His liberal tendencies guided his foreign policies, and in the aftermath of the First World War he would attempt to erect international institutions capable of resolving disputes between countries.

Wilson followed a similar idealism with regard to Latin America. His strong sense of Pan-Americanism presaged Franklin Roosevelt's Good Neighbor Policy. All American countries, Wilson claimed, were "spiritual partners."[100] He proposed a Pan American Pact and appointed a Liberal secretary of state, William Jennings Bryan, ready to carry out his idealistic motives. Both the Cuban leadership and the common people of Cuba hoped that these hints signalled a change from intervention to non-interference, and a possible abrogation of the Platt Amendment.

But Wilson had no such intention. His idealism was tainted with a sense of moral superiority, and he "self-riteously believed that America had to play a paternal role in Cuba." In that context he saw the Platt Amendment as a useful justification for interference in Cuban affairs, and a temporary, but necessary, substitute for complete Cuban self-government.[101] The United States continued to intervene in Cuban politics, and the Cubans to resent it.

In 1912, General Mario Menocal followed Gomez into office in Cuba. Immediately handicapped by charges that he was too favorable to American interests, Menocal would quickly establish himself as a corrupt and inefficient leader, and opposition groups became increasingly vocal. William Gonzales, the new, inexperienced U.S. minister, hurriedly warned Washington that a new revolution was imminent. He had exaggerated the threat to Menocal, however, and no revolt was forthcoming.[102]

Bryan nevertheless urged Wilson to offer troops to aid Menocal in putting down the "revolt." Menocal, not wanting to fan the flames of the anti-

American opposition that did exist, refused the offer. Bryan continued meddling in Cuban politics, intervening in the process of Cuban loans. That Bryan had the best interests of Cuba at heart is likely, however. No favorite of American business because of his progressivism, he argued strongly for special treatment of Cuba during the debates on the Underwood tariff bill.

In March, 1914, Bryan reiterated his requests for special treatment of Cuban trade. Bryan argued that when Cuban sugar—75 per cent of which was sold in American markets—lost its special protection, as was planned, the tariffs would devastate the Cuban economy. He asked an exemption for Cuba from the tariff bill. Wilson replied that the bill had been carefully assembled, and the compromises it embodied were finely balanced; it would be "a very great mistake," he insisted, to tamper with the legislation, and so he rejected Bryan's appeal. In the end, special treatment turned out to be unnecessary; World War One inflated sugar prices so much that the Cuban economy enjoyed an almost unprecedented boom.[103]

In June, 1915, Robert Lansing succeeded Bryan as Secretary of State. His policies essentially mirrored those of Bryan, but for different reasons; an international lawyer guided by a strong sense of *realpolitik* and national self-interest, Lansing favored use of the Platt Amendment to promote Cuban stability and, with it, American interests.[104] As Wilson became preoccupied with World War I, Lansing came to virtually control American Cuban policy, and continued the practice of "preventive interference."

THE ELECTION CRISIS OF 1916

Shortly before the 1916 elections Menocal shocked Cubans by announcing that he would run for another term of office. Re-election had always been a controversial issue. Cuban political observers feared the evolution of a dictatorial presidency, and sought to restrain that impulse by restricting presidents to one term. But such restrictions had not yet been formalized, and the crisis evoked by Estrada Palma's choice to run for a second term, when he had promised not to do so, had uncovered the underlying threat; Estrada Palma's corrupt second term had reinforced that threat in the minds of Cubans. Now Menocal, too, sought four more years.[105]

As Menocal began to gear up for the campaign, corruption became rife. Many Cubans, who had trusted Menocal's 1912 promise not to seek a second term, now turned against him. His vice-president declared he would not stand for re-election, and Menocal's own Conservative party was split over the issue. Those in favor of renominating him, however, used political schemes and fraud to maneuver his nomination through the party's convention in January

1916. Menocal thus stood for reelection "at the head of a demoralized party, without the unanimity of purpose or the organizational cohesion necessary to win the November balloting."[106] The Liberals, meanwhile, though they knew they held a sizeable numerical advantage among the voters, were not optimistic; they nominated Zayas and awaited the inevitable fraud in the upcoming election.

Events in Cuba would soon confront a novel aspect of Wilson's Latin American policy. The Wilson administration consistently gave precedence to governments in power and would not extend formal diplomatic recognition to revolutionary regimes. Designed to encourage stability in Latin American countries by promising U.S. hostility toward rebellions, and thus eliminating Roosevelt's feared "premium upon insurrection," this practice was called the "recognition" policy. Despite a number of dissenting voices—such as that of General Enoch Crowder, who wrote that "the right of a people to change their rulers. . .is essential to the preservation of a free government"— regimes brought to power by revolution enjoyed little favor in Washington. U.S. officials thus supported Menocal's government, viewing him as a superior alternative to his potentially radical opponents.

The United States thus remained wedded to support for the status quo, in stark contrast to its earlier support for revolutions. As a state itself born of revolution, the United States had long supported revolutions against despotism as an inherent right of oppressed peoples. Beginning to a large measure with Roosevelt, however, U.S. administrations gradually acquire a distaste for rebellions as America become an established power. This trend would trap later administrations into support for corrupt, brutal dictators, and hence foster the growth of anti-American sentiment throughout Latin America.

As most expected, government corruption became evident as the Cuban election approached in November 1916. Violence was also prevalent, and resulted in many deaths. Menocal appointed military supervisors to stop the violence, but they merely served as tools to implement his corrupt plans to steal the election. His pre-election tactics included arresting Liberal leaders and deploying troops to intimidate voters in various sections of the country.[107]

Early election results indicated a close race, with Zayas slightly ahead: the U.S. *charges d'affaires*, Gustave Scholle, actually reported to Washington that Zayas had won. But these expectations were premature: seeing he had begun to lose despite his plans to steal elections in the field, Menocal ceased all reporting of election results and screened them himself before they were released. And he adjusted them to suit his needs.

Records of the numbers of votes cast give some indication of the fraud involved. The entire country, which a later 1919 census showed to have less than half a million eligible voters, now in 1916 managed to cast more than 800,000 votes. Conservatives commonly emerged with 99 per cent of the vote cast, and in many cases well over 100 per cent of the registered vote.

With obvious reason, the Liberals charged Menocal with stealing the election. Conservative officials referred the case to the Cuban Supreme Court, expecting a quick decision in their favor. Instead, the court declared the elections void because of the evidence of corruption, and called for new contests.

If later re-elections in Santa Clara and Oriente had been won by the Liberals, Zayas could still have won. But again, the numbers tell the story of corruption. In Santa Clara, some 1,500 votes were expected to be cast, 1,200 of which, according to polls, were solidly Liberal. Come election day, however, 2,401 possible voters were counted, *2,427* of which—apparently every eligible citizen in the province and 26 of their friends—cast ballots for the Conservatives. The Liberals received a grand total of 33 ballots.

Liberal leaders, meanwhile, had not waited for these later elections. They felt that the time was ripe for revolt, both because Menocal was hugely unpopular and because it was sugar harvesting season, and the industry made a good target for guerrilla activities. In the first weeks of 1917, the Liberals appointed General Gomez to lead the opposition, and on February 4, they formally decided on revolution. General Gerardo Machado also played a significant role in the Liberal leadership. By mid-February the island was in a state of general revolt.

The United States made several fruitless efforts, albeit in good faith, to resolve the disputed election. On February 10, Secretary Lansing sent a note telling the two sides to resolve their differences, but as one subsequent commentator observed, the note failed in its purpose; ''ten days earlier it might have had some effect, but by the 11th the situation had gone beyond the point where any appeal to self-control could sway either party.'' Even Lansing's note, however, did not unambiguously spell out the U.S. position. Would it intervene? Would it stand by Menocal even if the elections were demonstrably stolen? None of this was clear.[108]

One U.S. note did make a certain priority obvious, however: the United States did not want a new war on the island to damage the extremely good economic conditions that the developing European war had created. U.S. companies now controlled almost half of Cuba's sugar industry, and a revolution could destroy this industry. The imminent war in Europe also made U.S. policy-makers wary of risking their primary sugar supply, and hence not overly receptive to the requests of the insurgent Cubans. Nor did rumors (eventually proven false) that the Germans were behind the revolt help its popularity in the United States.

On February 11 and 12, uprisings began in earnest all over the island.

Havana, Santa Clara, Camaguey, and Oriente were all racked with riots and various guerrilla activities. On the 13th Lansing, invoking the policy of non-recognition of revolutionary governments, sent a stronger note explaining that the United States was required to stand with the "constitutional" powers, i.e. Menocal's government. Lansing warned Gomez that the United States would never recognize his group even if it defeated Menocal in the field and took power.

On that same day, Minister Gonzales declared U.S. support for the "legal and constitutional" government of Cuba. Like Lansing's message, this firm statement came too late to prevent a resort to arms; had the Liberals known the United States would eventually stand against them, they might not have revolted. On February 18, the U.S. government declared its open support for Menocal's government, terming the revolt "lawless and unconstitutional" and holding the rebels responsible for all property damage. After that, Liberal representatives in New York and Washington attempting to obtain support for the revolt made little progress.[109]

The United States also aided Menocal materially. It did exert some pressure on him to reform, which he deflected by a series of symbolic moves (such as the appointment of a powerless "bipartisan commission" to investigate charges of fraud in the election) and outright refusals on nationalist grounds. But it also sold him 10,000 rifles and five million rounds of ammunition, and, as we have seen, discouraged Gomez with diplomatic rebuffs. This favoritism influenced all aspects of U.S. policy and all U.S. officials; when rebels at Santiago threatened to cut off the harbor, for example, U.S. naval officers on the U.S.S. *Petrel*, sent to protect U.S. property, declared that they could not accept such a move.

Liberal leaders, however, kept up the fight, hoping for an eventual American intervention that might set the stage for the honest elections they were confident they could win. Gomez ordered sugar mills to cease production, on punishment of destruction. The war temporarily devolved into a series of small guerrilla actions, which tested the mettle of neither side; the real test would come when the Cuban army as a whole was faced with a large action against the rebels, for its loyalty was somewhat in question and the fighting spirit it showed in its first large action would be a crucial indicator of its later performance.

By late February, all of Cuba was in a state of disorder, and the sugar industry had been significantly disrupted. The Santiago Chamber of Commerce asked Wilson to mediate and end the conflict. Wilson replied, through Lansing, that

the government of the United States has clearly defined its position in the present armed conflict against the Constitutional Government of Cuba and it will attribute any disturbance of economic conditions or ruin of crops to the action of those in rebellion against the Government. Moreover, it cannot hold communication with leaders of this rebellion while they are under arms against the Constitutional Government. No other question except the reestablishment of order throughout the Republic through the return of those in rebellion to faithful allegiance to the Government can be considered under the existing conditions.

Lansing offered the good services of the United States to negotiate a settlement, but such proceedings could only begin when "those persons who have revolted against the Government lay down their arms, declare allegiance to the Government and return to peaceful pursuits."[110]

Again, this sort of strong statement on February 3 or 4 might have ended the revolution in short order. But by the end of the month the Liberals were too heavily committed to turn back. Now realizing that their only hope of provoking U.S. intervention was to place U.S. property at risk, the Liberals on February 27 began destroying sugar mills and cane. U.S. property owners asked for protection, and hundreds of marines were landed at various points on the island. Gomez declared that he was ready to lay down his arms but wanted a U.S. guarantee of new, fair elections. The American preconditions, however, had been set.

On March 1, U.S. Minister Gonzales urged Menocal to arrange a truce and settle the dispute himself to prevent the need for U.S. intervention. Gonzales specifically urged the offer of new elections in Santa Clara and Oriente. Menocal refused, claiming that the rebel groups still in the field blocked a negotiated settlement. He also argued that Cuban army officers would desert if he offered an amnesty, and claimed he would win new elections in any case. Gonzales, apparently persuaded, recommended to the Department of State that the United States drop its pressure on Menocal, and the Department agreed, with the exception that it still insisted on elections in Oriente—which had never been held at all due to the conflict—after a truce.[111]

Gomez threatened to accelerate the campaign of property destruction, but before he could carry this out his army was destroyed and he was captured at the battle of Placetas on May 7-8. A few Liberals continued fighting, in part because they had received false encouragement from U.S. naval officers aboard ships lying off Cuba.[112] The Department of State subsequently told the naval officers to keep to their duties, and disavowed the negotiations. This, combined with other signs of the continuing U.S. hostility to their cause, led the Liberals to adopt an increasingly anti- American stance.

On March 9, Menocal, realizing that victory was near and hoping to placate his critics, agreed to new elections in Santa Clara. The United States sent General Crowder to oversee them, and continued to press for a cease-fire. On March 23 the State Department announced that if the remaining rebels in the field did not lay down their arms "the United States cannot hold communication with any of them and will be forced to regard them as outside the law and beyond its consideration."[113]

World War One, meanwhile, was finally reaching the United States, and the nation declared war on Germany on April 6. Cuban stability, and the sugar production it guaranteed, were more important to the United States than ever, and had the Liberals ever approached victory, the United States would almost certainly have intervened. As it was, the Liberal insurgents were near total defeat, and the Wilson administration backed Menocal more firmly than ever. On April 7 Menocal shrewdly came into the war on the American side, and the United States offered 1,000 troops to help Menocal put a final end to hostilities. He declined, but on May 15 the Department of State, anxious to have an insurance against further instability, asked Minister Gonzales to persuade Menocal to accept them. On the same day, Lansing issued a statement supporting the Cuban government and noting that, because of the World War, sugar production was crucial, and therefore "all disturbances which interfere with this production must be considered as hostile acts." The United States government, he continued, was forced to issue a warning that if the insurgents did not give up, "it may become necessary for the United States to regard them as its enemies and deal with them accordingly."[114] On the 18th, not waiting for Menocal's final approval, the Department of State requested that the War Department send 2 regiments of U.S. infantry to Cuba.

Menocal, meanwhile, largely through his usual corrupt tactics, and aided by the discouragement of the Liberals, won the Santa Clara and Oriente elections, and on May 20 was inaugurated as president, having been confirmed by the Cuban Congress twelve days earlier. Realizing they had lost, most Liberals still in revolt gave up; on the recommendation of the United States, Menocal publicly pardoned many and reduced the sentences of others. Quietly, however, he followed his own policies with regard to the surrendered insurgents. U.S. consul General Morgan wrote in late August that "a large number of murders...are being perpetuated in [Oriente] and Camaguey by hired assassins, the victims being members of the Liberal Party who took part in the last revolution."[115]

The United States did eventually send the troops that State had recommended. Two thousand regular infantry soldiers were deployed in Oriente and Camaguey to guard U.S.-owned sugar industries.

Clearly, the United States intervened heavily in Cuban politics during the crisis of 1917. But it had not intervened militarily, apart from the token provision of a few troops which was merely designed to affirm symbolically the U.S. commitment to Menocal. Nevertheless, the strong U.S. commitment to Menocal—in the form of diplomatic as well as military support—was crucial to the eventual defeat of the insurgency, on psychological as well as material grounds. And the revolt itself had a strong social content; many Cuban landowners and rural proletarians, forced off their land by U.S.-run *latifundia*, reacted violently against the outside economic domination. The resentment of the American economic presence in Cuba that underlay that reaction helped establish the context for later rebellions against U.S. influence.[116] For the time being, however, the pro- American Havana elite still held power.

Cuba in World War One

As we have seen, Menocal entered the war quickly, in large part as a political gesture toward the United States. Once in the war, Cuba took a number of actions to demonstrate clearly that it meant business, or as much so as such a tiny nation could. In a 1918 article in *Current History*, Menocal noted that the Cuban declaration of war "was soon vigorously put into practice." First, he explained, "a relatively considerable number of large German steamships were held by the war in Cuban ports." In fact, five small steamers were seized.[117] Menocal's government also raised money for the Red Cross, and offered to send troops abroad, though the latter request was politely declined by the United States. Menocal also offered the "mild climate" of Cuba for U.S. winter training, though this offer too was turned down. By far Cuba's most significant contribution to the war effort was its continued production of sugar.[118]

Menocal saw a number of benefits in a "vigorous" pursuit of the war effort. He was able to endear himself even further to the U.S. government, which regarded supplies of Cuban sugar as being of some importance. He was also able to blame the recent revolt on German scheming with the liberals, a charge which has never been borne out. Menocal thus shored up his greatly weakened domestic position.

END OF THE WAR: RETURN TO POLITICS AS USUAL, 1918

Not all memory of the elections was lost, however. Indeed, just after the war Cuban Vice President Nunez predicted that if the irregularities of the recent election were not resolved, the United States would be forced to intervene once again. Liberals and Conservatives, now united in their concern for order if nothing else—and each for its own reasons favoring election regularity—invited General Crowder back to revise the election code. He arrived March 18, 1919, and began his work; the U.S. Army, meanwhile, assisted with the Cuban census of 1919. Crowder recommended various procedural reforms to alleviate fraud, and the Cuban Congress overwhelmingly approved his work; on August 7, 1919, he left Cuba.

From 1918 to 1920, relations somewhat settled down. Small disputes over trade issues and whether the Cuban government was doing enough in health and sanitation—as the Platt Amendment demanded—were the only outstanding issues. Liberal leaders continued requesting new, U.S.-supervised elections, and the U.S. government kept declining.[119]

World War One and the period immediately afterward had been a period of unusual calm for Cuba. As a result of the destruction of the insurgency, the assassination of key Liberal leaders and the discouragement of the rest, high world sugar prices, and the presence of Cuban and U.S. troops, the island had enjoyed a period of relative stability. But this was accompanied by the graft and repression that had become hallmarks of Cuban government; the island's stability rested on the shifting sand of momentarily favorable conditions, and growing economic difficulties would soon plunge Cuba back into political anarchy. Another election crisis was imminent.

The 1920 Elections

Neither Crowder's reforms nor the legitimately good intentions of many Cubans, could prevent another election filled with fraud. For the 1920 election, the Liberals nominated General Gomez; Zayas, meanwhile, hated by the Liberals for his essential abandonment of their cause in the 1917 revolution after the defeat at Placetas, formed his own Popular party. It merged with the Conservatives and, supported by the existing government machinery, began to campaign.[120] Menocal and the United States joined in August, 1920 in calling for free and fair elections. U.S. Minister Long said American observers would monitor the election at various locations to ensure fairness.

Nevertheless, the election was again characterized by fraud, bullying, and various accusations. Zayas won narrowly, and the Liberals again claimed the election had been stolen. They appealed to the United States for mediation.

The U.S. State Department was now headed by Bainbridge Colby, and he was no more receptive to the Cuban requests than his predecessors had been. Guided by young men in the department such as Sumner Welles and Leo Rowe, Colby attempted to pursue a policy of non-intervention in Latin American affairs. Colby urged Wilson to argue that the primary responsibility for good elections lay with the Cubans. Besides requesting some small electoral reforms, Colby "favored a hands-off policy."[121]

Wilson approved this policy—his rhetorical commitment to non-intervention was long-standing in any case—and the United States announced that it would not interfere in the election. But already American observers had been present, attempting to preserve honesty, and after the election the Cubans again called in General Crowder to mediate disputes. Under Crowder's direction, a compromise between Menocal, Zayas, and Gomez was worked out, and partial new elections were held on March 15, which were again won by Zayas. Already, however, Colby's "hands-off" policy had been stretched beyond the point of credibility, and in fact the United States was entering a period of "diplomatic intervention" which would last for two years and make a mockery of Colby's intentions.

The end of the war also saw the development of a serious financial crisis in Cuba. After the war, as the world price of sugar fell precipitously—from 22 cents per pound to seven—the Cuban economy declined along with it. Many banks that had lent large sums to sugar industries went bankrupt, and in October, 1920 there was a run on Cuban banks. Menocal, a month before the 1920 elections, declared a moratorium on all debt payments until December 1.

The United States considered various measures to relieve the Cuban crisis, including a large-scale loan program. In November, 1920 a Cuban delegation came to Washington and requested financial assistance. The moratorium on loan payments was extended through January, 1921, but the failure of Cuban banks led to the involvement of foreign banks; the National City Bank of New York and the Royal Bank of Canada soon became the leading financial institutions in Cuba.[122]

Crowder had begun to exercise a significant amount of influence on Cuban politics. He remained for seven years, a period during which he enjoyed unprecedented access to the Cuban government. His *de facto* control of U.S. policy caused Minister Long, in what many regarded as a fit of pique, to resign, and the United States did not appoint another ambassador until Crowder left. Crowder came to dominate the Cuban government in a fashion mirrored by Sumner Welles a decade later. On many occasions Zayas merely followed Crowder's orders. While the United States did not formally intervene, then, it maintained basic control over the Cuban government.

Zayas's main problem remained the financial crisis. J.P. Morgan and Company loaned the Cuban government $5 million to help stabilize the situation, withholding further loans until the Cubans reformed their economic management system. Crowder used a broad interpretation of the Platt Amendment—which as we have seen could be used to justify interference in Cuban domestic affairs as well as military intervention—to demand the right to inspect Cuban government documents and records; Zayas, desperate for financial relief, had little choice but to assent. In the first months of 1922, Crowder sent his "fifteen memoranda" to the Cuban government, making recommendations on all aspects of its operations and of relations between the United States and Cuba.

The primary result of these suggestions was the appointment of the "Honest Cabinet" in June, 1922. Made up of men from inside and outside the government whose honesty was largely beyond question, the "Honest Cabinet" worked with Crowder to reduce patronage, cut government expenditures, eliminate needless public works programs, and make other reforms intended to clean up the Cuban government. Aided by Crowder's own efforts, these plans were formulated by the cabinet and passed through the Cuban Congress. Their implementation was aided, in part, by a flood of official and unofficial U.S. advisors who came to Cuba during 1922.

An implicit threat of U.S. intervention also motivated the Cubans. The Department of State urged in September, 1922 that to avoid a "serious situation" that might, the department implied, require intervention, Crowder's reforms should be adopted. Taking these and other threats to heart, the Cuban Congress complied, but continued to resent the U.S. presence. On June 20, 1922, it passed a resolution of protest urging the United States to keep out of Cuban domestic affairs.

During 1923, this process of U.S. intervention continued. J.P. Morgan and Co. followed their earlier loan with a new one of $50 million. Crowder was named the first Ambassador to Cuba, a position that replaced the earlier, less important ministerial office. Also during 1923, however, increasing Cuban resentment of Crowder and the U.S. presence caused Zayas to distance himself. In April of that year he began slowly to dismiss the "Honest Cabinet," and he made public statements critical of Crowder's role.

The United States, by 1923, was in no mood seriously to woo Zayas, because it had begun to pull back from diplomatic intervention. Many American policymakers were as tired of Crowder's meddling as were the Cubans. In the summer of 1923, to bolster these critics, the Cuban congress passed another resolution condemning the U.S. role in their country, but a more serious one than the year before; they threatened to break relations over the issue. In both the United States and Cuba, then, the time was ripe for a diminution of the U.S. role.

American economic interests, however, favored (and demanded) continued U.S. meddling. When, in August, 1923, the Cuban government proposed the Tarafa Law, designed to give the government control over all transportation industries on the island (including ports), U.S. companies protested and demanded that the American government prevent its passage. Not all Cubans favored the bill, and it was significantly watered down before it passed in September. But the incident demonstrated that the United States still had significant economic interests at stake, and could not easily pull back from its involvement in Cuban affairs.[123]

THE COOLIDGE POLICY: 1923-1929

U.S. officials were satisfied with these developments. Calvin Coolidge had become president, and his Latin American policy continued to emphasize, explicitly at least, non- interventionism. In August, 1923 he made references to intervention to correct Cuban instabilities, but the administration never seriously considered sending troops. Charles Evans Hughes, the secretary of state, was also committed to non-intervention, and even when provoked by Zayas's corruption felt compelled to avoid interference. Nevertheless the tacit mechanisms of control remained in place, and U.S. meddling continued. Coolidge responded to Cuban complaints about this continued interference with diplomatic niceties, making no substantive promises. American policy, it seemed, would remain essentially the same: the U.S. government sought the ability to control the policies of the Cuban government indirectly.[124]

Many Cubans were unhappy with this situation, and in April, 1924, Cuba was once again beset with a crisis of government. The Cuban Veterans Association, favoring progressive change and tired of Zayas's slow work, came out furiously for reform, arguing for changes even more extensive than those Crowder had proposed. The Veterans' movement (the Movimiento de Veteranos y Patriotas) was joined in opposition by radical student groups, such as the Federacion Estudiantil Universitaria (FEU), which also desired honesty in government and political reforms. In March, 1924, General Carlos Garcia Velez—son of the revolutionary hero Calixto Garcia—was appointed head of the Association, and organized a junta in New York to start a revolution against Zayas. He arrived in Cuba on April 30, and started an insurrection in Cienfuegos.

The United States needed to act and make its position clear; it was not about to repeat the mistakes of 1916-17, when a delayed response to insurrection had allowed the revolt to continue. Predictably, it stood by the elected government against the revolutionaries; though it recognized Zayas's shortcomings, the Coolidge administration also knew it held him in its pocket. On May 2 President Coolidge instituted an embargo on all arms sold to Cuban buyers other than the government, and later allowed the sale of $208,000 worth of war material to Zayas. By the end of August, the revolution was over; the insurgents had never possessed the necessary strength or popular or international support. On August 30, Coolidge lifted his arms embargo.[125]

The 1924 Elections in Cuba

Zayas, by now, was unpopular among the Conservatives; he had never been a true Conservative in any case, and merely struck a bargain in 1920 to get himself into the presidency for a term. The Conservatives' gave their nomination to Menocal, apparently believing his experience might count for something in the election. But he was still tremendously unpopular, and was easily defeated by the Liberal candidate, a man whose name would soon strike fear and hatred into Cuban hearts: General Gerardo Machado y Morales.

Machado, at the time, was an ambiguous personality, elected not out of his own popularity but because he was the only real alternative to Menocal. After serving in the 1895 revolution, Machado had fought against Menocal in 1917 with the Liberals. But his personal association with Cuban and American utilities corporations imbued him with a strong streak of conservative pro-Americanism. He vigorously opposed the Platt Amendment, as he was to do for his whole presidency; though he might have wanted it modified, however, he only displayed real anger for popular consumption in Cuba, and in fact he turned out to be a very pro-American president.

Machado's first term was relatively quiet. He developed relations with the United States to a fuller degree; various agreements were signed, including a sanitary convention, an extradition treaty, and an anti-smuggling treaty. A small dispute over cigar exports was quickly resolved.

At first, Machado's domestic programs were praiseworthy. He instituted public works plans, but programs with less corruption than had been the norm. He supported crop diversification schemes to reduce Cuba's dependence upon sugar. He promised he would not run for a second term, to quiet the constant fears of dictatorship; ''no power on earth,'' he had said, could keep him from relinquishing power at the appointed time.

Machado was also popular with the United States, for various reasons. He supported U.S. business, telling a banquet of American bankers that ''in my administration there will be absolute guarantees for all business, and there is no reason to fear the outbreak of disorders because I have sufficient force to suppress them.'' Machado's relative strength also allowed the United States to severely constrain its role in Cuban politics, a relief to Americans and—at first—Cubans alike.[126]

From late 1925 through 1927, however, Machado consolidated his power in a menacing fashion. A December, 1925 law he proposed made it enormously difficult to change the existing political parties or to form new ones, thus cementing the status quo. He gradually phased in huge patronage practices and more traditional levels of graft to bring all three existing political parties under his sway. In 1927, the Cuban Congress. also dominated by him, suggested lengthening Machado's term to six years.

These events represented a gradual shift on Machado's part from progressive leader to despotic, power-hungry dictator. Of course, Machado's true motives cannot be gauged with accuracy—he may have shown a gentle face early on merely to gather support as a prelude to authoritarian rule. In any event, a Cuban Constitutional Convention called in May, 1928 adopted a resolution arguing that Machado had done a fine job and was "unavoidably bound to accept a new presidential period." It did not accept the six-year term idea, but instead restricted all Cuban presidents to a single term of four years, a requirement to take effect *after* Machado's second term.

In the 1928 elections, then, Machado was the nominee of all three parties, and opposition was fragmented and ineffectual. His regime had become gradually more repressive, engaging in censorship, killings, torture, political arrests, and other brutalities. Labor leaders were killed by assassins inspired, if not actually sent, by Machado. The general anarchy led William Green, president of the American Federation of Labor, to remark on a visit in 1927 that "a condition of virtual terrorism existed." Meanwhile, Herbert Hoover was coming to power in the United States, and his Latin American policy would soon confront Machado's brutality.

Continuing claims by Americans in Cuba that the new government was brutal and corrupt led Senator Shipstead of New York to propose a resolution in 1928 calling for Congress to investigate the claims and determine their validity. A later resolution, also introduced by Shipstead, included a long list of specific charges against Machado. Cuban officials reacted angrily and U.S. Ambassador Judah made a few conciliatory comments to calm them down.

Various opposition groups sprang up in Cuba. The declining value of sugar and increasing American tariffs on the commodity, which wreaked havoc on the Cuban economy, combined with Machado's brutalities to create the context for a revolt. Menocal led opposition Conservatives, while Liberals arrayed against Machado were led by Miguel Mariano Gomez, the son of former president Gomez. Carlos Mendieta and other nationalists led the Union Nacionalista. When Machado shut down the University, which had become a hotbed of opposition, in 1929, many students and professors joined the ranks of the opposition.[128]

Another economic crisis struck in 1925, creating a huge depression. Big American milling companies pressed for production increases to make up the profit difference, but smaller planters favored production *controls* destined to reduce the sugar "glut" on the world market and drive prices up. In the Verdjeda Act of 1926, the Cuban Congress set quotas and grinding-time restrictions. Large American companies, however, merely used the slightly lower sugar flow as an excuse to sell off their own surpluses, and many Cuban producers were left with thousands of tons of unsalable cane.

This crisis was to last well into the 1930s, and the constant tensions it created were in large measure responsible for continuing political instability. Cuban officials made repeated attempts to negotiate world-wide sugar production controls, but to little avail. In attempting to adhere to their own restrictions, they often lost even more revenue. A 1931 attempt by the American Thomas L. Chadbourne to negotiate such a production quota scheme came to nothing, and the Smoot-Hawley tariffs, inspired by the deepening economic depression in the United States, further reduced Cuban exports.

One consequence of this export dearth was the growth of Cuban debts to banks in the United States. The 1923 Morgan loan of $50 million to Zayas was followed by a $9 million Morgan loan, and a $10 million Chase Bank loan, in 1927; by the early thirties Machado had borrowed over $100 million from various sources, in large part to support his public works programs and interest payments on previous loans. The money did not go into capital-producing projects, and so merely deepened Cuba's economic crisis, already exacerbated by a $50 million domestic budget deficit. Feeling that to default on the loans, or even to admit that a crisis existed, might end his usefulness to the Americans and thus doom his already teetering regime, Machado felt compelled to rape his own country's economy to make debt payments. He would eventually increase internal taxes and take other measures designed to maintain Cuba's credit. These policies established a new roadblock to the development of a legitimate Cuban owning/producing middle class.

The Cubans also engaged in constant discussions with American officials in attempts to establish a trade treaty between the two nations. In 1926-27 the Cubans asked the United States to renegotiate the existing treaty, with no success. Secretary of State Frank Kellogg essentially maintained that Cuba was running a trade surplus with the United States, so it ought not complain. In 1928 the U.S. Departments of State and Commerce did establish a commission to look into trade renegotiation, but again Kellogg and Hoover rejected the proposals. The Cuban ambassador, Orestes Ferrara, warned of possible Cuban protectionist retaliation, but nothing came of his threat. The growing crisis of 1931-32 spurred some in the United States to urge reconsideration of the policy, but before concrete action could be taken Franklin D. Roosevelt had come into office promising to reduce tariffs.[129]

CONCLUSION: SETTING THE STAGE FOR A CRISIS

American policy toward Cuba during the three decades after the military intervention of 1898 was generally a sorry combination of counterproductive lling in Cuban affairs and a damning fear of true intervention at key points.

rican business had come to dominate most aspects of the Cuban economy, but this short-term success concealed significant threats to U.S.
interests, threats that would continue to hold U.S. policy at risk for the next
three decades. But the ineffective damage-limitation schemes of "preventive" and "diplomatic" intervention had created a basis of Cuban nationalism
and anti-Americanism, guaranteeing a slow decline of American influence in
Cuba that would reach fruition in Castro's revolution.

More immediately, the declining health of the Cuban economy, the concen-
tration of what wealth was around in a few (mostly American) hands, and the
increasing brutality of Machado's regime were creating the context for a revolution. A new, progressive political consciousness, informed by the socialism
of Europe and the revolutions of other Latin American countries against
colonialism, was growing in Cuba. It provided the coming revolt with a strong
philosophical base. But the United States, worried at these developments,
opposed them, and the continued American domination of Cuban economic
life would hamper the development of an adequate, socially conscious and
concerned middle-class. The result was a revolution whose promise of true
reform would be lost, but which would set the stage for a much more violent
and total reaction against the status quo some two decades later. The social
and institutional context for Castro's rise to power was being established, and
American policy-makers ignored or downplayed its manifestations. An
American foreign policy catastrophe was brewing, and, as is so often the case,
no one seemed to notice.

6

A REVOLUTION DEFERRED

The Insurrection of 1933

"Make the Revolution a parent of settlement, and not a nursery
of future revolutions."
Edmund Burke, *Reflections on the Revolution in France*

"Remember that all of us, and you and I especially, are descended
from immigrants and revolutionists."
Franklin Delano Roosevelt, speech, 1938

"Never play at uprising, but once it is begun, remember firmly that
you have to go to the very end."
Karl Marx, attributed

Though underlying social and economic instabilities in Cuba
began to manifest themselves in 1933. For the first time, a serious, progressive challenge to American influence developed, born of decades of growing
labor strength and years of intellectual resentment of the American role.
Though American diplomacy succeeded in temporarily controlling the situation, the economic, political, and social tensions that lay at the base of Cuban
life remained unresolved. Twenty-five years later, the United States would
pay for its ignorance of these tensions with a diplomatic disaster of unprecedented regional proportions.[1] On the very eve of this revolution, Franklin
Roosevelt's administration undertook policies blatantly designed to protect

American business interests, policies that led the United States to become embroiled in Cuba's politics once again.

CRITIQUES OF MACHADO

By the early 1930s, a number of American commentators had begun to report seriously on the rights abuses practiced by Machado and his government. Writing in May 1931, Ernest Greuning noted that Machado was a "ruthless tyrant," that assassinations of opposition leaders were common, and that censorship of all organs of the press was the norm.[2] Russell Porter concurred, explaining in April 1933—on the verge of the revolution—that Machado "has imprisoned, exiled, deported or killed his political enemies," and that "under the Machado regime. . . assassination has risen to the dignity of a political art."[3] The killings were justified mainly by an old Spanish law, the *ley de fuga* (law of flight), which allowed policemen to shoot fleeing suspects; the law was terribly abused, and dozens of "suspects" who had no intention to flee were shot down. While the opposition claimed that over 2,500 people had been killed by the government, Porter noted, a more accurate figure was probably about 1,000—still a huge number.[4]

Charles Chapman also discussed the corruption of the Machado regime. Its graft and election fraud were legendary. Take the Chicago political machine, Chapman suggested, "season with a bit of San Francisco in the greater graft years after the fire, and multiply by New York under Boss Tweed, and you have but a respectable fraction of what Cuba has been under some of her recent rulers."[5] Machado himself was "arbitrary and dictatorial," and in one instance released murderers from jail for a day to serve as guards at the polls. As to election fraud, "we find that Christopher Columbus has voted early and often in practically all elections and in many towns of Cuba; and the town of Candelaria in 1922, with a total of 9,234 inhabitants, including many women and children, was able to muster a vote of 25,820!"[6] All but a few of those votes, no doubt, went to Machado. Other independent observers,[7] and many U.S. congressmen,[8] shared these perceptions.

These complaints about Machado's regime would grow as the revolt of 1933 neared. Whatever prospect Machado had of obtaining firm U.S. support during the crisis was eliminated by his reputation as a brutal dictator. As the year 1933 opened, then, Machado enjoyed support neither at home nor abroad, and the forces that would oust him from power were rapidly developing. This drama would be replayed a quarter of a century later.

* * *

Specific stories of Machado's brutalities appeared in the American press, and served to whip up public furor against the dictator. One, in *The Nation*, was written by "Lorenzo Alvarez," a pseudonym for the manager of an estate in Cuba. Apparently, the owner of the estate was involved with opposition groups; when government troops came to pick him up, he was gone, and they took his manager, Alvarez, instead. They brought him to the Castle of Atares, which was then, in Alvarez's words, "headquarters for a gang of uniformed malefactors": Machado's police. There he was met by an army officer named Crespo.

After having Alvarez tied to a chair in the middle of a small room, Crespo demanded information. "Where is the dynamite?" he asked.

Alvarez had no idea what the officer meant. "I don't know what dynamite you are talking about," he replied.

It was the wrong answer. For the next several hours, Alvarez was tortured: threatened with pistols, beaten, strangled with rope. Finally he fainted. When awakened, he found himself in a small, dank cell, its rickety cot stained by the blood of former inmates. Crespo came to him again, and again demanded to know the whereabouts of the dynamite; Alvarez again pleaded ignorance.

Now Crespo and his men applied what were called the "campaign stocks." Alvarez describes what this meant:

> In my case several rifles were passed under the bend of my knees after I had been forced to kneel; then my head was bent down until I kissed the ground, and with a cord, the two ends of which were tied to my wrists, my tormentors forced me down until my elbows and my knees were together in such a way that the rifles, at first two in number, formed an axle.

Alvarez responded with insults, and the torturers became furious and pulled the cords even tighter. Eventually Alvarez lost consciousness. Alvarez stayed fifteen days in the Castle of Atares, for the most part ignorant of what day it was or even whether it was day or night. He was served only rancid milk and bracken water. Eventually, when it was realized that he was innocent, he was given a bath and a shave; and a kindly sergeant, perhaps trying to make up in some small way for the indignities he had suffered, arranged for a taxi to take Alvarez from the castle. There were no release papers, no farewells. "Under the Machado regime," Alvarez wrote, "a person is less than a stray animal."

After staying a short time with some relatives in Havana, Alvarez fled to the United States, where he campaigned against the Machado government. He was a lucky one; as he noted, "other prisoners, before being killed, had suffered incredible things—hot irons in their eyes, needles inserted in the spinal cord, nails torn out with hooks, and jawbones dislocated after slow extraction of all the teeth.'' Like so many others, Alvarez, previously a quiet citizen, had been turned into a dedicated, revolutionary opponent of the Machado regime by its cruelty.

Ruby Hart Phillips' husband, Phil Phillips, was a *New York Times* reporter, and when he was assigned to Cuba, she had the opportunity she had hoped for— to study Cuban culture from the inside. She related the cold-blooded murder of a Cuban named Valdes Daussa, which, when reported by Phil, attracted much attention to the abuses of the *ley de fuga* under Machado's rule.

"It happened on Good Friday, April 14, 1933,'' Phillips notes. She and her husband were relaxing in their apartment when they heard a burst of rifle fire from the streets below, and ran to their balcony, squinting in the bright afternoon sun which made ''the streets and buildings seem much more white than they are.'' She explains what happened next:

> We saw a youth come running. He was alone in the street, his shadow the only other moving thing. He was weaving wildly from side to side, as if he did not know where he was going. Then I saw him halt, raise his arms and wave them. In the still hot afternoon his voice was perfectly audible as he cried, ''No tire mas, no tire mas.'' (Don't shoot anymore.) Several men posted on the cliff nearest our house raised their rifles. The first fusillade struck him in the back. He stumbled, falling. The second smashed through his head and shoulders.

The man fell in front of a statue dedicated to former president Jose Miguel Gomez. Phillips' husband had already burst from their apartment, and when he reached the sprawled figure, ''Phil saw that he was only a boy. He was breathing his last in a huge pool of blood. His chest was the only part of him that still moved. His eyes were no longer focused on anything.'' The boy did not seem to realize what had happened, and seemed, ''only to be trying desperately to catch his breath.'' After a time, a uniformed policeman came over and ordered Phillips away from the body: eventually, the newsman's stories about this and other incidents would provoke Machado's death squads, the *porristas*, into making an attempt on the American's life. But for the time being, only the Cuban boy named Valdes Daussa had been killed.[9]

* * *

U.S. POLICY UNDER HOOVER: 1929-1933

Herbert Hoover came into office calling for non-interventionism in Latin America. Hoover felt that the imposition of U.S. norms on Latin American countries only created resentment and propaganda for America's enemies, and that this problem could be cured through the use of an enlightened principle of non-interference in the affairs of other countries. He therefore pursued an essentially "laissez-faire" foreign policy and coined the phrase "good neighbor" to refer to cooperative economic and political relations and U.S. non- intervention in Latin America.[10]

Not all Latin Americans were enamored with this policy. Some Cubans called on the United States to exercise its duty under the Platt Amendment and intervene to oust Machado. Many U.S. congressmen agreed. Hoover had no desire to commit U.S. forces, however, and used the restrictive Root interpretation of the amendment to refuse. Once again the elasticity of the amendment served as rationale for a new policy: it could be used to justify intervention or isolation.[11]

Even the "preventive diplomacy" of previous and subsequent administrations was anathema to Hoover and his Secretary of State, Henry L. Stimson. Stimson believed that such meddling only created the necessity for later American intervention. If the United States interfered with elections and attempted to guarantee stability, the argument went, it could not refuse actual intervention when the necessity arose. For Stimson the way to break the cycle was to "abjure intervention at all costs."

One of the results of this practice was a continuation of the *de facto* recognition policy, which portrayed existing governments as legitimate, and revolutionary movements as necessarily suspect. If the United States were to pursue a truly non-interventionist policy, it could not take arbitrary stands for and against various governments on a diplomatic whim; it simply had to recognize the status quo and let the forces of change in Latin America take their course.[12]

Critiques of the Hoover-Stimson Policy

This last policy led to the most common (and probably soundest) criticism of the Hoover laissez- faire diplomacy: that it placed the United States too heavily on the side of the status quo, and failed to recognize that political change was inevitable. In an article in *Foreign Affairs*, Norman Davis, writing a Democratic critique of Hoover (in an article co-written with one Sumner Welles, who will become familiar to us later), argued that a hands-off policy led to American support for dictators, which in turn abetted resentment of the

United States in the hemisphere. Preventive diplomacy could aid progress toward democracy, Davis suggested, at a minimal cost in lives, money, and U.S. reputation.[13]

Charles Chapman, in an article which discussed changing interpretations of the Monroe Doctrine, also condemned the Hoover policy. By its silence the United States "virtually impose[d]" the Machado government on Cuba, he argued.[14] The "Wilson Corollary" of the Monroe Doctrine, he explained, was that the United States would recognize governments in power and refuse to recognize revolutionary regimes; Hoover followed the same policy, and it prevented Cubans from revolting against Machado, or against any other dictator. Bryce Wood has agreed, suggesting that an overcommitment to non-interference left Stimson "prisoner to his policy of strict adherence to the Root interpretation" of the Platt Amendment in dealing with Cuba. [15]

In 1929, Hoover appointed Harry F. Guggenheim ambassador to Cuba, and Guggenheim became another in the line of controversial figures in the Cuban-American relationship. Guggenheim belonged to an enormously wealthy family and brought with him to Cuba various advisors paid out of his own pocket. Some have contended that he was a selfish, indifferent aristocrat, and that he was in Cuba to promote his own interests at the expense of Cubans. He was also seen as the instrument in Cuba of the Hoover administration's hands-off policy, and of its apathy toward the rights violations committed by Machado's government. Carleton Beals, a leftist American journalist, for example, documented Guggenheim's ties to American financial interests in Cuba and argued that the ambassador helped American capital in its mission of reaping "the largest profits possible without regard for the welfare of the Cuban people."[16]

Guggenheim's defenders respond that he tried to pressure Machado into negotiations with the opposition and helped the moderate political opposition adopt a posture conducive to compromise. He requested permission from Stimson to indicate to Machado that U.S. support might not be permanent, and that the Cuban leader therefore ought to clean up his act. In all these efforts, however, Guggenheim was undercut by the Hoover administration's unwillingness to depart from its policy of recognition of established governments: it would not allow him to pressure Machado seriously or to open a dialogue which might result in opposition participation in the government. This situation frustrated Guggenheim. Eventually, Machado would negotiate with the opposition, but he undertook those talks largely as a result of growing unrest in his own country, not of American pressure.

Hoover, by committing himself firmly to non-intervention, at least initially did reduce suspicion and resentment of the United States in the hemisphere. His goodwill cruise to Latin American in 1928—after he was elected but before he assumed office—reassured many of America's southern neighbors that his intentions were benign. While his policy did not always have the intended effects, Hoover's defenders argue, at least his pledges of non-intervention set the United States on the right course in its dealings with Latin American.[17]

The Situation in Cuba

Meanwhile, in Cuba, unrest was growing day by day. Between 1930 and 1933, the various opposition groups— students, labor, left-wing militants, and others—grew and coalesced into serious challenges to Machado's rule. In late 1930, to help justify his responses to this unrest, Machado declared martial law; two efforts at negotiations failed. Finally, on August 9, 1931, rebellions broke out in Havana and Pinar del Rio.

The revolt was relatively small, however, and as the army stood firmly behind Machado, he was able to crush it easily enough. The Battle of Jibara annihilated most of the main body of insurgents. Machado's army was modern, well-trained, and equipped with advanced weapons and good transportation, and the insurgency was poorly organized.

As usual, the U.S. reaction to all these developments was to keep the Cuban situation at arm's length. In October, 1930, Stimson stressed that the United States would only intervene if absolutely necessary. In August, 1931, Acting Secretary of State William R. Castle said the United States had no intention of sending any troops, and that only "virtual anarchy" would necessitate intervention.[18] The American actions were strictly neutral—it did not even embargo arms to non-government sources in Cuba—but Machado clearly held the key cards in the situation, and the American silence continued to favor him.

The collapse of the 1931 insurgency allowed the government in Cuba to unleash the full fury of its wrath upon the opposition groups. Machado began to ignore even the window-dressing reforms he had been persuing; terrorism and political assassination became commonplace throughout 1932. Leaders of the moderate opposition, seeing no alternative, began to accommodate themselves to the regime to get what concessions they could; the opposition fragmented as more radical elements repudiated the compromise and began to turn to armed revolt.

DEVELOPMENT OF A NEW CUBAN CONSCIOUSNESS

In the late 1920s and early 1930s, a new political consciousness developed rapidly in Latin America, founded on nationalism, anti-imperialism, and progressive economic principles. Spurred in part by events in other Latin American countries—the Mexican Revolution of 1910, university reform in Argentina in 1918, and also indirectly by the Russian Revolution of 1917—the growing Latin American nationalism was colored by anti-Americanism, born of decades of American meddling. This political consciousness contributed heavily to the Cuban revolution of 1933 and later to Castro's 1959 revolt. Its essentials were far from new, as we have seen: they relied on intellectual and organizational roots stretching as far back as the eighteen century.

By the 1920s, this progressive thinking had influenced a number of distinct groups and political parties, organizations that had been developing in reaction to the succession of corrupt Cuban governments. One such group was the intellectual community, centered around the university in Havana and other centers of learning. Their nationalism was born of a frustrated desire for true independence from all outside interference, something they thought was denied by Machado's rule. In 1922, the "Protest of the Thirteen" attempted to expose Zayas's corruption; later artistic, literary, and scholarly intellectuals from the "Protest" and other organizations formed the "Minority Group" (*Grupo Minorista*) in Havana, claiming to represent the masses against American dominance. The *Grupo* included the best Cuban writers of the period: Juan Marinello, Jorge Manach, Felix Lizaso, and others. First merely a discussion group, it eventually engaged in political activities including protests. The idols of the intellectuals included, predictably, Jose Marti, as well as the poet Jose Varona.[19]

The students and professors of the university followed the lead of the independent intellectuals. Julio Antonio Mella, eventually leader of the Cuban Communist Party, formed his political views in the debates and protests at the university in Havana. Mella opposed Machado from the beginning of the latter's career in office and led student opposition to him, calling Machado a "tropical Mussolini." The radicalization of the students originated in the 1920s, a period of blossoming political and nationalistic consciousness in Latin America, and was fed by continued corruption of Cuban governments, economic malaise, and the rediscovery of Jose Marti's radical political thought.[20] The activities of Mella and other students eventually forced Machado to close down the university for various periods of time, and to arrest many of the student leaders; when Mella was arrested in 1925, he went on a hunger strike that caused protests lasting for weeks and led to his release and exile to Mexico. Eventually, Machado's agents hunted Mella down and assassinated him in 1929.

Students formed political groups (in particular, the *Directorio Estudiantil Universitario*, or DEU) and became heavily involved in protests, strikes and other expressions of opposition to Machado. As the American observer

Hubert Herring concluded, the students would furnish the "sin blood" of the opposition in the coming years. They were true id "thugs or Communists," Herring noted, but "the stuff of which gr are made. Their faith is almost fanatical in its intensity." Students tricably linked to all other opposition groups; they joined the AB the key opposition groups—and the Communist Party. They led strikes and generally formed the ideological and energetic core of the opposition. Student political thought was not entirely homogeneous, however. There were radicals and conservatives within the DEU, and their disputes diluted to some extent the movement's effect.[21]

Developed around a core of middle-class revolutionaries—the petty bourgeoisie, urban professionals, students—the ABC began as a secret terrorist organization, forming cells of operatives to carry out bombings and assassinations. Its original ideology was "generational, elitist, developmental, reformist, and corporatist," and its purpose was clear: "To destroy Machado, on middle-class terms."[22] Its economic program was nearly socialist, calling for national control of and aid to such industries as agriculture and manufacturing and for labor protection laws. Thus Antoni Kapcia notes that "ABC was revolutionary in two specific ways: in its commitment to violent activism, and in its clear break with conventional economic liberalism." Yet the ABC was not vehemently anti-American; it accepted, more than many other radical opposition groups, the necessity of operating (as Kapcia puts it) "within the inevitable U.S. orbit." This belief led to participation in U.S.-sponsored mediation schemes, participation that in turn discredited the ABC in the eyes of many Cuban nationalists.[23]

In the end, in fact, the ABC's essentially conventional origins would bring its character full circle. By late 1932, the repressive reactions of Machado, and the reactions of other revolutionary groups, created a situation of violence and anarchy, and this worried the leaders of the ABC. They attempted to convince the United States that the ABC was a legitimate nationalistic political organization, worthy of the governance of the country.

Like the intellectuals, Cuban workers began to develop political consciousness in the 1920s and 1930s. Large labor organizations had existed since the turn of the century, and they formed the base on which activists would build, and from which they would draw, as the opposition to Machado grew.

Labor groups had initiated a series of failed strikes in 1902; by 1907, however, better-organized and more determined, the unions managed to hold strikes lasting 145 days.[24] The post-World War One economic downturn in Cuba led the unions to become more radical, and by the 1930s the striking labor groups turned to violence. Machado responded with attempts to suppress the groups, using the Rural Guard and army to put down strikes and occasionally assassinating union leaders (such as Enrique Varona, who was shot and killed in Moron).

The Cuban Communists coalesced in the 1920s around a set of motivating factors and guiding principles: the Bolshevik Revolution and its international Communist aid organization offspring, the Comintern; opposition to U.S. hegemony; the radical student and labor movements in Cuba; and the already developed Cuban socialist movement. Initially led by Carlos Balino and Julio Antonio Mella, in 1925 the party received assistance from the Comintern (in the form of Enrique Flores Magon, a Mexican Communist), and soon a full-fledged Communist Party was at work in Cuba.[25]

Though small at first, the Communist Party was aided by Machado's repression of conventional labor groups. In 1927, Machado declared the PCC—as the Cuban Communist Party was known—illegal, but it continued to grow, bolstered by the conversion of members of other opposition groups. While by 1929, the PCC still had less than 100 official members, its non-official sympathizers numbered many more. The PCC also developed its own union, the Confederacion Nacional Obrero de Cuba (CNOC), which was formed in 1925 and undertook some strikes and promoted unrest from 1930 to 1932. By March 1930, Machado felt compelled to ban certain of its member unions outright.[26]

By 1932, the CNOC and the PCC had become a serious threat to Machado's rule, and the CNOC planned massive nationwide agricultural strikes as a first step toward bringing down his regime. Machado, trying to make the most of his new role as anti-Communist, provided the U.S. Department of State with evidence of these plots and claimed that, without U.S. help, the Communists would take over Cuba. State was rightly skeptical and felt that the biggest threat to Machado's regime still issued from more traditional opposition groups: the ABC and middle class, students, and so on. While the PCC continued to grow, the, the United States still refused to be drawn into open support for Machado.

THE ROOSEVELT ADMINISTRATION:
A RETURN TO MEDDLING

The 1932 election in the United States brought Franklin Delano Roosevelt into the White House. Roosevelt appointed Sumner Welles as his ambassador to Cuba, and Welles promptly declared that economic considerations would take precedence over political ones in American dealings with Cuba.[27] It would soon become apparent that Welles would not sit back, like Guggenheim, and allow Washington's indifference to scuttle his personal diplomacy.

In attempting to arrange a compromise in Cuba in accord with American interests, Welles would go far beyond his mandate from FDR and challenge the tolerance of his own Department of State.

FDR himself held a somewhat paternalistic view of Latin American nations, and was ready to admit that American diplomatic and even military intervention might be necessary to keep those countries in line. As early as 1917, he commented that Cuba needed a "continuation of orderly progress and not of radicalism." He was also enticed by the region's economic possibilities.

The Good Neighbor Policy

The best known aspect of Roosevelt's Latin American diplomacy was of course the Good Neighbor Policy. In fact, Hoover used the phrase before FDR, and pursued in many ways essentially the same broad policy Roosevelt would later advocate. But Roosevelt gave the phrase— and the policies it represented—a new prominence, while at the same time modifying them to allow American interference of the sort Hoover and Stimson eschewed.[28]

The basic keystone of the policy, though, was a rejection of the right of intervention in Latin American affairs. Roosevelt advocated an almost unconditional hands-off policy, and Sumner Welles, an architect of the policy, argued with the president that dictating norms and standards to other governments was fruitless, and indeed counterproductive. In part this was seen to be true because not all Latin American nations were ready for democracy. But at the same time, Welles (as we have seen) and FDR were wary of avoiding intervention to the point of supporting dictatorships. Cuba would constitute the severest test for this policy of non- intervention, as it had been for Hoover, and the administration clearly failed the test; Welles became intimately involved in Cuban political life in a manner that suggested U.S. meddling in, if not outright control of, the Cuban government's affairs.

On the economic level, the Good Neighbor Policy meant American financial and commercial cooperation with Latin American countries. In practice, this aspect of the policy was watered down as well; the Depression prevented the United States from granting really significant trade concessions, and in many cases renewed tariffs—including those on Cuban sugar—would ruin Latin American expectations of North American markets.

Roosevelt outlined the policy in an April 12, 1933, speech at the Pan-American Union emphasizing that the United States wanted to play the role of "Good Neighbor" in Latin American affairs. Intervention was generally criticized, but by the same token the United States could and should not sit by and allow the region to decay economically and politically. The Good Neighbor Policy thus offered cooperation and trade agreements to Latin American governments.[29]

In many ways, then, the Good Neighbor Policy was simply another incarnation of "preventive diplomacy." It can also be seen as a slightly modified reincarnation of Theodore Roosevelt's corollary to the Monroe Doctrine, which called for U.S. efforts to undercut the sources of Latin American instability. Jules R. Benjamin has noted that this sort of a paternalistic, international welfare program would serve as a model for later, post-World War Two aid programs such as the Marshall Plan. This trend "attests to the profundity of the expansionist impulse within the political economy of the United States," Benjamin argues, contending that the economic cooperation with Cuba was in many ways "more interventionist than New Deal domestic programs and certainly more aggressive than the Republican policy toward Cuba." In this sense, Roosevelt's New Deal with regard to Cuba represented intervention by another name, in that its purpose was to create within Cuba "the type of political regime and economic environment that would form the basis for further U.S. economic expansion."[30]

Roosevelt consulted frequently with Welles, and was strongly influenced by his ambassador's views on the Cuban issue. Both subscribed to a form of the "preventive intervention" school, believing that a little U.S. meddling in Cuban politics—to guarantee a fair election here, fix an appropriate compromise there—could prevent the need to intervene militarily. Roosevelt had no idea, however, just how far Welles would take this unwritten mandate.[31]

In 1932 and 1933, just before and just after their assumption of power, Roosevelt and the other New Dealers who swept into office in the 1932 elections prepared specific policies on a number of issued, including foreign affairs and, more specifically, Cuba. The Depression focused most attention on domestic concerns,[32] and the only issue of significance with regard to Cuba was the tariff debate; the Republicans were for a tariff, the Democrats against.

Welles met with president-elect Roosevelt and discussed what their Latin American and Cuban policies would be. They wanted to promote Latin American stability through a program of tariff reductions, American guidance, and the recognition of new regimes if they were validated by an election. Indeed this latter portion of the policy would turn the Wilson and Hoover practice of non-recognition on its head; Sumner Welles would end up campaigning to have Machado overthrown, a revolution that would produce a government capable of obtaining the sanction of the U.S. This was all to be implemented in a framework of "positive" and "preventive" diplomacy, whose end was the preservation of the stability of Republican governments in Latin America, but whose means could include temporary endorsement of instability or revolution.[33]

In all of these discussions, Roosevelt displayed an abiding interest in Cuba.

At a January, 1933 meeting with outgoing Secretary of State Stimson, Cuba was the first subject broached by FDR, and the next day he sent a representative back to Stimson to gather more details about America's Cuba policy. Roosevelt also expressed the prescient view that Cubans would soon revolt against Machado; Stimson disagreed. FDR and his special envoy, Charles Taussig—who was president of the American Molasses Company, and hence had a personal stake in U.S. sugar interests in Cuba—contemplated U.S. supervision of new elections to replace Machado, and other forms of American influence. Stimson, still a student of the ''laissez faire'' school of diplomacy, warned against this sort of interference, but FDR, Taussig and Welles had already made up their minds.

In January, 1933, as revolutionary sentiment ballooned in Cuba, Taussig visited the island and spoke with Guggenheim. He recognized that the U.S. ambassador had, in fact, been trying to implement a more active American role, but was stymied by the Hoover administration's unwillingness to endorse his actions, and Taussig sympathized with Guggenheim's position. Taussig's subsequent report to FDR outlined a U.S. policy shift away from Hoover's ''hands off'' diplomacy to a more activist role, and recommended that FDR find an energetic ambassador. This set the stage for the appointment of Sumner Welles to the position in April, 1933.

Sumner Welles: Architect of an Active Role

Upon his appointment as ambassador, Sumner Welles already had some experience with Cuban affairs. After several years of active interest in Cuba, he was appointed in 1923 as a middleman for the Morgan bank loans. Later, he served as administrator of the U.S. occupation of the Dominican Republic, where he acquired more knowledge of Latin American political habits.

Tall, thin and youthful, Welles had attended the same schools as FDR— Groton and Harvard—and he frequented the same social circles; Welles's interests in American business in the area were similar to the President's. While his rhetoric was non-interventionist (he said before arriving in Cuba that ''any policy tending towards intervention is to be avoided''), Welles was really an idealistic interventionist of the Wilsonian mold. And while well-intentioned—he wanted stability and prosperity for Latin American, and even went as far as distinguishing ''good'' American business influence from that which was exploitive— Welles's chief concern was in fact the protection of American business interests in Cuba. These two characteristics—a tendency to meddle and a goal of promoting U.S. business—guided Welles' actions throughout the subsequent months.[34]

Once the Roosevelt administration had taken up residence in Washington,

Welles was dispatched to Havana with a clear goal: promotion of American economic interests, with Cuban political stability as a necessary subsidiary goal. Many Roosevelt advisors had economic interests in Cuba, and combined with FDR's own desires to expand U.S. commerce in the region, created a powerful set of incentives for the protection of U.S. industry.[35]

Welles arrived in Cuba wielding "the stick of the Platt Amendment and the carrot of a new trade treaty." He quickly recognized that the Machado regime was near collapse, and put his "preventive diplomacy" into action by telling Machado to get his house in order. Maintenance of constitutional government, and hence the upholding of the Machado regime, was still the goal: but without reforms, and in the face of Machado's imminent overthrow, the American administration would be willing to shift allegiance; that became clear to both Machado and his opposition. But for the moment Welles rejected opposition demands that Machado be immediately deposed.[36]

Cordell Hull was Secretary of State at the time, and he issued instructions to Welles about the conduct of American diplomacy in Cuba. But it soon became apparent to many in the administration that Welles undertook actions, and made commitments, far beyond what he had been authorized to do. Welles's basic orders with regard to pressuring Machado were to engage in a friendly dialogue that firmly requested reforms followed by a truce, and eventual elections, a process promoted by U.S. economic assistance.[37] Welles would eventually go far beyond recommendations for a mere truce, and after a time even Machado began to suspect that the American ambassador was outstripping his authority.[38]

On May 11, just three days after his arrival, Welles privately expressed his opinion to the U.S. government that Machado must go. Though he still publicly opposed such a move, Welles noted—in a style that became typical—that he would proceed according to his belief unless "instructed to the contrary," which meant he was arrogating authority to himself and that if the administration didn't like it, they must specifically order him to change his policy.[39] Receiving no such countermanding order, Welles within two weeks had made extensive contacts with the Cuban opposition.

Machado was not ignorant of this process and wanted to forestall it if he could. On May 24, Welles met with Cuban Secretary of State Orestes Ferrara, and two weeks after that Machado announced a sweeping set of political reforms, including an offer to rewrite the electoral college laws—long a bone of contention between Machado and the opposition—under the direction of an American professor. Well aware that American backing, or at least American silence, was crucial to his rule, Machado was gambling that he could manage the reform process and avoid American disapproval. Also, believing as he did that much of the pressure for change came from Welles and not the U.S.

administration, Machado played along, hoping that the calls for reform had no real backing and would eventually subside, after which he could reinstate absolute control.

Pressure of FDR to resolve the Cuban crisis grew throughout 1933. In large measure it was sponsored by Cuban exiles in Florida, who launched a massive campaign to publicize Machado's crimes. Roosevelt was in a difficult situation, and the historian Charles A. Thompson has concluded that Cuba "represented Franklin D. Roosevelt's major challenge in the field of foreign affairs" in the spring of 1933.[40]

By early June, Welles's attempts to arrange talks between the government and the opposition were apparently beginning to bear fruit—both sides agreed to negotiations. Welles proposed a series of electoral reforms, the selection of a "neutral" vice- president, and full elections to choose a new president in 1934. While continuing to reject opposition demands for the immediate ouster of Machado, Welles nevertheless proposed a plan of action that would have the same result. On June 21, FDR officially approved the negotiations, and on July 1, 1933, they opened.

During the following weeks, negotiations would go on even as the cracks in Welles's ad hoc compromise became evident. Student, labor and Communist groups boycotted the sessions from the beginning, claiming that any compromise was insufficient. Leaders of the ABC did participate—continuing their shift from radicalism to conservative opposition—and this lost them a good deal of support among more radical opponents of the regime, fostering as well a significant split among ABC members themselves.

Machado had begun to tire of Welles's meddling some time before, but kept quiet to preserve American favor. But as Welles grew more outspoken—and as he dealt more and more with the opposition—Machado lost all tolerance for the American ambassador. Eventually Machado rejected the compromise demands for early elections; and on July 26, he repudiated Welles's role by stating openly that the latter was acting on his own and not on the orders of the U.S. government.

Welles now concluded that Machado must be removed from office, and he requested a statement of support from the Department of State. Though Welles's role was tentatively approved by Washington, however, Machado was not persuaded and the negotiations fell apart. In fact, on June 16, the State Department announced, in the words of one reported, that Welles's efforts in the negotiations were made in his "personal capacity" and not "as an official United States mediator."[41]

Not to be intimidated, Welles kept up the pressure: begging for support from Washington, claiming to Machado that he had such backing, and even personally threatening intervention on several occasions. Roosevelt agreed only to hint vaguely at intervention, and Machado refused to believe that Welles's statements reflected Roosevelt's sentiments. On most occasions, Welles was only bluffing; no American officials actually desired intervention. Despite the support of the Undersecretary of State William Philipps (who managed State's Cuban policy during this period, and who frequently claimed that FDR and Hull concurred with Welles's policies) Welles was unable to build the credible impression that his views were mirrored by Washington. Ironically, Welles's policy was hampered by a lack of support from Washington in the same way Guggenheim's had been. In practice, Roosevelt, preoccupied with domestic concerns, proved less willing to follow through with interference than his pre-election positions might have indicated.[42]

The basic causes of an eventual collapse of stability were now nearly in place. It remained for one crucial factor to enter the fray, the force that constituted Machado's bulwark against revolution and, now that the United States had been alienated, his last real source of support: the Cuban army.

Revolution Approaches: The Defection of the Army

Political violence and government repression continued throughout June and July, 1933. On June 1, after an argument in the Cuban senate, one senator was shot to death by the brother of another in the senate chamber. Skirmishes between rebels and Rural Guard forces in the outlying provinces continued. On June 7, Machado had announced some plans for reform, including limited press freedoms, but after what he considered an "overenthusiastic interpretation" of his announcement by the press, he reinstated harsh censorship measures the next day.

Desperate economic conditions contributed to the instability. Field workers were earning 25 cents for 10-12 hour days, and some received only food and shelter for their labor. A deepening depression drove more labor groups into the opposition, and from 1931 to 1933, Cuba was racked with widespread strikes. In August, 1933, a strike begun by bus drivers spread throughout the island, and the long-feared general strike was at hand. Guerrilla activity in rural areas continued, with frequent clashes between Rural Guard units and insurgents.[43]

Perhaps surprisingly, the PCC and the CNOC were not entirely happy with these developments. They saw the strikes as halfway measures, guided by businessmen and others opposed only to Machado's extreme brutalities, and not the Cuban capitalist system itself. They also feared U.S. intervention in the event of social unrest. Communist leaders therefore avoided supporting the strikes, and even discussed negotiations with the government designed to help crush them and prepare the way for what the Communists hoped would be a legitimate "proletarian revolution."[44]

On August 7, Machado met with the strike leaders, and the next day the ABC party's radio broadcast a false report of his resignation. Celebrating crowds surged into the Havana streets, thousands of them rushing to the presidential palace. Guards fired into the crowd, killing twenty and injuring many others; one observer noted that "there was no excuse for it [the killing]. It was sheer wanton murder." This and other incidents hardened the position of the strikers, and other groups joined it so that by August 9, the entire island was paralyzed.[45]

Through the days of August 7 and 8, Welles made more public his demands for the immediate resignation of Machado; he met with Cuban business and government leaders and argued for such a course, and suggested to the U.S. State Department that it withdraw its recognition of the Machado government. On the 7th, Welles also proposed directly to Machado that he step down in favor of a "neutral" secretary of state who would then assume the presidency: Machado's response was "blind fury" against interference by Welles.[46]

On the 9th, Machado, panicked by the general anarchy, declared a state of war, rallied his supporters in the Cuban congress and army about him, and asked for a censure vote against Welles in the Cuban legislature. Within two days, however, as his strength continued to crumble, Machado began to realize that he had to seek a way out. Many Cubans, meanwhile, hoped for American intervention, and actually resented Welles for not bringing it about.[47]

Crucial in prompting Machado to give up was the gradual defection of the Cuban army to the opposition. The army had always been somewhat ashamed of its oppressive role, and had feared the potential for U.S. intervention created by Machado's poor rule; Cuban officers had no desire to fight American troops, and feared that an American invasion might end in open hostilities. Since 1932, such officers as Col. Horacio Ferrer and Col. Julio Sanguily had plotted against Machado, and the events of 1933 lent new force to their arguments. On August 12, a group of officers urged Machado to resign; groups of military personnel seized various barracks and bases around the country.[48] It was becoming clear to Machado that he had little choice but to give in to Welles's demands.[49]

On August 9, FDR broke from Welles's positions in a manner that might have undercut some of the pressure on Machado, if the situation had not already been so desperate. He met with Cuban Ambassador Cintas, who assured the president that if the United States relaxed its pressure, Machado's government would initiate reforms on its own. Roosevelt instructed Welles to follow such a course, and at a press conference that day denied that his ambassador had given Machado an ultimatum, repudiating

Welles's claims of presidential backing on that issue.[50]

Now it was Welles who became worried. FDR's statements, combined with claims by Cuban Secretary of State Orestes Ferrara that America would not intervene and in fact supported Machado, had undercut his credibility. Welles was cornered, and instead of quietly following his orders he initiated on August 10 a final series of attempts to unseat Machado, attempts that contributed significantly to the impending revolution. Welles met with Ferrara, who demanded trade and loan concessions from the United States in exchange for pressuring Machado to step down. He met with opposition leaders and claimed that the U.S. government, whatever it said, really agreed that Machado should be ousted. He met with Cuban Secretary of War Herrera, whom he considered a possible successor to Machado, and secured Herrera's agreement to act as president when Machado resigned.[51]

Immediately after Welles left Herrera's office, Col. Ferrer went in and asked Herrera to join the coup against Machado. Herrera, perhaps to protect his own newly-acquired interest in Machado's resignation, refused. Indeed, Herrera actively opposed the coup, hoping to forestall it long enough for him to engineer a smooth resignation of Machado and his own subsequent ascent to power. On August 11, Herrera ordered the arrest of the coup leaders and later met with specific rebellious units, promising to speak with Machado and make their demands known. He eventually did this. Machado, who was now opposed by Welles, the radical and moderate opposition, the striking unions, and even large segments of his own officer corps, recognized that the situation was hopeless; he retired to his estate and requested safe passage out of the country.

On the evening of August 11, the Cuban military entered politics in a very open and crucial way. Many officers finally deserted Machado, primarily out of fear that his abuses would bring on a U.S. intervention, which none of them wanted. Welles had at first opposed Machado's resignation because the opposition was too fragmented to offer a stable alternative, but with the army offering one, Machado became expendable.[52]

On August 12, in the heat of the Cuban afternoon sun, Machado climbed into an amphibian plane at General Machado airport. Resentful of Welles's role, unhappy about this departure from power, Machado nevertheless recognized that his days were numbered no matter what he did. So, in the manner of so many Latin American dictators who would follow, Machado fled. The plane took off, bearing Machado and some of his closest aides, and headed for the Bahamas. Machado had abdicated.

Violent revelry quickly gripped Havana. Crowds tore down and destroyed everything remotely connected with Machado. Public buildings were sacked; particularly brutal members of Machado's police were hunted down and assassinated, as often as not by soldiers of the Cuban army. Machado's depar ture had not ended the violence.

Meanwhile, Herrera had his own problems. He had never been the military's first choice as Machado' successor, and reservations about his role immediately began to surface in that quarter. By August 11, it became clear that he was no longer acceptable to the military, and this worried the other opposition groups and Welles, who had grown accustomed to the thought of Herrera as president. Now the field seemed wide open; the liberal opposition coalesced around Col. Horacio Ferrer, one of the original leaders of anti-Machado organizations within the military, but Col. Ferrer was not interested in the presidency. Welles meanwhile tried to rally support behind Herrera.

When Welles saw that the military would not approve Herrera, he requested that it allow the Cuban officer to be president just long enough to appoint a secretary of state, who would then step up to the presidency. Col. Sanguily, Welles's contact with the rebellious officers, agreed to this proposal, as did Herrera. The problem was now to find the secretary-cum-next president, and Welles turned to Carlos Manuel de Cespedes, Cuba's ambassador to Mexico. Cespedes was a relatively conservative politician whom Welles had long respected. Loved by few, but respected by many and hated by almost no one, Cespedes seemed a reasonable enough choice.[53] On August 12, as the final details of the Herrera/Cespedes compromise were being hammered out, the Cuban congress was placed under siege. A few congressmen convened in the deserted chambers, joined by Welles, Herrera, Sanguily, and Cespedes. The congressmen noted the existence of a "quorum," and declared Cespedes president.

Unfortunately for Welles, the powerful political and economic forces swirling through Cuba doomed this project even before it began. The true, underlying tensions and causes of the revolt—economic deprivation, income disparity, American meddling—went unresolved. The situation demanded much more than ad hoc tinkering, but the result of Welles's machinations was "the artificial creation of a regime with neither social base nor nationalist appeal. Its rule was to be ineffective, its demise swift."[54]

The Cespedes Government

As expected, the Cespedes government, with its limitations, was strongly pro-American, indeed too much so for its own good. Instability had not subsided; the strike slowly ended, but urban violence blossomed as mobs hunted down those who had been associated with the Machado regime, especially the former *porristas*. Cespedes attempted some nationalistic reforms but the requirement of good relations with the United States prevented them from being substantive. He did manage to send many of Machado's congress packing, and to rescind the constitutional amendments of 1928 that institutionalized Machado's power. But he could not abandon many of the central policies of his predecessor for fear of losing American support. What was really necessary was a revolutionary government to do completely away with Machado's policies and institute reforms that would satisfy the opposition. The perception that Cespedes was a tool of the United States doomed his administration.[55]

Many of those associated with the government were tainted by the relationship, and lost favor with the radical opposition. The ABC, which continued to retreat from its more radical positions, supported the Cespedes government, and hoped by its participation to foster a compromise. But other opposition groups resented this "complicity" with American meddling, and the ABC gradually lost support and eventually destroyed itself with its attempt to influence the Cespedes government.[56]

Cespedes was also personally unsuited to the post of Cuban revolutionary leader. A relatively conventional diplomat, he had served under—and done nothing to oppose— Machado. He was not a Cuban native, but was born in New York while his father worked there as a leader of the exile Cuban revolutionary government in the late nineteenth century. And he was indecisive and somewhat lacking in leadership qualities.[57]

Nevertheless, the United States was obviously pleased with the Cespedes government. FDR and Hull congratulated Welles on his work, and the administration quickly recognized the new Cuban government. American officials and commentators were impressed with Cespedes's apparent honesty and his choice of a respected and expert cabinet.[58] (The American support for Cespedes continued an interesting pattern: American policy-makers seemed more comfortable dealing with Cubans who had lived in the United States for long periods of time, as exiles, students, or in some other capacity. The precedent for such favoritism was established with Tomas Estrada Palma and continued thereafter.)

Welles, for his part, was not so optimistic, and asked for two American destroyers to make a small show of strength and resolve. He also attempted to institute a number of reforms from the ABC program, but realizing that this would be difficult—and realizing also that his own connection with the Cespedes government tended to discredit it—Welles requested to be recalled. He also urged that his hand-picked successor, Jefferson Caffery, avoid political involvement as much as possible. FDR agreed and set the date of Welles's recall for September 15.

Whatever hopes Welles had for passing a quiet final month in Cuba, free of requirements of interference in Cuban affairs, were soon dashed. By the end of August, the situation there was again, in Welles' words, "almost anarchic." The continuing economic desperation of the Cuban people and rising anti-American nationalism combined to topple Cespedes's government.

The Revolt of the Sergeants

Cespedes's opponents could have been accurately characterized even before he was declared president; labor, student groups (especially the Directorio Estudantil), and the radical opposition all considered him too conservative and a stooge of the United States. Cespedes's reforms were paced too slowly for these groups, and his opposition to lawful (or unlawful) prosecution of Machado cronies further alienated the common Cuban people.[59] He had little true support, and his term in office was doomed to last only until the opposition could come up with a viable alternative. As it happened, the faction that would undertake this role was the army, which was rapidly becoming the dominant force in Cuban political life.

The noncommissioned officers of the Cuban army were unhappy with the state of affairs. Their chances for advancement, relatively good under Machado, dwindled under Cespedes's new military policies. Contacts with student radicals, moreover, politicized the noncoms to some degree, and their nationalism caused them to oppose Cespedes. They thus sought some means of asserting their independence and altering the situation.

Cuban officers, for the most part, lived in the cities, and stayed at the barracks only during the day. At night, most Cuban army installations were under the temporary command of noncoms. A better context for a coup of enlisted men could hardly have been imagined.

By mid-August, a group of Cuban noncoms had begun to meet and discuss their grievances. Led by Pablo Rodriquez and including the soon-to-be-famous Fulgencio Batista, the group dealt with simple matters like food, pay and promotion opportunities. By late August, this forum had developed into a formal interest group, the *Junta de Defensa*. At about the same time, Cespedes appointed Horacio Ferrer as secretary of war, and Ferrer acted quickly to break strikes and cut military force and pay levels. These and other actions contributed to the enlisted men's grievances, though at first the army personnel harbored few thoughts of revolt.

On September 1, a hurricane hit Cuba east of Havana; while Cespedes was out of the city inspecting the damage, the noncoms met to continue their discussions, but still gave no evidence they wished to overthrow him. Cespedes and his officer corps were aware of these meetings, but did not consider them a significant threat. Indeed, throughout the preceding weeks, Cuban officers had become more and more aware of the growing enlisted movement, but never acted decisively to head it off.

On September 4, the sergeants finally agreed to a revolt and joined with the radical opposition in drafting a "Provisional Revolutionary Government" manifesto. The document appointed five-persons (the "Pentarchy") to rule the country, though Sergeant Fulgencio Batista quickly emerged as the government's chief spokesman. On that night and over the next days, enlisted men seized all major military installations in the country. When Cespedes returned from his damage-inspection trip on September 5, he was greeted with the unhappy news that he had been deposed. That day he insisted to the new junta that he was a revolutionary too, and that they should allow him into their government. But they were not persuaded, and eventually, he gave up and left public life, retiring to his home.[60]

Welles was disturbed by these developments. When notified of the revolt, he immediately cabled Washington that "a revolutionary government has been set up, composed of the most extreme radicals in Cuba." Welles was wrong. The sergeants and their allies were not the "most extreme radical" groups in Cuba, and indeed, had the United States tried quickly to bargain with them, it might have found them agreeable, as Batista would later show himself to be. For the moment, however, Welles's fear of progressive regime colored his judgment; and his instinctive bias against any reformist Cuban government betrayed his overriding concern for American business interests in Cuba.

In his first interview with Batista after the coup, Welles did not receive what he perceived to be adequate assurances about the nature of the new regime. Batista wanted to obtain recognition, but Welles would not discuss that matter, preferring instead to query the sergeant on his provisions for public order. The answers were not entirely to Welles's liking, and this reinforced his doubts about the government.[61]

For its part, the Pentarchy had no program of action. Its membership was mostly moderate, and so was committed to neither radical reform nor reactionary conservatism. The sergeants, perhaps a little surprised at themselves for actually rebelling, merely wanted the Pentarchy to meet their demands for better treatment and pay, and beyond this suggested little in the way of governmental policy or direction. In fact, both the traditional opposition and the noncom group decided after all to pursue compromise; the Pentarchy wanted to arrange power-sharing with a re-inaugurated Cespedes government, the sergeants to place themselves back under the control of the officers, with some qualifications. But the demands by both Cespedes and his officers for full power—demands recommended by Welles—convinced the allied army and opposition groups that they needed to radicalize, not compromise.

Welles continued predictably to be skeptical of the new government, claiming that it was inadequate for the "protection of life, property, and individual liberty." In using the exact language of the Platt Amendment, he hoped to emphasize that if his views were borne out, the United States possessed the right and the duty to intervene. Again, Welles did not necessarily want intervention, but used the threat of it as a bargaining tool. Because massive new waves of violence and anarchy had not set in, Welles was forced to claim that they would. He met with representatives of both camps and tried to engineer Cespedes's return to power, even discussing a revolution inside Cuba, or the orchestration of an American intervention, to pull it off.[62] But none of the plans came to fruition, and Roosevelt and Hull continued to oppose intervention.

In fact, Cespedes and his cabinet, having had enough of Cuban politics, had resigned, and Welles was forced to look elsewhere for a "moderate" to support; and September 5 was the last official day of the Cespedes government. Welles chose Carlos Mendieta, a conservative Cuban politician. But Welles recognized that without the support of the Cuban army Mendieta would get nowhere, and he tried to secure their support. Welles also tried to turn U.S. policy against the Pentarchy and toward intervention by calling the ruling junta "Communist" (which it clearly was not) and asking for a "small" landing of Marines to protect U.S. property. Roosevelt would have none of it; he said intervention was "absolutely the last thing we have in mind," and on September 6, Hull instructed Welles to follow a policy of "strict neutrality" toward the new government.[63]

The End of the Pentarchy and the Beginning of the Grau Government

Any remaining prospects for compromise were completely eliminated when the Pentarchy promoted Sergeant Batista to colonel and appointed him head of the army. Accommodation with the officers was now nearly out of the question. The inexperienced young government would have to run the country on its own.

Leaders of the radical and moderate opposition soon began to fear that the Pentarchy was slipping into irrelevancy, and met on September 9. Afraid of the compromise proposals being bandied about and of the potential for a counter-coup, they appointed Dr. Ramon Grau San Martin as president, walked downstairs to a meeting of the Pentarchy (which was gathered in the same building) and presented their *fait accompli*. After a heated debate, the Pentarchy approved the plan and voted to dissolve itself. The next day, Grau became president as the leaders and members of opposition groups were informed of the decision. Many were angered by the lack of popular participation in it.[64]

Grau—a well-to-do doctor, professor, and former exile during Machado's regime—would head a government more progressive than any in Cuban history. He immediately denounced the Platt Amendment, and on September 20, announced legislation providing an 8-hour work day. He reopened the university, established a department of labor, and initiated other reforms. At first, they failed to satisfy anyone: the United States was shocked, and demanded caution; Cuban businessmen were distrustful of Grau's intentions and resentful of his restrictive legislation; and the left complained that the process had not gone far enough. In any case, the Grau government was at first too weak to make its reforms stick, or even to publicize them effectively.

From the start, American policy toward Grau was hostile, and almost immediately attempted to oust him from power. In fact, the first American response consisted of dispatching 29 warships on September 5 to emphasize American concern over the fall of Cespedes. The United States withdrew the political and economic support it had extended to Cespedes and began to cultivate an alliance with Batista that would last almost thirty years. On September 8, Roosevelt allowed Welles to express U.S. disapproval by noting that the administration was not even considering recognition of the Grau government. Welles wanted to go even further—to declare that the United States would *never* consider recognition—but Roosevelt rejected that idea.[65]

American rhetoric did not explicitly attack Grau, but its intent was clearly to unseat him and to promote a coalition government, which would include various moderate and conservative elements as well as Grau's people. On September 11, Hull announced that the United States was "prepared to welcome any government representing the will of the [Cuban] people," and that same day many Cuban opposition parties declared the Grau government unacceptable and called for a compromise regime.[66] On the 6th, Roosevelt had met with Latin American leaders to reassure them that the United States did not intend to intervene but that it wanted representative government, which seemed to confirm that the Grau government was not one.

Grau was also painted as incapable of responding to the threats facing the Cuban government.[67] Welles recounted stories of rebel attacks on American property, and Grau's apparent inability (or unwillingness) to stop them. Welles also argued that Grau was an ineffectual answer to the growing Communist threat—Welles had long exaggerated this danger— because he was too far to the left to actively oppose the PCC. Most U.S. corporations doing business in Cuba agreed. Clearly, The Roosevelt administration's opposition to Grau was based on its concern for U.S. economic interests.

Meanwhile, some 500 Cuban army officers, to protest the left-leaning Grau administration and its "traitorous" army of enlisted men, barricaded themselves in the posh Hotel Nacional, and threatened to resist with force any attempt to dislodge them. By coincidence, Welles was living at the same hotel, and the apparent (though misleading) connection did little to help his already damaged reputation. The situation remained tense until October 2, when a firefight broke out between the officers and the enlisted men who had surrounded the hotel. The officers finally surrendered, but not before killing 100 and wounding 200 of the soldiers, while themselves sustaining about 30 casualties. The situation was a complicated one: Batista's enlisted men were far more progressive than the officer corps, yet at the same time more conservative that Grau; the new Cuban "army" under Batista would soon emerge from the president's coalition to oppose him.

Gradually, a moderate opposition to Grau, calling themselves "responsible nationalists," emerged. They were wary, however, of the army, which Welles had made the centerpiece of his own alternative to Grau. This disagreement factionalized the opposition. Welles dismissed claims that Batista, were he to come to power, might institute a military dictatorship, and by the end of September had truly committed himself to Batista as an alternative to Grau; by September 21 he as calling the sergeant "extremely reasonable" and staunchly anti-Communist.[68]

Batista, meanwhile, was cementing his own power. The day after the October 2 clash ended in the officers' surrender, he met with Welles again and received the pledge that if he would act against radicals, he would obtain the support of "the very great majority of the commercial and financial interests in Cuba." Welles recommended that Batista use "the force of authority" he represented to take charge and resolve the continuing negotiations regarding a new government.

In early October, reading Batista's success as Grau's—since Batista was, after all, only the head of the army and under Grau's command— Roosevelt and Hull considered a *de facto* recognition of the Grau government. Welles would have none of it, and distinguished between Batista's power and reliability and that of Grau. Washington never followed up on the matter, and Welles effectively forestalled a policy change.[69]

Batista's U.S.- inspired conservatism in turn fostered a growing rift with the radical and student opposition. He eventually announced his support for Carlos Mendieta as Cuba's next president, falling more closely into line with Welles' opinions, and drifting further from his revolutionary origins. As with the ABC before him, Batista, somewhat of a populist, was being mellowed by the realities of power in Cuba and of American influence.[70]

Grau tried to moderate himself somewhat to conform to U.S. wishes; he broke a few strikes and qualified his reform plans. But these actions immediately angered the radical opposition, and in late October the students and the ABC dropped their support for the government, citing Grau's "submission to the army." Economic conditions remained terrible, and the Cuban polity fragmented, with various groups scurrying to different sources of perceived relief: the Grau government, the army, the radical opposition, even the United States. The Grau government was caught in the crossfire, insufficiently radical for the left and not conservative enough for the right.[71]

The Atares Revolt and the Departure of Welles

The ABC, returning to its earlier radicalism, began an uprising in Havana on November 9 aimed at securing the support of the military against the Grau government. The army, however, remained faithful to Batista—which again confirmed his importance—and confined the rebels to the Atares fortress, where they eventually surrendered. In the wake of this victory, confidence in the Grau government rose for a time. Charles Taussig, FDR's unofficial advisor on Cuba—again mistaking Batista's success for Grau's—called for recognition and, along with other observers of the Cuban scene, condemned Welles' role. Others, including Under Secretary of State William Philipps, pointed out that Welles was now so controversial in Cuba as to be of no use.[72]

The time for Welles's self-imposed recall, in any case, was at hand, and on November 19, he met with FDR and agreed to be replaced with Caffery provided Welles was assured that his policy of nonrecognition of Grau was continued. Welles returned to Havana, and in his last weeks there attempted to "solve" the Cuban crisis quickly before his replacement arrived. Negotiations bogged down, however, and Welles did not get his wish; but the eventual accession to power of Batista was by then almost inevitable. On December 18, Jefferson Caffery arrived in Havana, and he continued Welles's basic policies of opposition to Grau and support for Batista.[73]

Some Cuban government officials, especially Secretary of the Interior Antonio Guiteras, now tried to push Grau to the left, hoping to escape the middle ground which satisfied no one and to establish a firm base of support. At the same time, they were hoping to undercut Batista's support on the left. So the government returned to progressivism, and in some government circles socialist reforms were discussed openly. A number of U.S. companies were seized as part of a nationalization drive. In late December, as the negotiations fell into even greater disarray (in large part due directly to this shift to the left of the Grau government), Grau turned ever further to the left in a desperate bid to cement his power among the radicals.[74]

By January, 1934, Batista and the army had had enough, and they issued Grau an ultimatum: moderate or face ouster. Grau's days were clearly numbered. Batista had favored Carlos Mendieta as Grau's replacement, as had the United States; but Mendieta endorsed Carlos Hevia, Grau's progressive agriculture secretary and the choice of the left-wing opposition. On January

15, as the Grau government came apart, Hevia was appointed president. Strikes and instability continued to sweep the country.

Batista soon concluded that the left-leaning Hevia government must go, and his control of the army insured that he would eventually prevail. After a brief power struggle with Guiteras, it became clear that Batista had once again assumed the reins of true power. On September 18, having served as president for merely 39 hours, Hevia resigned. Batista, though he would later display some signs of his continuing progressivism, had now firmly committed himself to a moderate/conservative, pro-U.S. stance.[75]

THE REVOLUTION OF 1933: RAMIFICATIONS AND IMPLICATIONS

In retrospect it is perhaps clear that the United States should have tried to cooperate with the Grau government rather than topple it. The underlying problem with American policy toward Cuba continued to be the disastrous apathy toward the core of social problems of the country, and Grau was progressive enough to hold out some hope of solving them. By using threats of military aid cuts as a lever, Roosevelt could perhaps have enlisted Batista's grudging support for such a plan; Batista, after all, was a populist in his own way, sponsoring rural school and public-works programs. But it was not to be. The U.S. government decided that the continued rule of Grau was not in its interests and acted accordingly.

In the process, U.S. actions made a mockery of the Good Neighbor Policy's non-intervention pledge. Though he paid lip-service to non-interventionist principles, Sumner Welles interfered in Cuban political life to a degree virtually unprecedented for an ambassador. As one American commentator, Hubert Herring, concluded after Machado's downfall, "[The United States has] again intervened in Cuba. No marines walked the streets of Havana, but they would have done so had Machado resisted. Machado knew it." Josephus Daniels, the U.S. ambassador to Mexico, recognized the dangers of this path, and argued that the United States should encourage and assist social reform in Latin America and otherwise maintain a policy of strict noninterference. Subsequent critiques of Welles have been even more vitriolic; two recent American commentators described his role as a "new type" of intervention: "economic blackmail, political intrigue, [and] manipulation of the military, labor, and student groups," a process that produced "the succession of corrupt Cuban governments that ultimately led to the Castro revolution of the late 1950s."[76]

At the same time, not all observers viewed this interference as pejorative.

Herring himself concluded that his description of American interference was "not a criticism of Mr. Welles. There was an unpleasant job to be done, and he did it with the maximum of wisdom and good taste, with the minimum of affront to the pride of Cuba."[77] Irwin F. Gellman comes to essentially the same conclusions, noting through detailed analysis that Welles was simply trying to do the best job possible in a very difficult situation.[78] He was not corrupt, had no hidden agenda, and did his best to avoid, if not U.S. interference, then open intervention.

Even if that is true, Welles serves as an example of U.S. policy that tampered with the problems of Cuban society but did not solve them. He treated the Cuban leaders of the time as discrete phenomena, men who were corrupt or brutal and had to be done away with, but not as symptoms of far deeper disturbances within the Cuban national psyche. It was this ignorance of the deep social, economic, and national instability that justifies criticism of Welles,[79] for though these instabilities would remain dormant for some time, by the 1950s they would explode into a revolutionary fervor which had been simmering for decade. Like so much of America's policy toward the Third World before the 1980s, then, American actions in Cuba in 1933 were in large part attributable to a basic ignorance of the political, social, and economic forces at work. The United States would pay dearly for that ignorance.

American policy during this period, moreover, was clearly motivated by economic concerns. Whatever the faults of a universal, Marxist interpretation of U.S. foreign policy as aimed solely at promoting capitalists' interests, its analysis seems quite appropriate in this case. While the claim that a nation should direct its foreign policy toward supporting domestic economic interests should hardly come as a surprise in any context, the effects of such policies in Cuba, as in so many other places, worked against long-term U.S. interests.

Meanwhile the hope in Cuba for true social change and for an honest government had been dashed. Grau's reforms had begun a process of rising expectations that would later lead to revolution. As Ramon Ruiz has contended, "The reforms enacted by the Grau administration opened a Pandora's box of political passions and rivalries that were not stilled until 1944—and then only temporarily."[80]

Jorge Manach, a Cuban lawyer and writer and a member of the executive committee of the ABC, foresaw later developments with a good deal of prescience. The 1933 revolution, he argued, was only the "first phase" of a "genuine" revolution, which would come later. Manach noted that Jose Marti had commented that the revolution of 1895 was only a war for *emancipation*, and the battle for "internal liberty" would follow "as Marti prophesied, thirty years later."

But the Revolution of 1933 did not satisfy these requirements. It had been preempted and subverted by the United States in alliance with a number of conservative Cubans. As Manach noted, the true revolution thus remained to be fought:

> The events of August [1933] have been the initial steps in this effort to affirm and liberate the national will of the Cuban people. For that reason they constitute the first phase of a genuine revolution, for which the Machado tyranny has been only a stimulus. This revolution is animated by the purpose to restore the full liberty of the Cuban people. They must find their bearings in relation to their national problems, and solve those problems adequately and finally. For the first time since the war of independence, the people of Cuba experienced during those August days the emotion of control, the feeling that they were masters of their own destiny. We shall not inquire to what degree that experience was an illusion. The duty of loyal Cubans and the duty of all those who truly wish to help Cuba is to promote the translation of that illusion, if such it was, into reality.

Manach contended that the only way this could be accomplished was for the United States to remove itself from Cuban politics and to make more progressive commitments regarding the Cuban economy. America must, he noted, thus agree to "the simultaneous renunciation, for both present and future, of the privileges which power and proximity give." Only the pursuit of such a policy "will leave clear of all doubt. . .the friendship of the great Republic of the north for this young Republic of the Caribbean."[81]

Manach's conclusions were wise, his prescriptions sound. U.S. policy makers, however, could not find the wisdom to heed them; American economic domination of Cuba and political meddling in Cuban affairs continued. Fulgencio Batista, though distinctly less brutal, replaced Machado as the "lackey to Yankee imperialism," and none of the fundamental tensions within Cuban society were resolved.

For a time, at least, for a courageous, arrogant man would soon echo Marti's sentiments. "We are going to make the revolution," he would argue. "The revolution that never came about in 1898 or 1933. This time we're going to make it come true."[82] That man was Fidel Castro. The true Cuban Revolution, begun under the banner of Marti's rebellion for internal liberty, but brought to fruition as something for more radical, was on the way. And once it had occurred, nothing in Cuban-American relations would be the same.

7

SETTING THE STAGE

The United States and Batista, 1933-1956

"Powerlessness frustrates; absolute powerlessness
frustrates absolutely."
Russell Baker, *The New York Times*

"Revolutions are not made; they come. A revolution is as natural a growth
as an oak. It comes out of the past. Its foundations are laid far back."
Wendell Phillips, speech, Boston, 1852

"Dictators always look good until the last minutes."
Tomas Masaryk

The Cuban Revolution of 1933 had been largely still-born. Few significant changes took place in the way the Cuban polity functioned, or in the relationship between Cuba and the United States. In part, this return to business as usual—to corrupt and occasionally brutal Cuban governments, to American domination of Cuban markets and governments, and to the continued stagnation of the Cuban economy—would be responsible for a second, and far more sweeping, revolution a quarter of a century later. What happened in between those two revolutions is the subject of this chapter.

1934-1940: THE PUPPET PRESIDENTS

Carlos Mendieta was a former officer of the army of liberation, a well-known, honest and trusted man. His inauguration was greeted with "excitement and relief," at least among the upper classes, and bartenders "could hardly serve the drinks fast enough as the new president was toasted."[1] But a great leader he was not. Upon assuming the presidency, he proved immediately to be a weak head of government, and rather than striking out a firm path on his own he tried to ingratiate himself to all points on the political compass, a task that predictably proved impossible. The result was a struggle between the military and the ABC for influence in the shifting Mendieta government.[2]

Ruby Hart Phillips, an astute observer of the Cuban political scene of the 1930s, noted these flaws in Mendieta's character. The president, she noted

> does not seem to be taking hold like he should. Cuba needs a strong
> personality at the head of the government. . . . Really, nothing has
> been done. Strike after strike has been called. . . . Mendieta is
> apparently trying to please everybody and the result may bear out
> the fable of the man who tried to please everybody and only suc-
> ceeded in drowning his donkey.

By a "strong personality" she most explicitly was not referring to Batista, for whom the public had "no liking" and who "can never be popular, no matter what he does."[3]

This desire for a strong leader stemmed in part from the Cuban tradition of *caudillismo*, or the reverence for a *caudillo* or strong man. In many ways, Cubans were used to following powerful personalities—they had been doing so since the days of Gomez, Garcia, Maceo, and Marti of the nineteenth century—and in Latin America the cult of the strongman/leader (especially one from a military background) had developed into a powerful force. This continues, to some degree, to the present day, and helps to explain the undoubtedly strong support (especially among the peasantry) enjoyed by such ruthless dictators as Batista in Cuba and Trujillo in the Dominican Republic.

Ambassador Caffery, not recognizing the initial weakness of the Mendieta regime, recommended immediate U.S. recognition. It was granted on January 23, 1934. Most U.S. commentators approved of this action, and even some liberal Cubans agreed that backing the Mendieta government was the best thing to do under the circumstances. The U.S. press was also favorable, though recommending an abrogation of the Platt Amendment as a follow-up.[4]

As many recognized, Batista really remained in charge, his power only tempered by the ABC and its leader Martinez Saenz, who was able to wield influence by threats of withdrawing from the government. Mendieta, for his part, continued to pursue the path of reforms staked out by Batista himself, lifting various restrictions on freedoms while at the same time increasing his control over unions to prevent the sorts of strikes that disrupted earlier Cuban governments. But the problems that inspired the rebellion of 1933—chronic poverty, income disparities, an economy tied to sugar, and so on—had not been resolved, and would prove nearly intractable.[5]

Although the Mendieta government is correctly viewed as conservative, it did approve much of Grau's progressive legislation. Mendieta pursued significant labor reforms, the abrogation of the Platt Amendment, and the enfranchisement of women, leading to an "avalanche of legislation" in 1934-35 that "institutionaliz[ed] many of the revolutionary aspirations of 1933." Labor emerged as the most powerful interest group in Cuba, and within several years would achieve a set of labor reforms unequalled certainly in Latin America, if indeed anywhere: an 8-hour day, 44 hour week with pay for 48 hours, one month bonus at Christmas, paid leave for pregnant women, and tenure in jobs after six months—all guaranteed by law. Agricultural workers, too, felt the benefits of this trend; a land reform program after 1933 provided for a "law of permanency" that granted sugar tillers permanent ownership of the land they worked; this right could be sold or passed down to children. Later laws extended this right to all agricultural workers. The unemployed were also given some benefits, such as free health care in many areas of Cuba. As one former prominent mill owner puts it, "We had a very socialized society in Cuba."[6]

Political violence that had plagued Cuba for years, however, continued; the far left—Communists, students, and other groups—vehemently opposed Mendieta, and daily bombings, strikes, and assassinations became the norm. With supplies smuggled in from Florida, the opposition waged a war of terror against the government, and one observer estimated that over 2,000 bombings occurred during Mendieta's reign. One result was tension between Batista and Mendieta as the former pressed for a harder line and the latter refused to act. The growing death toll soon rendered Mendieta's policy untenable.

Cuba's economic difficulties continued, and provided the opposition with additional ammunition. Mendieta moved slightly to the left as part of his continuing attempts to satisfy everyone, instituting land redistribution schemes, cooperative farming programs, and other measures. But the left was not persuaded, and when Mendieta postponed the promised elections of 1934 until March 1935, the opposition increased the ferocity of its attacks. In June the ABC finally fulfilled its threats to leave the government; strikes returned and

Communist and student groups fomented instability. Only the disunity of the opposition allowed Mendieta to remain in control.[7]

By June, too, political assassinations and bombings had become commonplace, and nervous police started firing into crowds during riots. An attempt had even been made on Caffery's life late in May. Still, Mendieta took no action to calm the increasingly explosive situation. On June 15, he himself was almost killed by a bomb, and this seemed to spur him to action: he enacted a sweeping anti-terrorism law enforced by a court of no appeal.

The United States was clearly trying to help Cuba during this period. In November 1933, FDR promised that when Cuba became stable, the United States would consider abrogating the Platt amendment, and Cubans and Americans alike called for such action. In May of 1934, Roosevelt submitted a modified treaty of relations with Cuba to the Senate for ratification which replaced the Platt Amendment formula with a less interventionary American role. The Senate quickly ratified it, and on May 29, 1934, the Platt Amendment was officially abrogated. While this had few practical implications, it did improve America's image in Cuba, and one author called it a "master stroke of American diplomacy."[9] Even after the amendment was revoked, however, as Mario Lazo—an American-born lawyer working in Cuba—recognized later, Cubans continued to look to the United States for "tutelage" and to the U.S. ambassador "for solutions to major problems."[10]

A new Reciprocity Treaty was also signed at this time, the final version being approved in August 1934. It gave preferential treatment to 35 products from Cuba, in exchange for tariff concessions by Cuba on *400* U.S. exports. At the same time, the Jones-Costigan Act of May 1934 granted Cuba a quota of about 28 percent of the U.S. sugar market. In the short run, provisions for Cuban sugar exports to the United States allowed the Cuban economy to improve. But these treaties were disastrous from the long-range perspective, as they allowed American exports to dominate most non-sugar markets in Cuba and thus helped preserve the monocultural society. Many Cubans, including the ABC and the Communists, cried foul, but the short term sugar concessions were significant enough to mask the true implications of the treaty, and for the most part objections went unheeded.[11]

Besides these measures, the U.S. government also provided direct financial assistance, agreed to stabilize Cuban currency in relation to the dollar, and provided loans.[12] These efforts led Ruby Hart Phillips to conclude that the United States had "done everything possible to aid Cuba."[13]

American aid carried a political price as well. Jefferson Caffery, in Phillips' words, exerted "as much influence on the Mendieta government as did Ambassador Welles on the Cespedes administration."[14] Caffery was also beginning to turn increasingly to Batista as the only hope for stability in Cuba, and he dealt with the Colonel on a personal level, accompanying him on horse-back trips to inspect rural outposts, dining with him, and the like. And New Deal trade policies such as the Reciprocity Treaty, while supposedly to aid the Cubans, often worked more to the benefit of American than foreign trade.[15]

Even the short-term economic benefits of expanded sugar quotas proved fleeting, and the economic situation in Cuba continued to deteriorate. An American study group visited the island at about this time, and noted that the recession had created near-famine in various sectors of the country. Thousands were unemployed. This desperation led to growing instability, exploited by the left, and in March, 1935 the island was hit with a huge strike. The ABC and Autenticos turned against Mendieta, while Caffery turned more and more to Batista as the hope for stability. As Ramon E. Ruiz concludes, then, "King Sugar emerged from the crisis [of 1933] a strengthened lord of Cuba." The economic settlements of 1934 institutionalized Cuba's "lopsided economy," which Ruiz summarizes as

> One of the highest export rates in the world, but dependent totally on imports, including food; a high per-capita income for Latin America, in an economy burdened by seasonal and chronic unemployment; a sugar industry that kept the country alive, but survived on American markets and capital; a latifundia in the colonial mold, but heavily mechanized—these were the paradoxes of Cuba.[16]

Eventually the strike was broken, but in the United States and elsewhere, critics began to take Batista to task for rights violations occurring under Mendieta's regime. When a group of Leftist American commentators arrived in July 1935 to assess the situation, they were promptly arrested. Ex-president Grau made his own views known, views sharply critical of Roosevelt's support for Mendieta and, by extension, for Batista.[17]

The 1935 Elections and the Gomez Administration

Mendieta did reiterate his promise that elections would occur in December 1935, and Welles—now an assistant secretary of state—and Caffery declared the U.S. intention to avoid interference in the electoral process.[18] Various parties and groups jockeyed for position in Cuba in a confused political situation, and the government called in Dr. Harold Dodds, President of Princeton University, to make recommendations; he suggested that the elections be put off until January 1936 to allow the political scene to coalesce somewhat. Meanwhile, several opposition groups decided that their chances of winning were slim and pulled out, leaving Jose Miguel Gomez as the uncontested opposition candidate; Mendieta, realizing that he could not possibly win without open graft, resigned, leaving Jose A. Barnet y Vingares in charge of the government until election time. The pro-government candidacy devolved upon Mario Menocal, the former president of Cuba. In a relatively fair election, Gomez won.[19]

The election solved a few problems. The economic situation was still desperate; two observers described Cuba as a "Caribbean powder-keg."[20] Batista's support for the government was uncertain; few doubted that he could subvert Gomez's administration if he so chose. And the basic resentment of the Cuban people toward Batista's role in the government continued.

At first, the political scene seemed quiet enough. But the continued devotion of Cuban political leaders to corruption and personal gain rendered the new government stagnant throughout 1936. Problems regarding U.S. sugar policy, in part caused by New Deal Supreme Court decisions striking down some economic legislation, also hampered the Cuban economy, which slipped further into recession.[21]

Batista meanwhile continued to augment his strength. Increase in military pay and the provision of new military facilities guaranteed that the army would remain loyal to him. He proclaimed his fidelity to Gomez, but his role was as yet uncertain; an emerging split between Gomez and Batista was manifest in a December 1936 controversy over a rural school bill that Batista supported and Gomez opposed. The bill provided for military control of rural education and made additional appropriations for it. Gomez quietly asked the Cuban house to defeat the bill and threatened a veto, but when news of the plan leaked to the public, the popularity of the rural school measure caused a backlash against the president. Suddenly the Cuban public, media and military all seemed firmly behind Batista, and there was talk of impeaching Gomez.[22]

But Gomez did not back down. On December 21, 1936, he vetoed the sugar tax designed to fund the rural school bill. Gomez had already taken other actions that angered Batista—such as dismissing thousands of Cuban army reservists to cut down on government expenditures—and the veto proved to be the last straw.[23] Later that evening Gomez was indicted and impeached by the House, ostensibly for "inertia" and putting undue pressure on the Cuban Congress. On December 24 the Cuban Senate followed suit, and Gomez was out of office.[24]

In the United States, there were some claims that Cuba was now under the rule of a military dictator, but government officials had long favored Batista as a guarantor of stability. When terrorist radicals took over the land of some American companies, for example, Batista put down the small rebellion quickly and quietly, thereby earning the dedication of the U.S. corporate interests. Thus, the impeachment of Gomez was not thought to be a serious blow to U.S. interests. The U.S. role had been ambiguous; Caffery promoted the idea of free elections, but at the same time he once again ignored non-intervention pledges as he meddled in Cuban politics, giving private support to Batista and undertaking other measures designed to promote what he saw as American interests.[25]

The Bru Government

With the impeachment of Gomez, Vice President Federico Laredo Bru was inaugurated as the new president at noon on December 24. FDR quickly granted recognition; Batista pledged support, and Bru in return promised good relations with the army. Batista, however, still controlled the true reins of power; and while he courted U.S. favor and was willing on occasion to protect U.S. companies, he remained a populist at heart. He masterfully maneuvered a number of progressive reforms through the Cuban Congress, against the objections of a number of U.S. corporations. The United States government supported his plans against these complaints.[26]

In 1937, the United States appointed a new ambassador, J. Butler Wright, who continued to emphasize themes of non-intervention and regional cooperation, and returned U.S. relations with Batista too a more official, diplomatic level, in contrast to Caffery's personal favoritism. Though Batista did not follow all of the American suggestions, the Roosevelt administration was becoming increasingly concerned the German threat in Europe and the prospect of another world war. The administration's fear of Fascist influence in the Western Hemisphere led it to scale back its forceful promotion of U.S. business in Cuba in order to keep the favor of the government there.[27]

As the island's economy, tied to the world price of sugar, continued to stagnate, the United States sought to collect on the loans it had granted Cuba in preceding years. Cuban treasury officials, however were incapable of paying such debts as were incurred, for example, in the public works programs of Machado's government, and the result was a long, drawn-out series of negotiations finally resolved in 1940.[28] Batista, meanwhile, traveled to the United States in search of economic aid in 1938, and though he returned to Cuba promising big things, little aid was forthcoming.

The deepening financial crisis prompted a number of prominent Cuban political figures—Grau, Menocal, Gomez and others—to join in the opposition to Batista. 1940 witnessed worsening economic conditions, brought about in part by a 1939 suspension of the sugar quota by a Roosevelt administration under heavy domestic pressure. In 1940, a new ''Supplemental Reciprocity Treaty'' was signed, but the damage had been done.[29]

Despite the fact that the Cuban Communist Party—which had to a great degree evolved into a conservative, bourgeois organization—supported Batista, opposition groups won 41 of 76 seats in a November 1939 constituent assembly election. The stage was being set for the general elections the following year, and despite Cuba's economic problems, the electoral process seemed to have stabilized, though Batista retained firm control. Much of the rampant political violence had ended: Grau's reforms, bolstered by Batista's continuing progressivism, had mostly been institutionalized; and recent elections had been largely free of corruption.

The United States, moreover, made serious efforts to stay out of Cuban politics. Ambassador Wright died and was replaced by George Messersmith. The confused political situation led Messersmith to recommend a stronger U.S. role, but his suggestion was rejected. Welles, in his position at the State Department, declared that the United States would take no position on the election. Batista's representatives pressed U.S. corporations for campaign contributions, but the U.S. Department of State recommended that the companies stay out of the campaign.[30]

As the election approached, however, Batista turned more and more to fraud. Messersmith estimated that Grau would win a fair contest: a U.S. consular official in Cuba warned that Batista "is permitting himself to drift into a position where he will be rightly accused of having thwarted the popular will and in effect of having committed a *coup d'etat.*" Although the Roosevelt administration feared instability if the cruel Batista were to seize power, it nevertheless remained neutral; when Menocal inquired whether he should support Batista or Grau, for example, the administration refused to suggest a course of action.[31]

The elections occurred amid "mild" violence, which for Cuba amounted to 5 killed and 40 wounded. Batista won by a margin of roughly 800,000 to 580,000. Besides some claims of the pro-Grau press—and early indications that Batista was prepared to rig the contest—observers agreed that the elections were generally fair.[32] On October 10, 1940, Batista was inaugurated president of Cuba, and the United States thought that its guarantor of stability was in place.

Nevertheless, the underlying problems of Cuban discontent—income inequality, a monocultural economy disastrously dependent upon sugar exports, dependence on U.S. guidance—had not been solved. Trade agreements with the United States did little to help; the 1934 Reciprocal Trade Agreement, as we have seen, spurred more exports from the United States to Cuba than Cuban exports to America. Between 1933 and 1941, U.S. exports to Cuba rose from $23 Million to $147 million. Mass poverty and unemployment continued to plague Cuba, and the trend, begun earlier, of American influence hampering the development of the Cuban middle class continued. An American observer had concluded in 1931 that "the position of the Cuban *colono* is therefore desperate. . . . He is helpless. . . . his livelihood is dependent upon the patriarchal spirit of the foreign owners of the sugar industry."[34]

BORDERING ON DEMOCRACY: BATISTA AND HIS SUCCESSORS

Batista rapidly proved incapable, despite his reformism, of dealing with these issues. Corruption, by now a staple of Cuban political life, continued. Batista placed old cronies in key posts and graft was rife. Batista himself became rich while in office.[35]

In his efforts to appear as a reasonable civilian president—he refused to be seen in uniform, for example—Batista also alienated the military, which had thought it would enjoy unparalleled influence now that its leader was in office. In January 1941, a number of officers, led by Jose Pedraza, Chief of the Army, attempted a coup; but Batista, in a brilliant and daring move, drove directly to a rebel barracks and confronted the soldiers whom he had led—and protected—for so long. They immediately switched sides, abandoning Pedraza, who was promptly arrested and exiled along with two other coup leaders. For the time being, Batista's military flank was safe.[36]

Negotiations with the United States over economic aid and the dispensation of loans also continued. In December 1941, a second Supplemental Trade Agreement was signed, and in 1942 the Roosevelt administration granted Cuba a $25 million loan—both on the condition that Batista undertake economic reform—but Cuba's sluggish economy would not stir.[37]

The Cuban government also assisted the United States during the Second World War, providing training facilities, regional patrols, and the usual reliable sugar crops. (In fact, certain pro-U.S. mill owners insisted on holding the price down, and not speculating on skyrocketing world markets, to repay the United States for its preferential treatment.) Despite this, new U.S. Ambassador Spruille Braden constantly complained about the Cubans' war effort, and was accused by them of meddling in their politics. But military cooperation between the two countries continued.[38]

On the whole, during this period Batista preserved many of the rudiments of democracy. His rule was bad, but not too bad.[39] Cuban historian Hugh Thomas calls him "the democratic president," and notes that it was also during this period that the Cuban Constitution of 1940 was adopted. The document had flaws, but was nevertheless remarkably progressive on economic rights, guaranteeing an 8-hour day, 44- hour week, unemployment compensation, and many more of the measures referred to earlier.[40] By placing such controversial economic matters directly into the constitution, however, debate was encouraged on the legitimacy of the constitution itself, and because of the reaction against its progressivism, the constitution turned out to be the end, not the beginning, and a new "revolutionary" process.[41]

As the 1944 elections approached, all eyes were focused on Batista to see how well he would respect the democratic process. Once again, the United States remained neutral; so strongly did Braden, "vigorous, tough, forthright to the point of bluntness," press U.S. companies to avoid backing Batista that the latter demanded his recall. Though Batista put up a candidate of his own—Carlos Saladrigas, a conservative lawyer—he disavowed corrupt election tactics. Saladrigas ran against Grau, and the election boiled down to a contest between the Batista-led status quo and the *Autentico* party's promises for reform and honesty. Going into the election, Havana gambling men—basing their opinions largely on Batista's undeniable influence and wealth—cast Saladrigas a 5 or 6 to 1 favorite, but Grau's personal popularity began to narrow the margin, and by the time of largely free elections on June 1, there were rumors that Saladrigas might actually lose. Grau did in fact win, collecting about a million votes to Saladrigas' 840,000.[42]

U.S. Policy Under Truman and Eisenhower

With the death of Franklin Roosevelt and the end of the Second World War, American policy toward Latin America changed subtly. The Truman and early Eisenhower administrations were guided by a number of basic concerns. Latin America and the Caribbean were perceived, in many ways, as the 'soft underbelly' of the United States; and now that the Fascist threat to world peace had given way to a Communist one, American policy concentrated on eliminating Soviet and Chinese influence from the hemisphere.

The Wilson administration's recognition policy also became firmly entrenched with U.S. support for dictatorships throughout the hemisphere. Still ignorant of the disastrous long-term consequences of the policy, U.S. policy-makers threw American support behind brutal regimes; Batista's was one of the least odious of them. American military aid to these governments, which maintained themselves in power largely through force of arms, grew substantially.

American economic interests in the region also grew. U.S. investment in Latin America from 1946 to 1956 expanded by some 30 per cent, and the subsidiaries of U.S. multinationals based in the area grew faster than in any other region. U.S. economic policies toward Latin America and the Caribbean—the Export-Import Bank, the Point IV program, and others—were formulated as much to assist U.S. corporations with investments as to promote regional development.

In short, American policy toward the region during this period was anti-Communism informed by a strong concern for U.S. business interests.[43] It possessed both geo-political and economic motivations, but little sympathy for the people of the region.

The New Grau Regime

Grau came into office riding a wave of popular joy and hope for the future. Batista retired to Miami, and many hoped that the former sergeant's grip on Cuban political life had been broken. The nationalist, progressive Grau was charismatic and very popular, had been the symbol of reform and honesty in Cuban politics for many years, and Cubans expected a virtual new golden age of Cuban life.[44]

Grau would bitterly disappoint these hopes. A crafty, deflecting, man, Grau quickly displayed an inability to confront anyone about anything; he played enemies off one another or bought them off. His government rapidly devolved into one virtually as corrupt as any that had preceded it; perhaps it was a loss of idealism, but whatever triggered Grau's metamorphosis did so in a major and shocking fashion. He turned his presidency into an "orgy of theft,"[45] and "openly flaunted his disregard of constitutional restrictions."[46] He was, in the words of one conservative observer, "the most incompetent and corrupt [president] in Cuban history," and another, Teresa Casuso, wrote that "Grau, in his second term, was one of the very worst presidents we have ever had. He fomented group warfare by setting the student gangs against each other. Corruption spread throughout the island. . . .The country fell into one of its most shameful states in our history."[47] Many believed, however, that Grau himself was honest and that he was merely too weak to control those in his administration who were not.

Immediately, Grau called for good relations with the United States, but his rapid, apparently arbitrary, and sometimes contradictory reforms—replacing military and political leaders at his whim, purging Communists from labor unions, and so on—soon alienated many U.S. officials and Cubans alike. Braden continued cordial relations with Grau, but the latter's ineffectual and scattershot administration obstructed truly constructive U.S.-Cuban relations during this period. H. Bartlett Wells, the second secretary of the American embassy, wrote in September 1947 that

> Power. . . in inexperienced and visionary hands, under a system of governmental machinery insufficiently firm to canalize and mitigate the strong temperamental bias of the leader, has placed Grau's hostility or negativism in a position where, whatever be its cause, it

hobbles the conduct of business between the United States and Cuba.[48]

Other analyses by U.S. officials agreed, making clear that while the United States no longer considered Grau a significant threat, it did not hold much confidence in his ability to rule Cuba. Throughout his administration, the United States would press Grau to settle several outstanding loans and other financial matters, and considered him fiscally irresponsible for not doing so to American satisfaction. R. Henry Norweb, the American ambassador at this time, wrote in a memo to the Department of State in September 1946 that these fiscal problems and other signs of the continuing impotence of Cuban government caused him to worry about the future of Cuba. Grau's personal success, as the symbol of the revolution of 1933, was crucial; Norweb wrote that "the course of our future relations with Cuba will depend greatly on Cuba's own self- conducted experiment in democracy—and inevitably upon the future of sugar." Grau's inefficiency made the success of this process problematic: Norweb concluded in another dispatch that

> My general impression. . . is that President Grau is still fumbling, honestly and idealistically, with the tasks of government, and that despite a natural shrewdness in domestic politics he has little grasp of the long-range forces, economic and social, which are shaping the future of Cuba and the Western World. But even if his administration should decline into corruption, confusion and frustration. . . he would still remain a symbol of the best aspirations of Cuban democracy. Once can only hope that the moral values for which he stands will in time percolate throughout the body politic.

Unfortunately for the United States, Grau did soon decline into corruption and the moral values to which Norweb referred would be denied by a series of corrupt and eventually brutal Cuban governments. They would emerge later, to topple Batista and eliminate American influence in Cuba.[48]

True to these predictions, instability was soon rife. Political gangsterism, pursued by both the far left and the government itself, flourished. Labor disputes and strikes plagued the island, and the growing ascendancy of the Communist labor leadership, against which Grau's attitude—despite the passage of laws—was, the United States claimed, "passive and ineffective," began to worry the United States. Labor excesses "augured ill" for the future of a Cuban industry already crippled by international competition. While sugar prices were resilient enough to prevent a total collapse of the economy, no attempts were made to diversify Cuban crops. The great hopes of reform had suffered severely at the hands of reality.[49]

In 1947, open dissersion broke out within Grau's government. Eduardo Chibas, an emotional and occasionally irrational former student leader and supporter of Grau, broke with the Cuban president over the issue of corruption and started a campaign to "clean up" Cuban politics, taking a broom a his symbol. As the dispute between Chibas and Grau became more heated, Chibas's growing irrationality became more apparent. As Hugh Thomas has noted, he would "often fast, he would invite women to lunch with him and appear at five o'clock, he would remain in the bath under water for long periods, his telephoning of friends was frenetic, hi speeches had more and more the hysteria of madness as much as of genius."[50]

Another election was set for 1948, and as it approached Cuban political parties geared up for the contest. Dr. Carlos Prio Socorras was the candidate of the Autenticos; running against him were the peripatetic Eddie Chibas and his Ortodoxo party, dedicated to cleaning up Cuban politics, and Richardo Nunez Portuondo, Batista's representative. The Communist party also entered, though it was expected to do poorly.

Prio benefited from the work of the government's extensive political machinery, and he won a decisive victory, receiving a plurality in every province of Cuba. Chibas did receive about 12 percent of the vote, an impressive showing for him and he soon charged Prio with stealing the election.[51] Once Prio assumed power, Chibas continued his campaign against government corruption, including election fraud.

Prio for his part proved a well-meaning but corrupt leader. A former leader of the student opposition in the 1930s and a follower of Grau in 1933, Prio possessed seemingly strong liberal credentials, but his administration seriously challenged neither the corruption of the Cuban government nor the basic inequities of Cuban society. Throughout his term, gangsterism and government inefficiency were common, and the economy was only stable because of strong world sugar demand.

Prio did not serve completely without accomplishment. He established a National Bank, began to promote Cuban ownership of domestic industries (a trend that would continue over the next several years), and attempted to account for all government spending, an anti-corruption measure directed by a government agency that worked well up to a point in the government hierarchy, above which its authority was quickly exhausted. He also worked to bring domestic violence under control with measures such as a gun-control law, and succeeded to a certain degree. He was also in many ways a committed democrat, supporting democratic movements in other Latin American Countries and for a time at least allowing Cubans to exercise a wide gamut of personal freedoms.[52]

During Prio's administration, U.S. policy remained for the most part quiet and supportive. A secret U.S. Department of State "Policy Statement" on Cuba concluded in January 1951 that "President Prio's administration has shown a somewhat better disposition that that of his predecessor, President Grau, to work closely with the United States." Such cooperation was made possible by Prio's developed conservatism, in a sense a microcosm of that of the Cuban political system as a whole, which shaped itself to U.S. interests; the new U.S. ambassador, Willard Beavlac, concluded after a discussion with Prio that "he feels very close to the government of the United States. When he was younger he was a radical, but now he has changed. He used to be opposed to American capital, but now he is for it."[53] One aspect of this cooperation was Prio's promise to fight "on the side of the democracies" in any future war, thus firmly committing Cuba to the U.S. side of the Cold War.[54] In return the United States recognized and supported Prio's regime through diplomatic, military and economic means.

One source of continuing friction was Prio's campaign to bring "democracy" to Latin America. Groups of Cuban mercenaries attempted to topple the Trujillo regime in the Dominican Republic, and Trujillo argued that the Cuban government was behind the scheme. Tensions between Cuba and the Dominican Republic would continue into Batista's administration, and the United States expended a good deal of diplomatic energy keeping the two nations from each others' throats. In December 1949 Secretary of State Dean Acheson was forced to threaten U.S. military retaliation against regional adventurism.[55]

The American attitude toward economic issues in Cuba remained unchanged, and as a result little indigenous Cuban development occurred. The United States was trying to get Cuba to sign another inequitable commercial treaty, and the Department of State even attempted to use a provision of the Sugar Act of 1948 (providing for an elimination of the Cuban sugar quota if it did not sign the treaty) to enforce this desire; the attempt failed. A surprisingly revealing statement was made in this secret State policy statement: the department called on Cuba to "improve the climate for foreign capital investments"—as if those investments were not significant enough—and warned that "we shall discourage *whenever possible the creation or expansion of industries in Cuba* the existence of which is dependent on a degree of protection injurious to foreign trade and the interests of the Cuban consumer."[56] Reference to protectionism and the Cuban consumer were just smoke-screens, of course; what was really opposed was the development of any native Cuban industry competitive with American producers. It is hardly surprising that this attitude, enforced with American influence in Cuba, helped limit Cuba's economy to a seasonal sugar monoculture and thus to bring on revolution less than a decade later.

1952: The Return of Batista

In 1952, Prio's term in office was drawing to a close, and new national elections approached. Eduardo Chibas, using his regular radio broadcasts and anti-corruption campaign to good effect, had become enormously popular, and he was the early favorite as the candidate of the Orthodoxo party. Before the election, in fact, as Maria Lazo noted, "it was generally believed that [Chibas] would walk away with the presidency" because of his huge popularity, a function of his regular 8 p.m. radio broadcasts decrying government corruption.[57]

Before the election, however, Chibas accused the Minister of Education, Areliano Sanchez Arango, of improper use of government funds as part of a timber scheme in Guatemala. He also accused President Prio of stashing a huge, embezzled fund in Guatemala. When challenged by Arango to produce evidence of these charges, Chibas turned to Maria Lazo, who, in fact, knew of a secret trip Prio took to Guatemala in a military plane, which was a violation of a constitutionally required permission for such trips from the Cuban Senate.[58]

Before Lazo could get the proof to Chibas, however, the enigmatic Cuban political figure went of radio once again, speaking only in generalities and not mentioning his charge against Prio. Chibas apparently despaired of receiving the evidence. At the close of his broadcast, Chibas said "This is my last plea, I am knocking on the door for the last time, listen." whereupon he shot himself in the stomach. Unfortunately for Chibas, he was already off the air when he shot himself, so the popular effect of his act was muted. There is evidence that Chibas merely wanted to wound himself, but on August 16, 1851, he died.[59]

The Orthodoxo Party nominated Dr. Roberto Agramonte, a professor at the University, as his successor. The Autenticos, for their part— enjoying a significant lead in registered voters over their rivals—nominated Carlos Hevia, the thirty-six hour president of January 1934. And a third party entered the race—Fulgencio Batista, who had decided to return to politics. He was shunned by the established parties, however, and was given little chance of winning. The campaign promised to be controversial.

This election also offered a chance for real progress in establishing an honest, efficient Cuban government. Chibas' anti-graft campaign, and the recent loss suffered by Prio's corrupt brother in the Havana mayoral race, despite huge campaign spending, indicated that the Cuban people were tired of the lack of ethics in government. As Maria Llerena has concluded, "In the decade before 10 March 1952...the preaching of ethics & in public life, primarily in the campaigns and weekly radio broadcasts of Eddy Chibas, was carried to extremes that led to public fanaticism bordering on hysteria." The Autenticos, in response, nominated Carlos Hevia, a "rigid, honest man," according to one Cuban businessman, "tough and no-nonsense." Both major political parties were hence committed to strong, honest, progressive leadership, and had Hevia or Chibas won there is a strong possibility that later events would have unfolded very differently than they did.[60]

On March 10, 1952, however, Batista took matters into his own hands. He initiated a coup— another "barracks revolt"—and proclaimed himself president. Batista used the army to surround and neutralize potential centers of opposition, such as the Autentico and Ortodoxo headquarters. The reins of power in Cuba had once again been seized by an autocrat, and Batista would soon shed whatever reformist, progressive tendencies he had previously displayed. As Ramon Ruiz has concluded, "The Batista of 1952 no longer spoke as the ambivalent politician who accepted the rules of Cuban politics but granted concessions to labor, built schools, and kept the party hacks in check. The restored dictator stepped out of the Machado mold."[61]

THE EARLY YEARS OF THE BATISTA DICTATORSHIP: 1952-1954

The U.S. ambassador to Cuba at this time was Willard Beavlac,[62] and at first he responded slowly to Batista's coup. U.S. officials were understandably leery of this new Latin American strongman, and Ambassador Beavlac made U.S. fears clear in meetings with Cuban officials. Eventually, on March 24, 1952, Secretary of State Acheson recommended to the President that the U.S. establish diplomatic relations with Batista's government, which was done.[63]

The American government soon initiated programs of economic cooperation with Cuba designed to bypass the corrupt Cuban political machine and help develop indigenous Cuban industries. The programs included a joint fiber production project and overall the effort was called the "Point IV" program. Unfortunately, it made little headway.[64]

On July 14, 1953, Ambassador Beavlac sent the Department of State a progress report on the Cuban situation.[65] The "Point IV" program, he noted, was making some small progress, and the United States was supplying Batista with modest amounts of military aid. But Beavlac also noted that Batista had not been able to acquire any significant political support, and that this augured poorly for his future rule.

Batista had, in fact, moved quickly against the Communists whose support he had occasionally enjoyed. In October 1953, he declared the Communist

Party (PSP) illegal, and thus began a running war with Communists and other opposition groups which would gradually emerge as Batista's rule became more brutal. The United States helped with intelligence data from an anti-Communist agency in the Defense Department. It also provided military aid, in amounts rising from $400,000 in 1953 to $1.5 million in 1955 and $3.6 million in 1958.[66]

As with past Cuban leaders, Batista undertook significant public works projects; as usual, the purpose was to create as many government jobs as possible to provide patronage jobs for politically reliable Cubans.[67] The Korean War and the booming world economy kept the price of sugar stable, and the Cuban economy stayed at a decent level. Batista was, however, far lazier than he had been in the past, and seemed to let the Cuban polity drift aimlessly.

Among the population at large, the reaction to Batista's coup was not altogether negative. For the majority of Cubans the key consideration was stability, and Batista promised that. Nor did he immediately impose a harsh military dictatorship: unlike many other Latin American generals-cum- presidents, Batista saw himself as a politician first and a military man second. Although he did impose some new restrictions, Batista was much more likely to buy off his enemies than to shoot them.

At the same time, the urban intellectual opposition to Batista, though fragmented, began to coalesce around certain centers of protest, and it began the campaign of urban violence and terror that would provoke Batista into a repressive response. This in turn would plant the seeds of revolution. As Maria Llerena, a self-described "non-radical intellectual," later noted, immediately after Batista's coup many began to think of revolution, and there was a "mushrooming" of "militant revolutionary organizations." These included the Movimiento Nacional Revolucioinario (MNR), the Movimiento de Liberacion Radical (MLR), the Directorio Revolucionario (DR), and the Federacion Estudiantil Universitaria (FEU), in addition to Castro's own 26 July Movement. Labor and the Communists also turned irrevocably against Batista.[68]

On the whole, however, until the late 1950s, the United States kept the Cuban issue on the back burner. "Secretary of State John Foster Dulles thought Latin America uninteresting,"[69] and few others considered it crucial enough to devote significant effort to it. Most American policy-makers thought of Batista as a reliable, law-and-order leader who brought stability to the country. Gradually, the threat to his rule became apparent; by 1957 many American corporations were paying bribes to the guerrillas, and warned the State Department and the CIA of the rebels' success. Most such reports, however, were ignored until it was too late.

During this time, Havana was a top tourist attraction for American vacationers. Havana was dotted with modern hotels and casinos: under Batista the government helped build 28 new hotels and motels costing some $60 million. On the seamier side, illegal gambling, prostitution, and gangsterism were all relatively common. Police took bribes and even ran their own whorehouses; Errol Flynn called Cuba "a great place to get drunk." In the years leading up to the revolution, Cuba would be visited by tens of thousands of Americans, intent on vacationing and relaxing and only peripherally aware, for the most part, of the upheavals occurring in Cuban politics.[70]

Morris Morley has provided an insightful analysis of the motivations for U.S. policy during the Batista years. An explanation of U. S. actions tied to the perceptions of specific agencies or individuals is insufficient, he argues, to account for the "long-term continuities evident in imperial state policymaking toward Cuba." Rather, it was a combination of non-structural factors—national security considerations, ideology, domestic political and bureaucratic influences—and structural (i.e., economic) ones which produced the continuous U.S. meddling in Cuban politics.[71] Without the long-term economic interests created by U.S. investment, he implies, U.S. policy toward Cuba might have been different, as indeed it was in the early part of the 19th century, before significant U.S. investments in Cuba, when U.S. administrations enunciated a strict "no-transfer" rule but were unwilling to go farther.

The Moncada Incident

On July 26, 1953, the Cuban government was shaken by an assault on the Moncada barracks, led by a little known Cuban lawyer and activist named Fidel Castro. It had been preceded on April 11 by an attack led by Rafael Garcia Barcena, leader of the MNR, on Camp Columbia, which had failed totally, but Castro was not deterred. Castro led a small band of his followers against the Moncada army barracks; the attack failed miserably, and Castro and several of his top aides were captured.[72]

The Cuban government claimed that the attack was a blessing in disguise, as it confirmed the faithfulness of the Cuban military to Batista. Castro had been arrested and, for the time being, the threat embodied in his group had been dampened. Cuban leaders discussed more extensive plans to stop Communist influence.[73]

In October, Castro was placed on trial, and as the master of publicity and speaking that he was, he used the event to best advantage. He delivered his famous "History Will Absolve Me" speech, an hours-long rage against the Batista regime. The speech would later be published, and it added to the growing fame of Fidel Castro. Significantly, it was also relatively moderate, and along with various other restrained pronouncements it convinced many non-radical members of the opposition that Castro could be trusted.

Throughout the middle and late 1950s, debates over the Cuban sugar quota formed a major part of U.S. policy toward the island. Domestic American sugar cane producers and refiners wanted the quota restricted, while the State Department wanted it kept large to promote Cuban growth.[74]

Efforts to arrange a mediated settlement between the government and the opposition, led by such Cuban political figures as Cosme de la Torriente, bore little fruit. A military stalemate produced a situation in which neither side felt compelled to deal. Several of the opposition groups, such as the MLR, nearly disintegrated as a result, however, as accommodationist tactics divided their moderate and radical wings.

The 1954 Elections and After

In January 1953, Dwight D. Eisenhower became President of the United States. His policy toward Cuba would be essentially conservative, with the exception of the late revolutionary period. However, for the most part, Cuba was a minor issue during his administration: middle-level diplomats at the State Department would be responsible for Cuban relations. As we shall see in the next chapter, this led to a highly controversial early policy toward Castro.

For the time being, however, U.S. policy remained friendly to Batista. The new U.S. ambassador, Arthur Gardner, would become known (and despised by many Cubans) as a close friend of Batista, a man more intent on promoting U.S. economic interests than helping to solve the major underlying problems in the Cuban economy. Gardner was also staunchly anti-Communist, and suspicious of such groups as Castro's 26 July Movement. By his own admission, Gardner was the "father" of the Buro de Represion a las Actividades Communistas (BRAC), Batista's sometimes brutal anti-Communist agency.[75]

In October 1953, Batista announced that elections would be held in November of the following year. Grau, despite the objections of some of his supporters who felt he was accommodating himself to Batista, entered the elections and promised to unseat the dictator's regime. Batista himself resigned his post in August 1954 to run a huge and well-financed campaign.

Batista, however, demanded that the government retain control of the local election boards. Grau protested, arguing (rightly) that such a provision would make graft unavoidable and would guarantee a government victory. Batista refused to budge, and Grau pulled out of the election. On November 1, then, Batista was reelected without opposition.[76]

On the Eve of Revolution

The stage was now set for the success of Castro's revolution some four years later. Through 1958, Castro's guerrilla operations, and the terrorist attacks and strikes of the urban opposition, grew. The revolutionaries favored economic targets: transportation and communication lines, sugar crops, and so on. And despite the fact that 1957 was the best year yet for the Cuban economy, by then it was already beginning to feel the effects of this violence. By 1958 Castro's tactics combined with macroeconomic factors to drag the Cuban economy down.[77]

Cuban economic dependence on the United States continued. In 1955-56, 70 per cent of Cuba's imports came from the United States: U.S. interests controlled 40 per cent of Cuban sugar production, 90 per cent of the telephone and electric industries, and 50 per cent of the public railroads. U.S. banks held a quarter of all Cuban deposits.[78] This situation had already hampered the development of a stable Cuban middle-class, and now it helped foster resentment against American influence.

Contrary to what one might expect, moreover, the 1950s combination of economic prosperity and flirtation with elected democracy did not quell the demands of the Cuban middle- and lower-class opposition. In fact, the years before the revolution set the stage for the unrest by providing prosperity that led to rising expectations on the part of the population. When these expectations, of democratic reform and economic progress, were not met, ousting Batista presented itself as one remedy. The Communists had grown stronger under Carlos Rafael Rodriguez, Blas Roca, and Juan Marinello, and the thought of Antonio Guiteras encouraged progressivism and nationalism.[79]

By 1956, however, most analysts were still predicting that Batista would remain in power. Oden Meeker noted that a "diplomatic observer" had told him that "economic factors are not only important in Cuban politics, they might be decisive." The result of the healthy economy, therefore, was that there was "more apathy than disaffection" in Cuba. Barring an economic disaster, Batista would remain in power.[80]

Batista's lack of support and the emergence of significant opposition groups were nevertheless forcing the Cuban dictator to use ever more repressive means of holding power. In May of 1956, Assistant Secretary of State for Inter-American Affairs Henry F. Holland told the Secretary of State that resistance to Batista was growing and that "there is a danger that a resort to stronger measures may consolidate public opinion, which heretofore has been apathetic, against the regime." Especially because of a favorable economic situation, however, Holland, like Meeker, concluded that the Cuban government was secure for the time being.[81]

By October, U.S. Ambassador to Cuba, Arthur Gardner, concluded that the situation had not yet changed. Talk of revolution and insurrection was common, Gardner noted, and former Cuban president Prio was rumored to be active in the United States raising funds for an anti-Batista revolt. Several Cuban opposition groups—including the one led by Fidel Castro, who Gardner called "the Cuban attorney and activist"—had gained strength. But the relatively prosperous economic situation, Gardner concluded, kept the people apathetic.[82]

On November 21, 1956, Frank Pais, a regional 26 July Movement head, started an uprising in Santiago. His was not a random, unplanned act; it was the first step in a carefully coordinator strategy laid down by the Movement's popular and charismatic chief. Fidel Castro and his small band of revolutionaries had been training in Mexico, and now they sailed for Cuba in the overloaded yacht *Granma*, bought with money provided by the former Cuban president Carlos Prio. Batista's men knew Castro was on the way, and when he landed his force was almost immediately attacked by Cuban troops and almost wiped out. Castro and two of his men spent some time lying in a field of sugar cane to avoid capture. Eventually, Castro escaped to the Sierra Maestra mountains with a dozen or so men.[83]

But the big, loquacious Cuban lawyer and revolutionary had not yet begun to fight. For Castro was destined—as he is fond of pointing out—to change history.

PART
THREE

CASTRO'S REVOLUTION

Its Character and Cause

8

THE REVOLUTION

"Thinkers prepare the revolution; bandits carry it out."
Mario Azuela, *The Flies*

"The revolutionist despises and abhors the existing social ethic in all its
manifestations and expressions. For him everything is moral which
assists the triumph of the revolution. . . . All the tender and effeminate
emotions of kinship, friendship, love, gratitude, and every honor
must be stifled in him by a cold and single-handed passion for the revolutionary cause. . . . Night and day he must have but one thought,
one aim: merciless destruction."
Sergei Nechayev, *Catechism of the Revolution*

"In the last analysis, all the truths of Marxism can be summed up in the
sentence: To rebel is justified."
Mao Tse-tung, quoted in the London *Sunday Times,* 1967

Early in 1957, few in Cuba would have predicted an
imminent revolution in that small island nation. Arguably the most prosperous country in Latin American at that time, Cuba had enjoyed solid growth
under Batista's rule; 1957 would be the best year ever, statistically, for the
Cuban economy; and Cuba's powerful labor movement had secured a set of
rights and protection for workers unequalled elsewhere in the hemisphere,

even in the United States. Political repression was bothersome, but not odious. Continuing in the style of past leaders, Batista did not execute or imprison his enemies; he merely bought them off or exiled them.

Yet, shocking almost all observers of the Latin American scene, Cuba soon descended into violence and rebellion. Exactly *why* the revolution occurred is the subject of the next chapter; this present discussion seeks merely to lay out the developments in Cuba and Cuban-American relations from 1958 to 1961. In that short span of time one of the closest, most mutually supportive (or dependent, relative to one's perspective) relationships between two nations would be transformed into one of enmity and indeed open warfare; Cuba arguably went from been America's closest friend to its most dedicated adversary.[1]

REVOLUTION APPROACHES

Arthur Gardner still sat in Havana as ambassador. Gardner was a close personal friend of Batista, and though liked by wealthy, English- speaking Cubans, he was despised by almost everyone else on the island for his favoritism. Even the conservative, anti-Castro opposition had little respect for the U. S. ambassador.[2]

Urban terrorism was again on the rise, and, as predicted by U. S. officials, Batista's repressive measures grew along with actions by rebel groups in the cities and rural areas. Castro and others would later charge Batista with 20,000 killings, and while this figure was significantly inflated, the violence, imposition of martial law, repression of dissent, and undeniably cruel treatment of prisoners did little to endear Batista to the Cuban people. Just as the American analyses had predicted, as Batista was forced to adopt harsher tactics to deal with an increasingly brutal—and successful—rebellion, his support among the Cuban populace and armed forces crumbled.

Economic stagnation also contributed to the insurrection. To what degree the Cuban revolution was an economic, as opposed to social or political, phenomenon is a matter of some dispute, and this issue will be analyzed in depth in the next chapter. And, at first, the economy was not a problem— 1957 was its best year yet. But as rebel attacks and other factors combined to slow the economy in 1958, the primary factor keeping Batista in power— improving living standards—would be lost, and the consensus for revolution would be almost complete.

The stage for the revolution's denouement was set.

The Cuban Opposition

On the eve of Batista's fall, the Cuban opposition counted among its followers members of several different groups. Some of the organizations were offshoots of earlier political parties, others were newer creations. All had the same immediate goal—the overthrow of Batista—though their long-term perspectives diverged significantly.

Castro's own 26 July Movement was named, of course, for the date of his attack on the Moncada barracks in 1953. Castro claimed it to be an offshoot of what he perceived to be an insufficiently radical Ortodoxo party and the 26 July Movement was, at the time of Castro's landing, a largely urban phenomenon carried on by the group which was itself still tiny. Castro's group in 1956 was not its only, nor even its most powerful faction; his revolution in the Sierra was at first merely one of many insurgent activities carried on by the group. Later, Castro would have to beg for supplies from its urban directors.

The other large revolutionary group was the Directorio Revolucionario, or DR. Heir to the radical student and intellectual tradition of the 1920s and 1930s, the DR, was a mostly urban, middle-class group. Its two greatest leaders, Jose Antonio Echevarria and Frank Pais, were killed in 1957-58, and though this did not destroy the DR it did help Fidel Castro emerge as the undisputed leader of the revolution.[3] The DR, along with other revolutionary groups such as the student-based FEU and radical splinters of the Autenticos, hoped that their campaign of urban violence would create general anarchy and a repressive government response that would combine to topple Batista's regime.

The Cuban Communist Party was also functioning, though until 1958 it opposed violent revolution as a "Putschist" tactic and specifically attacked Castro. Led by Carlos Rafael Rodriguez, the Communist had little success, largely because they had become a notably conservative group. In 1945, seven years after purging purist Trotskyite elements, they had even called for more U.S. investment. This caused the party to "lose some of its revolutionary, intellectual and nationalist credentials."[4] In part the party adopted these tactics because of its belief that the Cuban revolution ought to be, in true Marxist fashion, one of the urban proletariat; calls for U.S. investment and opposition to strikes and labor reform were aimed at pushing Cuban workers into absolutely desperate straits and hence creating a "revolutionary condition."

In early 1956, a number of representatives of these groups formed the Dialogo Civico in an attempt to negotiate with Batista and achieve some concessions. The Ortodoxos and other traditional parties participated, but Batista, not yet feeling vulnerable, put off all the Dialogo's demands, saying he would not hold new elections until 1958. At this, Castro and many other radical dissidents formally split from the discredited Ortodoxos. An opportunity for a transition to a progressive Cuban government had been lost, in large part because of Batista's intransigence, in turn a result of strong continued U.S. support.[5]

The Matthews Stories

Until February, 1957, stories of Castro's death were still generally accepted. Rumors from the Sierra Maestras that the rebel leader was still alive were common, but there was no solid proof. But on February 17, 1957, *New York Times* correspondent Herbert Matthews was taken to Castro's stronghold, where he found Fidel alive, in good health, and predicting victory. Matthews wrote a series of stories for the *Times* that exaggerated the strength of Castro's movement (Fidel's brother Raul kept marching the same set of soldiers past Matthews) and firmly established Castro as a national and international hero and the primary threat to Batista.[6]

Matthews himself was an enormously controversial figure, and was often charged with having been used by Castro for the leader's own ends.[7] It is almost undeniably true that Matthews was strong-headed; he penned such claims as "[Castro] took criticism from me that no one else would have dared to utter."[8] His own role as journalist also impressed Matthews; he concluded another book with a good deal of self-righteous drivel about the nobel role of journalists, quoting from Tennyson and Hemingway. Theodore Draper pointed out in a letter to the reporter that Matthews had met Castro only a few times and "dozens of Cubans had infinitely more extensive and more intimate knowledge of him," yet "most of them lack your confidence that they really 'know' him or that he ever made it possible for them to 'know' him truly."[9]

Conservative observers also charge Matthews with a degree of political bias unfitting for a correspondent. He certainly had a history of following leftist movements, in the Spanish Civil War and elsewhere. One Cuban writer—a moderate member of the anti-Batista, anti-Castro opposition—wrote that Matthews was "opinionated to the degree of arrogance, politically naive, a presumed expert on Central America," who "seemed perfectly conditioned for the disastrous role he was about to play, however unwittingly."[10] Matthews has defended his role vehemently, however, and he was certainly adventurous in seeking out Castro.

The impact of the stories is difficult to exaggerate. Castro's legend grew, both in Cuba and internationally. Cubans who had thought of revolution but were discouraged by Castro's apparent death now reconsidered rebellion. And newspaper accounts combined with a number of television stories to establish a firm Castro following in the United States. The Cuban government at first refused to believe Matthews, and argued that he had fabricated the stories, but as more and more journalists traveled to Cuba and met with Fidel, that claim became untenable.

Through March, 1957, Castro's forces made little progress. Only about a half-dozen mountain peasants joined his group through the first several months in the Sierra Maestras, and Castro's actual guerrilla actions were strictly limited. For the time being, the brunt of the revolutionary burden was borne by urban groups such as the DR and the FEU. In April, a National Intelligence Estimate prepared by U. S. intelligence agencies summarized the situation. Batista was not yet in a desperate position, but he was being seriously challenged, especially by the urban opposition. The report referred to Fidel Castro as a "youthful leader of a self-styled reformist, anti-Batista revolutionary group."[11]

In June, Ambassador Gardner was replaced, largely because the Eisenhower administration was continuing to fill ambassadorial posts with its own appointees. Gardner was upset; although had tendered a *pro forma* resignation upon Eisenhower's victory, he did not expect it to be accepted, and now he feared that men in the State Department whom he suspected were pro-Communist would ruin U. S. Cuban policy. He need not have worried, for his replacement—the wildly controversial Earl E. T. Smith—shared his own vehement anti-Communism and violent distrust of Castro and his movement.

The Players

Obviously, Castro and Batista were the primary actors on the Cuban side in the unfolding revolutionary drama. But American policy makers would be just as important in shaping the coming events; indeed, some commentators contend that the U. S. Department of State unilaterally decided the outcome of the revolution. On the American side, the key personalities were all at State: Ambassador Earl Smith, R. Richard Rubottom, and William Wieland.

Smith became a hero of the Right and a bogeyman of the Left. Staunchly anti-Communist, Smith distrusted Castro and other radical opposition leaders and tried to assemble some sort of conservative "third party" government to replace the obviously flagging Batista. Smith himself was not a diplomat; he was a businessman, appointed (as with so many other U. S. ambassadors) as part of the political maneuvering of the president. Prior to leaving for Havana, on the suggestion of William Wieland, Smith was briefed by Matthews, whose recommendations—to dump Batista and back Castro—Smith promptly ignored. This perhaps accounts for Matthews hostile description of Smith, whom he considered unqualified and overly conservative.[12]

Rubottom, assistant secretary of state for inter-American affairs, was a cautious, thoughtful diplomat with little direct knowledge of Cuba. His primary concern was the strong criticism the department had been receiving for its open or tacit support of Latin American dictators. Secretary of State Dulles paid little attention to Cuba; his only real involvement would be the announcement of the arms embargo, and this policy had been virtually dictated from below. To a large degree, Rubottom was where the buck stopped on U. S. Cuban policy, and his overriding priority was to avoid the mistakes and criticisms of the past; that is, to avoid propping up another dictator. Rubottom's personal distaste for dictatorships intensified this feeling.[13]

The State Department's sensitivity to the rights issue was reinforced by the violent reaction in Latin America to Richard Nixon's mid-1958 goodwill tour. Expressing rage at U. S. support for various dictators, crowds chanted anti-American slogans and even stoned and spat upon Nixon's motorcade. A shaken Nixon returned recommending stronger American support for the development of democracy; in this he was joined by the president's brother, Dr. Milton Eisenhower.[14]

William Wieland was an enigmatic figure. Deputy Director of the State Department for middle American affairs (which later became the office of Caribbean and Mexican affairs), Wieland had risen rapidly in the State Department hierarchy. Not a diplomat by training, Wieland nevertheless parlayed a knowledge of Latin American politics into a successful career at State. Some critics later charged that he was unqualified, unprofessional, and had even secured his first job at the department by forging his credentials.[15]

Yet Wieland knew more of Cuba than almost anyone else at State. He had lived there for ten years as a child, spoke fluent Spanish with a Cuban accent, and had studied the island extensively. Recognizing that neither Batista nor Castro would adequately serve U. S. interests, he supported the idea of a "third force," a progressive government that he hoped would come to power through free elections. (However, by November 1958, Wieland accepted the idea that violence might be necessary to rid Cuba of Batista.)[16]

The strong and conflicting views of Smith on one hand, and Rubottom and Wieland on the other, were bound to come into conflict, and the three had been feuding almost from the day Smith arrived in Havana. Smith's main fear was that Castro was a Communist; while recognizing that Raul and Che Guevara might be, however, Rubottom and Wieland thought Castro was a nationalist first, and did not represent as much of a threat as Smith contended. The three also differed in their prescriptions for the "third force"; Smith generally favored anti-Batista army officers, who would take power after Batista or his successor continued in office; the State men talked with many opposition figures and generally preferred less conservative ones. Their assurance about Castro came from statements like the one of Civic Resistance leader Rufo Lopez-Fresquet to John Topping of the U. S. embassy: "Trust us, John, trust us," Lopez-Fresquet pleaded. "If Fidel turns out to be a problem, we politicians and moderates will be able to handle him once we get into office."[17]

Smith was also put on his guard by his old friend and fellow businessman-turned-diplomat Robert Hill, the newly appointed U. S. ambassador to Mexico. Hill said that based on his understanding, Smith was going to Cuba to "preside over the downfall of Batista," that State felt the Cuban dictator had to go.[18] Smith was angered by this report; he had many friends among the conservative, pro-U.S. Cuban business class, and would not look with favor on opposition demands for "social equity."

At one point, this feud became so heated that Smith stopped reporting regularly and completely on developments in Cuba, and State was forced to send CIA Inspector General Lyman Kirkpatrick to Cuba to emphasize the duty of all foreign service officers to report to their superiors. The department also took the extraordinary step of dispatching a U.S. consul, Park Wollam, to Santiago with orders to bypass Smith and report directly to State, a ploy designed to provide an alternate source of information to the unreliable ambassador.[19]

Upon arriving in Havana, Smith announced that he would meet with any group, but quickly made clear his commitment to anti-Communism; the new ambassador's anti-Castro sentiments were reinforced by discussions with some of the rebel leader's former friends, who described him as an "unstable terrorist." Smith did demonstrate his independence from Batista when he condemned an incident of police brutality at a demonstration, an action for which he received praise from the *New York Times*; the new ambassador was as a result immediately faced with the task of patching up relations with an angry Batista.[20]

By the early summer of 1957, Castro had not yet established dominance over the other opposition groups, and Batista was still firmly in control. When the 26 July Movement published its manifesto in July, therefore, it struck a relatively moderate tone. Castro-watchers in the U.S. Department of State and Central Intelligence Agency would use this manifesto and other signals to argue that Castro was a popular nationalist first, and not a Communist. The first Manifesto, called *Nuestra Razon* or "Our Course," was not signed by Castro, as was the later (equally moderate) version, drafted by Fidel in the Sierra and issued without the knowledge of his urban intellectual backers.[21]

Serious cracks in the Batista regime were becoming evident, even though Castro's forces had not engaged in any significant military operations. A September 5 revolt of naval officers at Cienfuegos demonstrated that support for Batista in the armed forces was crumbling; the second-ranking CIA man at the U.S. embassy may have contributed to the uprising by unintentionally implying to Cuban military personnel that the United States would recognize them if they overthrew Batista. Street violence, economic stagnation, and other signs of a declining regime were also in evidence.[22]

In the middle of September, Ambassador Smith provided several reports to the Department of State on the conditions in Cuba.[23] Smith noted that the United States was being criticized by some in Cuba for supplying arms to Batista, and recommended restraint and caution in the provision of arms under the Military Assistance Program, or MAP. At the same time, he warned that Castro was growing stronger, and that the Batista regime had displayed a total inability to stop the rebels. Smith's obsession with Castro's Communism was becoming clear; he recommended placing operatives in Castro's movement to determine, if possible, its ideological positions.

Policy Differences at State

Over the next several months, American support for Batista crumbled. There is little doubt that the officers at the Department of State responsible for Cuban policy—primarily Wieland and Rubottom—desired this; they openly advocated a policy designed to bring Batista down. These officials were not pro-Castro by any means, but they felt that continued American support for the Cuban dictator was a doomed policy. Smith, on the other hand, favored continued relations with Batista until a clear, stable alternative was discovered. These differences established the context for battles over U.S. Cuban policy within the State Department over the next several months.[24]

The opening salvos of this policy war were fired on September 23, when the State Department formally began its gradual withdrawal of support for Batista by deferring the sale of tanks to the Cuban army on the grounds of the bad publicity such a sale would produce. Rubottom personally ordered the deferral, and on September, 19 he had informed the Cuban Ambassador of his decision and the concurrence of the Department of Defense. On September 23, Smith met with Batista and explained the American rationale for the action.[25]

In December, 1957, as State's dissatisfaction with Batista grew, Smith and Wieland each wrote a set of policy recommendations for the United States in its relations with Cuba. They outlined the divergent positions the two men would take over the coming months as the debate over proper Cuban policy heated up within the State Department.

Smith's position was basically that Batista must go, but that Castro or those like him would be at least as bad, so the United States should work to assemble some sort of third- party government. Batista's brutality, the ambassador argued, was exacerbating the rebellion. Open, honest elections and a restoration of constitutional guarantees, leading to a stable democratic process, were necessary to quell the revolt, he believed. To this end, he recommended U.S. encouragement of a compromise between Batista and the opposition that might allow for an independent, interim government as a prelude to elections.[26] Smith's great fear was that if Batista fell without the provision of a U.S.-backed third force, Castro and his radicals would undoubtedly fill the power vacuum and seize control. Forestalling this outcome was Smith's obsession.

Wieland sent a memo to Rubottom on exactly the same subject about two weeks later. Wieland divided U.S. policy into four "phases." The first two involved U.S. pressure on Batista to hold elections and continued arms sales and aid to the Cuban regime, but in a cautious manner; and a gradual transition to a "favorable electoral climate" in which Batista would negotiate with the opposition and other independent groups. To that point, Wieland's proposals mirrored Smith's.

The differences emerged when Wieland discussed the options to be pursued in case his first two phases failed. Phase three would only be necessary if the "militant opposition remained intransigent" even after the offers of phases one and two, in which case the United States would step up support for Batista and press for elections even in the absence of opposition participation. Phase four, on the other hand, would be required if Batista would not cooperate, and it involved "taking action short of intervention designed to hasten the fall of the Batista regime" while encouraging a "responsible" opposition to fill the void. Wieland singled out termination of arms sales and a withdrawal of military missions as two such actions which could be justified by arguing that the Cubans were using MAP weapons for internal security; officially, weapons provided by this program were only to be used for "Hemispheric defense."[27]

In fact, this latter proposal would quickly become official Department of State policy. Within a month, Wieland had arrived in Havana bearing a paper arguing that the Cuban economy was on the verge of collapse and that the United States ought to hasten Batista's fall. Smith argued vehemently against this course; he felt so strongly that he paid his own way to Washington to make his case. It was in Washington that Smith made his famous remark that the United States "probably could not do business with" a Castro regime. Despite his protestations, the policy was adopted, though not of course publicly.[28]

It was implemented slowly, however, and its initial stages called merely for stepped-up pressure on Batista to restore constitutional guarantees. The Department still held out some hope that Batista would hold new, fair elections, for example, and it authorized Smith to offer Batista a shipment of armored cars if he would lift martial law. Against the objections of many conservative Cubans, Batista agreed, on the condition that the United States take action against Prio, who had ignored Wieland's warning and was still aiding the rebellion. The State Department acceded, and on January 25, 1958, Batista lifted the martial law regulations. State, however, failed to keep the primary component of its end of the bargain; the armored cars were never delivered.[29]

Even at this point, Wieland still favored keeping Batista until a third-party government could be assembled, though he believed this could be accomplished much more quickly than did Smith. Wieland's anti-Castro sentiments were reflected in comments to a reporter:

> I know Batista is considered by many as a son of a bitch. . . but American interests come first. . .at least he is our son of a bitch, he is not playing ball with the Communists. . . .On the other hand, Fidel Castro is surrounded by commies. I don't know whether he is himself a Communist. . . [but] I am certain he is subject to Communist influences.[30]

Wieland feared that unless Batista shaped up, it would become impossible to stop the revolution, and he and State used such tactics as withholding the armored cars to encourage Batista to democratize Cuba.

In February, 1958, though, as promised, various federal agencies did go after Prio. On February 13, he was indicted of Neutrality Act violations, another sign that State, while anti-Batista, was definitely not pro-Castro. Prio was released on bail, however, and some anti-Castro analysts argued afterward that the administration could have done much more to stem the supplies. In fact, he was only fined a few thousand dollars. But Wieland and Rubottom certainly did not harbor any secret hopes of indirectly assisting Castro by freeing Prio.[31]

That same month, Smith, sensing that Castro's strength was at a low ebb, pressed hard for a third-party government to take power before the scheduled 1958 elections. Some groups in Cuba supported similar solutions; a number of Cuban bishops, for example, in February, 1958, proposed a cease-fire and provisions for a new government, and later a "Joint Committee of Civic Institutions" suggested a similar plan. The Department of State, however, would not officially support these plans; it would no longer sanction the sort of political meddling practiced by Sumner Welles and others. It also feared that Ambassador Smith would undercut such efforts by being less than completely forthcoming in his attempts to pressure Batista. And Batista, still not desperate, resisted all these attempts to oust him from power.[32]

U.S. strategy toward Cuba during this period betrayed significant confusion. Many policy-makers agreed that Batista must be removed, but nearly everyone knew that Castro would be worse. Should the United States attempt to create a new Cuban government? Who would constitute it? That course was a risky one, too, as the events of 1933 had demonstrated. In essence the

United States was caught in a trap of its own making; Batista had been Washington's man in Havana for some time, and now that he was no longer acceptable, U.S. officials cast about for a suitable replacement.[33]

The Arms Cut

By March, pressure on the Eisenhower Administration to sever ties with the "brutal" Batista regime was growing. Some Congressmen, especially Rep. Adam Clayton Powell, denounced U.S. support for the dictator and called for an end to miliary aid. Mario Llerena, a Cuban active in the opposition, provided Powell with classified data on the military aid program that an employee of the Cuban embassy in Washington had acquired; Powell used the information in speeches on the House floor. Senator Wayne Morse referred to the Batista government as a "fascist dictatorship."[34]

The situation in Cuba was also growing more tense. One of the rebel groups attempted to assassinate Batista, and came close. Urban violence and attacks by Castro's group, among others, became even more commonplace. The campaign in the hills expanded rapidly.[35]

Finally, later in the month, the U.S. Department of State halted a shipment of Garand rifles intended for Cuba. This was done partly on Wieland's recommendation. On March 14, 1958, Secretary of State John Foster Dulles announced a total arms embargo, and apart from a few small deliveries of equipment that had already been paid for, the United States provided no more arms to the Batista government thereafter.[36] The Department of State also discouraged other suppliers of weapons, in Europe and elsewhere, to whom Batista turned.[37]

Opinions differ as to the effectiveness of this embargo. Earl Smith saw it as the key act in bringing the Batista government down, since Cuban and American businessmen alike began to lose confidence in the U.S. commitment to Batista. Certainly, however, the act did not cripple Batista's military; he still had plenty of guns, and despite some American efforts, he managed (with Earl Smith's help) to acquire more. Wayne Smith, a low-level embassy official at the time, has argued in fact that the effect of the embargo was "more psychological than substantive," and that it did not convince anyone that the United States was about to abandon Batista. Whatever the case, while the embargo was not necessarily the final straw in the revolutionary process, it certainly contributed to Batista's gradual loss of legitimacy.[38]

Earl Smith was nevertheless instructed to inform Batista that "there was no change in [the] basic attitude" of the United States toward the Cuban government. State argued that it was still ready to do business with Batista, but insisted on relaxation of the repression that made continued military assistance impossible from an American political standpoint. The United States also left its military mission in Cuba to train Batista's troops and the continued presence of American reviewing officers at Cuban military school graduations lent credence to State's claim that the United States continued to support Batista.[39]

As Wieland's memo had predicted, however, the Department of State, increasingly convinced that Batista was unwilling to compromise, refused further arms sales on the grounds that past weapons shipments had been used improperly. The military aid program was legally to be used for "Hemispheric defense," a requirement that allowed the United States to wash its hands of the domestic affairs of the recipients of its aid. The hemispheric defense provision was seldom enforced, but now State claimed Batista was using his aid to fight his internal war. This policy seriously damaged the morale of the Cuban army, which could no longer count on a steady supply of equipment.[40]

Meanwhile, the war continued. Castro's forces sabotaged many economic targets: transportation and communication lines, sugar combines, and the like. Corrupt soldiers in the Cuban army used their helicopters to meet Castro representatives in the mountains and to sell them guns. The CIA, meanwhile, spied on Castro through the use of journalists who traversed the Sierra Maestras.

In April, the opposition called a general strike that, while not completely effective, nevertheless helped hasten the decline of the Cuban economy. Castro also began attacking the water sources for the American naval base at Guantanamo Bay, but after numerous complaints from the Department of State he ended the attacks.[41]

Later, Smith succeeded in persuading Deputy Assistant Secretary of State for Latin American Affairs William Snow to overrule Wieland and order the delivery of several training planes Batista had already ordered. The planes, however, never arrived; Raul Castro had begun kidnapping American citizens and military personnel, and the Department of State claimed delivery of the planes might endanger the captives' lives. Even after the captives were released (at the urging of State, whose sensibilities the Castros did not want to offend) the planes were not provided.[42] (So well-treated were the captives, moreover, and so persuasive were the ideological arguments made by their captors, that a few of the American military men that had been taken hostage wanted to stay and fight Batista.[43])

Elections Approach

Batista delayed elections originally scheduled for June, 1958, until November, ostensibly because of continuing violence. The constitution of 1940 forbade Batista to hold two consecutive terms, and he agreed to step down in favor of the winner of the election. The top candidates were Grau, Dr. Carlos Marquez Sterling, and Dr. Andres Rivero Aguero, the latter being the government candidate. The campaign continued from the summer through October.

A measure of how important American backing for Batista remained was provided just before the elections. Cuban labor, which had backed Batista's candidate, was ready to withdraw its support of the United States was planning to drop its support for Batista. Ambassador Smith assured them that the United States had no such plans—a slightly disingenuous claim in light of what he knew of the State's intentions—and labor committed to Aguero.[44]

The State Department was pinning its hopes for Cuban stability on these elections. State, and Ambassador Smith, had for various reasons opposed most of the specific schemes so far floated to establish a third-party government; now both looked to the elections as a legitimate way to achieve the same end. Their desire was that the election would produce a suitable government, one bridging the gap between Batista and Castro.[45]

These hopes were quickly dashed; to the surprise of some observers, Aguero won. The opposition immediately charged fraud and refused to abide by the results; Castro, for his part, declared Revolutionary Law No. 2, calling for death to all candidates that had participated in the election. Some were indeed killed. Even Smith was disappointed with the results,[46] though he quickly began pressing for U.S. support if Aguero on the condition that the new president promise elections within a certain time.

Batista, meanwhile, remained adamant, rebuffing U.S. and opposition plans for a third party government. He refused to relinquish the presidency until it legally expired in February, 1959. He also demanded that Aguero take office as scheduled, and put off any discussion of new elections. The decision as to who would rule Cuba, however, would shortly be taken from his hands.

The End: November and December, 1958

At once, there were signs of trouble for Aguero. The United States refused to announce support for his upcoming administration, even after Smith recommended it; Rubottom and Wieland concurred that no good could come of such a move.[47] The economic situation in Cuba was deteriorating rapidly, particularly because of the attacks by Castro's bands of marauders. The Cuban army's will to fight had been all but exhausted.

The most crushing blow to the army came in the summer of 1958. It planned a summer offensive against Castro in the Sierra Maestras, using 14 battalions of infantry and other supporting ground, air, and naval forces—

some 12,000 men in all—confronting only about 300 guerrillas. On June 28, the first Cuban troops set off into the mountains. In a series of running battles over the next weeks, Castro's men—organized and in many instances led by Che Guevara, familiar with the terrain, and enjoying excellent communications—defeated an unprofessional, poorly led, and unmotivated army. Confidence among Cubans in Castro's chances of victory soared, and the army's material and moral collapse continued.[48]

At the same time, rumors of a U.S.-supported coup seeped out of Havana. A number of Cuban officers were caught plotting against Batista (who maintained effective control), and they claimed John Topping, the chief political officer at the embassy, had given them encouragement. Topping denied this to Smith, and there is good reason to believe he was telling the truth. But, like the supposed complicity of a CIA man in an earlier coup, even the suspicion of such activities now confirmed in the minds of many—especially Batista— that the United States had indeed turned against the Cuban leader.[49]

Meanwhile, the rift between Smith and State grew. Smith's anti-Communism became a running joke at the embassy, where relations between the ambassador and some of his staff were strained; Wayne Smith described the atmosphere there as "poisonous." Staff meetings were peppered with Ambassador Smith's demands to know what information State or CIA had about Communist influence in the 26 July Movement. The answer was always the same. There were Communists in the movement, including perhaps Raul Castro and Che Guevara; but it was not "Communist-dominated."[50] Smith's perspective was not clarified by the fact that he received most of his domestic information from Prime Minister Guell, other top government officials, and Cuban businessmen.

It was in this atmosphere that Ambassador William Pawley was sent to Cuba in a last-ditch attempt to form a third-party government. On his own initiative, Pawley, who knew Eisenhower, went directly to the president with a request to be allowed to go to Cuba and speak with Batista. He hoped to convince the Cuban leader to accept some sort of compromise that would bring a new government to power. Like Smith, Pawley was concerned that U.S. policy was undercutting Batista and providing the context for a Castroite— and hence Communist—takeover, and he wanted to forestall such a development. Eisenhower approved the idea and told Pawley to speak as his personal representative. Undersecretary of State Christian Herter, however, was uncomfortable with this arrangement and ordered Pawley to go merely as a private citizen; he was no longer authorized to speak for the president.[51] The proposal he bore called for Batista to step down in favor of an interim military junta of anti-Batista officers, who would take power until free elections could be held.

On Thanksgiving Day, Mario Lazo, a prominent Cuban lawyer, received word of Pawley's trip from sources in Washington. Knowing that the American ambassador had not yet been told, Lazo informed Smith of the plan. Smith was surprised, but not unhappy; Pawley was sternly anti-Communist, distrustful of Wieland and Rubottom, and favored exactly the sort of settlement Smith had been seeking.[52]

Pawley, however, made little headway with Batista. In his initial meeting with Prime Minister Guell, Pawley implied that he spoke for Eisenhower, and it was perhaps for this reason alone that Batista even saw him. But in his actual three-hour meeting with the Cuban president, Pawley reverted to this instructions and spoke only for himself. Both Batista and Pawley later said that the formula would have been accepted had Pawley been able to speak officially for Eisenhower,[53] but it should be borne in mind that they would have other motivations for saying this besides actually believing it. In any case, Batista rejected the plan.

The United States Withdraws Support

Ambassador Smith continued to hamper the full implementation of State's anti-Batista policy. In November, he had received Dispatch Number 292, which ordered him to inform the Cuban government that the United States would only support Aguero if he obtained widespread support from the Cuban population. It also emphasized that Batista's departure from the country was, in the U.S. view, a precondition for any other efforts to resolve the situation. But Smith made none of this known; in fact he congratulated Aguero on his victory. Not until Daniel Braddock of the U.S. embassy met with Prime Minister Guell and personally emphasized the dispatch's conclusions did the Cuban government receive some inkling of the current of thought in Washington.[54]

By mid-December, the State Department had completely given up on Batista. On the 14th, Smith received instructions from Rubottom to "disabuse" Batista of any ideas that the United States might recognize Aguero. Batista remained committed to Aguero, suggesting that the latter could hold free elections within two years. Smith requested U.S. support for such a plan, but State rejected it; in fact Smith was told at about the same time officially to inform the Cuban president that the United States no longer supported Batista's rule and hoped that he would resign. Smith accordingly told Cuban Foreign Minister Guell that it was his "unpleasant duty" to inform the Cubans that "the United States will no longer support the present government of Cuba and that my government believes that the President is losing effective control." On December 17, Smith relayed this message directly to Batista.[55]

Batista, quiet and calm to the end, asked if he could move to Daytona Beach with his family. Smith recommended that he stay in a neutral country, such as Spain, for at least one year before returning to the United States. The two spoke of plans for an interim government.

On December 23, Wieland provided details of these developments to Undersecretary Herter, who briefed Eisenhower later that day. It was the first time in a long while that the president had become involved in Cuban policy, and he was shocked by the situation there; he had apparently not been aware Batista's regime was in such desperate straits. Herter's memo was anti-Batista *and* anti-Castro; it stated that "the Department clearly does not want to see Castro succeed to the leadership of the Government [in Cuba]." Eisenhower approved a last, hasty search for a third-party government.[56]

With this and other motivations, a few final plans for provision of an independent government were pursued during the last days of the Batista regime. Wieland spoke with Tony Varona, a former prime minister of Cuba under Prio; Guell suggested that Batista's position had softened, that he would direct Aguero to hold elections within four months of assuming office. Smith reported this latter offer to State and once again requested support for Aguero; and once again he was turned down. In fact, on December 31 all argument on the matter was put to rest by a telegram from Robert Murphy, a top deputy undersecretary of state whose rank was high enough to grant him the last word: the United States would provide no aid to Aguero, he cabled Smith, and that was that. But it was all too little and too late. The revolution was moving too quickly to be stopped, and, unlike 1933, the Cuban people were not disposed to allow their rebellion to be co-opted at the last moment by American meddling.[57] In any case, it is probable that Fidel Castro would have won any truly fair elections at that point.[58]

Batista knew the writing was on the wall. The United States had deserted him, his army was crumbling, the opposition grew stronger every day. At the end of December, rumors flew as the Batista family and many of the president's closest friends requested updated visas from the American embassy. On January 1, 1959, he and his entourage boarded a plane waiting at the Havana airport and fled to the Dominican Republic, which, incidentally, did not expect him and was very surprised when the Cuban leader turned up at the airport. General Eulogio Cantillo was left to preside over what proved to be the last few hours of the Batista government.

Havana and other cities exploded at the news that Batista was gone and that the civil war was over. Symbols of corruption—parking meters, for example, and casinos—were destroyed or sacked. And many leaders of Batista's government and security forces who were unable to flee would meet their deaths at the hands of "revolutionary justice."

Fidel Castro immediately called a strike and moved to fill the power vacuum left by Batista. Nothing stood in his way, least of all the United States; on January 4, Wieland called Smith to Washington "because the State Department wanted to recognize the Fidel Castro government as soon as possible."[59]

Castro had been consolidating this power for some time, and now he began to dismantle the institutional structures, such as they were, of the 26 July Movement and the DR; his rebel army became the true repository of power. He forbade the DR from taking part in the victory march into Havana. During the revolution, he had prepared for the eventual victory by selecting regional guerrilla commanders strategically; he sent his brother Raul, for example, to establish a "second front." Significantly, many of these commanders were Communists. In January, 1959, however, Castro painted the revolution in moderate tones with the appointment of the non-radical Manuel Urrutia as president, the downright conservative Jose Miro Cardona as prime minister, and a collection of respected, moderate technocrats as the first cabinet.[60]

These machinations were still unknown to the average Cuban, who was merely happy that the bloodshed and the repression had ended. Marching into Havana, the revolutionary army was greeted by huge crowds. Fidel and his top commandantes arrived at Camp Colombia, which had been seized from the army; thousands of delirious Cubans surged toward the *leder maximo*, a tall, heroic, almost god-like figure. A path was cleared and Fidel strode confidently up to the platform; and as he gave his impassioned victory speech, a dove alighted upon his shoulder. It seemed that even the heavens had stopped to bless this revolution.

THE CASTRO REGIME AND PHILIP BONSAL: THE U.S. TRIES A SOFT LINE

On January 6, the Department of State proclaimed U.S. "good-will" and recognized the Castro government; the United States was the first government to do so. On January 7, Smith delivered the note of recognition to the officers of the new Cuban government in Washington.[61] The Soviet Union did not recognize Castro until the 10th, and it was not until a month later that its first official representative arrived in Havana, and he was merely a *Tass* correspondent. Diplomatic relations were not formally reestablished until May, 1960.[62]

The Department of State wished to follow an accommodating, friendly policy toward Castro, even though wary of him, and this meant first and foremost that Earl Smith must no longer be ambassador. He had already made

247

clear that he did not think the United States could "do business" with Castro. On January 19, he resigned and was replaced with Philip Bonsal.

Bonsal had clearly been appointed to signal a soft-line U.S. approach; in his past service in Bolivia, he had been noted for his sympathy for the left, and he defined his early policy as "benevolent, if nervous, watchfulness." He presided over an attempt by the State Department to establish cordial and regular relations with Castro. Yet Bonsal, who in 1952 as ambassador to Bolivia had succeeded in slowing the revolution of Paz Estensarro, was also sent to demonstrate the U.S. hope that Castro's policies would prove equally moderate in practice. As Smith had recognized, however, this policy was doomed to fail; it was indeed going to prove impossible for the United States to deal with Fidel Castro.[63]

Castro's Early Radicalization

Over the next several months Castro's hostility toward the United States grew. Though economic requirements and other pragmatic considerations might have recommended that he pursue an accommodation, Castro, for reasons that will be discussed, felt unable to maintain amicable relations. As the diplomatic storm brewed, Philip Bonsal's "benevolent watchfulness" proved impotent.

Carlos Franqui, a leader of the 26 July Movement and later editor of the newspaper *Revolucion*, has ably summarized the situation in Cuba at the time. Four centers of power had emerged from the revolution: the 26 July Movement and other radical groups of the bourgeoisie, whose urban leaders included David Salvador, Faustino Perez, and Franqui; democratic liberals— Raul Chibas, Huber Matos, and others—who were basically urban, middle-class moderates; conservative, pro-U.S. landowners; and pro-Soviet Marxist-Leninists, including Raul and Che. "So," Franqui concludes, "there were four major currents struggling for control of the nation. One was radically anti-imperalist, one was democratic-reformist, one was conservative and pro-U.S., and one was Marxist and pro-Soviet Union."[64] Castro moved quickly to resolve this situation by arrogating control of the revolution to himself.

Into this vortex plunged Philip Bonsal. Few observers have praised his work. Conservatives condemned him for lacking "forcefulness" and for pursuing a weak, fawning policy that misunderstood Castro.[65] Liberals such as Herbert Matthews argued that even though Bonsal might have meant well at first, he did not understand the revolution, and eventually he and the State Department, frustrated and angry, turned against it.[66] Most agree that Bonsal's quiet, official, precise, orderly manner was totally unsuited to dealing with the *barbudos*, the unorthodox "bearded ones" who led the new Cuban government.[67]

In any event, Bonsal pressed on, though to little avail. A March, 1959, meeting with Castro was cordial, but American offers of economic assistance were rebuffed. Castro also started rounding up and shooting *Batistianos*, and even by January, 1959, he had begun to rail against U.S. imperialism. In response to this, the United States in February pulled out its military missions; Castro in turn stepped up his rhetorical attacks against U.S. policy.[68] On March 4, 1959, the first nationalization of American property occurred; Castro's government seized the Cuban Telephone Company. This began a long process of nationalizations in which Castro would take the proper of American companies without reimbursing them. Cuban officials also harassed American citizens.

Until the middle of March, however, Eisenhower, following the recommendations of the State Department, tried to maintain cordial relations. He applauded the selection of the moderate Ernesto Dihigo y Lopez as Cuban ambassador to the United States. He expressed sympathy for the Cubans, and made more offers of aid. Bonsal, in Havana, followed a similar line, arguing that a hard-line approach would only drive Castro further into the Communist camp. It was still not certain, after all, that Castro was actually a Communist; in fact CIA chief Allen Dulles in January testified before a secret session of the Senate Foreign Relations Committee that Castro had no Communist leanings.[69]

By late March, however, Eisenhower began to lose patience. A CIA report noted that the Castro regime was moving further toward a dictatorship, with executions of *Batistianos* common and severe press and speech restrictions in effect. American business interests had also begun to exert pressure on the administration to moderate Castro's behavior. Eisenhower's statements reveal that he simply did not understand the virulent anti-Yankeeism of the Cuban psyche, molded by Jose Marti and others and brought to fruition in the long series of corrupt, U.S.-supported Cuban dictators; in fact at one point Eisenhower said Cuba's whole history "would seem to make it a puzzling matter to figure out just exactly why the Cubans and the Cuban government would be so unhappy" when the United States, their principle market, had treated them so well. "You would think," the president concluded, "they would want good relationships. I don't know exactly what the difficulty is."[70]

The April Visit

In April, 1959, at the invitation of the National Press Club, Castro visited the United States for the first time since assuming power. Charismatic and enigmatic, the Cuban leader made a favorable impression on the U.S. press.

Rubottom, on behalf of the State Department, offered to "help" Castro with his "economic plans," but Castro did not accept. In fact, Castro actually prevented his economic staff from meeting with American officials.[71]

Eisenhower, who did not wish to give Castro an implicit presidential stamp of approval, did not meet with the Cuban, but instead sent Vice President Nixon. Nixon was not enamored of Castro, and in fact was somewhat disturbed by the meeting. He wrote a memo warning of the dangers Castro posed, of which he said later: "I stated flatly that I was convinced Castro was either 'incredibly naive about Communism or under Communist discipline' and that we should treat him and deal with him accordingly."[72] Nixon's personal distrust of Castro strongly influenced his Cuba policy when he was himself president.

Meanwhile, Castro continued confiscating U.S. property. In May, he accelerated this trend with the radical Agrarian Reform Law, providing for the seizure of property and industry by the government and establishing a maximum land ownership level. It also provided for payments for the expropriated land (though these were in many cases never made) and created the Institute of Agrarian Reform (INRA), which would manage the coming economic revolution in Cuba.[73] Five moderate ministers resigned from the Cuban government in protest.

U.S. reactions to these seizures reflected the Department of State's concern at the leftward tilt of Castro's revolution. At first, as Philip Bonsal notes, the U.S. reply was "friendly and understanding."[74] Later, however, as the seizures expanded and Americans went uncompensated, U.S. ire was raised. Lowry Nelson concludes that here began "the verbal exchanges between the United States and Cuba that wold eventually end diplomatic relations."[75]

By June, Castro had begun fomenting revolutions throughout the region. Panama, the Dominican Republic, Nicaragua, and Haiti felt repercussions from the Cuban revolution. All were bloody failures, however, and these seemed to chasten Castro, to make him recognize that not all nations in Latin America were ready for the same sort of rebellion that was remaking the Cuban polity. His future adventures would be more measured.

On June 11, the United States, growing increasingly tired of Castro's seizures of property, made its official response to the Agrarian Reform Law by expressing "concern" over the lack of compensation for U.S. companies.[76] This was certainly a mild protest, but it was one of the first signals that the United States was losing tolerance for Castro. As such it has evoked the criticism that it came too soon, that the U.S. Government did not show enough understanding for Castro's situation. Castro's reaction was certainly violent, and he took the note as a provocation; after this time he held little trust even for the understanding Bonsal.[77]

Throughout the early summer Castro continued his process of radicalization. The National Bank of Cuba tried to rob Americans by collecting U.S. checks that Castro's people had stolen from the mails. Castro's revolutionary adventurism elsewhere in Latin America continued. On July 16, he ousted President Urrutia, whom Castro considered too moderate and whose appointment, along with that of Miro Cardona, had been largely for show. To achieve this end Castro resigned his own post in government and gave a speech opposing Urrutia; the resulting public outcry forced the latter to resign, and Castro was later appointed premier. Opposition to Castro among moderates increased markedly.[78]

By the end of the summer, Bonsal was no longer certain that Castro could be moderated. The Agrarian Reform Law had become a confiscation decree, and Castro brushed aside all outside criticism from the United States, the Organization of American States (OAS), or elsewhere. As summer moved into fall, Bonsal was caught in a difficult position, with Washington demanding that Castro moderate, and Castro responding violently to any American "intervention."[79]

In September 1959, the last signs of moderation emerged from Castro's government. Castro and his officials began to speak of some traditional economic ideas and development strategies. The State Department remained flexible and optimistic, and relations between the two countries seemed salvageable; Bonsal was even cheered at a Cuban baseball game.

By October, however, Castro had extinguished this brief glimmer of hope with a new set of radical measures. He increased duties on U.S. products by 30 to 100 percent, began to seize the assets of U.S. oil companies, and continued harassing Americans and nationalizing their industries. The United States responded by blocking the sale of British aircraft to Cuba, and by protesting the seizures. On November 5, Christian Herter of State made the first suggestion of the formation of an anti-Castro effort; four days later, Eisenhower approved the idea. In December Allen Dulles at CIA accepted a similar proposal, one that included suggestions of attempts to assassinate Castro. Even as it explicitly continued negotiations with the Cuban government, The United States' secret war against Castro had begun.[80]

The rupture in relations was complete by the end of October, fueled by a number of specific occurrences. Castro began a purge of moderate leaders, including Huber Matos, a popular former guerrilla commander who was arrested with 40 of his men on charges of treason. On October 21, Captain Pedro Diaz-Lanz, a Cuban defector, flew over Havana in a light plane and dropped leaflets opposing Castro's government, and a number of Cubans were killed when anti-aircraft fire fell on the city. Castro charged that Diaz had actually bombed the city on instructions from the United States; Bonsal, still trying to maintain an understanding tone, denied the accusation but expressed "sympathy" over the deaths. The appointment of Che Guevara to head the Cuban National Bank was another signal of radicalization.[81]

Castro's reforms centered on land redistribution and provision of better living standards for lower-class Cubans. Land holdings over 403 hectares and any small plots under 65 hectares were subject to confiscation. A redirection of crops, ostensibly away from the sugar monoculture, was begun but never consummated. Cooperatives were formed: 20 by July, 1959, and by May, 1960 they employed over 50,000 people. In December, 1960, the cooperatives were consolidated into *granjas del pueblo* (people's farms); later problems would scuttle these first steps toward cooperativization of agriculture.[82] Throughout, Castro's agricultural managers were hampered by a lack of technical expertise and equipment.

They were also blocked by the very people they were supposed to be helping. Cuban peasants, angered by the inefficiency of Castro's management and now by his increasing intolerance, began to rise up in sporadic insurrections. Small landowners also had no desire to give up portions of their land to the government, and during 1960 and 1961 a number of clashes occurred between Cuban citizens and Castro's forces. Castro responded in a fashion that would soon become common; he instituted mass arrests and confiscations to annihilate the opposition. Cuban farmers in turn cultivated their crops slowly and poorly to force a food shortage on the government, and this had some effect during the first years of Castro's rule. All these efforts did succeed in slowing the pace of nationalization; less than five per cent of Cuban property owners had their land seized during these early days.[83] Castro also termed the revolts counterrevolutionary, but most Cubans knew better and few perceived the rebels as traitors; it would take the later interference of the CIA to full discredit all anti-Castro feeling in Cuba.

Opposition to Castro was expressed in other ways as well. Urban bombings and shootings began again. Less violent means were also used; cheering in movie houses, for example, when U.S. officials or even symbols of the United States such as an eagle, were displayed. Castro's movie operators-cum-revolutionary zealots would respond immediately, switching on the lights in theaters and sending armed security troops down the aisles to quiet dissent. When the lights went out, however, the cheers would begin again.[84]

The Split is Cemented

Despite this trend, the Department of State had given up on the Cuban leader. It was hoped that, since Castro's power was not yet firmly set, the Cuban people might remold their revolution in a more moderate fashion.[85] But conservative pressure within the United States on Eisenhower to do something about Castro was mounting. Former ambassador Spruille Braden remarked in hearings in July, 1959 that Communist influence and poor socioeconomic conditions "unless eradicated at an early date, will convert the Caribbean into a Red Lake."[86] Conservative commentators in the U.S. press accused the administration of weakness and appeasement in the face of a clear Communist menace.

On January 10, Bonsal returned to Havana from Washington with a note from the Department of State that maintained the accommodative policy. The note was guardedly conciliatory while expressing some anger in regard to Castro's continuing seizures of U.S. property. In the end, this and other small diplomatic protests served little purpose; they were just provocative enough to anger Castro yet insufficiently forceful to cause him to reevaluate his plans.

At the end of the month, Bonsal once again persuaded Eisenhower to give Castro more time. At a meeting on the 25th, Bonsal expressed his belief that confrontation would only aggravate the problem. The next day, State announced that American tolerance for Castro would continue, and Eisenhower, at the suggestion of State, urged Congress to delay a cancellation of the Cuban sugar quota.[87] Conservatives in the United States were furious. "Still," wrote Ruby Hart Phillips, "Bonsal clung to the idea that we should be tolerant of Fidel Castro."[88] But the pledges of non-intervention and offers of help to Castro continued.

Yet at the same time, covert U.S. efforts to oust Castro were picking up steam. On January 18 Jake Engler, the CIA station Chief in Venezuela, was recalled to Washington to organize anti-Castro activities. Late in 1960 a small band of American instructors was sent to Panama to help train the first groups of anti-Castro guerrillas. During February and March, various discussions went on within the government; one option was to do away with the two Castros and Che Guevara "as a package." There was also talk of deposing Trujillo in the Dominican Republic first, as a gesture to liberals.[89]

Castro Opens Ties With the Soviets

That same month, Soviet Minister Anastas Mikoyan visited Cuba to open a scientific, cultural, and technical exhibition. He returned the next month and, as Castro rejected continued U.S. offers of aid, signed a major trade accord with Cuba.[90] The five-year commercial agreement provided for a plethora of Soviet aid, including promises to purchase large portions of Cuba's sugar crop.

Encouraged by these pledges of support, Castro accelerated the centralization of economic planning. He established the National Planning Board and purged more anti-Communists from the government. Inefficiency, caused in large part by the necessary resort to young, inexperienced revolutionaries in technical positions, was rife; the educated intelligentsia had either fled the country or had been rendered "ideologically unacceptable" because of their positions in the Batista regime. But the new Cuban government pressed ahead, guided as often as not by Fidel Castro's personal directives.

Castro took his own steps to forestall U.S. economic sanctions. Dr. Raul Roa, the Cuban minister of foreign relations, delivered a note to the U.S. embassy in late February suggesting once again that Castro might be willing to pursue a compromise, with the proviso that the United States not take any hostile actions such as cutting the sugar quota. But the United States was increasingly concerned over Castro's leftward surge, and Castro's radical actions belied his claims of a desire to negotiate.[91]

The two nations were rapidly approaching an irrevocable split. By March 1960, influenced by CIA Director Allen Dulles's fears of Castro, Eisenhower began searching for a tougher approach, possibly including economic sanctions and covert anti-Castro military operations. Eisenhower even suggested a blockade, and Herter's plans called for an ouster of Castro by the end of 1960. The Department of State began to block loans to Cuba and take other punitive economic measures. Castro fueled these plans with continued invective against U.S. "imperialism": he accused the United States, for example, of sabotaging the French munitions ship *La Coubre*, which blew up in Havana harbor on its way to delivering weapons to the Cuban government.[92]

Open Hostilities Begin

On March 17, following Vice President Nixon's recommendations, Eisenhower approved a specific plan to arm and train Cuban exiles for a possible attack on Castro. Eisenhower was not committed to this course of action and had doubts about its feasibility; he did not even keep close track of the program once it started. His intention was to examine its chances for success again in several months, when the Cubans were ready to be deployed. As we shall see, however, this program acquired an irresistible institutional momentum that would culminate in Kennedy's disaster at the Bay of Pigs.[93] And it served as a notice of Eisenhower's abandonment of any hope of dealing with Castro.

Throughout April and May, the State Department's rhetoric shifted from conciliatory to hostile, from sympathetic to condemnatory. State and other U.S. government agencies at once began to overestimate the domestic opposition to Castro, failing to understand his own role and status in the revolutionary process, his position as the *caudillo* heir to Jose Marti. A 1960 Princeton poll showed that 86 per cent of Cubans supported Castro, at least half of them strongly; but this and other such evidence was brushed aside in the overwhelming desire to believe Castro was vulnerable.[94]

On April 8, Eisenhower broke decisively from his soft-line policy of the past months with a letter to a Chilean student federation accusing Castro of betraying the revolution and bringing totalitarian Communism to Cuba. The image of Castro as a repressive, Communist "betrayer of the (authentic) revolution" would become a common justification for U.S. policy over the next decades. Secretary of State Herter added that the United States government was disappointed that "anti-Communism is being made synonymous with anti-revolution"; the United States, he claimed, was opposed to Communism, but not to revolution.

Castro responded on April 17 by charging U.S. officials at Guantanamo Bay with fomenting revolutionary sentiment among the Cuban populace. He also claimed that the United States was supporting counter-revolutionaries in the Sierra Maestras with aerial supply drops, and held a number of American citizens prisoner for various alleged crimes. On May 6, a Cuban coast guard ship fired on the U.S. submarine *Sea Poacher*, and it was clear that tensions had reached their peak.[95]

The Sugar Quota Cut and Severance of Relations

Early attempts in March, 1960 to establish presidential authority to cut the Cuban sugar quota failed, but with the growing Communist influence in Cuba and executive branch pressure, the Congress became more pliant. In late June, Eisenhower asked Congress to eliminate Cuba's sugar quota,[96] and on July 3, it voted him the power to reduce the quota. On July 6 he cut it from 3.1 million tons to 2.4. The effect was immediate, since what Eisenhower was actually doing was refusing to buy the last 700,000 tons of Cuba's 1960 allotment. Bonsal opposed this course and reported from Havana that Castro was surprised; the Cuban leader had expected a possible U.S. intervention, but not economic sanctions.[97] But he responded quickly, securing an agreement from the Soviet Union to absorb the slack in sugar exports and initiating a new round of nationalizations. Virtually all remaining U.S. enterprises in Cuba were now seized, including the facilities of U.S. oil companies that had refused to refine Soviet crude, agrarian operations, and banks. Eisenhower in turn froze all Cuban assets in the United States on July 8, and on the 14th U.S. officials reiterated their conviction that a Communist beachhead in the Western Hemisphere was intolerable and that the Monroe Doctrine applied to this case.[98]

The Soviet Union came increasingly to Castro's defense. On July 9, thinking that the rising tensions between Cuba and the United States might provoke

Eisenhower into military action, Khrushchev threatened that "Soviet artillery men can support the Cuban people with rocket fire, in case of a U.S. attack." On July 17, the first suggestion was made of direct military assistance from the USSR to Cuba. Emboldened by this support, Castro increased his rhetorical attacks on the U.S. government, calling Eisenhower a "gangster" and a "senile White House golfer."[99]

This pattern continued throughout the rest of 1960. In August, Castro seized the remaining U.S. property on the island. The Soviet Union dispatched an ambassador, Sergei M. Kudryavtsev, to Cuba. In September, Castro severed relations with the Republic of China on Taiwan and opened them with the People's Republic of China. On September 25, the State Department told U.S. Citizens to evacuate their families from Cuba; on October 12, the United States embargoed all exports to Cuba except food and medicine.

The United States also launched a huge effort to isolate Castro within the region. The administration used the OAS, which had been created as a counter-balance to growing anti-American sentiment in the UN, as a tool in this campaign and provided economic benefits to those nations that towed the U.S. line. Most Latin American governments, however, displayed a distinct desire to steer clear. The Eisenhower administration also began to establish the framework for what would become the multilateral economic boycott of Cuba.[100]

Opposition to Castro continued in Cuba. Resistance groups arose in a few disparate locations, and bombings and shootings began anew. New Year's Eve festivities planned by Castro were interrupted by bombs and arson. The most significant revolts took place in the Escambray mountains. Individuals against whom the revolution had turned or for whom it had done nothing staged bombings and attacked Castro's forces. Castro's commander on the scene, the Communist Felix Torres, set up his own feifdom, running the area with brutality and corruption surpassing the worst of the puppet presidents. The rebels, helped by Torres's cruel governance, were attracting some support until they killed a young black student. After a time Castro descended on the area with a vengeance, killing many rebels and rounding up thousands of peasants in a tactic Carlos Franqui compares to Weyler's policy of *reconcentracion*. The radicalization of the government was firmly accomplished: in November, 1960, Felipe Pazos, the moderate finance minister, was replaced with Che Guevara, and by the end of the year almost all the members of the original cabinet had been replaced with hard-line Castroites and Communists.[101]

While this was going on, Fidel still attempted to portray a respectable, human image to leaders of foreign press and governments. In September, 1960, he returned to the United States to speak at the U.N. General Assembly.

He was protected, ironically, by the CIA, which had no desire to have harm come to Castro while he was in the United States. Castro at first impressed, then bored the assembly with a rambling four-hour speech. But he did meet Khrushchev; they did their famous bear-hug on the floor of the U.N., and the Soviet leader invited representatives of the Cuban government to visit the Eastern Bloc. Soviet-Cuban ties were further cemented.[102]

Meanwhile, in the United States, presidential elections took place in November, 1960. Cuba became a significant issue, as the young John F. Kennedy struck a pose as a hawk and demanded action on the Communist regime there. Kennedy defeated Richard Nixon. The specifics of their debates on Cuba would have an impact on later U.S. policy; these will be addressed in Chapter Eleven.

"As the year 1961 opened," *New York Times* correspondent Ruby Hart Phillips noted, "Premier Castro's campaign against the United States rose to heights of hysteria."[103] He predicted that the United States would invade Cuba before Kennedy was inaugurated on January 20, and defied it to do so. On January 2, Castro demanded that the U.S. embassy reduce its staff to eight people within 48 hours, claiming that 80 per cent of the 300-odd employees were FBI or military intelligence agents.

Tensions had finally reached a fever pitch, and there was only one thing left for Eisenhower to do. On January 3, he formally severed relations with Castro's Cuba.[104]

CONCLUSIONS

The revolution in Cuba struck with devastating speed once it became clear that Batista's power would not last. Preaching slogans of democracy, initially appointing a moderate, respected cabinet, Castro seemed the answer to everyone's prayers; the fighting was over, at least in large part, and Cubans thought they could get back to the business of business. But they were wrong. For the revolution Fidel Castro had in mind for Cuba was not like past Cuban revolutions; it would not simply supplant one moderately progressive government with another. Indeed, the period leading up to January 1, 1959, was only the *rebellion*. The revolution, a true reformation of Cuba's entire socio-economic-political situation, was yet to come.

We will take up the story of the progress of the revolution and its relations with the United States in Chapter Eleven. But in 1959 and 1960, one question was on the lips of everyone who thought of Cuba: Why? Why had a revolution come to what was probably the most progressive and economically sound country in the Hemisphere? And why, after 1959, did Fidel Castro seem determined to lead Cuba into radicalization at home and abroad, and into the Soviet Communist orbit? What was the American role in all of this? These vexing questions are the subject of the next two chapters.

9

CAUSES OF THE REVOLUTION

"Thus it is manifest that the best political community is formed by
citizens of the middle class, and that those states are likely to
be well-administered in which the middle class is large, and stronger
if possible than both the other classes."
Aristotle, *Politics* Book IV chapter 11

"Those who make peaceful revolutions impossible will make violent
revolutions inevitable."
John F. Kennedy, March 12, 1962

"Hence it comes about that all armed Prophets have been victorious, and
all unarmed Prophets have been destroyed."
Niccolo Machiavelli, *The Prince*

In the almost thirty years since Castro's revolution,
debate over what caused it has never ceased. Analysts looking at the revolution have posited social, economic, political, military, personal, and "conspiracy" theories in attempting to explain why it occurred. As one of the prototypical examples of a Third World, anti-imperialist revolution, the Cuban case may offer some significant lessons about that revolutionary process. But scholars have disagreed vehemently over the primary cause of the revolution and, hence, about the lessons it offers future policy-makers.

Observers who have attempted to explain the Cuban revolution have done so with a dizzying number and variety of suggestions. Their theories range over a wide variety of political, social, and economic ground, and in many cases they defy easy classification. It is nevertheless necessary to arrive at some form of organization for the theories. This chapter will therefore examine ideas about the Cuban revolution in the context of three major models of its primary cause, models that deal with the role of various factors or actors: social/political forces, economic forces, and the role of the United States. Distinct sub-models will also be considered. (The role of Fidel Castro will be discussed in the next chapter.)

SOCIAL-POLITICAL FACTORS

For many analysts, political repression was the primary impetus to revolution, inspiring the Cuban people to rise up against Batista in 1959. Influenced by decades of radical political thought as well as by the more recent campaigns against corruption in government, Cubans rebelled against a tyrant and overthrew him. Radical sentiment had been temporarily capped after the frustrated revolution of 1933, but its re-emergence was inevitable. The leaders of this movement were the urban intellectuals.

In this sense, the Cuban revolution is seen as a primarily middle-class phenomenon. Theodore Draper, for example, has concluded that "there is no doubt that the revolutionary activity in the country as a whole was predominantly urban and middle-class." Draper argues that between one-fifth and one-third of Cuba's population was middle-class, and that this sector of society was crucial to Batista's rule. When this class became dissatisfied with the dictator's repressive measures, they rose up and overthrew him.[1]

Draper modifies this notion by granting that "this was not a revolution of the middle class," which was split in its allegiance. Yet the revolution was *led by* segments of the middle class; Draper concludes that "revolutions still issue *out* of the middle class but not *in behalf of* the middle class."[2]

Jose Manuel Casanova, a Cuban sugar mill owner who fled the island in the early 1960's has summarized this theory well. "The revolution," he argued,

> was a revolution of the bourgeoisie, not of the masses. It was the intellectuals, the professors, the university students that made the revolution. . . .The workers did not participate or support it; the farmers at the lower level of the spectrum did not support it.[3]

In many ways this revolutionary spirit originated in the disgust of the Cuban populace with the corrupt Grau and Prio regimes that had preceded Batista.

Cole Blasier argues that "the failure of [Grau and Prio] to come fully to grips with the nation's problems and establish a firm hold on the nation's loyalties, is fundamental to understanding the Cuban revolution."[4] The political gangsterism and denial of rights that accompanied these regimes—and the painful loss of hope after the reformist surge of 1933 was crushed and its leader, Grau, turned to corruption—contributed to the spirit of the rebellion.

This spirit was manifest in the writings of various Cuban political theorists. Such men as Julio Mella, Antonio Guiteras, and Eduardo Chibas led the fight against corruption and conservatism during the years prior to Batista's 1952 coup, and their ideas influenced the revolution significantly. Castro was particularly affected by Chibas' reformism and romantic idealism, and referred frequently to "Chibasismo."[5] Their thought was codified and made public by books, pamphlets, and articles, and the gradual radicalization of Cuban public thought continued.[6]

A crucial segment of the middle class rebellion was the student population. As previous chapters have documented, Cuban university students had already accumulated a long history of commitment to radical change, and in 1959 they came down firmly against the Batista regime. Student groups such as the FEU became intimately involved with the network of urban revolutionary activities.[7]

Importantly, too, this opposition was expressed in violent terms. It was middle-class intellectuals who, opposed to what they perceived as a corrupt, repressive regime dependent upon the United States, began a campaign of urban terrorism designed to create instability and topple the regime. This does not mean that Batista was not serving middle-class interests; in many ways he was, and many Cuban businessmen stayed away from the revolution (though some did support it with money). But a certain *segment* of the middle-class came to oppose him, and their terrorism provoked the government into every greater stages of repression; the totality of this violence destroyed the average Cuban's way of life and thus sealed the fate of the Batista regime.

Central to this theory is the idea that economic considerations—poverty, imbalance of wealth, and so on—played only a minor role in the revolution. To support this case, analysts cite the great relative wealth of Cuba in 1959. Cuba in 1958 had a literacy rate of 80 per cent, an infant mortality rate in the low 30's per thousand live births; Cubans owned 170,000 telephones, half a million televisions, 160,000 automobiles, and were served by 6,500 physicians; there were well over 300 university students per 100,000 citizens. All these figures were the best or among the best in Latin American, in some cases by huge margins; Cuba had as many doctors, for example, as the rest of the Caribbean republics combined.[8] Labor reforms were also significant, as summarized in Chapter Eight; Cuba was probably the most socialized country in the region.

Many analysts agree with this interpretation. Boris Goldenberg argues that middle-and upper-class intellectuals, reacting against Batista's repression, played a crucial role in the revolution.[9] Andrez Suarez concludes that "the overthrow of Batista was not due to any demand of the masses for the radical transformation of the socio-economic structure."[10] Frederico Gil ascribes the revolution to "a national feeling of revulsion towards existing political habit."[11] Jose Miro Cardona concurs that "the fight against Batista was a fight against political dictatorship, not against economic conditions."[12] In fact, Cole Blasier contends that "most authorities are in agreement that broad social and political issues were equally or more important than economic and fiscal ones."[13]

Another facet of this theory is that the middle class that supported the revolution was far more conservative than Castro, that they misinterpreted his determination and ideology, and that he may well have purposefully deceived them to achieve his own ends. Even by the middle of 1959, Castro's ideological colors were not clear, and the middle class thought his values were commensurate with its own. Castro was, after all, a product of that same class.[14] The perhaps intentionally vague program of the 26 July Movement fooled many moderate revolutionaries, as we shall see in the next chapter.

The notion of a revolution of rising expectations is also related to these considerations. As Ramon Ruiz concludes, "Social upheavals occur not where people have to grovel daily for a livelihood but, on the contrary, where economic development permits thinking and planning for the future."[15] Such analysis suggests why Cuba was in fact the Latin American country most ripe for revolution; its population was advanced enough to expect more than they had, in contrast to other nations. This was especially (if not only) true of the urban bourgeoisie, whose terrorist campaign brought the revolution to its denouement; as the rising expectations theory would predict, Cuban peasants and marginal workers did not join the revolution until late, and then not in particularly significant numbers. It was those on the forefront of social progress who were the first to demand more.

ECONOMIC CAUSES

Other analysts emphasize the crucial role played by various economic forces in fostering a revolutionary sentiment in Cuba. Cuba was not nearly the progressive, constantly expanding economic nirvana some have claimed, these observers argue, and underlying inequities and serious poverty in certain sectors of the country helped create revolution.

A Peasant or Proletarian Revolution?

The vast majority of recent analyses, however, have rejected two particular economic theories of revolt: that the revolution was either a *peasant* or an *urban proletarian* revolution, caused by the horrible economic deprivations of either group. Observes of the revolution have made cases for both models: Jean-Paul Sartre, Leo Huberman and Paul M. Sweezy, and C. Wright Mills have all stated or strongly implied that the revolution was one whose primary support lay among the peasantry.[16] Che Guevara characterized the revolution as a peasant's struggle.[17] And Castro has at various times argued that the revolution was one of the urban proletariat.

These theories no longer hold much validity, in large part because of the work of Theodore Draper. On the peasant revolution theory, he notes that between 1953 and 1956 no peasants at all joined Castro, and even when a "peasant influx" occurred in 1957-1958, "it was never very great."[18] Most of Castro's support was in the urban areas, and even if a significant percentage of Castro's guerrillas were peasants, only a tiny percentage of the peasants *became* guerrillas.[19] Draper also concludes that "an agrarian revolution implies a peasant party, a peasant leadership, and a peasant ideology, none of which the Cuban revolution had." The opposition groups, including the 26 July Movement, were born from, led and were supported by the urban middle class.[20]

Gil Carl Alroy, in an excellent essay on "The Peasantry in the Cuban Revolution," has made the important point that it is "futile" to try to characterize the Cuban revolution as a peasant revolt because even "to achieve a general agreement [on this]. . .would mean little more than promoting a painfully confused terminology."[21] Even though some of Castro's army did come from the Cuban peasantry, those peasants were fighting only because Batista's repressive measures—and his assumption that they were on Castro's side anyway—left them little choice. In this sense their support for Castro was more or less "involuntary," and Castro used the picture of a "victimized peasantry" to elicit sympathy from outside.[22]

This is not to say that peasant participation was irrelevant. Rural guerrillas were far more elusive than urban ones, and the peasant basis of support in the Sierra Maestras was Castro's *sine qua non* of survival.[23] Nevertheless, it seems relatively clear that the Cuban revolution was not a peasant revolution *per se*.

Working-class participation in the Cuban revolution has become even less credible as an explanation of the rebellion. Draper concludes that "one of the few things on which everyone seems to agree is that [the Cuban revolution] was not, at least as far as the conquest of power was concerned, a 'proletarian revolution.' " Even Blas Roca, secretary general of the Cuban socialist party, admitted that workers did not take a large part in the revolution.[24] Urban workers were few; Latin America had still not evolved any appreciable proletariat. Moreover, many of those workers were employed by the government, and this, combined with the strong position of labor, rendered those workers passive until the last moments of the revolution.

Other Economic Factors: Unemployment and Dislocation

Thus it seems unlikely that the Cuban revolution was a peasant or an urban working class phenomenon. More generally, however, economic factors such as poverty did influence events in Cuba. Recognizing that most authorities agree that economic motivations were not the original driving force behind the revolution, a number of writers have nevertheless emphasized that economics did play a role in ousting Batista.

Jorge Dominguez is one of the best spokesmen for this point of view. He admits that ''Perhaps no other hypothesis about the origins of the revolution has been held in such wide disrepute and treated with so much scorn as the possibility that economic conditions may have contributed to the fall of Batista.'' Most scholars, he notes, no matter what their larger preconceptions, reject that theory.[25]

Nevertheless, Dominguez emphasizes that economic concerns were a significant—though secondary—cause of the revolution. To support this claim he catalogues the depressed economic conditions that prevailed throughout much of the island by 1959. Unemployment ranged between 7 and 20 per cent, especially in mid-to late 1958. Seasonal and chronic unemployment struck at sugar workers and other groups.[26] The precipitous drop in the economy after 1957—caused in part by the rebels' sabotage—exacerbated these problems.

Other observers found similar problems with the image of Cuba as a prosperous, rapidly developing country. Boris Goldenberg has noted that many of the labor protection laws were not enforced throughout much of Cuba; many peasants, ignorant of their rights, simply never demanded their eight-hour day or forty-hour week. The average peasant lived in horrible poverty, and was ''usually in debt to local traders and was exploited by middlemen.''[27] Housing conditions were poor, and Cuban land was underdeveloped; only 30 per cent of available land was put to use, one-quarter of the total labor force permanently employed. Out of a working population of 2.2 million, 16.4 per cent were chronically unemployed, 6 per cent underemployed, and 7 per cent worked as unpaid laborers for their families. Over half of all forty-hour workers earned less than the minimum wage, and less that 40 per cent received more than a subsistence salary.[28]

This unemployment was in many ways the result of the cyclical nature of the sugar industry. Sugar could only be harvested for about four months, six at maximum during peak years; once the rains began to fall in the spring or summer, further harvesting became impossible. When the harvesting stopped, tens of thousands of agricultural workers lost their jobs. Some kept other jobs to make up the difference; some mill owners provided employment or advanced part of the seasonal salaries to the workers during the off-season. But vast numbers had no other source of income, and the problem was acute.

Cuba's economy was thus a very "lopsided" one, in Ramon Ruiz's term, not only in the sense that it was subject to seasonal and cyclical unemployment but also that it was dependent on sugar exports for its well-being. Cuba was hence subject to "chronic, seasonal, and cyclical unemployment," and Cuban producers were "at the mercy of forces outside [their] control," such as foreign quotas, tariffs, and the international market for sugar. American dominance of Cuban markets, as well as the "shaky nature" of sugar prices, served to destroy domestic Cuban confidence in their own economy, and, without a stake in development, most Cubans had little to lose in a revolution. Ruiz concludes that most Cubans were of the opinion that "Most national ills stemmed from the nature of the [sugar] industry and its reliance on the United States for survival."[29]

Acts of sabotage and terrorism by the insurrectionists also had an effect on the economy. Inflation grew, and some basic products became scarce. Prices of eggs rose from 4 cents to 10, for example; yucca went from 1 or 2 cents to 25; and meat, milk, potatoes, and even sugar became hard to get.[30]

Maurice Zeitlin, in his study *Revolutionary Politics and the Cuban Working Class*, has outlined a number of other problems in the Cuban economy that served to undermine national confidence and establish the context for a rebellion. Through a random sampling of workers in Cuba in 1962, Zeitlin concluded that chronic unemployment had created a "state of anxiety" among workers that "later became a significant determinant of their support for the revolution and its leadership." Zeitlin found, for example, that, statistically, the rate of pre-revolutionary unemployment for individual Cubans was a good indicator of their support for the revolution.[31] This worker estrangement aided Castro and his fellow revolutionaries. Zeitlin still concedes that these findings do not suggest that the revolution was primarily one of the proletariat; he concludes that while urban and rural workers became the "social base" of Castro's revolutionary process, the revolution against Batista "was not a workers' revolution in the classical Marxian sense. . . .The workers did not initiate the struggle for power."[32]

The problem of estrangement, of rootlessness and alienation, is a common one in revolutionary theory, and many classic texts on the subject have emphasized lack of social ties as an important contributor to rebellions. Eric Hoffer in *The True Believer* argued that a person dissatisfied with himself is more likely to join revolutionary movements to regain self-esteem; Albert Camus' *The Rebel* contends similarly that a revolutionary sees in his struggle the opportunity to cultivate close fraternity with his fellow rebels and to associate in a larger sense with the struggle of all mankind.[33] Certainly similar thoughts motivated the young Cubans who risked their lives to mold a new era.

Inequity

Two macroeconomic factors also contributed heavily to revolutionary feeling. One was the terribly inequitable status of Cuban wealth. Money in Cuba was concentrated in relatively few hands. The impressive figures for per capita television sets, automobiles, and telephones lose some of their luster when it is remembered that only a few Cubans possessed most of these luxuries. Nelson Amaro terms this "class disequilibrium."[34]

One example of such inequity is provided by general living conditions. Tens of thousands of Cuban peasants who owned no land—called *precaristas*— lived a marginal life, always threatened with evictions from the dirty huts they occupied on a landowner's property. A relatively stagnant job market, despite economic progress, meant that the unemployed and marginal workers remained in many cases a permanent underclass. Opportunities for advancement did exist, but only for a few.[35]

In earlier decades, the poor condition of Cuban peasants had led to revolts, the most prominent being the insurrection of 1917. The revolution of 1933 had been primarily an urban, intellectual phenomenon, and not since the early years of the century had the Cuban peasantry risen up against the government. This did not mean that they were content; from the beginning of the domination of Cuban agriculture by external powers, the Cuban peasants were dissatisfied. As Louis Perez has concluded, then, "What Fidel found in the Sierra Maestra mountains...were the descendants of many of the irreconcilable first generation *montuno* families," or those peasants that had been forced into virtual economic servitude at the hands of large agricultural combines. The decision of many of these peasants to support the revolution "was very much a function of the legacy of 1914-1917....The rage of 1917 [had] quickly transformed itself into an enduring enmity against the sugar latifundia, the foreigners that owned them, and the Rural Guards that protected them."[36] The revolution of 1959 is thus in some ways as much a child of the 1917 revolt as it is of the revolution of 1933; although, as we have seen, peasant participation was not its driving force.

Lack of a Rooted Bourgeoisie

The other macroeconomic problem in the Cuban economy lay in the under-development of its middle class. As has been discussed in previous chapters, the dominance of American capital and investment in Cuba robbed the island of the opportunity to develop a domestic, entrepreneurial, industrial class. Rather than owning their own land and managing their own businesses, Cuban upper-income groups were "something of a tail on the dog of the American business class," and even identified "with the United States rather than Cuba."[37] The result was that "Cuba did not possess a middle class worthy of the name,"[38] and that "more than most other Latin American countries Cuba lack[ed] 'rooted' classes."[39]

Writing in 1950, University of Minnesota sociologist Lowry Nelson recognized this phenomenon. Despite Cuba's material abundance, and though upper and lower classes undoubtedly existed, Nelson explained that he "was not at all certain that a middle class exists in Cuba." He divided Cuban society into two classes—upper and lower—and noted that while the "lower upper" and "upper lower" classes formed a sort of "middle" class, that class was not firmly established. "One has the general feeling," Nelson concluded, "that Cuban society has not set or jelled."[40]

This situation was far from new; Cuban governments had been dominated by the United States, and the Cuban middle class had hence been alienated from a significant interest in the country's development, for decades. Past chapters have documented this phenomenon. Irene A. Wright, writing in 1912, argued that "We have, then, in Cuba, a country owned by foreigners, the government of which is supported by foreigners, but administered by Cubans."[41]

Ramon Ruiz agrees that such alienation had become a pronounced factor of Cuban life by the late 1950's, something he calls the notion of a "splintered society." "No coherent society existed in Cuba in 1958, no stable or well-knit structure. . . . No permanent, homogeneous ruling class had evolved on the island," he writes. While there was certainly a class of wealthy Cubans, it was merely a "neo-entrepreneurial elite" that lacked any "consciousness of unity and class and exercis[ed] only a limited leadership." It "in no sense controlled society in the manner of the elite of Peru or Colombia, which dictated not merely the economic, but the social and political system." In sum, Ruiz concludes, "the middle class did not exist as a class. It was a collection of groups, none with a clear concept of its place in society, but each imbued with a set of *petit* ideals, the sum of which did not add up to an ideal of class."[42]

Also contributing to this phenomenon was the nature of Cuba's government. As we have seen, the corrupt governments were a source of thousands of relatively easy, well-paying jobs that were secure provided the government remained in power. Many talented young Cubans shared ambitions to serve in government rather than to go into business, and many Cubans who could have contributed technical or intellectual expertise to a Cuban economic renaissance chose instead to while away their hours in cushy government posts. "The purpose of government in Cuba," writes Jorge Dominguez, "in practice, was to advance the interests of the individual officeholder."[43] Hence Boris Goldenberg's conclusion that "Cuba did not have too much, but too little, capitalism."[44] Moreover, with no significant Cuban business sector to cater to, the government remained inefficient in its economic management.

The overall result was the lack of a rooted, powerful, business oriented middle class with strong interests in the status quo. "Fragmented and demoralized," James O'Connor concluded, the Cuban middle class "failed to systematically employ state power for its own ends; Cuban governments were made up of opportunists, pure and simple."[45] Certainly, there were those — the Cuban upper class — who strongly opposed radical change and whose interests demanded a continuation of U.S. business profits. But their number was small, and with stronger ties to America than to Cuba, their commitment to the Cuban polity was not overwhelming. The traditional Latin American national aristocracy, which gains control of much of the business and commerce of nations and opposes radical change, was notably absent in Cuba. In its place were a few enormously rich Americanophiles who preferred escaping to the United States to fighting for the Cuban government, and a large mass of "middle sector" businessmen, farmers, and the like whose loyalties to the status quo were ruined by the exploitative effect of U.S. capital, by Batista's growing repressiveness, and by the Cuban government's inability to maintain order beginning in about 1957.

Antoni Kapcia explains that this process consisted of replacing a once-strong middle-class sector of planters with a group of workers and small owners dependent on the United States. "The combination of restrictions on the colonial regime, the crises of the 1880's, the disruptive effects of the 1895-98 war, the departure of many Spanish landowners," and steadily increasing U.S. influence disrupted the traditional class of small planters. In its place arose a class dependent on the United States, which "now began to be squeezed out of the little space it occupied by the social and political system by the elite's transformation and steady subordination to external capital—i.e., to become an enclave elite." Unable to control its own destiny, much of the petit bourgeoisie turned to rebellion.[46]

Such analysis begins to point the way toward a compromise image of the role of the Cuban middle class: it did exist, but without the national roots or commitment to the status quo characteristic of other Latin American elites. American domination led the upper classes either to participate in corrupt, dependent governments or to turn to revolt. Again, the problem was not that Cuba totally lacked a middle class, but that it lacked a stable one with a sense of national identity.

This notion is related to a neo-Marxist theory of revolt. In the Cuban revolution, as we have seen, as in many modern revolutions, old Marxist and Maoist notions of proletarian or peasant revolution no longer apply. Today many revolutions issue out of the middle class, and to account for this fact Marxist theorists have built upon a thesis just barely mentioned in Marx: the notion of a "new working class" rebellion. This theory stresses the alienation caused by an atomistic, consumptive white-collar service economy; it sees the wasteful and often useless and hedonistic production of a service economy as a crime against the workers. Once they realize this, the workers, with the university often serving as a socializing agent, rise up to overthrow the system.[47] While not explaining the Cuban situation fully, these sorts of ideas are useful in examining the reasons for white-collar revolutions.

In rural areas, the lack of a true middle class had important implications for the success of the revolution. Ramon Ruiz argues that, "Nowhere was the weakness or nonexistence of the middle class more evident than in rural Cuba,"[48] and without landholding, business-oriented farmers about—only "semi-employed plantation worker[s] or land-hungry marginal farmer[s]," as two other writers have phrased it[49]—Castro and his allies encountered little resistance to their proposals for reform. Then, too, Castro initially made significant promises of land-ownership to the peasants; the early manifestos, such as *Nuestra Razon*, demanded that the individual peasant be given his own property. The peasants, most of whom had nothing to lose, thus eventually supported the revolution directly or indirectly.

The socio-economic base of Batista's support was undercut by the absence of middle-class interests. As two analysts have concluded:

> In summary, the weak character of the Cuban class structure helped shape both a political system without strong institutions and a political tradition without class consciousness. . . .The absence of class consciousness resulted in the absence of an effective defense of class interests by those groups threatened by the radicalization of the Cuban revolution.[50]

This was true after the revolution succeeded and during Castro's period of radicalization—1959-1962—as much as it was before Batista fled.

Not all analysts agree with this conclusion. Jorge Dominguez, while, as we have seen, emphasizing that economic factors such as poverty and unemployment contributed to the revolution, is not so sure about the weakness of

Cuba's middle class. Between 1933 and the late 1950's, he argues, the role of Cuban entrepreneurs pursuing domestic production "grew considerably." U.S. owners were expelled from some sugar and banking industries, and it is indeed true that the influence of U. S. capital in Cuba was in *decline* at the time of the revolution.[51]

Lowry Nelson has also qualified his own arguments about the middle class. He admits that, "in relation to its population, Cuba's middle class was probably the strongest in Latin America," although he admits feeling it was not quite "set."[52] But perhaps the key problem, he argues, was that "the disparity in well-being between the very wealthy and the very poor was great indeed." Thus Dominguez and Nelson might agree that income disparities and seasonal unemployment exercised a greater effect, proportionately, on the attitude of Cubans toward the revolution than did the strength or weakness of the island's middle class.

Of course, too, the revolution did issue from the middle class to the extent that it was bourgeois elements from the university and other urban centers that began the campaign of urban violence. In this sense, although a lack of a stable "ruling elite" might have made the society somewhat more susceptible to revolution, it was the opposition's terrorism and the government's brutal response that finally brought society to a standstill and compelled a change. Whether there was or was not a strong bourgeoisie was irrelevant; certain elements of it had created a situation that Cubans would not tolerate, and the gradual uprising against Batista was a product of this.[53]

THE U.S. ROLE: IMPERIALISM OR WEAK RESPONSE TO COMMUNISM?

Certainly, in one fashion or another, the policies of the United States toward Cuba since 1898 helped create the context for the revolution. Critiques of the American role differ completely, however, over what exactly U.S. officials did to foster a rebellion. Left-wing observers focus on the role of "imperialistic" U.S. corporations and the government officials beholden to them; right-wing analysts place the blame for the revolution on the shoulders of the U.S. State Department and other government agencies that refused to adequately support Batista against a Communist conspiracy. A number of diverging interpretations will be examined below.

The United States as Imperialistic Power

Liberal and Marxist historians most often view the Cuban revolution as a logical, and perhaps inevitable, response to the domination of Cuba's political and economic life by an outside power. These analysts point out that, even with the expansion of native Cuban industry, the United States still controlled a huge proportion of many industries: 40 per cent of sugar production, 90 per cent of public utilities, mines, and cattle ranches, 50 per cent of public railways, and 25 per cent of bank deposits. American investment robbed Cuba of much of the value of its natural resources and kept the mass of Cubans in a perpetual and destabilizing poverty from which only those willing to accommodate themselves to U.S. interests were allowed to escape.[54]

Ramon Ruiz lends a qualified concurrence to these general ideas. While not subscribing to all the liberal critiques of U.S. policy, he nevertheless agrees that American dominance of the Cuban polity helped delegitimize Cuban governments in the minds of many Cubans. "Foreign tutelage had had a deleterious effect on the Cuban mind," he concluded, as it "engendered frustration and rage, especially among the young, over the island's inability to travel alone on the road to nationhood."[55] Other analysts, such as Louis Perez, emphasize the destructive role played by dominant U.S. economic and political interests; some, such as James O'Connor, argue that this situation made the resort to socialism natural and inevitable.

Moreover, as we have seen, American dominance of Cuban markets arguably helped to hamper the growth of the Cuban ruling class, and hence to create a "splintered society" susceptible to revolution. American corporations controlled much of Cuba's sugar production and many of its public utilities and banks, and without a domestic elite managing these institutions and hence committed to stability, Cuba responded only weakly to radical calls for reform.

Many analysts, however, dispute the validity of this model of political control for the purposes of economic exploitation. Some writers have argued that the pernicious results of U.S. policy occurred by accident, that most American policy-makers, while naturally trying to protect U.S. economic interests, did want prosperity for the Cubans.[56] This issue goes to the heart of all American foreign economic policy. Do U.S. corporations really want to "exploit" the Third World? Or are they doing their best both to make a profit and benefit the nations in which they operate abroad? To what degree do U.S. business interests control public policy? All these questions are still hotly disputed, but one's answers to them significantly influence one's view of U.S. influence on the Cuban revolution.

As Dominguez notes, American dominance of Cuban markets was declining in the period before the revolution. While American industries still controlled most new fields of enterprise in Cuba—oil refining, for example, and concrete—traditional industries had come more and more under Cuban control. By the time of the revolution only a few fields—particulary public utilities—

were still firmly in American hands.[57]

In any case, even if the United States did dominate the Cuban market, this was not necessarily cause for revolution. Certainly, the Cuban economy had its problems, unemployment perhaps chief among them. But American capital need not have created the sort of violent hatred characteristic of Fidel Castro and his supporters, and sometimes attributed to the society as a whole. Naturally, America was sometimes painted as the enemy, and the wave of Cuban nationalism which preceded, inspired, and followed the 1933 revolution fostered some guarded anti-American feeling. But this was true of other nations that did not revolt, and there is no reason to assume American dominance of Cuba's economy uniquely created resentment that made revolution inevitable.

Some also question the general use of the term "imperialism." The economist John Strachey has argued that

> If. . .we extend the term [imperialism] to mean any bargaining advantage which the developed countries can exert against the underdeveloped, then indeed it is entirely true that this is one of the factors which tend to keep the poor countries poor and the rich countries rich. But if we extend the term imperialism as widely this it ceases to have any very clear meaning.[58]

Jorge Dominguez prefers the term "hegemony" in describing later U.S. influence on Cuban affairs, to distinguish the partial American control of Cuban affairs from earlier dominance. "Under imperialism," he argues, which was in place when the United States occupied Cuba, "policies had been imposed on the client, or dependent, state (in this case, Cuba); under hegemony, initiatives of the client state were resisted or reversed only when they were perceived as harmful."[59]

Other observers have pointed out that the successive, inefficient Cuban governments deserve just as much blame as any U.S. corporations. The natural resources of Cuba are impressive, and shrewd government management could have used American interests in Cuban investment to help create a diverse, export-oriented economy, one also capable of meeting Cuba's basic needs.[60]

Critics of the U. S. role would counter, with some truth, that Cuban governments were inefficient and corrupt *precisely because* of American meddling. Knowing both that the United States would intervene if the Cubans did not maintain order, and that any attempt to manage policy in a fashion that consistently placed Cuban interests above American ones would provoke retaliation, Cuban leaders had little incentive to become efficient. Cuban governments in the twentieth century, as has been noted, were largely patronage systems designed to ensure jobs for the educated classes; the corruption and poor management thus fostered certainly contributed to the revolution, but it is important to recognize to what degree American dominance of Cuban affairs actually created this situation. It could be argued that, once the Cubans decided the United States would not allow their government to operate as an independent entity promoting Cuban interests, they turned it into the next best thing: a source of lucrative jobs.

In this context, it is possible to discern a pattern of increasing conservatism among Cuban public officials through their periods of service. Both individuals and organizations consistently grew more status quo-oriented and pro-U.S. over time. Grau, Prio, and Batista all began their careers as radicals or populists, and ended far more pro-U.S. and conservative. These leaders also tended to become more corrupt in office, the second terms of Grau and Batista in particular being far worse than their first.

Organizations mirrored this development. The ABC was essentially a middle-class group to begin with, and it eventually resigned itself to accommodation with the government. The Autenticos began as the revolutionary party of the first decades of the twentieth century and ended as the conservative organization of the puppet presidents. Even the Ortodoxos, from whom Fidel Castro claimed to have taken much of his inspiration, had become deradicalized by the late 1950's, conceding that a compromise could be struck with the pro-U.S. government; this stance forced Castro to disavow officially the Ortodoxos and to repudiate his own membership in the party.

The cause of these trends is not hard to discern. American influence, which exercised a virtual veto power over any radical or progressive Cuban government, essentially drove Cuban political leaders and organizations into support for American capital and the status quo in Cuba. No doubt, American policymakers had no idea how dangerous this policy was; to them, the rapid economic development of Cuba was more than sufficient evidence of its success. By damming up the hopes of Cubans for a better order, however, and preventing the progressive evolution of the Cuban social, economic, and political systems—most directly in the subversion of the revolutions of 1917 and 1933—successive U.S. administrations created the context for a sudden and uncontrollable expression of the desire for progress.

It must be remembered that these effects were indirect and unintended; most U.S. officials—and, it should be admitted, many Cubans as well—viewed the U. S. role as a supportive one, providing Cuba with preferential economic treatment and favored status as a close ally. If the effect of U.S. policy was to stunt the political growth of Cuba, to chain its economy to an unreliable and cyclical sugar monoculture, to relegate tens of thousands of its citizens to poverty—even if this was the effect, it was certainly not the intention of U.S. policy makers.

The U.S. Role: Media

The American media strongly influenced the course of the Cuban revolution. Without it, Castro would not have become so well-known so quickly, and Batista's crimes would have gone unreported. This is certainly not a unique phenomenon. As we have seen, even in the nineteenth century, newspapers publicizing Spanish cruelties in Cuba helped fuel the eventual call for war, and similar effects can be found wherever U.S. policy affects other nations, from El Salvador to Vietnam to the Philippines.

Of greatest importance, of course, was the *New York Times* reporter Herbert Matthews' reporting on Castro. As one observer has concluded, "Seldom has a single writer so influentially set the tone—at least as perceived by a broad cross-section of its interested readership—toward a person, movement, or historical phenomenon."[61] Matthews was sympathetic to Castro, and he helped create the myth of "Fidel as Robin Hood" that in turn propelled Castro to fame in the United States.

Castro, for his part, was a master manipulator, and he knew just how and when to use the press to help create the image of himself he wanted the world to see.[62]

The U.S. Role: The Department of State

Perhaps the most controversial aspect of U.S. policy toward Cuba during the revolutionary period was the role of the Department of State. With Secretary of State John Foster Dulles and other top U.S. officials largely uninterested in Latin America before about 1958, control of U.S. Cuban policy devolved upon a handful of middle-level State Department officials. Roy Rubottom, William Wieland, and a number of other foreign service officers essentially shaped the United States, relations with Cuba. The actions of these men have come under intense scrutiny.

Ironically, critics from both political poles agree that State had a hand in inspiring the Communist revolution that had gripped Cuba by 1961: observers on the Right argue that State abandoned Batista in 1958, those on the Left that its harsh attitude toward Castro after 1959 forced him to radicalize. Each of these critiques bears a kernel of truth, but both are significantly overstated. The liberal argument, bearing as it does on events after 1959, speaks more to the leftward swing of the already victorious revolution than it does to the causes of the revolution itself; it will therefore be discussed in the next chapter, which examines Castro's radicalization. Here we will examine the conservative case.

Many conservative writers, both American and Cuban, have condemned

Rubottom and Wieland as naive, anti-Batista, pro-Castro fools who did irreparable damage to U.S. interests in the Caribbean by abandoning a proven American ally, thereby allowing a clearly Communist-dominated movement to take power.[63] Perhaps the most vitriolic of these analysts was Nathaniel Weyl. In *Red Star Over Cuba* Weyl argued that Castro's movement was part of a huge, well-financed Soviet subversive organization operating throughout Latin America. He portrayed Castro as cowardly and pitiless in battle. Most significantly for this discussion, he contended that the Department of State, filled with left-leaning idealists, gave Cuba to the Communists.[64]

Weyl possesses little credibility, however, even among conservative scholars of the revolution. Theodore Draper has criticized his arguments as "scapegoat history." The "recklessness with which Weyl uses his materials, good, bad, and dubious," Draper concludes, "is matched by that of his views."[65] Many of Weyl's assertions were demonstrably incorrect; the 26 July Movement was not part of any international Soviet organization, and Fidel Castro was occasionally very brave and almost always displayed great humanitarianism in battle. But Weyl's analysis of State's role in the revolution struck home with many conservatives in the United States, including Senators Thomas Dodd and Barry Goldwater.[66]

A somewhat more measured condemnation of State came from the prominent Cuban lawyer Mario Lazo in his 1968 book, *Dagger in the Heart.*[67] Lazo argued that Rubottom and Wieland overlooked clear evidence of Castro's Communism, including his participation in the *Bogotazo* affair in Colombia. Portraying State as pro-Castro and anti-Batista, Lazo charged Rubottom and Wieland with actively subverting the policies of Earl Smith, whose anti-Communism supposedly annoyed them. Like Weyl, Lazo believed that the Department of State was responsible for the success of the revolution.

Conservative U.S. policy makers who had dealt with Cuba, directly or indirectly, shared similar views. Earl Smith, of course, thought State had undercut his efforts and purposefully engineered Batista's fall. His personal account of his time in Cuba includes a chapter entitled, "What Does It All Mean?" that is, in essence, an extended diatribe against the Department of State. Indeed Smith called his book *The Fourth Floor,* a reference to the fourth floor of the State Department where the middle-level officers who were the subject of his wrath worked.

The revolution was not inevitable, Smith argued; "that it did happen was, to a surprising degree, due to the policy of many in critical positions in the State Department that a Leftist dictator was better than a Rightist dictator." Rubottom and Wieland knew Fidel was a Communist, Smith asserts, yet they allowed him to come to power. And the problem is bigger than those two men; because top officials, who presumably are trustworthy, cannot spend enough time on all international issues, many U.S. foreign policy decisions are made by middle-level bureaucrats at State, who are, according to Smith, not accountable. "I have reached the conclusion," he writes, "that the structure of organization in the State Department is faulty by law."[68]

Smith's friend, U.S. Ambassador to Mexico Robert Hill, agreed, and added his voice to the calls to emasculate State. Others added Herbert Matthews' name to the list of "co-conspirators" at State; William Pawley, the conservative U. S. eleventh-hour negotiator, later wrote that

> I believe that the deliberate overthrow of Batista by Wieland and [Herbert] Matthews, assisted by Rubottom, is almost as great tragedy as the surrendering of China to the Communists by a similar group of Department of State officials 15 or 16 years ago and we will not see the end in cost of American lives and American resources for these tragic errors.[69]

Former U.S. Ambassador to Cuba Spruille Braden concurred, and went even further. The Department of State, he claimed in 1959 hearings, was "infiltrated" with "relatively few Communists, a number of socialists, misguided idealists, and as I christened them, 'unidentifiable Theys.' "[70] Braden claimed the pro-Communist tilt at State went far back; he claimed the Department blocked a July 1945 memo to Truman recommending that he confront Stalin with the issue of Communist subversion. Braden's "evidence" of Communists at State amounted to the fact that some secret information had been leaked.[71]

Former Ambassador Arthur Gardner was more restrained. While arguing that Batista was a "great friend of the United States" who should have been supported, and that his own counsels were ignored, Gardner nevertheless admitted that State people were competent and well-meaning. They were, he insisted, "entirely off on the wrong track," and he referred to "Castro worship" at State, influenced in part by Matthews' opinions.[72] But he did not make the sort of blanket condemnations of the honesty or motives of the men at State that various other writers did.

All these analyses drew hevily on a series of hearings organized in the aftermath of the revolution by several conservative U.S. senators and chaired by Senator James O. Eastland. As Richard E. Welch concludes, "Eastland was prepared to use his subcommittee as a rival foreign office to the State Department, which he considered rife with Leftist sympathisers and homosexuals."[73] Anti-State witnesses such as Braden, Smith, and Gardner were called, as were anti-Castro Cuban exiles, some of whose claims that Castro was known to be a Communist in his early days were accepted without question. Later chroniclers of State's culpability, such as Weyl and Lazo, relied heavily on the statements made in these hearings and in Smith's account.

This war against State also involved a personal attack on William Wieland. In a senate hearing, Wieland's credentials were questioned, his opinions mocked.[74] Eastland even went as far as to imply (mostly in private discussions) that Wieland had only achieved his rank at State because of a clique of homosexuals within the Department that might have included then-Undersecretary Sumner Welles.[75]

What are we to make of these charges? To a great degree they are baseless. The release since 1959 of many classified communications and other previously secret information makes clear that the men at State did not trust Castro and had no desire to see him come to power. Wieland's own reference to Batista as "our son of a bitch" who was at least not surrounded with Communists, as Castro was, and the official State memo to Eisenhower of January 1959 recommending that Castro not be allowed to come to power, should allay most doubts on this point. Wayne Smith, at that time a low-level embassy staffer, reports a discussion in which Wieland said that while Batista was "bad medicine for everyone, Castro would be worse." Smith also notes that Wieland and Rubottom's search for a third-party government was designed precisely to prevent Castro coming to power; had they wanted that, they would have simply acted to topple Batista.[76]

Certainly, the men at State were anti-Batista. They considered him an inefficient leader and a butcher, but then many Cubans and independent observers did as well. The fear of Wieland and Rubottom was that Batista was doomed, and that if the United States continued to support him it would be caught in an anti-American revolutionary vortex. In this they were quite correct, for even without the American arms embargo it is likely that Batista's regime would have crumbled; the opposition was simply too widespread for him to remain in power much after 1958. Nor did Wieland and Rubottom make a great secret of their desire to see Batista gone; the official policy recommendations, and especially those of Wieland, openly advocated such a course as the best for American interests. Theirs was not a "hidden agenda." Where they went wrong was in assuming that the anti-imperialism (read anti-Americanism) of many Cuban revolutionary leaders was subject to easy redress; even when the United States abandoned Batista and quickly recognized Castro's revolution, it was unable to put to rest fears of renewed U.S. intervention.

One must also consider Wieland's qualifications. Rubottom was admittedly a relative novice to Cuban affairs, but Wieland had lived on the island for many years and knew Cuban politics well, far better than the series of pro-business U.S. ambassadors that preceded the revolution, men with no formal training in diplomacy or international affairs, let alone Cuban politics. Whatever Wieland's opinions, they were certainly based on a wealth of personal experience of the Cuban situation.

What of the charge that State officials knew Castro to be a Communist and foolishly ignored this fact? Both Wieland and Rubottom certainly had heard the rumors; both were in Colombia during the *Bogotazo*, and Rubottom in December 1956 received a message from Cuban Ambassador Campa informing him that Castro had participated in that episode and describing him as "a dangerous individual and a fanatic."[77] Wieland's own correspondence and policy recommendations show a knowledge of the 26 July Movement's Communist members, including Raul and Che. But these men made the simple observation that Fidel himself was not yet known to be a Communist, that he was merely a nationalist reformer who could perhaps be dealt with. And in any case they did not expect him to come to power; they had been assured by many in the moderate opposition that Castro could be "handled" once Batista fell. That they misjudged Castro's political skills and intentions is not evidence that Wieland or Rubottom willfully toppled Batista to bring a known Communist to power.

Contrary to the conservative analysts, Wayne Smith and others sympathetic to State's case place blame for the revolution on Earl Smith, for sabotaging early U.S. efforts to get rid of Batista, and less directly on Eisenhower and Dulles, for allowing amateur diplomats like Earl Smith to get away with such tactics. Earl Smith himself had no diplomatic experience, as has been noted; he, like Robert Hill and so many others in the U. S. ambassadorial corps, was a political appointee, chosen for his work on behalf of Eisenhower's campaign. This practice is still in force, and it occasionally has disastrous results for U.S. policy.[78]

The U.S. Role: The Views of Jose Marti

As we have seen, Jose Marti is a crucial figure in the historical development of the Cuban independence movement during the nineteenth century. But Marti's influence extends far beyond that century, indeed up to the present day; his ideas have been harnessed by almost every political party in Cuba since the 1920's. Fidel Castro's revolution was self-consciously based on Marti's ideas and ideals. Marti's views on the United States are controversial, and the interpretations of them serve as examples of the radically divergent subsequent models of American policy toward Cuba.

Marti's general ideas about society have been the subject of much writing. His economic ideal was an enlightened development of classical liberalism, drawing from Henry George's attempted reconciliation of liberalism and the utopian, democratic socialism of Edward Bellamy. Though not a Marxist, Marti wrote critiques of capitalism that shared many of the socio-political assumptions of Marxists, and grew from the same psychological soil: an overwhelming concern for the common worker. Politically, Marti was a democrat, and extolled the virtues of freedom and self-government. Like so many literary figures who became involved in politics, Marti was also a romantic who saw personal altruism and ethical responsibility as the hallmarks of a sound *polis*.[79]

It is Marti's views of the United States, however, which have had perhaps the greatest subsequent effect of the Cuban psyche. Marti's thought on the United States was complex, and it evolved to a considerable degree over time; the object here is merely to summarize its essentials.

Exiled from Cuba roughly from 1880-1895, Marti spent most of those years in the United States, and he wrote numerous essays on American society for U.S. newspapers. He was critical of the evolving capitalism he found, especially the pernicious effects of monopolies and the continuing poverty and racism. Yet he drew a generally positive impression of the rapidly advancing United States, in part because of its political democracy and the achievements of great U.S. statesmen and defenders of freedom, including Washington and Lincoln. The warmth and industriousness of the American people also impressed him.[80]

By the late 1880's, however, and particularly after the seminal years 1885-87, Marti became disillusioned with the American experience. As he traveled throughout the eastern and southern United States, Marti was shocked by economic inequalities and racism. The apparent control of the political process by predatory business interests, endangering at once the rights of American workers and those of citizens of the vulnerable countries to the south, worried Marti and led him to lose faith in the popular vote as a means of guaranteeing true freedom. The Haymarket Square riots and subsequent trial of workers in Chicago in 1886-87 also had an important effect on Marti, and were for him another reminder that the United States was run by and for an elite, not the common man. "The more that Marti got to know U.S. society," Jorge Ibarra has concluded, "the more he came to grasp the bitter realities that lay behind the facade of general prosperity," and his attacks on predatory capitalism increased.[81]

Marti also saw in American capitalism the seeds of a hemispheric imperialism. Between 1885 and 1887, he wrote the crucial "Nuestra America" ("Our America"), which urged the establishment of a non-U.S., inter-American economic and political alliance to resist U.S. imperialist penetration. Convinced that North American governments were dominated by business interests, and aware of the United States' huge military and economic potential, Marti feared it would descend on Latin America. His final letter, written just before his death and quoted at the beginning of Chapter Four, is probably the most succinct summary of this position.

Subsequent commentators have thus emphasized Marti's fear and distrust of the United States. Herbert Matthews has written that, "No one contributed more toward instilling a permanent anti-Americanism into the Cuban ethos that Jose Marti." The historian Hugh Thomas agrees that Marti's originality lay in his "hostility to any relation with the United States."[82]

These arguments, however, very slightly overstate the case, and they provide a mistaken impression to the extent that they suggest Marti was anti-*American*. He was, in fact, strongly anti-*imperialist*, and in this context viewed expansionist businessmen in the United States as a danger. But Marti had no quarrel with the American people as such, nor with capitalism *per se*, and viewed it as a corrigible, though then dangerous, system.

The historian Carlos Ripoll, while occasionally over-emphasizing this notion of Marti's respect for the United States, has nonetheless drawn an important distinction between Marti's views of the United States and those of traditional Marxists. Ripoll criticizes Marxists (he uses Philip Foner as his primary example) for neglecting Marti's favorable views toward the United States. Marti's concern over annexationist sentiment in the Untied States was only part of his general opposition to that phenomenon, by any power. He viewed the freedoms inherent in the Untied States as highly desirable, and felt that Cuba and the United States could enjoy friendly relations when the imperialist mood in North American had waned.[83]

Sheldon Liss essentially agrees. For Marti, the problems of capitalism could be cured; the accumulation of capital itself, anathema to Marxists, was perfectly acceptable to Marti; and while concerned with the average worker he showed no particular interest in the crucial Marxist notion of "surplus labor." Marti in fact criticized Marx for being overly strident and violent, and referred to socialism as another form of slavery of the worker. As for the United States, Marti "could never propagate hatred toward [it]; he believed Cuba's geographic and economic positions compelled it to pursue cordial relations, but without ties of servitude."[84]

Marti's views on the United States were perhaps best summed up in a statement on the subject by the Cuban Communist Party that appeared in a May 1947 issue of its journal, *Hoy*.[85] Marti, the CPC concluded, argued for "Respect for the great democratic tradition of the north, solidarity with its people, noble like all of the peoples of the world. But. . .no submission to the dictates of the Yankee government." Marti was not anti-American, *Hoy* concluded, merely anti-imperialist. "We love the country of Franklin Delano Roosevelt just as much as we fear and hate the country of Herbert Hoover," the editorial continued. "We love the country of the Good Neighbor just as much as we fear and hate the country of the Big Stick." *Hoy* concluded with a definition of Cuban Communists: "Anti-Americans, no. Anti-imperialists, yes. Exactly the same. . .as Jose Marti."

Marti's influence on the subsequent revolution is difficult to exaggerate.[86] Castro consciously mimicked Marti. Castro's *Granma* landing was even designed to imitate Marti's coming ashore in a similar fashion over six decades before. And Marti's vision of a humane Cuba struggling against tides of imperialism from the north became the official blueprint for revolutionary Cuba.

THE CUBAN REVOLUTION: RESPONSE TO CIVIL WAR AND VACUUM OF POWER

Each of the theses so far outlined bears an element of the truth. In the end, with the context for a revolution having been established by the various economic incentives discussed, the wave of violence that swept the country in the last year before Batista's flight served as the real trigger to the final revolutionary surge. Unable to function normally in society—unable to safely traverse the streets, work, or raise families—the Cuban people wanted Batista out. As Jose Manuel Casanova has concluded,

> [The Cuban people] had been tolerant of Batista, and now they were intolerant. They were not intolerant—and I'm speaking here of the majority—because Batista had not had a clean election; they were not intolerant because Batista was a very bad guy. They were intolerant because they couldn't function normally anymore, and because Batista could not control [the situation]. Therefore, the only solution was to move on to the next phase—Batista leaves, something else ensues, and we're back to normalcy.[87]

And when the Cuban people looked for that "something else," they found, waiting in the wings, speaking of elections and democracy and workers' rights, the big, loquacious lawyer who had so captivated their attention and how was now recognized even by the *New York Times* as a threat to Batista.

The purported "causes" of the revolution reviewed earlier—economic deprivation, societal inequities, lack of a rooted bourgeoisie, rising expectations and, resentment of American influence—combined to create a context in which Cuba was ready to oust Batista. As Jorge Dominguez recognizes, "Modernization without modernity, weak political institutions, and an economic depression in a context of political illegitimacy are the basic ingredients for the classic revolution,'' and they were all present in Cuba.[88] All that was then needed was a spark to set this revolutionary sentiment ablaze, and the widening campaign of urban terrorism, rural sabotage, and general civil war provided it.

The sum of the above analysis suggests a model of revolution that might be applicable to rapidly developing societies dependent on foreign capital and tutelage. Most basically the phenomenon is one of alienation, of an atomized society lacking a basic consensus on national symbols or values. Vast segments of the lower class are estranged from society by their poverty, their persistent or recurring unemployment, and their lack of opportunity for social mobility. The nation's intelligentsia is alienated from control of society by outside influence, and this alienation is accelerated by the waste production of a service economy.

From out of the bourgeoisie emerges a dedicated cadre of revolutionaries whose exposure (mostly in the university) to their country's literature of rebellion, often to a culture of political violence (again at the university as well as in the society at large), and to specific experiences that shape their individual personalities spur them to action. They pursue a strategy of terrorism and sabotage with a twofold aim: to provoke the government into ever-increasing rounds of repression in a counterproductive attempt to end the violence, and to make everyday life a dangerous prospect and so to create popular demand for change. Once this popular demand emerges, there is no facet of society willing to stem the revolutionary tide: peasants and proletarians, while not forming the nucleus of the revolution, are hopeful that a change might improve their condition; the radical bourgeoisie promotes the rebellion; and the moderate bourgeoisie hopes for a quick shift of governments that might return everything to normalcy once again. The only force capable of stemming the revolution is the outside power whose domination of the country's political and economic life is one of the real base causes of the revolution; if that power refuses to act, as the United States did in 1959, the revolution will inevitably come to fruition.

Once in power, of course, Fidel did not run the revolution exactly as most Cubans had expected; he turned out to be far more of a radical than anyone had suspected in 1958. Why exactly he developed into a Communist, pro-Soviet autocrat is the subject of much debate; many theories of the revolution speak directly to the motives and intentions of Fidel Castro, because he, in many ways, "made" the revolution after his own fashion. It is to the questions surrounding Fidel Castro and his role in the revolution that we now turn.

10

FIDEL CASTRO AND THE RADICALIZATION OF THE CUBAN REVOLUTION

"It is much safer to be feared than to be loved, when you have
to choose between the two."
Niccolo Machiavelli, *The Prince*

"What is good? All that elevates the feeling of power, the will to
power, the power itself in man. What is bad? All that proceeds from weakness. What is happiness? The feeling that power increases—that
resistance is being overcome. I preach not contentedness, but more
power; not peace, but war; not virtue, but efficiency. The weak
and defective shall perish; and they shall be given assistance:
that is the first principle of the Dionysian charity."
Friedrich Nietzsche, *The Anti-Christ*

Since he first appeared on the world stage, Fidel
Castro has undoubtedly been one of the most enigmatic figures on it. His
close associates admit that they don't know the "real" Fidel; some Western
journalists, after a few interviews, claim to understand him almost completely.
In many ways, Fidel *is* Cuba, and any American relations with his country are
in many ways merely relations with him.

Fidel's personal stamp on the revolution is undeniable and decisive, yet it
remains controversial. Why did he embark on a radicalized revolution in 1959?
Was it foreordained, chosen at the time, or forced by the United States?

Castro's own views and intentions crucially shaped that process, and they are the subject of this chapter.

FIDEL CASTRO RUZ THE MAN

Born August 13, 1926, Fidel Castro Ruz was the son of Angel Castro y Argiz, a Spaniard from Galicia who arrived in Cuba at the tender age of thirteen and eventually made his fortune as a worker and manager for the United Fruit Company. Fidel's mother was Lina Ruz Gonzalez, who was Angel's second wife; there is a strong suspicion that she was a housekeeper in Angel's house who became pregnant and whom Angel was forced to marry after divorcing his first wife. Angel was 25 years her senior.

Fidel's home life was turbulent. His father was violent and demanded hard work from his children. Fidel was constantly getting into trouble; he would threaten to burn down the house if he didn't get his way, and at times he even tried to organize Angel's farm hands into a union. But the notion that Fidel's childhood was uniformly miserable and that his father often beat him, is probably groundless.

At school, Fidel excelled at just about everything he attempted. As the son of a rich man, Fidel attended a Jesuit secondary school, an experience that had a significant effect on his life. Fidel loved the outdoors and was a superb athlete, participating in baseball, basketball, soccer, track and other sports.

In 1945, Fidel began his studies at the Havana University Law School. (As in many nations today, in Cuba, a student would go directly from secondary school—high school—into the professional school of his choice.) At the time, as we have seen, the University was probably the most politicized location in the country. Membership in the student group FEU was often a ticket to later political activism. Armed gangs roamed the campus, and Fidel, like many students, always carried a gun. He became well-known for his athletic, oratorical, and intellectual skills but never won election to a high post in the FEU.

At the University several themes of Fidel's later life emerged. He honed his persuasive skills to an amazing edge, and nearly everyone who knew him suspected that he was destined to be either another Jose Marti or a gangster. He also perfected his tactics of political maneuvering. While he didn't succeed in the FEU hierarchy, Fidel quickly recognized the value of concealing his true beliefs and remaining uncommitted to any political faction until a decisive moment. Finally, he began to realize the value of violent guerrilla warfare.

Castro later traveled to Colombia and the Dominican Republic, participating in revolutionary movements in both those countries. As we have seen, his role in the Colombian *Bogotazo* is controversial. But it is undoubtedly true that his penchant for violent, decisive action was reinforced during this period, and by the early 1950s he was ready to return to his homeland to lead his version of the "true" revolution for Cuban liberty.[1]

THE TURN TOWARD COMMUNISM: FOREORDAINED OR FORCED?

Why, then, once the revolution occurred, did Fidel Castro place Cuba on a path toward a one-party Communist state? Had he intended to do so all along, or was there some other reason?

Traditionally, there are two primary explanations for Castro's behavior. the first is termed the "imperialism" thesis: The United States, refusing to accept Castro's revolutionary transformation of Cuban society, soon opposed him and forced him to turn to the Soviet Union for aid. The second is the "conspiracy" theory: Castro had secretly been a Communist for quite a while and had always intended to transform Cuba into a totalitarian, Marxist-Leninist state on the Soviet model; once in power he quickly pursued this goal.

Both of these theories bear a kernel of truth, and each will be examined in turn. But, as will become apparent, neither tells the whole story. A number of observers of the Cuban scene have constructed subtler models of Castro's motivations, and these provide more sophisticated analyses of why Castro turned to the Soviet Union.

The Imperialism Thesis: Castro Reacts to U.S. Aggression

Many of the writers who see American imperialism—domination of Cuban markets and politics—as responsible for the revolution itself view the same processes as being at work on Castro. Although the United States seemed to accept Castro early on, its acceptance was heavily qualified, these analysts assert. Unable to accept Castro's nationalization of U.S. property (presumably because of the influence of capitalists on the government), the U.S. government quickly turned against him. Its June, 1959 letter protesting nationalizations is seen as a crucial turning point; once again the overbearing Colossus of the North was attempting to impose policies on the Cuban government. Faced with such hostility, Castro had no alternative but to turn to the Soviet Union. By March, 1960, the United States was already actively promoting Castro's downfall.[2]

There are variations on this theory. One prominent one is represented by former ambassador Philip Bonsal: Castro himself did spark the antagonism with nationalizations and hostile rhetoric, but the United States should have waited longer and given his revolution an opportunity to establish itself before severing relations.[3] Former Havana diplomat Wayne Smith has also recently expressed the opinion that the United States passed up several early opportunities to calm the mutually hostile rhetoric and preserve a workable relationship.[4] In these accounts, while Castro is depicted as a trouble-maker, the United States is faulted for not being more understanding.

Morris Morley has made a detailed effort to document when the United States turned against Castro, arguing that this occurred by early 1959 and that there was really no significant "wait and see" period during which the United States was willing to grant the Cuban leader the benefit of the political and economic doubt. Morley even views the appointment of Bonsal as an attempt to co-opt the revolution; in 1952, Bonsal was U.S. ambassador to Bolivia, and while there helped guide the Bolivian revolution to more moderate avenues. By sending him to Havana, Morley contends, the Eisenhower administration was sending the firm signal that it would not tolerate a radical transformation of the Cuban polity.[5]

Conspiracy Theory

Standing in stark contrast to the "imperialism" thesis is the "conspiracy theory." As a result of Castro's early conversion to Communism, conspiracy theorists conclude he harbored a secret intention to bring a radical social and economic revolution to Cuba rather than the sort of moderate social reform he preached from the Sierras. Once in power he pursued this path ruthlessly.

There is a variety of solid evidence to support this argument. It is undoubtedly clear that Castro, and not the United States, sought the break in relations: he pursued nationalizations and did not compensate U.S. companies; he launched a series of violent attacks against the U.S. role in the hemisphere; and he would not allow his economic ministers to pursue aid relationships.[6]

Further, there are significant indications that Castro by 1958 wanted to radicalize the revolution and place himself firmly at its autocratic head. At a very early stage, he rejected a unified opposition proposal that would have diluted his personal influence. He placed radicals and Communists in charge of his major units during the guerrilla war. On his victory, he refused to allow the DR and other opposition groups to march into Havana with him, thereby ensuring his personal control of the revolution. His first cabinet was clearly a fraud, consisting of moderates who were used to create an image and then discarded—in some cases shot.[7]

Efren Cordova has also chronicled Castro's machinations in the Cuban labor movement, control of which was crucial. Castro clearly made an organized effort to dominate labor shortly after January, 1959—he shot some fifteen labor leaders who would not follow his orders, placed his own people in top union posts, and generally infiltrated the unions with Communists. Cordova concludes that this campaign demonstrates that "the design to implant Communism in Cuba was already in Castro's mind in January 1959, and that everything he did afterwards corresponded in one way or another to that design.[8]

Castro was certainly familiar with Marxism. In his student days, and later in jail, he carefully studied most of the major Marxist-Leninist works. Revolutionary leader Juan Almeida later said that at the University Castro always had a volume of Lenin with him.[9]

Castro is depicted as making a bargain with the Communists early on. In 1958, Castro met with PSP head Carlos Rafael Rodriguez; what they said is unknown, but after that time Castro gave all the signals of being committed to a Communist path. Fidel certainly did not see eye to eye with the Communists—they had criticized his tactics, we have seen, as putschist, and he had condemned them as a bourgeois group—and he retained some suspicions. Hence, he did not embrace Rodriguez fully.[10] But Castro's own actions betrayed an intention eventually to socialize Cuba. Even his more liberal biographers, most notably Tad Szulc, recognize this.[11]

Once in power, Castro dumped the moderate intellectual baggage of the 26 July Movement and quickly shifted to the PSP, "eviscerat[ing] his own movement," as Theodore Draper concludes, because, "they were led to expect a different revolution from the one he was making."[12] He made attempts as early as June, 1959 to discuss relations with the Soviet Union, sending Ramiro Valdes, an important officer in the revolutionary army, to Mexico to consult with the Soviet ambassador.[13]

In this sense, Castro is seen as the "betrayer" of the revolution—he did not bring constitutional reforms and freedom, but rather a totalitarian dictatorship.[14] Theodore Draper, after a careful analysis of Castro's early commitments to democratic reformism and cautious socialization in a capitalist framework, concludes that "the revolution Castro promised was unquestionably betrayed."[15] Andres Suarez contends that the Cuban people rebelled only against the dictatorship and hence had little or no desire for the radicalized revolution they got.[16]

So there is good evidence that by the time he came to power, Castro was committed to transforming Cuba into a Communist country. Merely to say Castro wanted to turn to the Communists begs the question of his motivations: why did he feel this was necessary? An analysis of these motivations both provides a more sophisticated notion of Castro's machinations and serves to disabuse observers of the Cuban situation of the notion that the United States was blameless.

A Middle Ground

Even if Castro did secretly plan to bring Communism to Cuba, the Cuban people allowed him to pursue such a path, and once he was on it, at no point did any significant number of them attempt to halt or reverse the process. If the revolution was truly betrayed, why did the Cuban people not reject it? The answer to this question can inform a general analysis of Castro's motivations and the reasons why a radicalized revolution was possible in Cuba.

Castro's Communism was in many ways a function of his anti-imperialism and nationalism, which were in turn dependent upon his resentment of American influence in Cuba. Hence, the historical U.S. role in Cuba had created, at least for Castro, a context in which relations with the "Colossus of the North" were out of the question.[17] Castro's legitimacy in the eyes of other Cuban opposition groups also depended to a great degree on his independence from American control.[18]

Only in the most direct sense, then, was Castro's Communism a function of one man's ideological commitment—it was also, in Tad Szulc's phrase, a development "foreordained by the forces of history." Castro made his pact with the Communists; he radicalized Cuba's political economy and turned his nation into a Marxist state; he entered into a new, mutually dependent relationship with the Soviet Union. But he did this primarily because he was anti-imperialist and nationalist, and wanted to combat U.S. influence in the hemisphere.

Castro's general beliefs therefore called for certain actions: rejection of U.S. influence, radical transformation of the Cuban polity, and so on. And most importantly, Cuba was to become a beacon of support for revolutionary movements throughout the region. To pursue these actions safely, Castro needed a protector; thus, Wayne Smith sees Castro's foreign policy objectives as the primary motive for his turn to the Soviet Union. Castro is a crusader, Smith argues, a self-defined Messiah whose international revolutionary aspirations led him to seek Soviet protection.[19] Smith intelligently points out what is commonly forgotten, that Fidel's final claim (or admission) that he was a socialist came in April 1961, on the verge of the Bay of Pigs, an invasion Castro knew was coming. From his own knowledge of Marxist writings, Smith concludes, Castro knew of the doctrine of the irreversibility of Communist revolutions (which would later be codified in the Brezhnev Doctrine), and he suspected that once he wormed his way into the Communist camp, the Soviets would not be able to let his regime fall. In this he was enormously prescient. Andres Suarez agrees with this argument, and sees similar behavior by Castro in the Cuban Missile Crisis.[20]

This does not necessarily imply that Castro knew he was going to ally himself with the USSR in 1958. He did know that he wanted to spread Cuba's revolution to the rest of Latin America, and in doing so to undermine U.S. influence in the hemisphere; and he knew that the United States would react. But he probably also knew that placing himself under Soviet domination would not be particularly more desirable than being a victim of American imperialism. Castro perhaps delayed entering the Communist camp with finality as long as he could—announcing this move, as we have seen, literally as the United States launched its long-awaited invasion of Cuba.

In this sense, it might be possible to argue that the United States did spark Castro's alliance with the USSR, for if it had never actually threatened him, he might never have felt compelled to take that action. But for the United States to have adopted a non-provocative policy in 1961 would have required an immense amount of foresight. Kennedy would have had to remain patient while Castro seized American property, turned his island into a police state, and sent legions of revolutionaries forth to annihilate U.S.-backed governments throughout the region. It is incomprehensible to imagine the United States watching these developments without taking action, especially since it had no remaining evidence to contradict the version of a militant, Communist Castro intent on eventually entering the Soviet camp in any case. The Bay of Pigs was a mistake for its own reasons, but the general anti-Castro American policy that had emerged by 1961 is perfectly comprehensible given the context.

While these foreign-policy motivations were crucial in causing the radicalization of the revolution, it is important not to underestimate the domestic utility of Castro's shift. The well-organized PSP—much more structurally sound than the 26 July Movement—provided Castro with a ready basis for his revolutionary government, a cadre of radical leaders prepared to implement his dictates. In his meeting with Carlos Rafael Rodriguez in 1958, Castro may well have secured the sorts of concessions—mainly relating to his own personal control of the government—that he desired, and he could thus use the PSP without fearing its own leaders as rivals. His commitment to Communism thus established Castro as the best-organized leader on January 1, 1959, and along with his radicalized revolutionary army, it guaranteed that he would step into the power vacuum unopposed.[21]

As with many totalitarian rulers, however, Castro makes ample use of the threat from the United States in defending his actions. U.S. hostility, as Lee Lockwood has concluded, has provided Castro

> with the catalyst by which he has been able to consolidate and fuse the [support of the Cuban people], as well as with a foil against which to focus the thrust of his revolution. Indeed, it is not far-

fetched to conclude that Castro has derived much more benefit from the implacable enmity of the United States than he has suffered from it. As a master political tactician, Fidel fully understands the value of maintaining this tension.[22]

The assumption behind these analyses is that Castro's prime motivation is personal, not ideological, that he has used Marxism as it suited him to achieve and maintain his own position of power. Theodore Draper is the primary exponent of the Castro-as-power-hungry-opportunist thesis, but many others have agreed, including Philip Bonsal, whose own criticisms of U.S. policy are not altered by his conclusion that "Castro's major motivation since adolescence has been his drive for absolute personal power."[23] Tad Szulc, in his excellent and monumental work *Fidel*, characterizes the Maximum Leader as stern, uncompromising, arrogant, and autocratic; thus he writes that "Castro is the quintessential Spanish military caudillo, wrapped today in a Marxist-Leninist mantle of convenience."[24] Carlos Franqui, a former lieutenant of Castro's, has described Fidel's concern for *machismo* and his resulting arrogation of authority to himself.[25]

Castro's maintenance of power was made possible, in many ways, by the confusion in U.S. policy from 1959 to 1961. Unused to dealing with Third World revolutionaries, and unsure of what to think of the avowedly moderate Castro, many U.S. policy-makers were shocked by the Cuban leader's progressive shift to Communism; Lowry Nelson has described "a sort of bewilderment among the diplomatic personnel."[26] Certainly, many—including even the so-called "leftists," Rubottom and Wieland—knew of Castro's left-leaning thought and feared the influence of the Communists around him. But what to do? No one had any desire to intervene, and without that alternative, an attempt at cordial relations seemed the best and most natural path. In this sense, U.S. policy-makers were simply responding to the situation as they perceived it at the time; there were few options. And as American policy stagnated, Castro moved swiftly to seize an iron grip on the country and establish the context for close relations with the Soviets, if he needed them.

The unique circumstances surrounding the Cuban revolution then allowed a turn toward radical socialism as a solution for the nation's problems. James O'Connor is probably the best exponent of this view; rather than the result of Castro's conspiracy or American meddling, he argues, socialism was a necessary and inevitable response to Cuba's "permanent economic stagnation, economic degradation, and political do-nothingism and corruption." Without the radical transformation of society that socialism provided, the island's problems would have remained. Socialism was thus "an expression of hard economic, social, and political reality, as understood and acted upon by men whose guerrilla experiences conditioned them to act as revolution-aries as well as realists."[27]

In part, this milieu was created by the PSP itself. Through its calls for social reform and workers' rights, the Communist party established the context in which Castro's radicalization was possible, and perhaps even necessary. The flexibility of Castro and the Communists also supports this thesis, as it indicates that they used doctrinaire Marxist programs when that suited them, and avoided them when it did not; thus the situation in Cuba dictated the policies.[28]

Of course, this thesis makes a significant presumption: that Castro and his government were essentially honest, striving after certain altruistic and definable goals, especially promotion of the interests of the lower classes. And this also presumes that socialism was thrust upon Castro and his aides by the circumstances, that in a different context they might not have instituted a socialist economy. But if the previous thesis were correct—that Castro used the revolution, Communism, and all the other developments in Cuba at the time to augment his own personal standing—then O'Connor's suggestion is incorrect; Castro used socialism, not the other way around.

And indeed, there is much to suggest that this was the case. As we have seen, Castro's radicalization began even before he assumed power; once in charge of the government, he embarked on a well-planned scheme of nation-alization and centralization of the economy. If socialism were an inevitable product of social and economic forces at work on the island, not of an explicit policy, one would have expected it to take longer for Castro to radicalize. As it was, if socialism was indeed made inevitable by Cuba's situation, it had become so by 1958, and it was inevitable because of Fidel Castro, not the "realities of power."

Nonetheless, O'Connor's thesis suggests why Castro's radicalization was accepted in Cuba. O'Connor himself seems to hold that because of the ineq-uitable social conditions in Cuba before the revolution, the adoption of social-ism was a foregone conclusion; this is of course false, if only because of the many courses revolutions, by their nature, can take. The resentments against the existing social order catalogued by O'Connor were significant, and it was in large part due to their effect that Castro succeeded in socializing Cuba. This does not necessarily imply, of course, that, as O'Connor believes, socialism was an inevitable and necessary response to Cuba's political and economic problems.

Edward Gonzales has proposed other unique reasons for a radicalized revo-lution in Cuba: its revolution was *generational*, *nationalist*, and the *product of an armed struggle*. Each of these factors contributed to radicalization. The generational nature of the revolution contributed to radicalization and meant that its radical young leaders found it difficult to support older, politically tainted moderates. The strong anti-American nationalism of Cubans resentful of traditional U.S. influence established the context for Castro's foreign policy objectives, which, as we have seen, contributed to his split from the United States. Finally, the guerrilla leadership core of Fidel's government was accustomed to the absolute military rule of the Sierras; they did not view compromise, consensus, and other characteristics of democratic governments as particulary useful concepts. The product of all these influences was a government devoted to radicalization at home and abroad, and which viewed dictatorial rule as a necessary and justified means to achieve those ends.[29]

CONCLUSIONS

This discussion has made it clear that there are no easy answers to the riddle of Fidel Castro and his political commitments. When exactly he decided to mold Cuba into a Marxist-Leninist state, what deal(s) he made with the PSP to achieve this, to what extent he has merely used Communist ideology as a tool to maximize his own political power—these are mysteries that will probably never be solved.

Castro is no doubt a controversial personality; even books about him, like Szulc's *Fidel*, have become centers of bitter ideological debate. In one sense, however, it is possible to admire the *lider maximo*: he is a man of action, a world-historical personality, in the classical sense. His morality may be questionable; he is sometimes dishonest, scheming, and brutal. But he has lived a life few men can match: he organized, carried off, and secured a revolution in his country, and then proceeded to rule over it for thirty years (at the present writing); he has excelled in nearly every field of endeavor; he is enormously well-read, even a good cook. Whatever one thinks about his politics or policies, one must credit Fidel with living life like a true Nietzschean "superman"—changing history as he achieves nearly all he sets his sights on. If life is indeed "will to power," if "egoism" is indeed "the very essence of a noble soul," as Nietzsche contends, then Castro has come as close to anyone to leading a truly authentic existence.

Fidel Castro

Copyright Washington Post. Reprinted Permission D.C. Public Library (Washington Star Archive)

Alamenda wall in Cuba, against which the captured men from the *Virginius* were shot. *National Archives photo no. 111-RB-1780*

The El Caney battlefield. *National Archives photo no. 111-SC-100466*

Cuban sailors during the 1933 revolution. *National Archives photo no. 306-NT-1003-22*

Pools of blood in front of the Presidential Palace, which a delirious Cuban crowd had rushed in August, 1933 after a false report that President Machado had abdicated. *National Archives photo no. 306-NT-1003-21*

The Pentarchy; Grau is second from left. *National Archives photo no. 306-NT-1003-23*

U.S. Ambassador Caffery greets a Cuban politician. *National Archives photo no. 306-NT-1003-20*

Philip Bonsal, the American ambassador who failed in his
attempts to moderate Castro through understanding.
National Archives photo no. 306-PS-55-4099

John F. Kennedy during a speech after the Bay of Pigs debacle, as he is presented
the Brigade's battle flag. *National Archives photo no. 306-PS-C-62-7638*

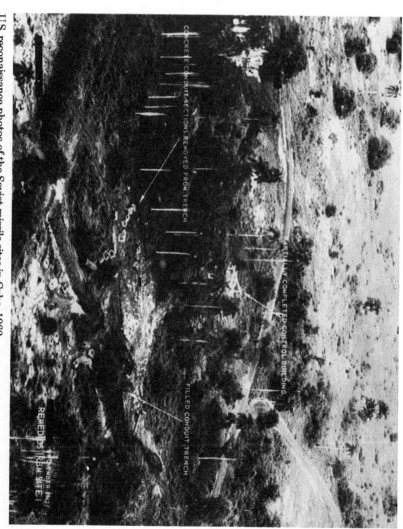

U.S. reconnaissance photos of the Soviet missile sites in Cuba, 1962. *National Archives photo no. 306-PSC-63-694 and 306-PS-62-6797*

Castro speaks at the Tricontinental Congress. *National Archives photo no. 306-PS-66-797*

PART
FOUR

RESPONSES TO REVOLUTION

Crises and Covert Action

11

KENNEDY AND THE BAY OF PIGS

"A state which has freshly achieved liberty makes enemies and no friends."
Niccolo Machiavelli, *The Prince*

"Any man can make mistakes but only an idiot persists in his error."
Cicero, *Philippics*

"The ill-fated invasion of Cuba in April, 1961, was one of those rare politico-military events: a perfect failure."
Theodore Draper, *Castro's Revolution: Myths and Realities*

John F. Kennedy came into office speaking loudly and promising to carry a big stick. Turning the tables on the Republicans—and himself strongly affected by the anti-Communism of the McCarthy era— Kennedy demanded a harder line on international Communism and on Cuba in particular. These promises emerged in policy, but policy that was ill-inspired and misguided; the result was the most explosive period of Cuban-American relations in history, and it would begin with perhaps the greatest American foreign policy blunder in history: the Bay of Pigs disaster.

THE EARLY COVERT WAR AGAINST CASTRO

Begun in 1959 under Eisenhower, the covert war waged against Castro by the United States included everything from "counterfeiting to biological warfare to assassination."[1] Kennedy continued the policy of attempting to destabilize Castro's regime, and top men at the CIA became particularly enamored of attempts on Castro's life. These efforts reached their peak in the period 1960 to 1963.

Desperate for a private army to fight this war—and one unconnected to the government—the CIA sought out leaders of the American mafia. Motivated primarily by the prospect of gaining back their Havana gambling houses, the mobsters were only too happy to cooperate. One was Johnny Rosselli, who arranged at least six attempts on Castro's life though 1963.[2]

The attempts on Castro's life sometimes assumed comical proportions. Would-be assassins tried to shoot him, poison him, and bomb him. Others hoped not to kill him but merely to incapacitate him; they treated his cigars with a depilatory which was supposed to make his beard fall off and bring his manhood into question. Some even attempted to spray his radio broadcast booth with a hallucinogen to render him incoherent on the air. All these plots failed.[3]

Private Americans were also involved. The billionaire Howard Hughes lent his services and money to the operations. Others, like Frank Sturgis, helped run supply missions to anti-Castro guerrillas in Cuba, who planted bombs and undertook other harassing actions, and who were supposed to form the nucleus of an anti-Castro underground to support the later invasion.[4] Others worked on the propaganda end in the United States and abroad. CIA intermediaries such as Howard Hunt, of later Watergate fame, paid and directed these Americans.

Within the government, Richard Nixon was the chief early advocate of programs designed to unseat Castro. Nixon became convinced in April, 1959 that Castro was a menace, either Communist or Communist-dominated, and from that time forward (until his own administration) he favored nearly every means of ousting the Cuban leader, including invasion. Nixon became a key proponent of the initial Bay of Pigs plans.[5]

Prominent Cuban politicians were also involved. Tony Varona, former vice president of Cuba and head of the Cuban Senate, was contacted by Rosselli and Sam Giancana, another mobster, about an attempt on Castro's life. Varona, living in Florida, was running a CIA-sponsored Cuban "exile government" at the time, but he agreed and had poison capsules brought into Cuba. In fact, this plot may have come close to working; Varona apparently had his people in place ready to slip the capsules into Castro's food. But Varona, with the other Cuban political exiles, was placed under house arrest during the Bay of Pigs operation to prevent security leaks, and he was unable to contact his agents to tell them to go ahead. Thus the CIA "destroyed its own best shot at Castro."[6]

KENNEDY'S PUBLIC POLICY

Of course, these covert efforts could not constitute the basis of an open public policy. Kennedy's position in the election of 1960 was a hawkish one, but his Democratic roots also lent him a sense of social progressivism. JFK's stiff anti-Communist line was thus combined with a call for economic aid and promotion of development for Latin America.[7] His inaugural address promised a war against poverty in the Hemisphere, and on the very eve of the Bay of Pigs he proposed his Alliance for Progress, a program designed to provide assistance to developing Latin American nations. Like several presidents before him, Kennedy hoped to cure the hemisphere of foreign intervention by removing what were seen as the causes of that involvement: poverty and underdevelopment. And like those presidents, Kennedy viewed these programs as means as much as ends.[8]

At the same time, Kennedy had no desire to see Cuba benefit from the fruits of regional prosperity, and he pursued a strict set of economic sanctions, including a sugar boycott. At first, however, he avoided direct pledges of support for Cuban exiles, hoping that his bluff and bluster in other areas would be sufficient to establish his hard-line credentials.[9] He also increased support for regional counterinsurgency efforts in an attempt to prevent more Communist revolutions.[10] In 1961, Washington was infected with Castroitis—and Kennedy was not immune.

THE BAY OF PIGS

All these well-considered public pronouncements, however, were undone by what, again, remains one of the greatest American foreign policy blunders in history. Critics of the left, right and center agree that the American-sponsored invasion of Cuba at the Bay of Pigs was a disaster. They disagree about whether it was ever a good idea, or about what should have been done differently; but there is complete unanimity that the operation as it was conducted was a tragedy. It stands perhaps as Kennedy's worst moment.

Development Under Eisenhower

The operation began, as Chapter Eight noted, under Eisenhower, who in March, 1960 authorized the organization and training of Cuban exile forces. Richard Bissell, deputy director of the CIA for plans, was the coordinator of the operation, and the CIA set up shop at Opa-Locka in suburban Miami. In a sense, the invasion was nearly inevitable from this point on; the very existence of what would become Brigade 2506, and those whose careers were staked on its success, created a huge institutional pressure to allow the operation to go ahead.[11]

The motivation for the invasion was clear enough: to rid Latin America of Castro and the Communist threat he embodied. The "success" of the CIA's 1954 Guatemala operations, which unseated the progressive Arbenz government, created the impression that such covert operations could be used as a reliable tool of national policy.[12] The appearance of anti-Castro groups in Cuba gave the U.S. government a tool that was "rationalized into national policy."[13] And Kennedy himself was "determined to demonstrate that the exemplars of the New Frontier were hard-nosed realists, capable of giving the containment policy a new vigor and success."[14]

Meanwhile, the Brigade itself was forming and training in Florida. Brigade members were recruited from the area and given identification numbers beginning with 2500. The sixth volunteer, Carl Rodriguez Santana, was killed in a training accident, and the Brigade took his number as its name: 2506. Later, many of the training facilities and bases would be moved to Guatemala.[15]

From the start, there were doubters. Secretary of State Christian Herter, for example, replacing the dying John Foster Dulles, thought at first that Castro was not a Communist and that measures directed against him were therefore wasted effort.

But the most damning trend during the early development of the invasion scheme was the failure to get all the relevant government agencies involved; from the beginning, the operation was planned and executed largely by a small organization within the CIA. The Joint Chiefs and their military branches, other executive branches and advisors, UN Ambassador Adlai Stevenson, even the intelligence arm of the CIA itself, all were brought into the operation at a later date, and all assumed that by the time that its consummation was *fait accompli*. None was thus in an adequate position to veto what many thought to be a foolhardy undertaking.

Fidel Castro, in fact, was better informed than many American policy makers about the upcoming invasion, and he would demonstrate this with a constant stream of accurate predictions about it. On April 22, 1960, he announced that the United States was formulating a well-organized plan to launch an invasion of his island with exiles; a week later he specified Guatemala as the training site for the invaders. Over the course of the next year, CIA planners would not be deterred by statements by Cuban officials, including Castro, which indicated they knew exactly when and how, if not where, the invasion would come.

On August 18, 1960, Eisenhower added steam to the CIA's operational engine with an allocation of $18 million for the Cuban invasion. He also authorized the use of Defense Department personnel and equipment to train the exiles, but—in a move that upset some CIA men—forbade the use of U.S. military personnel in combat.

This was the beginning of another dangerous facet of the mission's planning; the most senior U.S. officials refused to have the United States be drawn directly into the fighting, and indeed wanted the operation so removed from U.S. personnel that the United States could deny complicity. The mission's planners, however, not content to initiate the small guerrilla operations dictated by this limitation, began to expand the Brigade's mission into a full-scale invasion. There is some indication that CIA planners expected that, when worse came to worst, either Eisenhower or Kennedy would authorize the use of U.S. forces to pull the exile Cubans' fat from the fire, and that the CIA men thus convinced themselves that the invasion—with all its shortcomings— should go through. But if this was their belief they were mistaken, and what they ended up with was an invasion too large to be easily dispersed in case of failure but too small to achieve its objectives.[16]

The 1960 Election and Cuba

As the last chapter mentioned, the 1960 election brought the issue of a Cuban exile invasion into sharp focus. The Brigade was training before the election, and Nixon, running from the vice-presidential seat against Kennedy, hoped the invasion could go off before the election to give the GOP a boost. Nixon implied in several speeches that steps were already being taken against Castro. But Kennedy trumped Nixon on the issue, assailing the vice president for not doing anything about Castro's consolidation of power. On October 20, the eve of a televised debate between the candidates, Kennedy staffers handed out a press release arguing that anti-Castro forces should be "strengthened" with the "eventual hope of overthrowing Castro."[17]

It is impossible to estimate how much this electorally convenient act contributed to the later decision to approve the invasion, but there is no doubt that Kennedy was now firmly committed to the hawkish side of the fence on Cuba. He had perhaps created so much momentum on the issue that he would later feel compelled to allow the invasion to go on, despite the objections of some of his top advisers. Nixon, unable to reveal the existence of the Brigade, felt compelled to take a dovish line in the debates, arguing that support for the exiles or an invasion was contrary to international law and bad policy.

Just after the election, Kennedy was briefed on the growing operation by Bissell and Allen Dulles. The president-elect approved the project, and shortly after the election, the CIA unilaterally escalated support and accelerated the training of the Brigade and decided on the scope of the invasion. This decision was never made by a president. Ike had only endorsed the initial training, and wanted to review the project critically when it neared completion; and Kennedy was to be presented with a *fait accompli*, a fully trained and equipped Brigade of brave Cubans who could not be disbanded and whom he had promised vehemently to support.[18]

The concealment of the operation from U.S. officials continued. Bissell did not report to the NSC, the Joint Chiefs, or even the intelligence directorate of the CIA itself. Skeptical voices that might have succeeded in heading off the invasion were thus silenced by absence. In part, too, the operation was carried forward by the inter-administration momentum and lack of oversight that often occurs during a transition of power.

From the start, many of the CIA operatives involved were individuals whom no one would rationally trust with an important operation. One was Gerry Droller, a German-born agent who spoke English with a horrible accent, knew nothing of Latin America, and treated the Cubans under his command with contempt. Howard Hunt, the self-styled secret agent who would later be involved in Watergate, was known for his terrible judgement. Others had close ties to various Latin American dictators friendly to the United States. It was an odd, sinister, yet dedicated group.

Several experienced U.S. officials, convinced the operation would fail, attempted to distance themselves from it early on. Richard Helms, the well-respected CIA director of operations, failed to endorse the project and stayed out of it to the end. David M. Shoup, commandant of the Marine Corps, doubted the plan, as did Admiral Arleigh Burke and Arthur Schlesinger, Jr., at the time a young White House policy advisor. The Departments of State and Justice were also leery of the operation and pressured Eisenhower to avoid any violations of the Neutrality Act; these warnings went unheeded. In part, this was due to the fact that those who objected to the invasion did not make their feelings known, since the operation was already so far along that they felt unable to voice opposition.[19]

The Invasion Takes Form

Brigade 2506 therefore continued to train in Florida and Guatemala. A Cuban government in exile was established to be put ashore once a beachhead had been won. The CIA recruited Cuban pilots to fly air cover over the invasion—in some cases smuggling them out of Cuba for the purpose—and to train them, recruited volunteers from a U.S. Air National Guard unit in Alabama. The American pilots left homes, families, and jobs to take part in the operation.[20]

The United States had also established a propaganda radio station, Radio Swan, on an island in the western Caribbean near Honduras. This and other sources of information broadcast into Cuba the American rationale for the coming invasion: Castro, the Americans claimed, had betrayed the Cuban revolution. His totalitarian Communism was nothing like the progressive, social-democratic revolution most Cubans expected, and he was therefore a legitimate target for a new revolution. This would be the primary argument of an April, 1961 White Paper on Cuba written by Arthur Schlesinger to justify the administration's actions.[21]

Early on, CIA planners had envisioned merely establishing a modest guerrilla force in Cuba, which would then begin operations in one of the island's mountainous regions. But as the operation grew, its nature became more ambitious, and developed into a full seaborne invasion. On November 4, 1960, the CIA ordered that the 400-man guerrilla force of Cubans then in training be re-formed into a conventional military organization capable of conducting a beach landing. These late changes, among other problems, forced a delay of the invasion date, which had originally been set for November, 1960.[22]

Various American government and military agencies continued to express doubts about the operation. The Defense Department and the Army, in part because the CIA men, and not they, were running the show, were dubious. A Joint Chiefs of Staff committee—which had no knowledge of the CIA's plans— convened to examine alternatives for operations against Cuba. It concluded that only an invasion with considerable direct U.S. support would succeed, while the infiltration of a guerrilla force or a purely Cuban invasion would fail. These conclusions were made known to many top administration officials, including Robert Kennedy, Secretary of State Dean Rusk, Defense Secretary Robert McNamara, and others, all of whom chose to discount the JCS opinion that U.S. force would be necessary.

Proponents of the operation used other studies to make their case, studies that in fact were ambivalent at best. A JCS review of the CIA's actual plans made in late January, 1961 concluded that the operation could work—which the head of the study said meant they thought it had about a 30 per cent chance of success.[23] But the CIA people used this and other tentative endorsements to advance their cause. As noted in Chapter Eight, moreover, from the start many U.S. government officials had for various reasons been overestimating the Cuban domestic opposition to Castro, and this tendency provided a key motivation for the final approval of the Bay of Pigs invasion.

Senator J. William Fulbright, on hearing of the invasion plan, tried to persuade Kennedy to give it up. He prepared an extensive memo detailing his objections, in which he made the famous remark that Cuba was a ''thorn in the flesh; but it was not a dagger in the heart.'' But Kennedy was not persuaded.

As the invasion approached, secrecy was lost completely. Initially published in the Guatemalan paper *La Hora*, information about the Brigade leaked into the United States through articles in Stanford University's *Hispanic American Report* and the liberal newsweekly *The Nation*. Several reporters gained an almost complete knowledge of the operation, and while some journals — such as *U.S. News and World Report* — withheld their stories at the administration's request, others did not. In particular, the *New York Times* and reporter Tad Szulc printed most of what they knew, and the existence of a CIA-trained invasion force in Guatemala became common knowledge. Even the *Times*, however, held back some information. (Kennedy would later remark caustically that if the *Times* had only printed everything, it would have saved him from a great mistake.) Adlai Stevenson, U.S. ambassador to the United Nations, was forced to defend the United States against invasion charges without being informed of the operation's existence.[24]

Kennedy was skeptical from the beginning, but conveyed the idea that he was generally in favor of the invasion if it could be done without implicating the United States. As of January, 1961, however, the exiles were still in a poor state of readiness. Their new role as conventional soldiers, rather than guerrillas, had necessitated additional recruitment and training. And CIA analysts began to warn ominously of the need for air superiority over the beaches. If Castro's small air force of twenty planes or so were not completely destroyed, one report concluded, the invasion would be "courting disaster."[25]

Cuban officials, meanwhile, remained well informed of the operation's progress. In February, 1961 Cuban Foreign Minister Raul Roa told the UN that he expected an imminent invasion, and indeed, it was only two months away. Later, he accurately predicted that the United States planned to establish a provisional government within Cuba, and again named Guatemala as the staging base for the attack.

A sense of urgency had begun to affect the mission planners. Castro was getting stronger every day; massive military training programs were bringing thousands of new recruits into his militia and army, even at the expense of economic development plans. Soviet aid to Cuba had been stepped up, and now Castro had relatively modern tanks, anti-aircraft guns, and small arms. And there were rumors he would soon have a complement of MIGs; fifty Cuban pilots were being trained in Czechoslovakia, and the planes they would fly were said to be on the way to Cuba. The establishment of such an air force would eliminate any hope for the Brigade. Bissell and others at CIA also worried that Kennedy's resolve was flagging, that unless they carried the operation off soon he might cancel it altogether.

New intelligence estimates created more doubt about the plan. In February, a JCS team reported that, as a result of poor training and other deficiencies, the operation had only a 15 per cent change of success. One Castro plane, the group concluded, armed with a single .50 caliber machine gun, could wreak havoc on the Brigade's ships, whose decks would be loaded with ammunition and gasoline. This and other analyses also stressed the crucial role of the internal, anti-Castro rebellion that was expected to follow the Brigade's landing; without it, the operation was doomed to total failure. Yet on March 10, the JCS "approved" the operation—which did not mean they endorsed it, only that they would not veto it; but this crucial distinction, made (consciously or subconsciously) by so many of those who assented to the invasion, was lost on Kennedy since it was never spelled out.[26]

But what was that plan? The original operation had called merely for U.S. support of anti-Castro guerrilla operations in Cuba. Gradually this idea grew into a proposal for a full-scale invasion; the first idea called for a U.S.-supported assault at Trinidad, a city in southern Cuba near the coast. That area was reputed to harbor a great deal of anti-Castro sentiment, and bolstered by local volunteers, the Brigade was supposed to melt into the nearby Escambray Mountains, from which it would begin a guerrilla campaign not unlike Castro's own years earlier.

Kennedy, however, rejected this plan. It was too "spectacular," he felt, too controversial; a more modest operation was needed. The CIA was charged to find an alternative, and it finally determined on an attack at the Bay of Pigs, on the western side of Cuba's southern coast. This site was thought to have several advantages: it was surrounded by swamps, which could serve as an effective substitute for mountains in protecting the beachhead from Castro's attacks. CIA planners also assumed that the Brigade, if defeated, could melt into the swamps and initiate guerrilla actions, eventually making their way to the distant Escambray Mountains. On March 16, Kennedy tentatively approved this plan, though he reserved for himself the right to veto the landing up to 24 hours before it took place.

As it turned out, this second plan would have two primary drawbacks; one was that the Brigade now had no convenient mountains to which it could flee, and would therefore have to stand and fight on the beaches. The CIA's assertions that the Brigade could trek through nearly 100 miles of dense tropical swamps after being defeated by a numerically superior enemy, all the while harried by unopposed Castro air power and militia units, to reach the Escambrays, was pure fantasy. The other drawback would have a significant effect of the course of the coming battle: the Bay of Pigs just happened to be Fidel Castro's favorite fishing spot, and he knew its contours like the back of his hand.[27]

Castro's own information was almost completely up to date. On March 25, responding to what he felt was the American plan, he said he would not allow a provisional government to exist for even one day within Cuba. Foreign Minister Roa again warned the UN that a U.S. invasion was imminent.

On April 3, the State Department issued a White Paper on Cuba authored by Schlesinger. Designed as a theoretical justification for actions against Castro, the paper trumpeted the theme of "Castro as the betrayer" of the "true" Cuban revolution. Castro no longer represented the legitimate wishes of the Cuban people, it implied, and therefore could and should be deposed.[28]

Finally, on April 4, 1961, the final decision was taken to go ahead. Senator Fulbright, who had been invited to attend, and several others expressed doubts, but most present felt honor-bound to support the president. Schlesinger, who opposed the invasion, has noted that the "circumstances of discussion" prevented a real debate. Bissell and Allen Dulles argued very forcefully for the operation, and continued to emphasize the idea that the Brigade could just melt away into the swamps if its situation became untenable; Kennedy was apparently heavily influenced by this notion, as it obviated the need for any U.S.-run "rescue" of a defeated Brigade streaming back to the beaches.[29]

Once the decision was made, Schlesinger resigned himself to it and drafted a memo to JFK designed to help the president make the best of what Schlesinger considered a bad situation. He recommended a strategy of "plausible deniability." The United States had to be ready to "show that the alleged CIA personnel were errant idealists or soldiers of fortune working on their own." The president had to be isolated: "When lies must be told," Schlesinger recommended, "they should be told by subordinate officials. At no point should the president be asked to lend himself to the cover operation." Schlesinger noted merit in Rusk's proposal to have someone other than the president make the actual decision, "someone whose head can later be placed on the block if things go terribly wrong."[30]

At the same time, the date for Kennedy's final opportunity to veto the plan was set at April 16, about a day before the actual landings. But as Trumbull Higgins, a superb chronicler of the operation, has concluded, by this time Kennedy had "slid so far down the slippery slope toward the Bay of Pigs that for all practical purposes his approval for the operation had already been given."[31] Nothing could stop the invasion now.

The final nail was hammered in the coffin of the doubters when Col. Hawkins cabled on April 13 with an enthusiastic prediction of success and expression of confidence in the Cubans under his command. Robert Kennedy would later say this cable was the crucial influence on his brother, who had been demanding an "eleventh-hour veto" capability. The president would now let the operation go as planned.[32]

The Invasion

On April 15, 1961, the American-sponsored invasion of Cuba began with what was intended to be a diversionary attack at the mouth of the Mocambo River, some 30 miles east of Guantanamo Bay. But rocky reefs prevented the landing, and the ruse was never consummated. The U.S. Navy sent several ships to sail behind this feint and, using sophisticated electronic gear, to attempt to appear on Cuban radar as a large flotilla. As Peter Wyden notes, however, "the beauty of the CIA's great radar deception was lost on Castro and his defenders because *they had no radar.*"[33]

CIA-directed air attacks on Castro's airfields began the same day. The battle in the air would decide the invasion's outcome, and from the beginning the invasion air attacks were mismanaged. Though the CIA air force had 16 B-26 medium bombers available, only six were used in the initial attack. The American story was going to be that the planes were flown independently by Cuban defectors, and it was decided that 16 planes constituted an improbably large defector air force. The result was that the six bombers, although achieving complete surprise and doing their jobs bravely and well, could not disable all of Castro's planes in the initial attack.[34]

Dean Rusk and McGeorge Bundy further hampered the invasion force's air support by cancelling, at the last minute, a second set of air strikes scheduled for the immediate pre-invasion hours. These second strikes might have destroyed Castro's remaining air power, but the two U.S. officials felt an adequately plausible deniability required that Cuban bombers operate from captured Castro airfields. Accusations against the United States directed at ambassador Stevenson at the UN were a decisive influence in persuading Rusk and Bundy to scale down the operation. They thus ordered air strikes held up until the invasion force captured an airfield on Cuban soil.

Immediately, a number of the operation's chief planners protested. These last-minute changes seriously damaged the operation's chances of success, and Bissell and General Cabell, deputy director of CIA, went to see President Kennedy to plead for a change in the decision. Neither, however, would seriously challenge JFK, and nothing was done. A parade of military officers filed into Cabell's office screaming, yelling, pounding fists, and demanding the right to launch air strikes. Colonel Hawkins called the decision, "criminally negligent"; General Shoup "damn near choked." General Lemnitzer, head of the JCS, termed it "absolutely reprehensible, almost criminal." Arleigh Burke was "horrified."[35]

But the decision stood; the invasion force would be deprived of its dawn air-support strikes and would thereafter be vulnerable to attacks from Castro's aircraft.

In Cuba, Castro reacted to the clear signals that an invasion was underway. On April 15, speaking at the funeral of the victims of the air raids, Castro for the first time declared Cuba a fully "socialist" country, explicitly placing himself in the Soviet camp. The following day, he received the first word that an invasion force was steaming for Cuba when reporters from the *New York Times* called Carlos Franqui, editor of *Revolucion*, and requested information about the assault they knew to be underway. Franqui passed the word on to Castro.[36]

At that moment, the invasion force itself was indeed heading toward Cuba. The old ships which carried the troops and their equipment were slow, and ammunition and fuel were piled high on their decks. Apart from troubles with coral reefs—which CIA intelligence men had assured the Cubans were "clouds" on photographs—the initial landings went well enough. Unfortunately, the two ships carrying most of the ammunition ran out to sea to avoid imminent attacks from Castro's planes.

They had left in response to a fateful message received at 1 a.m. on the invasion eve: "Castro still has operational aircraft. Expect you to be hit at dawn. Unload all troops and supplies and take ships to sea as soon as possible." Unfortunately, the message did not mention that the dawn air strikes had been cancelled and the CIA commanders on the scene assumed they were still on.

Grayston Lynch and William "Rip" Robertson, two American volunteers with ties to the CIA, were in charge on the beaches. Lynch, who enlisted in the Army at fifteen by lying about his age, eventually gravitated to the Special Forces. In 1960 he joined the CIA. Robertson had fought in World War II as a Marine officer and worked with the CIA in Guatemala in 1954. Later he had pursued business ventures in Nicaragua, where he became friends with dictator Anastasio Somoza. Both were physically large men and tough soldiers.

At dawn, while the Brigade became embroiled in a few fire fights with scattered bunches of Castro troops, several Cuban Air Force aircraft appeared over the beaches and promptly sank two ships, the *Houston* and the *Rio Escondido*. The men ashore made some progress, but their supplies were already beginning to run low, and the ammunition ships showed no sign of returning. The situation was already beginning to look desperate.

* * *

When the invasion force's B-26s finally returned, they were met by Castro's fighters and well-prepared anti-aircraft units. Castro's units had Sea Fury propeller planes and T-33 jets, more than a match for the Brigade's old, slow medium bombers.

A number of the Brigade's bombers did not come back. Jose Crespo, one of the Brigade pilots, had been hit over the beaches on a bombing run and was trying to nurse his wounded B-26 home when he came upon Jose Ferrer. Ferrer, a former Cubana Airlines pilot, was heading toward Cuba in a transport plane, hoping to drop supplies to the Brigade.

Crespo immediately told Ferrer to stay back, that two T-33s and a Sea Fury were prowling the beaches and had already downed one B-26. Only the intercession of two U.S. jets, which had flown between the Cuban planes and his B-26, had saved Crespo, but his plan was severely damaged. Peter Wyden, whose *Bay of Pigs* is by far the best account of the invasion itself, described what happened next:

> Ferrer identified himself to Crespo by his code name, Falcon One, and asked for Crespo's situation. The stricken plane's left engine was destroyed. Most of the navigation equipment wasn't working. Crespo couldn't tell what else was wrong; something was, because he was losing air speed steadily. He wanted Ferrer to fly back to base within sight of him 'so if I fall in the water you know where I am and they can pick me up tomorrow.' Ferrer agreed. It was getting dark. He did not want to abandon his comrade.

Two hours later, Crespo was still flying but losing air speed and altitude steadily. A priest came on the radio from the planes' base, and Crespo and his co-pilot gave confession. Ferrer and others on the line removed their headsets so the men could speak privately.

After another hour, Crespo's plane was clearly about to crash. He called Ferrer on the radio and said, "Eddie, the situation is bad. I'm three or four hundred feet from the water. I'm going to have to ditch in about two or three minutes."

Ferrer replied, "God bless you. I hope you make it all right. You have been very brave, and your co-pilot too. I will try to look for you tomorrow. Give me a last holler just before you get in the water."

Ten minutes later Ferrer heard Crespo shout, "Hitting the water!"

A day later, Ferrer returned to where Crespo had gone down, but he found nothing.

During the invasion, as the number of Cuban pilots willing or able to fly missions dwindled, Washington allowed a number of the American Alabama Air National Guard volunteers to fly missions. Two who went were Lt. Col. Joe Shannon and Maj. Riley Shamburger. Shannon and Shamburger were old friends who frequently visited each other's homes in Alabama for meetings and parties. They were eager to fight, having seen too many of their Cuban friends killed in an operation whose irrationality enraged them. Now they had a chance to do something about it.

Five B-26s were sent, four with U.S. crews. They would take off at 3 a.m., fly to the Bay of Pigs and penetrate just past the beaches, bombing and machine-gunning whatever of Castro's troops and equipment they could find.

The planes arrived at Cuba without incident. On the first pass, however, as Shannon went after a column of Cuban trucks, Shamburger yelled over the radio, "I'm hit and on fire!"

"What'd you hit?" Shannon asked. But there was no answer; Shamburger's plane was diving out of control, and it hit the water in a shallow dive at about three hundred miles an hour.

Shannon quickly noticed the T-33, or "T-bird," which had hit his friend off to his right. Wyden continues:

> Shannon pulled right toward the T-bird as hard as he could. Instinctively, he knew that if he turned away from the jet it would hit his lumbering old plane too. As it was, the Cuban pilot had no choice, he had to evade. And he did, pulling up abruptly. Shannon slid by directly under him. Less than two hundred feet separated the planes.

As Shannon turned to shoot at the plane, however, it disappeared into the sun, and he did not see it again. He sped off home "inches above the water," hoping for revenge. But later missions were scrubbed.

Other Americans died that day, including Thomas Ray and Leo Francis Baker. They were under attack from Castro's planes when U.S. naval aircraft from the *Essex* appeared; Ray and Francis begged for help, but the Americans, as reported by another Cuban pilot who overheard the exchange, could only reply that they were unable to engage. "I am a naval officer and I must obey my orders," the pilot said. Ray and Baker's B-26 was caught by Castro's planes and exploded in a ball of fire.

But the Americans were not dead. Their plane had crashed in a fiery wreck, yet they had somehow survived. Cuban militiamen rushed to the crash site, under orders to take any prisoners alive; but neither Ray nor Baker would surrender; Ray tried to lob a hand grenade at the Cubans, and Baker apparently shot at them. Both were killed. As late as 1978, Wyden was informed that Baker's body still lay in a Havana morgue because the Cubans were "waiting for the U.S. government to claim it."[37]

* * *

Meanwhile, American ships and planes were in the area, but were unable to help. U.S. pilots flying new A-4 Skyhawk aircraft with their markings painted out, were allowed to chase away a few of Castro's planes but never to engage. The American pilots were repeatedly moved to tears at the tragedy that began to unfold before their eyes and which they were powerless to avert.

Two U.S. destroyers, the *Eaton* and the *Murray*, almost got more action than they bargained for. Steaming close to the Cuban shoreline, hoping to be allowed to pick up survivors of invasion ships that had been sunk, they were targeted by both tank and artillery units of Castro's forces. Most of the Cuban commanders on the scene, however, held their fire, though a few tanks did shoot at the ships. But the American captain did not return fire, and a direct confrontation was avoided.[38]

The Invasion fails

Castro directed an immediate counterattack at the Brigade. Roads leading through the swamps to the beach had not been adequately blocked, another consequence of the Brigade's insufficient air support, and several thousand Castro Militia and regular troops, supported by tanks, soon engaged the invaders. Castro had long suspected that if the rebels gained a significant foothold, they might be able to establish a permanent beachhead and a provisional government, and thus become a serious threat to his regime. Rounding up cadets from a military academy and various militia units, Castro hurled them at the Brigade, and followed this assault with heavily-armed units of Cuban regular forces.[39]

Perhaps the motives of the men of the Brigade can be questioned, but their bravery under fire is beyond dispute. Many fought stubbornly with little ammunition, food, or water, with virtually no air support, against eventually overwhelming odds, and under the dark cloud of the CIA's broken promises. They exacted a grave toll on Castro's forces, both on the ground and in the air; by this time Castro only had about 5 planes left, but his little air force had already done its damage. As the Brigade's ammunition gradually gave out, they had no choice but to fall back, and Castro's forces began to overrun the beachhead. A few Brigade members made it back to the beaches and attempted to escape in small boats; some of these parties starved at sea, others perished in the swamps into which the CIA had claimed they could "melt."[40]

By April 19, some 20,000 Castro troops were involved in the battle, and the Brigade's position was hopeless. Its inexperienced troops had failed to conserve ammunition during the early stages of the battle, and now they ran out. Their resupply ships—ironically bearing tens of thousands of rifles for the anti-Castro guerrillas that were supposed to have joined the Brigade—had been sunk or had fled the incessant air attacks. The Brigade was defeated.

Finally, the remaining Brigade members were captured or killed, and the battle was over. 114 Brigade members had died; Castro captured some 1,189. U.S. ships picked up a few survivors. President Kennedy called in Nixon—his old adversary—and asked his advice; Nixon recommended invasion, but Kennedy demurred, fearing that if he did invade the Russians would seize West Berlin. The American commanders involved were distraught and furious. The Cuban Revolutionary Council begged to be put ashore with the Brigade to die with them, but their request was denied and they were put under house arrest to prevent them from taking rash actions. (It was at this point that Tony Varona was unable to contact the men he had hired to kill Castro.) Castro gave an impassioned and lengthy televised speech in which he interrogated and tried the Brigade.[41]

Later, Kennedy secured the release of the prisoners. Most of them were treated tolerably well by Castro, and eventually he agreed to a ransom of $53 million worth of food and drugs, which were donated by U.S. corporations. In late December, 1962, the Brigade returned to Florida.

ASSESSING THE INVASION

Why, in the end, did the Bay of Pigs occur? Who was to blame? Why was it such a disaster?

John F. Kennedy bears the lion's share of the blame for the operation. He failed to adequately assess the dangers involved; he allowed himself to be strung along by CIA men he considered bright; he did not follow the planning closely enough to realize when the operation had become unstoppable; and he allowed top officials with no knowledge of the operation requirements to dictate last-minute changes that doomed the invasion. Kennedy certainly accepted the blame himself. He must be credited, however, with rejecting late appeals to use U.S. forces, which would only have turned a disaster into a calamity.[42]

Lucien S. Vandenbrouke has applied Graham Allison's models of decision making—which were originally formulated to analyze the Cuban Missile Crisis, as we shall see in the next chapter[43]—to the Bay of Pigs operation in an attempt to determine why it occurred. These models postulate rational decision-making, bureaucratic politics, and governmental or domestic politics as motivation for foreign policy decisions. Vandenbrouke notes that none of these models satisfactorily explains the Bay of Pigs: policy-makers ignored rational reasons why the invasion would fail[44]; bureaucratic politics (that is, the role of the CIA and other government agencies) fails to explain Kennedy's approval[45]; and while domestic pressure certainly created an atmosphere in which action seemed necessary, it did not dictate the form of that action nor did it require an invasion.[46]

Vandenbrouke concludes that these three models are collectively insufficient to explain the decision to go ahead in the face of significant probability of failure. Finally, he analyzes the "cognitive" theory of decision-making, which suggests that individuals tend to seek "cognitive consistency," rejecting information that disturbs their "congruence of beliefs." In essence, this model argues that individuals delude themselves into believing what they want or feel compelled to believe.[47]

Here, the Bay of Pigs decision becomes more comprehensible. President Kennedy perhaps deluded himself into believing that the plan would succeed, feeling that he had to launch it in any case because of political and bureaucratic pressure. Infused with what Arthur Schlesinger has called an "enormous confidence in his own luck,"[48] he went ahead. Bissell, for his part, wanting an operation to improve his own position, might have done something similar. In short, Allison's cognitive theory would suggest that the planners of the Bay of Pigs believed it would succeed because they wanted it to.

Post-operations critiques and reports took different positions. Hard-liners complained that Kennedy should have sent in U.S. troops; perhaps the best exposition of this position is the Taylor Committee report, which was highly classified but parts of which have been made available. Though it recognized that the operation as it was conducted should have been abandoned, the report's general conclusions were enormously hard-line, talking up the renewed Communist threat to Latin American rather than investigating the true causes of the Bay of Pigs failure. It also included testimony of some of the Cubans and Americans who had taken part.[49]

On the other end of the political spectrum, there were those who lamented the "abuses" of the CIA and harshly criticized the administration for its "folly." The Bay of Pigs, in the view of some, was merely another confirmation of the militaristic nature of the U.S. government and its agencies, especially the CIA. Some argued that failure was in fact the best thing that could have happened in the circumstances, because, had the invasion succeeded, the United States would once again have been placed in the role of imperialistic arbiter of Cuba's political fortunes.[50]

Lyman Kirkpatrick, inspector general of the CIA, also wrote a confidential post-operation report, but his was designed to analyze the flaws in American decision-making. He argued that there had been no serious consideration of the level of opposition to Castro in Cuba. He blamed CIA operators for bad policy decisions and implementation, and essentially contended—unlike many

CIA men—that the operation had been a mistake from the start. His report was never released.[51]

The invasion had different effects in Cuba. As Carlos Franqui relates, the Bay of Pigs operation convinced Castro once and for all that radicalization and dependence on the Soviet Union were his only alternatives. He undertook mass arrests to round up suspected U.S. agents; he clamped down on what little freedom of speech and press remained; and he replaced many government officials, even his most trusted Celia Sanchez, with hard-line Communists. "The long, expert Soviet repressive arm," Franqui explains, "was now joined to the Castroite military body, which meant total repression." Fidel's victory at the Bay of Pigs

> unleashed Fidel's repressed hatred of anything that wasn't obedience, work, official Communism, and military strength based on the cult of one man. The unions were eliminated, the militiamen were made into regular army troops, and an elite Communist party came into being. How could a living culture exist in such a society? The historical death of a new and free revolution had already taken place.

CIA meddling with the anti-Castro forces also made any criticism of the regime impossible. "For the Cuban People," Franqui concludes, "opposition and counterrevolution became synonymous."[52]

Why, then, did the operation fail? The common refrain is that "lack of adequate air cover" was the reason, and this certainly has some merit. Castro's planes made a crucial difference on the first day of the battle. But Trumbull Higgins has correctly pointed out that even with adequate air support capable of knocking out Castro's entire air force, there is no guarantee the outcome would have been any different.[53] The thousand or so exile raiders were outnumbered twenty to one, or more, and, as the CIA's own pre-invasion polls indicated, support for Castro in Cuba was high; the exiles could expect no significant support from the Cuban population, certainly not as the representatives of an obviously American-initiated and financed operation. Besides, the Soviet Union might well have felt compelled to rush Castro large amounts of new military aid, including the MiGs CIA planners so feared. Even under the best of circumstances, then, without U.S. backing, the Brigade would probably have been ground down slowly and finally destroyed.

The real problem with the invasion was that it was half-hearted, too small to succeed without U.S. assistance but too big to constitute an easily scrapped guerrilla operation. The political requirements of U.S. distance from the operation, as Higgins has aptly pointed out, conflicted exactly with the military requirements for U.S. support.[54] The CIA's planners, Dulles concluded, recognized this; as Dulles later conceded, he went ahead with the operation because he felt that "when the chips were down . . . any action required for success would be authorized rather than permit the enterprise to fail."[55]

THE AFTERMATH

For the remainder of 1961, the Kennedy administration, chastened by its abject failure at the Bay of Pigs, returned to its earlier patterns of diplomacy toward Cuba. There was some pressure to follow up the invasion with hard-line measures: U.S. invasion or an assassination of Castro. But the intensity of covert operations slowed down and, in fact, Bissell was actually called to task by the president and his brother for not doing enough about Cuba. Eventually, some further attempts at assassinations were made.[56]

Kennedy ordered a number of studies to determine what to do about the post-Bay of Pigs Cuba. At the end of 1961, the CIA developed "Operation Mongoose," an attempt to overthrow Castro from within by turning Cubans against him. The operation was directed by new CIA operations director Richard Helms and encompassed hundreds of agents in Miami and elsewhere and hundreds of millions of dollars. (Bissell had left of his own choice, though CIA Director Allen Dulles was fired on November 28.) The University of Miami helped out by lending some land and false personas for agents, and U.S. law enforcement agencies were instructed to ignore neutrality act problems.

Soon, ships were being sent out of Florida on regular runs to Cuba. They dropped leaflets and brought in guns, equipment, and agents for the anti-Castro underground. Some also shelled waterside towns and resorts. Many of the Cubans and Americans who had been involved at the Bay of Pigs were part of this operation.[57]

It is unclear whether Kennedy ever actually approved of an assassination attempt against Castro. He certainly knew such attempts were underway; at one point he made reference to them in an interview with the reporter Tad Szulc. He probably never ordered an actual "hit," but given his phraseology — "getting rid of Castro" — it is unreasonable to believe he didn't recognize what the practical effects of his orders would be. One U.S. official later said that "no limitations" were placed on the order to remove Castro.[58]

In any case, with the Bay of Pigs Kennedy adopted Castro as his personal enemy. Robert Kennedy, protecting his brother, after the disaster, even attacked those urging the president not to make the issue "personal." As Thomas Powers has concluded, after the Bay of Pigs, "Castro ceased to be an enemy inherited from Eisenhower, and became [Kennedy's] own."[59]

At the same time, President Kennedy's connection to the anti-Castro operations had got him into trouble of a different sort. He had begun to have an affair with one Judith Exner (or Campbell), a former companion of mobsters Rosselli and Giancana. J. Edgar Hoover's FBI discovered the affair, and after Hoover discussed it with the President, JFK ended the relationship.[60]

The United States continued to impose economic and political sanctions on Castro's Cuba. Pressure was put on regional powers—Argentina, Mexico, Ecuador, Chile, Brazil, and others—to isolate Cuba diplomatically and economically. Alliance for Progress funds were made conditional upon agreement to the anti-Cuban stance. The administration attempted to have Cuba ousted from the Organization of American States, and paid Haiti a $5 million bribe for its vote. Yet already many regional governments were becoming uncomfortable with the American position, in large measure because of their own growing nationalism and resultant desire to strike out a path independent of Washington; the seeds of collapse of the regional anti-Castro consensus were already being planted.[61]

Nevertheless, by early 1962, Cuban-American relations had apparently settled back into the hostile but relatively predictable pattern they had followed since 1960. But rumors were already rife that the Soviets had begun installing nuclear missiles in Cuba, and the Kennedy administration, as it turned out, had not heard the last from Castro's Cuba.

12

THE MISSILES OF OCTOBER

"There was danger in standing still or moving forward. I thought it was
the wisest policy to risk that which was incident to the latter course."
James Monroe, letter to Thomas Jefferson

"A low capacity for getting along with those near us often goes hand in
hand with a high receptivity to the idea of the brotherhood of men."
Eric Hoffer, *The Ordeal of Change*

As 1962 opened, tensions between Cuba and the
United States were high, but did not seem to offer the immediate prospect
of conflict. Fidel Castro had rapidly consolidated power, and was basking in the
glow of his victory over the United States at the Bay of Pigs; John F. Kennedy
languished in the shame of that same defeat, and had just two months before
launched an enormous effort to destabilize Castro's regime. Neither expected
or desired a new round of hostilities, least of all the Kennedy administration,
then confronted with problems in Berlin, Laos, and elsewhere. But a third
actor—the Soviet Union—had its own agenda, and in the summer of 1962 it
embarked on a gambit that brought the superpowers closer to nuclear war
than they had ever.

SOVIET BUILDUP AND AMERICAN RESPONSE:
THE TENSIONS GROW

Kennedy's rhetoric and actions toward the new, hostile Cuban government were becoming increasingly bellicose. On January 3, the State Department released a document entitled, "The Castro Regime in Cuba," which referred to the island as "a bridgehead of Sino-Soviet imperialism within the inner defenses of the Western Hemisphere," one that represented, "a serious threat to the collective security of the American republics."[1] On February 3, Kennedy initiated an embargo on all U.S. trade with Cuba with the exception, "on humanitarian grounds," of medicine and food. The embargo would cost Cuba about $35 million in exports to the United States. Two weeks later, the United States called on all its allies to institute similar embargoes against Cuba.

Fidel Castro hardened his own anti-Yankee stance. At the beginning of January, *Tass* announced the signing of a Soviet-Cuban trade protocol, which provided for arrangements increasing Soviet-Cuban trade 40 per cent over 1961. It was announced that Cuban schools would teach only strict Marxist-Leninist doctrine, and Castro condemned the embargo as, "another economic aggression." But the practical effects of Cuba's growing isolation were also becoming clear: on March 12, Castro announced the rationing of various products, caused, as news reports of the time pointed out, as much by his regime's economic mismanagement as by the American actions.[2] The expanding conduit of Soviet military aid to Cuba also became evident; at the end of March, the State Department issued a report estimating that the USSR had supplied Cuba with $100 million in military aid, a package including training, aircraft, and supplies for the army, including hundreds of tanks and hundreds of thousands of small arms. By mid-August reports of huge influxes of Soviet aid—20 ship dockings in the five days between July 27 and 31, for example—make the level of aid more clear. Up to 5,000 Communist advisors and technicians were reported to have been provided as well.[3]

During August, the Soviets started emplacing medium-range nuclear missiles in Cuba, though this act remained unknown to the United States.[4]

By late August, hard-liners in the United States had already begun to pressure the Kennedy administration to respond to Soviet military deployments in Cuba, though the presence of missiles had not yet been detected.[5] Kennedy responded on August 29 by denying an intention to intervene "at this time." To clarify, he noted that his words should not be interpreted to mean he might invade later; he stated conclusively that, "I think it would be a mistake to invade Cuba." As if encouraged by Kennedy's pledge, the Soviet Union announced on September 2 that it would formally provide arms to the Cuban government. The *New York Times* called it a "watershed in hemispheric history" and a "power move in the cold war by the Soviet Union," one which redoubled the complications of invading Cuba.[6]

Forced again to respond, Kennedy declared on September 4 that the United States would use "whatever means may be necessary" to prevent Cuba from exporting its revolution to other regional countries. To support his pledge, he asked Congress for the authority to call up 150,000 reserves for a year of duty. Kennedy added, prophetically, that there was no evidence of, "any organized combat force [in Cuba] from any Soviet-bloc country; of military bases provided to Russia. . . . [or] of the presence of offensive ground-to-ground missiles. . . .Were it to be otherwise the gravest issues would arise."[7]

Pressure on JFK to stand firm continued—former Vice President Nixon, on the 18th, urged even harsher measures, including a naval blockade; on the 20th, the Senate passed a resolution 86-1 stating that the United States was determined, "to prevent by whatever means may be necessary, including the use of arms, the Marxist-Leninist regime in Cuba from extending by force or threat of force its aggressive or subversive activities to any part of this Hemisphere." The House soon adopted the same amendment by a vote of 384 to 7.[8]

The discovery of missiles in Cuba would not come as a complete surprise to all analysts. CIA director John McCone had thought for some time that the Soviets would install missiles in Cuba. The October 1 issue of *Aviation Week and Space Technology* quoted "Pentagon strategists" as believing that the Soviets would put missiles in Cuba because the defenses being built on the island at the time were to prevent photo reconnaissance and not an attack; in other words, the Soviets were going to put something in Cuba that they wanted to keep hidden.[9]

DISCOVERY: THE CRISIS BEGINS

On October 14, 1962, American U-2 reconnaissance planes flew over Cuba and photographed equipment and construction patterns common to Soviet medium-range nuclear missile sites. *Time* magazine later reported: "Chillingly clear to the expert eye were some 40 slim, 52-ft., medium-range missiles, many of them already angled up on their mobile launchers and pointed at the U.S. mainland." This description was incorrect; by October 14, the full set of missiles was not yet visible, and many of the component parts had not yet been assembled. But to the trained eyes of photointelligence specialists, launching stations for Soviet medium-range (1,020 nautical miles) SS-4 and intermediate-range (2,200 nautical miles) SS-5 missiles were clearly being constructed. By October 19, the CIA concluded that 12 SS-5 launch pads were under construction at Guanajay and Remedios, which would become operational in December; and more ominously, that 3 SS-4 launch sites, with 4 launchers each, were already operational at San Cristobal and Sagua la Grande. 42 Il-28 medium bombers, capable of carrying nuclear weapons, were also observed.[10]

Later, the developed photos were shown to a deputy director of the Department of Defense, Roswell Gilpatric. McGeorge Bundy, the president's national security advisor, and others were also notified, but Bundy decided to wait a day to tell Kennedy; by that time the president would have taken in a good night's sleep, and photointelligence officers would have verified the accuracy of the pictures.

At 8 o'clock on the morning of October 16, Kennedy was notified of the existence of the missiles by Bundy. Kennedy immediately called a staff meeting for slightly after eleven and specified those to be present; this group of top officials would serve as a unit throughout the crisis and become known as the "Executive Committee" or ExComm. The consensus at that early meeting was that Khrushchev would use the missiles in Cuba as bargaining chips, either to get U.S. missiles out of Turkey and Italy or to force the U.S. to withdraw from West Berlin.[11]

At this meeting, and throughout the crisis, debates raged over what would constitute a proper U.S. response to the provocation. Dean Acheson soon became the primary advocate of military action; Robert Kennedy favored restraint, at most a naval blockade of Cuba. On the 18th, President Kennedy met with Soviet foreign Minister Andrei Gromyko, but did not tell him the administration knew of the missiles; some critics of JFK's policy later argued that had he made the U.S. information known, he would have given the Soviets a chance to back down quietly at an early stage without risking humiliation.[12]

The presence of missiles in Cuba had been publicly revealed by Senator Kenneth Keating (R.- N.Y.), who told the Senate on October 10 that he had accurate information about the placement of medium-range missile sites in Cuba by the Soviet Union. He called on the administration to respond. "Construction has begun on at least a half dozen launching sites for intermediate-range tactical missiles," he said. "Mr. President, let us have all the facts, and have them now."[13]

Kennedy attempted to dampen the war-mongering in Congress to preserve his own freedom of action. On the 13th he lashed out at Senator Homer Capehart of Indiana, who had called for an invasion of Cuba. "These self-appointed generals and admirals who want to send someone else's sons to war," Kennedy said, "ought to be kept at home by voters and replaced by someone who has some understanding of what the twentieth century is all about."[14]

The pressure to respond, however, was enormous. Congressional elections were just a few months away and many candidates had made the Cuba issue into a test of American will for the Democrats. JFK and the ExComm discussed a number of options. After eliminating a nuclear strike on Cuba as a viable option, two alternatives were developed that defined the parameters of the debate for days to come: launching an air strike against Cuba followed by an invasion, or merely instituting a blockade of the island. Supporters of the former course, including Acheson, Paul Nitze, and JCS Chief Maxwell Taylor, argued that it was the only way to truly eliminate the Soviet threat, and that the missile crisis provided a good opportunity to expand on the Bay of Pigs and get rid of Castro. Those favoring a blockade, including Robert Kennedy, Undersecretary of State George Ball, and Defense Secretary McNamara, noted that their course was less provocative, and that if necessary it could later be upgraded to direct military action. The debate was far from resolved, but President Kennedy had the Department of State draw up a program of occupation for Cuba, in case an invasion became necessary.[15]

Perhaps influenced by memories of the Bay of Pigs disaster, JFK from the start leaned toward the blockade camp. The influence of his brother was particularly telling. Kennedy also suspected that an air strike alone would not accomplish much besides killing Russians, and therefore guaranteeing a true crisis. By October 18, the ExComm was backing away from support for a strike. The JCS continued to demand military action, but Kennedy's preference for caution had become evident.[16]

On the 19th, the true mechanics of the crisis became operative. American troops in the Caribbean area were put on alert. High U.S. government officials, involved in ExComm sessions or other crisis-related operations began to miss previously scheduled meetings and appointments. By this time, too, Kennedy had almost decided on a blockade, and by that evening most members of the ExComm agreed, in part influenced by the fact that an airstrike might not succeed in knocking out all the missiles.

On Saturday, October 20, President Kennedy feigned illness and returned to Washington from mid-term campaigning in Chicago. On the same day, U.S. military commanders around the globe were warned to prepare for action. Kennedy finally decided upon a blockade as his opening move, and U.S. ships—many bearing hodge-podge crews borrowed in part from other ships in the emergency of the moment—were sent off under secret orders without being told what was truly afoot.[17]

Final preparations for the announcement of U.S. policy were made the next day. A presidential speech was scheduled for the 22nd, and aides worked over drafts of the speech through Sunday. American emissaries—including Acheson, Robert Kennedy, and other members of ExComm—were sent off to various key foreign countries to canvass support for the policy once it was declared. As the morning papers of the 22nd went to press, they reported a crisis atmosphere and noted that something was about to break, probably about Cuba; but as the crisis entered its ninth day, the American people were still ignorant of its essentials. Some newspapermen had made accurate conclusions about what the Kennedy administration was about to do, but at the urging of top officials withheld their speculations.

The Quarantine

Finally, On October 22, Kennedy made his famous "quarantine" broadcast. He noted that, "a series of offensive missile sites is now in preparation" in Cuba, whose purpose could be none other than, "to provide a nuclear strike capability against the Western Hemisphere."[18] He referred to the congressional resolutions that had been passed regarding U.S. responses to the Soviet military buildup in Cuba, and the powers he was granted by them.

Kennedy then announced his remedy: a "strict quarantine on all offensive military equipment under shipment to Cuba," continued surveillance, and a policy that, "any nuclear missile launched from Cuba against any nation in the Western Hemisphere [shall be considered] as an attack by the Soviet Union on the United States." Kennedy also said he would reinforce the U.S. naval base at Guantanamo Bay, called for consultation with the Organization of American States and the United Nations, urged Khrushchev to, "eliminate this clandestine, reckless, and provocative threat to world peace," and noted his hope that the Cuban people would oust Castro. Kennedy concluded that, "our goal is not the victory of might but the vindication of right—not peace at the expense of freedom, but both peace and freedom, here in this hemisphere and around the world."[19]

That evening, President Kennedy met with congressional leaders and was surprised to find out that many recommended further action. Senators Russell and Fulbright argued that a blockade was not enough and complained that by potentially drawing out the conflict, a blockade might be more risky than a "quick" airstrike. But they pledged to support the president and avoided public criticism.[20]

The next day, Adlai E. Stevenson, the U.S. representative to the United Nations Security Council, made the same charges and threats directly to the Soviets. Stevenson reiterated the U. S. commitment to the U.N. Charter, and noted that the Soviet Union had waged war against the U.N. goals of democracy and openness. He surveyed the extensive history of Soviet expansion and the Communization of Cuba. He then submitted a resolution providing for the removal of the Soviet missiles. "If we do not stand firm here," Stevenson concluded, "our adversaries may think that we stand firm nowhere—and we guarantee a heightening of the world civil war to new levels of intensity and danger." That same day, the OAS voted a unanimous resolution approving the use of force to consummate the blockade.[21]

The Soviets were somewhat slow to respond. On the 23rd, Khrushchev did claim that the USSR would not respect the blockade. But the Soviets did not make any rapid military or diplomatic moves; for whatever reason, they had apparently either not expected the Americans to find the missiles, or not expected Kennedy to react as he did.

As October 24 dawned, the crisis was at its height. The U. S. Defense Department notified the president that some 25 Soviet ships were still on their way to Cuba. That day, the cordon was firmly drawn around Cuba by about two dozen U. S. warships. American commanders feared a confrontation in which U.S. ships would be forced to fire upon Soviet vessels to compel them to stop. The blockade line was set between 500 and 800 miles around the Cuban coast.[22]

World opinion was apprehensive and ambivalent. UN Secretary U Thant made an "urgent" plea to both sides to suspend hostilities, as did the British philosopher and peace activist Bertrand Russell. Support for Kennedy was limited to a few quarters: France and Latin American, for the most part. Other nations joined the Soviet Union in condemning *American* aggression, and many painted the superpowers as equally culpable.[23]

The next day Khrushchev agreed to UN negotiations, but Kennedy remained committed to his demands, arguing that the Soviets had provoked the crisis with the installation of missiles and demanding the removal of those missiles.

Just after 10 p.m. on the night of the 24th, McNamara announced that the two Soviet ships nearest Cuba, the *Gagarin* and *Komiles*, would hit the blockade line by noon the next day. There were disturbing reports of Soviet submarines in the area, and the U.S. carrier *Essex* was ordered to find the Soviet sub and force it to surface. No one knew what the reaction from the Soviet side would be when their ships ran into the blockade, or when their sub was harried by an American warship. Tension ran high among members of the ExComm. As Robert Kennedy recalled,

> I think these few minutes were the time of gravest concern for the president. Was the world on the brink of a holocaust? Was it our error? A mistake?. . .His hand went up to his face and covered his mouth. He opened and closed his fist. His face seemed drawn, his

eyes pained, almost gray. We stared at each other across the table. For a few fleeting seconds, it was almost as though no one else was there and he was no longer the president. Inexplicably, I thought of when he was ill and almost died; when he lost his child; when we learned that our older brother had been killed; of personal times of strain and hurt. The voice droned on, but I didn't seem to hear anything. . .[24]

True to McNamara's prediction, on the 25th the first true contact occurred: the U.S. Navy intercepted a Soviet tanker and, after the Soviets replied that they carried no weapons, allowed it to continue through the blockade line. Kennedy had given specific orders that Soviet vessels which ran the blockade were not to be stopped and boarded; his priority was avoiding a shooting confrontation. At the same time, most other Soviet ships, after many had halted dead in the water for some time, were reported to be turning away from Cuba.

That same day, political scientist Walter Lippman wrote an article in the *Washington Post* that would significantly influence events. In it, he suggested the very sort of Cuba-for-Turkey superpower missile trade that the ExComm feared the Soviets were trying to engineer. Soviet officials reporting to Khrushchev may have read the message as a trial balloon from Kennedy, an indirect suggestion of a possible compromise through a neutral source. This interpretation would have been false, but some commentators argue that it influenced Khrushchev's suggestions throughout the coming days.[25]

Also on the 25th, responding to U Thant's urgent pleas, both sides agreed to avoid each other in the Caribbean as much as possible; Soviet vessels would not try to run the quarantine line, and the Americans would be as deferent as possible in dealing with Soviet ships. The next day, Kennedy ordered the Navy to board a vessel, but as a non- provocative example he chose a Soviet-chartered ship of neutral Lebanese registry.[26] The boarding went off without incident.

While the Soviets were not getting any new missiles into Cuba, they made a feverish dash to complete the bases already there. U.S. intelligence reported that construction of the MRBM sites continued at a "rapid pace." U.S. officials threatened harsher sanctions if this work continued, and Robert Kennedy warned Soviet Ambassador Dobrynin that President Kennedy needed to act firmly within two days—if the Soviets had not accepted a compromise, that action might not be to their liking. The American military, meanwhile, was placed at Defense Condition (or DefCon) 2 status (DefCon 5 is normal peacetime operations; DefCon 1 is a state of war; the Cuban missile crisis is the only known time the U.S. military has been as high as DefCon

2) and made hurried preparations for war in all theaters.

On October 26, the first of a series of confusing developments began. On that day, Khrushchev apparently sent a personal message to Kennedy. The White House received a letter suggesting that the Soviets, "will declare that our ships bound for Cuba are not carrying any armaments," in exchange for a U.S. pledge not to invade Cuba or to "support any other forces which might intend to invade Cuba." A further communication was transmitted through ABC News correspondent John Scali, who received it at lunch from a Soviet embassy employee, Alexander Fomin. Fomin was widely believed to be the head of the KGB in the United States, and Scali had suspected that the lunch might not be purely social. Indeed, it wasn't: Fomin elaborated on the Khrushchev letter and made clear that the Soviets were willing to remove their missiles from Cuba for the U.S. non-intervention pledge.[27]

Khrushchev's letter bore the distinct tone of an author who was worried and almost desperate, and who wanted badly to pull back from the brink of war. Later commentators are unanimous in describing its language as confused and indicative of someone under a great strain. It also possessed what were believed to be unmistakable Khrushchevian traits, including earthy stories and grammatical mistakes. Some later analysts interpreted the letter as being personally sent by a worried Khrushchev to bypass hard-liners in the Kremlin, who wanted to press the confrontation to its denouement.[28]

On the 27th, however, Kennedy received a second message from Khrushchev, broadcast over Radio Moscow at 9 a.m. Washington time. This hardened the Soviets' line, proposing the trade-off expected by many U.S. officials: if the United States would dismantle its missile bases in Turkey, the Soviet Union would do the same in Cuba. The United States has some 15 aging Jupiter intermediate range missiles deployed in Turkey, and as Walter Lippman's proposal had suggested, the Soviets were offering a trade.

It has long been assumed that this deal would have imposed little actual cost on the United States, as Kennedy had already ordered missile bases in Turkey, Italy, and Britain dismantled; the old missiles were thought to be of marginal military value, and they were difficult to maintain. The conventional version of the crisis contends that bureaucratic delays and Turkish opposition— they wanted to keep the missiles as an assurance of U.S. commitment— obstructed a quick enactment of Kennedy's order, and by the time of the missile crisis, the U.S. missiles were still in place.[29] Now, of course, Kennedy could not give them up without appearing to back down. JFK, it is therefore argued, was angry that his order had not been carried out and now opposed the Cuba/Turkey deal.

More recent evidence suggests otherwise. Transcripts of the October 27 ExComm meeting and statements by Dean Rusk indicate that Kennedy was more than prepared to give up the Jupiters if he had to. He felt the trade was reasonable. Moreover, the considerable Turkish opposition to removing the missiles before the crisis left the administration in no hurry to pull them out; their surrender in a trade would therefore have been a significant concession, yet one that JFK was prepared to make. He even had Rusk give Professor Andrew Cordier of Columbia a Statement for U Thant to make, if necessary, suggesting the trade; Kennedy could then agree to what would seem a fair international solution, without (publicly) "giving in" to Khrushchev's demands. Kennedy kept this plan secret from the ExComm, another indication of how badly he wanted to keep the trade option open.[30]

Meanwhile, American analysts were scrambling to find reasons for this Soviet volte-face; most felt that a weak Khrushchev had been overruled by hawks in the Politburo and forced to recant his earlier proposal. Kennedy was ready to accept Khrushchev's earlier plan, but the Turkey deal was a different matter, and the small opening provided by Khrushchev's strange letter had quickly been closed. Later on the 27th, the administration publicly rejected the proposed swap, arguing that the Cuban situation had to be resolved first. Later negotiations dealing with "properly inspected arms limitation" outside the Western Hemisphere, a State Department release said, could "continue as soon as the present Soviet-created threat is ended."[31]

That same day, the U.S. Defense Department announced that a U-2 spy plane had been lost over Cuba. It was piloted by Major Rudolf Anderson, Jr., and it had been downed by Soviet anti-aircraft missiles. Tension continued to mount.

The Crisis Continues

Saturday, October 27, was the high point of the crisis. The Russians had given their ultimatum; a U-2 spy plane had been shot down; and Kennedy knew he could not hold the nation perpetually on the brink of war, that he had to act by Sunday. McNamara held American forces on alert, and an airstrike could have been arranged in less than 48 hours. The JCS and many of the ExComm members now returned to their demands for an immediate airstrike, arguing that the purpose of the blockade—to give the Soviets a chance to back down—had been served but had not ended the crisis. Kennedy demanded one more day's wait.

Several members of the ExComm had an idea. They suggested accepting Khrushchev's *first* offer, promising to end the blockade and not invade Cuba if the Soviets would pull the missiles out. JFK liked the idea and said so in a public announcement. In a private meeting with Dobrynin that evening, however, at the urging of his brother, Robert Kennedy did stress that the United

States had been "anxious to remove those missiles from Turkey and Italy for a long period of time" and that, if the Soviets would back down, his brother just might go through with the plans.[32] In essence, the Kennedys offered a two-part plan: a public retreat for the Soviets, as they agreed to remove the Cuban missiles and a private American concession.

This was called the "Trollope Ploy" for Victorian novelist Anthony Trollope, whose heroines were known to take lukewarm praises as true marriage proposals, just as Kennedy would do with Khrushchev's first offer. And the major reason Kennedy tried this ploy, rather than immediately resorting, as he was inclined to do, to trading the Jupiters, was that former ambassador to Moscow Llewellyn Thompson suggested the Soviets might accept the lesser offer. Thompson was the only recognized Soviet expert who took part in the discussions, and his influence was crucial. As two analysts of the crisis have concluded, "it was only after [Thompson's] argument that the Soviets might *not* insist on the Jupiter trade that the President approved the Trollope Ploy."[33]

The Soviets accepted. The next day, Sunday, October 28, Dobrynin made known that the proposal was acceptable, and a radio broadcast from Moscow at about 9 a.m. Washington time said that the Soviet government "has given a new order to dismantle the arms which you described as offensive, and to crate and return them to the Soviet Union." The Soviets also offered to allow U.N. supervision of the process, though Fidel Castro would later take issue with that pledge. But the crucial implication of the message was clear to everyone in Washington: the Cuban Missile Crisis was over. The Soviets had given in.

Aftermath of the Crisis

Various arguments and disputes related to the Soviet military buildup continued into 1963. Castro maintained a hard line, refusing to admit international inspection teams, including the U.N. and Red Cross personnel the Soviets had approved. The missile bases were soon dismantled, but Soviet Ilyushin-28 medium bombers remained in Castro's hands, and he said he intended to keep them. By November 8, however, U.S. intelligence services reported that all known missiles had been removed from Cuba.

On November 19, probably under heavy Soviet pressure, Castro relented and, calling the Il-28s "antiquated equipment," agreed to give them up. He still threatened to shoot down U.S. reconnaissance planes, though no more were lost. On the 21st, the crisis finally wound down as U.S. ships were taken off station from the blockade and as U.S. and Soviet military units stood down around the globe.

In December 1962, President Kennedy spoke before a rally of 40,000 Cuban exiles in Miami. He was presented with the battle flag of Brigade 2506, and he gave an impassioned address calling for the liberation of Cuba and the restoration of freedom on the island. Kennedy did virtually everything but commit himself to an invasion. Predictably, the Soviets and Cubans both denounced the speech as bellicose and imperialist.

Some American congressmen, meanwhile—Senators Kenneth Keating and John Sherman Cooper, among others—were dissatisfied with the Kennedy administration's handling of the crisis, and demanded stricter verification procedures. Some argued that the Soviets had merely engaged in a temporary halt, and were planning to continue their military buildup in Cuba at an ever more rapid pace. Cuban exiles reported that the Soviets were hiding missiles in caves, and had not removed them all; conservative U.S. congressmen used these and other reports as evidence in their call for an investigation.[34]

Kennedy tried his best to calm these fears while pursuing a cautious policy toward Cuba. Far from emboldening the young president, the missile crisis brought home the risks of war in the modern world, and his later policies— toward Cuba and elsewhere—became more restrained. A *New Republic* editorial characterized his policy at the time as "watch and wait, in the hope that...Castro is losing prestige, and the Soviets will eventually prove unwilling to pay their $1 million a day bill for supporting Castro's economy." The *Washington Post* agreed, editorializing on January 12, 1963 that "the insurgent traditions of Cuba, and the distance from the Soviet Union, make it unlikely that in the long run a widely-detested regime in Havana can survive."[35] American observers of the Cuban situation still seemed incapable of recognizing the true depth of feeling underlying Castro's revolution; and if Kennedy—or American analysts—actually anticipated such developments, they would be in for a long wait indeed.

Ramifications of the Crisis

The Cuban Missile Crisis still represents the moment when the superpowers came closest to actual nuclear conflict, and as such it has been studied and discussed by scholars and analysts ever since. The results and implications of this brush with Armageddon continue to inform most of the debate on nuclear crisis management. The lessons that have been drawn, however, are as divergent as were the initial responses to Kennedy's actions.

Within a year, Khrushchev had been deposed. There are various theories about the reasons why, though by far the most common rationale relies on the idea of Khrushchev as anti-establishment reformer and dove forced out by traditional Kremlin hawks.

Some claim that another result of the crisis was a huge Soviet military build-up. Chastised by their humiliating concessions, the argument goes, the Soviets embarked on the greatest peacetime military buildup in history. There is little debate over the fact that the Soviets built up, and did so quickly; however, some scholars question whether the Missile Crisis was a unique motivation. Some observers argue that the parameters of the Soviet military buildup were spelled out in Soviet doctrinal writings years before the crisis, which affected Soviet military spending only marginally, if at all.

In the United States, Kennedy adopted the role of peacemaker, apparently chastened by his brush with annihilation. In June, 1963, he gave a speech at American University calling for an end to the arms race, and made a conscious attempt to temper his rhetoric from then on. Democrats, buoyed by reinvigorated American pride, did well in November elections. Kennedy's softer line toward the Soviets eventually led to the negotiation of a number of treaties designed to reduce the risk of nuclear war, including the Hot Line and Limited Test-Ban Treaties.

In Cuba, Castro was predictably furious with the Soviets for letting him down; he was reportedly so angry that he kicked and broke a mirror, and later exclaimed that Khrushchev had no *cajones* (balls).[36] For a time, he turned to the Chinese for assistance in his ideological attacks on the Soviets; the People's Republic of China was certainly disappointed in the Soviets, and the *People's Daily* proclaimed on October 31, that Khrushchev had yielded to a "U.S. imperialist attempt to browbeat the people of the world into retreat at the expense of Cuba."[37] The Chinese, however, simply did not have the sort of funds to contemplate supporting Castro, and though the Cuban leader was angry, there was little he could do. Soviet aid continued to constitute his economic lifeblood.[38]

Cuban-Soviet relations were thus strained for a time. In mid-November, the Soviets nevertheless proclaimed their continued support for Cuba, and eventually Castro, recognizing the inevitability of his position, abandoned his harsher criticisms of the Soviets. In time, the relationship returned to relative normalcy, although Castro would from 1962 on, harbor few illusions about the reliability of the Soviet Union.

RETROSPECTIVE ASSESSMENTS

Since the crisis, dozens of analysts have speculated about its true implications. Did it mean that Kennedy was a hawk, and Khrushchev a dove? Did it prove the absolute value of nuclear superiority? Did it mean that Castro was expendable to the Soviets if the price were high enough?

Causes of the Crisis

The most common assessment of the reason for the Cuban Missile Crisis is that the Soviets took a risk because they felt they were confronted with a young, callow American leader. Kennedy's perceived weakness—which had caused him to back down on both the Berlin Wall and Bay of Pigs issues—were seen by some as an irresistible temptation for the Soviets.[39] CIA Director John McCone blamed Kennedy for a "climate of inaction" which contributed to Soviet risk-taking.[40]

Khrushchev's poor impression of Kennedy was supposedly confirmed when the two met in Vienna. James Reston, whose November 15, 1964 article in the *New York Times Magazine* in many ways originated the theory of a weak Kennedy, argued in that piece that Khrushchev thought he was "dealing with an inexperienced young leader who could be intimidated and blackmailed." The introduction of missiles into Cuba, Reston concludes, was "the final gamble of this assumption."[41]

Not all analysts share this belief, however. Richard Ned Lebow, in particular, has made a strong case that "Kennedy's youth, the Vienna meeting, and the Bay of Pigs are at best ambiguous in their implications."[42] The Vienna conversation was reported at that time to be mutually tough and uncompromising.[43] With regard to Cuba, the Soviets could just as easily have believed that the Bay of Pigs created a requirement for a crisis as that it pointed to Kennedy's weakness. Kennedy, moreover, had "acted firmly, even belligerently" during the Berlin crisis of 1961 and at other times,[44] and the Soviets had by no means a clear picture of a weak American leader.

Lebow emphasizes that this evidence does not point to the "correctness of any particular interpretation of the meaning of these events,"[45] but it certainly dooms the common theory of Kennedy's weakness. Perhaps, as one writer has pointed out, the Soviets expected a weak response regarding Cuba, because several American officials had made statements disparaging the significance of the Soviet military buildup there; the process could have been analogous to the way in which Allan Dulles' exclusion of Korea from the list of American interests had encouraged a North Korean attack.[46] As Lebow and others have suggested, Khrushchev, unable to prove objectively that Kennedy was weak, may have convinced himself that the young president would back down simply because he (Khrushchev) wanted to believe it.[47] If this is indeed the case, then the world came close to nuclear annihilation in 1962 simply because Nikita Khrushchev intentionally misread signals from Kennedy.

Most important, the underlying assumption of this "orthodox" interpretation of the crisis is that the Soviet Union was basically responsible for it. It took the risks, the assessment goes; it put the missiles in Cuba, it dared the United State to react.[48]

A contrary view has emerged, however, and it is commonly termed the "revisionist" approach. These are various such analyses, all of which ascribe significant, if not total, responsibility for the crisis to the United States. One form, which might be termed "broad" revisionism, argues that the United States caused the crisis by provoking the Soviet Union on a worldwide basis and forcing it to react. American nuclear superiority and worldwide belligerency, especially with regard to Cuba, prompted a response from a worried USSR. As Thomas Peterson has concluded, for example, "It is plausible to argue that had there been no economic embargo, no Bay of Pigs, no Operation Mongoose, no hit-and-run raids conducted by CIA-assisted Cuban exiles, no ouster of Cuba from the OAS and no assassination attempts, there would have been no missile crisis."[49] Another form of revisionism suggests that, once the crisis developed, the Kennedy administration exaggerated its importance for domestic political effect.

With regard to this latter model, however, which posits Kennedy as a warmonger determined to re-establish his image as a tough leader after the Bay of Pigs debacle, the historical evidence is mixed. Transcripts of ExComm meetings show little concern with domestic political results, only an overwhelming desire to avoid war. Kennedy's willingness to trade the Jupiters, for example, as two students of the crisis have concluded, means that "some of the Cuban missile crisis 'revisionists' will have to rethink their views."[50]

Another likely motive for the emplacement of the missiles was a fear of U.S. invasion, on the part of both Castro and Khrushchev. Whether the Cubans or the Soviets first suggested that the missiles be emplaced is a matter of historical dispute; even Castro has vacillated on this point. But both would have strong interests in avoiding another U.S. invasion, Castro for obvious reasons, and Khrushchev to protect his reputation as a friend of socialist revolutions. For if the United States intervened, given the proximity of Cuba and the U.S. nuclear superiority, there would have been very little the Soviets could have done about it. In this sense, the emplacement of nuclear missiles might have been seen as a deterrent to U.S. intervention, and given the U.S. missiles in Turkey, the Soviets might not have expected the sort of vehement reaction they got. The eventual lone Soviet condition for withdrawing the missiles—that the U.S. cease planning or aiding invasion attempts—reinforces this model of Soviet motivations.[51]

Perhaps the most persuasive explanation for Khrushchev's emplacement of the missiles is simply that his move was a calculated gamble, aimed at shifting the geopolitical situation. The Soviet leader was concerned about Communist China, whose respect and allegiance he wanted to preserve lest it strike out on an independent path. He could also have seen the deployment as a counter to the U.S. military deployments that ringed the Soviet Union from Western Europe to Turkey to the Middle and Far East.

The Khrushchev Letters: Who Were the Doves?

As discussed earlier, one common interpretation, both contemporary and retrospective, of the two Khrushchev communications to Kennedy runs roughly thus: Khrushchev was the soft-liner in the Kremlin, arguing for small defense budgets and thus angering the Soviet miliary. In the crisis he sent a personal note, bearing signs of stress, to Kennedy trying to concede, but hawks in the Kremlin discovered his ploy and overruled him, proposing a stiffer compromise—the Jupiter trade—over Radio Moscow. Not all analysts, however, share this view.

The most obvious problem with the model is that the Soviets *did* eventually accept American agreement to the less stringent of their two proposals. If the "hawks" in the Kremlin had really taken over by that point, such an outcome seems unlikely. There are a number of possible explanations. Perhaps the hawks lost their enthusiasm for war at the last moment, for example, and reminded again of the U.S. nuclear superiority (it possessed over 200 ICBMs while the Soviets had just a few dozen), backed down. Or Khrushchev might have regained control after a time and reasserted his intention to agree to his first proposal. The eventual secret U.S. pledge regarding the Turkish missiles might not have been sufficient.

Other interesting suggestions come from historian John L. Scherer. He admits that a split obviously existed in the Kremlin, and that apparent weakness had endeared him to few: during the crisis, Khrushchev's name was de-emphasized, for example, appearing only alphabetically in state dinner invitations. On October 25, the only town in the USSR called "Khrushchev" had its name changed to "Kremges." Khrushchev was being isolated. But by whom and why?

Scherer argues that Khrushchev, and not Brezhnev or others, may have been the hawk during the crisis. Though he had argued for smaller military budgets, Khrushchev was still a bellicose country man, prone to outbursts and unpredictable confrontationalism. He could easily have inspired and orchestrated the crisis.

In such a context, the two Soviet communications to Kennedy take on different meanings, though exactly what they imply is unclear. Khrushchev's first letter did not explicitly offer to remove the missiles; it only said that should the United States end the blockade "the question of armaments. . . would look different," and promised that no ships then on their way to Cuba held weapons. Scherer also notes that the Russian linguistic techniques used in that portion of the letter intentionally create ambiguity.

Given that it was only when Fomin lunched with Scali that the Soviet offer became one to *remove* the missiles already in Cuba, it is possible to speculate that Fomin's communication was ordered by Kremlin *doves* fearful of Khrushchev's actions. After all, why would Khrushchev have chosen Fomin as a means to relay information, when he had already sent a letter? Moreover, sending the message through the newsman Scali ensured that, if not at the time then later, the Soviet offer would become public, and it seems unlikely that a terrified Khrushchev, under pressure from Kremlin hawks to stand tough but desperate to end the crisis, would use such a mechanism. Kremlin doves, on the other hand, attempting to undercut a bellicose Khrushchev, would have incentives to publicize their offer. Once in the open, it would be difficult for Khrushchev to reject; he would at once appear as the warmonger and reveal the splits in his own government.

In this hypothetical context, the radio broadcast of the 27th becomes easier to understand. Khrushchev, having been informed of Fomin's ploy and afraid he was losing control, acted quickly to overrule his earlier offer and—broadcasting over Radio Moscow, a guarantee of public awareness—sought to put the Cuba/Turkey deal firmly in the open before Fomin's plan became common knowledge.[52]

An interesting confirmation of the thesis that Khrushchev personally initiated the crisis comes from Carlos Franqui, who was an early associate of Castro's and had been involved in the Cuban government since the revolution. He notes that in 1962, Aleksei Adzubei, Khrushchev's son-in-law and prominent figure in the Soviet press, came to Cuba bearing the warning that the United States intended to invade Cuba and the Soviet Union was unable to persuade it otherwise. Castro, obviously upset, began a series of close consultations with the Soviets that resulted in the installation of the missiles. In wondering why Khrushchev used this unusual channel to talk with the Cubans, Franqui concludes that, "It seems that the missile business was one of Khrushchev's pet projects, one he worked out with the Soviet military, but one from which he excluded both the Party and the Soviet government." Later, when speaking with Khrushchev, Franqui became convinced that the missile ploy was Khrushchev's way of establishing a bargaining chip to negotiate the removal of some of the American bases that ringed the Soviet Union in 1962—in Western Europe, Turkey, Japan, the Middle East, and elsewhere.[53]

Whether or not this interpretation is accurate, it is certainly interesting, and it challenges some commonly accepted notions of the mechanics of the crisis. Subsequently, the notion that Khrushchev himself ordered the emplacement of the missiles has become relatively well-accepted. But the exact machinations going on in the Kremlin during that period will probably never be known.

Lessons of the Crisis: Models of Analysis

Commentators on the Cuban Missile Crisis have used a wide variety of analytical models to explain the decisions of both sides. While analysts discussed earlier in this section propose logical reasons for the superpowers to have acted as they did, other writers have attempted to explain those actions with more plausible models of behavior.

There are a great number of such systems. Conventional, "rational" policy analysts simply look at the actions of decision-makers in pure rational-decision frameworks,[54] Jack Snyder and others have advocated the "cognitive dynamics" model that views decision-makers as trapped or locked into strategies based on "compellance"; in this case Kennedy, Snyder contends, feared impeachment if the missiles were not removed, and this "compelled" his tough reaction.[55] Proponents of the bureaucratic politics notion see the power-based maneuvering of the bureaucracies of both sides as responsible for the decisions of their leaders.[56] Some commentators focus on the personalities of the participants.[57] Observers of domestic politics note Kennedy's requirement to be seen as taking a harder line in the wake of the Bay of Pigs and Berlin crises.[58]

Blema Steinberg takes a different approach, analyzing the divergent goals of the superpowers with regard to Cuba before the crisis as predictors of subsequent events. This method allows Steinberg to straddle the "orthodox" and "revisionist" approaches discussed earlier: the crisis was neither side's fault, but was "a product of a mixture of prior incompatible objectives and conflict behavior" and that "both sides contribute[d] mutually to escalating the conflict." The Soviet Union wanted to prevent an attack on Cuba and enhance its own prestige, the United States to block Soviet inroads into the hemisphere and preserve its nuclear superiority. In fact, Steinberg concludes that "the effort to assign responsibility to one side or the other appears overly simplistic."[59]

Stuart Thorson and Donald Sylvan used a complex computer program to examine the decisions taken in the crisis; the conclusions are interesting. A shorter crisis time, they report, might have proved disastrous insofar as it would have forced Kennedy to react more quickly, in which case he probably would have taken military action. Kennedy, moreover, wanted firm action, they contend, and the blockade course was the absolute lowest rung on the escalation ladder at which he was willing to start; in other words, his "belligerency coefficient" was quite high.[60]

Charles Lockhart has applied the theory of incremental policy-making to the crisis and agrees that the gradual nature of decision-making—spread out as it was over two weeks or more—helped temper American reactions. "Incremental steps," he concludes, "allowed flexibility" in American decisions, and also gave the soviets time to hit upon an acceptable, face-saving way out of the crisis. Incrementalism, Lockhart concludes, might therefore hold more promise as a decision-making technique that the sort of preemptive action taken in the invasion of the Dominican Republic in 1965, or Grenada in 1983.[61]

Kennedy's Role

Commentators differ sharply in assessments of President Kennedy's role in the crisis. The conventional view of the period, encouraged by the sense of relief and national pride, was that Kennedy's decisions were prudent and courageous, and that he had managed the crisis as well as could be expected. Many subsequent analysts essentially agree, noting that Kennedy avoided unnecessary provocations.[62]

Left-wing analysts, however, have argued that Kennedy's actions bordered on irresponsible brinkmanship, guided most saliently by a desire to bolster his domestic political reputation.[63] Kennedy did not have to take the immediate, provocative action that he did; a blockade was unnecessary, these analysts argue, and Kennedy in fact only narrowly avoided endorsing an airstrike, an action that almost definitely would have brought on a war. Perhaps most ominously, however, Kennedy's actions reinforced the emerging notion that credibility was all in international relations, a notion which would later lead the United States into an unnecessary war fought almost solely to maintain America's "image."[64] This is the second model of "revisionism" referred to earlier.

Kennedy was also criticized from the right. David Lowenthal, among others, argued that the crisis was a "lost opportunity," that the blockade constituted "the weakest response open to us." Kennedy should have seized the excuse, Lowenthal argues, to topple the Castro regime once and for all. Presuming that the Soviets were rational, they would have realized that the American nuclear superiority, and the proximity of a Cuban battlefield to American forces and supplies, would have rendered a conflict over the island a disastrous undertaking, and would therefore not have interfered. Kennedy's explicit adjuration of intervention constituted something close to an "explicit retraction of the Monroe Doctrine."[65] In short, Lowenthal and other conservative commentators argue, Kennedy had been too weak in the crisis.[66]

Those predisposed against American intervention in Cuban affairs and unafraid of Soviet influence in the hemisphere saw Kennedy's action as an overreaction. Those who believed the United States should bend Latin American countries to its will, and that such actions constituted a necessary response to dangerous Communist advances in the region, believed he should have gone further. Many who were strong proponents of neither view were simply happy to have weathered the crisis, and applauded the young president for his at once cautious and resolved policies.

American Versus Soviet Perceptions

Peter W. Rodman has emphasized the divergent lessons drawn by American and Soviet policy-makers.[67] One involved the relative importance of nuclear and conventional weapons. The Kennedy administration had come into office warning of the dangers of an overemphasis on nuclear weapons, and Kennedy officials drew supporting lessons from the crisis. McGeorge Bundy argued at the time that "what was most important here was not the strategic nuclear balance, but the immediate and effective impact of the conventional forces of the United States in the Caribbean." George Ball concurred, as did McNamara, who said shortly after the crisis: "Nuclear force...was in the background. Non-nuclear forces were our sword, our nuclear forces were our shield."[68] Soviet planners, on the other hand, believed that the crisis again demonstrated the overwhelming importance of strategic nuclear missiles, and continued their buildup of those weapons.[69]

Another divergence of perception was related to the implications of the crisis for peace-making. The brush with nuclear war had terrified U.S. leaders, including Kennedy, and afterward they pressed hard for various symbols of peace: a superpower Hot Line agreement to improve communications, a nuclear Test Ban Treaty, and so on. The Soviet opinion, on the other hand, was summed up by the remark of First Deputy Foreign minister Vasily Kuznetsov: "You American will never be able to do this to us again."[70] The Soviets continued their military buildup in the aftermath of the crisis, determined to reach a parity that did not admit the kind of American bullying that took place, in their eyes, during the crisis.

The Key Lesson: A Fragile Peace

Perhaps the most significant lesson of the crisis is that models of analysis that claim to predict superpower behavior, but which rely for their accuracy on a presumption of nearly perfect rationality, are doomed to break down. Former Defense Secretary Robert McNamara has stated this lesson neatly in an expression that he calls "McNamara's Law," and that he sees as having been vindicated, not only in the missile crisis, but in all international crises with implications for the superpowers. "It is impossible to predict with a high degree of confidence," he argues, "what the effects of the military use of force will be because of the risks of accident, miscalculation, misperception and inadvertence."[71]

In the Cuban Missile Crisis, for example, the United States did not have a clear idea of why the Soviets had emplaced the missiles in Cuba, nor did American leaders have any idea how Moscow would respond to U.S. action. The blockade could have provoked war; an air strike might not have. There was simply no way to know. In the situation, with its international prestige — and perhaps more than one high-level Kremlin career—on the line, the Soviet Union might have felt compelled to begin an escalatory process which would have resulted in general war. That it did not was furtuitious, but decision-makers in a crisis cannot be confident that such a favorable conclusion will result from every crisis. As Meg Greenfield has pointed out, complex analytical models of the crisis are dangerous to the extent that they fool us into believing that all crises are manageable, that if everyone merely acts rationally, everything will work itself out. "Less rational influences" can often determine the end of a crisis, she notes; "accident, one man's strength of will, another's folly."[72]

The miscalculations which led to the First World War, ably summarized in Barbara Tuchman's *The Guns of August*—to which, incidentally, Kennedy referred often during the crisis—stand as probably the prime example of the inadvertent initiation of hostilities. But the fact that it could happen again, anywhere and at any time, urges caution in the employment of military force. Since the Cuban Missile Crisis, at least, both superpowers have proven capable of skillfully pursuing their interests while avoiding even indirect military confrontation. One can only hope that this admirable restraint will continue to characterize superpower decision-making in the future.

KENNEDY'S LATER POLICIES

The last months of the Kennedy administration were mostly devoted to responding to charges that Cuba still constituted an offensive threat, that the agreements reached to end the Missile Crisis were insufficient. In February 1963, for example, at a news conference, Kennedy rebutted claims that some missiles remained in Cuba and that the Komar guided-missile patrol boats Khrushchev had given Castro were a serious threat.[73]

Kennedy also applied increasingly tight clamps to Cuba in the form of various sanctions. An economic embargo was in force, and in July, 1963, the State and Treasury Departments blocked transfers of funds to Cuba and froze all Cuban assets in the United States [74]

Throughout the Cuban Missile Crisis, covert operations against Castro had continued. In April 1962, the CIA renewed its contracts with the mob to kill Castro, though there is some evidence that the mob never seriously attempted to kill the Cuban leader, and that in fact it informed him of CIA plans in exchange for concessions on smuggling. Robert Kennedy was particularly interested in Operation Mongoose and other aspects of the secret war against Castro, and wanted these tactics vigorously pursued. By the spring of 1963, the NSC was still recommending an increase in operations against Cuba. After the Missile Crisis, however, the agreement by the United States to cease hostile acts against Castro as a precondition for the removal of the missiles suggested that the covert war was doomed.[75]

Cuban exiles continued to attack the island from locations in Florida, and the Kennedy administration was forced to respond. On March 30, 1963, the Departments of Justice and State announced that "these acts are neither supported nor condoned by this government." The announcement did express understanding for the exiles, but was clear in the intention of the United States to prosecute violations of its Neutrality Act. Jose Miro Cardona, a Cuban exile leader, disparaged this act and charged that Kennedy had reneged on a post-Bay of Pigs promise for an invasion with six U.S. divisions; Kennedy denied the claim, and there is no evidence to suggest he ever made such a promise.[76]

Covert Operations Continue

Nevertheless, at the same time it was publicly stopping Cuban exiles from attacking Castro, the Kennedy administration continued its covert war against the Cuban regime. The CIA supported its own raids on the island, and sometimes aided the same independent groups State and Treasury had told to stop. Certainly, the volume dropped off in the aftermath of the crisis, and in many instances Cuban exile groups organized and trained by the CIA simply continued operations without U.S. approval. The Soviet Union charged that the United States was violating its pledge to cease attacks on Cuba, but Kennedy— citing his public positions—denied this. Nevertheless, attacks and assassination attempts (aimed at Castro and others) continued.[77]

One independent Cuban exile group attacked Soviet ships near Cuba in 1963, hoping to precipitate another Soviet-American crisis that might lead to an invasion of Cuba by the United States. The CIA did not direct this group, which called itself "Alpha 66," though some have claimed that the Agency did wink at its activities. The U.S. Coast Guard attempted to stop the Cubans, but in March 1963, they attacked and sank the Russian merchantman *Baku* in shallow water near Cuba. Kennedy, responding to angry demands from the USSR, stepped up his enforcement of the neutrality laws, and some Cubans came to hate him for his "coexistence" policy. The United States was placed in the ironic position of stopping Cubans who were following U.S. orders; as one writer in the *Washington Post* phrased it, "How could persons doing the bidding of an arm of the United States government be prosecuted for violating a United States law?"[78]

The CIA also maintained more conventional intelligence-gathering operations inside Cuba. It placed agents in various locations, including within the Cuban government.[79] All the tools of a continued policy of hostility towards the revolution were in place.

1963-1964: Castro's "Olive Branch"

In the fall of 1963, the Cuban United Nations delegation made known that Fidel Castro desired an accommodation with the United States. It was the first of what would be many such suggestions of rapprochement made by Castro, and it caught the Kennedy administration by surprise. Some analysts immediately suggested that it was a ruse, designed to win a few economic and diplomatic concessions from the United States while Castro continued his revolutionary activity. Others, however, argued that a number of factors—including Castro's plunging economy and the demonstrated unwillingness of the Soviets to go to war for him in the Missile Crisis—created legitimate motives for the Cuban leader to seek an accommodation.

The administration pursued these contacts through a special advisor to its U.N. delegation, Bill Atwood. He told the Cubans that the United States would send a representative to meet with Castro in Havana as long as the Cubans agreed to set the agenda in advance. The Cubans, in turn, said they would talk to their people in Havana and get back to him.[80]

Meanwhile, Kennedy was making known his own desire for closer relations. In October, 1963, he met with French journalist Jean Daniel, whom he knew was travelling to Cuba. Kennedy made some surprising statements and concluded that

> I believe that there is no country in the world, including any and all the countries under colonial domination, where economic colonization, humiliation and exploitation were worse than Cuba, in part owing to my country's policies during the Batista regime. I believe that we created, built, and manufactured the Castro movement out

of whole cloth without realizing it. . . . I will go even further: to some extent it is as though Batista was the incarnation of a number of sins on the part of the United States. Now we shall have to pay for those sins.

Kennedy then admitted that, even though this was the case, the Cuban-American conflict had taken on an international dimension with the addition of Soviet influence. Nevertheless, he suggested that, if Castro moderated his revolutionary activities, an accommodation might be possible. "The continuation of the blockade," he said, "depends on the continuation of [Castro's] subversive activities."

In Cuba, Daniel met with Castro, who came to his hotel room without warning one evening. On hearing Kennedy's remarks, Castro calmly and thoughtfully reflected that "I believe Kennedy is sincere. I also believe that today the expression of his sincerity could have political significance." He meant that Kennedy had initially been pressured into a hard line on Cuba because of the political realities of his campaign against Nixon, and only now was ready to express his true feelings. But Castro also said he believed that the monied classes in the United States would prevent Kennedy from significantly altering American policy. Castro merely asked, as he put it, for nothing "but peace, and to be accepted as we are," a socialist country that could coexist peacefully with the United States. "So far as we are concerned, everything can be restored to normalcy on the basis of mutual respect of sovereignty."[81]

These contracts were abruptly ended, however, when John Kennedy was killed on November 22, 1963. No one knows what would have happened had he lived; Wayne Smith, a former head of the U.S. interests section in Cuba, argued that "had John Kennedy lived, he might have reached a *modus vivendi* with the Cubans," but it is impossible to be sure. Castro himself, on hearing of Kennedy's death, remarked that, "this is bad for Cuba." Secretary of State Dean Rusk would later deny that Kennedy actually sought better relations.[82]

Before Kennedy's death, however, the stage seemed set for talks. Lisa Howard, an ABC newswoman, served as an intermediary. Castro sent word that he wanted Atwood to come to Cuba, and JFK expressed an interest in this proposal. McGeorge Bundy told Atwood that the president would make a decision on the policy "after a brief trip to Dallas."[83]

* * *

Kennedy, of course, did not return from that trip. On November 22, as his motorcade rolled slowly through Dallas's Dealey Plaza, John F. Kennedy was killed by a gunshot wound to the head. Besides these basic facts, however, as later investigators have demonstrated, little about the assassination of JFK is clear. Researchers have amassed a huge volume of evidence suggesting that Kennedy was killed by one or more of various groups with something to gain from the president's death, and Cubans figure prominently in nearly all these discussions. Just what role pro- or anti-Castro Cubans enacted in the assassination, of course, is a mystery, and will probably ever remain so. The evidence of conspiracy, once so fresh and subject to analysis, was ignored by early official investigations, and now lies buried by time and inattention. At least two things are apparent, however: Lee Harvey Oswald did not kill JFK acting alone; and Jack Ruby did not kill Oswald acting alone.

The Evidence

The official version of what happened on those fateful days in Dallas is quite straightforward, and, many critics contend, riddled with evidential and legal holes. Lee Harvey Oswald, the story goes, acting alone and out of a desire to protect Castro's Cuba from the ''militaristic'' JFK, killed the president and wounded Texas Governor John Connally with three shots from an aging Italian Manlicher-Carcano 6.5mm rifle, fired from the sixth floor of the Texas School Depository Building (TSDB). Fleeing the scene, Oswald ran across Dallas policeman J.D. Tippit and killed him with four shots from a revolver. Acting suspiciously and fitting a police description of the assassin, Oswald was reported to police and arrested in a theater. Days later he was gunned down by Jack Ruby, acting alone out of pity for the Kennedy family.

Since 1963, however, researchers have (in a staggering number of books and articles) made an impressive case that neither Oswald nor Ruby acted alone. Consider, for example, the actual shooting. Oswald was using an old, bolt-action rifle, probably firing aged ammunition and with a sighting scope that was mounted improperly. A former Marine, Oswald was recalled by his friends in the service as a terrible shot. Kennedy's car was moving away from Oswald, downhill, several hundred yards away. Yet Oswald was able to squeeze off three shots in less than six seconds—with a rifle he had to cock after each shot—and achieved two hits out of three with stunning accuracy. In subsequent tests, using a refurbished rifle and firing at *stationary* targets, top government rifle experts have not been able to match Oswald's accuracy; working the bolt and firing simply takes too much time. As one assassination researcher, Henry Hurt, concludes, ''The fact remains that, to this day, *no expert marksman has ever duplicated Oswald's shooting skills in any official test or demonstration.*''

There has also been much speculation about the theory of a second gunman, firing from in front of President Kennedy's car in the area of the ''grassy knoll." Indeed, after the assassination. while 32 witnesses said the shots had come from the TSDB, 51 said they had come from the grassy knoll, and others said they heard shots from both areas. The famous motion of Kennedy's head on the film of the assassination—moving distinctly backwards—would indicate a shot from the front. Acoustical evidence examined by a 1979 House committee on the shooting concluded that there was a "high probability" of a second gunman firing from the front. Witnesses standing in front of the grassy knoll—including a soldier on leave, just returned from live-firing exercises—testified that there was gunfire immediately behind them, and that the shots whistled past their ears. And Governor Connally, himself an experienced rifleman, was absolutely convinced that there were two gunmen, that he and the President had been hit with separate shots—not one, as the official version suggests. Of course, as soon as the necessity of a second gunman is accepted, the assassination of JFK becomes, by definition, a conspiracy.

Perhaps casting the greatest shroud of doubt over the single-assassin theory, however, is the nature of Kennedy's wounds. Kennedy had received a massive wound in the right side of his head, and wounds in the back and front of the neck. In early reports, the back wound was reported in the lower neck, a necessary presumption if it were to exit the front of the neck and then travel into Connally's body.

Difficult as it is to believe that autopsy reports were mistaken, it seems clear today from a vast wealth of evidence that the wound in Kennedy's back was further down, five to six inches from the back of the neck. Kennedy's suit and shirt both show holes in this location. If this is true, it would be impossible for a bullet fired from *above* to enter Kennedy's mid-back, suddenly turn upward and exit through his throat, then spin downward again and strike Connally. Doctors in the first autopsy, moreover, noted that the path of the bullet entering Kennedy's back was a downward slope, between 45 and 60 degrees; while possible for a bullet fired from Oswald's location, this would make it impossible for the bullet to exit through Kennedy's neck or for it to strike Connally. And if *that* is true, then that last bullet cannot account for all the wounds, and there must have been a second gunman.

Complicating the picture is the testimony of various witnesses who claim to have seen *two* men, or more, on the sixth floor during the shooting. Many observers described the men has having dark complexions, like Latins or Cubans. And a film discovered in 1978 taken of the building by a spectator just before the assassination, in the view of photographic experts, shows two and possibly three men on the sixth floor.

What does all this mean? Oswald claimed that he was "just a patsy," that he had shot no one. Three possibilities present themselves. Either Oswald *was* in the TSDB that day and shot Kennedy; or he was in the TSDB and did not shoot Kennedy; or he was not in the building at all. In the second scenario, Oswald, the "patsy" of a conspiracy designated to take the fall for Kennedy's murder, might have remained in the lunch room, or been elsewhere, during the shooting, which was performed by others on the sixth floor and from the grassy knoll. As some researchers have suggested in positing the third scenario, however, there is good evidence that at various times before the assassination someone was *posing* as Lee Harvey Oswald in various places in the world—an Oswald double—and that it might have been this double in the TSDB that day, not Oswald himself. (This last possibility is a little farfetched, given that Oswald definitely did come to work that day—a co-worker gave him a ride—and that it would be unlikely that people who worked with him for some time would not recognize an imposter.)

Of all the portions of the official version of the assassination, perhaps the most difficult to accept is that Jack Ruby gunned down Lee Harvey Oswald out of pity for the Kennedy family. Ruby was a criminal, a pimp, a small-time hoodlum who had connections to the mob. That this man would have killed Oswald to protect the Kennedys is beyond belief.

Ruby had strong connections to the mob in New Orleans and other areas in which he operated. He went to Cuba several times, and once asked for an introduction to Fidel Castro in a failed attempt to establish a gun-running operation to the beleaguered dictator. There is little doubt that Ruby was strongly bound up with both the mob and anti-Castro exiles in New Orleans.

Of the evidence casting doubt on Ruby's spontaneous act of passion, perhaps the strongest is the undeniable fact that Ruby stalked Oswald from the time of the assassination. He made visits to Dallas police headquarters trying to find out when and how Oswald would be transferred, and later bothered a TV news crew whose cameras were in the basement of the building where Oswald was shot. If Jack Ruby intended to kill Oswald from the time of the assassination, he must have had a reason.

Perhaps most unsettling are the statements Ruby made after being arrested. Like Oswald, he claimed to have been a mere pawn in a conspiracy. "Geez," he said to a friend when he was in jail, "they're going to find out about Cuba, they're going to find out about the guns, find out about New Orleans, find out about everything." Later he more pointedly claimed that he had been used to silence Oswald; "The people [who] have so much to gain and had such an ulterior motive to put me in the position I am in," he said, "will never let the facts [be known] to the world."

The Cuban Question

Threads of Cuban involvement are common to the many varied tapestries of conspiracy woven by critics of the official version of JFK's assassination. Many groups of Cubans—pro-Castro, anti-Castro—as well as Americans with a significant stake in events in Cuba wanted Kennedy dead. Yet official investigators have been unwilling to pry open the Pandora's box of possibilities inherent in "the Cuban Question."

Of the groups that had reasons to want Kennedy dead in late 1963, almost all were bound up with Cuba and the events there since 1959, especially the Bay of Pigs. Pro-Cubans, including Castro himself, may have wanted to kill Kennedy in retaliation for the CIA's many attempts at killing *Castro.* As we have seen, Kennedy probably never actually ordered an assassination campaign per se, but his instructions to "get rid of Castro" were interpreted by his CIA subordinate to mean that, and he definitely had some inkling about what they were up to.

Many anti- Castro exiles, along with their allies in the CIA, openly called for Kennedy's assassination in the wake of the Bay of Pigs fiasco. Feeling betrayed, especially after Kennedy reneged on subsequent veiled promises to stage another invasion, these groups wanted to kill Kennedy for revenge's sake.

The mob also wanted to kill Kennedy, and in typical gangster fashion, a number of them publicly predicted that the president "would be hit." Bobby Kennedy's war on organized crime had the mob worried, and there was some suggestion that in order to "get" Bobby, the mob would first have to kill JFK, for if they killed the president's younger brother first, his rage would intensify the war against them. The mob was also heavily involved with Cuba; it had enjoyed large gambling, prostitution, and drug operations there before the revolution. How exactly motives involving Cuba would have figured in the mob hit on the President is unclear.

As noted, too, both Oswald and Ruby had close ties to Cuba, Oswald through his "Fair Play for Cuba Committee" and Ruby through his mob contacts. Either could have been working for any of the groups mentioned above. Either the CIA or anti-Castro exiles, or both working together, could have set Oswald up to take the fall by promoting him as a *pro*-Castro radical; this would explain Oswald's ties to anti-Castro groups holding offices in the same building where he based in own pro-Castro group. Or Castro himself could have set in motion a plot that eventually spun Oswald into its web, again to take the fall. Or the mob could have combined with any of those three groups with the same result.[84] None of this discussion, of course, is intended to provide any final conclusions about the Kennedy assassination. It is provided merely to illustrate that Cuban-American relations have had implications for both countries that sometimes go unnoticed in the more staid accounts of diplomacy. In one form or another, Cubans were probably involved in John F. Kennedy's assassination.

13

THE ELEPHANT IN THE LIVING ROOM

Relations During the Johnson and Nixon Administrations

Nikita Khrushchev told a story about a poor Russian peasant who learned by necessity to live with his unsanitary goat. Cuba, he said, was America's goat. ''You are not happy about it, you won't like it, but you'll learn to live with it.''

''The Americans won't do anything [about Cuba]. It's as if you had entered the house and suddenly found an elephant in the living room. You immediately begin to shout: An elephant in the living room! You try to get it out of the house but, if you don't succeed, after a while you start to ignore it. In the end it becomes an inconvenient but familiar fixture, an elephant in the living room.''
Elderly Cuban Peasant, 1960s

''There'll be no change toward that bastard
while I'm President.''
Richard Nixon[1]

After the Cuban Missile Crisis, the issue of Cuba faded from the news for a time. The Kennedy administration ended not with a bang, but with a whimper—with talk of accommodation, of ''learning to live'' with Castro. Lyndon Johnson would not follow up on accommodation, but would rather institutionalize and set firmly in place the hard line economic, political, and military policy toward Cuba that has been followed more or less to the present day. Along the way, he would deal with a number of small crises. But Cuba had become, as the wise old Cuban peasant suggested, an elephant in the living room of the Americas.

THE JOHNSON ADMINISTRATION

With the death of John Kennedy, Lyndon Baines Johnson became the 36th president of the United States. Johnson would prove generally more willing than Kennedy to commit U.S. troops abroad—in Vietnam and the Dominican Republic, for example—but with regard to Cuba his policy was decidedly less ambitious: he made significant efforts neither to overthrow Castro nor to woo him. One result of this policy was that Johnson put an end to Kennedy's accommodationist drift.

The notion of accepting Castro's government as an established fact developed slowly, however, and would only come to more complete fruition during the Nixon administration. Underlying Johnson policies, for example, was the stated conviction that Castro's regime was temporary, and that U.S. policy could help unseat him. Recognizing that the embargo and other U.S. anti-Castro efforts would not alone topple the Cuban regime, the administration nevertheless saw value in damaging and discrediting Castro. It therefore continued to seek sanctions and condemnations.[2] In short, the United States would not admit that Castro had firmly established himself. Leonard Meeker, a State Department official, explained in 1964 that the United States had settled the issue of the claims of American nationals against Castro for his nationalizations by seizing Cuban assets in the United States. But he cautioned that

> [While] that, in turn, could foster the impression that the United States accepts the Castro regime as a permanent feature of international life [, in fact] nothing could be farther from U.S. policy. Our program is to apply continuing political and economic pressure on the Castro's regime. . . . All of these measures bear witness to our refusal to accept the Castro regime as a permanent fact of international life.[3]

In part, Johnson's position was dictated by pressure from the Right. The evolving Communist threat in Vietnam and elsewhere had come hard on the heels of the McCarthy era, and a soft line on a Communist government anywhere was politically suicidal.[4] Republican presidential candidate Barry Goldwater in particular called for tough, immediate action on Cuba, at various times favoring a U.S. naval blockade of the island, a new exile invasion, and American air support for both.[5] Richard Nixon favored using "all means short of war" to unseat Castro. And in 1968, the governor of California, Ronald Reagan, criticized the Johnson administration for not supporting Cuban exile groups.[6]

Johnson was not above flexing U.S. muscle in the region, moreover, to show Castro who was "boss." On February 3, 1964, the United States searched and seized a number of Cuban vessels operating in U.S. territorial waters near Cuba. The boats had apparently been spying; four boats were taken, and two of the crew members requested asylum in the United States. On February 4, the administration sent a note to the Cuban government explaining this act.[7] The Cubans protested in the U.N., and on February 7, the U.S. government responded with a statement by Ambassador Stevenson to the General Assembly.[8]

In retaliation, the Cuban government shut off the water supply to Guantanamo Bay, and there was some concern in Washington that Cuba was prepared to re-open the entire issue of an American base on Cuban soil. Barry Goldwater called for the use of U.S. Marines to keep the water flowing, but other observers—including Goldwater's rival for the GOP presidential nomination, Nelson Rockefeller—argued that this would be a dangerous course. In the end, after a few days, the Cubans turned the water on again.[9]

Johnson's commitment to economic and diplomatic sanctions against Castro, however, was already being severely tested. More and more nations— including U.S. allies like Spain, Japan, the Netherlands, and Morocco— ignored the embargo and traded with Cuba. By late January, 1964, one U.S. official was already admitting that, "for all practical purposes the U.S. blockade of Cuba has failed."[10]

The administration took a number of steps to head off this trend. In February, Secretary of State Dean Rusk waned that nations trading with Cuba might face a "public boycott" in which U.S. consumers would refuse to buy products from countries violating the embargo.[11] Finally, several days later, the United States curtailed military aid to five nations that ignored the embargo: Britain, France, Yugoslavia, Spain, and Morocco. (This did not affect U.S. military commitments, only direct military aid—which in the case of Britain, France, and Yugoslavia amounted to only about $100,000 apiece annually. But Spain and Morocco received some $30 and $20 million annually, respectively.) Within days, however, citing national security concerns, the administration backed down and removed the sanctions from Spain.[12] The others remained i n force temporarily, but merely demonstrated the growing American embarrassment over the Cuban embargo issue.

These problems signaled the beginning of the end of national and international consensus on sanctions against Castro. In March, 1964, Senator William Fulbright became one of the first to call for an end to the embargo, declaring the Castro was not a true threat to the hemisphere. Cuba was an OAS problem, he argued, not an American one. Rusk and Johnson responded quickly and angrily, contending that Castro was indeed a menace to regional security.[13] Both within the United States and among other governments, however, support for the isolation of Castro was crumbling-a collapse that would be complete by the early 1970s.

For the time being, however, the Johnson administration stuck to its guns. In April, responding to concerns about the nature of the weapons possessed by the Cuban Armed forces, the Department of State argued that overflights of Cuba by U.S. reconnaissance platforms were necessary for verification of Missile Crisis agreements, and noted that the flights would continue. President Johnson himself promised that the missions would not be dropped, despite Cuban objections.[14]

On April 23, 1964, Undersecretary of State George Ball gave a speech on U.S. policy toward Cuba that reiterated the administration's goals. Cuba, he claimed, was not a military threat to the United States. The real threat represented by Castro "is the menace of *subversion.*" Ball also established two preconditions to rapprochement talks with Castro: the Cubans must loosen or cut their ties to Moscow and surrender their support for revolutionary movements in Latin American and elsewhere. Without such actions, Ball outlined a two-part strategy for dealing with Cuba comprised of strengthening other countries in the region against Communist subversion and waging an economic and diplomatic war against Castro. This has been termed the "denial policy."[15]

Meanwhile, Cuban exiles, in some cases aided by the CIA, continued operations against Cuba. These groups caused problems in the United States as well, robbing armories and engaging in terrorist acts against Cuban government officials visiting the United States. In December, 1964, one group fired a bazooka at the United Nations in New York during a visit by Che Guevara; the terrorists were later arrested. In June, a British warship, the destroyer *Decoy*, had seized a shipment of arms bound for exiles inside Cuba near the British territory of Anguilla, and with it five Cuban exile fighters and three of their American compatriots.[16]

New Accommodationist Winds From Havana

Given such a context, it is not surprising that Castro's continued efforts at obtaining an American compromise were rejected. Throughout the winter and spring of 1964, the Cubans continued making noises about possible rapprochement; in April, for example, Che Guevara indicated that Cuba was again willing to discuss issues of disagreement between the two countries.[17] Finally, in July, Castro outlined his plan in detail to visiting *New York Times* reporter Dick Eder. For the first time, Castro admitted that both the United States and Cuba were responsible for the mutual hostilities. He expressed a desire to open relations, and claimed he was impressed with the U.S. Alliance for Progress. And he offered a deal: he was ready to stop fomenting revolution in Latin America if the United States would begin a normalization process and end support of Cuban exile raiders, and to remunerate U.S. corporations for their properties in Cuba that had been nationalized if the Johnson administration would lift the economic embargo. Castro also made promises regarding the release of political prisoners and a pledge not to shoot down U.S. reconnaissance planes over Cuba.[18]

The Johnson administration, however, rejected the proposal. Publicly, its officials claimed the policy was still to wait Castro out, that to accede to the normalization plan would cement the Cuban leader in power when the United States still held some hope of unseating him. Privately, too, some government analysts concurred with this judgement. But with the 1964 elections approaching, many observers speculated that the administration simply did not want to appear soft on Communism. In any event, the administration reiterated Ball's theme of loosened ties with the USSR as a precondition for any talks.[19]

To sound a conciliatory note on Castro, moreover, would have undercut the administration's efforts in the OAS to obtain regional sanctions against Cuba. On July 22, Secretary of State Dean Rusk issued a hard line statement at a meeting of foreign ministers of the American states. Thus encouraged by the United States, and in many cases threatened themselves with Cuban-supported insurgent movements, the countries at this meeting voted on July 26 a "Final Act" condemning Cuba. This suspended trade and diplomatic relations with Cuba, and provided for regional economic agreements to help alleviate the poverty that was seen as an ally of Castro's revolutionary groups. Mexico, Peru, Colombia, Bolivia, Venezuela, Brazil, and other Latin American countries signed the act; the final vote was 15-4.[20]

On that same day, Castro, in his annual speech commemorating the date of the Moncada attack, called for better relations with the United States, and essentially formalized his earlier offer by calling for detente and respect for "international norms." This last condition explicitly included a renunciation of revolutionary activity. But the United States held the key cards—it now had the region firmly on its side—and it again rejected the Cuban proposal. [21]

Whether Castro was sincere with these offers is a matter of serious dispute. Liberal commentators have concluded that economic and political pressures made Castro honestly desirous of better relations. Wayne Smith, for example, who opposed normalization in 1964, has concluded that

> the Castro overtures of 1964 may have been only a ploy, Perhaps we ought indeed to have rejected them. In retrospect, however, I have read over the Eder interviews and Castro's July 26 speech many times, and I have often looked back on those discussions with Eder. . .with the painful suspicion that they were right and I was wrong.[22]

Other writers at the time called for normalization, and many since have argued that the United States should not have burned its bridges so quickly after 1962. More skeptical observers, however, view Castro's proposals with great suspicion, arguing that Castro occasionally makes proposals of accommodation when his revolution needs some breathing space. They cite Castro's later interventions in Angola and Ethiopia at the height of conciliations with the United States as evidence that Castro's international ventures mean much more to him than amicable relations with the United States.

In any case, the Johnson administration was not about to play into the hands of the Republicans by appearing conciliatory toward Castro. The CIA continued its covert operations against Cuba.[23] Through 1965 and 1966, the administration reiterated the need for sanctions and praised their effectiveness. In 1966, the United States secured from the OAS a condemnation of the Havana Tricontinental Conference, a meeting of Communist government officials.[24] Only one issue arose to disturb this routine process of hostilities: the problem of Cuban immigration.

The Immigration Crisis of 1965

The growing radicalization of the Castro government and the sagging Cuban economy encouraged many Cubans to leave in the early 1960s, and since the revolution thousands of them had fled by boat or plane to the United States and elsewhere. Perhaps angered by the continuing stream of defections, Castro on September 28, 1965, declared that participation in the revolution was "voluntary" and that anyone who wanted to flee Cuba could do so. He told those who wanted to leave to congregate at the beach of Camarioca, where they would be allowed to leave, presumably picked up by friends from other countries.

Thousands of Cubans soon rushed to the beach; during the first month alone, more than 5,000 secured transportation and left. But the trip to Florida was a dangerous one, especially in small boats, and despite the best efforts of the U.S. Coast Guard some Cubans died. After a month, the United States, hoping to control the rate of immigration and register those coming in, as well as to end unnecessary deaths, proposed an airlift; the Cubans who wanted to leave would be flown to the United States. Somewhat surprisingly, Castro accepted.

The arrangement went on for some time. A part of the U.S. Immigration Bill of 1965 provided for the entry of the Cubans. Both countries, however, emphasized that the plan was merely adopted to satisfy mutual needs, not as an attempt to ease tensions. And a precedent of sorts had been set; the issue of immigration would be one on which U.S. and Cuban leaders, with common interests, would forge most of the few agreements reached between the two governments over the next decades.[25]

Continuing Tensions: 1966-1968

During the last three years of the Johnson administration, its "denial strategy" remained in place as conservatives in the United States pressed for even harsher sanctions while governments abroad continued to cozy up to Castro in ways that made the United States furious. An example of the former phenomenon occurred in 1966, when congressional Republicans attempted to pass an amendment eliminating food aid to any nations that failed to observe the embargo of Cuba. The measure elicited a great amount of criticism, and the administration opposed it. Standing firm, however, the Republicans did manage to pass a version of the amendment, one that did cut food aid but allowed the president to make exceptions for reasons of national security.[26]

In 1967, responding to the continuing trend—especially in Latin America—to regard Castro's threat as muted, the administration again emphasized the insurrectionary activities financed by Cuba in the hemisphere. At an OAS meeting in Washington, the United States succeeded in eliciting a few supporting resolutions that condemned Castro.[27] But on the whole, the grip of the United States on Latin American Cuban policy was beginning to slip. A rising hemispheric nationalism, expressing itself occasionally in anti-American fashion, would also help make continued enforcement of the sanctions impossible.

Small tensions continued to plague the U.S.-Cuban relationship. On May 27, 1966, the United States protested "armed incursions" of the Guantanamo naval base by Cubans.[28] Castro still complained about attacks from exile Cubans based in the United States. And hijackers began to use Cuba as a place to fly their captive charges; dozens of hijackings occurred, and at one point two large passenger planes were taken to Cuba on the same day.[29]

The Johnson administration thus ended quietly. In a sense, Fidel Castro posed such a problem for American policy that U.S. leaders dealt with him by not dealing with him; they harassed him and hoped he would go away. Despite all his explosive rhetoric about support for Cuban exiles, Richard Nixon's policies would amount to the same thing. The problem for U.S. policy was that Fidel Castro would *not* go away. And the presence of a hostile, repressive, Communist nation ninety miles from American shores—paradoxically one that would make repeated gestures of accommodation—created dilemmas for American policy that have still not been truly addressed. But the process of at least tacitly recognizing Castro's government as a permanent fixture in the hemisphere was under way, and it would come to fruition in the mid-1970s.

CUBAN FOREIGN POLICY, 1962-1968

During this period, Castro's foreign policy underwent several significant changes. In many ways, Castro viewed his foreign adventures as his most important policies; he viewed himself (and indeed all of Cuba) as an international liberator, providing assistance to oppressed peoples in their struggle against colonialism and imperialism. The policies that flowed from this belief would have significant impact on relations with the United States.

The first years after the revolution were a time of internationalist fervor. Until 1962, fear of American intervention limited the expression of this sentiment to support for a few modest operations. Castro allegedly supported small revolutionary cells in a number of Latin American countries, though his primary emphasis was on dictatorships that had already showed some signs of weakness; such as Trujillo's Dominican Republic and Somoza's Nicaragua. Haiti, Panama, and Guatemala were also infiltrated by guerrillas. Small bands of dedicated revolutionaries left Cuba to start revolutions throughout the region.[30]

These practices were in line with Fidel Castro's thinking on revolution, which is commonly called the *foco* theory. As explicated by Che Guevara (and also the revolutionary theorist Regis Debray in *Revolution in the Revolution*), the *foco* theory asserts that, contrary to Marxist-Leninist doctrine, one need not wait for a "revolutionary condition" to arise before starting an insurrection. Rather, a small band of dedicated men—the *foco*—can *create* the conditions for a revolution.[31]

This theory is classic Castro. Men of action need not wait patiently for the right time to revolt, it boldly asserts; men can indeed change history. Fidel Castro had done just that—and he knew it and like to boast of it. Now he would send groups of revolutionaries forth as his personal agents to liberate the whole hemisphere, in the manner of Simon Bolivar. Fidel's early, personal involvement in revolutions in the Dominican Republic and Colombia left him sympathetic to that form of warfare.

Cuba's internationalism was based in a number of historical influences. A revolutionary messianism, informed by Marti's internationalism and Castro's own ambition, encouraged interventions in other countries. A growing desire to strike out an independent course—distinct from both American and Soviet policy—also recommended support for revolutions, as did a legitimate ideological commitment to such movements.

By 1963, influenced by these factors, Castro had become more ambitious. Not content to merely complete the destabilization of unstable regimes, he went after regional heavyweights, traditionally secure governments: Argentina, Brazil, Bolivia, Colombia, and Chile, to name a few. His February, 1962 Second Declaration of Havana sounded the regional clarion call to revolt, and open Cuban support for Latin American insurgency movements grew significantly. Even Venezuela's Social Democratic President Romulo Betancourt, who had refused Castro's requests for economic assistance, was targeted; in February, 1962, about two dozen Venezuelans, trained and armed by Cuba, began an insurgency. Castro also spread his efforts more broadly, beginning an involvement in Africa that would later culminate with huge commitments to Angola and Ethiopia; as early as 1960, he had sent some aid to the Algerian National Liberation Front, and in the next several years he trained guerrillas in Ghana and supported the new revolutionary regime in Algeria.[32]

These efforts, and his *foco* theory, quickly got Castro into hot water with traditional Latin American Communist parties. Many of them, as had been the case with the PSP in Cuba, had become conservative, reformist, even bourgeois; they were dedicated to the idea of awaiting the "revolutionary condition," and Castro's bold advocacy of violent revolution angered them. It also created the first of many policy rifts with the Soviet Union, whose conservative leaders had been wary of supporting Castro in the first place·and were increasingly upset with the Caribbean upstart's failure to toe the socialist line. Meanwhile, the military dictatorships and semi-democracies of the region, for internal as well as external reasons, had turned to the United States, and Cuba was soon isolated within the hemisphere. By 1964, most of the guerrilla movements supported by Castro had been crushed.[33]

The Soviet Union was soon forced to intervene in an attempt to mediate this dispute. At a 1964 Conference of Communist Parties in Havana, Soviet leaders essentially forced the two sides to shake hands and make up. Both agreed to respect the tactics of the other, and in exchange for this recognition, Castro said he would restrain his revolutionary adventurism. And he did, for a while, shifting support in some cases, for example, from violent revolutionary cells to more traditional Communist parties.

By the following year, however, Castro had given up this accommodation. American interventions in Vietnam and the Dominican Republic, and the lack of an adequate Soviet response, perhaps convinced him that he must again assume the role of Third World leader. He stepped up his support for revolutionary groups. He used the 1966 Tricontinental Congress in Havana as a forum to promote the need for armed revolts against colonial power and the illegitimate governments they had left in their wake. Through 1966 and 1967, his commitment to insurgencies grew.[34]

These activities led to serious rifts in the communist alliance in Latin America. In the spring of 1967, for example, Castro formally split with the Venezuelan Communist Party, and he again engaged in a verbal feud with Moscow, whose drift toward detente and peaceful coexistence made him fear that he might be left out in the cold. In March of that year, Castro took the shockingly bold action of announcing that being pro-Soviet was not enough; to be a true Communist, one must also support revolutionary movements in the Third World. Castro's dissatisfaction with the increasing Soviet emphasis on peaceful coexistence was evident; he had no desire to "make his peace" with the capitalists. "By 1967," according to H. Michael Erisman, "Cuban-Soviet relations were at an all-time low."[35]

Yet by 1968 Castro had again moderated his revolutionism. His support for insurgencies dropped off, he endorsed peaceful evolution and diplomacy as means to achieve socialism, and he expressed a desire to establish peaceful and conventional relations with his non-socialist neighbors, making anti-imperialism, not Marxism-Leninism *per se*, the key qualification for Cuban friendship. A number of plausible explanations of this shift have been advanced.

Che Guevara's death in Bolivia was a serious blow to Castro, and along with the failure of all the insurgencies Castro had set up, this may have convinced him that his efforts were coming to naught. No other revolutionary governments had arisen in Latin America in response to Castro's calls, and it was apparent that he was wasting a huge amount of resources on a losing cause. The rise to power of leftist governments in Chile and Peru through non-revolutionary means may also have suggested that armed insurgency was not as necessary as had once been thought, and Castro determined to take advantage of the rising Latin American nationalism to encourage a gradual leftward trend rather than support violent revolutions.

Resources had become especially scarce, moreover, as 1970 approached. Cuba was experiencing an economic crisis, and Castro needed to turn his attention inward. The 1960s had been a period of stagnant growth, and the economic disaster of 1970 would render support for hemispheric revolutions impossible for the time being.

Castro also needed more military and economic aid from the Soviet Union, and his ideological rift with Moscow made the acquisition of such assistance problematic; his moderation allowed him to patch up the differences.[37] "Rapprochement with the USSR represented the Fidelistas's most dramatic turnabout during this phase," Erisman concludes. Soviet leaders probably exerted great pressure on Castro to set revolutionism aside for a time, as it was incompatible with peaceful coexistence, and when he complied they boosted their aid; the USSR's 1968 aid package to Cuba, totaling $2.6 billion, surpassed all previous aid combined, and through the early 1970s Soviet aid would continue to grow, from $3.2 billion in 1969 to $5.3 billion in 1973. In 1972, Cuba also became the first non-European country to be admitted to the Council for Mutual Economic Assistance (CEMA), the Communist world's common market.[38]

By 1970, then, Castro had significantly moderated his foreign policy. After that time, there would be no more of the total commitment to hemispheric revolutions so characteristic of his first years in power. His later major foreign commitments were more often products of local threats to countries with which he was allied than the result of Castro's personally-initiated meddling.

THE NIXON ADMINISTRATION

Long known as a hard-line hawk, Richard Nixon came into office in 1969 bearing a significant amount of rhetorical baggage about foreign policy, having played up the Communist threat for many years. In regard to Cuba, he called for support for Cuban exiles, and during the Bay of Pigs disaster, he told Kennedy to invade. Once in office, however, Nixon sought detente with the world's two most powerful Communist governments, withdrew from Vietnam, and generally followed policies of restraint. This would hold true to a certain degree with regard to Castro,, for whom Nixon had nothing but enmity but against whom the president was willing to direct no new hostile acts.[39]

Generally, Nixon's Cuban policy was a continuation of that of the later Kennedy and Johnson administrations. He kept the embargo and other sanctions in place and urged Latin American and Caribbean governments to support them. Repeatedly, moreover, the position expressed by Nixon and his Secretary of State, Henry Kissinger, was that until Castro moderated his international behavior, Washington would not consider any appreciable form of rapprochement. Continuing American demands for compensation for nationalized land were also still a barrier to improved relations. Robert Osgood has defined the "Nixon strategy" as "military retrenchment without political disengagement," and this is an apt summary of Nixon's Cuba policy as well; military measures were out of the questions, but the administration would use every political and economic lever in its power to discredit Castro's regime.[40]

In many ways, U.S. policy toward Cuba during Nixon's tenure was dictated by the mutual antipathy felt by the two leaders. In fact, one commentator has concluded that, "there is still much confusion over the extent to which American policy under Nixon was based on rational considerations and the extent to which it derived from personal spleen."[41]

A New Policy: Accepting Castro

Yet the trend toward a grudging acceptance of Castro was unmistakable. While the United States still refused to accept Cuba's revolutionary activity throughout the world and its close military ties to the USSR, Cuba's internal policies—and thus presumably the very existence of a Castro government— were no longer an issue of dispute. For the first time, the United States began to accept the notion that Castro would not go away, and sought only to influence his foreign policy.[42]

This new position was reflected in a number of administration statements. Deputy Assistant Secretary of State Robert A. Hurwitch became the chief spokesman for American policy, and on a number of occasions he noted that the administration no longer refused to recognize Castro himself. "I wish to invite the committee's attention," he said in one hearing, "to the fact that...our concern is based upon the external, not internal, policies and activities of the Cuban government."[43] Hurwitch also noted that by harassing Castro, "the United States has not sought the overthrow of the present Cuban regime," merely, "the reduction of Cuba's capacity to export armed revolution and the discouragement of Soviet adventures in this hemisphere."[44]

At the same time, Hurwitch explicitly rejected proposals for rapprochement. American conciliation, he argued, would encourage more Cuban adventurism; the sanctions were hurting Castro, moreover, and the requirements of world peace did not demand good American relations with Cuba as they did with such nations as the USSR and the People's Republic of China. Additionally, "from the economic standpoint," he argued, "the United States has little, if anything, to gain." It acquired sugar from other suppliers, and "the absence of Cuban tobacco or the few other Cuban export products has also not had significant effect upon our economy."[45] In short, the United States perceived no immediate need to reach an accommodation with Castro, and the risks of such a course recommended adherence to standard patterns of harassment and hostility.

Opposition to Cuban foreign adventures, in fact, became "the linchpin of the Nixon administration's policy toward Cuba."[46] Nixon's argument in this regard was clear; Castro, he said, "thrives. . .in stirring up trouble in other countries. He couldn't possibly survive, in my opinion, unless he had this policy of 'foreign' devils." Hence Nixon's policy in Chile, which he feared would become another Cuba, spreading revolution throughout the hemisphere.[47] By calling for unilateral foreign restraint on Castro's part—and toughening this call with economic and political warfare—Nixon hoped to one day eliminate Castro's opportunities to create such devils.

Developments in Cuba

Meanshile, in Cuba, Castro was expending great efforts in fixing firmly the revolutionary process. 1970 was a watershed year for Cuba; it failed to reach Castro's stated goal of a 10 million ton sugar harvest (getting only 8.5), and this, combined with other economic problems, caused Castro to re-evaluate his course. Massive dislocations occurred throughout the entire Cuban economy, since many industries were stripped of funds and workers to help the sugar effort. The poor economic performance of the 1960s, stemming in part from crippling experiments with egalitarian wage scales and other socialist economic measures, also finally caught up to the Cuban government.

The period that followed is commonly called the 'institutionalization of the revolution,'" during which Castro's personal influence declined somewhat as efficiency-minded technocrats began to take control of policy. Attempts were made to lessen the arbitrariness and bad planning of what was essentially a personal dictatorship, and to transform Cuba into a more conventionally institutionalized planned economy. Soviet pressure on Cuba to moderate its foreign policy and concentrate on internal reform in an evolving era of detente also encouraged this process.[48]

Tensions with the United States remained at a high level throughout this period. In May, 1969, a confidential Department of State memorandum urged a continuation of the U.S. arms-length policy toward Castro, and Nixon complied.[49] Although some in the United States began to call for warmed relations—in December, 1969, for example, Senators Mathias and Mansfield argued that the United States should "disenthrall" itself with Cuba[50]—no rapprochement was forthcoming.

One issue that kept tensions high was again that of anti-Castro Cuban exiles in the United States. These groups—including the most famous one, Alpha 66—kept up raids on Cuba, in many cases launching them from U.S. soil. In April, 1970, Castro reported that a particularly large group of exiles had landed in Oriente province and were waging guerrilla warfare against his regime. The following month, in part due to domestic and international pressure to deal with the Cuban exile problem, the FBI in May, 1970, raided the Alpha 66 headquarters in Miami. The raid achieved little, but continued pressure in 1971 against the exile groups helped reduce their operations to nuisance levels.[51]

Members of these groups came from the extensive population of Cubans in Florida and elsewhere in the southern United States. These Cubans had fled their homeland between 1959 and 1973 in the ''greatest mass migration in the history of the Western hemisphere,'' totaling some 560,000. The U.S. airlift program begun in 1961 was finally cancelled by Castro in 1973, by which time it had cost the U.S. government some $727 million. Exiles thus brought into the United states served as the nucleus of various anti-Castro groups, including Alpha 66 and the Peoples Revolutionary Party.[52]

Nixon did continue the CIA's secret war against Castro, though at a lower level than in the past. Various tactics were used to disrupt Castro's government: the CIA tried to use weather-modification techniques to ruin Cuba's crops; the introduction of swine fever into Cuba caused a large pork shortfall. A plan to provoke an American invasion of Cuba by using Cuban exiles masquerading as Cuban air force fliers to attack Nixon at his residence in Key Biscayne was never put into effect. It was at about this time too that the CIA hunted down and killed Che Guevara in the jungles of Bolivia.[53]

Castro responded with some secretive operations of his own. It was later revealed that during the 1970s Castro supported subversive groups in the United States, such as the Weather Underground, in their campaign against U.S. worldwide policies.[54] Castro also aided Vietnam during the American intervention, and as we have seen, continued to assist revolutionary groups throughout Latin America.

The Cienfuegos Base

Another sticking point in relations centered around Soviet submarines, which were using Cuba as a port. Soviet-American disagreements over this issue quickly escalated to crisis proportions, and the Nixon administration was faced with a crucial test of its Cuban policy.

The first inklings that the Soviets were up to something in Cuba came at the end of July, 1970, when secretary of State Kissinger received a call from the Soviet charge, Yuli M. Vorontsov. Vorontsov wanted a U.S. reaffirmation of the post-Missile Crisis pledge not to invade Cuba. Nixon and Kissinger, searching for reasons why this might be the case, decided that the Soviets sought another signal of the evolving strength of detente. On August 7, therefore, Kissinger reiterated the pledge that as long as the Soviets did not introduce offensive weapons into Cuba, the United States would not invade.

Later in August, U.S. photoreconnaissance suggested that Vorontsov's request might have meant something more. A major new naval base was under construction at Cienfuegos in Cuba, and a Soviet flotilla was on its way to the island, a flotilla including ships usually used to service nuclear submarines. These early indications strongly suggested that the Soviets were constructing a submarine base in Cuba, though whether it was for attack submarines (which carry only torpedoes) or missile-carrying boats was unclear.

On September 2, U.S. Defense Secretary Melvin Laird informed American reporters of the flotilla, and admitted that it might carry offensive weapons, including nuclear ballistic-missile carrying submarines. He declined to predict a crisis, but events moved quickly to indicate one was afoot: by the middle of the month, increasingly vitriolic Cuban threats to down American U-2 reconnaissance planes led Kissinger to warn the USSR against basing nuclear missile submarines in Cuba. This, he said, would be a violation of the Soviet side of the post-Missile-Crisis agreement. The same day as Kissinger's announcement, September 16, U-2 photos showed that construction on the Cienfuegos base had been sped up. A later CIA analysis suggested that such a base would increase the Soviet submarine-based missile threat to the United States by over 40 per cent.

The Nixon administration was faced with a number of other serious foreign policy problems at the time: the Suez crisis, problems with leftist government in Chile, and others. Meanwhile, mid-term elections were approaching, and plans for a U.S.-Soviet summit were well advanced; the Soviets agreed to a meeting on September 25. In this complex atmosphere, Nixon hoped to defuse the Cuban issue, and the Department of State, on the advice of Soviet specialist Llewellyn Thompson, supported such a course, arguing that Nixon should negotiate quietly with Soviet leaders. The Joint Chiefs of Staff and Defense Department made a case for stronger measures, and demanded that whatever the means, the United States must force the submarines to leave Cuba.

On September 25, a bureaucratic mistake significantly affected the determination of U.S. policy. A DOD press briefer, instructed to provide only a few select details of Soviet submarine deployments in Cuba, instead released virtually all the information held by the U.S. government. The press quickly reported these developments, and the public and congressional outcry was immediate and forceful. Nixon had been backed into a corner; he had to insist that the base be dismantled, and he did so, sending Kissinger to tell Soviet Ambassador Dobrynin that the basing of Soviet nuclear missile submarines in Cuba was unacceptable.

Fortunately for Nixon, the Soviets, perhaps not expecting such a serious reaction, quickly backed down, and agreed to dismantle the base and not to give ballistic missile submarines an operational capability in Cuba. The result was a formal understanding that sea-based missiles fell under the provisions of the post-Missile-Crisis agreement of 1962, which prohibited the stationing of offensive weapons in Cuba. Through late 1970 and early 1971, the Soviets tested American resolve be sending a few submarine tenders to visit Cuba, using the loophole of "port visits" to keep some (symbolic) submarine capability in Cuba at all times. The Soviets never sent any ballistic missile submarines to the island after the 1970 agreement, however, and the other Soviet actions, while provocative, posed no particular danger, and the issue faded from public consciousness. But for Nixon its implication was clear: "The events at Cienfuegos Bay convinced me that I had chosen the right course in dealing with another Communist threat in Latin American—this one in Chile. . . ."[55]

More Rumors of Accommodation

In part, the result of this continuing tension was an unwillingness on either side to consider a normalization of relations. In 1971, Nixon said that the United States would not consider normalization "as long as Cuba adopts an anti-American line." Castro countered by ruling out accommodation in his July 26 commemoration speech that same year, and expressed anger at Communist China for pursuing ties with the United States.[56]

Nevertheless, in the summer of 1971, rumors again began to circulate that the United States was prepared to soften its stance against Castro. The OAS continued to press the United States to loosen its sanctions, as did various American policy makers, including Senator William Fulbright. In the fall, Fulbright proposed a sense of the Senate resolution that called for a rapprochement, and Senator Edward Kennedy called Nixon's Cuban policy counterproductive and outdated.[57]

Once again, however, the administration rose to quash these stirrings. In September it declared that U.S. policy was unchanged, and administration officials stressed continuing Cuban-Soviet ties and Cuban support for violent revolutions, both in Latin American and elsewhere.[58] Castro's close contacts with Allende in Chile and his continued harsh attacks on U.S.policy helped cement the hostile U.S. attitude.

Cuban Worries About Detente

At about this time, the United States and the Soviet Union were beginning to consummate their new policy of detente, and Fidel Castro was understandably worried by this process. Through 1971, the USSR assured him that detente would not mean less support for Cuba.[59] But this was apparently not enough, and in late June, 1972—barely a month before Nixon himself arrived in Moscow—Castro traveled to the Soviet Union to obtain direct assurances of support. That same month, Cuba joined CEMA, and he was clearly attempting to make his position as a chief Soviet ally "detente-proof."[60]

Tensions between the United States and Cuba continued. An embarrassing development occurred in October, 1971, as 19 Cubans flew into New Orleans to attend an international sugar cane production meeting. They had not received permission to come, and the United States immediately demanded that they leave. While the Cuban government refused to bring them back, the delegation had a wonderful time in the United States, talking to newspeople and tossing cigars to reporters from their hotel balcony. The Nixon administration, to forestall some of the huge embarrassment the delegation was causing, moved them to the Bachelor Officer Quarters at the U.S. Naval base in Belle Chase, Louisiana. Eventually, the Cuban sugar experts went home, but not before serving as microcosmic examples of what many saw as the growing foolishness of U.S. policy toward Cuba.[61]

In December, the Cuban Coast Guard seized two ships—the *Lyla Express* and the *Johnny Express*—that were known to be active in anti-Castro exile operations. Nixon pledged to work for the release of the crew, and as he made threatening noises about possible U.S. responses to future such seizures, hostility rose.[62] Eventually, except for the captain, the crews were released, but again, U.S.-Cuban relations had reached a nadir of acrimony.

The 1972 Election and Cuba

In early 1972, Secretary of State Rogers hinted that the United States would reconsider its policies toward Cuba if the Cubans would alter their own international behavior. This was not a particularly bold offer—it only placed the traditional U.S. demand for Cuban restraint in a somewhat more conciliatory light—but nevertheless, the Department of State immediately cautioned that Rogers' offer was not a blanket one, and later officials and observers would deny any significant change in U.S. policy.[63]

As the election approached, both Republican and Democratic candidates staked out clear positions on the issue of Cuba. George McGovern, the Democrat challenging Nixon, urged a reconsideration of U.S. Cuban policy, and Nixon felt he was under some significant pressure.[64]

Nixon remained firm. On November 5, he noted that his policy toward Cuba would not change, "unless Fidel Castro changes his attitude." Earlier in the year, he had made some tough statements for political effect; in April, for example, he ordered U.S. warships in the Caribbean to prevent—by force if necessary—Cuban seizures of merchant vessels of the United States and its allies.[65]

* * *

Nixon, of course, won that election. But he would not remain in office for his full term, and the reasons why were bound up surprisingly closely with Cuban-American relations.

On June 17, 1972, 5 men carrying cameras, electronic equipment, burglary tools, and walkie-talkies were arrested in the Democratic National Committee headquarters in Washington's Watergate Hotel. Two were Cuban born. At the time, few in the nation's capitol understood the full story behind the break-in, and those who did, weren't talking.

In fact, as we now know, the break-in was part of a conspiracy by members of Nixon's Committee to Re-Elect the President (CREEP) to spy on and subvert the efforts of the Democratic party in the 1972 elections. The result of the Watergate crisis would be a national scandal and, eventually, Nixon's resignation.

Cubans were involved in the operation from the beginning. As G. Gordon Liddy put it, Nixon operative Howard Hunt claimed he could get manpower by "call[ing] upon some loyal Cuban-American friends from his Bay of Pigs days." Former American intelligence people who had been involved in that invasion, like Frank Sturgis, also worked for the Nixon group. Cubans were used as locksmiths, surveillance operatives, and investigators. Cuban-American prostitutes were interviewed for possible work at the Democratic National Convention; they were to pose as rich, lonely women and elicit information from delegates. Liddy planned to use one team of Cubans to sabotage the air conditioning at the convention.

Indeed, to a large extent, the whole operations was discovered because of one of the Cubans caught at the Democratic headquarters. He was carrying a check from Howard Hunt, who was known to have White House connections. Though the Nixon administration quickly denied any involvement, the threads of conspiracy were already beginning to lead back to the president's closest advisors.[66]

Of course, the Cubans involved in the Watergate scandal did not plan or initiate it; they were merely used as pawns by administration officials. The involvement of the Cubans testifies to the dedication of the Cuban exile community in the United States and to the fact that America's Cuban policy, since the influx of tens of thousands of Cubans after 1959, has become a domestic as well as a foreign policy concern.

* * *

1973: The Hijacking Issue

Strategies for dealing with the continuing rash of airline hijackings dominated the U.S.-Cuban agenda in 1973. Both nations had interests in a workable anti-hijacking agreement—the United States to prevent its planes from
being seized, and Cuba to prevent both an influx of unwanted and embarrassing criminals and an exodus of exiles. Negotiations on a potential hijacking
agreement which had been going on for some time, stalled because of disagreements over the status of Cuban defectors. Finally, on February 15, 1973,
the urgent necessities of the times overrode reservations on both sides and
an agreement was signed.[67]

Some observers saw the agreement as a first step toward improved relations, and encouraged it as such. Senator Edward Kennedy urged normalization, as did some Republican representatives in a message to Nixon. But the
administration spurned these requests, and made clear on several occasions
that the hijacking agreement was not meant to serve as a catalyst for improved
relations.[68]

Nevertheless, in March the administration showed concern for Cuban sensibilities by refusing asylum to two Cuban fishermen who attempted to defect.
Undoubtedly, this refusal was meant to satisfy an understanding of hijacking
accord; in return for sending back criminals who seized American aircraft, the
Cubans expected the United States to support its position on defectors. The
two fishermen subverted the American policy, however, by jumping from their
ship about a mile off Florida and swimming to the coast, where they were
taken in by a Cuban exile group.[69]

Nixon's Last Year: 1974

Until August 9, when Richard Nixon became the first American president
to resign from office, his administration, though preoccupied with domestic
concerns stemming from Watergate, pursued its stated foreign policies in a
normal fashion. No significant alterations in Cuban policy would occur, but the
domestic and international pressure for an accommodation would reach its
apex. Though Nixon was too preoccupied to respond to this pressure, his successors would feel its effects in major ways; the urge to normalize set the
stage for the Ford and Carter administrations' efforts at an accommodation
with Castro.

Various incentives coalesced in early 1974 to create an overwhelming case
for rapprochement. In the U.S. Congress, Senator Claiborne Pell and others
led the fight for normalization; on April 23, the Senate Foreign Relations Committee voted 12-0 on a resolution proposed by Senator Jacob Javitz to end the

U.S. embargo and normalize relations. In early January, the Cubans had declared a willingness to talk, and the U.S. Department of State, calling the Cuban announcement a significant change of policy, expressed "cautious interest." On January 11, in fact, Castro reportedly sent a cablegram to the administration requesting bilateral talks, though State Department sources denied this report.

In February, U.S. industrialist Cyrus S. Eaton visited Cuba and reported that if Secretary of State Kissinger would initiate a negotiating process, relations could be re-established; Eaton argued that the American business stake in an end to the embargo was significant. Also in February, Kissinger met with Latin American and Caribbean foreign ministers, many of whom expressed hope that the United States would end the embargo; later, in April, the United States partially conceded to these sentiments by granting Argentina official permission to violate the embargo and sell automobiles—produced by subsidiaries of American companies—to Cuba. George Ball, among other prominent observers, urged that the United States follow up this move with a total abrogation of the embargo.

The Nixon administration continued to wade against this tide. In March, Kissinger insisted that the United States would only change its policies when Castro surrendered his adventurist practices. Speaking to a meeting of OAS ministers in April, he further opposed an invitation to Cuba to join the organization, though in addition to granting the auto sales concession, the Secretary of State was also forced to drop the U.S. opposition to the inclusion of Cuba in a 1975 meeting of regional foreign ministers.[70]

In the Summer of 1974—on the eve of Nixon's resignation—the control of American Cuban policy seemed to have spun firmly out of his grip. Frank Mankiewicz of the National Executive Conference traveled to Cuba to interview Castro about potential business opportunities after the resumption of relations; the chief of staff of the Senate Foreign Relations Committee, Pat M. Holt, also went to Cuba and argued against a continuation of hostility. Castro made known his desires for better relations, and the consensus both within the United States and in Latin America to accept these overtures had now become significant. Even Nixon administration officials now began to admit they were losing effective control of policy.[71]

With Nixon Gone, the Stage is Set

But all these discussions were drowned out by the national furor over the Watergate affair. On August 9, 1974, Richard Milhouse Nixon became the first U.S. chief executive ever to resign from office. A number of U.S. policies would be altered by his successor, the more relaxed Gerald Ford. U.S.-Cuban relations would shift considerably; the forces impelling the United States and Cuba toward a reconsideration of their mutual hostility reached fruition in 1974. Both Gerald Ford and Jimmy Carter would take advantage of this atmosphere to attempt limited rapprochements. For complex reasons that will be assessed in the next chapter, these overtures came to naught. But with the resignation of Richard Nixon, the last major barrier to improved U.S.-Cuban ties was removed, and the next several years would witness the most serious Cuban and American flirtations with accommodation since 1959.

PART
FIVE

RELATIONS SINCE 1974

14

THE FAILED RAPPROCHEMENT

Relations Under Ford and Carter 1975-1980

"International incidents should not govern foreign policy, but foreign
policy, incidents."
Napoleon I, *Maxims*

"The friendships of nations, built on common interests, cannot survive
the mutability of those interests."
Agnes Repplier, *Under Dispute*

"The fact is that a man who wants to act virtuously in every way necessarily comes to grief among so many who are not virtuous."
Niccolo Machiavelli, *The Prince*

Cuban policy during the Ford and Carter administra-
tions was highly controversial when it was implemented, and it remains so to
this day. An initial glance at the overtures to Cuba and expression of willingness to reach an accommodation with Castro indicates that a significant shift
in emphasis had taken place; The United States was through trying to topple
Castro and now wanted to make the best deal with him it could. This is the
traditional interpretation of Ford/Carter policies.

Some observers, however, most prominently Morris Morley in his recent
book *Imperial State and Revolution*, are not so sure that U.S. policy toward

Cuba changed much at all. To them, American offers of rapprochement were made with the most stringent of conditions on Cuba's external behavior. No major changes took place in policy, as it turned out, and skeptical analysts view the continuing economic blockade and hostility to Castro's foreign policy as symbols of an American policy that remained essentially the same as it had been since 1959: hostile to Castro.

In a sense, these views of Ford and Carter diplomacy toward Cuba are two sides of the same coin, and how one views American policy during this period depends largely on one's preconceptions. It is undoubtedly true that the Ford and Carter administrations significantly altered at least the rhetorical American attitude toward Cuba, and made real and significant offers of accommodation. It is also true that they attached conditions to these offers, conditions mainly relating to Castro's policy of exporting revolutions to pro-Western countries; when those conditions were not met, the efforts at rapprochement fell apart. For U.S. policy-makers pursuing American geostrategic interests, such an approach makes perfect sense. In short it could be fairly argued that while the Ford and Carter administrations were prepared to reconsider the hostile American stance toward Cuba, they were not ready to allow Castro a free revolutionary hand in the Third World. And Castro, for his part, was not willing to give up that crusade. The net result was that U.S.-Cuban relations at the end of the Ford/Carter period were just as strained, if not more so, than they had been at the beginning.

THE FORD ADMINISTRATION:
A FIRST TRY AT NORMALIZATION

Gerald Ford entered office amid the unprecedented controversy of Richard Nixon's resignation and Ford's subsequent pardon of the disgraced former president. Generally, Ford's diplomacy would continue in the tradition of geopolitical maneuvering established by Nixon and Henry Kissinger, who stayed on as Secretary of State. With regard to Cuba, however, Ford possessed less of the violent distrust of Castro that made an accommodation impossible during Nixon's administration. To be sure, Ford was no fan of Castro, but the new American leader would prove more susceptible to the significant pressures for rapprochement that had been building for over a decade.

The incentives for accommodation with Cuba that had been accumulating since the Johnson administration reached their apex in 1975. Individuals from divergent perspectives argued for normalization: U.S. congressmen, political analysts, and businessmen; leaders of Latin American countries; and Fidel Castro himself.

A number of congressmen, leading "special study missions" or going alone, traveled to Cuba and returned recommending increased relations. In January 1975 Senator John Sparkman, chairman of the foreign relations committee, announced that "Our policy of isolating Cuba has been a failure, and it is time to reexamine that policy with a view toward ending the futile economic boycott and restoring normal relations."[1] In September 1974 Senators Jacob Javits and Claiborne Pell went to Cuba and claimed that it was "a propitious moment" to begin the normalization process.[2] Rep. Stephen Solarz reported the following year that the Cuban GNP was growing, its foreign trade was blossoming, and Cubans supported Castro; in short, the U.S. embargo had failed, and ought to be ended.[3] Charles W. Whalen, a congressman from Ohio, submitted a report in July 1975 recommending normalization.[4]

Perhaps the most ardent congressional advocate of normalization, however, was Senator George S. McGovern. He traveled to Cuba and met with Castro. Like many Western politicians, he was captivated. McGovern recommended an end to the embargo; "At the earliest possible moment," he wrote in his report, "I believe the United States should end its trade embargo against Cuba and explicitly acknowledge an interest in establishing normal diplomatic relations with the government of Fidel Castro."[5] McGovern also wrote articles for the *New York Times Magazine* and other opinion-making journals advocating such a course.[6]

These pro-normalization congressmen called hearings to examine the effects of the boycott and of a potential resumption of trade.[7] Not all participants at these hearings agreed that normalization was the best course; some Cuban exiles and anti-Castro academics called to testify argued that normalization would only legitimize a brutal and illegal regime and would serve the designs of a "foreign despot," in Rolando Bonachea's phrase.[8] But many congressmen used the meetings as forums to rail against what they felt to be an anachronistic, failed policy of isolation.[9]

Legislation was also introduced. House and Senate resolutions expressed the congressional desire to normalize relations and end the embargo, and these put additional pressure on the Ford administration.[10]

Many academics who studied Cuba agreed the American boycott had failed, and there was no good reason to keep it in force. Many liberal critics of U.S. policy toward Cuba since 1960, sensing that the United States was on the verge of a major policy shift, now accelerated their efforts to promote the idea of a rapprochement with Cuba.[11]

U.S. businessmen, too, argued for normalization of relations. A number of companies that had lost property or equipment during the Cuban nationalizations of 1959-60 believed that a settlement with Cuba might include provisions for reparations. Others looked to the business possibilities renewed trade with Cuba might bring.[12]

Many Latin American nations and other countries also pressed for improved U.S.-Cuban ties. As we have seen, during the Johnson administration the American international boycott effort began to crumble, and a number of U.S. allies and Latin American nations began trading with Cuba. During Ford's term this trend continued.[13] In January, 1975 West Germany reestablished diplomatic relations with Cuba; in March Colombia followed suit, and soon a number of OAS governments were pressing the United States to modify its position.[14]

Fidel Castro soon added his own voice to this growing chorus. In January, 1975, at an impromptu press conference, Castro explained that "We have always had some visitors from the United States, such as congressmen, economists, workers, students, young Americans. But I can assure you that in different U.S. circles there is a growing interest in Cuba and *we receive this with pleasure*, of course."[15]

The Administration Responds

Not blind to these developments, the Ford administration made clear its own willingness to pursue discussions with Cuba, provided certain conditions were met. In February 1975, President Ford claimed that if Cuba would "reevaluate and give us some indication of a change in its policy toward the United States, then we certainly would take another look." Echoing this sentiment, in March, 1975 Secretary of State Henry Kissinger said in a major Houston speech that "We see no virtue in perpetual antagonism between the United States and Cuba," and that "we are prepared to move in a new direction if Cuba will." The onus was placed on Castro to stop supporting anti-U.S. revolutionary movements throughout the hemisphere.[16]

Thus the Ford administration established the basic U.S. policy on normalization, one that would be generally followed through the Reagan years: the United States expected Cuba to moderate its foreign policy in exchange for an end to hostility. At times, the U.S. demand would be phrased more broadly, calling for Castro to renounce his ties with the Soviet Union; at times more narrowly, demanding only an end to subversion in the Western Hemisphere. Either way, the U.S. policy, which attempted to mold Cuban behavior in accord with U.S. interests, was controversial; liberals argued that the conditions American policy-makers tried to impose on Cuba's external policies were examples of continuing American diplomatic imperialism of the sort that had dominated Cuba for decades. American policy-makers viewed their actions as merely a defense of U.S. interests throughout the world, interests that outweighed any prospective benefits of normalization with Castro.

By May, the administration's general views began to be formalized in policy. Kissinger said that the United States and the OAS had reached "a general understanding" on ending diplomatic and economic sanctions against Cuba; by June he declared the United States ready to improve relations. White House Press Secretary Ron Nessen, responding to statements by Senator George McGovern about normalization, also said in May that the United States saw "no advantage in perpetual antagonism" with Cuba.[17]

Substantive changes soon followed. On July 29, 1975, the United States voted with the 15 other OAS nations to remove hemispheric sanctions on Cuba; each member nation was now free to act as it wished. The United States did not reestablish diplomatic relations, as did many other countries, but its action demonstrated a novel tolerance for regional acceptance of Castro's Cuba. Indirect U.S. sanctions were lifted; for example, foreign subsidiaries of U.S. corporations were granted the right to trade with Cuba. Also that summer, Castro and Kissinger exchanged messages on establishing formal negotiations. In November the Department of Commerce eased more trade restrictions.

In September 1975, U.S. Secretary of State William D. Rogers indicated that the United States now desired to more formally increase relations with Cuba. The Cuban response was promising; in December the First Party Congress concluded that Cuba was "willing to discuss the normalization of relations with the United States, something which will also contribute to a necessary international detente." U.S. officials began meeting with Cubans; Kissinger's assistant Laurence Eagleburger spoke with members of Cuba's UN mission in November 1974 to clarify a number of issues. From February 1975 Rogers himself was involved.[18]

Even more rapid progress was restrained by U.S. electoral politics. Primary elections for party nominations to the presidency were almost at hand, and Ford was receiving heavy pressure from the right in the person of California Governor Ronald Reagan. As one Kissinger aide said later, "Kissinger definitely wanted to go ahead [with the Cuban rapprochement]. But something stayed his hand. It was Reagan."[19] Thus delayed, the normalization process stalled at the end of 1975, and in early 1976, another issue arose to destroy any hopes of rapprochement and return U.S.-Cuban relations to acrimony and hostility: Castro's Angolian adventure.

Angola

In May 1975, the first Cuban units arrived in Angola to help train the pro-Communist MPLA guerrillas there. This was merely the latest in a series of

African commitments made by Castro, but it would soon become his most ambitious—and costly—venture to date.

From an initial level of about 200 advisors, the Cuban presence grew rapidly, and by the end of 1975 more than 5,000 Cuban troops were in the country. The situation in Angola and Cuban motives for intervening will be examined below, but both were largely irrelevant to U.S. policymakers; what was important was that Castro was again throwing his revolutionary weight around. At the same time, evidence of a growing Cuban role in the Puerto Rican separatist movement was revealed. The Ford administration warned Castro that further adventurism would jeopardize the emerging accommodation; in a November 24 speech in Detroit Kissinger warned that "A policy of conciliation [toward Cuba] will not survive Cuban meddling in Puerto Rico or Cuban armed intervention in the affairs of other nations struggling to decide their own fate." Congressional support for rapprochement declined; Representative Johnathon Bingham, for example, citing Cuba's interventionism, dropped his efforts at ending the U.S. boycott. Many other congressmen who had been cautiously in favor of normalization followed suit.

On December 20, at a surprise news conference, President Ford drove the final nail in the coffin of rapprochement by announcing that "I want it on the record, and as forceful as I can say, that the effort of the Cuban government to get Puerto Rico free and clear of the United States and to involve itself in Angola ends any efforts as far as I am concerned to have friendlier relations." [20]

In the first months of January the problem escalated. U.S. news and intelligence sources reported that by January Cuban forces in Angola approached 15,000. Castro referred to a withdrawal as an "absurd price. . . [to] pay for an improvement in relations." At the end of January Kissinger termed the Angolan invasion a "willful, direct assault upon the recent constructive trend in U.S.-Soviet relations and our efforts to improve relations with Cuba." [21] In February, Kissinger noted that the Cubans were again in the business of "exporting revolution," and emphasized that this policy made a rapprochement out of the question; he also warned Cuba that "the United States will not tolerate" Cuban interventionism in the Western Hemisphere. [22]

Tensions reached an apex in late February. President Ford, fresh from a narrow primary victory over Reagan, called Castro an "international outlaw" during a campaign trip in Florida,. "My administration will have nothing to do with the Cuba of Fidel Castro," he said, and warned that the United States "would take appropriate action" to combat Cuban interventions in Latin America. [23] In early March Kissinger repeated this warning in hearings before the House International Relations Committee, and on March 6, referring to potential Cuban support for Rhodesian guerrillas, he extended it to the rest of the world. At the end of the month the Secretary of State stated conclusively that "The United States will not accept further Cuban military interventions abroad."[24]

Later in March, the Ford administration even began considering specific military options to pursue in case Castro did not heed the warnings. Blockades, demonstration bombings, and outright invasions were listed as alternatives, although few believed any of these would become necessary.[25]

New tensions emerged in March with attacks on Cuban fishing boats by anti-Castro exiles based in the United States. The Ford administration announced that it was attempting to locate an stop the exiles, but the damage was done, and Castro threatened to cancel even the anti-hijacking accord he had reached with Nixon in 1973. In October, a civilian airliner was hijacked by exiles, and 73 people, including 57 Cubans, were killed; in response Castro on October 15, 1976, did abrogate the hijacking agreement.

Meanwhile, the Angolan situation continued to obstruct U.S.-Cuban relations. In April, Kissinger firmly established a Cuban withdrawal from Angola as a precondition for any further talks.

By May, 1976, Castro's involvement in Angola was winding down. The Cuban-backed MPLA had emerged victorious, and Castro began a slow withdrawal of his forces. Nevertheless, U.S. officials and politicians were in no mood to cozy up to Castro again; the Republic Party Platform seemingly reverted even to pre-Nixon policies by arguing that "We shall continue to share the aspirations of the Cuban people to regain their liberty," hence presumably refusing to recognize Castro's legitimate rule.[26] Whatever Kissinger said about "preconditions" for further talks, it was clear that President Ford's small reservoir of trust in Castro had been exhausted. Any normalization of relations would have to await a change of administrations, and one was not long in coming.

THE CUBAN ANGOLAN ADVENTURE: REASONS AND MOTIVES

Since 1968, Castro's moderate trend in foreign policy had largely continued, up until his massive commitment to Angola. Castro initiated further relations with nonsocialist governments, especially Japan, Canada, and Western Europe. Cuban trade with non-Communist countries rose from 32 per cent of its total trade to 41 per cent. In April 1975, the OAS voted to lift all sanctions on Cuba; that same month, Mexican President Luis Echevarria became the first non-socialist leader to visit Castro.[27]

The reasons for this moderation were similar to those that had prompted the initial recourse to reduced emphasis on violent revolution. Economic problems mandated closer ties with the Soviet Union, which demanded closer adherence to the USSR's own policy of peaceful coexistence. The rise to power of socialist leaders through non-violent means—Velasco in Peru, Allende in Chile, Peron in Argentina—provided the convenient explanation that armed revolt was not always necessary to promote Communism. The failure of Castro's early attempts at fomenting revolutions still haunted Cuban planners, and made recourse to other such ventures less likely.[28]

Yet all this would change dramatically with the Cuban intervention of Angola. A survey of the situation in Angola in the early 1970s is necessary to understand Cuban motives.

The Conflict in Angola

The Angolan war has included elements of wars of national liberation, civil wars, regional wars, and global power struggle. In the early 1970s Angola was a Portuguese colony; various national liberation movements—the MPLA (mostly Kimbundu tribesmen), FNLA (the Bakongo), and UNITA (Ovimbundu tribesmen)—had been fighting the Portuguese since 1961 without success. Inequitable economic conditions, discriminatory treatment, and occasional brutality characteristic of the Portuguese occupation continued unabated; in 1975, for example, nearly 90 per cent of the population was illiterate.[29]

During this period, the MPLA, which would later become a Communist movement, was still not avowedly Marxist. It appealed to the United States for aid, and was predictably rebuffed. During the late 1960s and early 1970s, the Soviet Union funneled some $60 million in aid to the MPLA, but the Portuguese remained in power.

In 1974, however, a coup occurred in Portugal. On April 25, a group of liberal army officers with broad national support seized power and immediately began a series of reforms; they abolished the secret police, released political prisoners, and restored many civil rights. the new, leftist government was also determined to withdraw from Portugal's colonial possessions. They called a meeting in January 1975 of the major opposition groups in Angola—UNITA led by Jonas Savimbi, Holden Roberto's FNLA, and Agostinho Neto's MPLA (Daniel Chipenda also ran an MPLA faction, but he was not invited to the meeting)—to establish procedures for a Portuguese pullout. Meeting at Alvor, Portugal, the three groups signed the Alvor Agreement, providing for a transitional government (which in fact came to power on January 31), equal ceilings on the three groups' armed forces, and a Portuguese withdrawal on November 11.

What happened next is the subject of much dispute. The three groups quickly began fighting again, and the agreement fell apart; Portuguese troops proved incapable of halting the civil war, and a Portuguese request for assistance from the United Nations went unanswered. In September, 1975 Portugal announced that it would leave in any case, bequeathing sovereignty over the country to the "people of Angola." On November 10, the Portuguese colonial government fled.

Bolstered with aid from the United States, Roberto made quick progress, but soon the Soviet Union and Cuba entered the fray decisively on the side of the MPLA. By February, 1976, 15,000 Cuban troops had come into the country; a year later that figure stood at over 30,000. In response, the United States increased aid to Roberto and Savimbi, and considered more direct action. President Ford encouraged both Zaire and South Africa to intervene against Neto, and both did; but the Cuban backing proved decisive. The U.S. Congress was meanwhile angered over the Ford administration's meddling, and on December 19, 1975, it approved the Clark Amendment, which ended all U.S. support for UNITA and the FNLA. In response to this South Africa withdrew, and the forces facing the MPLA quickly collapsed. Neto's group soon won the war, and it emerged as the new, Communist, government of Angola, a government that the United States has yet to recognize.[30]

Controversy rages about who broke the Alvor agreement first. John Stockwell, head of the CIA's Angolan Task Force at the time, later revealed that the U.S. National Security Council's secret "40 Committee" had approved some $300,000 in aid for the FNLA after the Alvor accord was signed, thus encouraging Roberto to violate the agreement and renew the civil war.[31] Many subsequent analysts have thus blamed the United States for sparking the renewed civil war that prompted the Cuban response, concluding that the United States was responsible for the collapse of U.S.-Cuban relations in 1975, since it broke the Alvor accord.[32]

Not all observers agree with this interpretation. Some have contended that the Soviets provided Neto with aid in March and April of 1975, before the U.S. "40 Committee"-approved funds arrived, and in any case the Soviets, Cubans, and Chinese had all aided at least one of the three groups in late 1974. Nathaniel Davis, Undersecretary of State for African affairs in 1975, though he argued against covert U.S. intervention in Angola at the time, has noted that many sources were funneling arms and funds into the conflict. He concludes that the does not believe "the case is [yet] made" that the United States caused a renewal of the conflict.[33]

Nor is it certain that, had the United States honored the agreement, the Soviets and Cubans would have done likewise; the massive Cuban troop commitment was made in response to Roberto's successes, but smaller (yet still significant) aid might well have been provided even had the United States remained clear of the conflict. Even without any outside interference, moreover, any thought that the Alvor accords would have held up is problematic; the personal ambitions of the three leaders involved, the ready armies they possessed, and the volatile situation suggest otherwise. Finally, since the Ford administration, and Henry Kissinger in particular, viewed the Angolan situation as a crucial test of America's strength in opposing Communist revolutions, it is unlikely that any Cuban involvement in Angola would have been looked upon favorably.[34]

One can only conclude with certainty that all sides in the conflict received arms, and that the Alvor truce soon dissolved in a new round of civil conflicts.[35] Blaming the United States for the conflict is no more accurate than blaming Cuba or the Soviet Union; all had a hand in prompting a new civil war. Thus the collapse of U.S.-Cuban relations issuing from Cuba's Angolan intervention can most properly be ascribed to the unfortunate convergence of a certain set of circumstances. It was no one's fault; each actor believed it was acting in its own best interests, and given what was known to each at the time, they may indeed have been doing just that. One result, as we have seen, was an end to the process of U.S.-Cuban rapprochement.

Why Did the Cubans Intervene?

But why did the Cubans commit themselves so heavily to the Angolan cause? There is no doubt that the intervention was costly in terms of resources, men, domestic development, and relations with the United States (although Castro did claim surprise when finding out that his intervention would scuttle the normalization trend). A number of theories have been adduced to explain the Cuban intervention.

The one that is probably at once most common and also the most simplistic suggests that the Cubans intervened into Angola on orders from Moscow. This is unlikely, given the cautious Soviet behavior since 1968 and Moscow's emphasis on peaceful coexistence. Soviet support for Cuba's Angolan operations was limited; their behavior suggests they tolerated, and perhaps even encouraged, but did not order, the Cuban moves. Certainly Cuba did not need to intervene to obtain more Soviet aid. Since Castro had fallen into line with Moscow's Third World restraint in 1968, the USSR had been quite forthcoming with economic and military assistance. Nor, in any case, is the model of Cuba as a mere puppet of Soviet interests valid; Cuban foreign policy is dictated as much (and probably far more) by its own internal and external concerns. As Michael Erisman has recognized, "convergence of interests" is a better explanation than the "Soviet surrogate" thesis.[36]

Abraham Lowenthal wrote an interesting article in 1977 suggesting possible internal Cuban motives for the Angolan intervention.[37] Lowenthal spelled out the goals of Cuban foreign policy, and how each would be met, or at least not significantly damaged, by the Angolan operation. The primary goals were: (1) to protect the revolution—not a significant concern since the United States would not attack Cuba over Angola; (2) to support national liberation movements—accomplished by aiding the MPLA; and (3) to strengthen the alliance with the USSR while asserting independence—achieved by pursuing a course the Soviets would favor without explicitly doing the Soviets' bidding. Castro could also expect that long-term relations with the United States would not suffer because of Angola, since Ford, in an election year, was unlikely to be more forthcoming in any case, and his likely Democratic successor would probably press for a rapprochement almost regardless of what the Cubans did. Hence, as Lowenthal concludes, Cuba's Angolan intervention could well have been dictated by "consistent and sensible calculations of Cuba's interests as perceived by its national leaders." Importantly, such adventures allowed the Cubans to achieve bargaining leverage with both the United States and the Soviet Union.[38]

Of the considerations outlined by Lowenthal, perhaps the most significant was the traditional Cuban commitment to support of revolutionary movements. Though not always a decisive force, ideological motivation certainly had some effect. This motive became especially operative after October 23, when South Africa intervened into Angola; Castro had now virtually been challenged to support his African allies, and he was quick to respond. This commitment also stemmed from a rapidly evolved Cuban nationalism, which is often overshadowed by Marxist-Leninist ideology but which nevertheless is an important motivation for Cuba's foreign policy.[39]

Institutional developments within the Cuban government also occurred that allowed these ideological motives to be given expression. After a short period of decreased influence in the early 1970s, occasioned by a series of government reforms magnifying the power of planners, technocrats, and managers, Fidel, Raul, and their followers (Fidelistas and Raulistas) had reasserted complete control of the government by 1975. Thus Fidel's concern for international revolutionary activity, and Raul's desire to augment the importance of the Cuban military, encouraged a renewed set of foreign adventures. This established the atmosphere in which Cuba responded quickly to the MPLA's plight.[40]

In truth, Castro undoubtedly intervened in Angola for a combination of these reasons. No one of them is necessarily enough to have caused him to risk so much. Whatever the motive, though, Castro had played his hand, and in doing so had ruined any chances for a U.S.-Cuban accommodation during the Ford administration. Only a change in the U.S. government could rekindle hopes for a rapprochement, and just such a change occurred in 1976 with the election of Jimmy Carter.

THE CARTER ADMINISTRATION

Under Jimmy Carter, American foreign policy would enter a phase of internationalist idealism. He would continue (for a time) Nixon's policy of detente toward the Soviet Union and would expand the opening to the People's Republic of China, finally shifting U.S. recognition from Taiwan to the PRC. But the novel aspect of Carter's approach was its focus on the Third World as its overarching commitment to the promotion of human rights around the globe, even at the temporary expense of traditional U.S. national interests.

A New Internationalism: Mainsprings of the Carter Policy

The Carter administration's desire to seek a limited rapprochement with Castro was part of this new set of priorities in foreign policy. Carter's foreign policy leaders were well aware that Castro would not surrender his own international agenda, but they felt that a limited accommodation could give the United States some leverage over Cuban actions while establishing the context for a possible full resumption of relations at a later date.[41] Over time, the more conservative elements of the administration, most notably the National Security Council, would reassert the traditional U.S. demand for changes in Cuban external behavior, but at least at first, such demands were muted.

These two particular foreign policy goals—an increased awareness of Third World concerns and a desire for accommodation with Castro—translated into a more understanding position on Angola. Before the election Carter said that the United States had "missed the opportunity" to serve as a "positive and creative force for good" in Angola, and that the Soviet and Cuban presence there was not a significant threat to U.S. interests. Once in office, Carter appointed as Andrew Young, UN Ambassador who had advocated recognizing the MPLA. New Secretary of State Cyrus Vance also urged "affirmative" as opposed to negative (or anti-Cuban) policies in Angola.[42]

Early Progress

All early signs from the Carter administration pointed toward a resumption of rapprochement with Cuba. On January 10, during Senate confirmation hearings, Secretary of State designate Cyrus Vance said he hoped to work for improved U.S.-Cuban relations. On taking office Carter suspended the recon- naissance flights over Cuba, and in March he ended the travel ban prevent- ing U.S. citizens from going to Cuba. Both of these acts had mixed motivations—satellites had made overflights unnecessary and U.S. courts were having constitutional problems with government travel bans—but both nevertheless served to reduce tensions with Cuba. On January 25, Andrew Young made it clear that the United States was no longer in a fury over Africa when he said that "The Cubans bring a certain stability and order to Angola." At a January 31 press conference, Vance expressed a hope that the United States "could begin the process of moving toward normalization" with Cuba.

The Cubans were not deaf to these overtures, and responded with interest. On February 2, 1977, Cuban Vice President Carlos Rafael Rodriguez (the head of the PSP before the revolution) said that Cuba was willing to discuss all issues of bilateral relations, though it would not change its ideological posi- tions. On February 9 Castro himself said that Carter was a "man of morals" and that it might be possible to normalize relations.

Both sides quickly expressed an interest in direct talks. In January the Cubans quietly made known their desire for negotiations on fishing rights; on February 4 the Department of State acknowledged this request and depart- ment spokesman Fred Brown referred to a "whole range of issues we want to discuss with the Cubans." State's director of Cuban affairs, Culver Gleysteen—long an advocate of a rapprochement—met in early 1977 with Nestor Garcia, the first secretary of the Cuban mission to the UN, to discuss possibilities for a formal conference of officials.[43]

Carter soon displayed some degree of inconsistency with regard to two basic issues: human rights and the Angolan situation. Carter's general emphasis on human rights and foreign policy did not exempt Communist governments, and he would occasionally place pressure on Castro to release political prisoners and grant Cuban citizens greater freedoms. Castro natu- rally resented such pressure, and at other times Carter would back off. On Angola, the administration position on whether a Cuban withdrawal was necessary for talks varied; all early official statements said it was not, but on February 16 Carter implied he would not talk with the Cubans unless they withdrew. Carter and Vance both clarified that statement to mean that a *full* rapprochement was impossible while the Cubans were in Angola, but that lower-level talks were not. Nevertheless, Carter had already begun to display the sort of incoherence and poor policy enunciation that would plague his administration throughout its tenure.[44]

The Department of State quickly worked out its position on Cuba. It would press for a gradual improvement in relations, prompted by agreement on a number of small measures. Full removal of the embargo would be conditional on Cuban provision of compensation for the property seized after the revolution. Finally, a strong emphasis would be placed on the promotion of human rights.

These plans were put into effect in a series of meetings with the Cubans in March. On March 16 Vance said the United States was in direct contact with Cuban representatives; on March 24, a U.S. delegation began meetings with Cuban officials in New York City. The topic of discussion was the fishing and navigation agreement, but both sides expressed a hope for broader progress as well. At the end of the talks, the Cuban delegation proposed a follow-up meeting in Havana.

In April, Senators George McGovern and James Abourezk visited Cuba. Cuban officials insisted to the senators that the United States end the embargo as a prelude to the signing of new agreements, such as a renewal of the anti-hijacking accord. But Raul Castro implied that small steps—such as exemption to the embargo for food and medicine—might get relations rolling.[45]

Continuing in the pattern established in the Ford administration, a number of congressmen followed McGovern and Abourezk to Cuba and returned recommending a rapprochement. In February Representative Jonathon B. Bingham returned from Cuba calling for an end to the embargo.[46] Senator Frank Church wrote in a committee report that the U.S. policy of hostility had failed "monumentally. Instead of isolating Cuba from the world at large, we have managed only to isolate ourselves from Cuba."[47] Other congressmen, such as Jacob Javitz and Claiborne Pell, followed these groups to Cuba.[48]

Other pressures for improved relations with Cuba developed. U.S. businessmen hoped for export opportunities when relations were normalized.[49] In December 1976, moreover, the U.S. Commission on Latin American Relations had issued its second report—called the Linowitz report for the Commission's head, former OAS Ambassador Sol Linowitz—which urged the Carter administration to normalize relations with Cuba, and the Commission's recommendations carried significant weight.

First Signs of Hesitation

By March, however, despite the snowballing talks, the first signs of hesitation from the American side began to emerge. The U.S. press reported on continued Cuban involvement in Africa. Castro had troops in Angola, Somalia, Mozambique, Congo, and other countries. The "Shaba" wars, in which Angola invaded Zaire in retaliation for Zaire's earlier opposition to the MPLA, were in full swing, and although the Cubans denied it many sources reported that Cuban troops were leading the Angolan assault. (Actually the invading forces were primarily Katangese: well-traveled soldiers of fortune who had received approval from Angolan leaders, still smarting from Zaire's intervention in their own civil war, but little direct support.) On March 17, already hesitating in his call for rapprochement, Carter omitted the phrase "We are prepared to seek reconciliation with Havana" from a UN speech.[50]

Throughout the Carter administration, the role of National Security Advisor Zbigniew Brzezinski was crucial and controversial. Much more hawkish than most administration officials, Brzezinski engaged in a running feud with Secretary of State Vance over various aspects of U.S. foreign policy, and their disagreements often centered around relations with Cuba. Critics of Brzezinski's role have labeled him a schemer who surreptitiously undercut administration policies he disagreed with, such as the opening toward Cuba;[51] his defenders argue that he was the only hard-nosed realist among a group of foreign policy amateurs was one of the few saving graces of the Carter years.[52]

In April, more signs that the accommodation was faltering developed. The leader of the South West African People's Organization (SWAPO) said that Castro had promised to help them overthrow Namibia. Zaire on April 4 broke diplomatic relations with Cuba; the same day Castro arrived on a solidarity visit to Moscow. The following day he criticized the U.S. "double standard" on Africa. On the 8th, a *Chicago Tribune* article reported that Raul Castro was now saying the closure of the United States's Guantanamo Bay naval base in Cuba was a precondition to further negotiations.[53]

The spring also saw a renewed Cuban commitment to Africa. Neto was facing hard going against Zaire in the conflict over Zaire's Shaba province; Zairean leader Mobutu had received aid from a number of countries including Belgium, France, Egypt, and most substantially Morocco. In response to Mobutu's successes, Cuba in June and July halted the downgrading of their presence in Angola and sent reinforcements. In May, Castro had implied to Barbara Walters in an interview that he planned to do this.[54]

Interestingly, the Cubans at this point may have been working *against* the Soviets. The coup against Neto was led by a group of pro-Soviet black nationalists. In all probability, Soviet leaders at least had knowledge of the coup attempt, and may have materially aided it. Once it occurred, Castro intervened decisively to protect Neto, whom the Soviets from that point supported openly.[55] Meanwhile, the Angolan civil war continued, with Roberto and Savimbi waging a guerrilla war against Neto for control of the country.

While recognizing the Cubans' perceived need to intervene, the United States was nevertheless wary of these actions. With a controversial situation in Namibia to deal with, however, and still hoping to expand the accommodative trend toward Havana, the administration muted its complaints. Still, another potential thorn in the U.S.-Cuban relationship had been introduced.[56]

Nevertheless, officials on both sides continued negotiations. On April 14, Carter said at an OAS meeting that he wanted improved relations; the next day he agreed with Andrew Young's suggestion that the Cuban presence in Angola "stabilized" the situation. On April 19, he told McGovern and Abourezk that he would not oppose an exemption to the embargo for food and medicine. A Gallup poll at about the same time found that 53 per cent of the U.S. public felt that the United States should formally reestablish relations with Castro; only 33 per cent were opposed.[57]

On April 25, as suggested by the Cubans the previous month, a U.S. delegation traveled to Havana. Led by Assistant Secretary of State for Inter-American Affairs Terence Todman, the U.S. group signed agreements on fishing rights and maritime boundaries. On the 28th Todman predicted a "constant improvement" in relations.

On May 5, Andrew Young met with the Cuban UN delegate; on the 10th the Senate Foreign Relations Committee voted 10-6 to allow sales of food and medicine to Cuba. Senator McGovern had favored full provisions for two-way trade in foodstuffs, but his proposal was rejected. On May 30, an agreement was signed opening interest sections; on August 20 Lyle Franklin Cane was appointed as the head of the U.S. interests section, which opened in Havana on September 1. On June 1, Carter proclaimed that his goal was still a full friendship with Cuba, but predicted it would be some time in coming.

There were a number of qualifications to this general progress. On May 12 the House, in a measure primarily aimed at Vietnam but also designed to counter the Senate's action, passed an amendment banning aid or trade with Cuba and Vietnam. On May 31, Roslynn Carter said during a visit to Costa Rica that the administration still had problems with Cuba's human rights record. It was proving difficult in practice to work out the sort of understanding both Havana and Washington seemed to want. While a series of minor, mutually beneficial agreements (on emigration, exchange of weather and air-traffic control information, and so on) were in force, the United States and Cuba seemed to have largely irreconcilable interests in a larger geopolitical sense.

The Collapse: Brzezinski and the "Secret Study"

By November, the African issue reasserted itself. A "secret study" in the Carter administration recommended slowing the rapprochement because of Castro's actions in Africa.[58] A high administration official said that "The Carter White House is seriously disturbed by the steadily expanding Cuban military presence in [Africa] . . . and sees no possibility of re-establishing formal diplomatic relations with Havana under these circumstances."[59] Castro the following month said he would not end his commitment to Africa, and it seemed that the trend toward accommodation had been dealt a death blow.[60]

The "high official" in question was Zbigniew Brzezinski. He had made known the contents of a CIA "study" suggesting a massively increased Cuban commitment to Angola; in fact the study itself proved little, and CIA analysts later denied that their evidence supported Brzezinski's conclusions. Moreover, Brzezinski had taken the unusual step of intervening in the diplomatic process without informing the State Department, which now scrambled for a way to prevent its Cuban efforts from coming to naught.[61]

Brzezinski's role in this matter is controversial. Critics, such as Wayne Smith, contend that the national security adviser's fear of a worldwide Communist conspiracy led him to intentionally undermine State's diplomacy with politically calculated leaks of information.[62] Undoubtedly, the administration wanted to portray a somewhat harder line to assist passage of the SALT II treaty; though why leaks such as Brzezinski's would assist this process, when they merely served to reinforce the image of Carter as a patsy of the Soviets, is unclear. The *New York Times* called the ploy "a cheap way to score political points."[63] In any case, whatever his motives, Brzezinski had placed a temporary damper on the drive for improved relations.

Castro would end it more forcefully—and finally—three months later.

A New Intervention: Ethiopia

Trouble had been brewing in Africa in the Ethiopian-Somalian relationship for some time. Dedicated enemies, the two had for some time been clients of different superpowers. Ethiopia, even under the new Marxist leader Mangistu Haile Mariam, was friendly to the West, which backed its political conflict with Eritrean secessionists; Somalia, under Siad Barre, was a client of the Soviet Union. In 1977, however, all of that changed.

The United States, citing concerns about Ethiopian rights violations, began reducing its aid to Mengistu. The Ethiopian leader retaliated by closing U.S. military bases in Ethiopia, and the Carter administration then eliminated all aid. A dedicated Marxist in any case, Mengistu was perfectly content to turn to the Soviet Union for assistance.

Now, however, the Soviets were financing two sworn rivals: Ethiopia and Somalia. Fidel Castro and Soviet President Podgorny visited both countries pleading for peace, but Siad Barre, dedicated to the "reunification" of Somalia, was planing to invade Ethiopia. Recognizing that the Soviets might well sever their relationship with him if he did so, Siad Barre turned to the United States for assistance.

Quickly, seizing what was seen as an opportunity to draw a nation out of the

Communist camp, the Carter administration informally suggested that military aid might be provided, though it made no specific commitments. Apparently encouraged, and utilizing the equipment the Soviets had already provided him, Siad Barre invaded Ethiopia in July 1977, an invasion that the Soviets, Cubans, and Ethiopians alike understandably perceived as American-inspired.[64]

At first, Somalian forces, better equipped and trained than their Ethiopian counterparts, made good progress. Their attack bogged down for a time, then Siad Barre directed a new thrust; at the same time he expelled all Soviet and Cuban personnel and broke relations with Havana, hoping thus to cement relations with the United States and ensure aid from that quarter. Somalia seemed on the verge of winning the war, especially if it actually received U.S. military assistance.[65]

No U.S. aid was forthcoming, however. Siad Barre's actions had shocked the Carter administration, which backed down from its earlier suggestions. Meanwhile the Ethiopians pleaded for Soviet assistance, and in late 1977 the Cubans started providing it; by February, 1978 they had committed 15,000 troops, led in many cases by Soviets. Soon Somali forces were on the defensive. Cuban and Ethiopian units drove them out of the country, but did not invade Somalia.

Once again, too, Castro differed with the Soviets. As noted, a group of Eritrean rebels were fighting for independence from Ethiopia, and Castro had supported them rhetorically and materially for some time. When the USSR began supplying Ethiopia with arms to fight the Eritrean separatists, Castro declared that he would not do the same. The Eritreans, he claimed, were fighting for their own national independence, and though he would help Ethiopia in its war against Somalia he would supply no arms or advisors for use against the Eritreans. Castro continued to call for "just political solutions" to the Eritrean issue for some time.[66]

The increased Cuban commitments in Africa, meanwhile, led to a military buildup within Cuba itself, as the Soviet Union supplied an ever-increasing number of weapons and advisors for use in Africa and elsewhere. While they might have minor disagreements with the Cubans over particular issues, the Soviets still found their Caribbean ally enormously useful, and their high levels of aid reflected this.[67]

The Carter administration reacted angrily; the Cubans had, it seemed, disturbed the process of rapprochement with another foreign military adventure. Many U.S. policy-makers began seriously to question the long-term possibilities for an accommodation with the Cubans, who seemed determined to continue their military adventurism. Even the *New York Times* was furious, referring to Cubans as "tools of Soviet imperial purposes."[68]

Meanwhile, the conflict between Angola and Zaire continued. In May 1978, Katangese troops once again invaded the Shaba province of Zaire. Castro immediately made known Cuba's desire to work with the United States to end the conflict; there was no evidence that Cubans had approved or participated in the invasion, and Castro argued that it merely endangered Angola's security. South Africa also intervened again.[69]

Again the United States reacted harshly. Carter called Castro a liar; Brzezinski made threatening noises about the invasion being part of the global Soviet-Cuban conspiracy for world domination.

Negotiations Continue

During the same period, Castro made known his desire for more talks with the United States on the subject of political prisoners. In April and May of 1978, Cuban officials, in meetings with Undersecretary of State David Newsom and other U.S. representatives, explained that Castro desired to release several thousand political prisoners, presumably to the United States. The Department of State immediately expressed an interest in taking the prisoners. There was also some indication that the Cubans wanted to get the rapprochement process moving again, and that the prisoner issue was a strategic concession based on an analysis of U.S. desires.

But the continuing feud over Cuban policy between State and the NSC continued. Initially, Attorney General Griffin Bell hampered the process with technicalities, demanding to review each case personally. But when the blind Cuban political prisoner hero Antonio Cuesta arrived in Miami and excoriated the attorney general for his foot-dragging, the process speeded up. Still, however, Brzezinski and others at the NSC harbored doubts about the program, and although the United States had planned to receive over 400 prisoners a month, the NSC refused to admit the immigrants. Eventually, some prisoners would be allowed to emigrate.[70]

By late 1978, U.S.-Cuban talks were stalled on all fronts. U.S. officials suggested that the Cubans release the last four American citizens held in Castro's jails—for obviously criminal activities—and the Cubans showed some interest. They reacted angrily, however, to a set of Anglo-American air maneuvers off Cuba's northern coast and the resumption of reconnaissance overflights; Castro called off the release and put his country on a full war alert. The four prisoners were later released.

The MiG Controversy

Another minor controversy over the Soviet presence in Cuba erupted in the fall of 1978 when it was revealed that the Soviets were supplying two squad-rons of MiG-23 aircraft to Cuba. The MiG-23 was a more capable aircraft that anything the Cubans possessed, but most importantly, it was capable of car-rying nuclear weapons. If the Soviets supplied the nuclear-capable version, they would arguably have been in violation of the 1962 Kennedy-Khrushchev agreement banning offensive weapons from Cuba. The issue was a significant one, if for no other reason than principle; in 1962 the United States had insisted Castro give up his Il-28 medium bombers, whose capabilities were far less than the MiG-23. It would be hard now to support that action while claiming the MiG-23s were no threat, despite the fact that the Cubans had possessed MiG-21s—whose capabilities also far exceeded the Il-28's—for some time without U.S. objection.

American officials were confident of their ability to detect the presence of nuclear weapons, and various intelligence sources confirmed that there were none in Cuba. On close inspection, moreover, it was decided that the MiG-23s were not the nuclear-capable version. The USSR claimed it would not provide either the nuclear-capable version or nuclear weapons. In January 1979, the Department of State issued a small statement downplaying the role of the MiGs and arguing that they had no offensive capability against the United States, and the diplomatic flap was over.[71]

Conservatives in the United States, however, would not let the issue die.[72] They claimed that the administration was once again failing to respond to the Communist military buildup in Cuba. They demanded various responses to this threat, but most ominously, they tied the administration's weakness to the ongoing debates over SALT II; a president too vacillating to adequately confront Communist expansion could not be trusted to negotiate a fair treaty, it was argued. This domestic pressure from the right would set the stage for the Carter administration's later, nearly hysterical reactions to Cuban moves.

The Soviet Brigade

The Carter administration's gradual shift to a hard line was solidified through early 1979. It seemed clear that the Soviet Union was seizing the stra-tegic initiative: revolutions brought Communist governments to power in Grenada and Nicaragua; Cuba assumed a leadership role in the Non-Aligned Movement (NAM), and continued its activities in Africa; and later that year, Soviet troops would invade Afghanistan. A revolution in Iran brought a vio-lently anti-American government to power which, while also anti-Soviet, did enormous damage to U.S. interests in the Persian Gulf.

Castro was consciously playing the moderate, but no one seemed to notice. His speech to an NAM meeting condemned American policy but called for unity and conciliation within the movement, not the revolutionary fervor he had been expected to demand. His initial advice to the new leaders of Grenada and Nicaragua was pragmatic; he urged them not to burn their bridges to the United States, but to develop their own revolutions as they saw fit. He also congratulated the United States on its early provision of aid to the Nicaraguans.[73]

In the poisonous atmosphere of the times, however, with Soviet allies and proxies apparently on the march throughout the world, these statements were largely ignored. Concerned about the Soviet military buildup in Cuba, Brzezinski requested an assessment from U.S. intelligence of the Soviet presence there.[74] The results created a minor crisis in superpower relations: U.S. reconnaissance photos revealed the presence of a Soviet unit seemingly configured in a combat, rather than training, role. On August 17, 1979, the brigade was photographed in combat maneuvers; on August 23 Carter was briefed. The U.S. intelligence community's *National Intelligence Daily*, a classified briefing on world events for a select group of policy-makers, referred to the unit as a "combat brigade."[75]

This information came to light in an atmosphere already clouded with controversy over Soviet troops in Cuba. Senator Bernard Stone of Florida, pressing for a tough line on Cuba in response to political pressure from his state, had as early as July charged that the Soviets had a full combat brigade in Cuba. Secretary of Defense Harold Brown and Secretary of State Vance, however, both denied the charge, and argued that there had been no significant increase in Soviet forces in Cuba. Nevertheless, Stone expressed his doubts. The United States made known to Soviet officials that it was watching their Cuban deployments carefully.

In late August, the issue suddenly exploded with the public revelation of the existence of the brigade. Clarence Robinson, a staff member of *Aviation Week*, called Richard Baker, a staff member of Undersecretary of State for Political Affairs David Newsom. Robinson told Baker that he had acquired a copy of the *National Intelligence Daily*, and was planning to publicize the information.[76]

Newsom informed Vance of this development, and the secretary of state was immediately worried about the disclosure's impact on SALT II. At issue were the Kennedy/Khrushchev post-Missile Crisis agreements about Soviet troops in Cuba; the Soviet leader had pledged not to install offensive weapons in Cuba. A fully-equipped combat brigade capable of offensive operations might, under a loose definition, constitute such a force, although it is clear that the general assumption in 1962-63 was that Khrushchev's pledge applied only to nuclear delivery systems such as missiles and bombers. (In fact, when confronted with the existence of the brigade the Soviets would make reference to a specific portion of the 1962 agreements that allowed them to keep the brigade at its then-current location.)[77]

Nevertheless, the revelation of a "new" Soviet combat brigade in Cuba would be politically damaging, and Vance immediately assembled his aides to formulate a response. These events unfolded during Congress's August recess, and most top policymakers were out of town; many congressmen and executive department officials, including President Carter himself, were on vacation. Vance decided that there was no basis for the United States to demand that the brigade be removed; Newsom was sent to inform Soviet charge Vasev (Ambassador Dobrynin was in Moscow) that the United States was concerned about the brigade, although it admitted that "as currently configured and supported the unit poses no threat to the United States."[78] Newsom also informed many influential congressmen of the brigade; most expressed a hope that the affair would not be blown out of proportion.

The reaction of one senator was not so sanguine. Frank Church had been wounded politically by Cuban issues in the past; already facing an Idaho constituency more conservative than himself, Church had been vilified in many parts of his state for an April, 1977 good will trip to Cuba. He had also strongly supported the administration against Stone's charges, and now risked being made the fool again. Church was understandably disturbed about the news.

Church called Vance from his home and argued that if no other official would make the issue public, he felt he ought to. Vance merely said that "We'll trust you to use your judgment on that, Senator," though he emphasized that he hoped Church would keep it relatively quiet. Church, however, quickly called a press conference and demanded that the brigade be removed.[79]

Media attention over the issue soon peaked. On August 31, Press Secretary Hodding Carter was besieged with questions on the brigade at his normal State Department Friday briefing. By the early days of September, however, press coverage was waning, despite Church's hastily convened hearings on September 4 to discuss the issue, and despite the fact that hawks like Senator Henry Jackson were using the brigade as an argument against SALT II. The following day, Vance called a press conference to further defuse the issue; he claimed that the existence of the brigade was a serious matter, but that it posed no threat to the United States. When asked about whether the United States would demand a withdrawal of the unit, however, Vance sounded a somewhat tougher line, saying that he would "not be satisfied with the maintenance of the status quo."

That same afternoon, the Soviet charge delivered their answer: the brigade was part of a 17-year old training center for Cubans, designed to familiarize them with Russian equipment. Throughout the first days of September it became apparent that the Soviets were confused and angry that the Carter administration seemed intent on manufacturing a crisis; it could not see the problem with a small training unit in Cuba that had been there since 1962.[80]

It was now clear to most American policy makers that the Senators and administration officials who had trumpeted the brigade's significance had overstated the case. It had probably been in existence in its then-current form for some time, and it certainly posed no threat to the United States. Only the broadest possible interpretation of the 1962 Kennedy-Khrushchev pact would invalidate the presence of a ground combat unit. But the administration had backed itself into a corner with its harsh rhetoric; Carter now sought a way out.

On September 7, President Carter maintained the administration's ambiguous stand in a televised speech. Urging restraint and pointing out that the brigade did not pose an immediate threat, Carter nevertheless condemned the Soviets for not respecting U.S. "interests" and "concerns." What Carter actually expected them to do now was unclear.

Over the next several weeks, U.S. and Soviet officials conducted meetings aimed at resolving the impasse over the brigade. The public Soviet position was tough, refusing even to consider a withdrawal and (somewhat justifiably) blaming the United States for blowing the issue out of perspective to achieve political ends. Vance met several times with Dobrynin; on September 20, he put forward the official U.S. proposal, which amounted to the dissolution of the brigade and the transfer of its heavy equipment to Cubans.

Initially, little progress was made. On September 22 and 27, Vance met with Soviet Foreign Minister Gromyko in New York without achieving anything. On the 23rd, Brzezinski warned of a possible U.S. "retaliation" if the Soviets did not make some concessions, though what that retaliation would be was unclear. Carter called Brezhnev on the Hot Line, but even this top-level intervention did not get the stalled talks moving.

Finally, recognizing that the Soviets were not going to budge, the Carter administration decided unilaterally to extricate itself from its dilemma. On October 1, Carter made another televised speech that essentially assembled various Soviet assurances and U.S. actions into a package designed to minimize the brigade's significance. He catalogued Soviet reassurances that the brigade was only a training unit and its reaffirmation of the missile crisis pledge regarding offensive weapons in Cuba. He then announced that the United States would increase reconnaissance of Cuba, establish a military task force headquarters in Key West, and bolster economic assistance to other Caribbean nations. None of this addressed the actual complaints that had been made about the unit, of course; Carter merely wanted a way out.[81]

Reaction to this speech was mixed. Hard-liners charged the administration with backing down.[82] One critic even went so far as to claim that "The Kremlin can hardly fail to conclude from President Carter's speech on October 1 that it stands to reap handsome dividends from its decision to defy the United States" on the presence of the brigade. The Soviet Union, this analyst concluded, was positioned "for new success in its global strategy."[83]

Liberal critics were no more generous. To them, the crisis represented the dangerous political maneuverings of an administration desperate to rescue SALT II. Raymond Garthoff, in one of the more moderate phrasings of the argument, has concluded that "it is befitting the essentially internal American political process that generated the whole incident" that it is possible to outline roughly the first two weeks of the "crisis" with "almost no reference to American relations with the Soviet Union—except in terms of the consequences of the internal U.S. political dynamic."[84] Other critical observers painted Brzezinski as the culprit, as he had been in the Ethiopian affair; his concerns about Soviet global ambitions, in the view of less hawkish analysts, caused him to unilaterally subvert the U.S. policy of rapprochement with Cuba and to invent a potentially fatal crisis out of thin air to "challenge" the Soviets.

In the frightening atmosphere of the times, however, those emphasizing the immediacy of the Soviet and Cuban threat won out. Influenced by hard-line arguments, the Senate on October 2 passed a resolution making SALT II hostage to the non-combat nature of the brigade. The detente and arms control policy begun under the Nixon administration and carried on by Carter was beginning to unravel, and Cuba, along with the Soviet Union, was largely responsible.

Lean Years for Castro

For Castro, meanwhile, the 1970s had been a time of disruption. After the failed 1970 sugar harvest, significant reforms were undertaken in the government with the goal of efficiency and improved production. Certain high government officials were dismissed and replaced by more pragmatic planners. As recent analyses have suggested, these reforms succeeded, and Cuba experienced a period of impressive growth in the first half of the 1970s.[85]

By the mid-1970s, however, Castro and his close associates had reasserted a more direct control over Cuba's affairs of state, and perhaps partly as a result Cuba's economic performance dropped significantly. Starting in the late 1970's, falling prices for oil, which Cuba re-exported to acquire hard currency, also hurt. From the mid-1970's to 1980, growth was sluggish. Poor crops and other economic problems, along with the increasing unpopularity of Castro's calls for "socialist energy" and renewed efforts for the revolution, combined to create poor productivity and worker diffidence and dissatisfaction.

The visits of some 100,000 Cuban-Americans, allowed by the more open emigration laws, caused problems. They were allowed to visit primarily so

Cuba could benefit from their hard currency expenditures, but the primary effect was to spread the word in Cuba about how much better life was in the United States. Unrest among the population grew even more, as did the desire of thousands of Cubans to emigrate.

The emigration of released political prisoners and others from Cuba had become a relatively steady stream, and after ironing out some initial bureaucratic problems the United States ran its own immigration process smoothly. U.S. officials also granted citizenship to many Cubans who fled the island in boats and landed in Florida, a practice that enraged Castro because the United States appeared to be encouraging illegal emigration from Cuba. Particularly troublesome for Cuban officials was the fact that, as in the past, those who left were very often the cream of Cuban society: highly educated specialists such as doctors and lawyers.

1980: The Mariel Crisis

These various pressures combined to create a huge surge of unhappiness in Cuba and a desire to emigrate. Cuban citizens began flooding various foreign embassies, seeking entry visas. In April, 1980, a crisis occurred when Cuban guards at the Peruvian embassy were withdrawn; one had been shot in a near-riot by Cubans demanding the right to go to Peru, and the Cuban government removed the rest for reasons of "safety." Some 10,000 Cubans immediately occupied the embassy grounds, essentially living on the lawn there in the hope that Peru eventually would allow them in.

President Carter was sympathetic to the desires of the Cubans, and on April 14 he signed an order providing for the legal immigration of 3,500 Cuban refugees. An airlift was organized, and from the 14th to the 18th it carried out some 1,000 Cubans, but on the 18th Castro cancelled it. Costa Rica offered to take the rest of the refugees.

On April 20, Castro, once again furious over the desire of thousands of his countrymen to flee, made a familiar offer: any Cubans who wanted to leave could, he said. All they needed to do was obtain transportation to the United States or elsewhere from the port of Mariel.

Tens of thousands of Cubans took Castro at his word. Within a month, some 115,000 Cubans had fled to the United States alone. They came in boats of every size and description, and, as in past such exoduses, a number of Cubans died during the transit.

Carter was stunned at the scope of the migration. In mid-May, concerned over continuing reports of deaths at sea, he instituted a four-part program. The United States would (1) begin an airlift and sealift to bring the Cubans to Florida safely, (2) open a family registration center in Miami, (3) provide help to Cuban boats via the Coast Guard and Navy, and (4)exclude known criminals. The last provision soon took on a special importance as it became clear that Castro was attempting to empty many of his jails and dump the criminals on the United States, in some cases forcing families to take convicted criminals with them in their boats.[86]

The administration established immigration processing facilities in Florida. The vast majority of the refugees were law-abiding Cubans, and they were duly processed through Immigration and Naturalization Service offices and granted citizenship. The administration faced a serious problem in dealing with Cubans known to be criminals—since the United States still had no formal diplomatic relations with Cuba, it could not deport them, and Castro refused to take back those he had specifically sent away.

For the Carter administration, the "Mariel boatlift," as it quickly became known, was another in a string of foreign policy disasters. The administration was in the midst of a series of crises: revolutions in Nicaragua, Iran, and Grenada, the Soviet invasion of Afghanistan, and others. It was being challenged at home by Sen. Edward Kennedy's strong bid for the democratic nomination in the next election. In this atmosphere, Carter's reaction to the boatlift was seen as another example of his inefficiency: Castro had dumped his worst criminals on the United States, critics argued, and Carter let him get away with it.[87]

Legacy of the Carter Administration

Whatever the truth, the Carter administration was rapidly drawing to a close. Ronald Reagan had won a landslide victory over Carter in an election that was in large part a reflection of the desire of most Americans to shed its image of incompetence and weakness and to reassert American power abroad. Reagan's policies toward Cuba would be a reflection of his larger geopolitical priorities: anti-Communism and a flexing of American military might. The trend toward rapprochement so evident in the Ford and Carter administrations, temporarily restrained by Castro's African adventures, was about to come to a screeching halt.

The Carter administration left a mixed legacy. Its foreign policy, at least in the initial stages of the administration, placed renewed emphasis on responsible international behavior and on honesty, a welcome change in the aftermath of Watergate and revelations about sinister CIA activities during the previous decades. For many Latin American nations the new American emphasis on nonintervention and Third World concerns was refreshing. Many of the so-called "Carter disasters," moreover, such as the Nicaraguan, Grenadian, and Iranian revolutions, and the Soviet invasion of Afghanistan, were in many respects merely the results of long-standing problems that finally manifested themselves during the Carter years.

Yet Carter's Cuba policy serves as a microcosmic example of the failures of his foreign policy generally. His slightly confused early tactics were well-intentioned enough but fell victim to the contradictions within Carter's diplomacy. His emphasis on human rights soon came into conflict with important goals in foreign policy; and where conflicts arose, they were usually resolved in favor of national security concerns and to the detriment of the explication of values in foreign policy. Later, Cuban and Soviet actions stunned the foreign-policy novice Carter; his famous remark that he had "learned more about the Soviet Union in the two weeks" after the invasion of Afghanistan than in his whole life speaks as much to what he didn't know beforehand as to what he learned in 1979. Shocked by apparent world-wide Communist crusades, and struggling to obtain approval for the controversial SALT treaty at home, the Carter administration overreacted to certain Cuban and Soviet moves and staked American "credibility" on meaningless issues such as the Soviet brigade controversy.

Most significantly from the perspective of U.S.-Cuban relations, Carter's failed attempt at normalization, like his stillborn efforts at creating a new era of detente, set the stage for a reaction against the essentially passive American diplomacy of the Ford and Carter years. That reaction took the form, in 1980, of a Republican challenger for the presidency so conservative many political analysts had been saying for years he could never get elected: Ronald Wilson Reagan.

15

GOING TO THE SOURCE

The Reagan Years, 1980-1988

"The efficiency of the truly national leader consists primarily
in preventing the division of the attention of a people, and always in
concentrating it on a single enemy."
Adolf Hitler, *Mein Kampf*

The end of the Carter administration brought to a close
a nearly unique period in American foreign relations. The overwhelming
emphasis on values in foreign policy, on promoting human rights abroad came
to a sharp halt with the election of Ronald Reagan. Gone were the accommodating policies toward Communist states and the harsh criticisms of right-
wing dictatorships; in their stead, Reagan brought a hard-line anti-Communism that tended to depict all foreign policy questions (especially those in
Latin America) as East-West issues.

Reagan's Cuban Policy

Reagan's general foreign and defense policy was a tough one that emphasized military power and an adequate response to the Soviet threat. Based on
an essentially bipolar world view, and hence viewing most Third World conflicts in East-West terms, the Reagan policy encouraged strong support for
pro-U.S. developing nations and active opposition to established Communist
governments. Military solutions were to be considered, if not favored.[1]

Such a black-and-white concept of global politics informed Reagan's view of Cuba. As earlier chapters have documented, Reagan's distrust of Castro had a long history. As late as 1980, moreover, Reagan still felt that Cuba might be taken from Castro, that the Cuban regime might be vulnerable to outside pressure.[2] His policy toward Cuba was designed to apply just such pressure.

During the Carter administration, Reagan made a number of radio addresses on the subject of Cuba, painting Castro as a deceitful dictator and criticizing Carter for his light-handed treatment of Cuban African adventures. Reagan pointed to Castro's political prisoners and to Cuba's support for revolutionary governments from Vietnam to North Korea to Nicaragua.[3]

As president, then, it was hardly surprising that Reagan immediately adopted a tough line toward Cuba. A February 1981 Department of State White Paper made it clear that the new administration viewed Latin American issues in a distinctly East-West framework. Cuba was seen as a primary conduit of Soviet influence in the hemisphere; there was even talk of support for a "war of national liberation" against Castro.[4] The administration also bolstered aid to El Salvador and other regional allies battling Communist insurgencies. Reagan demanded unilateral changes (really reversals) in Cuban behavior; in an April 1982 interview, when asked if he would consider normalizing relations with Castro, Reagan replied:

> What it would take is Fidel Castro, recognizing that he made the wrong choice quite a while ago, and that he sincerely and honestly wants to rejoin the family of American nations. . . . And it would take more than words. I think there are some deeds that if he performed those deeds it would prove his sincerity.[5]

Similar themes were present in early administration policy statements. Assistant Secretary of State for Inter-American Affairs Thomas O. Enders outlined the administration response to the Cuban challenge in a June 1981 speech. "Both Central America and the Caribbean are exposed to an effort at armed subversion by Cuba of great subtlety and sophistication," he argued, cataloguing Cuban involvement in Nicaragua, El Salvador, Guatemala, Colombia, and Jamaica. Enders outlined a four-point U.S. response: (1) "We will help threatened countries to defend themselves," (2) "we will help threatened countries to preserve their people's rights to self-determination," (3) "we will help countries of the basin to achieve economic success," and (4) "we will focus on the source of the problem."

This last statement echoed the eventual position of Secretary of State Haig, who would suggest that the United States "go to the source" of Central American instability. Enders went on:

Cuba has become a misshapen society, poorer now than it was at the time of the revolution. A fifth of its citizens may wish to emigrate. It is dependent on $8 million of Soviet aid a day. Yet it plays Gurkha to the Soviet imperialists in Africa and threatens nearly all its neighbors. . . .Cuba has declared covert war on its neighbors. *The United States will join with them to bring the costs of that war back to Havana.*[6]

What exactly Enders meant by that last statement was a mystery, as much to the Cubans as to observers of American policy. Later administration statements, however, by White House advisor Edwin Meese and Undersecretary of State Walter Stoessel emphasized that the administration ruled out no option in dealing with Cuba. The implicit threat of military action was clear.[7]

Enders' solutions to regional problems, moreover, signaled the Reagan administration's focus: three dealt directly or indirectly with the Communist menace, only one with economic development. These priorities reflected the administration's emphasis on Communist subversion as the primary cause of regional instability.[8]

Within the administration, the chief proponent of the tough stance on Cuba was Secretary of State Alexander Haig. The former military head of NATO, Haig was accustomed to forceful solutions to problems, and he made repeated references to military operations against Cuba. His early claim that the administration intended to ''go to the source'' of Central American turmoil was interpreted in Havana as a near threat of invasion. In January, 1981 Haig rejected improved ties with Cuba, and in March Reagan was forced to clarify his secretary's position by conceding that no invasion was planned.[9] Castro responded harshly to these provocations, in February declaring that Reagan intended to initiate a blockade; that same month Soviet leader Leonid Brezhnev declared that the Soviet Union was dedicated to supporting Cuba.[10]

Viewing Castro as dangerous, duplicitous Marxist-Leninist, the Reagan administration consistently rejected Cuban offers of negotiations. The administration's policy involved putting enormous pressure on Castro to force him to make concessions on support for revolutions and other aspects of his policies viewed as unacceptable in Washington. Reagan administration officials quite simply did not believe Castro would negotiate in good faith; they saw his invasions of Angola and Ethiopia in the midst of rapprochement talks with the Ford and Carter administrations as evidence of the Cuban leader's capacity for double-talk. Given this predisposition, the only alternative was to contain Castro and render foreign adventures costly.[11]

Throughout the Reagan administration, two specific issues would dominate Cuban policy, issues that were often in conflict. One was the continuing refugee problem. A series of court decisions suggested that the administration could not legally hold Cuban refugees in prison who had committed no crimes other than entering the United States "illegally." In April 1981, a U.S. court ordered the release of Pedro Rodriguez, one such inmate, and the administration feared the decision would set a precedent for many others.[12]

The logical solution to this problem was an immigration agreement with Cuba that would provide for the deportation of unwanted emigres. But such an accord was rendered problematic by the other major theme of U.S. policy under the Reagan administration: a constant series of apparently ad hoc punitive measures against Cuba. The administration would attempt to impose tougher economic sanctions, begin broadcasting anti-Castro radio into Cuba, ban the importation of Cuban periodicals into the United States, and take other actions that, while not significant enough to do Castro any serious damage, demonstrated the administration's opposition to the Cuban leader and his policies.[13]

Besides such small actions, however, the more general administration policy was unclear. At different times, various administration officials would make conflicting claims about the actions Castro would have to take for the United States to consider a limited rapprochement; sometimes the condition was an end to intervention in the hemisphere, at other times a complete shift from the Communist camp. But a general policy did emerge over time, one apparently adopted as much out of necessity as anything else; as Wayne Smith has recognized, it was that

> The United States would not even talk to the Cubans until they
> ceased all interventionist activity in Latin America and withdrew
> their troops from Africa. If they refused to do so, Washington would
> exclude no option, including a U.S. blockade or invasion of Cuba.
> Meanwhile, the administration adopted measures to signal its dis-
> pleasure and to underline that there could be no business as usual.[14]

in essence, then, the administration had no real goal other than to harass Castro and to make his foreign adventures as costly as possible.

CUBA IN THE 1980S:
STAGNATION AND MODERATED INTERNATIONALISM

When Ronald Reagan came into office in the United States, Fidel Castro was facing a unique set of problems in Cuba. The economic expansion of the early 1970s had been replaced with slower growth in the later 1970s and an actual contraction in 1980. The regime's tight control of daily life was producing resentment, worker diffidence, and international censure. Soviet support, so strong since the late 1960s, also began to dry up somewhat.

This section will examine Castro's Cuba as it had evolved during the 1980s. As a self-proclaimed model of revolutionary development, Cuba has become one of the most controversial nations on earth, and its domestic and foreign policies have been subject to microscopic observation and analysis. A few results of those examinations are presented below.

The Cuban Economy

Deciphering the Cuban economy is an enormously difficult task. As a centrally planned economy, its performance is measured in distinctly different terms than those to which Western economists are accustomed. Cuban statistics were for a time notoriously unreliable, and although this situation has improved significantly, problematic figures can still be uncovered. The Cuban economy, moreover, is measured in terms of "Global Social Product," which excludes such "non-productive" sectors as education and defense and is hence smaller than Western GNP figures; few accurate conversions of GSP to GNP have been made. Any conclusions about Cuban economic performance must necessarily be tentative.[15]

With this in mind, a number of aspects of the Cuban economy can be examined. The official Cuban budget for 1982 and 1983 is presented below:

Table One
Cuban Budget, 1982 and 1983 (in millions of dollars)

	1982	1983
Total Budget	11,900	31,200
Production	4,000	4,500
Housing/Commun. Service	618	650
Education/Health	2,600	2,700
Cultural/Scientific	2,000	2,000
State Administration	794	813
Defense	1,200	1,450

Source: Pamela S. Falk, *Cuban Foreign Policy: Caribbean Tempest* (lexington, MA: Lexington Books, 1986).

The Cuban government controls about 87 per cent of all land, and essentially 100 per cent of all other business: industry, communications, transport, banking, education, and so on.[16]

These sorts of expenditures are only made possible by enormous Soviet aid, estimated at between $4.5 billion and $5 billion annually. This aid takes several forms: direct aid; provision of oil, which Cuba then re-exports to obtain hard currency; and purchases of upwards of 70 per cent of Cuba's sugar crop at five to six times the world market price. Cuba currently owes the Soviet Union some $22 billion. (It also, incidentally, owes Western banks some $3.4 billion, a debt it has succeeded in renegotiating several times.)[17]

Cuba also obtains hard currency through its international "aid" ventures. Partly this comes from soldiers sent abroad; over 2 per cent of Cuba's population is in the military, a rate three to ten times that of virtually every other Latin American nation, and when Cuba provides these troops to foreign governments it gets what hard currency it can in return. Cuban doctors and teachers sent to Africa or Latin America also help Castro with his severe balance-of-payments problem.

Cuban economic performance is difficult to measure, precisely for the reasons outlined above. Nevertheless, a number of economic studies have reached some general conclusions about its performance. Annual growth seems to have run at between 3 and 5 per cent until 1980, when the economy actually contracted; this is slightly below the general Latin American average of about 6 per cent. The early 1980s witnessed essential stagnation, and by 1987 the Cuban economy shrank again. Productivity in most sectors of the economy, in particular agriculture and industry, declined significantly. One Soviet scholar in 1986 ranked Cuban economic prospects 20 on a scale on which the Soviet Union was 100 and East Germany 140; even Mongolia had better prospects than Cuba.[18]

This poor economic performance can be attributed to a number of factors. The decline in the world price of oil put a severe crimp in Cuba's balance of payments situation; in 1984 it acquired more than 40 per cent of its hard currency through oil re-exports. Soviet aid has slowed, especially under Gorbachev. Worker dissatisfaction has contributed to poor productivity. The American embargo, honored by other nations as well, has undoubtedly hurt Cuba's situation.[19] (It is instructive, however, that Cuba's primary export is still sugar, and since the Soviet Union pays many times the world price for it, the relative benefit to Cuba of opening up the United States once again to Cuban sugar would be questionable.) And poor economic planning and implementation of economic goals by Cuba's planners have also helped to stagnate growth.

Despite the relatively poor performance of the Cuban economy in traditional terms—growth, productivity, and so on—Marxist economists claim that such standards judge Communist economies based on capitalist measures. To accurately gauge the economic success of Cuba's revolution, the argument goes, credit must be given for social progress. An analysis of Cuban achievements in such areas reveals progress, but, except in basic indices of distribution of wealth, no more impressive progress than many other Caribbean nations.[20]

Income Equity

Of undoubted success has been the revolution's attempts to reduce income inequity. While the Cuban government has issued few official figures on this, there is no question that a significant income redistribution has occurred since 1959.[21] As Claes Brundenius, one of the most ardent chroniclers of Cuban economic performance, summed it up: ''It is quite clear that there had been a radical redistribution of income in Cuba since the revolution with the major transfer of income going to the bottom quintiles during the first years after 1959 and more moderate transfers during the latter part of the 1960s and the 1970s.''[22]

More specifically, a reduction of inequities between town and country has occurred. Arthur MacEwan has defined the conflict between urban industry and rural agriculture as key to Cuba's economic situation,[23] and in this sense Castro has responded relatively well. Many development, health, and literacy programs have been focused specifically on rural areas. Brundenius contends that the resulting decreases in rural/urban discrepancies is ''the revolutionary government's most spectacular success.''[24]

Cuba's egalitarianism also stands up in a comparative context. Despite significant economic growth in Brazil since 1960, for example, per capita income of the poorest 40 per cent only doubled, while that of the same group in Cuba grew by 500 per cent. In other Latin American nations, such as Peru, where economic growth has been slower or nonexistent, the poor have gotten poorer, both relatively and absolutely, with per capita incomes, in many instances, falling under $200.[25]

Cuban economic reforms of the early 1970s altered this situation somewhat. The radical egalitarian wage policies of the 1960s were replaced by a more conventional, Soviet-model sliding scale of wages. Other incentives, such as bonuses, earned vacations, overtime, and so on were also introduced to help boost productivity. As Carmelo Mesa-Lago concludes: ''In the 1970's, the previous egalitarian policies were criticized as idealistic mistakes and more realistic distributive policies, which take into account skills and productivity rather than needs, were implemented.''[26] As has been noted, these reforms, along with other changes, were effective, and the Cuban economy experienced significant growth in the first half of the 1970s.

Yet one inevitable result of this more capitalistic procedure was a reduction in income equity. Wage rates varied significantly: workers in agriculture made from $64 a month to $514; industrial workers' monthly salaries ranged from $85 to $264, which technical and executive positions were the most lucrative of all, paying $272 to $844 a month.[27] In other words, the best paid agricultural worker made roughly half of what the poorest technical worker did.

Because of such wage systems, in 1973 the wealthiest 10 per cent of Cubans earned some seven times what the poorest ten percent did. Still, those levels were far behind the income disparities of other Latin American nations, and less than pre-revolutionary disparities by a factor of 100 or more. [28]

A price-control system also protects poor Cubans from the vagaries of the market. For some time, however, many goods have been rationed, and since 1973 an official parallel (or "red") market has operated that offers the same goods at three to eight times their set price. There are also elite "diplo-stores" that cater to foreign and Cuban officials. And there is, of course, the black market, offering everything from food to blue jeans and American music. With an average monthly wage of 140 pesos, most Cubans can afford more than their required amounts of necessities, but few amenities from the expensive "red" or black markets.[29] The table below illustrates rationed items and their prices:

Table Two
Items Rationed in Cuba, June 1987

Monthly rations:

Item	Quantity per person	Official price (pesos/pound except as noted)	Parallel price/3
Bath soap	1 bar	0.25/bar	1.70-1.85/bar
Beans (any kind)	20 oz.	0.24	1.80-2.00
Bread	15 pounds	0.15	—
Chicken/1	2 pounds	0.70	3.00
Cigarettes (black) /2	3 packages	0.25/package	1.60-2.00 pkg.
Cigarettes (mild) /2	1 package	0.30/package	1.80/package
Cigars (males only) /2	4	0.15/each	0.60-1.50
Coffee	4 oz.	0.96	24.00
Detergent	7 oz.	0.60	1.15-2.50
Lard	1 pound	0.30	—
Meat, Beef /1	—7 oz. top grade	0.65	—
—5 oz. second grade		—	
Milk, canned	3 cans	0.30/can	—
(6 cans for over 65)	0.30/can	—	
Milk, fresh (under 7)	30 liters	0.25/liter	1.00
Oil, cooking	8 oz.	0.40	3.20
Rice	5 pounds	0.24	1.50
Sugar	4 pounds	0.14	—
Tomato sauce	1 can	0.25/can	2.00/can

Notes to monthly rations:

1. Meat products are available approximately every 9 days. Monthly beef rations must be purchased all together; chicken rations are sold one pound at a time.

2. Cigarettes and cigars are rationed to those born before 1955—younger people must buy at the parallel market prices.

3. Rationed items may be purchased when available at official prices. Quantities beyond the allowed amounts must be bought at parallel market prices. Canned milk, lard, sugar, laundry soap, and beef are not generally available in the parallel market.

Potatoes, bananas, sweet potatoes, malangas, onions, garlic, tomatoes, and other fresh vegetables are rationed according to availability. For example, potato rations have varied from zero to eight pounds a month.

The average monthly wage in Cuba is currently 140 pesos.

45 Day Rations:
1 case of beer per household at rationed prices

Quarterly Rations:
Men's socks, handkerchiefs, shampoo, deodorant, talc, thread, toothbrushes, zippers, needles, dishes, glasses, cups, shoe polish, and other assorted products according to availability.

Semi-Annual Rations:
1 bra or 2 bloomers—for women only
1 brief or 1 undershirt—for men only

Annual Rations:
1 pair of shoes
1 pair of tennis shoes
1 sheet or towel
4 meters of cloth (more than 1 meter wide) or
6 meters of cloth (less than 1 meter wide)—for women only
2 shirts—for men only
2 trousers—for men only

All the 45-day, quarterly, semi-annual, and annual rations are also available in parallel and black markets at steep prices.

Source: U.S. Department of State

The more capitalistic procedures of the 1970s also had a deleterious effect on employment. Cuba had always had near-total employment, but as Mesa-Lago notes, this was only achieved "by transforming open unemployment into underemployment at the expense of a sharp decrease in labor productivity."[30] The new policies of the 1970s have created significant unemployment; the official government figures vary from 4 to 5 per cent, or about 100,000 individuals, plus some 6.7 per cent termed a "potential labor force"; the real numbers may be much higher. Productivity has improved somewhat, but the official rate of absenteeism is still near 40 per cent.[31]

Literacy and Health

One of the primary efforts of the Castro government has been a huge literacy campaign. Officially, literacy rates in Cuba rose from 79 per cent in 1959 to 87 per cent in 1970 and within a few points of total literacy by 1979. Post-1979 figures, however, benefit from a change in definitions: while figures until then covered everyone 15 and above, from 1979 the Cuban figures cover only those 15-49. Some experts judged that the true rate of illiteracy in 1980 was about 10 per cent.[32]

These gains are significant, but not unique. Dominica, Trinidad-Tobago, Martinique, and Puerto Rico all made arguably more significant percentage gains over the same period. Chile, Costa Rica, Panama, and other regional nations have roughly matched Cuban performance. Since Cuba was already so highly literate in 1959, its relative gains were more difficult at the margins, but still it can be fairly stated that it has not demonstrably made the best progress in reducing illiteracy in the hemisphere.

Health figures reflect similar moderate progress. One of the best measures of health is infant mortality, and in this realm Castro's government has again made strides, reducing mortality from about 38 per thousand live births in 1958 to 19 in 1979 and less than 17 today. Again, however, the low current rate is comparable to many other Caribbean countries: Costa Rice (18.0), Grenada (15.4), Guadeloupe (15.5), Puerto Rico (16.0), Martinique (16.0), and so on. Cuba's rate of progress has again been similar to other countries, such as Chile.[33]

There is some evidence, moreover, that the Cuban figures are of questionable validity (as indeed may be those of Chile and a few other countries). Infant mortality is commonly computed in two ways: directly, through census data, and indirectly through "life tables" that apply demographic data to census information. These latter figures are usually more accurate, since no censi are complete and life tables can account for their omissions.

Cuba's life tables tell an interesting story. In 1970, they squared with the official figures at about 40 infant deaths per one thousand live births. But as the 1970s progressed, and official figures showed a decline in mortality, the life tables indicated increases or constant rates; the life table for 1974, for example, shows a rate of 45, 50 per cent higher than the government's figure of 29.

The incidence of diseases commonly associated with infant mortality— acute diarrhea, respiratory infections, hepatitis, chicken pox, measles, and syphilis—increased during this period by up to 500 per cent. That these diseases would become more common while infant mortality fell is unusual.

Also casting doubt on Cuban figures are the official reporting techniques for them. Since 1972 all infant mortality figures are treated as tentative and hence subject to revision at any time. Cuba's State Statistical Committee cannot review the figures, which come directly from the Ministry of Health; "whose performance," Nick Eberstadt notes, "they implicitly measure."[34] Cuba's

1981 census also grouped all people under 16 together without differentiating them by age of sex, a process that makes the construction of life tables impossible. Again, even the official Cuban figures for infant mortality betray a performance merely matching that of many other regional countries.

Undoubtedly, Castro's government has spent an enormous amount of money on the construction of hospitals, training of physicians, and provision of medical care to all Cubans. Cuba life expectancy is about equal to that of many other Caribbean nations, and medical care has become more equitable under the revolution. Economist Sergio Diaz-Briquets estimates that ''the gain in life expectancy in Cuba between 1953 and 1970 exceeded by about 2 to 3 years what might have taken place without the revolution.''[35]

Disparities still exist. Cuba's current ratio of about 1,100 persons per physician is roughly the same as pre-revolutionary figures, but that ratio varies from 263: 1 in large cities to 1,750: 1 in rural areas.[36] Still, progress has been made from pre-revolutionary statistics.

Housing figures provide another indication of the revolution's real but limited gains. In the immediate aftermath of the revolution, housing was made more equitable by the reduction of rents and homeowner payments and the confiscation of large homes or buildings from wealthy Cubans. Huge construction programs were undertaken; the government built 55,000 new units in the first five years after the revolution, 26,000 of them in rural areas. Actual rates of housing construction fell from pre-revolutionary times, but the distribution of housing among the population became much more egalitarian. Housing quality is often poor by Western standards, but quite good compared to that of pre-revolutionary rural Cuba, where poor peasants lived mostly in *bohios*, or thatched-roof huts.[37]

The Economy in the 1980s

As noted elsewhere, Castro's emphasis in the 1980s has returned to one of socialist commitment and discipline, as opposed to rational economic reforms. For a variety of reasons, an analysis below will document, he has been reluctant to mirror Mikahil Gorbachev's policy of economic restructuring and has contented himself with the belief that a new round of socialist work brigades and voluntary overtime can relieve Cuba's economic woes. A number of capitalistic profit schemes introduced in the 1970s to improve production in agriculture and other areas have been abandoned. Castro knows he has a luxury that the Soviets do not: an outside subsidy that finances over a third of his budget—in the form, of course, of direct and indirect Soviet aid.[38]

A few salient economic figures as of 1985 are given below.

Table Three
The Cuban Economy in 1985

Average Annual Growth Rate: 1.1%

Population: 9.946 million; 70% urban, 30% rural

Disposable National Income: $15.8 billion

Per Capita Income: $1,590

Exports: 75% sugar, 9% petroleum re-exports, 4% seafood

Source: U.S. Department of State, *Background Notes: Cuba*, August 1985

Religion

Until very recently, the practice of religion was severely circumscribed in Cuba. Castro's crackdown on churches was dictated in many ways by their conservatism; in 1960 several Catholic Church leaders declared that they might support the United States against Castro, and in 1961 when Brigade 2506 landed it was accompanied by several priests. There is also evidence the churches did actually participate in counter-revolutionary activities. In any case, in 1961, as part of his general crackdown on internal dissent in the wake of the Bay of Pigs, Castro expelled 2,800 nuns and exiled or imprisoned many priests. He also shut down dozens of churches and church schools.

From that time until 1986, the Cuban government engaged in a series of anti-religious efforts. Children of religious families were harassed, at school and elsewhere. Church property and assets were confiscated. Occupational discrimination was practiced against believers, and access to select schools was also used as a tool to discourage belief. In 1970 Christmas was abolished and Christmas trees banned as "counterrevolutionary symbols." Religious broadcasts and publishing were prohibited.

By 1982, Cuba's churches were in a poor condition. Only some 200 priests remained, compared to over 700 before the revolution. Cuba had the lowest ratio of priests to parishioners in the hemisphere, and the lowest rates of religious marriages and baptisms. The Catholic Church had never been overwhelmingly strong, in part because of its association with the former Spanish rulers; but under Castro's rule it wa severely emasculated. By 1987 only 1 per cent of the population were practicing churchgoers.[39]

In 1986, however, a new dialogue between the church and the state was begun. After a series of interviews with Friar Betto, a leftist Cuban priest, Castro held three public meetings with church leaders and expressed a desire to provide the church more leeway. In return, he seemed to expect assistance in his drive to create a renewed sense of purpose among the Cuban people, something necessary as the Cuban economy began to sag with no real prospect of relief. A group called the National Congress of the Church pressed for an end to the discriminatory practices against believers, and some progress was made—the church secured the release of 300 political prisoners, permission to rebuild several churches, and visas providing for visits by a few foreign priests and nuns. Cuban exiles in the United States and elsewhere bitterly criticized this "accommodation" with the regime, and highlighted the danger that Castro was merely taking advantage of the church in a period of economic failure.[40]

Human Rights

The major failure of Castro's revolution must be its almost total denial of all basic human rights and political freedoms, and its occasional resort to brutality, torture, and violence to maintain control. From the start, Castro has valued loyalty highly and has refused to tolerate any dissent, which he views as "counter-revolutionary agitation." There is no freedom of press in Cuba, nor of assembly, religion, or speech. Arbitrary arrests are common, and thousands of political prisoners are held.[41]

In 1986, Cuban exile dissident Armando Valladares published *Against All Hope*, his account of 22 years in a Cuban jail. While imprisoned Valladares suffered all manner of psychological and physical abuse.[42] His horrifying account galvanized criticism against Castro's record on human rights.

After several recent amnesty programs, the number of political prisoners left in Cuban jails is probably about 1,100. Executions still occur—during 1983 and 1984 Cubans were killed by the government for spreading anti-government propaganda and producing illegal religious literature. In November, as two Cuban youths—boys aged 16 and 8—tried to gain access to the Venezuelan embassy compound to request asylum, they were shot by Cuban guards. The elder boy was killed, the younger wounded. Since 1974, 21 Cubans have been killed on the doorsteps of the Venezuelan embassy alone.[43]

The Political Situation in Cuba

In the period after the 1970 re-organization, the government did become somewhat more accountable with provisions for limited elections. Through the 1960s, Castro had claimed that Cuba's "direct democracy" made democratic symbols—elections and political freedoms—unnecessary. In the late 1960s, a few small-scale schemes for local participation in government were attempted. After 1970, these models were implemented more generally, on a trial basis in 1974 in Matanzas and nationwide in 1976. Termed "Organs of Peoples' Power," the local bodies thus elected had some input into government decision-making at lower levels, and their presence improved government accountability.[44]

The early 1980s witnessed a recentralization of power at the top in the hands of Fidel and Raul and their close associates. The Third Party Congress in 1986 showed Castro firmly in control, having dismissed a few economic managers, such as Humberto Perez, for "inefficiency." Stress was laid on the pursuit of "revolutionary values" as motivation for higher productivity.[45]

Relations with the Soviet Union

This centralization of decision-making was another in a series of clues that Castro was not entirely enamored with Mikhail Gorbachev's call for reforms in all socialist countries. Castro argued that "we are not obliged to copy. . .the socialist countries' experience," and indeed for some time Cuba was seen as one of the few Communist governments moving further away from Gorbachev's program of reform.

Castro for his part emphasized "rectification," again the call for socialist "moral commitment" to work and the development of Cuba. Castro's opposition to reform may have been motivated by a concern for maintenance of internal power, and also fear of U.S. actions during the tough-talking Reagan presidency. These feelings were manifest in the dismissal of the economist Perez, Moscow-trained and perhaps swayed by the new Soviet economic ideas, and in Castro's refusal to attend the funeral of Soviet leader Konstantin Chernenko in 1984-85. The Cuban leader also continued his opposition to Ethiopia's Soviet-supported war against its Eritrean separatist rebels.

By mid-1986, however, Cuba and the Soviet Union were once again on cordial terms. Perhaps recognizing that importance to each of the other's continued good offices, Cuban and Soviet leaders embarked on a new round of negotiations and friendly discussions. Castro's Third Party Congress speech mirrored Gorbachev's own to his 27th Party Congress, excoriating the inefficiency in the Cuban economy and calling for change. (Castro's change, however, as we have seen, is of a different variety.) In April 1986 the Soviet Union signed an accord promising $3 billion of additional aid for 1986-1990, representing an increase of 50 per cent over existing amounts. Once again, Havana and Moscow were reasserting their socialist brotherhood.[46]

Cuban Foreign Policy in the 1980s

Cuba's commitment to "worldwide revolutionary solidarity" slowed somewhat in the 1980s, due primarily to two factors. First, the Soviet Union's invasion of Afghanistan in 1979 and other foreign adventures reflected poorly on Cuba's status as an independent protector of the Third World's interests. Second, the Reagan administration's tough policies in Latin America both stiffened military resistance in the hemisphere to Communist insurgencies and created fear in Havana that the United States might again be prepared to undertake direct military action against Cuba.

One result was that Cuba's activity in the Non-Aligned Movement slackened. After Afghanistan and with the ascendance of the moderate wing of the movement, led by Indira Gandhi, the radicalizing effect of Cuba's presence was less noticeable.

Another implication of Cuba's moderation was a more conditional commitment to Latin American revolutionary movements. As Michael Erisman has noted, "Havana did not (contrary to statements by some U.S. officials) develop and pursue a coordinated regional master plan. Instead it proceeded rather deliberately, reacting cautiously to developments as they occurred (especially in volatile Centra America) and trying to tailor each response to each individual situation.[47] Castro's assistance to the guerrilla movement in El Salvador, for example, rose and fell according to his priorities with regard to the United States. His commitment to defend Nicaragua against American aggression was also subject to revision, especially in the aftermath of the Grenada invasion.[48]

Cuba has cultivated new allies in Africa, and maintained old friendships. It has certainly not withdrawn from the world stage, but its economic crisis at home and the challenge of Reagan's military threat have led it to adopt a distinct, though possibly temporary, revolutionary realism.

RELATIONS WITH THE UNITED STATES: THE REAGAN ADMINISTRATION REFUSES TALKS

Meanwhile, in mid-1981, as its client guerrilla movements in El Salvador and elsewhere in Latin America fell on hard times, the Cuban government (along with its Nicaraguan allies) sought negotiations with the United States. Castro was also a little unnerved at the statements of Haig and others in the Reagan administration that seemed to hint at the possibility of intervention, and though he was not about to be intimidated into changing his policies, he might offer to do so in exchange for American concessions. These desires for talks were communicated to Wayne Smith, chief of the U.S. interests section in Havana, who recommended that the administration accept the offer.

Smith's cables, however, were ignored by the administration which had no desire to talk with Castro. As already noted, Reagan foreign policy managers believed there was little reason to trust Castro, and whatever one feels about this policy it must be admitted that there was credible evidence to support it. Thus, despite the fact that Cuba and Nicaragua both scaled back their support for El Salvadoran Communist guerrillas, the administration did not respond to the Cuban overtures. In February 1981, this position began to become clear with the position of the controversial Department of State White Paper that purported to prove Cuban involvement in financing Salvadoran guerrillas.[49]

In fact, in June, 1981 an administration interagency task force on Cuba produced a report advocating a continued hard line. The proposal for a radio station broadcasting into Cuba—a Caribbean equivalent of Radio Free Europe (first termed Radio Free Cuba, it was later officially named Radio Marti)— was first broached at this time. The report advocated continued economic and political pressure on Castro.

Castro quickly organized a half-million militia members and virtually dared the United States to take the military action it seemed to be planning. Throughout the late summer and early fall, Secretary of State Haig continued to charge the Cubans with regional subversion and a huge military buildup, and the Cubans kept challenging him to prove his charges—which, because the Cubans had actually (for their own reasons) scaled back support to El Salvador, he had difficulty doing. In September 1981, at a meeting of a UN group, the Inter-Parliamentary Union, in Havana, Castro again lambasted the United States for its renewed militarism.[50]

Haig's Threats

Toward the end of the year, the administration's Radio Marti proposal began to come under fire from both Congress and the U.S. Information Agency, but the administration's hard line did not recede. On October 29, Haig made his most confrontational comments yet: Cuba continued to be responsible for regional insecurity, he said, and the United States was finally prepared to act. On the 31st, Castro mobilized his reserve and placed his nation on a near war-footing, claiming that an invasion was imminent. Ten days later, Reagan denied that the United States was contemplating intervention, but tensions had risen to a level rivaling that before the Bay of Pigs.

Nevertheless, the administration, partly at the urging of other Latin American countries, engaged in some dialogue with the Cubans. On November 23,

Haig met with Cuban Vice President Carlos Rafael Rodriguez; Haig merely recited a list of Cuban actions that the administration found unacceptable; Rodriguez did not volunteer to alter them, and little progress was made. In March 1982, Gen. Vernon Walters, an administration special envoy, spoke with Castro in Havana and adopted essentially the same position.

During and immediately after these exchanges, the administration hardened its position on Cuba further. Assistant Secretary of State Thomas Enders presented a paper in December 1981 to the Senate arguing that Cuba was once again exporting revolution and calling for a tougher policy; the same day, a State special report was released cataloguing Cuba's involvement in regional revolutionary movements. The administration rejected a February-March 1982 Mexican peace plan for Central America as insufficiently attentive to Communist subversion. Finally, in April 1982 it allowed the 1977 fishing agreement to lapse and blocked U.S. citizens from going to Cuba. (U.S. courts had declared outright travel bans unconstitutional, but the administration circumvented this problem by instituting regulations against spending money in Cuba, which at least discouraged any Americans from going and which were later upheld by the courts.)[51]

That these talks accomplished so little, that the administration officials involved merely repeated obviously unacceptable demands to the Cubans, and that Reagan hardened his stance on Cuba so soon after them have caused critics to argue that the meetings were intended as pure deception. Wayne Smith and others have suggested that, in order to claim it had "tried talking" with Castro, the administration arranged a few cursory exchanges; Wayne Smith said the talks were "simply a way to parry domestic and foreign criticism."[52] In those meetings, U.S. representatives made absolutely no concessions and virtually no attempt to be forthcoming on bilateral issues. Once the talks had "failed" to change Cuban behavior, the administration could strike out with further reprisals.[53] Given the administration's larger agenda, however, the unproductive outcome should hardly have come as a surprise: it was demanding substantial changes in policy that the Cubans were unwilling to make, and this impasse made any substantial negotiations impossible.

In late 1982, Haig still expressed hope that Castro might be persuaded to drop his close connections to the Soviet Union and to adopt a more "responsible" position in the region. In May he made statements implying that an end to Cuban interventionism in the hemisphere would be sufficient evidence of good intentions for the United States to begin talks with Havana, but in April he reverted to calling for a full Cuban shift from the Communist camp, a proposal over which, he claimed, Castro was "agonizing." The Department of State later backed away from these ideas, and later in April Reagan himself restated the notion that Castro would have to surrender his Soviet ties to get better relations with Washington.[54] Continued American insistence on such radical change as a precondition for improved U.S.-Cuban relations ensured that no such improvement would occur, though whether this result is desirable is a matter of debate.

By 1982, the Reagan administration began to run into problems in achieving a regional consensus on its hard line toward Cuba. In 1981 Mexican President Jose Lopez Portillo became one of the first Latin American statesmen to desert the hard line when he stressed Mexico's close relations with Cuba. In August he met with Castro, and in 1982 he would call for closer U.S.-Cuban ties as a means to ease regional tensions. Later in 1982 and 1983, Brazil, Venezuela, Argentina, and to some degree Colombia would all improve relations with Cuba, contrary to the Reagan administration's wishes.[55] Congress was uncooperative, failing for a time to fund Radio Marti and refusing to renew a 20-year-old pledge to use military force if necessary to deal with Cuba. The head of the U.S. interests section in Havana, Wayne Smith, resigned in protest over the administration's failure to seek negotiations with the Cubans, and wrote a number of articles criticizing the administration's position.

Still, through 1983 the administration kept up its tough line, and had some success. It halted the flights of the Cuban-operated American Airways Charter, stranding 2,000 Cuban nationals in the United States. It began construction of Radio Marti even without congressional approval, and after some delay in the Senate obtained funding from both the House and the Senate. The Justice Department indicted four high-ranking Cuban officials on charges of conspiracy to smuggle drugs. The Senate, in a reversal of its earlier position, agreed to a resolution promising to stop Cuban aggression by any means, "including the use of arms." The Treasury Department banned travel to Cuba by preventing American tourists from spending money there. In April 1983, an SR-71 reconnaissance plane was sent over Cuba during Castro's Ba` of Pigs celebrations. Finally, in May 1983, Reagan addressed the Cuban American National Foundation, an anti-Castro group, and pledged that someday Cuba would be free.[56]

A small dispute over the Soviet presence in Cuba was quickly resolved. The United States was beginning to emplace Intermediate Range Nuclear Forces (INF) in Europe to counter Soviet SS-20 deployments; the Soviets said they would honor their 1962 pledge and wold not emplace INF in Cuba. The Reagan administration expressed its satisfaction but noted that if the Soviets did take such action, the American reaction would be similar to what it had been in 1962. Reagan actually claimed that the Soviets had violated the 1962 accord and had emplaced offensive weapons in Cuba, but White House spokesman Larry Speakes quickly qualified this claim, noting that Reagan only meant the Soviets had violated the "spirit" of the agreement.[57]

The Caribbean Basin Initiative

In February 1982, President Reagan had launched his Caribbean Basin Initiative. In the tradition of the Good Neighbor Policy and the Alliance for Progress, Reagan's initiative hoped to promote regional economic development, but was far more modest in scope than the earlier programs had been. It contained provisions for a one-way free trade zone for Caribbean countries (an offer the U.S. Congress never accepted), tax incentives and investment insurance for U.S. businesses investing in Latin America, bilateral trade treaties, and direct aid, mostly aimed at agricultural modernization. Critics immediately pointed to the distinction between ends and means: Was the economic vitality of the region a goal in itself, or merely a tool to prevent Communist influence? It is probably impossible to separate out the motives of various administration officials, though the initiative itself has had only modest effects.[58]

1983: Grenada

Since the 1979 revolution in Grenada, Castro had supported the Marxist government there with significant amounts of aid. Grenadian leader Maurice Bishop was no a hard-line Communist, but when American ambassador Frank Ortiz visited in April 1979 bearing threats of sanctions if Bishop accommodated himself to Cuba and the insulting offer (reportedly) of $5,000 in aid, Bishop turned to Cuba. Castro saw in Grenada an opportunity to cultivate a tiny Caribbean ally in which he would recreate the achievements of the Cuban revolution; in a sense, Grenada would be to Cuba what Cuba was to the Soviet Union, in a modified form. Eventually Cuba provided assistance to Grenadian literacy and health programs, and 350 construction-cum-military workers.

In October 1983, however, Bishop's revolution spun out of control. Radical Marxists seized control of the New Jewel Movement from Bishop on the 12th and imprisoned him. A week later his supporters freed him, but he was quickly recaptured and executed. Taking advantage of the fragmented situation, and using the safety of a number of American medical students as its justification, the Reagan administration staged a quickly organized intervention on the 25th. It was aided by troops from a number of nations of the English-speaking Caribbean: Jamaica, Barbados, Antiqua, Dominica, St. Lucia, and St. Vincent. In a short, somewhat confused battle, American troops captured the island; the Cubans suffered 24 dead and 59 wounded, the Americans 18 dead and 113 wounded.[59]

The invasion was a clear blow to Castro's regional credibility. Christopher Dickey later concluded that

[The invasion] showed that the hard-line policy [of the Reagan administration] was capable of intimidating not only Nicaraguans, but Cubans. The invasion of Grenada seemed to strip Cuban President Fidel Castro of an ally and protege. Not only did Castro make no move to come to its rescue, he seemed to back away from the Sandinistas as well, noting that 'we do not have the means' to give direct military assistance to allies attacked by the United States.[60]

Cuba's allies in the region, no longer able to dismiss the Reagan administration's tough rhetoric and unable to count on Castro or the Soviet Union, moderated their statements and actions. Suriname and Nicaragua, for example, pulled away from support for Castro and support for El Salvadoran guerrillas, respectively.[61]

1984: New Winds of Accommodation?

From 1982 through 1984, there had been some signals from Havana that Castro was ready to negotiate with the United States on a series of issues. Cuban Vice President Carlos Rafael Rodriguez, among others, had declared that the Cubans were willing to talk, though they would not sacrifice their ties to the USSR. Other Cuban officials, in meetings with Luis Burstin, a former Costa Rican official, made clear their desire for a "Yugoslavianization" of the Cuban economy, a process that required more openings with the United States. Cuban officials apparently stood ready to agree to end their support for new revolutionary movements in exchange for an end to the embargo and trade with the United States.[62] Many observers were leery of these offers—the Cubans had made them before, and broken their promises—but nevertheless an interested skepticism prevailed in Havana and Washington.[63]

In July 1984, Castro himself declared that he would welcome increased relations with the United States. The Department of State noted that Castro had not changed his policy, however, and in August Reagan himself said he was not optimistic about the prospects for an accommodation.[64] Still, general speculation about a warming in the relationship continued.

As if to confirm this trend, on December 14, 1984, it was announced that the United States and Cuba had reached a new immigration agreement. The United States would allow 20,000 Cubans to immigrate annually, and in return the Cuban government agreed to accept the criminals who had come into the United States in 1980, the so-called "Mariel excludables."[65]

But the administration's tough line on Cuba soon re-emerged to put an end to any speculation about accommodation. Director of the State Department Office of Cuban Affairs Kenneth Skoug qualified the progress of the immigration agreement by noting that, "welcome as this agreement is, however, it should not be taken as indicating change in our resolve to deal firmly with Cuba's aggressive foreign policy."[66] It was quickly apparent that as long as the United States remained committed to its demands for substantial change in Cuban foreign policy as a precondition to talks, and as long as Cuba remained intransigent on those issues, little would change.

A continued skepticism of Castro was also in evidence in the administration's response to a 1984 visit by Rev. Jesse Jackson to Cuba. Jackson met with Castro and secured the release of 48 prisoners, 22 American and 26 Cuban. The Department of State pointed out that many of those released were common criminals, and indeed several were arrested immediately upon returning to the United States. Secretary of State George Shultz called the trip a "propaganda victory" for Castro, and while Reagan himself later softened his tone and declared himself "grateful" to Jackson for bringing the prisoners out, the administration obviously thought little of Jackson's personal diplomacy.[67]

In early 1985, this non-conciliatory policy remained in effect. U.S.-Cuban relations dropped to a new low on May 20 when Radio Marti finally went on the air. The Cuban government, in addition to attempting to jam the signal, immediately suspended the 1984 immigration agreements. President Reagan retaliated by banning visits to the United States by Cuban officials. Tensions with Cuba were once again running at a high level.

THE REAGAN ADMINISTRATION AND ANGOLA

Soon after the suspension of the immigration act, in July 1985, the Clark amendment, which barred U.S. aid to groups in Angola, was repealed. Immediately, various resolutions were afoot in Congress to provide Jonas Savimbi's UNITA with non-lethal or military aid for his war against the MPLA government. Castro promised a renewed commitment to his socialist brothers in Luanda, and Angola and once again moved to the forefront of U.S.-Cuban relations.

Angola Since 1975

In 1978, UN Resolution 435 provided for the independence of Namibia, a South African withdrawal from that state and from Angola, and a SWAPO pledge to end its warfare against South Africa. Angolan leader Jose Eduardo dos Santos, who had succeeded Neto, promised that all Cuban advisors and troops in Angola would leave once the resolutions was successfully implemented. South Africa, however, called for the withdrawal of the Cubans as a first step, and this issue would prove a significant stumbling block in the years ahead.

Little movement in the situation occurred until 1981, when the United States became involved, offering to mediate talks between Angola and South Africa. Secretary of State Haig met with the Angolan foreign minister, and discussed timetables for a Cuban withdrawal. South Africa, skeptical of Angola's intentions, continued to raid into southern Angola and to support Jonas Savimbi's UNITA, which held large portions of the country.

By the mid-1980s, the crucial issue remained Namibian independence. A U.S. negotiating team, led by Assistant Secretary of State for African Affairs Chester Crocker, made significant progress in achieving a cease-fire and general agreement on an independence scheme for Namibia, and eventually UN Secretary General Javier Perez de Cuellar offered to supplement U.S. mediation efforts with his own. Finally, in February 1984, the Lusaka accord provided for Namibian independence and for a South African agreement to withdraw from Angola. In November of that year, Angola promised to send up to 20,000 Cubans home over a three-year period, provided the agreement held up.

It did not. South Africa once again pointed to the three-year timetable as inadequate. It feared that the Angolans and Cubans intended to use that time to wipe out UNITA, and this suspicion was confirmed during 1984 when the Soviet Union and Cuba pumped enormous new amounts of military aid into Angola, including $2 billion worth of military equipment and 7,000 new troops. A major offensive was launched against Savimbi in the summer of 1985, and Luanda was clearly banking on his defeat within the three-year grace period.

The Lusaka agreement was never fully implemented. In March 1985 South Africa named its own Namibian government and stepped up its attacks into Angola as well as its support for Savimbi. The United States also surrendered its neutral role; in July 1985 the Clark Amendment was repealed, and the following year the U.S. Congress approved $15 million for Savimbi. A 1986 House resolution to cancel the aid failed, and despite serious controversy over the policy in the United States, Savimbi received modern U.S. arms, including highly effective Stinger anti-aircraft missiles.

In 1987, a new series of talks was held aimed once again at achieving a cease-fire. Congolese President Denis Sassou-Nguesso, chairman of the Organization of African Unity (OAU), organized a meeting between the United States and Angola. Little progress was achieved, however; it seemed that the Angolans were unwilling to let the Cubans leave until Savimbi had been neutralized, while South African would agree to no formula that did not call for the immediate withdrawal of the Cubans.[68]

In the fall of 1987, Angolan and Cuban troops launched a major new offensive at Savimbi. Many Cubans assumed combat roles as Soviet equipment arrived that was too sophisticated for the Angolans to handle. UNITA was forced to deploy in conventional military fashion to defend the ground it held, rather than in the guerrilla manner to which it had become accustomed. It had received, however, a good deal of modern equipment in recent shipments from the United States and South Africa, and with South African backing it dug in to await the assault of some 20,000 Cubans and Angolans.

In bitter fighting, Savimbi's forces pushed combined Angolan and Cuban units back from the town of Cuito Cuanavale, which lay at the heart of Savimbi's stronghold in southeastern Angola. The Angolan government and their Cuban advisors had suffered a major defeat.[69]

In early 1988, the Reagan administration made one final effort to convince the Angolans to send their Cuban protectors home. With Savimbi firmly established in the south, however, and with the prospect of unending South African and American aid to the UNITA leader, Luanda was in no mood to renounce Castro's military aid. Chester Crocker traveled to the Angolan capital once again. At the time there were some 37,000 Cubans in the country, and Crocker was suggesting a plan that would require the Angolans to send 20,000 Cubans home immediately and restrict the rest to the far northern part of the country. But the Angolans were understandably confused at administration policy that provided aid to its major internal opposition while demanding that it send the real core of its available military forces away; Crocker himself reportedly argued against the aid to Savimbi but was overruled by administration hard-liners.[70]

TENSIONS INSTITUTIONALIZED:
THE END OF THE REAGAN YEARS

Through 1986 and 1987, relations between Cuban and the United States continued at their previous low level. In the summer of 1986, talks in Mexico City aimed at reestablishing the immigration agreement fell apart because of a Cuban demand for clear-channel broadcasting rights in the United States to counteract Radio Marti. The administration once again attempted to tighten the economic embargo.[71] On August 22, 1986, Reagan extended the ban on official Cuban visits and suspended all immigration from Cuba.[72]

Verbal attacks on Castro's role in the hemisphere also continued, and indeed escalated, during 1986. In November 1986 U.S. UN Ambassador Vernon Walters made the first of a series of speeches sharply critical of Castro's record on human rights; he made another such statement in March 1987 before the UN Commission on Human Rights in Geneva. In February 1987, Secretary of State George Shultz gave a speech before the American Bar Association in which he stressed Cuba's role as a "Soviet proxy" in the hemisphere.[73]

At the same time, the Reagan administration launched an international diplomatic effort to achieve a condemnation of Castro's record on human rights in the UN. Ambassadors in 42 capitals solicited support for the resolution, and more than 400 diplomatic cables were sent out. Reagan personally contacted President Francois Mitterand of France and President Abdou Diouf of Senegal to request their votes. In the end, the United States lost; on March 13, 1987, a vote to bring the resolution to a full vote lost 19 to 18 with six abstentions. The last-minute defections of Colombia and Venezuela to the Cuban side were crucial.[74]

Relations remained anything but cordial. In early 1987, the Reagan administration withdrew the head of its Havana interests section, Curtis W. Kamman, for what were termed "administrative reasons." In December 1986, the Cubans claimed a U.S. SR-71 reconnaissance plane sped over Cuba at relatively low altitude, breaking the sound barrier and causing several large sonic booms. Cuba, for its part, continued jamming Radio Marti, and attempting to broadcast high-power radio signals into the United States.[75]

Yet despite all these jabs and counter-jabs, actual acrimony between the United States and Cuba did not seem to rise.[76] The Cubans artfully accepted Washington's explanation that Kamman was not recalled to prove a point, and Castro even invited Kamman to a meeting before he left. No actual threats were traded. Nevertheless, diplomatic contact was at a near-minimum.

1986 and 1987 also saw the defection of some high-level Cuban officials. General Rafael del Pino, a high-ranking Cuban air force officer, Major Florentino Aspillaga Lombard, and others defected in 1987 bearing stories about growing dissatisfaction in Cuba, Castro's management of the Cuban economy, and successful Cuban intelligence penetration of the CIA.[77]

November 1987: The Prison Riots

In November 1987, the United States and Cuba came to an agreement on the reactivation of the 1984 immigration accords. Castro would accept the return of 2,746 "undesirables" then held in U.S. prisons, and the Reagan administration would again begin allowing 20,000 Cubans to immigrate annually. The new agreement was reached in Mexico City between State Department deputy legal adviser Michael G. Kozak and Cuban Deputy Foreign Minister Ricardo Alarcon. Cuban had been insisting on a broad range of radio broadcasting rights within the United States, but dropped that demand and agreed to re-establish the immigration system in exchange for some smaller broadcasting concessions.[78]

The reaction of the Cuban "undesirables" was immediate and violent. Groups of Cuban inmates seized control of two prisons—one in Oakdale, Louisiana, only hours after the immigration agreement was signed, and one in Atlanta two days later—taking hostages and burning buildings. They demanded not to be sent back to Cuba, where they were certain they would face severe punishments, in some cases including death.

The Cuban-American community rallied around the inmates. Cuban-Americans, including many who had come in during the 1980 Mariel boatlift, feared that the deportation of inmates was merely a prelude to the expulsion of over 7,000 *Marielitos*. Groups such as Huber Matos, Jr.'s *Cuba Independiente y Democratica*, and individuals such as Cuban-American Bishop Augustin Roman, traveled to the prisons to mediate between the inmates and the U.S. government.

On November 24, as rioting broke out in the Atlanta penitentiary, U.S. Attorney General Edwin Meese III offered to declare a moratorium on deportations, and to review each case fully and fairly. His offer was delivered to inmates at Oakdale by Louisiana Senator John B. Breaux, but no immediate progress was apparent.

Negotiations with the inmates were touchy. The Cubans did not trust U.S. officials, and only the efforts of Cuban-American mediators prevented a total collapse of the situation. Agreements were finally signed for the release of the prisoners at both institutions, although afterwards the inmates and the Justice Department differed over the interpretation of the terms of the agreement.[79]

The 1988 Presidential Campaign

As the 1988 presidential campaign heated up, various Republican candidates jockeyed for position for toughness on Cuba, although the issue was not a prominent one. In May 1987, just before giving a speech to the Cuban American National Foundation, Senator Bob Dole introduced a bill in the Senate to again stiffen economic sanctions on Cuba; this was amid general attempts in the Congress to reopen trade channel to Havana. Alexander Haig, before withdrawing from the race, re-emphasized the importance of dealing with Cuba.

But the candidate who elicited the greatest controversy was Rev. Pat Robertson. During his early campaigns, Robertson made reference to the fact that he had knowledge of the deployment of Soviet SS-4 and SS-5 missiles in Cuba, presumably left over from 1962. There had been some minor press reports that missiles might still be there, but no analyst had publicly claimed to have knowledge of such deployments—until Robertson did.[80]

After hedging somewhat because of the issue's limited appeal in early primaries in liberal Iowa and New Hampshire, Robertson in late February 1988 firmly committed himself to the issue and vowed to do something about it if he became president. Reagan administration sources denied the validity of Robertson's claim, but he nevertheless pressed the issue, hoping to gain votes from conservative Southern Democrats and Republicans, in particular from the Cuban-American community.

THE REAGAN ADMINISTRATION'S LEGACY

As the 1988 presidential campaign unfolded, Ronald Reagan's legacy to the United States began to come under close scrutiny. As with his predecessor, Reagan's Cuba policy serves as an accurate microcosm of his foreign policy in general, and one's impressions of that foreign policy will largely determine one's reaction to Reagan's treatment of Cuba.

Determined to reassert American military and diplomatic power in the face of what he saw as an overwhelming Soviet threat, Reagan built up American defenses and increased support to pro-American and anti-Soviet movements and nations around the globe. It was thus logical for his administration to attempt to isolate Cuba diplomatically and economically, although it was unclear how much fruit those efforts bore. Cuba was seen primarily as a Soviet proxy power spreading revolution, especially within the Americas' "soft underbelly": Central America and the Caribbean. Reagan's emphasis on military power translated into the use of military intimidation against Castro, which did apparently have some moderating influence on Cuba's behavior.

Given the general worldview of the Reagan administration, then, its Cuba policy is perfectly logical. But the frustration of Reagan policy-makers illustrates the dilemma of dealing with Cuba in the modern era. Receiving as it does massive subsidies from East Bloc nations, and enjoying some amount of trade with a few Western countries whose own interests prevent them from honoring the U.S. embargo, Cuba is relatively immune to economic pressure. The growing nationalism tinged with Anti-Yankeeism of Latin America and the Caribbean has rendered any diplomatic moves against Cuba in the region problematic. And, both because of the costs involved and the lack of a clear and immediate rationale, military action is out of the question. In short, there is little today the United States can do to Cuba that holds any real hope of creating enough discomfort to force Castro to change his ways.

Of course, such a change, either in the form of explicitly moderated revolutionism or in a true shift from the Communist camp, is not a necessary result for Reagan supporters to claim success for their policy. Pointing to the emergence of several new Latin American democracies and to the fact that no nations have been lost to Communism since 1980, conservatives argue that their strategy—isolating Cuba and Nicaragua, supporting regional allies with military aid, using American military power in certain instances—has worked.

In many respects this view is perfectly accurate. But there is today, apart from its own economic problems, nothing to prevent Cuba from invading another African nation, or stepping up its support for Communist guerrilla movements in Latin America or—in a seldom-discussed possibility—in the Philippines, arguably its partner in turn-of-the-century American colonial exploitation. The United States simply has no leverage over Cuba. Castro would certainly not willingly grant it any, and it is debatable whether any set of economic and diplomatic relationships would provide the United States with a veto over Cuban foreign policy; which, in the end, is what most U.S. Cuban policy since 1959 has been aimed at acquiring. If, as Reagan claims the Ford and Carter experiences suggest, Castro is and will remain more dedicated to support for revolutionary solidarity than to acquiring U.S. concessions, then there is indeed little the United States can do to bring Cuban policies more into line with American interests. Given such an assumption, the Reagan administration's general policies toward Cuba may be the only remaining answer: to make foreign adventures costly for Castro and look toward the day when he will be gone and perhaps a more moderate, pragmatic government will come to power in Havana. This again harks back to the early-60s policy of refusing to recognize Castro's legitimacy.

By the end of the Reagan administration, however, a number of commentators had begun to speculate that the United States *did* have a choice, that it could achieve a partial accommodation with Castro that would provide Washington with some limited leverage over Cuban behavior. Ford and Carter, they argued, had overreacted to two very unique Cuban moves that were dictated by conditions in Africa, and they point out that no American president has ever really tested a long-term accommodation with Castro, one that would put up with a few revolutionary adventures. (It is important to remember that as long as Castro undertakes ventures to express his independence from the Soviet Union, he will certainly do so during the early stages of a rapprochement with the United States.) But as of 1988 these voices represented a minority position. Only time—and perhaps American electoral politics—will tell if the United States will ever truly accept the irreversibility of Castro's revolution and act accordingly.

PART
SIX

ASSESSMENTS

16

LOOKING BACK

U.S. and Cuban Foreign Policy in Historical Perspective

''Every attempt to explain human behavior, especially the irrational,
must as a matter of course end in simplification.''
Morton Irving Seiden, *The Paradox of Hate*

''But men generally decide upon a middle course, which is most hazardous,
for they know neither how to be entirely good nor entirely bad.''
Niccolo Machiavelli, *The Prince*

''That men do not learn very much from the lessons of history is the
most important of all the lessons of history.''
Aldous Huxley, *Collected Essays*

The last fifteen chapters have outlined an enormously
complex and important relationship, that of the United States and Cuba, over
a period of over 350 years. I hope that the reader has not discerned any blatant political bias, or any attempt to foster one particular view of Cuban or
American policy. In certain instances, when relatively clear and objective facts
have come to light that discredit a particular theory, a more critical approach
has been taken. On the whole, however, the relationship has been allowed to
speak for itself.

The history of U.S.-Cuban relations, however, if examined more judgementally, does seem to offer certain lessons regarding the behavior of nations over time. It is these lessons that the present chapter seeks to illuminate. The following analysis is not original; it draws from many sociological and political perspectives. Its central concept is that the behavior of nations is both simple and complex: simple, because it is based purely in a drive for power and security, and complex because that drive is shaped and conditioned by a host of factors relating to the particular nation's cultural history and domestic situation and to the international environment in which it operates.

The implication of such a model is that black-and-white portraits of national behavior—theories that paint the United States as "business-dominated and imperialistic" or the Soviet Union as an "expansionist Marxist-Leninist state" or Cuba as a "personalized, messianic Communist dictatorship"— over-simplify the issue. Only through a detailed examination of a nation's history, its current political culture, and the world in which it makes its policies can any analysis arrive at reasonably sophisticated conclusions about that nation's behavior. Attempting to squeeze all of a given nation's policies, or most of them, into one narrow category of explanation may serve personal or ideological purposes, but it is a poor substitute for more sophisticated analysis.

Within this general framework of analysis, an examination will be made of two key themes in U.S.-Cuban relations: U.S. dominance of Cuban affairs, and the rise of Cuban radicalism. These two trends were on a collision course almost from the first U.S. intervention into Cuba, and the conflict, put off temporarily in 1933, finally reached a head in 1958.

A MODEL OF NATIONAL BEHAVIOR

An examination of the behavior of U.S. and Cuban leaders and officials over the course of the relationship illustrates, to repeat, that the behavior of nations is at once a complex and deceptively simple process: nations behave in their own self-interest, nothing more, but their specific choices are conditioned by the shared experiences of their culture(s) and influenced by a variety of specific momentary factors. All of these influences are then focused in an often improvised manner on fleeting policy issues.

A schematic representation of this notion might look something like this:

GOAL: Security and Power
In the context of a response to the country's unique security dilemma

POLICY DECISIONS AND ACTIONS

CONDITIONED BY:
Past experiences of the nation or culture; the general
national milieu and shared societal standards

CONSTRAINED BY:
Domestic Political Considerations
Ideological Considerations
Economic/Resource Constraints
Personal/Psychological Aspects of Leaders

AS APPLIED TO:
Specific policy decisions in a given context

   This is, of course, not an original theory, nor one that necessarily pretends
to be able accurately to predict national behavior. What it does suggest is that
the policy decisions of a country are influenced by a whole range of factors:
the underlying assumptions of leaders, established by part experience and the
national political culture; political, ideological and resource constraints at a
given moment; personal quirks of officials or leaders; and of course pure
chance. Foreign policy therefore cannot be ascribed to a particular, overwhelming factor: domestic political influences, ideology/world conquest
goals, influence of business interests, or any other.
   It thus becomes extremely difficult to predict accurately the behavior of a
nation with regard to a given issue. At any time, one influence may emerge as
dominant and outweigh others. For example, while it may not have been a
rational pursuit of power and security for the United States to support the Bay
of Pigs operations, several factors—political pressure on the Kennedy
administration, poor decision-making organizations, inertia—combined to
override any completely objective analysis of the situation. During the Franklin Roosevelt administration, support for American business in Cuba was the
chief concern, while during the Reagan years a lack of domestic support
prevented the administration for pursuing as hawkish a line as it would have
liked.
   Specific reference to this model was not made in earlier discussions, but,
due to the nature of the analytical framework, it need not have been; each
event could be discussed essentially in isolation, within its own context and
with a recognition of the particular influences most at work. For example, the
United States' entry into the Spanish-Cuban-American war was prompted
by domestic pressure on McKinley from humanitarian interests, McKinley's

own anger with the obdurate Spanish, the messianic vision present in America at the time, and of course the specific historical accident of the *Maine* disaster. McKinley's decision and those of others who supported it was based on a rational calculus of the United States' best interests at the time, and nothing more; though that somewhat simple formula is, as noted, quite complex, as it involves a series of interconnected influences and motivations.[1]

THE POVERTY OF POLAR TRUTH

Since the foreign policy of a state is conditioned by such a diverse set of factors, it would seem obvious that simplistic, one-dimensional explanations for the foreign policy of a state are flawed. Yet writers persist in applying them.

Perhaps the favorite theme in U.S.-Cuban relations is the role of expansionist and ruthless U.S. business interests in dictating the occupation of Cuba. Successive U.S. administrations, it is argued, filled with former leaders and representatives of businesses with interests in Cuba, catered to those businesses, intervening when the Cubans threatened to get out of hand. Similarly, in the rest of Latin America, the United States propped up corrupt dictators like Trujillo and Somoza in a futile attempt to keep the people of the region in chains and rob them of the natural resources of their nations.

The preceding chapters have demonstrated that this suggestion is facile. Certainly, American business interests did have a strong influence on U.S. policy, and, as Louis Perez has suggested, stability in Cuba was often seen more as a "means" to U.S. profit than as an end in itself. In specific periods, such considerations were, indeed, overriding. But they often took second place to the sort of strategic/geopolitical goals referred to above as the primary ones of any state. In many instances, businesses were ambivalent—in 1898, for example, or 1959—and gave little guidance to policy, which was determined on other grounds. At other times, strong business pressure to change geopolitical strategies fell on deaf ears, as with the Reagan administration's refusal to allow trade with Cuba.

In any case, that the United States government has occasionally worked to support the interests of domestic American businesses should hardly come as a surprise. One often wonders, reading critiques of "imperialist" U.S. policy, whether the U.S. government exists to serve someone besides its own citizens. Certainly, there is a good case to be made that the blanket favoritism to U.S. business in Latin America through the middle of this century was disastrous long-term policy; as we have seen with regard to Cuba, the actions of the United States as often as not fomented revolutions that eventually undermined U.S. interests. But regardless of their advisability, policies that favor U.S. businesses at the expense of foreign interests are most definitely those one would expect an American government to follow.[2]

No more appealing are the ideological bromides of analysts on the right. To them, the Cuban revolution is just another example of the well-concerted worldwide Soviet advance—and of American moral absenteeism to boot. If one thing should be clear from chapters eight through ten, it is that painting the enormously complex Cuban revolution, which finally came about for reasons having very little to do with Communism, in this light, distorts the reality.

Such left-or right-wing analyses are not objective history, but rather ideological history, theses in search of supporting evidence and universal truths in search of application. In fact, the interpretation of the foreign policy of states by both ideological poles is somewhat similar: both posit immutable, single motives, whether imperialism or Marxism-Leninism. In this sense such theories can be seen as a secular attempt to explain the world according to basic, reliable rubrics, to account for national and individual behavior in a manner that provides reassurances through simplification about man's ability to understand the pattern of his existence.

The model of decision-making outlined above gives the lie to all such interpretations; foreign policy is made, not in the one-dimensional vacuum of "imperialism" or "Communism" but in a confusing forest of numerous, each potentially decisive, influences. In this sense it seems defensible that with regard to each significant historical event, the compromise position is closest to the truth. For each even a crop of left- and right-wing analysts must expound their fringe theories about the absolute domination of policy by group x or y, and more objective scholars are left to sift through the often contradictory and always complex historical evidence to assemble a more accurate version of events, one sharing fragments of both polar interpretations but relying completely on neither.

THEMES IN THE U.S.-CUBAN RELATIONSHIP

After all is said and done, however, a number of themes in the U.S.-Cuban relationship have emerged as significant. These have been developed through the chapters, but a small reassessment here seems in order.

1. *U.S. Dominance of Cuban Affairs*. Perhaps the most constant theme is that of American control of Cuban economic and political matters. Before 1898, this control took the form of warnings to European powers to leave Cuba

in the hands of Spain's decaying colonial administration: the no-transfer resolution, the "ripe fruit" policy, and of course the Monroe Doctrine. From 1898 to about 1918, the United States exercised a more direct control over Cuban affairs, intervening on several occasions and using the threat of intervention to mold Cuban policy to its wishes. The Platt Amendment served as the legal justification. From 1918 to 1959, American officials utilized mechanisms of indirect influence—trade laws, for example, and threats or implications of renewed intervention—to influence Cuban leaders. Throughout this period, American economic interests dominated the Cuban scene, though this was on the decline before the revolution.

The implications of this domination were examined in Chapter Nine. Resentment against American influence and an image of the United States as the cause of Cuba's problems were the psychological results. Economically, U.S. business interests robbed Cuba of the opportunity to develop an expanding, diverse middle class of entrepreneurs, owners, and the like. Politically, Cuban leaders and parties—until 1959—were repeatedly steered away from progressive solutions to the country's problems and in the end were forced to adopt conservative, pro-U.S. stances.

One example of U.S. domination is its use of economic treaties and aid plans to promote its own interests. Many of the commercial treaties that Cuba signed with the United States, while providing Cuba with a certain percentage of the U.S. sugar market, gave preferential treatment to hundreds of U.S. exports to Cuba. This was certainly true of the 1934 treaty; by 1947, however, Cuban nationalism had developed to the point where Cuban leaders were unwilling to accede to U.S. demands. American aid schemes were used in a similar way. The Open Door, the Alliance for Progress, the Caribbean Basin Initiative, and other such programs were developed as much to promote U.S. economic interests as Latin American ones, and in the bargain, it was hoped, to reduce the threat of outside intervention in the hemisphere.

U.S. officials and businessmen did not pursue these policies out of any malice for the Cuban people. American governments and businesses were merely acting in what they perceived were the best interests of the country. Admittedly, these was a certain callousness toward the Cubans at times, but it must be remembered that many of these policies were adopted in eras when social concern, equality of races and sexes, and other forms of national altruism were largely unknown, at least as we understand them today. The United States of the early twentieth century was no more "imperialist" than any of the European powers.

Indeed, it was far less so; the United States never acquired the sort of colonial possessions the Old World had. Naturally this is in large part due to America's late entrance onto the international scene, but this alone cannot explain it. In fact, U.S. foreign policy has displayed a consistent ambiguity towards expansion and foreign involvement. American leaders have been uncomfortable with their increasingly pivotal role in the world arena, an ambivalence apparent ever since the country assumed that role in 1898 and confirmed it in 1917.[3]

Thus with regard to Cuba, we find a desire on the part of U.S. officials to avoid interventions, and once forced to intervene to withdraw as quickly as possible. Certainly, the United States wanted to exercise control, and it provided itself with such tools as the Platt Amendment to ensure that it could protect its interests when it had to. But the views of Teddy Roosevelt perhaps come closest to summarizing the overall U.S. opinion: he hoped to let the Cubans alone, to allow them to develop and grow, under American tutelage, into a system mirroring America's own. When the Cubans failed to achieve this goal, American governments grew angry and once again began to treat Cuban leaders like children. The resulting inefficiency and corruption of Cuban governments seems hardly surprising.

This ambiguity can be seen in specific policies toward Cuba. In the first decades of the twentieth century, the U.S. administrations wanted to maintain order in Cuba but did not want to intervene. In 1933, Sumner Welles meddled just enough to alter the situation but not enough to decide it completely. In 1958-59, the Department of State made several futile efforts to assemble a third-party government without ever actually considering merely imposing one on Cuba. At the Bay of Pigs, Kennedy made perhaps the prototypical fence-straddling decision: yes, the United States would arm and train Cuban exiles; yes, it would deliver them to the beaches; but it would not support them with its own military.

In many cases this uncertainty regarding America's role is more a part of the public consciousness than that of national leaders. During the Reagan administration, for example, a government that might have considered more militaristic solutions to its Cuban problems (though intervention was probably out of the question) was restrained by a Congress distrustful of the administration's policies in Latin America.

While in 1898 the American people demanded greater world influence, then, they adopted almost immediately afterward a decidedly ambivalent attitude toward their eventual role as self-proclaimed "world policeman." Even the American entry into the two world wars in the face of a clear and unambiguous expansionist threat to U.S. national interests was achieved only over the objection of large, isolationist portions of the American populace. The Korean conflict remained a "police action" in part because American leaders knew their constituents would never support a full-scale war against China. The development of the media magnified the effect of public opinion; Vietnam became the self-defeating quagmire that it did in large measure due to opposition to the war at home, opposition that eventually forced an American withdrawal. In the modern world, it may well be that the only sorts of wars the American people are willing to tolerate—aside from simple defense against attacks on the United States itself—are short, relatively painless conflicts like the intervention into Grenada.

2. *The Rise of Radical Thought in Cuba*. Partly as a result of the U.S. role in Cuba, intellectuals on the island from an early date turned to radical and progressive thought. Not adopting any single European school of thought as a whole, Cuban thinkers evolved a world-view distinct to the island, which eventually came to be represented by Jose Marti's thought. Concern for the individual, altruism, respect for the worker and the peasant, and opposition to imperialism and colonialism were the hallmarks of this philosophy, as we have seen. General Cuban support for these concepts has been manifest in the traditionally strong position of labor in Cuba, in the respect for intellectuals, and in reverence of Marti.

American dominance prevented the true manifestation of this thinking in policy, however, most especially in the aborted revolution of 1933. Cuban intellectuals were thus forced to turn elsewhere for a satisfaction of their vision of a new Cuba, a true *Cuba libre*, and they turned to violent revolution. Most did not radicalize their ideology; they retained the essentially moderate yet progressive reformism characteristic of the liberal Cuban parties of the time. The revolutionary situation, however, created the context for the ascendance to power of a group that would turn out to be quite radical: Fidel Castro and his close associates.

Combined with the traditional Spanish/Cuban respect for the *caudillo* or strong-man, and the unique set of circumstances in 1958, such radical thought helped Fidel Castro consolidate the revolution in the period after January, 1959. Cubans were accustomed to dictatorial leaders, and had a history of enthrallment with such men; most Cubans were willing to allow them to rule as long as they served the national interest in a very general sense, preserved order, and cared for the average Cuban. Hence while Castro's government has exercised a heavier repressive hand than earlier Cuban governments, it has also done far more to promote Cuba's international image, provide for Cuban independence from American dictates, and guarantee in many ways the dignity of the common worker or peasant. Cuba's history of radical thought and the traditional acceptance of socialist ideas, established the groundwork that made Castro's initial radicalization legitimate; after that, his personality and his government's programs of internal and external nationalism kept his government secure.

Cuban foreign policy can be seen in a similar light. Through the early decades of the twentieth century it was for the most part hostage to American opinion; even as late as 1941 Cuba felt compelled quickly to enter the war on the American side. Beginning in the late 1940s, however, and especially during the Grau administrations, Cuba began fitfully to assert its independence abroad; a good example is its refusal to abide by the 1947 commercial treaty and its support for anti-American thought in the Hemisphere as a response. But these nationalist inklings remained isolated until 1959, when, with Fidel Castro's rise to power, Cuban activities abroad became both the essential ingredient of his regime and the primary point of dispute with the United States.

Then too there is the long history of Cuban exile activity in the United States. From the anti-Spanish revolutionaries of the nineteenth century to the anti-Castro groups of today, the United States has served as a refuge and organizing point for thousands of Cuban insurrectionists. At times, as with CIA-supported anti-Castro exiles, the United States has aided these groups; at others it has remained neutral; and sometimes, under strong pressure from the Spanish or the Castro government, it has been forced to curtail the activities of the Cubans.[4] The importance of the United States as a staging point for exiled Cuban revels, however, cannot be overestimated.

CONCLUSION: A CRUCIAL RELATIONSHIP

These two themes were clearly on a collision course from the beginning of this century. From 1900 until 1933, Cuban nationalism and radicalism gradually grew and finally produced a revolution against corruption in the government and against U.S. influence. Neither was done away with, and it would take Castro's "total revolution" of 1959 to force more permanent changes in the Cuban polity and the Cuban-American relationship.

That relationship historically has been one of the most important for both nations; clearly the most important from the Cuban perspective, at least until 1959 and arguably thereafter as well. There is no reason to believe that this situation will change. Indeed, as the world balance of power shifts from a stark and hostile bipolarity based on military force to a less ideological, more economic and political multipolarity, as Fidel Castro passes from the scene and is replaced by more pragmatic technocrats, as American administrators become disenthralled with Communism—if and when these developments occur in full or in part, America's relationship to Cuba could again come to the forefront of the foreign policy of both states. Because of the long history of American domination of Cuban affairs, perhaps it took a total revolution—

against the United States as much as anything else—and a long, uninterrupted expression of pure Cuban nationalism and internationalism to cleanse the Cuban polity of the effects of political and economic servitude. When that experiment will end, when Cuba and the United States can enjoy (for the first time) relations as amicable if ideologically divergent neighbors, only time will tell.

Notes

Chapter One

1. For an analysis of early U.S. foreign policy along these lines, see James H. Huston, "Intellectual Foundations of Early American Diplomacy," *Diplomatic History* 1 (Winter 1977): 1-19.

2. See Hugh Thomas, *Cuba: The Pursuit of Freedom* (New York: Harper and Row, 1971), pp. 12-24, and Charles E. Chapman, *A History of the Cuban Republic: A Study in Hispanic-American Politics* (New York: Octagon Books, 1969), Chapter 1.

3. Jaime Suchlicki, *Cuba From Columbus to Castro* (Washington, D. C.: Pergamon-Brassey's, 1986), p. 5.

4. Suchlicki p. 78; Philip Foner, *A History of Cuba and Its Relations With The United States* (New York: International Publishers, 1962), Volume I pp. 17ff; M. R. Harrington, *Cuba Before Columbus* (New York: AMS Press, 1979; reprint of 1921 edition, 1 volumes).

5. Terence Cannon, *Revolutionary Cuba* (New York: Thomas Y. Crowell, 1981), pp. 10-12; Foner, I, pp. 20-26; and Rafael Fermoselle, *The Evolution of the Cuban Military 1492-1986* (Miami: Edciones Universal, 1987), p. 28. See also Willis Fletcher Johnson, *The History of Cuba* (New York: B. F. Buck and Company, 1920), Vol. I, for a general description of early Cuban history.

6. Suchlicki p. 28.

7. Ibid. p. 36.

8. Irene A. Wright, *The Early History of Cuba, 1492-1586* (New York: Octagon Books, 19780, reprint of 1916 edition); Douglas E. Leach, *Roots of Conflict: British Armed Forces and Colonial Americans, 1677-1763* (Chapel Hill: University of North Carolina press, 1986), pp. 43, 46-47. For a summary of the benefits reaped by Spain, see John Fisher, "The Imperial Response to 'Free Trade': Spanish Imports From Spanish American, 1778-1796," *Journal of Latin American Studies* 17 (May 1985): 35.78.

9. Foner, I, pp. 37-39

10. Allan J. Kueth, *Cuba, 1753-1815: Crown, Military, and Society* (Knoxville: University of Tennessee Press, 1986), pp. 132, 175.

11. Johnson, II, pp. 130-36.

12. David Turnbull, *Cuba and the Slave Trade* (New York: Negro University Press, 1969, reprint of 1840 Longman edition), pp. 498-527; Leach pp. 175 (n. 57).

13. James M. Callahan, *Cuban and International Relations: A Historical Study in American Diplomacy* (Baltimore: Johns Hopkins Press, 1899), pp 45-50.

14. Nelson Vance Russell, "The Reaction in England and America to the Capture of Havana, 1762," *Hispanic American Historical Review* 9 (August 1929): 312-13; Gonzalo de Quesada and Henry Northrop, *The War in Cuba* (New York: Arno Press, reprint edition 1970), pp. 277-96.

15. Thomas pp. 1-11. Lord Albemarle, the leader of the expedition, and his two younger brothers—Commodore and Major General Keppel—were down on their luck financially. It was common practice for officers in European armies of the period to obtain a large portion of the spoils of their victories, and Albemarle and his relatives expected big results from their Cuban foray. By all accounts, they were not disappointed.

16. Ibid. p. 313; for an account of the English occupation, see Turnbull, pp. 528-35, and G. de Zendegui, "When the British Captured Havana," *Americas* 16 (March 1964): 21-28.

17. Callahan p. 51.

18. Chapman p. 31, Foner, I. p. 42.

19. Foner, I. p. 42

.20. Fermoselle, p. 33: cf. pp. 33-35. See also Johnson, Ii, pp. 145-46.

21. Foner, I. pp. 41-44.

22. Kathryn Trimmer Abbey, "Spanish Projects for the Reoccupation of the Floridas During the American Revolution," *Hispanic American Historical Review* X (August 1929): 266-67.

23. Ibid. p. 270.

24. Ibid. p. 271. Many members of Congress agreed, but Henry Laurens argued vehemently against an expedition to Florida. He said such proposals were based on "vague and indigested plans and predispositions, adopted by a few and apparently acquiesced in by a great majority." His arguments helped defeat the proposals.

25. Ibid. p. 278. The British reinforced their southern forces in April, 1780, and the Spanish were gradually severing ties to the developing colonial army. Some Spanish troops under Glavez did make an expedition against parts of Louisiana and the surrounding territories in August, 1779, and made some progress, capturing a few forts along with several hundred British soldiers. Later plans for invasions of Florida were eventually given up.

26. Roy S. Nichols, "Trade Relations and the Establishment of U.S. Consulates in Spanish America, 1779-1809," *Hispanic American Historical Review* XIII (August 1933): 290.

27. James W. Cortada, *Two Nations Over Time: Spain and the United States, 1776-1976* (Westport, CT: Greenwood Press, 1978), pp. 8-11.

28. Foner, I, p. 44.

29. Nichols pp. 292-93.

30. Ibid. p. 296. The U. S. exported mostly foodstuffs to Cuba: flour, rice, butter, fish, and meat, along with some lumber, tar and other construction materials.

Don Luis de Las Cases, then governor of Cuba, aided this trade by using his discretionary powers to open Cuban ports to American shipping in 1793.

31. Ibid. p. 300.

32. Ibid. p. 302.

33. Samuel Flagg Bemis, *The Latin American Policy of the United States* (New York: Harcourt, Brace, and World, 1943), p. 19.

34. Johnson, II, pp. 265-66.

35. Saul K. Padover, *The Complete Jefferson* (New York: Tudor Publishing Company, 1943), p. 175; Thomas A. Bailey, *A Diplomatic History of the American People* (Englewood Cliffs, NJ: Prentice-Hall, 1980), p. 165; Samuel Flagg Bemis, *A Diplomatic History of the United States*, 5th Ed. (New York: Holt, Rinehart, and Winston, 1965), pp. 196-97.

36. I. J. Cox, "The Pan-American Policy of Jefferson and Wilkinson," *Mississippi Valley Historical Review* I (September 1914): 215; Foner, I, p. 125.

37. Basil Rauch, *American Interest in Cuba: 1848-1855* (New York: Octagon Books, 1974), p. 15.

38. Rauch pp. 16 7; Cox pp. 213-214.

39. John P. Foley, ed., *The Jefferson Cyclopedia* (New york: Russell and Russell, 1967), volume I, p. 222.

40. Chapman p. 47; Foner, I, p. 125; Thomas pp. 87-88.

41. Bemis p. 23; Graham Stuart, *Latin American and the United States (New York: The Century Co., 1928), pp. 173-75.*

42. Bemis p. 27.

43 Chapman p. 49; Henry Adams, ed., *The Writings of Albert Gallatin* (New York: Antiquarian Press Ltd., 1960), Vol, I, p. 387; Callahan pp. 98-99.

44. Bemis p. 27; Bailey p. 286. As Bailey notes this declaration "foreshadowed the no-transfer principle of the Monroe Doctrine." At another time Jefferson wrote that "We shall be well satisfied to see Cuba and Mexico remain in their present dependence [upon Spain]; but very unwilling to see them in that of either France or England, politically or commercially. We consider their interests and ours as the same, and that the object of both must be to exclude all European influence from the is hemisphere." Foley p. 222.

45. Cox p. 214.

46. Nichols, p. 310; regarding the embargo itself, see Richard Mannix, "Gallatin, Jefferson, and the Embargo of 1808," *Diplomatic History* 3 (Spring 1979): 151-72.

47. James Madison, *Letters and Other Writings* (New York: R. Worthington, 1884), Volume II, p. 440.

48. Adams, I, p. 490; Madison p. 488.

49. Foner, I, p. 127.

50. Rauch p. 18.

51. Accounts from Franklin W. Knight, *Slave Society in Cuba During the Nineteenth Century* (Madison: University of Wisconsin press, 1970), pp. 48-49; Hudson Strode, *The Pageant of Cuba* (London: Jarrold's Publishers, 1935), p. 97-98; David Turnbull, *Cuba, With Notes of Porto Rico, and the Slave Trade* (New York: Negro

University Press, reprint of 1840 Longman edition, 1969); Alexander Humboldt, *The Island of Cuba* (New York: Negro University Press, reprint of 1856 Derby and Jackson edition, 1969). See also Julia Ward Hower, *A Trip to Cuba* (New York: Frederick A. Praeger Publishers, 1969; reprint of 1860 edition), pp. 217-19; Thomas pp. 156-92, 278-92; and Laird W. Bergad, "Slave Prices in Cuba 1940-1875," *Hispanic American Historical Review* 67 (November 1987): 631-57.

See also Gordon K. Lewis, *Main Currents of Caribbean Thought: The Historical Evolution of Caribbean Society in Its Ideological Aspects, 1492-1900* (Baltimore: Johns Hopkins University Press, 1983), which contains many excellent passages on the nature and implications of slavery in the region. See especially pages 205-13 for a description of the British and French abolitionism of this period.

52. Foner, I, p. 129.
53. Bemis p. 29; Foner, I, p. 130.
54. Fermoselle pp. 43-45; Callahan p. 105.
55. Bemis p. 39.
56. Foner, I, p. 132.
57. Halford L. Hoskins, "The Hispanic American Policy of Henry Clay, 1816-1828," *Hispanic American Historical Review* VII (November 1927): 460-78; Bemis, *Latin American Policy* pp. 40-41.
58. Hoskins p. 476.
59. Thomas p. 104.
60. Stanislaus Murray Hamilton, *The Writings of James Monroe* (New York: G. P. Putnam's Sons, 1902), Vol. VI, pl. 35; Bemis *Latin American Policy* p. 67.
61. Chapman p. 49.
62. Jaime Suchlicki, *Cuba From Columbus to Castro* (Washington: Pergamon Brassey's 1986) pp. 58-59; Thomas p. 111; Arthur F. Corwin, *Spain and the Abolition of Slavery in Cuba, 1817-1886* (Austin: University of Texas Press, 1967), pp. 3-35.
63. Foner, I, p. 140.
64. Charles Francis Adams, ed., *Memoirs of John Quincy Adams* (Philadelphia, 1874-1877), Vol. IV, p. 188.
65. Rauch pp. 20-21; Johnson, I, p. 259.
66. Hamilton p. 313.
67. Johnson, II, p. 262.
68. Callahan p. 129, Fermoselle p. 49.
69. Cortada pp. 42.51. Information on threat of French involvement: Bailey pp. 178, 286.
70. Stuart pp. 169-170; Ruhl J. Bartlett, ed., *The Record of American Diplomacy* (New York: Alfred A. Knopf, 1948), pp. 231-34; *American State Papers: Foreign Relations*, vol. V, pp. 408ff.
71. Bemis p. 62. For more information of the U. S rejection of the joint declaration plan see Bailey p. 286; Samuel Flagg Bemis, ed., *The American Secretaries of State and Their Diplomacy* (New York: Alfred A. knopf, 1928), Vol V, pp. 107, 124-37, 184.

72. Ibid.

73. Hamilton p. 340.

74. Federico Gil, *Latin American-United States Relations* (New York: Harcourt, Brace, Janovich, 1971), pp. 63-64.

75. Ibid. pp. 76-78.

76. Ernest R. May, *The Making of the Monroe Doctrine* (Cambridge, MA: Belknap Press of Harvard University Press, 1975), p. 255-60.

Harry Ammon, in a direct critique of May's work, has warned against overemphasizing the domestic political influences on Monroe. He cites historical evidence to confirm the thesis that the primary motives of most members of the administration were geostrategic, based in a fear of European influence. See Ammon, "The Monroe Doctrine: Domestic Politics or National Decision?" *Diplomatic History* 5 (Winter 1981): 53-70, and May's "Response," pp. 71-74.

77. Cecil v. Crabb, Jr., *The Doctrines of American Foreign Policy: Their Meaning, Role and Future* (Baton Rouge: Louisiana State University Press, 1982), p. 9; cf. also pp. 1-42.

78. Callahan pp. 139-40.

79. Gordon K. Lewis, *Main Currents of Caribbean Thought: The Historical Evolution of Caribbean Society in its Ideological Aspects, 1492-1900* (Baltimore: Johns Hopkins University Press, 1983), p. 6. See also William Rex Crawford, *A Century of Latin American Thought* (Cambridge, MA: Harvard University Press, 1961); Arthur P. Whitaker, ed., *Latin American and the Enlightenment* (Ithaca, NY: Great Seal books, 1961); and German Auciniegas, *Latin America: A Cultural History*, trans. Joan MacLean (New York: Alfred A. knopf, 1967), esp. pp. 3-285.

80. Lewis p. 114.

81. Lewis p. 36.

82. Sheldon Liss, *Roots of Revolution: Radical Thought in Cuba* (Lincoln: University of Nebraska Press, 1987), pp. 3-5.

Chapter Two

1. Daniel O'Leary, *Bolivar and the War of Independence* (Austin: University of Texas Press, 1970), pp. 8-21-.

2. Jesus Maria Henao and Gerardo Arrubla, *History of Colombia*, trans. J. Fred Rippy (New York: Greenwood Press, 1969), p. 234.

3. Harold A. Bierck, ed., *Selected Writings of Bolivar, Vol. II: 1823-1830* (New York: The Colonial Press, 1951), pp. 434-35.

4. Ibid. p. 499.

5. Philip Foner, *A History of Cuba and Its Relations With the United States* (New York: International Publishers, 1962), Volume I, p. 164.

6. Ibid. p. 169; John Lloyd Mecham, *Survey of U.S.-Latin American Relations* (Boston: Houghton-Mifflin, 1965), pp. 28-47; Leland Jenks, *Our Cuban Colony: A Study in Sugar* (New York: Vanguard Press, 1928), pp. 9-10; Graham Stuart, *Latin American and the United States* (New York: The Century Co., 1928), pp. 175.

7. Charles E. Chapman, *A History of the Cuban Republic: A Study in*

Hispanic-American Politics (New York: Octagon Books, 1969), p. 54.

8. Henry Adams, ed., *The Writings of Albert Gallatin* (New York: Antiquarian Press Ltd., 1960), Vol. II, p. 352; Stuart p. 171.

9. John M. Belohlavek, *"Let the Eagle Soar!" The Foreign Policy of Andrew Jackson* (Lincoln, NE: University of Nebraska Press, 1985), p. 74.

10. For an interesting portrait of Cuba during this year see Sophia Peabody Hawthorne—a painter and Nathaniel's wife—*The Cuba Journal, 1833-35* (Washington, D.C.: Library of Congress copyright, 1981).

11. Callahan 181. See also B. D. Gooch, "Belgium and the prospective Sale of Cuba in 1837," *Hispanic American Historical Review* 39 (1959: 413-27). Gooch discusses British attempts to purchase the island and also notes that Belgium was interested.

12. James M. Callahan, *Cuba and International Relations: A Historical Study in American Diplomacy* (Baltimore: Johns Hopkins Press, 1899) p. 186; Samuel Flagg Bemis, ed., *American Secretaries of State and Their Diplomacy* (New York: Alfred A. Knopf, 1928), Vol. V, pp. 56-57, 139-44.

13. Chapman p. 55; Jenks pp. 11-13.

14. Amos Aschbach Ettinger, *The Mission of Spain of Pierre Soule, 1853-1855: A Study in the Cuban Diplomacy of the United States* (New Haven: Yale University Press, 1932), p. 338.

15. Basil Rauch, *American Interest in Cuba: 1848-1855* (New York: Octagon Books, 1974), pp. 49-50; Charles H. Brown, *Agents of Manifest Destiny: The Lives and Times of the Filibusters* (Chapel Hill: University of North Carolina Press, 1980) pp. 21-33.

16. Rauch pp. 56-57.

17. Rauch p. 60.

18. Rauch pp. 67-71

19. Chapman p. 57; Bemis, *American Secretaries*, V, pp. 298-300; Ruhl Bartlett, *The Record of American Diplomacy* (New York: Alfred A. Knopf, 1948), pp. 234-37 reprints the June Buchanan to Saunders letter authorizing purchase attempts. Bailey p. 288 discusses the same.

20. Foner, II, p. 28; Arthur F. Corwin, *Spain and the Abolition of Slavery in Cuba, 1817-1886* (Austin: University of Texas Press, 1967), pp. 93-106.

21. Robert G. Caldwell, *The Lopez Expeditions to Cuba, 1848-1851* (Princeton, NJ: Princeton University Press, 1915), p. 313.

22. See Chapter Three, "Manifest Destiny," in *Readings in the Latin American Policy of the United States*, Thomas Karnes, ed. (Tucson: The University of Arizona Press, 1972). *De Bow's Review* [VI (July 1848)] wrote that "We *will* have old Mexico and Cuba!" See also Bailey pp. 287-88; Bemis, *American Secretaries*, Vi, pp. 102, 147, 176-87, 216; Chapman pp. 54-56; Hugh Thomas, *Cuba: The Pursuit of Freedom* (New York: Harper and row, 1971), pp. 207-17.

23. Rauch p. 84. Buchanan continued to subvert plans to purchase Cuba, in the summer of 1848 denying that U.S. Minister Saunders had the authority to offer a purchase proposal.

24. Rauch p. 98-100.

25. Fillmore rejected the multilateral non-intervention pledge by writing: "It might take a few years, but in the end, with the encouragement derived from the free institutions of the United States, Cuba would either be free from Spanish rule, or annexed to the United States." William Elliot Griffis, *Millard Fillmore: Constructive Statesman, Defender of the Constitution, President of the United States* (Ithaca, NY: Andrus and Church, 1915), p. 109. See also Rauch p. 103. The U.S. was at the same time negotiating with Spain over various issues, including the treatment of U.S. sailors arrested for smuggling *La Verdad* and other revolutionary literature into Cuba. The U.S. minister to Cuba Mr. Campbell, pursued these issues with such vigor that the Spanish government asked Taylor to recall him claiming that he might even "bring on a contest between the two Governments" which Spain otherwise wished to avoid. Taylor declined, but asked Campbell to resign, though the latter would not leave his post.

26. *New York Times*, October 22, 1852.

27. Rauch p. 107.

28. Brown p. 42; J.C. Davis, *The History of the Late Expedition to Cuba* (New Orleans: Daily Delta Press, 1850), pp 27-28. The Lopez quote comes from Gordon K. Lewis, *Main Currents of Caribbean Thought: The Historical Evolution of Caribbean Society in Its Ideological Aspects, 1492-1900* (Baltimore: Johns Hopkins University Press, 1983), p. 156. for a pro-Spanish version of events, see Thomas William Wilson, *An Authentic Narrative of the Piratical Descent Upon Cuba Made by Hordes From the United States* (Havana: 1851).

29. Caldwell, footnote, p. 4.

30. Sheldon Liss, *Roots of Revolution: Radical Thought in Cuba* (Lincoln: University of Nebraska Press, 1987), pp. 5-7. See also Lewis, pp. 94-154, for a good description of the pro-slavery attitudes in Cuba at the time, and the growing conflict among Cubans over whether to support abolitionism.

31. "The Late Cuba Expedition," *De Bow's Review* 9 (August, 1850): pp. 164-77. See also Caldwell pp. 19, 49, 54; Foner, II, p. 44.

32. Caldwell P. 61. It was a consistent feature of the filibustering expeditions that, in order to avoid being stopped for violation of the Neutrality Act, they claimed to be going somewhere besides Cuba, and had to receive their war supplies once at sea.

33. Ibid. p. 105; Griffis pp. 104-9; Brown pp. 87-88.

34. Descriptions from: Caldwell pp. 107-10, Brown pp. 85-88; Richard Henry Dana, *To Cuba and Back: A Vocation Voyage* (Boston: Ticknor and fields, 1859), pp. 223-24; Hudson Strode, *The Pageant of Cuba* (London: Jarrold's Publishers, 1935), pp. 104-5. See also Bailey pp. 288-90; Bemis, *American Secretaries*, VI, pp. 37-40, 103-5.

35. Caldwell, p. 121 Griffis pp. 107-8; Stuart p. 181. In the end, the Lopez forays may have had counterproductive results for the freedom of Cuba. Captain General Concha used the invasions as a pretext to solidify his autocratic rule. The U.S. government's indifference also disappointed annexationists both in

Cuba and in the United States.

36. Suchlicki p. 59; Brown pp. 89-144.

37. Rauch pp. 183-187; Stuart pp. 182-84. For a more detailed description of trade during this period, see Roland T. Ely, "The Old Cuba Trade: Highlights and Case Studies of Cuban-American Interdependence During the 19th Century," *Business History Review* 38 (Winter 1964). For some examples of *De Bow's Review* stories, see "Cuba, Its Present Condition," Vol 18 (February 1855): 163-67; "The Island of Cuba—Past and Present," Vol. 14 (February 1853): 93-122; and "Cuba—Its Position, Dimensions, and Population," Vol. 8 (April 1850): 313-23.

38. Rauch p. 266.

39. Brown p. 109. for a description of Pierce's continuing no-transfer policy, see Bailey pp. 185-87. For information on Quitman, see G. B. Henderson, "Southern Designs on Cuba, 1854-1857, and Some European Opinions," *Journal of Southern History* V (1939); R. E. May, *The Southern Dream of a Caribbean Empire, 1854-1861* (Baton Rouge: Louisiana State University Press, 1985); Dona Sue Luskin, "The Annexation Designs of the United States Towards Cuba, 1853-55, and Their International Repercussion," MA Dissertation, Georgetown University, February 1972; C. S. Urban, "The Abortive Quitman Filibustering Expedition, 1853-1855," *Journal of Mississippi History* 18 (1956).

40. Ettinger pp. 220-29;0245. Bartlett provides the text of an April Marcy to Soule letter discussing purchase plans, pp. 239-40.

41. Ettinger pp. 257-90; Bailey pp. 293-94. See also H. C. Haynes, "The Black Warrior Affair," *American Historical Review* 12 (1907); Bemis, *American Secretaries*, VI, pp. 189-92.

42. Stanley J. Urban, "The Africanization of Cuba Scare, 1953-1855," *Hispanic American Historical Review* 37 (February 1957): 29-45; Rauch pp. 280-82; Bemis *American Secretaries*, VI, p. 202.

43. Ettinger pp. 291-338. This has been called the "purchase or detach" policy; see Bemis, *American Secretaries*, VI, pp. 192-95, 209-14.

44. Ettinger pp. 339-412; quote from "commentator" from Stuart p. 183.

45. Henry Steele Commager, ed., *Documents of American History* (New York: Appleton-Century-Crofts Inc., 6th Edition, 1958), pp. 333-35-4; Foner, II, p. 101.

46. Foner, II, p. 104.

47. See David Turnbull, *Cuba, With Notes of Porto Rico and the Slave Trade* (New York, Negro University Press, reprint of 1840 Longman edition, 1969), and Alexander Humboldt, *The Island of Cuba* (New York: Negro University Press, reprint of 1856 Derby and Jackson edition, 1969), for a description of Cuba during this period.

48. William O. Scroggs, "William Walker's Designs on Cuba," *Mississippi Valley Historical Review* I (September 1914). See also Lawrence Green, *The Filibuster* (New York: Bobbs-Merrill, 1937), and William O. Scroggs, *Filibusters and Financiers: the Story of William Walker and His Associates* (New York: Russell and Russell, 1969, reprint of 1916 edition).

49. Rauch p. 118.

50. Rauch p. 211; he concludes that Douglas "offered one [issue] as his only specific platform: Cuba."

51. John G. Nicolay and John Hay, eds., *The Complete Works of Abraham Lincoln* (New York: The Lamb Publishing Company, 1894), pp. 28-28, emphasis mine.

Chapter Three

1. James M. Callahan, *Cuban and International Relations: A Historical Study in American Diplomacy* (Baltimore: Johns Hopkins University Press, 1899), p. 330.

2. Clifford L. Egan, "Cuba, Spain, and the American Civil War," *Rocky Mountain Social Science Journal* 5 (1968), p. 58. See also E. J. Pratt, "Spanish Opinion of the North American Civil War," *Hispanic American Historical Review* 10 (1930), pp. 14-26. Pratt argues that Spain was forced by domestic politics to end up favoring the North; liberals in Spain desired that outcome, and reactionaries, already besieged, could not afford the political cost of opposing it. See Ibid. 18-19.

3. Egan p. 59.

4. Philip Foner, *A History of Cuba and Its Relations With the United States* (New York: International Publishers, 1962), Vol. II, p. 131.

5. Rebecca Scott, *Slave Emancipation in Cuba: The Transition to Free Labor, 1860-1899* (Princeton: Princeton University Press, 1985), pp. 37-39; Foner II, pp. 128-33.

6. John G. Nicolay and John Hay, eds. *The Complete Works of Abraham Lincoln* (New York: The Lamb Publishing Company, 1894, Vol. VI, p. 93.

7. Callahan p. 336; "Cuba: The March of Empire and the Course of Trade," *De Bow's Review* 30 (January 1861): 30-42. This latter article concluded that annexation would be no guarantee of security because "to defend Cuba we must annex the West Indies," and to defend them required more expansion, ad infinitum; it concluded that "the Southern States, rounded off with the Indian territory, will constitute a splendid empire." Also, instability in Cuba, which might result from a Southern invasion, would reflect poorly on slave societies in general, and to annex Cuba would bring into the South a strange, alien—and presumably inferior—
people.

8. Egan pp. 60-61. The Spanish continued to favor the Confederacy, and continuing arguments over violations of Cuban Waters by Federal ships pursuing Confederate raiders plagued Federal-Spanish relations. The man forced to argue this difficult case was Carl Shurz, U.S. minister in Madrid. The Federal Navy had blockaded Cuba, and Shurz spent much of his time papering over disputes regarding this blockade.

9. Scott esp. pp. 35-41; and Arthur F. Corwin, *Spain and the Abolition of Slavery in Cuba, 1817-1886* (Austin: University of Texas Press, 1967), pp. 43, 84, 129-89, 203, 209, 241-45, 276-77.

10. Callahan pp. 365-67.

11. Dennis B. Wood, "The Long Revolution: Class Relations and Political Conflict in Cuba, 1868-1968," *Science and Society* 34 (Spring 1970): 4-5; C.A. M.

Hennessy, "The Roots of Cuban Nationalism," *International Affairs* (london) 39 (July 1963): 348; Callahan p. 369. Roberto Fernandez Retamar has noted that in 1868 "the most radical and least slave-dependent fraction of the creole landowning class unleased in eastern Cuba the war of independence," which was confronted with "the hostility of the richest slave-owning landowners in the West." He concludes that "To a considerable extent the slave-owners' opposition contributed to the failure of the struggle." See Retamar, "The Modernity of Marti," in Christopher Abel and Nissa Torrents, eds., *Jose Marti: Revolutionary Democrat* (Durham: Duke University Press, 1986), p. 5. See also Scott, pp. 45-62. She notes the ambiguity of the revolt's position on slavery: though Cespedes freed his own slaves and called for "gradual and indemnified emancipation," the leaders of the revolution still "respected the basic principle of slaveholding" and "in November 1868 Cespedes decreed the death penalty for anyone inciting the slaves to rebellion." Eventually the rebel leaders promised that abolition would occur if the rebellion were (p. 46) successful.

Another excellent source on the revolutionary position on slavery is Gordon K. Lewis, *Main Currents of Caribbean Thought: The Historical Evolution of Caribbean Society in Its Ideological Aspects, 1492-1900* (Baltimore: Johns Hopkins University Press, 1983), esp. pp. 1257-59. See also Sheldon Liss, *Roots of Revolution: Radical Thought in Cuba* (Lincoln: University of Nebraska Press, 1987), pp. 24-25.

For details of Cuban exile communities in the United States during the Ten Years' War, see Gerald E. Poyo, "Key West and the Cuban Ten Years War," *Florida Historical Quarterly* LVII (January 1979): 289-307, and Poyo, "Cuban Revolutionaries and Monroe County Reconstruction Politics, 1868-1876," *Florida Historical Quarterly* LV (April 1977): 407-22.

12. Foner, II, p. 174.

13. See Chapter three of Alexander Gallenga, *The Pearl of the Antilles* (New York: Negro University Press, 1970; reprint of 1873 Chapman and Hall edition); Graham Stuart, *Latin American and the United States* (New York: The Century Co., 1928), pp. 185-87.

14. Gallenga pp. 51.

15. Foner, II, pp. 176-79, Corwin pp. 230-32. Regarding the Volunteers, see also "Life in Cuba," *Harper's New Monthly Magazine* XLIII (August 1871): 355-56, and W. J. Sparks, "Cuba and the Cuban Insurrection," *Schribner's Monthly* 6 (May 1873): 14-16.

16. Richard H. Bradford, *The Virginius Affair* (Boulder: Colorado Associated University Press, 1980), pp. 1-2.

17. See Allan Nevins, *Hamilton Fish: The Inner History of the Grant Administration* (New York: Dodd, Mead, and Co., 1936). Nevins is one of Fish's ablest defenders, and the volume contains a superb and enormously detailed account of U.S. diplomacy toward Spain during the Ten Years' War. See also Joseph Fuller, "Hamilton Fish," is Samuel Flagg Bemis, ed., *American Secretaries of State and Their Diplomacy*, Vol 7, (New York: Pageant Book Co., 1958), pp. 125-214; and

James b. Chapin, "Hamilton Fish and American Expansionism," PHD dissertation, Cornell University, 1971.

18. Bradford pp. 18-20.

19. Corwin pp. 233-37.

20. See Nevins pp. 176-278.

21. Thomas A. Bailey, *A Diplomatic History of the American People* (Englewood Cliffs, NJ: Prentice-Hall, 1980), pp. 379-80, has a good description of the pressures for recognition. He argues that the June Grant message to Congress "probably spike the [belligerency] resolution and possibly averted war over Cuba." *Ibid*. p. 380. For the British perspective see J.C. Bartlett, "British Reaction to the Cuban Insurrection of 1868-1878," *Hispanic American Historical Review* 37 (1957): 296-312.

22. References from Bradford, pp. 46-47, 52-53. See also Stuart pp. 187-88; Nevins pp. 667-694; Bailey pp. 380-81; "The Virginius Case," *The American Law Review* 8 (April 1874); James D. Hill, "Captain Joseph Fry of the S.S. *Virginius*," *The American Neptune* 36 (April 1976): 88-100; and Henry H. Beck, *Cuba's Fight for Freedom and the War With Spain* (Philadelphia: Globe Bible Publishing Co., 1898), pp. 173-84. For counsels of caution, see two articles in *The Nation*, Volume 17: "Now Should We Fight Spain," December 4, 1873, p. 364; and "The Reasons for Keeping Cool About It," November 20, 1873, pp. 332-34.

23. Joseph Smith, *Illusions of Conflict: Anglo-American Diplomacy Toward Latin American, 1865-1896* (Pittsburgh: University of Pittsburgh Press, 1979), p. 59; Bradford p. 134.

24. James W. Cortada,*Two Nations Over Time: Spain and the United States, 1776-1976* (Westport, CT: Greenwood Press, 1978), p. 96.

25. Foner, II, p. 250.

26. Philip Foner, *Antonio Maceo: The 'Bronze Titan' and Cuba's Struggle for Independence* (New York: Monthly Review Press, 1977).

27. Callahan p. 418.

28. Callahan p. 419. For the text of a November letter by Fish emphasizing the stronger U.S. stance, see Ruhl Bartlett, ed., *The Record of American Diplomacy* (New York: Alfred A. Knopf, 1948), pp. 370-71. Regarding the November 1875 attempts to get Europe to censure Spain, see Bailey p. 389.

29. *Papers Relating to the Foreign Relations of the United States, 1875* (Washington, D.C.: GPO), Vol. I, pp. i-xxvii. for Grant's Cuba message, see *Congressional Record*, 44th Congress, 1st Session, Vol. 4, December 7, 1875, pp. 176-77. Grant wrote that "no such civil organization exists [in Cuba] which may be recognized as an independent government," and that "I fail to find in the insurrection the existence of such a substantial political organization, real, palpable, and manifest in the world [etc]. . .to which a recognition of belligerence would aim to elevate it."

30. Callahan p. 442.

31. Foner, II, p. 271.

32. Liss pp. 7-8, 24-32.

33. See *Foreign Relations of the United States* for the following years: 1877, pp.486-92, 525-31, 1878, pp. 789-91, 809-15; 1879, pp. 941-54; 1880, pp. 889-93; 1883, pp. 773-76, 781-85, 788-89, 796-99; 1884, pp. 471, 476, 483-86, 496, 504-21; 1885, pp. 767-83; 1888, Vol. II. pp. 1471-73. See also *Congressional Record*, 45th Cong. 2d Sess., Vol. 7, December 6, 1877, p. 51 for a sample resolution demanding investigation of the way.

34. Callahan pp. 455-56; Smith, *Illusions* p. 123; Michael J. Devine, *John W. Foster: Politics and Diplomacy in the Imperial Era, 1873-1917* (Athens, Ohio: University of Ohio Press, 1981), pp. 30-33, 40-42.

35. Charles e. Chapman, *A History of the Cuban Republic: A Study in Hispanic-American Politics* (New York: Octagon books, 1969), p. 72.

36. Earl R. Beck, ''The Martinez Campos Government of 1879: Spain's Last Chance in Cuba,'' *Hispanic American Historical Review* 56 (May 1976): 288.

37. The literature on Jose Marti is extensive. One of the best short introductions is the chapter in Ramon Eduardo Ruiz, *Cuba: The Making of a Revolution* (New York: W. W. Norton, 1968), pp. 58-75. See also Felix Lizaso, *Marti: Martyr of Cuban Independence*, trans. Esther Elise Shuler (Albuquerque: University of New Mexico Press, 1953); richard Butler Gray, *Jose Marti: Cuban Patriot* (Gainesville: University of Florida Press, 1962); Peter Turton, *Jose Marti: Architect of Cuba's Freedom* (London: Zen Books, 1986); Manuel Pedro Gonzales, *Jose Marti: Epic Chronicler of the United States in the Eighties* (Chapel Hill: University of North Carolina Press, 1953); and Jorge Manach, *Marti: Apostle of Freedom*, trans. Coley Taylor (New York: Devin-Adair, 1950). Interesting journal articles include John M. Kirk, ''Jose Marti and the United States: A Further Interpretation,'' *Journal of Latin American Studies* 9 (November 1977): 275-90, and Jon S. Vincent, ''Jose Marti: Surrealist of Seer?'' *Latin American Research Review* 13 (No. 1 1978): 176-81

For a view of Marti in the context of the history of Caribbean thought, see Lewis pp. 290-303.

38. Quotes are from Jose Marti, *Thoughts on Liberty, Government, Art, and Morality*, Carlos Ripoll, ed. (New York: Eliseo Torres and Sons, 1980), pp. 27, 43 93. for more of Marti's writings see Marti, *Our America*, trans. Elinor Randall, ed. Philip Foner (New York: Monthly Review Press, 1977).

39. For more information on Marti, see the section in Chapter Nine that discusses his views.

40. Louis A. Presz, Jr., *Cuba Between Empires, 1878-1902* (Pittsburgh: University of Pittsburgh Press, 1983), pp. 12-13.

41. Ibid. pp. 14-16.

Chapter Four

1. Lester D. Langley, *The Cuban Policy of the United States: A Brief History* (New York: John Wiley and Sons, Inc., 1968), pp. 85-86.

2. Samuel Flagg Bemis, *The Latin American Policy of the United States* (New York: Harcourt, Brace, and World, 1943), pp. 123-24.

3. Philip Foner, *The Spanish-Cuban-American War and the Birth of American Imperialism, 1895-1902* (New York: Monthly Review Press, 1972), Vol. I, pp. xx-xxv. for outstanding summaries of Marti's work with the exile groups, see Gerald E. Poyo, "Jose Marti: Architect of Social Unity in the Emigre Communities of the United States," and Jacqueline Kaye, "Marti in the United States: The Flight from Disorder," both in Christopher Abel and Nissa Torrents, eds., *Jose Marti: Revolutionary Democrat* (Durham, NC: Duke University Press, 1986), pp. 16-31 and 65-82.

On the activities of the exiles more generally and the U.S. response, see Gerald E. Poyo, "Cuban Patriots in Key West, 1878-1886: Guardians at the Separatist Ideal," *Florida Historical Quarterly* LXI (July 1982): 20-36. Poyo notes that President Chester Arthur, seeking a trade treaty with Spain,, was forced to replace pro-Cuban customs officials, who often winked at neutrality act violations and illegal trade in order to placate Madrid. Many Florida congressmen at the time were distinctly pro-Cuban, as many remain today. (pp. 27-28).

4. Harry F. Guggenheim, *The United States and Cuba: A Study in International Relations* (Freeport, NY: Books for Libraries Press, 1934), p. 30; Christopher Abel, "Concluding Perspectives," in Abel and Torrents, eds., *Jose Marti*, pp. 192-93.

5. Guggenheim p. 30; Jorge Manache, *Marti: Apostle of Freedom*, trans. Coley Taylor (New York: Devin Adair Co., 1950), pp. 347-48.

6. Foner, I, p. 2.

7. David F. Healy, *The United States in Cuba, 1898-1902: Generals, Politicians, and the Search for Policy* (Madison: University of Wisconsin Press, 1963), p. 8. See also Dennis B. Wood, "The Long Revolution: Class Relations and Political Conflict in Cuba, 1868-1968," *Science and Society* 34 (Spring 1970): 5. As Wood and others have noted, the original "middle class" in Cuba was made up almost entirely of the wealthy Spanish who bankrolled Cuban planters. Later, numbers of Creoles and other native Cubans joined the middle sectors, but just as they were beginning to have some true influence, they were overwhelmed by the power of huge, U.S.-backed industrial combines. For a description of American land policy during the occupation and how it furthered this process, see Louis A. Perez, "Insurrection, Intervention, and the Transformation of Land Tenure Systems in Cuba, 1895-1902," *Hispanic American Historical Review* 65 (May 1895): 229-54.

8. Foner, I, p. 8.

9. The fish/water analogy comes from Mao.

10. the numbers deployed on each side would indicate a tough battle: the rebels usually numbering about 30,000; Spain in December 1895 had 100,000 regulars and 63,000 irregulars—Volunteers, home guards, etc.—on the island. By 1897 the Spanish had committed nearly a quarter of a million regular troops. Foner, I, pp. 16-17.

11. Foner, I, p. 74.

12. Joseph E. Wisan, *The Cuban Crisis as Reflected in the New York Press (1895-1898)* (New York: Columbia University Press, 1934), p. 88.

13. Ibid. p. 90.

14. Grover Flint, *Marching With Gomez* (Boston: Lamson, Wolfe and Co.,, 1898), pp. 104-109. See also U.S. Congress, Senate, *Consular Correspondence Respecting the Conditions of the Reconcentrados in Cuba, the State of War in the Island, and the Prospects of the Projected Autonomy,* 55th Cong, 2d. Sess., S. Doc. 230 (Washington, D.C.: GPO, 1898); and Senor Gonzalo de Quesada and Henry Northrop, *The War in Cuba* (New York: Arno Press, 1970, reprint of 1896 Edition) for a summary of the hostilities from a pro-Cuban point of view; Gonzalo de Quesada was head of the "Republic of Cuba" office in Washington in 1896. for the organization of Cuban armies at the time, see Rafael Fermoselle, *The Evolution of The Cuban Military 1492-1986* (Miami: Ediciones Universal, 1987), pp. 75-92.

15. Foner, I, p. 13. For a less anti-imperialist view of the quote, see Carlos Ripoll, *Jose Marti, The United States, and the Marxist Interpretation of Cuban History* (New Brunswick: Transaction Books, 1984).

16. *Foreign Relations of the U.S., 1895,* Part 2, pp. 1214-20; Ibid. *1896,* pp. 670-76, 695, 702-4, 710, 746-7-847. also Edwin F. Atkins, *60 Years in Cuba* (New York: Arno Press, 1980; reprint of 1926 edition), pp. 221-23.

17. *Foreign Relations of the U.S. 1895,* Part 2, pp. 1177-85.

18. Wisan pp. 71-73. The *Congressional Record* of 1895-1898 contains dozens of examples of resolutions demanding investigations of the war and recognition of the belligerents. On Cleveland's resistance see Robert Leckie, *The Wars of American (New York: Harper and Row, 1968), pp. 543-44, and Norman A. Graebner, Foundations of American Foreign Policy: A Realist Appraisal from Franklin to McKinley* (Wilmington,DE: Scholarly Resources, Inc., 1985), pp. 326-28. Regarding the Spanish intransigence over economic issues see Tennant S. McWilliams, "Procrastination Diplomacy: Hannis Taylor and the Cuban Business Disputes, 1893-97," *Diplomatic History* 2 (Winter 1978): 63080.

19. *Foreign Relations of the U.S. 1895,* Part 2, pp. 1191-1209; Ibid. *1896,* pp. 711-45 for description of *Competitor* episode.

20. Not all Cubans did support the war, however; some landowners and others still opposed it, and the mayor of Havana wrote in a U.S., journal in 1898 that the war was unpopular because many Cubans feared that annexation to the United States would be the inevitable result; Langley pp. 89-90.

21. Guggenhcim p. 31.

22. Healy p. 11.

23. Horatio Rubens, *Liberty: The Story of Cuba* (New York: Arno Press, 1932), pp. 140-41; for accounts of these filibustering expeditions see same, pp. 140-201. Rubens' arguments should be taken in context; he was a lawyer for the *Junta Cubana* in New York during the Spanish-Cuban-American War.

24. For example, one Cuban commentator argued at the time that The North American state was always the enemy of Cuban independence. It obstructed or annulled the efforts of the Cuban patriots in their attempts to send to the island expeditions with materials of war and medicines. It stubbornly resisted recognizing a state of war. On the other hand, at various times it offered material support

to Spain in order to keep the island under its domination, even volunteering to help recover it if the island were lost by Spain.

See Emilio Roig de Leuchsenring, "Ideas, Ideologies, and Attitudes," in Robert F. Smith, ed., *Background to Revolution: The Development of Modern Cuba* (Huntington, NY: Robert E. Krieger Publishing Co., 1979), p. 65. See also Foner, I, pp. 178,207.

25. Healy, p. 9.

26. Langley p. 93.

27. Guggenheimm p. 33.

28. Wisan p. 100

29. Philip S. Foner,*Antonio Maceo: The 'Bronze Titan' and Cuba's struggle for Independence* (New York: Monthly Review Press, 1977), pp. 249-51; Magdalen M. Pando, *Cuba's Freedom Fighter, Antonio Maceo: 1845-1896* (Gainesville, FL: Felicity Press, 1980); Patricia Weiss Fagen, "Antonio Maceo: Heroes, History and Historiography," *Latin American Research Review* XI (No. 3 1976): 69-93.76): 69-93.

30. Guggenheim pp. 34-35. In the United States, supporters of the Cuban cause claimed Maceo had been killed by Spanish treachery during negotiations, and this provided emotionally charged material for the pro-Cuban papers.

31. Guggenheim. p. 35.

32. Langley p. 98.

33. Healy p. 13.

34. James D. Richardson, ed., *Messages and Papers of the Presidents* (New York: 1897-1927), Vol. XIII,m p. 6261.

35. Lewis L. Gould, *The Spanish-American War and President McKinley* (Lawrence: University of Kansas Press, 1982), p. 29.

36. Guggenheim p. 36. Regarding the Red Cross role, see Clara Barton, "Our Work and Observations in Cuba," *North American Review* 166 (May 1898).

37. Gould, p. 30.

38. Samuel Janney and John McCook, a Wall Street financier and a New York lawyer, headed up this purchase attempt, and even got the support of Toma Estrada Palma, the Cuban rebel delegate to the United States. These parties also agreed that, if Spain would not sell, Janney and McCook would use their considerable resources to pay off U.S. leaders to invade and annex the island. But the plot was revealed and came to naught. *Foreign Relations of the U.S. 1897*, pp. 483-540.

39. Gould pp. 30-31; Julius Pratt, *America's Colonial Experiment* (New York: Prentice-Hall, 1951), pp. 45-46.

40. Julius Pratt, *Expansionists of 1898: The Acquisitions of Hawaii and the Spanish Islands* (New York: Quadrangle Books, 1936), p. 3.

41. See John Fiske, "Manifest Destiny," *Harper's New Monthly Magazine* LXX, pp. 578-90.

42. Pratt, *Expansionists* p. 3.

43. Walter Mills, *The Martial Spirit: A Study of Our War With Spain* (Boston: Houghton-Mifflin Co., 1931), pp. 1-10.

44. Ernest R. May, *American Imperialism: A Speculative Essay* (New York: Atheneum Books, 1968).

45. Richard Hofstadler, *The Paranoid Style in American Politics and Other Essays* (New York: 1966).

46. Walter LeFeber, *The New Empire: An Interpretation of American Expansion, 1860-1898* (Ithaca, NY: Cornell University Press, 1963), pp 403-5.

47. Ibid. p. 408.

48. May pp. 193-94. For an interesting advocacy of trade with Cuba to cure just such export needs, see the statement of Mr. Caldwell, *Congressional Record*, 45th Cong., 3d Sess., Vol. 8, February 28, 1879, pp. 3224-15.

49. William Appleman Williams, *The Roots of the Modern American Empire* (New York: Random House, 1969); see Also Williams, *The Tragedy of American Diplomacy* (New York: Dell, 1962).

50. Charles Beard, *An Economic Interpretation of the Constitution of the United States* (New York: Macmillan, 1929).

51. Leland Jenks, *Our Cuban Colony: A Study in Sugar* (New York: Vanguard Press, 1928), p. 2.

52. Foner, I, pp. 281-310.

53. John M. Dobson, *America's Ascent: The United States Becomes a Great Power, 1880-1914* (Dekalb, IL: Northern Illinois University Press, 1978), pp. 13, 17-18.

54. Foster Rea Dulles, *Prelude to World Power: American Diplomatic History, 1860-1900* (New York: Macmillan and Co., 1965), pp. 68-69.

Julius Pratt, in *America's Colonial Experiment*, concurs. ''The demand for intervention,'' he wrote, ''arose plainly from humanitarian rather than economic conditions.'' While Protestant journals and others in sympathy with the Cubans pushed for war, ''mouthpieces of business-trade journals and resolutions of boards of trade and chambers of commerce—with few exceptions advocated a hands-off policy. American business in general. . .was fearful that a war with Spain would interrupt its upward march to prosperity.'' Pratt concludes that ''Practically the only business interests that agitated for intervention were seaboard firms normally engaged in trade with Cuba''; many other companies warned the Department of State that they feared a war with Spain would do more harm than good to American business. (pp. 342-43).

55. David Healy, *U.S. Expansionism: The Imperialist Urge in the 1890's* (Madison: University of Wisconsin Press, 1970), p. 113. Alfred Thayer Mahan, *The Influence of Sea Power Upon History, 1660-1783* (Boston: Little, Brown, 1890). See also Mahan, *Lessons of the War With Spain and Other Articles* (Boston: Little, Brown, 1899), and Russell F. Weigley, *The American Way of War: A History of United States Mililtary Strategy and Policy* (Bloomington: Indiana University Press, 1973), p. 176.

56. Frederick Merk, *Manifest Destiny and Mission in American History: A Reinterpretation* (New York: Alfred A. Knopf, 1963).

57. Robert L. Beisner, *Twelve Against Empire: The Anti-Imperialist, 1898-1900* (New York: McGraw Hill, 1968), pp. 5-17.

58. Ibid. pp. 216ff.

59. Mils, *Martial Spirit* p. 409.

60. See Thomas R. Hietala, *Manifest Design: Anxious Aggranzement in Late Jacksonian America* (Ithica, NY, New York: Cornell University Press, 1885).

61. Hence the Platt Amendment, which as we shall see was a clear attempt to institutionalize indirect control of Cuban economic and political affairs.

62. Dobson pp. 15-16.

63. Guggenheim p. 38.

64. Thomas A. Bailey, *A Diplomatic History of the American People* (Englewood Cliffs, NJ: Prentice-Hall, 1980), pp. 455-65. H. Wayne Morgan, "The deLome Letter: A New Appraisal," *The Historian* 26 (November 1963): 36-49.

65. Hyman G. Rickover, *How the Battlship 'Maine'Was Destroyed* (Washington, D.C.: Department of the Navy, Naval History Division, 1976), p. 1.

66. See Rickover.

67. Healy, *U.S. in Cuba* p. 17; Pratt, *America's Colonial Experiment* pp. 47-48.

68. Ibid. p. 18.

69. Charles G. Dawes, *A Journal of the McKinley Years* (Chicago: The Lakeside Press, 1950), pp. 146-53, gives an account of the Spanish reform proposals and McKinley's responses.

70. Guggenheim p. 43.

71. James Truslow Adams, *The March of Democracy* (New York: Charles Scribner's Sons, 1932), Vol. 2, p. 249.

72. Flint pp. 19-21, 119, 140-46. Frederick Funston, *Memories of Two Wars: Cuban and Philippine Experiences* (New York: Charles Scribner's Sons, 1914), pp. 31. 63-64, 71-79. William White *The Autobiography of William White* (New York: Macmillan, 1946), for description of funston; see also Thomas W. Crouch, *A Yankee Guerillero: Frederick Funston and the Cuban Insurrection, 1896-1897* (Memphis, RN: Memphis State University Press, 1975), esp. pp. 63-81.

A different perspective of the war is provided by George Bronson Rea in *Facts and Fakes About Cuba* (New York: George Munro's Sons, 1897). The New York *Herald*'s correspondent in Cuba and a man distinctly favorable to Spain, Rea was totally unimpressed with what he considered to be an inefficient rebel organization. Gomez, Rea argued, also possessed an arrogant yet lackadaisical command style. The lack of discipline among the rebels was unbelievable, Rea wrote, and their conduct of the war was alternately cowardly, lazy and brutal. Even Rea, however, held nothing but respect for Maceo, who, as Rea wrote, "heroically endeavored to attain his ideal by fighting for it." Unlike the other "opera-bouffe" Cuban generals, Rea believed, Maceo and his men carried the brunt of the way, leaving the other famous chiefs to lay around the hills and plains," where they passed the time "wrangling among themselves instead of trying to fight the Spaniards." Maceo, on the other hand, "devoted himself strictly to the campaign," and "never refused a fight." (pp. xix, xvi.).

73. Healy p. 22; all Healy cites hereafter are from *U.S. in Cuba*.

74. *Foreign Relations of the U.S., 1898*, pp. 750-60; also in *House Ex. Doc.*

(3743), 55th Cong., 3d Sess., No I, p. 704-712; Pratt, *America's Colonial Experiment* pp. 47-49.

75. Paul S. Holbo, "Presidential Leadership in Foreign Affairs: William McKinley and the Turpie-Foraker Amendment," *American Historical Review* 72 (July 1967): 1328.

76. Ibid. p. 1320. See also the Foraker speech on "Cuba," Wednesday, May 19, 1897, in the U.S. Senate. Published independently with floor debate in Washington, D.C.: no publisher, 1897.

77. Holbo pp. 1334 = 35.

78. Foner, I, p. 216.

79. LaFeber p. 400. The historical treatment of McKinley's role is enormously complicated and progressed through several distinctly recognizable phases. A superb history of these phases can be found in Joseph A. Fry, "William McKinley and the Coming of the Spanish-American War: A study of the Besmirching and Redemption of an Historical Image," *Diplomatic History* 3 (Winter 1979): 77-98.

The early history after the war was generally hostile to McKinley's role. Most scholars depicted him as caving in to popular and business pressure for an unwise war. See Albert G. Robinson, *Cuba and the Intervention* (London 1905), pp. 67-72, and Albert J. Enton, *International Law and Diplomacy of the Spanish-American War* (1908, reprint edition, Gloucester, Mass., 1968), pp.65-108. Such critical historians note that the Spanish had acceded to almost all of McKinley's demands and that, at the last minute and having almost solved his problem without war, McKinley, in the words of James Ford Rhodes, "abandoned his policy and went over to the war party;" see Rhodes, *The McKinley and Roosevelt Administrations, 1897-1909* (1922; reprint edition, Port Washington, NY, 1965), pp. 61-64; Ernest R. May, *Imperial Democracy: The Emergence of American as a Great Power* (new York, 1973), and Gerald F. Linderman, *The Mirror of War: American Society and the Spanish-American War* (Ann Arbor, 1974), Linderman concludes that in the end McKinley "did not choose war. . . he simply slipped over the line between peace and war in moving as slowly as possible to accommodate demands he could no longer resist" (p. 34). Robert Leckie points out that "by April 9 Spain had acceded to every American request except Cuban independence: she had released every prisoner, recalled General Weyler, recalled her offending ambassador, revoked the reconcentration order, agreed to furnish food for Cuba and finally granted an armistice"; Lecki p. 546.

A number of historians who emphasized economic motives saw McKinley as particularly dominated by business interests. This is true of Beard, LaFeber, Jenks, and some other economic historians cited earlier. See also Scott Nearing and Joseph Freeman, *Dollar Diplomacy: A Study in American Diplomacy* (New York, 1925), esp. pp. 250;-51.

Even the realist school of historians prominent in the late 1930s and 1940s condemned McKinley, in this case for pursuing an unnecessary war that began the process of overextension of American influence so dangerous to the country. See Hans J. Morgenthau, *In Defense of the National Interest: A Critical Examination of*

American Foreign Policy (New York, 1952), p. 23; and George F. Kennan, *American Diplomacy, 1900-1950* (Chicago, 1951), pp. 12-13. A later realist critique of U. S. foreign policy concluded that McKinley's harsh conditions "offered Spain no choice except capitulation to Cuba's request or war with the United States"; see Graebner pp. 327-29.

80. Gould p. 136. Other influential defenders of McKinley are Charles S. Olcott, *William McKinley* (Boston and New York, 1916), esp. 1: 394-400; John Layser Offner, "President McKinley and the Origins of the Spanish-American War," (PhD diss., Pennsylvania State University, 1957); and H. Wayne Morgan, *William McKinley and His America* (Syracuse, NY: Syracuse University Press, 1963). See also Morgan "William McKinley as a Political Leader," *Review of Politics* 28 (October 1966): 417-32, and Morgan, *America's Road to Empire: The War With Spain and Overseas Expansion* (New York: 1965).

Ironically, some later economic historians such as William Appleman Williams concede that McKinley, though eventually collapsing to business pressure, courageously withstood it for quite a while. See Williams, *The Tragedy of American Diplomacy* pp. 29-30, 37-38, 41-45.

81. Maurice Matloff, general editor, *American Military History* (Washington, D.C.: Office of the Chief of Military History, U.S. Army, revised edition 1973), pp. 322-42. The best independent history of the war is probably G. J. A. O'Toole, *The Spanish War: An American Epic—1898* (New York: W. W. Norton and Co., 1984). Nathan C. Green, *The War With Spain and Story of Spain and Cuba* (Baltimore: International News and Book Co., 1898), contains many interesting accounts and photographs.

82. Arthur H. Lee, "The Regulars at El Caney," *Scribner's Magazine* 24 (1898): 403-13. George Kennan, *Campaigning in Cuba* (New York: The Century Co., 1899), pp. 120-23. Theodore Roosevelt, *The Rough Riders* (New York: Charles Scribner's Sons, 1901), gives information about the battle at San Juan Hill, but Roosevelt's version must be taken with care. Naval engagement details can be found in Charles H. Brown, *The Correspondent's War: Journalists in the Spanish-American War* (New York: Charles Scribner's Sons, 1967), pp. 381-83.

83. Healy pp. 39-40; Charles Johnson Post, *The Little War of Private Post* (New York: Little, Brown, 1961), pp. 91-94; Fermoselle pp. 93-94. For an interesting description of the treatment accorded Cubans by Spanish troops after the surrender but before American troops and officials had taken over governance of the islands, see T. H. Slavens, *Incidents of Cuban Occupation by U. S. Troops, 1898* (no citation; Washington, D. C.: Library of Congress collection). Slavens, a retired U.S. Brigadier General, reported that Cuban rebels arriving in Havana before U.S. troops were treated harshly by the Spanish, and one boy was shot for shouting "Viva Cuba Libre." Other Cubans were killed in rioting that swept the city.

84. Louis A. Perez, Jr., "Supervision of a Protectorate: The United States and the Cuban Army, 1898-1908," *Hispanic American Historical Review* 52 (May, 1972): 250-71. for a summary of Spain's lost business see R. J. Harrison, "Catalan Business and the Loss of Cuba, 1898-1914," *Economic History Review* XXVII

(August 1974): 431-41. Regarding end of war see John Offner, "The United States and France: Ending the Spanish-American War," *Diplomatic History* 7 (Winter 1983): 1-21.

85. Healy p. 64.

86. Perez, "Supervision," op. cit. See also U.S. Army, *Annual Report of Brigadier General Fitzhugh Lee*(Quemados, Cuba, Adjutant General's Office, 1899), and Perez, "The Pursuit of Pacification: Banditry and the United States Occupation of Cuba, 1899-1902," *Journal of Latin American Studies* 18 (November 1986): 313-32.

87. J.D. Whelpley, "Cuba of To-Day and To-Morrow," *The Atlantic Monthly* 86 (July 1900): 45-52.

88. Herbert Pelham Williams, "The Outlook in Cuba," *The Atlantic Monthly* 83 (June 1899): 827.

89. Ibid. pp. 828-29; 834.

90. Ibid. p. 836.

91. Healy, p. 87.

92. Healy pp. 100-106.

93. Guggenheim p. 53.

94. Healy p. 114.

95. Philip C. Jessup, *Elihu Root* (New York: Dodd, Mead and Co., 2 Vols, 19398), vol, I., pp. 289, 303, 314-15, 318-20, 325. Emphasis mine.

96. Healy p. 121.

97. John G. Home, *The Life of Leonard Wood* (Garden City, NY: Doubleday, Page and Co., 1920), pp. 6-7. See also Ray S. Baker, "General Leonard Wood," *McClure's Magazine* XIV (February 1900): 368-79.

98. Healy p. 128, Guggenheim p. 62.

Chapter Five

1. Louis A. Perez, Jr., *Cuba Under the Platt Amendment, 1902-1934* (Pittsburgh, PA: University of Pittsburgh Press, 1986), p. 32, hereafter cited as Perez, *Cuba*; George Kennan, "Cuban Chaos," *Outlook* 63 (December 23, 1899): 1021-22; Walter Millis, *The Martial Spirit: A Study of Our War With Spain* (Boston: Houghton Mifflin, 1931), p. 362.

2. Perez, *Cuba*, p. 38.

3. Christopher Abel, "Concluding Perspectives," in Abel and Nissa Torrents, eds., *Jose Marti: Revolutionary Democrat* (Durham, NC: Duke University Press, 1986), p. 195. See also Orville H. Platt, "The Pacification of Cuba," *Independent* 53 (June 27, 1901).

4. Perez, *Cuba*, p. 40. Emphasis mine.

5. James Hitchman, "U.S. Control Over Cuban Sugar Production, 1898-1902," *Journal of Inter-American Studies and World Affairs* 12 (January 1970): 99.

6. Ibid. p. 106. In 1902 and 1903, U.S. companies controlled only 10 and 13 per cent, respectively, of the Cuban sugar market. This situation would change by the

1930s, however; see William O. Scroggs, "The American Investment in Latin America," *Foreign Affairs* 10 (April 1932): 502-4.

7. John G. Holme, *The Life of Leonard Wood* (Garden City, NY: Doubleday, Page and Co., 1920), p. 100.

8. Ibid. p. 130.

9. Ibid. pp. 90-97.

10. Hermann Hagedorn, *Leonard Wood: A Biography* (New York: Harper and Brothers, 1931), vol, I., p. 389. See both volumes for the general portrait of Wood.

11. Louis A. Perez, Jr., "Supervision of a Protectorate: The United States and the Cuban Army, 1898-1908," *Hispanic American Historical Review* 52 (May 1972): 250-71.

12. Philip c. Jessup, *Elihu Root* (New York: Dodd, Mead and Co., 1938), Vol. I, p. 323.

13. Louis L. Gould notes that the Democrats, after some debate at their convention, "decided that imperialism, 'growing out of the Spanish war, involves the very existence of the Republic. . . .We regard it as the paramount issue of this campaign." Gould, *The Presidency of William McKinley* (Lawrence: The Regents Press of Kansas, 1980), p. 220. Some U.S. commentators pointed to a post-office scandal to prove the evils of expansionism: over $100,000 had been embezzled from the Havana office alone, and those opposed to intervention said this and other scandals were evidence of the morally corrupting nature of imperialism.

14. Whitney T. Perkins, *Constraint of Empire: The United States and the Caribbean Interventions* (Westport, CT: Greenwood Press, 1981), pp. 7-12.

15. Louis A. Perez, Jr., *Cuba Between Empires, 1878-1902* (Pittsburgh, PA: University of Pittsburgh Press, 1983), pp. 303-28; Perez, *Cuba*, pp 214-332.

16. Charles Warren Currier, "Why Cuba Should Be Independent," *Forum* 30 (October 1900): 139-46. Wood also had private motives for speeding the convention process: he wanted to go to China fight the Boxers.

17. Ibid, pp. 145-46; Horatio Rubens, *Liberty: The Story of Cuba* (New York: 1932), p. 400.

18. Quoted in Philip Foner, *The Spanish-Cuban-American War and the Birth of American Imperialism, 1895-1902* (New York: Monthly Review Press, 1972), Vol. 2, pp. 541-421 See same source, pp. 540. For a description of these faults with the convention.

19. foner, II, p. 566.

20. Lejeune Cummins, "The Formation of the Platt Amendment," *The Americas* (April 1967): 386-87.

21. Ibid. p. 389; see also Jessup for a general description of Root's motives.

22. Foner, II, pp. 567-68.

23. Harry F. Guggenheim, *The United States and Cuba: A Study in International Relations* (Freeport, NY: Books for Libraries Press, 1969 reprint of 1934 edition) p. 71.

24. *Foreign Relations of the U.S., 1902*, pp. 320-22.

25. Perez, *Cuba*, p. 53.

26. James Scott, "The Origin and Purpose of the Platt Amendment," *American Journal of International Law* 3 (July 1914): 590-91.

27. Cosme de la Torriente, "The Platt Amendment," *Foreign Affairs* 8 (April 1930): 369.

28. Foner, II, pp. 585-887.

29. Guggenheim p. 192.

30. See Harry F. Guggenheim, "Amending the Platt Amendment," *Foreign Affairs* 12 (April 1934): 451. Guggenheim, like Torriente, recommended alterations in the amendment's wording and suggested abolishing articles two through six, including the intervention clause, altogether.

31. Torriente, p. 366.

32. Ibid. p. 378.

33. Pedro Capo-Rodriguez, "The Platt Amendment," *American Journal of International Law* 17 (October 1923): 764; Antoni Kapcia, "Cuban Populism and the Birth of the Myth of Marti," in Christopher Abel and Nissa Torrents, eds., *Jose Marti*, p. 35.

34. Ibid. p. 765.

35. "O." (Anonymous), "Cuba and the United States," *Foreign Affairs* 6 (January 1928): 231-45.

36. Ibid. p. 244-45.

37. Perez, *Cuba*, pp. 49. xvii.

38. Albert G. Robinson, *Cuba and the Intervention* (New York: Longmans, Green and Co., 1905), pp. 139-83. See also James H. Hitchman, *Leonard Wood and Cuban Independence, 1898-1902* (The Hague: Matinus Nighoff, 1971), and John M. Hunter, "Investment as a Factor in the Economic Development of Cuba, 1899-1935," *Inter-American Economic Affairs* 5 (Winter 1951): 82-100. An interesting description of the U.S.-established educational system in Cuba, which made strong attempts to Americanize the Cuban children and was thus a "cultural component of annexation," can be found in Louis A. Perez, Jr., "The Imperial Design: Politic and Pedagogy in Occupied Cuba, 1899-1902," *Cuban Studies* 12 (July 1982): 1-20.

39. See Louis A. Perez, Jr., "Insurrection, Intervention, and the Transformation of Land Tenure Systems in Cuba, 1895-1902," *Hispanic American Historical Review* 65 (May 1985): 229-54. Quote is from Dennis B. Wood, "The Long Revolution: Class Relations and Political Conflict in Cuba, 1868-1968," *Science and Society* 34 (Spring 1970): 17.

40. Kapcia pp. 35-36. for further descriptions of the phenomenon, see Fernando Ortiz, *Cuban Counterpoint*, trans. Harriet de Onis (New York: A. A. Knopf, 1947), pp. 53-54; Ramiro Guerra y Sanchez, *Sugar and Society in the Caribbean: An Economic History of Cuban Agriculture* (New Haven: Yale University Press, 1964); Lowry Nelson, "The Evolution of the Cuban Land System," *Land Economics* 25 (1949): 365-81; and Robert A. Batchelder, "The Evolution of Cuban Land Tenure and Its Relation to Certain Agro-Economic Problems," *South West Social Science* 22 (1952-53): 239-46. Lisandro Perez has documented that other

industries displayed a similar pattern; see "Iron Mining and Socio-Demographic Change in Eastern Cuba, 1884-1940," *Journal of Latin American Studies* 14 (November 1982).

Jorge Dominguez has concluded that U.S. corporations served to alienate power and interest from Cuba, "weakening not only the incumbent administration but the general authority of the state as well." Dominguez, *Cuba: Order and Revolution* (Cambridge, MA: Harvard University Press, 1978), p. 19; cf. p. 19-24.

41. Sheldon Liss, *Roots of Revolution: Radical Thought in Cuba* (Lincoln: University of Nebraska Press, 1987), pp. 58ff.

42. *Foreign Relations of the U.S. 1902*, pp. 322-38.

43. David A. Lockmiller, *Magoon in Cuba: A History of the Second Intervention, 1906-1909* (Chapel Hill: University of North Carolina Press, 1938), p. 18.

44. Charles E. Chapman, *A History of the Cuban Republic: A Study in Hispanic-American Politics* (New York: Octagon Books, 1969), pp. 152-75; *Foreign Relations of the U.S. 1902* pp. 338-58, 36068.

45. Lockmiller pp. 19-21. Kapcia (p. 33) concludes that "the consequences of the treaty were ambiguous, leading to security and prosperity on the one had, especially for the leading sugar sector, but also, on the other, to restrictions (of possible agrarian diversification and growth in manufacturing), [and] to a further 'Americanization' of the economy." He argues that the imbalance and "dislocations" thus caused helped spur the economic collapses of the 1920s.

46. Dana G. Munro, *Intervention and Dollar Diplomacy in the Caribbean, 1900-1921* (Princeton, NJ: Princeton University Press, 1964), p. 33.

47. Disputes over the Isle of Pines and sanitation laws were also resolved. *Foreign Relations of the U.S. 1903* p. 365; *1904*, pp. 240-45; *1905*, p. 286; *1906*, pp. 510-15; *1911*, pp. 135-37. For information on the health conditions—which U.S. Officials claimed proved the Cubans were not living up to their Platt Amendment responsibilities, see *Foreign Relations of the U.S. 1903*, pp 363-64; *1904*, pp. 242, 247-53; *1905*, pp. 262-76; *1906*, pp. 503-510; *1907*, Vol. I, p. 301.

48. See Albert Hart, ed., *Theodore Roosevelt Cyclopedia (New York: Roosevelt Memorial Association, 1941),* for this and other quotes on the issue.

49. Munro p. 65. The doctrine was enunciated in Roosevelt's December 6 annual message; see *House Documents* (4780), 58th Cong. 3d Sess. No. 1, pp. xli-ii.

50. *House Documents*, Ibid.

51. Howard C. Hill, *Roosevelt and the Caribbean* (New York: Russell and Russell, 1965), p. 69. Roosevelt's statements indicate that he was unwilling to simply cast Cuba loose when the island had no experience with self-government; he once remarked that "After having delivered the island from its oppressors, we refused to turn it loose offhand, with the certainty that it would sink back into chaos and savagery." At another time he said that "until order and liberty are secured, we must remain in the island to ensure them." While there, the United States attempted to educate Cubans about the processes of governing; then, "when we had laid deep and broad the foundations upon which civil liberty and national inde-

pendence must rest, we turned the island over to the hands of those whom its people had chosen as the founders of the new republic." See Hart, *Theodore Roosevelt Cyclopedia*, p. 127.

52. Munro pp. 65-66; Frederick W. Marks, "Morality as a Drive-Wheel in the Diplomacy of Theodore Roosevelt," *Diplomatic History* 2 (Winter 1978): 43-62.

53. Ibid. pp. 113-14.

54. *Foreign Relations of the U.S. 1905*, pp. 263-91.

55. Perez, Cuba, p. 92.

56. Hugh Thomas, *Cuba: The Pursuit of Freedom* (New York: Harper and Row, 1971), p., 480.

57. Lockmiller p. 28.

58. Lockmiller pp. 31-32; Chapman pp. 177-94. For a general summary of the period and details of U.S. occupation, see William H. Taft and Robert Bacon, "Cuban Pacification," Excerpt from the Report of the Secretary of War, 1906 (Washington, D.C.: GPO 1907).

59. See Gen. Faustino Guerra Puente, "Causes of the Cuban Insurrection," *North American Review* CLXXXII (September 21, 1906): 538-46.

60. Allen Millett, *The Politics of Intervention* (Ohio State University Press, 1968), p. 65; Lockmiller p. 49.

61. Hart p. 126.

62. Guggenheim, *The United States and Cuba*, p. 205 (all subsequent references to this author are to this book, unless otherwise noted); see also *Foreign Relations of the U.S. 1906, Vol. I, pp. xliv-xlv, 454-94; 1907*, vol. I, p. xliv.

63. Millett p. 60.

64. Millett pp 65-67. Funston estimated that the army would need a numerical advantage of five to one or more to achieve victory; Bell urged the immediate establishment of a network of spies to report on the movements of rebel units in case intervention proved necessary.

65. Millett pp. 72-73; Guggenheim p. 198; *Foreign Relations of the U.S. 1906*, pp. 480-88.

66. Guggenheim p. 199.

67. Millett P. 81. Of course, all sides wanted intervention because each thought the U.S. government would be on its side. Interestingly, the commander of the U.S. naval force, CDR William F. Fullam, had long advocated the abolishment of the Marines and their replacement with landing parties of sailors. He put his theory to the test in Cuba by landing men from the *Denver*, and this may have accounted for his over-enthusiasm. Dominguez, p. 15.

68. Ralph Eldin Minger, "William H. Taft and the U.S. Intervention in Cuba in 1906," *Hispanic American Historical Review* XLI (February 1961): 79-80; Hart pp. 126-27.

69. Henry F. Pringle, *The Life and Times of William Howard Taft* (New York: Farrar and Rinehart, Inc., 1939), Vol. I, pp. 305-10; Millett pp. 90-91; Perez, *Cuba*, p. 95.

70. Perez, *Cuba*, p. 100; Lockmiller p. 53; Minger p. 81.

71. Taft-Bacon *Report*, pp. 461ff, 507-512; Lockmiller p. 53; Millett p. 96-97.

72. Millett pp. 96-99.

73. Taft-Bacon *Report*, pp. 463-64.

74. For a pessimistic view of the Cuban situation, see William Inglis, "The Future in Cuba," *North American Review* 138 (November 16, 1906): 1037-40.

75. Millett p. 107; Lockmiller p. 59.

76. Millett p. 102.

77. Minger pp. 88-89. For other descriptions of the Cuban political scene at the time, see Frederick Adams, "Cuba, Its Condition and Outlook," *World's Work* CIII (November 1906): 8237-42; Charles Aguirre, "A Struggle for Cuban Liberty," *Independent* LXI (September 20, 1906): 664; Atherton Brownell, "The Cuban Republic on Trial, " *Review of Reviews* XXXIV (October 1906): 424-25; John G. Rockwood, "Rescuing Cuba from the Cubans," *World To-Day* XI (November 1906): 1199-1203; John W. Foster, "The Annexation of Cuba," *Independent* LXI (October 25, 1906): 965-68; and Aldama Carrillo, "The Cuban Government's Side," *Independent* LXI (September 10, 1906): 664.

78. Lockmiller p. 98.

79. Lockmiller pp. 93-121, 146-73; Millett pp. 196-215.

80. Millett pp. 161-89, esp. p. 172.

81. See Perez, "Supervision of a Protectorate," op. cit.

82. Millett pp. 247-48.

83. Millett pp. 248-49.

84. Charles E. Magoon, *Report on the Law of Civil Government in Territory Subject to Military Occupation by the Military Forces of the United States* (Washington, D.C.: GPO 1902), pp. 9-10

85. Hudson Strode, *The Pageant of Cuba* (London: Jarrold's Publishers, 1935), p. 221.

86. Lockmiller pp. 197-223; Thomas pp. 483-86.

87. Lockmiller p. 214; Millett p. 149.

88. "The Restoration of Cuban Self-Government," *The American Journal of International Law* 3 (April 1909): 4431-34.

89. Hill p. 105.

90. Millett P. 254.

91. Chapman, "New Corollaries," p. 174.

92. Wilfrid Hardy Callcott, *The Caribbean Policy of the United States, 1890-1920* (New York: Octagon Books, 1977), pp. 258-59.

93. Munro, p. 163; Bemis, *American Secretaries*, Vol. 10, pp. 337-40. See also Burton I. Kaufman, "United States Trade and Latin America: The Wilson Years," *The Journal of American History* 58 (September 1971): 342-63.

94. Louis A. Perez, Jr., "Dollar Diplomacy, Preventive Intervention, and the Platt Amendment in Cuba, 1909-1912," *Inter-American Economic Affairs* 38 (Autumn 1984): 22-44.

95. Perez, *Cuba*, 118.

96. Ibid. p. 136. See also Perez, "Dollar Diplomacy," p. 44.

97. Dominguez pp. 48-49; Thomas pp. 514-24; Munro pp. 476-80.

98. *Foreign Relations of the U.S. 1910*, pp. 416-17.

99. Lester D. Langley, *The Cuban Policy of the United States: A Brief History* (New York: John Wiley and Sons, 1968), p. 130.

100. *Foreign Relations of the U.S. 1915*, p. xi.

101. George Baker, "The Wilson Administration and Cuba, 1913-1921," *Mid-America* 46 (January 1964): 49.

102. Ibid. p. 50.

103. :Cuban Observations," *Review of Reviews* 49 (April 19141).

104. Baker p. 54. See also Joseph C. Gilligan, "The Cuban Sugar Industry and the American Market, 1914-1922: A Study in Economic Dependence," MA Dissertation, Georgetown University, May 1964.

105. Louis A. Perez, Jr., *Intervention, Revolution, and Politics in Cuba, 1913-1921* (Pittsburgh, PA: University of Pittsburgh Press, 1978), pp. 5-6.

106. Ibid. P. 10.

107. Leo J. Meyer, "The United States and the Cuban Revolution of 1917," *Hispanic American Historical Review* 10 (February 1930): 139; Baker pp. 53-56.

108. Meyer pp. 141-43.

109. Russell H. Fitzgibbon, *Cuba and the United States, 1900-1935* (Menasha, WI: George Banta Publishing Co., 1935), pp. 158-59.

110. *Foreign Relations of the U.S. 1917*, p. 366.

111. Meyer p. 153; Baker p. 53.

112. Meyer pp. 155-56.

113. *Foreign Relations of the U.S. 1917*, pp. 387-88.

114. Ibid. p. 407.

115. Fitzgibbon p. 160.

116. See James Brown Scott, "The Attitude of the United States Toward Political Disturbances in Cuba," *The American Journal of International Law* 11 (April 1917): 422-23. This article provides a benign view of the intervention, noting that "the United States did not wish to intervene in Cuba" and did not "intend to allow itself to be forced to intervene." Scott argues that the avoidance of a full-scale invasion would help "Cuba settle its own differences without calling in the guarantor of its independence."

Regarding the insurrection itself, see Louis A. Perez, Jr., "'La Chambelona': Political Protest, Sugar and Social Banditry in cuba, 1914-17," *Inter-American Economic Affairs* XXXI (Spring 1978): 3-28. The Liberals were so confident of success in its early stages, he notes, that they viewed the revolution as "something of a musical jamboree, in which street dancing, strolling musicians, and minstrel orchestras would lead the triumphant liberal advance on Havana." (p. 5).

117. Mario G. Menocal, "Cuba's Part in the World War," *Current History* 9 (November 1918): 315; Fitzgibbon pp. 161-62.

118. Meyer p. 163; see also Leland Jenks, *Our Cuban Colony: A Study in*

Sugar (New York: Vanguard Press, 1928), pp. 175-205, and Rt. Rev. H.R. Hulse, "The Crisis in Cuba," *North American Review* 230 (July 1930): 72.

119. *Foreign Relations of the U.S. 1918*, pp. 276-358.

120. *Foreign Relations of the U.S. 1919*, Vol. II, pp. 1-84, contains the Crowder report and correspondence; see also Ibid. *1920*, pp. 1-69; Meyer p. 163.

121. Baker p. 61; Jenks pp. 229-245.

122. Fitzgibbon pp. 165-70. The financial crisis also created a huge capital shortage i n Cuba. Ships bearing imports sat in Cuban ports, unable to unload their cargoes because no one on the island had the cash to pay for them. This situation was aggravated by the fact that American companies, relieved of the burdens of World War I, finally began delivering thousands of backlogged Cuban orders for which no one was able to pay.

See also Louis A. Perez, Jr., "Capital, Bureaucrats, and Policy: The Economic Contours of United States-Cuban Relations, 1916-1921," *Inter-American Economic Affairs XXIX* (Summer 1975): 65-80. Perez stressed the role of Norman Davis, a prominent Democrat who had made a fortune in Cuba and who retained close ties to business interests on the island. By 1920, with Wilson paralyzed, control over many sub-areas of policy was devolving upon lower officials, and Davis influenced U.S. choices. Perez also notes that the man in charge of the 1919 American census in Cuba—Maj. Harold Stepheson—set up a sugar corporation there with $25 million in capital from investors: Stephenson aided the Conservatives, who courted his favor, with irregularities in the census. See also Normal H. Davis, "Wanted: A Consistent Latin American Policy," *Foreign Affairs* IX (July 1931).

123. Ibid pp. 170-81.

124. See George Navarrette, *The Latin American Policy of Charles Evans Hughes* (Ann Arbor, MI: University Microfilms, Inc., 1974; copy of PhD dissertation at University of California at Berkeley, 1965), pp. 145-230; David Danelski and Joseph S., Tulchin, *The Autobiographical Notes of Charles Evans Hughes* (Cambridge, MA: Harvard University Press, 1973); *Foreign Relations of the U.S. 1923*, Vol. I, pp. 837-854.

125. Kapcia pp. 39-40; Fitzgibbon p. 184.

126. Fitzgibbon P. 187; Jules Benjamin, *The United States and Cuba: Hegemony and Dependent Development, 1880-1934* (Pittsburgh, PA: University of Pittsburgh Press, 1977), p. 50. Others gave favorable reviews to Machado after one term. Graham Stuart wrote that "President Machado has made an extraordinary effort to give Cuba an honest and efficient administration." *Latin America and the United States* (New York: The Century Co., 1928), p. 25. Chester Lloyd Jones argued that "Machado. . .has brought about a decided improvement in the conduct of public affairs which is to be hoped is earnest of what may be expected in future administrations;" see "The Development of the Caribbean," in *The United States and the Caribbean* (Chicago: University of Chicago Press, 1929), pp. 20-21. Ramon Ruiz recognized that many said this at the time, and he himself concludes that Machado's early accomplishments were "impressive, a point almost always overlooked by his critics. Later financial crises forced Machado to rule with an "iron

fist." Ruiz, *Cuba: The Making of a Revolution* (New York: W. W. Norton and Co., 1968), pp. 77-78m 101-2.

127. Fitzgibbon pp. 1888-89.

128. Hulse pp. 72-73; Fitzgibbon p. 191. For a description of the Pan-American conference held at this time and resulting in U.S. policy, see Walter Lippman, "Second Thoughts on Havana," *Foreign Affairs* 6 (July 1928): 541-54.

129. Benjamin pp 34, 43; Hulse pp. 71-75. For a general summary see Thomas Clemens, "U.S. Diplomatic Relations With Cuba, 1928-1934," MA Dissertation, Georgetown University, January 1965.

Chapter Six

1. For a short summary of this period. see Raymond C. Buell, "The Caribbean Situation: Cuba and Haiti," *Foreign Policy Reports* 9 (June 21, 1933).

2. Ernest Gruening, "Cuba Under the Machado Regime," *Current History* 34 (May 1931): 214-19.

3. Russell B. Porter, "Cuba Under President Machado," *Current History* 38 (April 1933): 29.

4. Ibid. p. 30; see also Carleton Beals, *The Crime of Cuba* (Philadelphia: J.C. Lippincott and Co., 1933), pp. 237-335. Beals concluded that the "hands-off" U.S. Policy wa a farce; in fact, the "policeman's club" of the Platt Amendment prevented independence. U.S. business and financial interests, he argued, dictated national policy. And Guggenheim, who had close ties to American business, wa a tool of this policy.

5. Charles E. Chapman, "New Corollaries of the Monroe Doctrine, With Especial Reference to the Relations of the United States With Cuba," *University of California Chronicle* 33 (April 1931): 180.

6. Ibid, pp. 181-82. See also Francis Jackman, "America's Cuba Policy During the Period of the Machado Regime," PhD Dissertation, Catholic University, 1964.

7. Orestes Ferrara and William Walling, "President Machado's Administration of Cuba," *Current History* 32 (May 1930): 257-67.

8. See *Congressional Record*, 72nd Cong., lst Sess., Vol. 75, Part 7, p. 7874; 73rd Cong., lst Sess. Vol. 77, Part 3, pp. 289lff.

9. Lorenzo Alvarez (pseudonym), "'Where is the Dynamite?' An Incident of Life Under Machado," *Nation* 136 (June 14, 1933); Ruby Hart Phillips, *Cuba: Island of Paradox* (New York: McDowell, Obolensky, n.d.), pp. 7-8.

10. Alexander DeConde, *Herbert Hoover's Latin-American Policy* (New York: Octagon Books, 1970), pp. 13-24.

11. Jules Robert Benjamin, *The United States and Cuba: Hegemony and Dependent Development, 1880-1934* (Pittsburgh, PA: University of Pittsburgh Press, 1977), pp. 67-68; DeConde pp. 103 10.

12. For a text of a Stimson statement on non-intervention, see Ruhl J. Bartlett, ed., *The Record of American Diplomacy* (New York: Alfred A. Knopf, 1948), pp. 549-50.

13. Norman Davis, "Wanted: A Consistent Latin American Policy," *Foreign Affairs* 9 (July 1931): 547-68. Note the similarity of this debate to the Carter-Reagan human rights debate of the late 1970s and early 1980s. Davis' motivations are open to question, inasmuch as he was the same person mentioned in Chapter Five who had strong economic ties to Cuba. It could well have ben that Davis urged an interventionist U.S. approach because of his tie to those interests.

14. Chapman, "New Corollaries," p. 161. See also Robert H. Ferrell, *American Diplomacy in the Great Depression: Hoover-Stimson Foreign Policy, 1929-1933* (New York: Archon Books, 1969), esp. Chapter 13, "Latin America."

15. Chapman, "New Corollaries," pp. 180ff; Bryce Wood, *The Making of the Good Neighbor Policy* (New York: Columbia University Press, 1961), p. 55; cf. pp. 51-59 of same for Stimson's role.

16. Beals pp. 323, 327-54; Ramon E. Ruiz, *Cuba: The Making of a Revolution* (New York: W. W. Norton and Co., 1968), pp. 97-99.

17. Ferrell pp. 215-16.

18. Russell H. Fitzgibbon, *Cuba and the United States, 1900-1935* (Menasha, WI: George Banta Publishing Co., 1935), p. 193.

19. Luis Aguilar, *Cuba 1933: Prologue to Revolution* (Ithaca, NY: Cornell University Press, 1972), pp. 69-72; Sheldon Liss, *Roots of Revolution: Radical Thought in Cuba* (Lincoln, University of Nebraska Press, 1987), pp. 62-103.

20. Aguilar p. 76; Jaime Suchlicki, "Stirrings of Cuban Nationalism: The Student Generation of 1930," *Journal of Inter-American Studies* 10 (July 1968): 350-68; Antoni Kapcia, "Cuban Populism and the Birth of the Myth of Marti," in Christopher Abel and Nissa Torrents, eds., *Jose Marti: Revolutionary Democrat* (Durham, NC: Duke University Press, 1986), pp. 37-47.

21. Hubert Herring, "Can Cuba Save Herself?" *Current History* 39 (November 1933): 153; Kapcia p. 48.

22. Benjamin pp. 60-61; Hugh Thomas, *Cuba: The Pursuit of Freedom* (Nw York: Harper and Row, 1971), p. 594.

23. Kapcia pp. 50-51; Buell pp. 86-87; Benjamin p. 61. Buell notes that the key emphasis of the ABC's program was economic reformism, designed in part to counter the dominance of U.S. corporations; the ABC called for a complete redistribution of wealth to "place[e] the wealth of the island in the hands of the Cuban people." Another commentator, however, has written that the ABC was a "bourgeois-landowner opposition" to Machado, and that it "served the reactionary bourgeoisie"; see Fabio Grobart, "The Cuban Working Class Movement From 1925-1933," *Science and Society* 39 (Spring 1975): 93-94.

24. Aguilar p. 80; Grobart pp. 73-103.

25. Aguilar p. 84; se also Luis Aguilar, ed., *Marxism in Latin America* (Philadelphia, PA: Temple University Press, 1978); and James O'Connor, *The Origins of Socialism in Cuba* (Ithaca: Cornell University Press, 1970), pp. 1-36.

26. Benjamin pp. 62-63; Aguilar, *Cuba 1933*, pp. 85-87. All Subsequent references to Aguilar are to this work.

27. Fitzgibbon p. 195.

28. Edward O. Guerrant, *Roosevelt's Good Neighbor Policy* (Albuquerque: University of New Mexico Press, 1950); Wood; and Alan Nevins, *The New Deal and World Affairs: A Chronicle of International Affairs, 1933-1945* (New Haven, CT: Yale University Press, 1950), esp. pp. 26-39.

29. Irwin F. Gellman, *Roosevelt and Batista: Good Neighbor Diplomacy in Cuba, 1933-1945* (Albuquerque: University of New Mexico Press, 1973), p. 11.

30. Jules L. Benjamin, "The New Deal, Cuba, and the Rise of A Global Foreign Economic Policy," *Business History Review* LI (Spring 1977): 57-78.

31. See cite above at n. 28. and also Franklin D. Roosevelt, "Our Foreign Policy: A Democratic View," *Foreign Affairs* 6 (July 1928): 573-86.

32. Gellman pp.11-12.

33. Benjamin, *The United States and Cuba*, p. 85. All subsequent references to Benjamin refer to this book.

34. Gellman p. 14.

35. Benjamin pp. 73-77.

36. Benjamin pp. 90-92.

37. *Foreign Relations of the U.S. 1933*, V, pp. 283-85.

38. Benjamin pp. 90-95; Aguilar pp. 129-31; Wood, p. 59; *Foreign Relations of the U.S. 1933*, V, p. 278.

39. Aguilar pp. 132-33; Wood pp. 62-69.

40. Thompson is cited in Ruiz, p. 86; Ruiz agrees. See also Aguilar pp. 134-35.

41. Charles W. Hackett, "Cuban Peace Prospects," *Current History* 38 (August 1933): 594; see also by the same author "American Mediation in Cuba," and "Cuba Lives Through Another Revolt," in *Current History*, September 1933 and January 1934, respectively.

42. E. David Cronon, "Interpreting the Good Neighbor Policy: The Cuban Crisis of 1933," *Hispanic American Historical Review* 39 (November 1959): 540; Aguilar pp. 140-43.

44. Benjamin pp. 101-2.

45. Hubert Herring, "The downfall of Machado," *Current History* 39 (October 1933): 14; Phillips, *Sideshow*, pp. 51-58.

46. Herring, "Downfall," p. 14; *Foreign Relations of the U.S. 1933*, V, pp. 336-37; Cronon pp. 540-41.

47. Aguilar pp. 148-49; Herring, "Downfall," p. 16; Phillips, *Sideshow*, pp. 58-62; Jorge I. Dominguez, *Cuba: Order and Revolution* (Cambridge: Harvard University Press, 1978), pp. 25-33.

48. Aguilar pp. 149-50.

49. See Louis A. Perez, Jr., "Army Politics, Diplomacy, and the Collapse of the Cuban Officer Corps: The 'Sergeants Revolt' of 1933," *Journal of Latin American Studies* 6 (May 1974): 59-76. Perez ably explicates the army's motives in this act, and notes the social divisions between offices and enlisted, and the close civilian/enlisted relations, which prompted a military repudiation of the government. Perez also notes that U.S. pressure was key in persuading senior officers

not to rejoin the army and to maintain a stiff line in compromise talks.

50. Cronon pp. 543-44.

51. *Foreign Relations of the U.S. 1933*, V, pp. 354-59; Cronon p. 544.

52. Herring, "Downfall"; Gellman pp. 18, 30-31; Phillips *Sideshow* pp. 63-77.

53. Wood pp. 68-69.

54. Benjamin p. 111.

55. Aguilar p. 153; Gellman pp. 34-38; Wood pp. 69-71.

56. Aguilar pp. 154-55.

57. Gellman p. 37.

58. Herring, "Downfall," p. 19.

59. Herring, "Can Cuba Save Herself?" p. 152.

60. Benjamin p. 137; Gellman p. 44. The Pentarchy was composed of Grau, Porforio Franco, Jose Miguel Irisarri, Sergio Carbo, and Guillermo Portela.

61. Benjamin p. 139; Wood p. 71; Gellman pp. 44-45.

62. Gellman pp. 46-48; wood pp. 72-76.

63. *Foreign Relations of the U.S. 1933*, V, p. 389; Cronon pp. 547-49. As these sources document, Welles for the next several days continued to promote the idea of intervention, first calling for the landing of a "considerable force" at Havana, and later contending that the Cuban army mutiny constituted a Platt Amendment-based grounds for interference. Later, believing questionable reports about a renewed upsurge of support for Cespedes, Welles asked for a small "policing force" to assist Cespedes' return to power. These requests were either ignored or rejected by Washington.

64. Gellman p. 56.

65. Wood pp. 81-98; Herring, "Can Cuba Save Herself?" p. 154; Cronon pp. 553-55; *Foreign Relations of the U.S. 1933*, V, pp. 396-410; Benjamin pp. 153-55.

66. Gellman p. 60.

67. Herring "Can Cuba Save Herself?" pp. 154-56, explains that the U.S. government had two primary doubts about Grau: first, he seemed to lack majority support, especially among the ABC, the Communists, left-wing labor, and of course conservatives and business; and second, Grau seemed clearly unable to maintain order. The administration cited these and other reasons when explaining its decision not to grant recognition.

68. *Foreign Relations of the U.S. 1933*, V, pp. 451-49; Cronon pp. 554-55; Benjamin p. 161; Gellman pp. 62-64.

69. *Foreign Relations of the U.S. 1933*, V. pp. 469-71; Wood pp. 93-94.

70. *Foreign Relations of the U.S. 1933*, V. p. 489.

71. Aguilar p. 176; Gellman pp. 65-83.

72. Charles Hackett, "Cuba Lives Through Another Revolt," *Current History* 39 (January 1934): 4462-64.

73. Cronon pp. 562-63; Wood pp. 98-100.

74. Gellman pp. 57-58, 84-85; Aguilar p. 181; Benjamin p. 168. Guiteras founded a radical group Joven Cuba. Guiteras' ideas were not as systematically expressed as those of Marti or others; Joven Cuba possessed a vaguer, more

romantic flavor than many other opposition groups. It was radical and anti-imperialist in its economic outlook, and favored income redistribution and demilitarization in Cuba. Guiteras would remain an influential figure in Cuba long after hi death in 1935, and his ideas strongly influenced Castro. Kapcia, pp. 51-52.

75. Aguilar p. 182; Gellman pp. 84-85; Benjamin p. 169.

76. Cronon pp. 565-67. Quote from recent analysts is from Warren Hinckle and William W. Turner, *The Fish is Red: The Story of the Secret War Against Castro* (New York: Harper and Row, 1981), p. 11.

77. Herring, "Downfall," p. 24.

78. See generally Gellman pp. 8-84.

79. Benjamin pp. 148-49. Ruiz (p. 90) argues that Welles followed the policies de did because he had "no empathy with the revolution:' he was a "cold, phlegmatic man" who had "nothing in common with the bold, brash, and youthful rebels." These same critiques would later be leveled at Philip Bonsal, a quiet and proper diplomat totally out of his element trying to deal with Castro and the *Barbudos*.

80. Ruiz p. 84.

81. Jorge Manach, "Revolution in Cuba"', *Foreign Affairs* 12 (October 1933): 49-50, 55-56.

82. Quoted in Carlos Franqui, *Family Portrait With Fidel* (New York: Vintage Books, 1984), p. 5.

Chapter Seven

1. Ruby Hart Phillips, *Cuban Sideshow* (Havana: Cuban Press, 1935), pp. 289-90.

2. Hubert Herring, "Another Chance for Cuba," *Current History* 39 (March 1934): 660.

3. Phillips pp. 307, 293.

4. See "Quick Action Needed in Cuba," *The Christian Century* 51 (January 31, 1934): 140; "Mendieta Lacks Support," *The New Republic* 77 (January 31, 1934): 319-20; and "Cuba: Mendieta's Inauguration," *Newsweek*, January 27, 1934, p. 15.

5. Hugh Thomas, *Cuba, Pursuit of Freedom* (New York: Harper and Row, 1971), pp. 691-97.

6. Quotes are from Jorge I. Dominguez, *Cuba: Order and Revolution* (Cambridge, MA: Harvard University Press, 1978), pp. 78-79. Information on labor laws from Jose Manuel Casanova, Executive Director of the Inter-American Development Bank, and a former mill owner in Cuba; Casanova's father had been head of the sugar industry in Cuba for many years. Interview with the author, January 15, 1988. James Monahan and Kenneth O. Gilmore, *The Great Deception* (New York: Farrar, Strauss and Co., 1963), pp. 40-41, which, despite its partisanship, contains some quite good interview materials with Cubans who fled Castro's radicalization; and International Commission of Jurists, *Cuba and the Rule of Law* (Geneva: ICJ, 1962). See also Richard Barry, "Cuba Boils Again—With Two Dictators," *Literary*

Digest 118 (October 20, 1934): 17.

7. See "Mendieta's Government," *The New Republic* 77 (March 21, 1934): 142; Charles Hackett, "The Cuban Turmoil," *Current History* 40 (June 1934): 333-34; Hackett, "Cabinet Trouble in Cuba," *Current History* 40 (September 1934); and Hubert Herring, "Cuba's Election Campaign," *Current History* 41 (February 1935): 602-4.

Hugh Thomas has noted that the prevalence of violence in Cuba after 1933 had strong roots in the failure of that year's revolution. "The events of 1933," he explains, "finally created a revolutionary generation which, despite some real achievements, regarded itself as thwarted, and its appetite whetted for both power and social change, carried on its desires and its methods," especially "the use of weapons. . . For the revolutionary organizations which helped to overthrow Machado never properly disbanded or laid down their arms." (p. 688).

8. Irwin F. Gellman, *Roosevelt and Batista: Good Neighbor Diplomacy in Cuba, 1933-1945* (Albuquerque: University of New Mexico Press, 1973), pp. 997-112; Thomas p. 695.

9. Edward O. Guerrant, *Roosevelt's Good Neighbor Policy* (Albuquerque: University of New Mexico Press, 1950) p. 5. See also Lester H. Woolsey, "The New Cuban Treaty," *American Journal of International Law* 28 (July 1934): 530-34; Julius W. Pratt, *Cordell Hull*, Vol. I, which is Vol. XII of Samuel Flagg Bemis, et., *American Secretaries of State and Their Diplomacy* (New York: Coopers' Square Publishers, 1964), pp. 153-54, 164-65; Gellman pp. 105-7.

10. Mario Lazo, *Dagger in the Heart: American Policy Failures in Cuba* (New York: Funk and Wagnalls, 1968), p. 37.

11. Pratt, *Cordell Hull*, pp. 113-114, 119; Gellman pp. 113-16; Ramon E. Ruiz, *Cuba: The Making of a REvolution* (Nw York: W. W. Norton and Co., 1968), p. 95.

12. Gellman pp. 101-3; Hugh Thomas, *Cuba: The Pursuit of Freedom* (New York: Harper and Row, 1971), p. 696; Robert F. Smith, *The United States and Cuba: Business and Diplomacy, 1917-1960* (New York: Bookman Associates, 1960), pp. 144, 163; John Lloyd Mecham, *Survey of U.S.-Latin American Relations* (Boston: Houghton-Mifflin, 1965), p. 122.

13. Phillips, *Sideshow*, p. 312.

14. Ibid. p. 315.

15. Lazo p. 56; Mecham pp. 123-24.

16. Raymond Buell et al., *Problems of the New Cuba: Report of the Commission on Cuban Affairs* (New York: Foreign Policy Association, 1935), esp. pp. 42-128 and 443-502; Ruiz pp. 97-99; Gellman p. 126; Thomas p. 699.

17. See Hubert Herring, "Cuba Regains a Constitution," *Current History* 41 (August 1935): 526-28; Carleton Beals, "New Machado in Cuba," *Nation* 141 (August 7, 1935): 152-54; and three other *Current History* articles by Herring: "The Kettle Simmers," 43 (October 1935): 79-80; "Cuba's Political Parties," 43 (December 1935); and "Cuban Politics," 43 (Janaury 1936): 415-16.

18. *Foreign Relations of the U.S. 1935*, Vol. IV, pp. 476-77.

19. See Gellman pp. 134-37; Thomas pp. 701-2; and Russell Fitzgibbon and

Max Healy, "Cuban Elections of 1936," *American Political Science Review* 30 (August 1936): 724-35.

20. Fitzgibbon and Healy, p. 735.

21.*Foreign Relations of the U.S. 1936*, V, pp. 446-48, 893-900, 906-7, and 914-30.

22. Gellman pp. 147-49. The rural school bill showed Batista's populism— though he wanted to augment the strength of his army he also wanted to help poor Cubans, and he was a "reformer in practice"; Ruiz p. 104. These progressive tendencies were also displayed in Batista's 1949 criticism of Prio's loans from the United States and by Batista's endorsement of the anti-U.S. Peace Congress in Mexico; Thomas pp. 762-63.

23. Lazo p. 53.

24. One result of this process was the arrogation of power in the hands of the president; Batista's strength meant that unchecked executive power became the norm. Jorge Dominguez has argued that this worked to "facilitat[e] corruption and the abuse of power" and to further undermine the already questionable legitimacy of the political process; Dominquez pp. 79-82.

25. Gellman pp. 154-58; Hubert Herring, "Cuba Under a New President," *Current History* 43 (March 1936): 636.

26. Gerald K. Hains, "Under the Eagle's Wing: The Franklin Roosevelt Administration Forges an American Hemisphere," *Diplomatic History* 1 (Fall 1977): 373-88; Gellman pp. 160-63.

27. Lazo pp. 56-57.

28. *Foreign Relations of the U.S. 1938*, V, pp. 472-90; *1940*, V, pp. 763-72; Smith pp. 171-75.

29. Gellman pp. 169-72; Mecham pp. 133-34.

30. Willard L. Beulac, *Career Ambassador* (New York: The McMillan Company, 1951), pp. 144-51.

31.*Foreign Relations of the U.S. 1940* V, pp. 737-40.

32. Gellman pp. 182-83; Thomas pp. 718-19; Lazo p. 61. Ruiz contends that Batista ruled "probably. . .with no more fraud than usual;" p. 109.

33. Smith pp. 165-76.

34. Philip G. Wright, *The Cuban Situation and Our Treaty Relations* (Washington, D.C.: The Brookings Institution, 1931), p. 173.

35. Gellman pp. 185-86; Thomas p. 736.

36. Gellman pp. 187-88; Thomas pp. 724-26; Lazo pp. 61-62.

37. *Foreign Relations of the U.S. 1941*, VII, pp. 127-95; *1942*, VI, pp. 290-315; *1943*, VI pp. 240-59: *1944*, VII, pp. 405-71; *1945*, IC, pp. 917-5.

38. Ibid. *1941*, VII, pp. 97-115, 214-16, 222; *1942*, VI, pp. 253-89; *1943*, VI, pp. 135-51; *1944*, VII, pp. 892-905; *1945*, IX, pp. 896-916; Casanova interview, January 15, 1988; Gellman pp. 193-201; Mecham pp. 210, 213, 218-19, 226; Cosme de la Torriente, "Cuba, American and the War," *Foreign Affairs* 19 (October 1940): 145-55; Lazo pp. 62-63.

39. Gellman p. 4; Luis E. Aguilar,*Cuba 1933: Prologue to Revolution* (Ithaca, NY: Cornell University Press, 1972), pp. 225-26.

40. Thomas pp. 719-21, 724-36; Lazo pp. 59-61; Ruiz p. 102.

41. Thomas p. 720.

42. Lazo pp. 64ff; William S. Stokes, "The 'Cuban Revolution' and the Presidential Elections of 1948," *Hispanic American Historical Review* 31 (February 1951): 38-40; "Cuba Elects Grau," *Life*, June 26, 1944, pp. 81-84; W. A. Roberts, "Cuba Goes Democratic," *American Mercury*, October 1944 pp. 450-56; and "Cuban Upset," *Newsweek*, June 12, 1944, p. 52.

43. Morris H. Morley, *The Imperial State and Revolution: The United States and Cuba, 1852-1986* (Cambridge: Cambridge University Press, 1987), pp. 40-46.

44. Aguilar p. 240.

45. Thomas p. 737.

46. Lazo p. 61.

47. Ibid p. 65; Teresa Casuso, *Cuba and Castro*, trans. Elmer Grossberg (New York: Random House, 1961), p. 85; Stokes pp. 41-42. About Grau's personal innocence, Jose Manuel Casanova remarked:

> No one used to say that Grau got the millions. Grau always lived in his same house—he was a professional, and he had a nice house, but he always lived there, before and after [he was president] and always. He was a modest man. So if someone who knew the story told me that that man didn't steal, I would accept it as true. But everyone else stole, and he was so weak that he never intervened in anything that happened around him.
>
> (Interview with the author, January 15, 1988)

48. See information from *Confidential U.S. State Department files, Cuba, 1945-1949* (Frederick, MD: University Publications of America, 1987). This is a microfilm collection, hereafter referred to as *State Department Files*, the years (e.g. 1945-49), and reel and frame number on the microfilm. See September 21, 1945 letter to State from U.S. Ambassador R. Henry Norweb, reel 28 frame 496; January 11, 1946 embassy memo, reel 28 frame 506; Norweb dispatch to State, September 12, 1946, reel 28 frames 520-28; and H. Bartlett Wells (the second secretary of the embassy in Havana), "A Study in Cuban-American Relations: Some Causes of Tension and Suggested Approaches," September 8, 1947, reel 28 frames 541-70.

Casanova tells an interesting story about one mechanism used the United States to make its desire known.

> I remember at one point the United States embassy called my father, whom they considered a friend, to a meeting, and he took me there. They gave us a lecture on U.S. interest and so on, and [how they] hoped that the president [Grau] would get the message. My father had me take everything down. Then he took me over to see President Grau. I was about fourteen. And my father said,] "Oh, I'm so proud of my son, United States educated, speaks English so well. As a matter of fact, we were just at the American embassy, and he understands everything. Why don't you tell him what you heard over there!" So here was Grau, smiling, a very sociable call we were making here, and all of a sudden I started talking, translating into Spanish, and his face started changing as the message came. And when I finished, my father said quickly, "Well, Mr. President, I think we have to go, we've infringed on your time." We quickly said good-bye, and took off. The mes-

sage was laid, and I was the conduit at fourteen years old.

(Interview with the author, January 15, 1988.)

49. Thomas pp. 739-47; *Foreign Relations of the U.S. 1945*, IX, pp. 969-73.

50. Thomas p. 751; Stokes pp. 42-44.

51. Lazo p. 70. See Stokes generally for an in-depth analysis of the election. Writing in 1951, he noted that the Cuban "revolution" of 1933 had not yet been a revolution at all, but merely a reform of the status quo. But if "reform zeal" could be practiced by the Autenticos, he argued, "It is possible that. . .Cuba might yet experience revolution, but by the slower process of evolution." (p. 79) But this did not occur, and within two years after these words were written Castro had attacked the Moncada barracks.

52. Aguilar P. 243; Thomas pp. 757-61; Casanova interview; Casuso p. 88.

53. *State Department Files*, 1945-49; dispatch from Lansing Collins at embassy to State, August 17, 1948, reel 28 frame 85. *State Department Files*, 1950-1954; embassy dispatch to State, January 16, 1951, reel 38 frames 3-4; "Department of State Policy Statement: Cuba," January 11, 1951, reel 39 frames 158-69; Beaulac dispatches, October 19, 1971, reel 39 frames 191-92, and November 15, 1951, reel 39 frame 213-15.

54. Ibid.

55. *State Department Files*, 1945-49, general dispatches on the Dominican Republic issues, reel 28 frames 94ff.

56. "Department of State Policy Statement: Cuba," Ibid. from note 54, p. 3. Thomas J. Heston has made an excellent analysis of the 1948 Sugar Act decision; see "Cuba, the United States, and the Sugar Act of 1948: The Failure of Economic Coercion," *Diplomatic History* 6 (Winter 1982): 1-21. Heston notes that treaties served the same indirect control function as the Platt Amendment and other political mechanisms; the 1934 treaty was signed, he notes, because "The United States wanted greater cooperation from Cuba without the stigma of overt intervention" (p. 4).

American corporations, Heston notes, were by the late 40s angry with Cuba's wide panoply of worker protection laws, and wanted them to be repealed; hence the United States attempted to force Cuban assent to a new commercial treaty in 1947. At about the same time, the Sugar Act of 1948 was being passed, that provided Cuba with 98.64 per cent of all U.S. sugar demand over 5.22 million tons—about 2 million tons; guaranteed that Cuba would not have less than 28.6 per cent of the American market; and granted Cuba 95 per cent of the Philippine sugar deficit, which was total since the Philippines were importing sugar at this time. In sum, Cuba was granted some 3 million tons worth of the American market, subsidized at prices a few cents per pound above the world rate.

The State Department, to obtain leverage on the treaty issue, attempted to insert Section 202(e) of the Act, allowing the Secretary of Agriculture to reduce a country's quota if that country "denies fair and equitable treatment to the nationals of the United States, its commerce, navigation, or industry." Cuba protested strongly, made its case in international forums, and even stirred up anti-

American feeling in Latin America. It also forwarded the "Grau Doctrine," a proposal to outlaw "economic aggression" in international law. In the end, State agreed to eliminate 202(e), and the crisis ended.

57. Lazo pp. 70-71.

58. Thomas p. 769, Lazo p. 71.

59. Lazo pp. 71-73, Thomas p. 770.

60. Mario Llerena, *The Unsuspected Revolution: The Birth and Rise of Castroism* (Ithaca: Cornell University Press, 19778), pp. 35-36; Casanova interview.

61. Ruiz p. 110; Aguilar pp. 245-47; Thomas pp. 775-86.

62. See Beaulac's book for details of his ambassadorship.

63. *Foreign Relations of the U.S. 1952-54*, IV, pp. 868-80. Casuso noted that the United States recognized Batista "immediately" because it was "still more interested in 'friends' than true democracy." Casuso, pp. 87-88. See also *State Department Files*, 1950-54; March 24, Acheson memo, reel 39 frames 227-30; Beaulac dispatch regarding meeting with Batista, June 25, 1952, reel 39 frame 247.

64. *Foreign Relations*, Ibid. pp. 881-82.

65. Ibid. pp. 892-95.

66. Cole Blasier, *The Hovering Giant: U.S. Responses to Revolutionary Change in Latin American, 1910-1985* (Pittsburgh, PA: University of Pittsburgh Press, 1985), p. 22; Lazo p. 77; Phillips, *Paradox*, pp. 263ff; Hugh Thomas, "Cuba, the United States, an Batista," in Irving Louis Horowitz, ed., *Cuban Communism* (New Brunswick, NJ: Transaction Books, 1987), p. 5.

The crackdown on Communists was not necessarily very harsh, however. Batista still allowed Communists to support him, and his undersecretary of labor, Arsenio Gonzales, was a Communist. There are also reports that the BRAC did not work very hard at its appointed task; Ruiz pp. 132-3.

67. Lazo p. 77. for Batista's own account of these programs and his term in general see Fulgencio Batista, *The Growth and Decline of the Cuban Republic* (New York: Devin-Adair, 1964).

68. Llerena pp. 38-39; Thomas, *Cuba*, pp. 789-802. See also Harold D. Sims, "Cuban Labor and the Communist Party, 1937-1958: An Interpretation," *Cuban Studies* 15 (Winter 1985): 43-58. Sims adequately summarizes the change of heart of labor and the Communists, which by the mid-fifties were seriously opposed to Batista but which largely distrusted Castro until February 1858 when, recognizing that the writing was on the wall, they joined him.

69. Thomas, "Cuba, the United States, and Batista," p. 6; Morley pp. 46-58.

70. See J.H. Durston, "America's Favorite Offshore Resorts," *House and Garden*, May 1956, pp. 92-95; E. Aguilara, "Cruising Around Cuba," *Yachting*, December 1956, pp. 47-50; P. Andrews, "Mademoiselle Says Let's Go," *Mademoiselle*, December 1956, p. 46; John Dorschner and Roberto Fabricio, *The Winds of December*, (New York: Coward, McCann and Geoghegan, 1980), p. 20; and Ramon L. Bonachea and Marta San Martin, *The Cuban Insurrection 1952-1959* (New Brunswick, NJ: Transaction Books, 1974), pp. 31-34; Morley p. 50.

71. Morris Morley, "The U.S. Imperial State in Cuba, 1952-1958: Policy

Making and Capitalists' Interests," *Journal of Latin American Studies* 14 (May 1982): 143-70.

72. Llerena, pp. 51, 54; Dorschner and Fabricio p. 33; Bonachea and Martin pp. 10-28.

73. *Foreign Relations of the U.S. 1952-1954*, IV, pp. 899-902.

74. See *Foreign Relations of the U.S. 1955-1957*, VI, pp. 777-89, 791-820, 821-31 832-35; and M. Stephen Kane, "Reassessing the Bureaucratic Dimension of Foreign Policy Making," *Social Science Quarterly* 64 (March 1983): 46-65.

75. See Morris H. Morley, *Imperial State and Revolution: The United States and Cuba, 1956-1986* (Cambridge: Cambridge University Press, 1987), for a good description of Gardner's policies and those of his successors.

76. Thomas pp. 854-62; Bonachea and Martin pp. 29-31; "Cuba: Batista and the Outlook," *Newsweek*, November 15, 1954, p. 67; "Caribbean's Troubled Waters," *Newsweek*, March 12, 1956, p. 61.

77. "Cuba: Creeping Revolt," *Time*, January 7, 1957m p. 33; "Cuba: Hit-and-Run Revolt,"*Time*, December 10, 1956, p. 42.

78. U.S. Department of Commerce, Bureau for Foreign Commerce, *Investment in Cuba: Basic Information for United States Businessmen* (Washington: GPO 1956).

79. Sheldon Liss, *Roots of Revolution: Radical Thought in Cuba* (Lincoln: University of Nebraska Press, 1987), pp. 108-51.

80. Oden Meeker, "Cuba Under Batista: More Apathy Than Disaffection," *The Reporter* 11 (September 14, 1954): 21-23.

81.*Foreign Relations of the U.S. 1955-1957*, VI, pp. 831-32; Llerena, pp. 65-69.

82. Ibid. pp. 835-37.

83. Bonachea and Martin pp. 65-66, 85-86; Tad Szulc, *Fidel: A Critical Portrait* (New York: Avon Books, 1986).

Chapter Eight

1. For bibiographised of writings on the revolution, see Louis A. Perez, Jr., *The Cuban Revolutionary War, 1953-58: A Bibliography* (Metuchen, NJ: The scarecrow Press, Inc., 1976;) Jaime Suchlicki, *The Cuban Revolution: A Documentary Bibliography, 1952-1968* (Coral Gables, FL: University of Miami Center for Advanced International Studies, October 1968); and probably the most complete, Ronald H. Chilcote, *Cuba, 1953-1978: A Bibliographical Guide to the Literature* (White Plains, NY: Kraus International Publications, 1986), 2 volumes.

2. Herbert Matthews, *The Cuban Story* (New York: George Braziller, 1961), p. 20; Mario Lazo, *Dagger in the Heart: American Policy Failures in Cuba* (New York: Funk and Wagnalls, 1968), pp. 125-26.

3. Carlos Franqui, *Family Portrait with Fidel* (New York: Vintage Books, 1984), pp. 4-5.

4. Antoni Kapcia, "Cuban Populism and the Birth of the Myth of Marti," in Christopher Abel and Nissa Torrents, eds., *Jose Marti: Revolutionary Democrat* (Durham, NC: Duke University Press, 1986), p. 57.

5. Hugh Thomas, *Cuba: The Pursuit of Freedom* (New York: Harper and Row, 1971), pp.873-75, 950.

6. Mario Llerena, *The Unsuspected Revolution: The Birth and Rise of Castroism* (Ithaca: Cornell University Press, 1978), pp. 92-95; Lazo pp. 109-20; Matthews pp. 15-44.

7. Cole Blasier, *The Hovering Giant: U.S. Responses to Revolutionary Change in Latin America 1910-1985* (Pittsburgh, PA: University of Pittsburgh Press, 1985), p. 21.

8. Matthews p. 121.

9. Theodore Draper, *Castro's Revolution: Myths and Realities* (New York: Praeger, 1962), pp. 189-90.

10 Lazo p. 109. There is some chance that the story would have been different had it been written by Ruby Hart Phillips, the *Times*'s primary correspondent in Cuba and a conservative anti-Communist suspicious of Castro and his movement. The *Times* only sent Matthews because it judged that it needed a visiting correspondent to do the story and get out, lest the author become a target either of the government or the rebels. A story written by Phillips would have differed significantly from the one Matthews produced.

11. *Foreign Relations of the United States, 1955-57,* Volume 6, p. 633; Llerena p. 99; Lazo pp. 107-8.

12. Matthews pp. 69-71; Earl E.T. Smith, *The Fourth Floor: An Account of the Castro Communist Revolution* (New York: Random House, 1962), pp. 5-6.

13. John Dorschner and Roberto Fabricio, *The Winds of December* (New York: Coward, McCann and Geoghegan, 1980), pp. 51-52; Thomas p. 948.

14. Wayne S. Smith, *The Closest of Enemies: A Personal and Diplomatic History of the Castro Years* (New York: WW Norton, 1987), pp. 46-47.

15. See Morris H. Morley, *Imperial State and Revolution: The United States and Cuba, 1956-1986* (Cambridge: Cambridge University Press, 1987).

16. Dorschner and Fabricio pp. 52-54.

17. Ibid. p. 73.

18. Thomas p. 949.

19. Dorschner and Fabricio pp. 54-55.

20. Earl Smith, *Fourth Floor*, pp. 11-13, 19-29.

21. Carleton Beals, ''Rebels Without a Cause,'' *Nation* 84 (June 29, 1957): 560-68; Llerena p. 124-27, Thomas pp. 954-55.

22. Earl Smith, *Fourth Floor* pp. 31-37.

23. *Foreign Relations of the United States, 1955-57,* VI, pp. 845-49.

24. Ibid. pp. 850-51; at this time Wieland had already begun to pressure Prio to cease his support for Castro. In late September Wieland warned Prio that continued assistance to Castro would constitute violations of U.S. neutrality laws.

25. Ibid. pp. 844-45, 852-54.

26. Ibid. pp. 865-70; Earl Smith, *Fourth Floor* pp. 45-51.

27. *Foreign Relations of the United States, 1955-57,* VI, pp. 870-76.

28. Lazo pp. 140-42; Earl Smith, *Fourth Floor* pp. 58-61; Thomas p. 976.

29. Lazo pp. 145-46; Earl Smith, *Fourth Floor* pp. 61-64.

30. Wieland hearings, *op. cit.* pp. 1-4.

31. Matthews pp. 85-86; Blasier pp. 20-22; *Foreign Relations of the United States, 1955-57,* VI, pp. 633, 820, 858-63; Earl Smith, *Fourth Floor* pp. 64-65.

32. Wayne Smith, *Closest of Enemies* pp. 20-27.

33. Morley pp. 61-71.

34. Llerena pp. 176-83; *Congressional Record,* 55th Cong., 2d sess., Vol 104, March 20 1958, pp. 4407-8; Ibid. March 26 pp. 4797-99; Earl Smith, *Fourth Floor,* pp. 85-86; Morley pp. 58-61.

35. Ramon L. Bonachea and Marta San Martin, *The Cuban Insurrection 1952-59* (New Brunswick, New Jersey: Transaction Books, 1974), pp. 106-133. For a memoir of Castro's evolving battles from an American who took part in them see Neill Macaulay, *A Rebel in Cuba: An American's Memoir* (Chicago: Quadrangle Books, 1970). See also Che Guevara's memoir, *Reminiscences of the Cuban Revolutionary War,* trans. Victoria Ortiz (New York: Monthly Review Press, 1968).

36. Blasier p. 22; see also Lazo p. 174, Thomas A. Bailey, *A Diplomatic History of the American People* (New York: Appleton-Century-Crofts, various editions), p. 860; Bonachea and Martin pp. 198-201. For Batista's version see his book, *Cuba Betrayed* (New York: Vantage, 1962).

37. Lazo p. 149. Morley, who interprets U.S. policy in a Marxist fashion— attributing most decision to the pursuit of economic interests by an "imperial state"'—contends that the boycott was "always framed by the basic commitment to a secure environment to American business in Cuba"(p. 61). While the general American pro-business policy was clear enough, strategic concerns involving Communism and worldwide U.S. image also played a large role in the decision; indeed a solely pro-business perspective might have backed Batista completely in expectation that he could keep order. Morley's claim seems overstated.

38. Earl Smith, *Fourth Floor* p. 107; Wayne Smith, *Closest of Enemies* pp. 16-17; Blasier p. 23; Matthews pp. 82-84; Lazo pp. 148-49.

39. Wayne Smith, *Closest of Enemies* pp. 17-18. While this may have been the case, Earl Smith contended that in fact "it was no longer possible to engender any support in the State Department for the Batista government" after March 12. Smith, *Fourth Floor* p. 98.

40. *Foreign Relations of the United States, 1955-57,* VI, pp. 856-58; Lazo p. 151; Earl Smith, *Fourth Floor* pp. 97-99; Wayne Smith *Closest of Enemies* p. 20; Morley p. 59.

41. Earl Smith, *Fourth Floor* pp. 109-27; Bonachea and Martin pp. 198-255.

42. Earl Smith, *Fourth Floor* pp. 137-51. For an impressively precise analysis of the kidnappings and the tactics involved, see Roberta Wohlstetter, "Kidnapping to Win Friends and Influence People," *Survey* 20 (Autumn 1974): 1-40.

43. Dorschner and Fabricio p. 93.

44. Earl Smith, *Fourth Floor* pp. 153-54; Lazo pp. 1556-56.

45. Wayne Smith, *Closest of Enemies* pp. 29-30.

46. Earl Smith, *Fourth Floor* pp. 154-57.

47. Earl Smith, *Fourth Floor* pp. 157-60; Dorschner and Fabricio pp. 50-51.

48. Bonachea and Martin pp. 226-265; Wayne Smith, *Closest of Enemies* pp. 18-19.

49. Dorschner and Fabricio pp. 69-74.

50. Wayne Smith, *Closest of Enemies* pp. 33-34; Dorschner and Fabricio pp. 144-52.

51. Blasier p. 26; Earl Smith, *Fourth Floor* p. 165; Lazo pp. 158-63; Dorschner and Fabricio pp. 152-54.

52. Earl Smith, *Fourth Floor* pp. 165-66.

53. Blasier p., 26; Lazo pp. 163-64.

54. Wayne Smith, *Closest of Enemies* pp. 35-36.

55. Earl Smith, *Fourth Floor* pp. 169-72; Dorschner and Fabricio pp. 189-93.

56. Dorschner and Fabricio pp. 244-47.

57. Blasier p. 27.

58. On December 31, after hearing a bizarre report from CBS radio that the United States was contemplating intervention in Cuba, Senator Wayne Morse convened an emergency meeting of the Latin American subcommittee of the Senate Foreign Relations Committee. Rubottom was the only witness, and he denied the report. He also stressed State's continuing convictions about the hope for an independent government andr the lack of certainty about Fidel Castro's Communist leanings.

59. Earl Smith, *Fourth Floor* p. 193.

60. Franqui pp. 6-7, 12-13.

61. Philip Bonsal, *Cuba, Castro, and the United States* (Pittsburgh, PA: University of Pittsburgh Press, 1971), p. 25; Richard Welch, *Response to Revolution: The United States and the Cuban Revolution, 1959-61* (Chapel Hill: University of North Carolina Press, 1985), p.29; Earl Smith, *Fourth Floor* pp. 196-207.

62. Blasier p. 188. See also George J. Boughton, "Soviet-Cuban Relations, 1956-60," *Journal of Inter-American Studies and World Affairs* 16 (November 1974): 436-53. Boughton chronicles the general contacts, mostly through mutually-admiring government press pieces, that began to evolve once Castro came to power.

63. Welch p. 29; Bonsal pp. 25-31; Morley pp. 73-74.

64. Franqui pp. 21-24.

65. Ruby Hart Phillips, *The Cuban Dilemma* (New York: Ivan Obolensky, 1962), p. 31; Lazo pp. 177-226.

66. Matthews pp. 179, 231.

67. Matthews p. 248; Welch p. 33.

68. Andres Suarez, *Cuba: Castroism and Communism, 1959-1966* (Cambridge: MIT Press 1967), pp. 45-47. American citizens were so anxious to get along with the Cuban government that they paid their taxes early, and paid back taxes. Cubans did the same thing, but out of a desire to make a fresh start with an honest regime. Phillips pp. 23-30, 55-58; Jose Manuel Casanova, interview with the author, January 15, 1988.

69. Trumbull Higgins, *The Perfect Failure: Kennedy, Eisenhower, and the CIA at the Bay of Pigs* (New York: W.W. Norton and Co., 1987), p. 42; Bonsal pp. 58-61.

70. *Public Papers of the Presidents of the United States: Dwight D. Eisenhower 1959* (Washington, D.C.: GPO, 1960), p. 751; *Department of State Current Documents* No. 101, October 28, 1959.

71. Bonsal pp. 62-69; Suarez pp. 47-50; Phillips pp. 70-73; Tersa Casuso, *Cuba and Castro*, trans. Elmer Grossberg (New York: Random House, 1961), pp. 204-9; Franqui pp. 31-32; Blasier p. 181; Wayne Smith, *Closest of Enemies* p. 47; Morley pp. 79-80, who notes that Felipe Pazos told him in a letter that the U.S. attitude at this time was "that of a most willing lender."

72. Richard Nixon, *Six Crises* (Garden City, NY: Doubleday, 1962), pp. 351-52. Stephen E. Ambrose, in *Nixon: The Education of a Politician, 1913-1962* (New York: Simon and Schuster, 1987), pp. 515-16, paints Nixon as more "ambivalent" with this decision that Nixon's later statements would indicate; Nixon respected Castro as a great leader who "may change his attitude" and recommended that the United States try to "orient him in the right direction."

73. Phillips pp. 81ff; Blasier pp. 90-91, 190; Jose Manuel Casanova, interview, January 1988. See also Lowry Nelson, *Cuba: The Measure of a Revolution* (Minneapolis, MN: University of Minnesota Press, 1972), pp. 25, 77-78.

There were actually two agricultural reform laws, the radical one—which was written by Che Guevara—and a moderate one formulated by the first minister of agriculture, Sori Marin. Sori Marin had no idea Che was writing a separate plan, which was later forced on an unwilling (and increasingly concerned) cabinet. Franqui p. 37; Casanova interview.

This radicalism took place often with the support of the still-conservative PSP; see Suarez for a good summary of the PSP's role in the early government.

74. Philip Bonsal, "Cuba, Castro, and the United States," *Foreign Affairs* 45 (January 1967): 268.

75. Nelson p. 25. See also Susan Fernandez, "The Sanctity of Property: American Responses to Cuban Expropriations, 1959-1984," *Cuban Studies* 14 (Summer 1984): 21-34; Morley pp. 81-83.

76. Phillips pp. 85-86; Blasier p. 91.

77. For the liberal view, see Marice Zeitlin and Robert Sheer, *Cuba: Tragedy in Our Hemisphere* (New York: Grove Press, 1963); Matthews pp. 233-34.

78. Phillips pp. 88-104; Blasier pp. 180-81.

79. Welch pp. 36-38; Bonsal pp. 97-99; Blasier pp. 91-93, 182-83; Higgins pp. 45-46.

81. Bonsal pp. 100-109; Welch pp. 39-40; Franqui pp. 52-55; Phillips pp. 115-17.

82. James O'Connor, *The Origins of Socialism in Cuba* (Ithaca: Cornell University Press, 1970), pp. 91-113. Claes Brundenius, in *Revolutionary Cuba: The Challenge of Growth With Equity* (Boulder, CO: Westview Press, 1984), pp. 41-49, has ably catalogued the early economic policies of the revolutionary government.

83. O'Connor pp. 91-99; William L. LeoGrande, *The Development of the Party System in Cuba* (Pennsylvania: Northwest Pennsylvania Institute for Latin American Studies, Mercyhurst College, 1978), p. 4.

84. Wayne Smith, *Closest of Enemies* pp. 59-60; Casanova, interview, January 1988.

85. Bonsal pp. 109-16; Phillips p. 142.

86. U.S. Senate, Judiciary Committee, Subcommittee to Investigate the Administration of the Internal Security Act and Other Internal Security Laws, *Communist Threat to the United States Through the Caribbean*, Part V, July 17, 1959, p. 245.

87. *Department of State Bulletin* 42 (February 15, 1960); Bonsal pp. 121-28.

88. Phillips p. 149; see also Blasier p. 190; Wayne Smith, *Closest of Enemies* pp. 54-55.

89. Higgins pp. 46-49.

90. Welch pp. 44-45; Bonsal pp. 129-32; Nelson p. 27; Franqui pp. 66-67.

91. Wayne Smith, *Closest of Enemies* pp. 55-56; Morley pp. 87-88.

92. Bonsal p. 134; Blasier p. 188; Welch p. 45; Franqui pp. 69-70; Morley pp. 85-88, 94-95.

93. Bonsal pp. 133-44.

94. Ibid. p. 141.

95. Phillips pp. 196-204; Nelson p. 29; Morley pp. 102-7.

96. *Congressional Record*, 86th Cong., 2d sess., Vol. 106 1960, Part 11 pp. 15228ff; Blasier p. 192.

97. Welch pp. 50-51; Nelson pp. 303-1; Bonsal pp. 145-55. Even Bonsal had given up by now. He wrote that "I am as convinced as anyone could be that we cannot do business with Castro and the people who currently control him"; Morley, p. 112. That statement mirrors Smith's earlier one to the same effect.

98. *Department of State Bulletin* XLIII (August 1, 1960): 170-71; Bonsal pp. 18-61; Wayne Smith *Closest of Enemies* p. 57.

99. Bailey p. 863; Blasier pp. 195-99.

100. Morley pp. 113-26.

101. Wlech pp. 55-57; Phillips pp. 223-86; Franqui pp. 111-15.

102. Franqui pp. 83-90.

103. Phillips p. 285.

104. Bailey p. 863; Welch pp. 59-60.

Chapter Nine

1. Theodore Draper, *Castroism in Theory and Practice* (New York: Frederick A. Praeger, 1965), pp. 78-83; see also Richard J. Heggen and Alfred G. Cuzan, "Legitimacy, Coercion, and Scope: An Expansion Path Analysis Applied to Five Central American Countries and Cuba," *Behavioral Science* 26 (April1981): 143-52.

2. Emphasis mine; Draper pp. 111-12.

3. Jose Manuel Casanova, interview with the author, January 1988.

4. Cole Blasier, "Social Revolution: Origins in Mexico, Bolivia, and Cuba," in Rolando E. Bonachea and Nelson P. Valdes, eds., *Cuba in Revolution* (New York: Anchor Books, 1972), p. 28.

5. Nelson P. Valdes, *Ideological Roots of the Cuban Revolutionary Movement* (Glasgow: University of Glasgow Occasional Papers, No. 15, 1975). See also William Rex Crawford, "The Development of Cuban Thought," in Robert F. Smith, ed., *Background to Revolution: The Development of Modern Cuba* (Huntington, NY: Robert E. Krieger Publishing Co., 1979), pp. 38-46.

6. Sheldon B. Liss, *Roots of Revolution: Radical Thought in Cuba* (Lincoln: University of Nebraska Press, 1987).

7. Jaime Suchlicki, *University Students and Revolution in Cuba, 1920-1968* (Coral Gables, FL: University of Miami Press, 1969), pp. 58-86; Rolando E. Bonachea and Marta San Martin, *The Cuban Insurrection 1952-1959* (New Brunswick, NJ: Transaction Books, 1974), pp. 41-60.

8. Draper pp. 98-103.

9. Boris Goldenberg, *The Cuban Revolution and Latin America* (New York: Praeger, 1965), p. 144.

10. Andres Suarez, *Cuba: Castroism and Communism 1959-1966* (Cambridge: MIT University Press, 1967).

11. Frederico Gil, "Antecedents of the Cuban Revolution," *Centennial Review* 6 (No. 3 1962): 385.

12. Maurice Zeitlin and Robert Scheer, *Cuba: Tragedy in Our Hemisphere* (New York: Grove Press, 1963), p. 12.

13. Blasier p. 25

14. James O'Connor, *The Origins of Socialism in Cuba* (Ithaca, NY: Cornell University Press, 1970), pp. 47-48.

15. Ramon E. Ruiz, *Cuba: Making of a Revolution* (New York: W.W. Norton and Co., 1968), p. 10.

16. See Jean-Paul Sartre, *Sartre on Cuba* (Westport, CT: Greenwood Press, 1974); Leo Huberman and Paul M. Sweezy, *Cuba: Anatomy of a Revolution* (New York: Monthly Review Press, 1961); and C. Wright Mills, *Listen, Yankee* (New York: McGraw Hill, 1960). See also Paul Boran, "Reflections on the Cuban Revolution," *Monthly Review* (January 1961): 467, who concludes that peasants "made the revolution."

17. Che Guevara, *Reminiscences on the Cuban Revolutionary War*, translated by Victoria Ortiz (New York: Monthly Review Press, 1968), pp. 192-196

18. Draper pp. 71-72.

19. Theodore Draper, *Castro's Revolution: Myths and Realities* (New York: Praeger, 1962), pp. 6-15.

20. Draper, *Castroism* p. 74; Goldenberg pp. 145-46; Brois Goldenberg, "The Cuban Revolution: An Analysis," *Problems of Communism* (September-October 1963): 4; Ruby Hart Phillips, *The Cuban Dilemma* (New York: Ivan Obolensky, 1962), p. 95; Bonachea and Martin, *Insurrection* p. 103.

21. Gil Carl Alroy, "The Peasantry in the Cuban Revolution," in Bonachea

and Valdes, *Cuba in Revolution*, p. 4.

22. Ibid. pp. 7, 16.

23. Ibid. pp. 8-10.

24. Draper, *Castroism* p. 76; Draper, *Myths* pp. 42-48; Goldenberg, *Cuban Revolution* pp. 144-45 (all subsequent references are to his book).

25. Jorge Dominguez, *Cuba: Order and Revolution* (Cambridge: Harvard University Press, 1978), pp. 120-21.

26. Ibid. p. 121; Goldenberg p. 133.

27. Goldenberg p. 125.

28. Ibid. pp. 126-33; see also Wyatt McGaffey and Clifford Barnett, *Cuba: Its People, Its Society, Its Culture* (New Haven: American University Press, 1962), for a pessimistic view of the economic situation in Cuba at the time.

29. Ruiz pp. 44-51.

30. John Dorschner and Roberto Fabricio, *The Winds of December* (New York: Coward, McCann, and Geoghegan, 1980), p. 89.

31. Maurice Zeitlin, *Revolutionary Politics and the Cuban Working Class* (Princeton, NJ: Princeton University Press, 1967), pp. 45-65.

32. Ibid. pp. 185-210, 278.

33. See Eric Hoffer, *The True Believer: Thoughts in the Nature of Mass Movements* (New York: Harper and Row, 1951); Albert Camus, *The Rebel* (New York: Alfred A. Knopf, 1956). Lucian Pye has also stressed rootlessness as a cause of revolution in his *Guerrilla Communism in Malaya: Its Social and Political Meanings* (Princeton, NJ: Princeton University Press, 1956).

34. Nelson Amaro, "Mass and Class in the Origins of the Cuban Revolution," in Irving Louis Horowitz, ed., *Cuban Communism* (New Brunswick, NJ: Transaction Books,1987), p. 13.

35. Carlos Franqui, *Family Portrait With Fidel* (New York: Vintage Books, 1984), pp. 34-35, 71-72.

36. Louis A. Perez, Jr., "La Chambelona" Political Protest, Sugar, and Social Banditry in Cuba, 1914-1917," *Inter-American Economic Affairs* XXXI (Spring 1978): 3-28.

37. Gilbert Merks and Nelson Valdes, "Revolution, Consciousness, and Class: Cuba and Argentina," in Bonachea and Valdes, *Cuba in Revolution*, p. 99.

38. Robin Blackburn, "Prologue to the Cuban Revolution," *New Left Review* No. 21 (October 1963).

39. Goldenberg, *Cuban Revolution* p. 134. See also James O'Connor, "Cuba: Its Political Economy," in Bonachea and Valdes, *Cuba in Revolution*, pp. 52-81.

40. Lowry Nelson, *Rural Cuba* (minneapolis: University of Minnesota Press, 1950; reprint edition, Octagon Books, 1970), p. 139; cf pp. 159-61.

41. Irene A. Wright, "The Illusion of Democracy, Reform, and Self-Government," in Smith, *Background*, p. 81.

42. Ruiz pp. 142-46; see also Louis Gotshalk, "Causes of Revolution," in Claude E. Welch, Jr. and Mavis Taintor, *Revolution and Political Change* (North Scituate, MA: Duxbury Press, 1972), pp. 176-82.

43. Goldenberg pp. 127-31; O'Connor, "Cuba," in Bonachea and Valdes, p. 67; Dominguez p. 35. Dominguez refers here to Max Weber's patromonial political system; see Weber, *The Theory of Social and Economic Organization* (New York: Free Press, 1965), esp. pp. 347-55.

44. Goldenberg, p. 135.

45. O'Connor, "Cuba," in Bonachea and Valdes, p. 81; Merkx and Valdes p. 99.

46. Antoni Kapcia, "Cuban Populism and the Birth of the Myth of Marti," in Christopher Abel and Nissa Torrents, eds., *Jose Marti: Revolutionary Democrat* (Durham, NC: Duke University Press, 1986), pp. 34-35. Kapcia has called this phenomenon "plattism," and he also notes the lack of a Cuban "nationaist mythology: the consensus on a coherent set of symbols to express a real or imagined collective national identity" (p. 36). He also recognizes that it was this lack of commitment to the country that led to the corrupt Cuban governments of the time. The American independent elite "was faced with a clear imperative: to fill the void, to disguise its lack of real pwer and its lack of real reform program, and to provide a safe distraction." It pursued these goals by creating an "establishment nationalism" that channeled real desire for change into minor issues: renegotiating a reciprocity treaty or a quota and so on (p. 55).

47. William H. Friedland et al., *Revolutionary Theory* (Totowa, NJ: Allanheld, Osmun, and Co., 1982), pp. 53-62.

48. Ruiz pp. 145-46.

49. Merks and Valdes p. 103.

50. Ibid. p. 107.

51. Dominguez p. 69; Goldenberg pp. 122-24.

52. Lowry Nelson, *Cuba: The Measure of a Revolution* (Minneapolis: University of Minnesota Press, 1974), p. 46.

53. Draper, *Castroism* p. 110.

54. Liss p. 111.

55. Ruiz p. 7.

56. Goldenberg pp. 137-41.

57. Interview with the author, January 1988.

58. John Strachey, *The End of Empire* (New York: Random House, 1960). The sort of broad definition to which Strachey refers has been proposed by a number of writers, including J.A. Hobson, who argues that imperialism is "the use of the machinery of government by private interests, mainly capitalists, to secure from them economic gains outside their country." The definition is cited by Liss (p. 60), who notes that it "fit the United States' role in Cuba."
It is easy to see that such a definition is useless, just as Strachey argues. Every nation on earth pursues the policy outlined by Hobson—Communist as well as capitalist—although the "private" interests in Communist countries are the ruling elite.

59. Dominguez p. 59.

60. Goldenberg p. 142.

61. William Ratliff, "The *New York Times* and the Cuban Revolution," in Rat-

liff, ed., *The Selling of Fidel Castro: The Media and The Cuban Revolution* (New Brunswick, NJ: Transaction Books, 1987), pp. 3-4.

62. John P. Walach, "Fidel Castro and the United States Press," in Ibid. pp. 129-56.

63. Nathaniel Weyl, *Red Star Over Cuba* (New York: Devin-Adair Co., 1960).

64. Ibid. pp. 155-84.

65. Draper, *Myths* pp. 34-42.

66. Richard E. Welch, *Response to Revolution: The United States and the Cuban Revolution, 1959-1961* (Chapel Hill: University of North Carolina Press, 1985), p. 107.

67. Mario Lazo, *Dagger in the Heart: American Policy Failures in Cuba* (New York: Funk and Wagnalls, 1968).

68. Earl E.T. Smith, *The Fourth Floor: An Account of the Castro Communist Revolution* (New York: Random House, 1962), pp. 225, 231.

69. Cited in Lazo pp. 163-64.

70. Braden testimony, Senate Judiciary Committee, Subcommittee to Investigate of the Internal Security Act and Other Internal Security Laws, *Communist Threat to the United States Through the Caribbean*, Part 5, July 17, 1959, p. 246.

71. Ibid. pp. 246-58.

72. Gardner testimony, Ibid. hearings, Part 9, August 27 and 30, 1960, pp. 667-68.

73. Welch p. 105.

74. Senate Judiciary Committee, *The Case of William Wieland*, 1962.

75. Welch p. 106.

76. Wayne Smith, *The Closest of Enemies: A Personal and Diplomatic History of the Castro Years* (New York: W.W. Norton and Co., 1987), pp. 36-37. See also Morris J. Morley, *Imperial State and Revolution: The United States and Cuba, 1956-1986* (Cambridge: Cambridge University Press, 1987), pp. 56 and 63 for a defense of State officials. Morley reports an interview with a former State official who said that "nobody in the State Department wanted Castro to get in."

77. *Foreign Relations of the United States, 1955-57*, Vol. 6, p. 838.

78. Wayne Smith, *Closest of Enemies* p. 37.

79. For a general summary see Valdes, *Ideological Roots*, and Christopher Abel and Nissa Torrents, eds., *Jose Marti*.

80. Roberto Fernandez Retamar, "The Modernity of Marti," in Abel and Torrents pp. 6-7.

81. Jose Ibarra, "Marti and Socialism," in Abel and Torrents, p. 85; Christopher Abel, "Marti, Latin America and Spain," in *Ibid.*, pp. 125, 140-41.

82. Herbert Matthews, *Revolution in Cuba: An Essay in Understanding* (New York: Scribners, 1975), p. 21; Hugh Thomas, *Cuba: The Pursuit of Freedom* (New York: Harper and Row, 1971), p. 317.

83. Carolos Ripoll, *Jose Marti, the United States, and the Marxist Interpretation of Cuban History* (New Brunswick, NJ: Transaction Books, 1984).

84. Liss pp. 51-55.

85. Translation can be found in *State Department Documents: Secret State Department Files on Cuba, 1945-49* (Frederick, MD: University Publications of America, 1987); State Department Dispatch No. 2863.

86. Maurice Halperin, *The Rise and Decline of Fidel Castro* (Berkeley, CA: University of California Press, 1974), p. 6; Ruiz pp. 58-75; Liss pp. 56-57; Mario Llerena, *The Unsuspected Revolution: The Birth and Rise of Castroism* (Ithaca: Cornell University Press, 1978), p. 275. Llerena concludes that "The ideological source of the 26 July Movement is Marti." For a good general summary see *Jose Marti and the Cuban Revolution Retraced* (UCLA: UCLA Latin American Center Publications, 1986).

87. Interview with the author, January 1988.

88. Dominguez p. 133.

Chapter Ten

1. For general bibliographic information about Fidel Castro, see Tad Szulc, *Fidel* (New York: Avon Books, 1986).

2. For proponents of this view see Maurice Zeitlin and Robert Scheer, *Cuba: Tragedy in Our Hemisphere* (New York: Grove Press, 1963).

3. Philip Bonsal, *Cuba, Castro, and the United States* (Pittsburgh: University of Pittsburgh Press, 1971), p. 154.

4. Wayne S. Smith, *The Closest of Enemies: A Personal and Diplomatic History of the Castro Years* (New York: W.W. Norton, 1987); see also Richard E. Welch, *Response to Revolution: The United States and the Cuban Revolution, 1959-1961* (Chapel Hill: University of North Carolina Press, 1985), p. 118, who cites the liberal writer I.F. Stone; Stone, writing on Castro's denial of rights, concludes that "again for this, the United States shares responsibility."

5. Morris H. Morley, *Imperial State and Revolution: The United States and Cuba, 1956-1986* (Cambridge: Cambridge University Press, 1987).

6. Cole Blasier, *The Hovering Giant: U.S. Responses to Revolutionary Change in Latin America 1910-1985* (Pittsburgh, PA: University of Pittsburgh Press, 1985), p. 187; Lowry Nelson, *Cuba: Measure of a Revolution* (Minneapolis: University of Minnesota Press, 1972), p. 33.

7. See Ramon L. Boncahea and Marta San Martin, *The Cuban Insurrection 1952-1959* (New Brunswick, NJ: Transaction Books, 1974), pp. 166-72; Carlos Franqui, *Family Portrait With Fidel* (New York: Vintage Books, 1984).

8. Efren Cordova, *Castro and the Cuban Labor Movement: Statecraft and Society in a Revolutionary Period (1959-1961)* (Lanham, MD: University Press of America, 1987), pp. 16-17.

9. Cordova pp. 325-26.

10. Andres Suarez, *Cuba: Castroism and Communism 1959-1966* (Cambridge, MA: MIT Press, 1967), pp. 28-29.

11. See Szulc.

12. Theodore Draper, *Castro's Revolution: Myths and Realities* (New York: Frederick A. Praeger, 1965), pp. 24-26; see also Franqui.

13. Daniel James, "Castro Unmasked," *Global Affairs* 2 (Summer 1987): 168-69.

14. See Paul D. Bethel, *The Losers: The Definitive Report, by an Eyewitness, of the Communist Conquest of Cuba and the Soviet Penetration in Latin America* (New Rochelle, NY: Arlington House, 1969); James Monahan and Kenneth O. Gilmore, *The Great Deception: The Inside Story of How the Kremlin Took Over Cuba* (New York: Farrar, Straus and Co., 1963).

15. Draper p. 20. See also Manuel Urrutia Lleo, *Fidel Castro and Company, Inc.: Communist Tyranny in Cuba* (New York: Praeger, 1964).

16. Suarez p. 34.

17. Richard E. Welch, *Response to Revolution: The United States and the Cuban Revolution, 1959-1961* (Chapel Hill: University of North Carolina Press, 1985), pp. 35-36.

18. Ramon E. Ruiz, *Cuba: The Making of a Revolution* (New York: W.W. Norton and Co., 1968), p. 4.

19. Wayne Smith pp. 45-54.

20. Suarez pp. 85, 119-24; see also Jacques Levesque, *The USSR and the Cuban Revolution* (New York: Praeger, 1978), p. 10.

21. William L. LeoGrande, *The Development of the Party System in Revolutionary Cuba* (Mercyhurst College, PA: Northwest Pennsylvania Institute for Latin American Studies, 1978), p. 2.

22. Lee Lockwood, *Castro's Cuba, Cuba's Fidel* (New York: Vintage Books, 1969), p. 337.

23. Bonsal p. 55.

24. Szulc p. 87; see also Suarez, whose book is an excellent summary of this thesis.

25. Franqui pp. 150-51.

26. Nelson p. 33.

27. James O'Connor, *The Development of Socialism in Cuba* (Ithaca: Cornell University Press, 1970), pp. 6, 11.

28. Samuel Farber, "Cuban Communists in the Early Stages of the Cuban Revolution: Revolutionaries or Reformists?" *Latin American Research Review* 18 (No. 1 1983): 76.

29. Edward Gonzales, *Cuba Under Castro: The Limits of Charisma* (Boston: Houghton Mifflin, 1974), pp. 21-110.

Chapter Eleven

1. Warren Hinckle and William W. Turner, *The Fish is Red: The Story of the Secret War Against Castro* (New York: Harper and Row, 1981), p. 13; Morris H. Morley, *Imperial State and Revolution: The United States and Cuba, 1956-1986* (Cambridge: Cambridge University Press, 1987), pp. 94-99.

2. Hinckle and Turner pp. 23-28; Bradley Ayers, *The War That Never Was: An Insider's Account of CIA Covert Operations Against Cuba* (New York: Bobbs-Merrill, 1976).

3. *Alleged Assassination Plots Involving Foreign Leaders*, Senate Report No. 94-465, November 20, 1975 (Washington, D.C.: Government Printing Office, 1975); Trumbull Higgins, *The Perfect Failure: Kennedy, Eisenhower, and the CIA at the Bay of Pigs* (New York: W.W. Norton, 1987), pp. 55-56.

4. Hinckle and Turner pp. 71-73; Peter Wyden, *Bay of Pigs: The Untold Story* (New York: Simon and Schuster, 1979), pp. 109-14.

5. Higgins p. 51.

6. Hinckle pp. 70-77; Senate Assassination Plots Report.

7. Richard E. Welch, *Response to Revolution: The United States and the Cuban Revolution, 1959-1961* (Chapel Hill: University of North Carolina Press, 1985), p. 64.

8. *Department of State Bulletin*, February 27, 1961, pp. 175, 298. See also Morley p. 131, who quotes Chester Bowles of the State Department as concluding that the Alliance for Progress "in large measure grew out of the Cuban situation."

9. Welch p. 67.

10. *New York Times*, December 11, 1963, p. 16.¼

11. Karl E. Meyer and Tad Szulc, *The Cuban Invasion: The Chronicle of a Disaster* (New York: Praeger, 1962), pp. 77-84; Wyden p. 20; Haynes Johnson, *The Bay of Pigs: The Leaders' Story of Brigade 2506* (New York: W.W. Norton and Co., 1964), pp. 53-63.

12. Higgins pp. 15-38.

14. Welch p. 67.

15. Wyden pp. 35-38, 51.

16. Higgins pp. 40-55.

17. Richard Nixon, *RN: The Memoirs of Richard Nixon* (New York: Grosset and Dunlap, 1978), pp. 220-21; Stephen E. Ambrose, *Nixon: The Education of a Politician, 1913-1962* (New York: Simon and Schuster, 1987), pp. 590-95; "Necessary Lies, Hidden Truths: Cuba in the 1960 Campaign," *Diplomatic History* 8 (Winter 1984); "John F. Kennedy on the Cuban Sitution, Presidential Campaign of 1960," *Inter-American Economic Affairs* XV (Winter 1961); Hinckle and Turner pp.38-39; Meyer and Szulc pp. 65-71; Higgins p. 59.

18. Arthur Schlesinger, *A Thousand Days: John F. Kennedy in the White House* (Boston: Houghton Mifflin, 1965), p. 233; Wyden pp. 69-73; Higgins pp. 60-61.

19. Wyden pp. 33-34, 45, 90-103; Higgins pp. 83-85.

20. For a general description of the training, see E. Howard Hunt, *Give us This Day* (New Rochelle, NY: Arlington House, 1973).

21. Welch pp. 74-77; Higgins p. 51.

22. Schlesinger pp. 233-34; Higgins pp. 61-65.

23. Schlesinger pp. 238-39; Wyden p. 89; Higgins pp. 82-83.

24. Wyden pp. 142-46, 153-58; Higgins pp. 66-67; Meyer and Szulc pp. 98-99; Schlesinger p. 235.

25. Schlesinger pp. 236-37; Higgins pp. 67-73.

26. Schlesinger p. 239; Higgins pp. 91-93.

27. Schlesinger pp. 240-43.

28. Ibid. pp. 245-49.

29. Ibid. pp. 249-52.

30. Wyden pp. 160-61; Higgins p. 117; Schlesinger pp. 252-26.

31. Higgins p. 123.

32. Wyden pp. 168-69.

33. Ibid. p. 172; see Schlesinger pp. 267-97 and Johnson pp. 74-153.

34. Wyden pp. 174-76; Meyer and Szulc pp. 116-46.

35. Wyden pp. 198-206.

36. Carlos Franqui, *Family Portrait With Fidel* (New York: Vintage Books, 1985), pp. 120-21.

37. Wyden pp. 234-40; "Cover-Up," *Time*, March 8, 1963, pp. 23-24; *Life*, March 15, 1963, p. 44.

38. Wyden pp. 261-64, 282-83.

39. Wyden pp. 248-64; Johnson pp. 154-72; Franqui p. 122.

40. Johnson pp. 181-202; Franqui pp. 124-25; Wyden pp. 272-88.

41. Nixon, *RN* pp. 232-37; Ambrose, *Nixon* pp. 631-33; Johnson pp. 203-84; Higgins pp. 149-50; Wyden p. 303.

42. Welch pp. 84-86; Philip Bonsal, *Cuba, Castro, and the United States* (Pittsburgh: University of Pittsburgh Press, 1971), p. 182; Franqui p. 126; Theodore C. Sorenson, "Kennedy's Worst Disaster," *Look*, August 10, 1965; Higgins pp. 173-74.

43. Graham Allison, *Essence of Decision* (Boston: Little, Brown and Co., 1971).

44. Lucien Vandenbrouke, "Anatomy of a Failure: The Decision to Land at the Bay of Pigs," *Political Science Quarterly* 99 (Fall 1984): 471-73.

45. Ibid. pp. 474-80.

46. Ibid. pp. 480-87.

47. Ibid. pp. 488-91.

48. Schlesinger p. 259.

49. *Operation Zapata: The 'Ultrasensitive' Report and Testimony of the Board of Inquiry on the Bay of Pigs* (Frederick, MD: University Publications of America, 1981), esp. pp. 36-53.

50. Welch pp. 84-85, Bonsal p. 185.

51. Hinckle and Turner pp. 98-99.

52. Franqui pp. 135, 115.

53. Higgins p. 104.

54. Ibid. p. 120.

55. Allen Dulles, *The Craft of Intelligence* (New York: Signet, 1965), pp. 157-58; Higgins p. 103; Schlesinger p. 234.

56. Tad Szulc, "Cuba on our Mind," *Esquire*, February 1974; Hinckle and Turner p. 110; Senate Assassination Plots Report p. 142.

57. Hinckle and Turner pp. 113-32; Taylor Branch and George Crile, "The Kennedy Vendetta: How the CIA Waged a Silent War Against Cuba," *Harper's Magazine*, August 1975, pp. 49-63.

58. Morley p. 154.

59. Thomas Powers, *The Man Who Kept the Secrets: Richard Helms and the CIA* (New York: Alfred A. Knopf, 1979), p. 133.

60. Wyden p. 44, Hinckle and Turber p. 125.

61. Morley pp. 155-75.

Chapter Twelve

1. *Cuban Crisis on Record* (New York: Keynote Publications Inc., Deadline Data on World Affairs Vol. 1 No. 1, 1963), pp. 22-23, hereafter referred to as CCOR.

2. CCOR p. 25; *Economist*, March 17, 1962.

3. CCOR p. 27.

4. Raymond Garthoff, *Reflections on the Cuban Missile Crisis* (Washington, D.C.: The Brookings Institution, 1987).

5. Hugh Thomas has referred to a ''xenophobia of rare proportions'' to describe the national feeling at the time. Thomas, *Cuba: The Pursuit of Freedom* (New York: Harper and Row, 1971), p. 1399.

6. CCOR p. 29; *New York Times*, September 9, 1962.

7. CCOR p. 30.

8. David A. Larson, ed., *The. 'Cuban Crisis' of 1962: Selected Documents, Chronology and Bibliography* (Lanham, MD: University Press of America, 1986), pp. 33-34.

9. Elie Abel, *The Missile Crisis* (Philadelphia: J.B. Lippincott Co., 1966), pp. 14-18.

10. David A Welch and James G. Blight, ''The Eleventh Hour of the Cuban Missile Crisis: An Introduction to the Ex-Comm Transcripts,'' *International Security* 12 (Winter 1987/88): 7; ''The Backdown,'' *Time*, November 2, 19672, pp. 16-17.

11. Abel pp. 47-48; David Detzer, *The Brink: Cuban Missile Crisis, 1962* (New York: Thomas Y. Crowell, 1979), pp. 110-11; Fred J. Cook, *The Cuban Missile Crisis October 1962* (New York: Franklin Watts, 1972), pp. 25-32; Robert F. Kennedy, *Thirteen Days: A Memoir of the Cuban Missile Crisis* (New York: W.W. Norton, 1969), pp. 23-31.

12. Abel pp. 76-77.

13. *Congressional Record*, October 10, 1962, p. 22957.

14. CCOR p. 35.

15. Ambrose p. 194; Cook pp. 18-25; Kennedy pp. 34-38, 54-55.

16. Abel pp. 72, 80-81; Kennedy pp. 38-39, 43-46.

17. Abel pp. 86-89, 96-99, 114; Kennedy pp. 40-49.

18. ''The U.S. Response to the Soviet Military Buildup in Cuba,'' Report to the People; Department of State Publication No. 7449, U.S. GPO, October 1962, p. 1; Cook pp. 1-6.

19. ''The U.S. Response,'' pp. 7-12. Cubans also heard Kennedy's speech, which was broadcast into Cuba through a network of commercial radio stations in the southern United States. Those stations had allowed the government to use

their facilities for an evening, and the speech was translated into Spanish and read over these stations. Just before the speech, many ambassadors of foreign nations were also notified of its contents, including Dobrynin and those of U.S. allies in NATO, SEATO, and CENTO.

20. Abel pp. 19-20; Robert Albright, "Key Legislators of Both Parties Back Blockade," *Washington Post*, October 23, 1962, p. A14; Kennedy pp. 53-54. For Fulbright's view of his own positions see "Fulbright's Role in the Cuban Missile Crisis," *Inter-American Economic Affairs* XXVII (Spring 1974): 86-94.

21. "U.S. Charges of a Soviet Military Buildup in Cuba," Department of State Publication No. 7458, November 1962, p. 22; Abel pp. 128-38.

22. See Dan Caldwell, "A Research Note on the Quarantine of Cuba, October 1962," *International Studies Quarterly* 22 (December 1978): 625-34. Robert Kennedy said the quarantine line was moved in to 500 miles from the original plan of 800 at the suggestion of British ambassador David Ormsby-Gore, to give the Soviets more time to think before their first ship hit the line; Kennedy p. 67.

23. Welch and Blight, "Introduction," pp. 8-9.

24. Kennedy pp. 69-70.

25. Abel p. 160; Kennedy pp. 69-73.

26. Abel pp. 173ff.

27. John L. Scherer, "Reinterpreting Soviet Behavior During the Cuban Missile Crisis," *World Affairs* 144 (Fall 1981): 111; Abel pp. 177-80; Detzer pp. 235-40; Cook pp. 73-76; Welch and Blight, "Introduction," p. 10; R.R. Pope, *Soviet Views of the Cuban Missile Crisis* (Lanham, MD: University Press of America, 1982), p. 48.

28. Larsen pp. 178-80.

29. Abel pp. 192-93; Ambrose p. 196.

30. Welch and Blight, "Introduction," pp. 12-18; Richard Harwood, "Kennedy Secretly a 'Dove' in Cuba Crisis, Letter Shows," *Washington Post*, August 29, 1987, p.1; James G. Blight, Joseph S. Nye, and David A. Welch, "The Cuban Missile Crisis Revisited," *Foreign Affairs* 66 (Fall 1987): 178-79.

31. Larson p. 187.

32. Barton J. Bernstein, "The Cuban Missile Crisis: Trading the Jupiters in Turkey?" *Political Science Quarterly* 95 (Spring 1980): 97-126; Cook pp. 79-80; Blight et al., "The Crisis Revisited," pp. 177-78. Welch and Blight in the "Introduction" (p. 19) make clear that, while Bobby Kennedy later said he had come up with the idea of trading the Jupiters, in fact the notion was raised by several members of the ExComm before him.

33. Abel p. 204; Welch and Belight, "Introduction," pp. 12, 19.

34. See Walter Lippman, "On the Cuban Question Today," *Washington Post*, February 12, 1963; John Herbert, "Cooper Urges New Blockade," *Washington Post* , February 12, 1963; and "Keating and Cuba," *Washington Posat* editorial, February 20, 1963.

35. *The New Republic*, February 16, 1963; *The Washington Post*, January 12, 1963.

36. Detzer p. 260.

37. CCOR p. 45.

38. *Christian Science Monitor,* November 1, 1962.

39. See Abel and Arnold L. Horelick, "The Cuban Missile Crisis: An Analysis of Soviet Calculations and Behavior," *World Politics* 16 (1964): 380-82.

40. Abel p. 35.

41. *The New York Times Magazine,* November 15, 1964.

42. Richard Ned Lebow, "Correspondence: Deterrence Failure Revisited," *International Security* 12 (Summer 1987): 203. See also Lebow, "The Cuban Missile Crisis: Reading the Lessons Correctly," *Political Science Quarterly* 98 (Fall 1983): 431-58.

43. Lebow, "Correspondence" p. 204; Arthur Schlesinger, *A Thousand Days: John F. Kennedy in the White House* (Boston: Houghton, Mifflin, 1965), p. 361.

44. Lebow, "Correspondence" p. 205.

46. Detzer pp. 53-54.

47. Lebow, "The Cuban Missile Crisis," p. 456; see also Herbert S. Dinerstein, *The Making of a Missile Crisis: October 1962* (Baltimore: Johns Hopkins University Press, 1976), pp. 152-53.

48. See Abel, Horelick, and Ulam for this perspective.

49. Thomas G. Paterson, "Lost Opportunities," *The Nation,* March 7, 1987, p. 300. For advocates of the second model of revisionism, see Barton Bernstein, "The Cuban Missile Crisis," in *Reflections on the Cold War,* Lynn Miller and Ronald Pruessen eds. (Philadelphia, PA: Temple University Press, 1974), pp. 111-42; Ronald Steel, "The Kennedys and the Missile Crisis," *New York Review of Books* , March 13, 1969, pp. 15-22; and I.F. Stone, "The Brink," *New York Review of Books,* April 14, 1966, pp. 1-4.

50. Welch and Blight, "Introduction," p. 16.

51. Paterson, "Lost Opportunities." For an analysis of other motives involved in the crisis—Soviet, American, and Cuban—see Albert and Roberta Wohlstetter, *Controlling the Risks in Cuba,* Adelphi Paper No. 17 (London: International Institute of Strategic Studies, April 1963).

Another interesting explanation is put forward by Adam Ulam and others. They suggest that Soviet posturing was directed in large part at the Communist Chinese, who had long demanded that the USSR stand up to the imperialist United States. The Soviets may in part have been trying to get tough; and in the process to persuade the Chinese to put themselves under Soviet nuclear protection, foregoing the development of their own nuclear weapons. See Stephen E. Ambrose, *Rise to Globalism: American Foreign Policy Since 1938* (New York: Penguin Books, 1985), pp. 192-93; Adam Ulam, "Khruschev's Grand Design," in *The Cuban Missile Crisis,* Robert A. Devine ed. (Chicago: Quadrangle Books, 1971), pp. 139-52.

52. Scherer pp. 113-17.

53. Carlos Franqui, *Family Portrait with Fidel* (New York: Vintage Books, 1985), pp. 185-88.

54. Graham Allison *Essence of Decision: Explaining the Cuban Missile Crisis*

(Boston: Little, Brown and Co., 1971) pp. 39-66.

55. Jack L. Snyder, "Rationality at the Brink: The Role of Cognitive Processes in Failures of Deterrence," *World Politics* 30 (April 1978): 345-65.

56. Allison pp. 185-244. Donald L. Hafner has criticized the interpretation that JFK was "bureaucratically entrapped" by his failure to remove the Jupiters. See "Bureaucratic Politics and 'Those Friggin Missiles': JFK, Cuba, and the U.S. Missiles in Turkey," *Orbis* 21 (Summer 1977): 307-34. The transcripts of ExComm meetings that have become available, however, suggest that such influence was marginal at best; Welch and Blight, "Introduction," pp. 23-24.

57. See Thomas Mongar, "Personality and Decision-Making: John F. Kennedy in Four Crisis Decision," *Canadian Journal of Political Science* 2 (1969): 200-225.

58. See Stone and Steel for this perspective. Again, however, transcripts indicate little concern with domestic politics; Welch and Blight, "Introduction," p. 25.

59. Blema S. Steinberg, "Goals in Conflict: Escalation, Cuba, 1962," *Canadian Journal of Political Science* 14 (March 1981): 83-106.

60. Stuart J. Thorson and Donald A. Sylvan, "Counterfactuals and the Cuban Missile Crisis," *International Studies Quarterly* 26 (December 1982): 539-71.

61. Charles Lockart, "The Varying Fortunes of Incremental Commitment: An Inquiry Into the Cuban and Southeast Asian Cases," *International Studies Quarterly* (March 1975): 46-66.

62. See Schlesinger and Sorenson for sympathetic accounts.

63. See Bernstein in Miller, *op. cit.*; Leslie Dewart, "The Cuban Crisis Revisited," *Studies on the Left* 5 (Spring 1965): 24-40; Roger Hagan, "Triumph or Tragedy," *Dissent* 10 (Winter 1963): 13-26; and Ronald Steel, "End Game," *New York Review of Books*, March 13, 1969, pp. 15-22.

64. James A. Nathan, "The Missile Crisis: His Finest Hour Now," *World Politics* 27 (1975): 280-281.

65. David Lowenthal, "The Lost Opportunity," in *The Cuban Missile Crisis*, Robert A. Divine ed., *op. cit.*, pp. 90-93.

66. See also Mario Lazo, *Dagger in the Heart: American Policy Failures in Cuba* (New York: Funk and Wagnalls, 1968), pp. 322-78; and Ruby Hart Phillips, *Cuban Dilemma* (New York: Ivan obolensky, 1962), p. 357.

67. Peter W. Rodman, "The Missiles of October," *Commentary* 74 (October 1982): 39-45.

68. Cited in Rodman, reprinted in Irving Louis Horowitz, ed., *Cuban Communism* (New Brunswick, NJ: Transaction Books, 1987), pp. 79-80.

69. Ibid. pp. 81-82.

70. Ibid. pp. 83-34.

71. Cited in Blight et al., *op. cit.* p. 186.

72. Meg Greenfield, "Time to Recall This Model?" *Washington Post*, September 15, 1987, p. A23.

73. Richard P. Stebbins, ed., *Documents on American Foreign Relations 1963* (New York: Council on Foreign Relations, 1964), pp. 370-74.

74. Ibid. pp. 388-389.

75. Henry Hurt, *Reasonable Doubt: An Investigation into the Assassination of John F. Kennedy* (New York: Holt, Rinehart, and Winston, 1986), pp. 319-23.

76. Stebbins pp. 385-88.

77. Hurt pp. 308-16, Warren Hinckle and William W. Turner, *The Fish is Red: The Story of the Secret War Against Castro* (New York: Harper and Row, 1981), pp. 137-97; Morris H. Morley, *Imperial State and Revolution: The United States and Cuba, 1956-1986* (Cambridge: Cambridge mG}University Press, 1987), pp. 146-55.

78. David Kraslow, "Exile Raider Ban Baffles Cubans and Compounds Irony for FBI," *The Washington Post*, April 8, 1963, p. A15.

79. The story of one is told in *Cuban-American Spy for Freedom* (New York: Vantage Press, 1982), the story of Geraldine Shamma.

80. Wayne Smith, *Closest of Enemies: A Personal and Diplomatic History of the Castro Years* (New York: W.W. Norton, 1987), p. 85; William Atwood, *The Reds and the Blacks* (New York: Harper and Row, 1967), pp. 142-44; Hinckle and Turner pp. 195-97.

81. Jean Daniel, "UnofficialEnvoy: An Historic Report From Two Capitals," *The New Republic*, December 14, 1963, pp. 15-20; Maurice Halperin, *The Taming of Fidel Castro* (Berkeley, CA: University of California Press, 1981), p. 110.

82. Wayne Smith, p. 86; Hinckle p. 218; *New York Times*, January 3,1964, p. 8.

83. Atwood p. 144.

84. There are of course a huge number of sources on the Kennedy assassination. In this author's opinion the best is the Hurt volume already cited. See also Anthony Summers, *Conspiracy* (New York: McGraw Hill, 1980), esp. pp. 253-368; Albert H. Newman, *The Assassination of John F. Kennedy: The Reasons Why* (New York: Clarkson Potter, 1970); Jean Davison, *Oswald's Game* (New York: W.W. Norton, 1983); and Edward Jay Epstein, *Legend: The Secret World of Lee Harvey Oswald* (New York: McGraw Hill, 1978).

For an excellent summary of the possible Cuban role in the assassinatio, see Donald E. Schulz, "Kennedy and the Cuban connection," *Foreign Policy* No. 26 (Spring 1977): 57-64, 121-39. Schulz concludes that Castro probably would not have killed Kennedy since the two were seeking a rapprochement at the time.

Chapter Thirteen

1. The quotation from the Cuban peasant is from Carlos Alberto Montaner, "Toward a Consistent U.S. Cuban Policy," in Irving Louis Horiwitz, ed., *Cuban Communism* (New Brunswick, NJ: Transaction Books, 1987), p. 526; the Nixon quote is from Roger Morris, *Uncertain Greatness: Henry Kissinger and American Foreign Policy* (New York: Harper and Row, 1977), p. 106

2. *New York Times*, March 14, 1964, p. 5; U.S. Department of State, *U.S. Policy Toward Cuba*, DOS Publication No. 7690, 1964; Lynn Darrell Bender, *Cuba vs. the United States: The Politics of Hostility* (San Juan, Puerto Rico: Inter-American Universities Press, 1981), pp. 22-26.

3. House Committee on Foreign Affairs, Subcommittee on Inter American

Affairs, *Claims of U.S. Nationals Against the Government of Cuba*, 1964, p. 142.

4. See Thomas J. Dodd, "Vietnam and Latin America: The Danger of a Hemispheric Vietnam," *Vital Speeches* 31 (September 15, 1965): 706-9.

5. *New York Times*, January 6, 1964, p. 17; January 16 p. 21; January 25 p. 9; February 13 p. 19.

6. Ibid., March 4, 1964, p. 18; May 22 1968 p. 28.

7. Jules Davids, ed., *Documents on American Foreign Policy 1964* (New York: Council on Foreign Relations with Harper and Row, 1965), p. 280.

8. See *Department of State Bulletin*, February 24, 1964, p. 279.

9. *New York Times*, February 7, 1964, p. 1; February 9, Part IV pp. 1, 7; February 8 p. 24; February 17 p. 19.

10. *New York Times*, January 28, 1964, p. 6; for an analysis of the pressures on the U.S. government from its allies see Morris H. Morley, "The United States and the Global Economic Blockade of Cuba: A Study in Political Pressures on America's Allies," *Canadian Journal of Political Science* 17 (March 1984): 25-48.

11. *New York Times*, February 16, 1964, p. 1.

12. Ibid., February 19, 1964, p. 1., February 23, 1964, p. 1.

13. Ibid., March 26, 1964, p. 1; March 27 p. 4; March 28 p. 1; March 29 p. 1.

14. *Department of State Bulletin*, May 11, 1964, p. 744.

15. Robert D. Crassweller, *Cuba and the United States: The Tangled Relationship* (New York: Foreign Policy Association Headline Series No. 207, October 1971), pp. 28-30; *Department of State Bulletin*, May 11, 1964, pp. 738-44; Department of State Press Release No. 180, April 23, 1964.

16. *New York Times*, December 12, 1964, p. 1; December 23 p. 1; June 4, 1964, p. 1.

17. Ibid., April 1, 1964, p. 1.

18. Ibid., July 6, 1964, p. 1; "Cuba: Variation on a Theme," *Newsweek*, July 20, 1964, pp. 49-50; Wayne Smith, *Closest of Enemies* (New York: W.W. Norton and Co., 1987), p. 87.

19. Some observers have also suggested that Johnson originally intended to continue Kennedy's search for a rapproachement but was drawn away by advisors and domestic pressure; see Leslie Dewart, "A Negotiated Settlement: Toward Ending the Cuban Stalemate," *Commonweal* LXXXII (October 1, 1965): 717.

20. *Department of State Bulletin*, August 10, 1964, pp. 174-79; *New York Times*, July 26, 1964, p. 1.

21. Smith pp. 87-88.

22. Ibid. p. 89.

23. Warren Hinckle and William W. Turner, *The Fish is Red: The Story of the Secret War Against Castro* (New York: Harper and Row, 1981), pp. 198-285.

24. *Department of State Bulletin*, March 7, 1966, pp. 383-85; Stebbins, ed., *Documents of American Foreign Relations 1966* (New York: Council on Foreign Relations, 1967), pp. 323-25.

25. Smith pp. 90-92; Stebbins pp. 33-34; "Cuba: Fidel's Challenge," *Newsweek*, November 15, 1965, p. 70; *New York Times*, September 30, 1965, p. 1;

October 4 p. 1; October 8 p. 14; October 19 p. 13.

26. *New York Times*, May 23, 1966, p. 5; September 20 p. 13; September 29 p. 19; October 6 p. 1; October 8 p. 14; October 19 p. 13.

27. Ibid., July 3, 1967, p. 5; July 6 p. 34; September 24 p. 1; September 25 p. 1.

28. *Department of State Bulletin*, June 13, 1966, pp. 934-35.

29. "Troubles U.S. is Having with Cuba," *U.S. News and World Report*, July 15, 1968, p. 11; *New York Times*, November 24, 1968, p. 83; November 25 p. 16; December 4 p. 1; December 20 p. 30.

30. H. Michael Erisman, *Cuba's International Relations: The Anatomy of a Nationalistic Foreign Policy* (Boulder, CO: Westview Press, 1985), pp. 19-20; Paul D. Bethel, *The Losers* (New Rochell, NY: Arlington House, 1969), pp. 11-30; Pamela S. Falk, *Cuban Foreign Policy: Caribbean Tempest* (Lexington, MA: Lexington Books, 1986), pp. 24-27.

31. Carla Anne Robbins, *The Cuban Threat* (New York: McGraw Hill, 1983), pp. 39-41.

32. Robbins pp. 61-62; Erisman pp. 20-21; Falk pp. 30-35; Juan M. del Aguila, *Cuba: Dilemmas of a Revolution* (Boulder, CO: Westview Press, 1984), pp. 101-10.

33. Robins pp. 23-30; Jorge I. Dominguez, "Cuban Foreign Policy," *Foreign Affairs* 57 (Fall 1978): 83-108; Erisman pp. 21-25; M. Michael Kline, "Castros's Challenge to Latin American Communism," in Jaime Suchlicki, ed., *Cuba, Castro, and Revolution*, (Coral Gables, FL: University of Miami Press, 1972), pp. 190-220; Anthony T. Bryan, "Cuba's Impact in the Caribbean," *International Journal* XL (Spring 1985): 331-47.

34. Robbins pp. 31-39; David A. Crain, "Guatemalan Revolutionaries and Havana's Ideological Offensive of 1966-68," *Journal of Inter-American Studies and World Affairs* 17 (May 1975): 175-206.

35. Robinns pp. 42-43; Erisman pp. 25-31.

36. Erisman p. 30.

37. Erisman pp. 33-36, quote from p. 35; Robbins pp. 54, 169-206.

38. U.S. Central Intelligence Agency, *The Cuban Economy: A Statistical Review, 1968-1976* (CIA, December 1976).

39. See generally Robert E. Osgood, et al., *Retreat from Empire: The First Nixon Administration* (Baltimore: Johns Hopkins University Press, 1973); Richard Nixon, *RN: The Memoirs of Richard Nixon* (New York: Grosset and Dunlap, 1978); Franz Schurmann, *The Foreign Politics of Richard Nixon: The Grand Design* (Berkeley: Institute of International Studies, 1987); and Tad Szulc, *The Illusion of Peace: Foreign Policy in the Nixon Years* (New York: The Viking Press, 1978).

40. Robert E. Osgood, "The Nixon Doctrine and Strategy," in Osgood et al., *Retreat from Empire*, p. 9; Bender, *U.S. vs. Cuba* pp. 26-27; Lynn Darrell Bender, "U.S. Claims Against the Cuban Government: An Obstacle to Rapproachement," *Inter-American Economic Affairs* 27 (Summer 1973): 3-14.

41. Rober Fontaine, *On Negotiating With Cuba* (Washington, D.C.: American

Enterprise Institute for Public Policy Research, December 1975), p. 60.

42. Fontaine p. 61; Bender *U.S. vs. Cuba* pp. 28-29.

43. Senate Foreign Relations Committee, *U.S. Policy Towards Cuba*, 1971, p. 4. See also Senate Foreign Relations Committee, *Aircraft Hijacking Convention*, 1971, pp. 76-77; *Washington Post*, April 13, 1972, p. A23; and *Department of State Bulletin*, October 11, 1971, p. 392.

44. Senate, *U.S. Policy Towards Cuba*, p. 4.

45. Ibid. p. 7.

46. Bender, *U.S. vs. Cuba* p. 29.

47. *Department of State Bulletin*, January 25, 1972, p. 84; Szulc, *Illusion* pp. 353-69, 481-82.

48. del Aguila pp. 135-43; Edward Gonzales, *Cuba Under Castro: The Limits of Charisma* (Boston: Houghton-Mifflin, 1974), pp-. 190-216; Sergio Roca and Roberto E. Hernandez, "Structural Economic Problems," in Suchlicki, ed., *Cuba, Castro, and Revolution*, pp. 23-42; Arthur MacEwan, *Revolution and Economic Development in Cuba* (New York: St. Martin's Press, 1981), pp. 93-120; Claes Brundenius, *Revolutionary Cuba: The Challenge of Growth of Equity* (Boulder, CO: Westview Press, 1984), pp. 54-56. On the Venceremos brigades see Sandra Levinson and Carol Brightman, *Venceremos Brigade: Young Americans Sharing the Life and Work of Revolutionary Cuba* (New York: Simon and Schuster, 1971).

49. *New York Times*, May 4, 1969, p. 1; May 11, Part VI p. 133.

50. Ibid., December 9 1969 p. 4.

51. *New York Times*, April 20, 1970, p. 1; April 26 Part IV p. 2; May 27 p. 29; January 6, 1971, p. 24; April 18, 1971, p. 26.

52. Lynn Darrell Bender, "The Cuban Exiles: An Analytical Sketch," *Journal of Latin American Studies* 5 (November 1973): 271, 274.

53. Hinckle and Turner pp. 286-313.

54. Nicholas M. Horrock, "Cuba Aided Weather Underground in War Protest Years, FBI Says," *New York Times*, October 9, 1977.

55. Nixon, *RN*, p. 489. On the crisis see Henry A. Kissinger, *White House Years* (Boston: Little, Brown, 1979), pp. 632-52; House Committee on Foreign Affairs, *Soviet Naval Activities in Cuba*, September, October, and November 1979, September 1; October 19 p. 9; November 15 p. 1; January 5, 1971, p. 1; January 6 p.d 14. See also Lynn Darrell Bender, *The Politics of Hostility: Castro's Revolution and United States Policy* (Hato Rey, Puerto Rico: Inter-American University Press, 1975), pp. 66-72; Barry Blechman, "Soviet Sub Visits to Cuba," *U.S. Naval Institute Proceedings* 101 (September 1975); Raymond L. Gartoff, "Handling the Cienfuegos Crisis," *International Security* 8 (Summer 1983): 46-128; and Tad Szulc, *Illusions* pp. 364-66.

56. *New York Times*, April 20, 1971, p. 11; July 27 p. 10.

57. Ibid., September 17, 1971, p. 4; October 13 p. 19.

58. Ibid., September 17 p. 14.

59. Ibid., October 20, 1971, p. 3; October 21 p. 11; November 13 p. 8.

60. See Jacques Levesque, *The USSR and the Cuban Revolution: Soviet Ideo-*

logical and Strategical Perspectives, 1959-1977 (New York: Praeger, 1978), p. 1966.

61. *New York Times*, October 27, 1971, p. 1; October 28 p. 1; October 29 p. 1; November 6 p. 17.

62. Ibid., December 17, 1971, p. 1; December 18 p. 1; December 19 p. 7; December 20 p. 10.

63. Ibid., April 13, 1972, p. 2; April 20 p. 44.

64. See McGovern's *New York Times* magazine articles, cited in Chapter Fourteen.

65. *New York Times*, November 10, 1972, pp. 1, 20; April 14, 1972, p. 1; April 16, Part IV p. 2.

66. The Watergate accounts with the most information on the involvement of Cubans are logically the first-hand narratives. See G. Gordon Liddy, *Will* (New York: St. Martin's Press, 1980), pp. 164-72, 191-99, 218-42, 299-311; and John W. Dean III, *Blind Ambition: The White House Years* (New York: Simon and Schuster, 1976), pp. 90-93, 97, 171, 182, 203.

67. *New York Times*, January 11, 1973, p. 3; February 16 p. 1

68. Ibid., November 16, 1972, p. 1; November 17 p. 1; December 3, Part IV p. 3; January 14, 1973, Part IV p. 16; January 30 p. 8; February 14 p. 7; February 17 p. 12.

69. Ibid., March 20, 1973, p. 1.

70. Ibid., January 12, 1974, p. 10; February 10 p. 12; February 13 p. 5; February 23 p. 4; February 24 p. 1; April 24 p. 64; April 26 p. 55; March 21 p. 41; April 21, Part IV p. 2.

71. Ibid., July 6, 1974, p. 2; July 13 p. 1; July 14, Part IV p. 4; August 3 p. 3.

Chapter Fourteen

1. Much of the information is from a chronology in House Committee on International Relations, Special Study Mission to Cuba, *Toward Improved U.S.-Cuban Relations*, May 23, 1977 (Washington, D.C.: GPO, 1977), p. 72. Hereinafter cited as *TIR*. See also Morris H. Morley, *Imperial State and Revolution: The United States and Cuba, 1952-1986* (Cambridge: Cambridge University Press, 1987), pp. 279-87.

2. Senate Foreign Relations Committee, *The United States and Cuba: A Propitious Moment*, 1974.

3. *U.S Relations with Cuba: Report of a Special Study Mission to Cuba, August/September 1975* (Washington, D.C.: GPO, 1975).

4. House International Relations Committee, *Cuba Study Mission: A Fact Finding Survey, June 26-July 2, 1975.*

5. Senate Foreign Relations Committee Report, *Cuban Realities: May 1975*, August 1975, p. 1.

6. For an analysis of trade ramifications of rapproachement see U.S. Department of Commerce, "On Resumption of Trade With Cuba: The Issues Defined," *Inter-American Economic Affairs* 29 (Autumn 1975): 59-78.

7. See, for example, House International Relations Committee, Subcommittees on International Trade and Commerce and International Organizations, *U.S.*

Trade Embargo of Cuba, May 8-22, June 11 and 26, July 9, and September 23, 1975.

8. For another cautionary voice see Roger Fontaine, *On Negotiating With Cuba* (Washington, D.C.: American Enterprise Institute for Public Policy Research, December 1975).

9. See also House Committee on International Relations, Subcommittee on International Trade and Commerce, *U.S.-Cuba Trade Promotion*, July 22, 1976.

10. See, for example, Senate Resolution 230, *Congressional Record*, 94th Cong., 1st sess., No. 126, Part II, Vol. 121, August 1, 1975.

11. See Kalman H. Silvert and Frieda M. Silvert, *Fate, Chance and Faith: Some Ideas Suggested by a Recent Trip to Cuba* (Hanover, NH: American Universities Field Staff Report, Vol. 2, No. 2, September 1974), and Abraham Lowenthal, "Cuba: Time for a Change," *Foreign Policy* 20 (Fall 1975): 65-86.

12. Morley pp. 287-97.

13. See "Cuba's Influence Rises in the Caribbean," *Wall Street Journal*, March 22, 1976, and Morley pp. 266-78.

14. *TIR* pp. 70-72.

15. Emphasis mine; Ibid. p. 72.

16. Ibid. p. 71.

17. Wayne Smith, *The Closest of Enemies: A Personal and Diplomatic History of the Castro Years* (New York: W.W. Norton, 1987), p. 93

18. Smith pp. 93-94; *TIR* pp. 62, 66-68.

19. David Binder, "Angola is Only the Latest Cause of U.S.-Cuba Friction," *New York Times*, April 25, 1976.

20. *TIR* pp. 62-63.

21. Ibid. pp. 59-60; "Cautioning the Cubans," *The Washington Star*, February 29, 1976; "Castro's Imprint," *The Washington Post*, February 29, 1976.

22. David Binder, "Kissinger Believes Cuba 'Exports' Revolution Again," *New York Times*, February 5, 1976.

23. Edward Walsh, "President Brands Castro an 'International Outlaw,'" *The Washington Post*, February 29, 1976.

24. Bernard Gwertzman, "Kissinger Says U.S. Will Not Tolerate Any Further Cuban Intervention Abroad," *New York Times*, March 23, 1976; Gwertzman, "Kissinger Repeats Warning to Cuba," *New York Times*, March 24, 1976.

25. Drew Middleton, "Military Analysts Consider the Deterrence Options the U.S. Has Against Cuba," *New York Times*, March 24, 1976; Murray Marder, "White House, Pentagon Weigh Military Action Against Cuba," *The Washington Post*, March 25, 1976.

26. Smith p. 99; William LeoGrande, *Cuba's Policy in Africa, 1959-1980* (Berkeley: Institute of Interiational Studies, 1980), pp. 13-34; *TIR* p. 51.

27. Edward Gonzales, "Institutionalization, Political Elites, and Foreign Policies," in Cole Blasier and Carmelo Mesa-Lago, *Cuba in the World* (Pittsburgh, PA: University of Pittsburgh Press, 1979), pp. 190-206.

28. Ibid.

29. Arthur Jay Klinghoffer, "The Angolan War: A Study in Regional Insecurity," *Jerusalem Journal of International Relations* 8 (June 1986): 149; Pamela S. Falk, "Cuba in Africa," *Foreign Affairs* 65 (Summer 1987).

30. Mark N. Katz, "The Soviet-Cuban Connection," *International Security* 8 (Summer 1983): 94-95; William J. Durch, "The Cuban Military in Africa and the Middle East: From Algeria to Angola," *Studies in Comparative Communism* 9 (Spring-Summer 1978): 34-74; and Raymond L. Garthoff, *Detente and Confrontation: American-Soviet Relations from Nixon to Reagan* (Washington, D.C.: The Brookings Institution, 1985), pp. 502-37.

31. John Stockwell, *In Search of Enemies: A CIA Story* (New York: W.W. Norton, 1978), esp. pp. 66-69.

32. Smith pp. 94-98; LeoGrande, *Cuba's Policy in Africa* pp. 16-17; and John A. Marcum, *The Angolan Revolution: Exile Politics and Guerrilla Warfare, 1962-1976* (Cambridge, MA; MIT Press, 1978), pp. 257-59.

33. Jiri Valenta, "The Soviet-Cuban Intervention in Angola, 1975," *Studies in Comparative Communism* 11 (Spring-Summer 1978): 10; Nathaniel Davis, "The Angolan Decision of 1975: A Personal Memoir," *Foreign Affairs* 57 (Fall 1978): 110, 120-23.

34. See John A. Marcum, "Lessons of Angola," *Foreign Affairs* 54 (April 1976): 407-9.

35. Carla Anne Robbins, *The Cuban Threat* (New York: McGraw Hill, 1983), p. 216; Klinghoffer p. 151.

36. H. Michael Erisman, *Cuba's International Relations: The Anatomy of a Nationalistic Foreign Policy* (Boulder, CO: Westview, 1985), pp. 3-5; Robbins p. 221; Susan Eckstein, "Structural and Ideological Bases of Cuba's Overseas Programs," *Politics and Society* 11 (1982): 102-8; Richard Fagen, "Cuba and the Soviet Union," *Wilson Quarterly* 2 (Winter 1978): 72-78.

37. Abraham Lowenthal, "Cuba's African Adventure," *International Security* 2 (Summer 1977).

38. Ibid. p. 4; Wolf Grabendorff, "Cuba's Involvement inAfrica: An Interpretation of Objectives, Reactions, and Limitations," *Journal of Inter-American Studies and World Affairs* 22 (February 1980); Jorge I. Dominguez, "The Armed Forces and Foreign Relations," and Nelson Valdes, "Revolutionary Solidarity in Angola," both in Cole Blasier and Carmelo Mesa-Lago, eds., *Cuba in the World* (Pittsburgh, PA: University of Pittsburgh Press, 1979). Erisman emphasizes that these motives are based in an essential nationalism; Erisman pp. 68-69.

39. Eckstein pp. 88-102; Pamela S. Falk, *Cuban Foreign Policy: Caribbean Tempest* (Lexington, MA: Lexington Books, 1986), pp. 83-91; Erisman p. 9-11.

40. Gonzales, "Institutionalization," pp. 4-24; see also Edward Gonzales, "Complexities of Cuban Foreign Policy," *Problems of Communism* 26 (November-December 1977): 1-16.

41. Smith pp. 17-18.

42. Gerald J. Bender, "Angola, the Cubans, the American Anxieties," *Foreign Policy* 31 (Summer 1978): 5-6.

43. Smith pp. 101-3; *TIR* pp. 44-48; see also "Chronology of U.S.-Cuban Rapproachement: 1977," *Cuban Studies* 8 (January 1978): 36-43.

44. Smith pp. 102-3.

45. Smith pp. 103-9; *TIR* pp. 36-42.

46. House Committee on International Relations, *Report of a Special Study Mission to Cuba, February 10-15 1977,* May 23, 1977.

47. *Delusions and Reality: The Future of U.S.-Cuba Relations,* Report to the Senate Committee on Foreign Relations, October 1977.

48. Karen De Young, "Rave Review for Castro: Cuban President Regains Media Stardom in U.S.," *Washington Post,* August 28, 1977; George McGovern, "A Talk With Castro," *New York Times Magazine,* March 13, 1977; William F. Buckley, "McGovern and Castro: What's Going On?" *The Washington Post,* April 30, 1977.

49. See Irving Louis Horowitz, "The Cuba Lobby," *The Washington Review of Strategic and International Studies* 1 (July 1978): 58-71; Sarita Skidmore, "Cuba: When the Door Opens," (Menlo Park, CA: SRI International, December 1977).

50. Bender pp. 14-15; Garthoff, *Detente and Confrontation* pp. 623-30.

51. See Bender; Smith; and LeoGrande for general critiques. See also Gloria Duffy's article on the brigade issue, cited below; Morley pp. 242-43; and Simon Serfaty, "Brzezinski: Play in Again, Zbig," *Foreign Policy* No. 32 (Fall 1978): 3-21.

52. The ablest defender of Brzezinski is the former national security adviser himself. See his *Power and Principle: Memoirs of the National Security Adviser, 1977-1981* (New York: Farrar, Straus, Giroux, 1983). In this volume he makes no bones about the fact that he was more conservative than most in the administration. While Carter's goal, he writes, was to "make U.S. foreign policy more humane and moral," Brzezinski felt that "power had to come first" (pp. 48-49). Brzezinski also documents the pressures on heads of the various departments to defent their institutional "turf"—Vance and himself especially—from middle-level bureaucrats concerned about the relative position of their agency (pp. 37-38).

53. *TIR* pp. 38-39.

54. Barbara Walters, "An Interview with Fidel Castro," *Foreign Policy* 28 (Fall 1977); Bender pp. 12-13.

55. William M. LeoGrande, "Cuban-Soviet Relations and Cuban Policy in Africa," *Cuban Studies* 10 (January 1980): 16-17; Katz pp. 94-95.

56. See Cyrus Vance, *Hard Choices: Critical Years in America's Foreign Policy* (New York: Simon and Schuster, 1983), pp. 70-72, 89-91, 272-76; David S. McClellan, *Cyrus Vance* (Totowa, NJ: Rowman and Allanheld, 1985, volume 20 of American Secretaries of State and Their Diplomacy), pp. 48-52.

57. *TIR* pp. 36-37; Skidmore p. 5.

58. "Cuban Buildup Alarming, Study Finds," *The Washington Post,* November 17, 1977.

59. Hedrick Smith, "U.S. Sees Cuba's Africa Buildup Blocking Efforts to Improve Ties," *New York Times,* November 17, 1977; Karen De Young, "'Troops' Role in Africa Given Cubans at Home a Cause," *The Washington Post,* June 25, 1978.

60. Dusko Doder, "Castro Vows to Continue Africa Push," *The Washington Post*, December 26, 1977.

61. Smith pp. 122-23.

62. Smith pp. 123-27.

63. Smith p. 171; "The Cubans are Coming!" November 23, 1977.

64. Smith pp. 128-34; Roger W. Fontaine, "Cuba on the Horn," *The Washington Journal of Strategic and International Studies*, Special Supplement, May 1978; Vance pp. 72-75; LeoGrande, *Cuba's Policy in Africa*, pp. 35-57.

65. Robbins pp. 227-33; Falk pp. 95-106; and Steven David, "Realignment in the Horn: The Soviet Advantage," *International Security* 4 (Fall 1979): 69-90.

66. Katz pp. 96-97.

67. Jorge I. Dominguez, "U.S.-Cuban Relations in the 1980s: Issues and Policies," *Journal of Inter-American Studies and World Affairs* 27 (February 1985): 21-22.

68. "Soviets as Pilots, Cubans as Tools," *New York Times*, February 15, 1978; Fontaine p. 40.

69. Smith pp. 137ff; Bender pp. 15-19.

70. Smith pp. 143-63.

71. Raymond L. Garthoff, "American Reaction to Soviet Aircraft in Cuba, 1962 and 1978," *Political Science Quarterly* 95 (Fall 1980).

72. See, for example, Rowland Evans and Robert Novak, "Those Cuban MiGs," *The Washington Post*, December 8, 1978.

73. Smith pp. 170-82; regarding Grenada see Robert A. Pastor, "Does the United States Push Revolutions to Cuba? The Case of Grenada," *Journal of Inter-American Studies and World Affairs* 28 (Spring 1986): 1-34.

74. David D. Newsom, *The Soviet Brigade in Cuba: A Study in Political Diplomacy* (Bloomington: Indiana University Press, 1987), p. 11; Gloria Duffy, "Crisis Mangling and the Cuban Brigade," *International Security* 8 (Summer 1983): 71-72.

75. Smith pp. 182-87.

76. Newsom pp. 11-22; Duffy pp. 75-76.

77. Newsom p. 31.

78. Ibid. pp. 32-33.

79. Duffy pp. 76-79; Newsom pp. 34-39.

80. Newsom pp. 39-40; Duffy pp. 79-82.

81. See Department of State, Bureau of Public Affairs Current Policy Paper No. 93, "Background on the Question of Soviet Troops in Cuba," October 1, 1979.

82. See Ray S. Cline, "History Repeated as Force," *The Washington Post*, October 15, 1979. Brzezinski was also angry about the soft-line approach. He explains that this was the only time he "thought seriously of resigning;" Brzezinski pp. 344-53.

83. Mose L. Harvey, *Soviet Combat Troops in Cuba: Implications of the Carter Solution for the USSR* (Miami: Advanced International Studies Institute Monographs on International Affairs, 1979), p. 1.

84. Garthoff, *Detente and Confrontation* p. 837; see generally 828-48 for a summary of the events surrounding the brigade. See also Wayne Smith, "Dateline Havana: Myopic Diplomacy," *Foreign Policy* No. 48 (Fall 1982): 158-59; Duffy pp. 86-87.

85. See Jorge F. Perez-Lopez, *Measuring Cuban Economic Performance* (Austin: University of Texas Press, 1987); Edward Gonzales, "Political Succession in Cuba," *Studies in Comparative Communism* 9 (Spring-Summer 1976): 82-84; Carmelo Mesa-Lago, "Conversion of the Cuban Economy to Soviet Orthodoxy," *Journal of Economic Issue* 8 (March 1974): 41-66.

86. See Alejandro Portes et al., "The New Wave: A Statistical Profile of the Cuban Exiles to the United States," *Cuban Studies* 7 (January 1977): 1-32; Department of State Current Policy No. 183, "Cubans Seek Asylum in the United States," May 14, 1980 (the Carter statement); Department of State *Gist*, "Exodus from Cuba," May 1980; Gaston A. Fernandez, "The Freedom Flotilla: A Legitimacy Crisis of Cuban Socialism?" *Journal of Inter-American Studies and World Affairs* 24 (May 1982): 183-209; House Committee on the Judiciary, Subcommittee on Immigration, Refugees, and International Law, *Caribbean Migration*, May 13, June 4 and 17, 1980; and Senate Committee on the Judiciary, *Caribbean Refugee Crisis: Cubans and Haitians*, May 12, 1980.

86. John Scanlon and Gilbert Loescher, "U.S. Foreign Policy: 1959-1980—Impact on Refugee Flow From Cuba," and Ronald Copeland, "The Cuban Boatlift of 1980: Strategies in Federal Crisis Management," both in *Annals of the American Academy of Political and Social Sciences* 467 (May 1983): 116-50.

Chapter Fifteen

1. On Reagan's foreign policy, see generally Kenneth A. Oye et al., eds., *Eagle Defiant: United States Foreign Policy in the 1980s* (Boston: Little, Brown, 1983); John A. Vasquez, ed., *Evaluating U.S. Foreign Policy* (New York: Praeger, 1986).

2. Morris H. Morley, *Imperial State and Revolution: The United States and Cuba, 1956-1986* (Cambridge: Cambridge University Press, 1987), p. 319; *Newsweek*, November-December 1984, Special Issue on the Election, p. 32.

3. See *Reagan on Cuba* (Washington, D.C.: Cuban American National Foundation, 1986), pp. 7-18. Reagan has also accused Cuba of drug trafficking; see House Committee on Foreign Affairs, *U.S. Response to Cuban Government Involvement in Narcotics Trafficking and Review of Worldwide Illicit Narcotics Situation*, February 21 and 23, 1984; see especially testimony of James H. Michel, deputy assistant undersecretary of state, pp. 20-29.

4. Wayne Smith, *The Closest of Enemies: A Personal and Diplomatic Account of the Castro Years* (New York: W.W. Norton, 1987), p. 239.

5. *Reagan on Cuba* p. 21; *New York Times*, May 1, 1982, p. 3.

6. Thomas Enders, "Tasks for U.S. Policy in the Hemisphere," Department of State Current Policy No. 282, June 3, 1981; emphasis mine.

7. Morley p. 322.

8. For summaries of this position see Mark N. Katz, "The Cuban-Soviet Connection," *International Security* 8 (Summer 1983): 88-112, and Robert Leiken, "Eastern Winds in Latin America," *Foreign Policy* No. 42 (Spring 1981): 94-113.

Enders's position was spelled out more fully in congressional hearings; see, for example, House Committee on Foreign Affairs, Subcommittees on International Economics, Politics, and Trade and on Inter-American Affairs, December 14, 1982, pp. 1-26. By keeping Cuba at "arm's length," Enders argued, the United States has "denied it the legitimacy. . .normal relations with us would confer." The efforts at rapproachement in the 1970s not only failed, but "arguably [they] resulted in or at least [were] followed by even bolder, more aggressive action by Castro" (p. 4).

9. *New York Times*, January 11, 1981, p. 26; march 4, 1981, p. 22. For Haig's views see *Caveat: Realism, Reagan, and Foreign Policy* (New York: Macmillan, 1984). This volume contains the same sort of veiled threats of action made while Haig was in office; at one point, after assurances from the Soviet Union that "Cuban activities in the Western Hemisphere were a matter between the United States and Cuba," Haig argues that the administration was ready to solve the Cuban "problem" through the "unequivocal application of pressure." Haig concludes that "Castro had more reason to be nervous than he knew." (p. 131) But never is there an explicit, detailed account of what form the administration's "unequivocal pressure" would take; one imagines the ommission is caused by the lack of any feasible option and the unwillingness to admit of that truth, an unwillingness still present when Haig wrote his book.

10. *Ibid.*, February 25, 1981, p. 3; February 27 p. 2.

11. Morley pp. 334-36.

12. *New York Times*, April 22, Part II, p. 6; April 24 p. 12.

13. Morley, pp. 337-55, has a good summary of the administration's efforts to reassert the economic blockade.

14. Wayne Smith, "Dateline Havana: Myopic Diplomacy," *Foreign Policy* No. 48 (Fall 1982): 160.

15. See Jorge Salazar-Carrillo, "Is the Cuban Economy Knowable?" *Caribbean Review* 15 (Spring 1986): 24-25, and Carmelo Mesa-Lago, "Cuba's Centrally Planned Economy: An Equity Tradeoff for Growth," in Irving Louis Horowitz, ed., *Cuban Communish* (New Brunswick, NJ: Transaction Books, Sixth Edition, 1987), pp. 163-64.

16. For a good set of statistics, see the appendices in Pamela S. Falk, *Cuban Foreign Policy: Caribbean Tempest* (Lexington, MA: Lexington Books, 1986).

17. See "Cuba is Living on Borrowed Time," *Business Week*, December 14, 1987, pp. 52-53; Donald P. Henry et al., *An Analysis of Cuban Debt* (Santa Monica, CA: The Rand Corporation, May 1984); Jorge F. Perez-Lopez, "Cuba as an Oil Trader: Petroleum Deals in a Falling Market," *Caribbean Review* 15 (Spring 1986): 26-29, 43-44; Wilson P. Dizard III, "Cuba in the Red," *Worldview* 26 (March 1983): 17-20.

18. Kenneth N. Skoug, Jr., "Cuba's Growing Crisis," Department of State Current Policy No. 976, May 27, 1987; Mesa-Lago, "Cuba's Centrally Planned Economy," pp. 165, 68; and Nancy Forster, "Cuban Agricultural Productivity," in Horowitz, ed., *Cuban Communism*, pp. 196-216.

19. Susan Eckstein has done extensive analyses of Cuba's participation in the world economy. See her "Capitalist Constraints on Cuban Socialist Development," *Comparative Politics* 12 (April 1980): 253-74; "The Socialist Transformation of Cuban Agriculture: Domestic and International Constraints," *Social Problems* 29 (December 1981): 178-96; and "Revolutions and the Restructuring of National Economies: The Latin American Experience," *Comparative Politics* 17 (July 1985): 473-94.

20. For a guide to writings on this subject see Larry Oberg, compiler, *Human Services in Postrevolutionary Cuba: An Annotated Bibliography* (Westport, CT: Greenwood Press, 1984). Antonio Jorge has done a good (if skeptical) general summary of Cuban economic performance in "Ideology, Planning, Efficiency,a nd Growth: Change Without Development," in Horowitz, ed., *Cuban Communism*, pp. 289-311. He concludes that "Whichever way one looks at the Cuban economy, it is evident that the traditional goals that contemporary nation-states usually define as desirable have not been reached," goals such as "self-reliance, stability, and balance." In fact he contends that "The Cuban economy has failed the test in every important respect, even in its self-avowed and much-touted quest for equality, from which a sharp reversal is by now definitive." (p. 310).

21. Carmelo Mesa-Lago, *The Economy of Socialist Cuba: A Two Decade Appraisal* (Albuquerque: University of New Mexico Press, 1981), pp. 142-44.

22. Claes Brudenius, *Revolutionary Cuba: The Challenge of Economic Growth With Equity* (Boulder: Westview Press, 1984), p. 110; see also Brudenius, *Economic Growth, Basic Needs, and Income Distribution in Revolutionary Cuba* (Sweden: University of Lund Research Policy Institute, 1981). See also U.S. Central Intelligence Agency, National Foreign Assessment Center, *The Cuban Economy: A Statistical Review* (March 1981).

23. Arthur MacEwan, *Revolution and Economic Development in Cuba* (New York: St. Martins Press, 1981), pp. 213-14.

24. Brudenius, *Revolutionary Cuba* (all subsequent references are to this work), p. 120; Mesa-Lago, *Economy of Socialist Cuba* pp. 144-45.

25. Brudenius p. 122.

26. Mesa-Lago, *Economy of Socialist Cuba* p. 191; cf. 191-92.

27. Carmelo Mesa-Lago, "Farm Payment Systems in Socialist Cuba," *Studies in Comparative Communism* IX (Autumn 1976): 275-84.

28. Mesa-Lago, *Economy of Socialist Cuba*, p. 192.

29. *Ibid*. p. 194.

30. *Ibid*. p. 188.

31. R. Bruce McColm, "Castro's Ambitions Amid New Winds from Moscow," *Strategic Review* 14 (Summer 1986); Mesa-Lago, "Cuba's Centrally

Planned Economy," pp. 177-78.

32. Nick Eberstadt, "Did Fidel Fudge the Figures?" *Caribbean Review* 15 (Spring 1986).

33. *Ibid.*

34. *Ibid.*

35. Sergio-Diaz Briquets, *The Health Revolution in Cuba* (Austin: University of Texas press, 1983), p. 125.

36. Lrrin Philipson, "Castro's Tarnished Silver," *Policy Review* 29 (Summer 1984): 84-87.

37. Jill Hamberg, *Under Construction: Housing Policy in Revolutionary Cuba* (New York: Center for Cuban Studies, 1986); Mesa-Lago, "Cuba's Centrally Planned Economy" p. 178.

38. See McColm; Lawrence H. Theriot, "Cuba Faces the Economic Realities of the 1980s," Study for the Joint Economic Committee, U.S. Congress, March 22, 1982 (Washington, D.C.: GPO, 1982).

39. Juan Clark, *Religious Repression in Cuba* (Miami: Institute for Inter-American Studies, University of Miami, 1985); Margaret E. Crahan, "Cuba: Religion and Revolutionary Institutionalization," *Journal of Latin American Studies* 17 (November 1985): 319-40.

40. Paul E. Sigmund, "Fidel and the Friars: Castro Confesses to Friar Betto," *Caribbean Review* 15 (Spring 1986): 30-31; Fidel Castro, *Fidel and Religion* (New York: Simon and Schuster, 1987); Tennant C. Wright, "Cuba: The Church is Open," *America* 157 (October 24, 1987): 266-69; Joan Frawley Desmond, "Fidel and Religion," *National Catholic Reporter,* September 20, 1987, pp. 1, 6-7.

41. Andrew Borowizc, "Walters Turns Up Heat on Cuba for Violating Rights," *The Washington Times,* March 6, 1987, p. 3; Kenneth N. Skoug, Jr., "A Spotlight on Cuba," Department of State Current Policy No. 881, October 22, 1986; Richard Schifter, "Human Rights Violations in Cuba," *Catholicism in Crisis,* March 1985, pp. 26-29; Lucy Keyser, "Cubans Recall Horror of Fidel's Gulag," *The Washington Times,* September 25, 1986, p. 1B; Jeane J. Kirkpatrick, "Cuba's Crimes," *The Washington Post,* March 23, 1987, p. A11; Organization of American States, Inter-American Commission on Human Rights, *Sixth Report on the Situation of Political Prisoners in Cuba* (Washington, D.C.: OAS, December 1979); U.S. Department of State, Human Rights in Castro's Cuba," *Department of State Bulletin* 87 (February 1987): 62-67; Amnesty International, *Political Imprisonment in Cuba* (Washington, D.C.: The Cuban-American National foundtion, 1987); "On Human Rights: A Report on the Human Condition in Cuba" (Washington, D.C.: On Human Rights organization, Georgetown University; editions 1984-1986).

42. Armado Valladares, *Against All Hope* (New York: Alfred A. Knopf, 1986).

43. Department of State, "Human Rights in Castro's Cuba," Special report No. 153, December 1986.

44. William M. LeoGrande, "The Theory and Practice of Socialist Democracy in Cuba: Mechanisms of Elite Accountability," *Studies in Comparative Communism* XII (Spring 1979): 39-62; Edward Gonzales, "Castro and Cuba's New

Orthodoxy," *Problems of Communism* 25 (January-February 1976): 1-19; LeoGrande, "Civil-Military Relations in Cuba: Party Control and Political Socialization," *Studies in Comparative Communism* XI (Autumn 1978): 278-91.

45. Juan M. del Aguila, "Cuba's Revolution After Twenty-Five Years," *Current History* 84 (March 1985): 122-26, 133-34; Sergio Roca, "Cuba Confronts the 1980s," *Current History* 82 (February 1983): 74-78; Jorge I. Dominguez, "Cuba in the 1980s," *Foreign Affairs* 65 (Fall 1986): del Aguila, "Political Developments in Cuba," *Current History* 85 (January 1986): 12-15, 36-37; Roca, "Economic, Political and Institutional Change in Socialist Cuba," *Journal of Economic Issues* 17 (June 1983): 405-14; "Policy Split in Cuba," *The Latin American Times*, March 11, 1986, p. 1.

46. Peter Ford, "Despite Close Ties with Moscow, Havana Balks and Pursuing *Glasnost*," *Christian Science Monitor*, June 22, 1987, pp. 7, 10; McColm; W. Raymond Duncan, "Castro and Gorbachev: The Politics of Accommodation," *Problems of Communism* 35 (March-April 1986): 45-57.

47. H. Michael Erisman, *Cuba's International Relations: The Anatomy of a Nationalistic Foreign Policy* (Boulder, CO: Westview Press, 1985), p. 135.

48. See generally Erisman pp. 126-52; Falk, *Cuban Foreign Policy* pp. 57-80.

49. Smith, *Closest of Enemies* pp. 241-44; Smith, "Dateline Havana," pp. 160-61; "Communist Influence in El Salvador," Department of State Special Report No. 80, February 23, 1981.

50. Smith, "Dateline Havana" pp. 163-64.

51. Strategic Situation in Central America and the Caribbean," Department of State Current Policy No. 352 (Enders statement), December 14, 1981; "Cuba's Renewed Support for Violence in Latin America," Department of State Special Report No. 90, December 14, 1981; "Tips for Travelers to Cuba," Department of State Bureau of Consular Affairs, September 1987.

52. Smith, "Dateline Havana" p. 169.

53. Smith, *Closest of Enemies* pp. 249-60.

54. *New York Times*, April 23, 1982, p. 9; April 24, 1982, p. 2; "No Offer to Cuba, State Official Says," *The Washington Post*, April 24, 1982, p. A25.

55. *New York Times*, February 21, 1981, p. 1; August 8, 1981, p. 22; March 12, 1982, p. 1; Morley pp. 355-63.

56. Radio Marti and Cuban Interference," Department of State Current Policy No. 392, May 10, 1982; "Cuban Armed Forces and the Soviet Military Presence," Department of State Special Report No. 103, August 1982; "Cuban Support for Terrorism and Insurgency in the Western Hemisphere," Department of State Current Policy No. 376, March 12, 1982; "Dealing With the Reality of Cuba," Department of State Current Policy No. 443, December 14, 1982; *New York Times*, August 11, 1982, p. 4; August 20, 1982, p. 4; August 21, 1982, p. 3.

57. *New York Times*, April 2, 1982, p. 4; April 19, 1982, p. 5; September 15, 1982, p. 11.

58. "Background on the Caribbean Basin Initiative," Department of State Special Report No. 97, March 1982; Reagan address, "The Caribbean Basin Initia-

tive," Department of State Current Policy No. 370, February 24, 1982; more cities on CBI.

59. Erisman pp. 145-57; Falk pp. 45-47; Gordon K. Lewis, *Grenada: The Jewel Despoiled*, (Baltimore: Johns Hopkins University Press, 1987).

60. Christopher Dickey, "Central America: From Quagmire to Cauldron?" *Foreign Affairs* 62 (America and the World 1983), p. 666.

61. Erisman pp. 145-50.

62. Luis Burstin, "My Talks With the Cubans," *The New Republic* 190 (February 13, 1984); *New York Times*, May 6, 1982, p. 27; June 17 1983, p. 3.

63. Jaime Suchlicki, "Is Castro Ready to Accomodate?" *Strategic Review* 12 (Fall 1984): 22-29.

64. *New York Times*, July 27, 1984, p. 1; July 28, 1984, p. 3; August 5, 1984, Section IV, p. 5.

65. Department of State Press Statement and attached information package, "Agreement Signed on Mariel Excludagles," December 14, 1984; *New York Times*, July 14, 1984, p. 4; August 5, 1984, p. 14.

66. "The United States and Cuba," Department of State Current Policy No. 646, December 17, 1984, p. 5.

67. *New York Times*, June 3, 1984, p. 32; June 24, 1984, p. 1; June 27, 1984, p. 1; June 28, 1984, p. 4; June 30, 1984, p. 1; July 7, 1984, p. 8.

68. Pamela S. Falk, "Cuba in Africa," *Foreign Affairs* 65 (Summer 1987); William Claiborne, "Cuban, Soviet Advisors Key to Angolan Regime," *The Washington Post*, July 9, 1987, p. 31; "Reagan Facing Challenge to U.S. Role in Angolan War," *Congressional Quarterly Weekly Report*, September 6, 1986, p. 2065; Patrick Tyler, "Rebel Success Turns on South African Aid," *The Washington Post*, July 30, 1986; Sheila Rule, "Angolan Head Seeks Reagan Talks," *New York Times*, August 19, 1986; Edward Walsh, "House Votes Renewed Aid to Savimbi," *The Washington Post*, September 18, 1986, p. 14; David B. Ottaway, "U.S. Oil Firms Ignore Reagan Policy," *The Washington Post*, July 31, 1986.

See also John A. Marcum, "Angola," *Survival* 30 (January-February 1988): 3-13. He notes that Savimbi is also supported by Morocco and Saudi Arabia, and that the Cuban troops in Angola cost Luanda $400-$500 million annually.

69. William Claiborne, "Angolan Rebels Prepare for Expected Offensive," *The Washington Post*, August 6, 1987, p. A23; Margaret Knox, "Battle for a Tiny Town 'At the End of the Earth'," *The Washington Post*, March 1, 1988, p. a14.

70. Neil A. Lewis, "U.S. Urging Angola on Cuban Pullout," *The New York Times*, January 30, 1988, p. 2.

71. *New York Times*, August 11, 1986, p. 1; August 23, 1986, p. 3.

72. Presidential Proclamation No. 5617, *Federal Register* Vol. 51, No. 165, August 26, 1986.

73. American Bar Association Law and National Security Report, March 1987, pp. 1-2, 6-8.

74. U.S. UN Press Release, USUN 169 (86), November 26, 1986; Elaine Sciolino, "Reagan's Mighty Effort to Condemn Cuba," *New York Times*, March

24, 1987; Vernon Walters, "Castro's Gulag Should Burden UN," *New York Times*, March 21, 1987; John McCaslin, "Cuba's Threats Saved Face at UN," *The Washington Times*, May 13, 1987, p. 3; Vernon Walters (March 5 Geneva statement), "Human Rights in Cuba," Department of State Current Policy No. 954, March 5, 1987.

75. "Cuban Broadcasts Interfere With Two U.S. Stations," *The Washington Post*, July 23, 1987, p. 17.

76. Joseph B. Treaster, "Downward Spiral for U.S.-Cuban Ties," *New York Times*, May 2, 1987, p. 1.

77. Lewis H. Diguid, "Cuban Officials Wastes Funds, Defector Says," *The Washington Post*, August 11, 1987, p. A18; "the War of the Spies," *Economic Foreign Report*, August 20, 1987, p. 2; Michael Wines and Ronald Ostrow, "Cuban Defector Claims Double Agents Duped U.S.," *The Washington Post*, August 12, 1987, p. A8; *General Del Pino Speaks: An Insight into Corruption and Military Dissention in Castro's Cuba* (Washington, D.C.: Cuban-American National Foundation, 1987).

78. John M. Goshko, "U.S. and Cuba to Reactivate Migration Pact," *The Washington Post*, November 21, 1987, p. A1.

79. John M. Goshko, "For Detainees, Exile May Come Full Circle," *The Washington Post*, November 24, 1987, p. AQ; Art Harris, "Meese Offers to Delay Cuban Deportations," *Ibid.*; David Maraniss, "Cuba Exiles Holding 20 as Hostages," *The Washington Post*, November 23, 1987, p. A1; "News Analysis," *NewsCuba*, December 1987.

80. Peter Samuel, "Cubans Digging Tunnels That Could Hide MIssiles, Analysts Say," *New York City tribune*, February 10, 1988, p. 1; "Covert Basing of Missiles on Cuba Called Possible," *FPI International Report* VIII (February 12, 1988): 1-2.

Chapter Sixteen

1. The literature on the motivations for U.S. foreign policy is, of course, immense. Several sources that were particularly helpful in preparing this chapter were: Gene Rainey, *Patterns of American Foreign Policy* (Boston: Allyn and Bacon, 1975); Stephen E. Ambrose, *Rise to Globalism: American Foreign Policy Since 1938* (New York: Penguin Books, 1985); and Arnold Wolfers et al., eds., *The Anglo-American Tradition in Foreign Affairs* New Haven, CT: Yale University Press, 1956).

2. Morrel Heald and Lawrence S. Kaplan, in *Culture and Diplomacy: The American Experience* (Westport, CT: Greenwood Press, 1977), makes the important point that "From the beginning, Americans had considered it the responsibility of diplomacy to advance the interests, economic or otherwise, of private citizens." (p. 347) Thus it should hardly be surprising that twentieth-century American administrators have continued in the same pattern.

3. On the notion of an ambiguous commitment to empire, see Edmund Stillman and William Pfaff, *Power and Impotence: The Failure of America's Foreign Policy* (New York: Random House, 1966), pp. 3-14; and Simon Serfaty, *American*

Foreign Policy in a Hostile World: Dangerous Years (New York: Praeger, 1984), pp. 3-36.

4. Joan Didion has superbly chronicled the history and present status of the Cuban exile community in *Miami* (New York: Simon and Schuster, 1987).

Select Bibliography

It would be difficult, and not extremely useful, to reiterate citations for all the works to which this volume refers. If the reader desires a specific list of citations, he or she should consult the notes. This select bibliography has been included to suggest a few particular works in each period of Cuban-American relations.

Quotations
The quotations that begin each chapter are drawn from a number of sources. These include Georges Seldes, *The Great Thoughts* (Ballantine Books, 1985); *The Oxford Dictionary of Quotations* (Oxford University Press, various editions); Rhoda T. Tripp, *The International Thesaurus of Quotations* (Thomas Y. Crowell Company, 1970); Michael Jackman, *Crown's Book of Political Quotation* (Crown Publishers, 1982); John Bartlett, *Familiar Quotations*, 15th edition (Little, Brown, 1980); and *The International Encyclopedia of Quotations* (J.C. Ferguson Publishing Co., 1978).

Early Relations: To 1823
There are a few volumes that deal specifically with Cuban-American relations during this period. James M. Callahan's *Cuban and International Relations: A Historical Study in American Diplomacy* (Johns Hopkins, 1899), is one of the best, although unfortunately its sources are not documented. Philip Foner's two-volume *A History of Cuba and Its Relations With the United States* (International Publishers, 1962), is quite excellent; Foner is a Marxist, and some of his critiques of U.S. policy are a little one-sided, but his information is good. Two general histories of Cuba also yield considerable insight into this period: Charles E. Chapman's *A History of the Cuban Republic* (Octagon, 1969) and Willis Fletcher Johnson's multi-volume *A History of Cuba* (B. F. Buck, 1920). Various journal articles provide the best detail of specific issues; see Fisher, Russell, Abbey, Nichols, Cox, and Hoskins, all cited in the notes for Chapter One. Of course, Hugh Thomas's *Cuba, or the Pursuit of Freedom* (Harper and Row, 1971) is superb in this period as in all others.

The Monroe Doctrine
Many of the works cited above contain discussions of the Monroe Doctrine in the context of Cuban-American relations. Of course, there is a vast literature on the Doctrine apart from its U.S.-Cuban context. For several interesting discussions see Ernest R.

May, *The Making of the Monroe Doctrine* (Belknap, 1975); Dexter Perkins, *A History of the Monroe Doctrine* (Little, Brown, 1963); and Albert Bushnell Hart, *The Monroe Doctrine: An Interpretation* (Little, Brown, 1916).

Relations to the End of the Century

Foner, Chapman, and Callahan continue to be relevant here. See also Basil Rauch, *American Interest in Cuba: 1818-1855* (Octagon, 1974), a superb study of a discrete period. Amos Ettinger's *The Mission to Spain of Pierre Soule* (Yale, 1932) examines the U.S. Minister's policies, while Allan Nevins, *Hamilton Fish: the Inner History of the Grant Administration* (Dodd, Mead, 1936), provides outstanding details of U.S. policy during the Ten Years' War. The filibusters are able studies in Charles H. Brown, *Agents of Manifest Destiny: The Lives and Times of the Filibusters* (University of North Carolina, 1980). Richard H. Bradford, in *The Virginius Affair* (Colorado Associated University Press, 1980), gives details both of that expedition and of the context of U.S.-Spanish relations that surrounded it.

Once again, journal articles are good on specific points. See, in Chapter Two notes, Ely, Henderson, Luskin, Urban (two articles), Haynes, and Scroggs. Cuba's relevance to the U.S. Civil War is considered in Egan and Pratt, both cited in Chapter Three notes.

End of the Century and the American Occupation

For the best single account of the war, see G. J. A. O'Toole, *The Spanish War: An American Epic—1898* (W. W. Norton, 1984). There are a vast number of books chronicling America's rise to world power status and the motivations for the intervention in Cuba; some of these are catalogued in the Chapter Four notes.

For details of the American occupation and after, David F. Healy, *The United States in Cuba, 1898-1902* (University of Wisconsin, 1963), is good. But by far the best chronicler of this period is Louis A. Perez, Jr. See his *Cuba Between Empires, 1878-1902* (University of Pittsburgh, 1983), and his articles cited in Chapter Four and Five notes.

Post-Occupation Relation to 1933

Once again, Louis Perez is the best; see *Intervention, Revolution, and Politics in Cuba, 1913-1921* (Pittsburgh, 1978) and *Cuba Under the Platt Amendment, 1902-1934* (Pittsburgh, 1986), and also his article cited in Chapter Five. See also Russell H. Fitzgibbon, *Cuba and the United States, 1900-1935* (George Bantam, 1934); Harry F. Guggenheim, *The United States and Cuba: A Study in International Relations* (Books for Libraries Press, 1969); and Jules Benjamin, *The United States and Cuba: Hegemony and Dependent Development, 1880-1934* (Pittsburgh, 1977). Jorge I. Dominguez' excellent *Cuba: Order and Revolution* (Harvard, 1978), is also excellent on this period, and it is through the following decades.

On the 1909 intervention, see David Lockmiller, *Magoon in Cuba* (University of North Carolina, 1938), and Allen Millett, *The Politics of Intervention* (Ohio State University, 1968).

On Wilson's policies, see three journal articles cited in Chapter Five notes: Kaufman, Baker, and Meyer.

The 1933 Revolution

Benjamin, Fitzgibbon, Thomas, Guggenheim, and Dominguez are all good on this issue. See also Luis Aguilar *Cuba: 1933* (Cornell University, 1972), and several journal articles from Chapter Six notes: Cronon, Manach, Buell, Perez, and Hubert Herring's excellent series in *Current History*.

1933-1958

The secondary literature here is a little thinner. See Irwin F. Gellman, *Roosevelt and Batista: Good Neighbor Diplomacy in Cuba, 1933-45* (University of New Mexico, 1973). Dominguez and Thomas also have good detail, as do the books of Ruby Hart Phillips: *Cuban Sideshow* and *Cuban Dilemma*. See also Robert F. Smith, *The United States and Cuba: Business and Diplomacy, 1917-1960* (Bookman Associates, 1960. For journal articles, see in Chapter Seven notes Fitzgibbon and Healy, Stokes, and again Herring's good articles.

The Revolution

The literature naturally explodes at this point. Two general summaries of U.S. policy from about 1956 are Morris Morley, *Imperial State and Revolution* (Cambridge, 1987) and Wayne Smith, *The Closest of Enemies* (W. W. Norton, 1987). Both are critical of U.S. policy, but Smith's is by far the more honest; Morley's Marxist analysis causes him to ignore a good amount of evidence and to distort certain events.

A number of books written by participants or observers have interesting information. See Mario Lazo, *Dagger in the Heart* (Funk and Wagnalls, 1968); Mario Llerena, *The Unsuspected Revolution* (Cornell, 1978); Carlos Franqui, *Family Portrait with Fidel* (Vintage, 1984). Earl Smith's *The Fourth Floor* (Random House, 1962) must be treated with caution but is indispensible.

John Dorschner and Roberto Fabricio's *The Winds of December* (Coward, McCann, and Georghegan, 1980), is a superb volume that combines personal stories with a good general summary of events and some new archival material. It is perhaps the most readable accurate version of the revolution.

In terms of analyses of the revolution, Chapter Nine notes contain most of the best sources. The works of Draper, Ruiz, and Dominguez are particularly helpful.

The Bay of Pigs

Here only two books need to be mentioned. Peter Wyden's *Bay of Pigs* (Simon and Schuster, 1979) is by far the best narrative of events, while Trumbull Higgins's *The Perfect Failure* (W. W. Norton, 1987) is the best account of the American decision-making process. See also the Vandenbrouke article cited in Chapter Eleven notes.

Warren Hinckle and William Turner's *The Fish is Red* (Harper and Row, 1981) is an excellent summary of the secret war against Castro during the Eisenhower, Kennedy, Johnson, and Nixon administrations.

The Cuban Missile Crisis

Once again there is a huge volume of literature. Graham Allison's *Essence of Decision* (Little, Brown, 1971), is a classic of decision- making theory. More recent journal articles—two with transcripts in *International Security*, and one reporting the results of new information in *Foreign Affairs* (all cited in Chapter Twelve notes)—provide indispensable up-to-date declassified revelations. The small volume edited by Robert A. Divine, *The Cuban Missile Crisis* (Quadrangle, 1971), is a superb collection that has selections from all perspectives. The Abel and Dinerstein books provide a decent general summary of events, as does Robert Kennedy's *Thirteen Days*.

Johnson and Nixon Administrations

There is a dearth of secondary source material for this period. The best information on U.S. policy toward Cuba comes from congressional hearings and newspapers. Wayne Smith and Morris Morley, however, both discuss the period. Lynn Darrell Bender is the best chronicler of Nixon's policies; see *The Politics of Hostility* (Inter-American University Press, 1975) and her articles.

Ford Administration to the Present

Once again Wayne Smith and Morris Morley are major sources on this period. See also the numerous congressional reports on relations with Cuba outlined, especially, in Chapter Fourteen notes. The memoirs of those involved are also useful: Kissinger, Brzezinski, Haig, Carter, Vance, etc. Beyond that, the various journal articles cited in Chapter Fourteen and Fifteen notes are helpful.

Cuban History, Economy, and Society

The two best works on this subject are almost undoubtedly Hugh Thomas's *Cuba: The Pursuit of Freedom* (Harper and Row, 1971) and Jorge Dominguez's *Cuba: Order and Revolution* (Harvard, 1978). Both deal with a wide span of history—especially Thomas's mammoth work—and do so with accuracy and sophistication.

On the development of Cuban thought see Sheldon Liss, *Roots of Revolution* (Nebraska, 1987) and Gordon K. Lewis, *Main Currents of Caribbean Thought* (Johns Hopkins, 1983)

On the Cuban economy see Carmelo Mesa-Lago, *The Economy of Socialist Cuba: A Two-Decade Appraisal* (New Mexico, 1981); Claes Brundenius, *Revolutionary Cuba* (Westview, 1984); Lawrence H. Therlot, "Cuba Faces the Economic Realities of the 1980s," Study for the Joint Economic Committee, U.S. Congress, March 22, 1982 (GPO, 1982); and Arthur MacEwan, *Revolution and Economic Development in Cuba* (St. Martins, 1981). Of great interest in terms of literacy and health is Nick Eberstadt's short article, "Did Fidel Fudge the Figures?" in *Caribbean Review* 15 (Spring 1986).

On recent Cuba generally, Juan M. del Aguila's short book *Cuba: Dilemmas of a Revolution* (Westview, 1987) is an excellent introduction.

The literature on Cuban foreign policy is of mixed quality. Michael Erisman's *Cuba's International Relations* (Westview, 1985) is probably the best text, though short. Carla Anne Robbins's *The Cuban Threat* (McGraw Hill, 1983) has some good information, but is ideologically biased and contains numerous factual errors, especially on the pre-Reagan years. Pamela S. Falk's *Cuban Foreign Policy* (Lexington, 1986) is a good enough text, with solid basic information, but is somewhat scattershot in its approach; it is also quite short, though its set of historical and economic appendices is almost worth the price of the book itself. See also the journal articles cited in Chapter Fourteen and Fifteen notes.